Retailing

Retailing
environment
& operations

Andrew J. Newman

Peter Cullen

THOMSON

LEARNING

Australia • Canada • Mexico • Singapore • Spain • United Kingdom • United States

Retailing: environment & operations

Copyright © Andrew J. Newman and Peter Cullen 2002

British Library Cataloguing-in-Publication Data
A catalogue record for this book is available from the British Library

ISBN 1–86152–533–8

First edition 2002

Typeset by Saxon Graphics Ltd, Derby

Printed in Great Britain by TJ International, Padstow, Cornwall

To my son Michael (AJN)

For my family (PC)

Contents

Preface   xi
List of figures   xiv
List of tables   xv

PART 1   MANAGING THE RETAILING ENVIRONMENT   **1**

1   Introduction to the Retailing Environment   **3**
   1.1   The Functions of Retailing   5
   1.2   The Retail Industry in the UK   6
   1.3   Retail Formats   16
   1.4   Successful Retailing   19
   1.5   The Context of Retail Business Planning   25

2   Structural Change in the Retail Environment   **31**
   2.1   Changes in the Retail Environment   33
   2.2   Sociodemographic Change   38
   2.3   Technology and Economic Change   40
   2.4   Socio-economic Changes   43
   2.5   Impact on the Retail Industry   48

3   Market Structure and Control: Retailing Structures   **51**
   3.1   Environment and Competition   53
   3.2   The Competitive Environment in Different Retail Sectors   59
   3.3   Government Policy, Competition and Consumer Demand   64
   3.4   Retail Development and Competition   66
   3.5   Additional Theories of Conflict and Development   71

4   Managing in Good Times and Bad: Dealing with Booms and Slumps   **77**
   4.1   The Mood of the Nation   79
   4.2   Maintaining the Balance in the Economy   82
   4.3   Government Macroeconomic Policy   84
   4.4   The Impact of Economic Fluctuations on the Retailing Industry   88
   4.5   Managing Fluctuations   89

PART 2   RETAIL MARKETING: PLANNING AND DEVELOPMENT   **93**

5   Strategic Marketing Planning for Retailing: Setting up the Business   **95**
   5.1   The Strategic Planning Process: A Framework   97
   5.2   Objectives to Position the Business   101
   5.3   The Integrated Marketing System   110

5.4	Forging Relationships for Success	113
5.5	The Role of Retail Formats and Merchandise	115

6   The Customer and the Retail Business: Knowing your Customers   **119**

6.1	Focusing on the Consumer	121
6.2	Mapping Out Society: Psychographics	124
6.3	Postmodern Consumers	126
6.4	Learning Attitudes, Motivation and Perception	128
6.5	Modelling Consumer Behaviour	133

7   The Fundamentals of Merchandising: Product   **139**

7.1	Merchandise Strategies	141
7.2	Planning	144
7.3	Sourcing	151
7.4	Arranging and Displays	157
7.5	Space Management	163

8   Establishing a Pricing Strategy   **167**

8.1	Pricing Objectives	169
8.2	Pricing for Markets	172
8.3	Pricing Calculations	175
8.4	Pricing Policies	183
8.5	Pricing Strategies	185

9   Promoting the Store: Sending Out the Correct Sort of Messages   **191**

9.1	Communicating the Image	193
9.2	Promoting the Retailer as a Brand	197
9.3	Selecting the Promotional Mix	202
9.4	Advertising and Sales Promotions	206
9.5	Publicity, Personal Selling and Relationship Marketing	209

10 Locating the Store in the Retail Environment   **213**

10.1	Developing a Location Strategy	215
10.2	Evaluating the Trading Area	219
10.3	Locating: A Practical Guide for all Retailers	221
10.4	Researching the Proposed Trading Area	225
10.5	Defining the Catchment Area	229

PART 3   RETAIL MARKETING: OPERATIONS   **237**

11 Store Design and Layout: Producing the Right Format   **239**

11.1	The Store and its Image	241
11.2	The External Store: Structure as Part of Image	246
11.3	Internal Store	249
11.4	Display	256
11.5	Visual Merchandising and Atmospherics	262

12 Managing Retail Services: Creating Quality Retail Services   **267**

12.1	Retail Services	269
12.2	Service Characteristics	273
12.3	Branding: Perceptions of Service Quality	277
12.4	Managing the Service Setting and the Service Encounter	284
12.5	Analyzing Service Problems: Some Techniques	291

13 Services Retailing: Creating Tangibility **293**
13.1 From Service Provider to Service Retailer 295
13.2 Service Retail Sectors 299
13.3 Developing and Promoting the Service 303
13.4 Managing the Store 305
13.5 Delivering the Service 310

14 Business Operations: Financial Development **315**
14.1 Risks and Financial Requirements of a Business during Development 317
14.2 The Growing Firm 322
14.3 The Structure of the Business 325
14. 4 Investment Decisions 331
14.5 Financial Evaluation 335

15 Logistics and Distribution: Shipping the Goods to Market **339**
15.1 The Distribution Process 341
15.2 The Stages of Distribution 343
15.3 Trends in Supply Chain Management 348
15.4 Physical Distribution and Inventory Management 354
15.5 Warehouse Management 359

PART 4   DELIVERING THE PRODUCT **365**

16 Rolling Out the Goods: Developing New Relationships **367**
16.1 Retail Information Systems 369
16.2 Category Management 373
16.3 Integrating the Supply Chain 376
16.4 Customer Relationship Management 379
16.5 Retail Security and Information Systems 383

17 People in Retailing: Making People Matter **389**
17.1 Retail Employment 391
17.2 Planning the Workforce 399
17.3 Management and Organizational Culture 402
17.4 Personnel Management and Administration 406
17.5 Health and Safety 407

18 Out-of-Store Retailing: Buy by Wire **413**
18.1 Out-of-Store Retailing 415
18.2 Retail Strategy and the Internet 421
18.3 Mail Order Catalogue Shopping 426
18.4 Television Shopping 430
18.5 The Future of Out-of-Store Retailing 434

19 International Retailing Internationalization and Globalization **439**
19.1 Shopping at World Stores 441
19.2 Internationalization and Globalization 446
19.3 Going International 451
19.4 The Internationalization Process 454
19.5 Culture, Business and International Management 459

20 A Review of Retailing: Environment and Operations **465**
20.1 Retail Change: A Review 467

20.2 Cultural Transformation and Retailing   470
20.3 New Approaches in Retailing   473
20.4 Emerging Themes and Niches   476
20.5 Building for the Future: Learning from the Past 479

Index   485

Preface

To Students of Retailing

This book is for you, the student. You may be on a retailing course or studying retailing as part of a course in marketing, distribution or business studies. It does not assume any previous study of retailing. You will also find it useful for understanding developments in retailing in hospitality services, financial services and other areas of service management.

Retailing is a vibrant part of our changing society and a major source of employment. It is closely tied to the changing moods of the consumer and new ways of doing business, spurred on by the impressive developments in technology and management theory. As the title of the book implies, we look at the interaction of social and technical change with retail operations. We continue this theme in our treatment of topics throughout the book.

The book provides a comprehensive grounding in many facets of retailing, including logistics and distribution, merchandising, store layouts and design, pricing and location strategy. We have also included major new areas of importance, including managing retail services and out-of-store retailing. In recent times these issues have emerged as crucial determinants of success, and major areas of differentiation between competitors. This allows you to use the text selectively, as a complete reader or as instructed by your tutors.

The first few chapters in 'Part 1: Managing the Retail Environment' discuss the external (macro) environment. We recommend you read these chapters before tackling the operational issues that are covered later. This should aid intellectual progression and develop a more integrated knowledge of retailing before considering in-store or other microenvironmental issues.

Modern retailing is increasingly an expression of consumer consciousness in society. Societies, however, differ in the expression of that consumer consciousness. Retailing has developed a more international flavour because of closer cultural and social interaction between various countries. The spread of some retail formats, such as the supermarket, across the world also implies a greater cultural similarity. However, there are still significant differences in retailing patterns even within Western Europe. Consequently, we feel it right that an introduction to retailing should be grounded in the study of retailing within a specific country, in this case the UK. However, you will notice, we move steadily outwards during the later chapters to a more international view of developments.

We have provided cases from accessible material such as *Retail Week* and other sources that you should find easily accessible on-line through your university or college. We encourage you to use such material regularly to keep up to date and to obtain a good feel for the changes that are taking place in the industry. Reading this book will help you put these changes in context of the wider influences affecting decisions within the retail industry.

To Retail Educators

From the beginning, the aim of this book has been to provide a very accessible and easy-to-understand route to the subject of retailing. Perhaps the greatest challenge was to achieve this goal without sacrificing the theoretical and intellectual content. Moreover, the extent and scope of the subject area necessitated a great deal of time and research if our goal was to be achieved. Nevertheless, we both agreed during our numerous discussions and deliberations that a textbook of this type was badly needed.

We do explicitly recognize several other high-quality retailing texts that are available, and cite them where we feel it would be useful for students to consult them. These texts have undoubtedly influenced our own exposition. However, we keenly felt the need for a text for the European market and the UK in particular that provided the content, context and examples required by British students. We also wanted to provide a book with the breadth and scope that reflected UK retailing. This presented us with a considerable challenge that took us on an unforgettable journey when we first compiled the subjects and main areas of this textbook.

Our target market has clearly influenced the style and structure of the book. We designed the book to be both an aid to student learning and a template for the instructor. We have written the book within a strict format. Twenty chapters provide material that can be completely covered in a one-year course, or selectively chosen to compile two one-semester courses in introductory retail studies and retail operations. Each chapter is based around a theme and contains five linked sections. This, we believe, represents an appropriate focused format for student learning. It also provides instructors with the clear option of deleting and combining sections, as they feel appropriate. We have deliberately restricted the content to what we feel the student at this level can cope with effectively and which provides a framework within which continuing developments in retailing can be placed.

Where possible we have used a blend of material from both commercial and academic sources. This has created a mix of views that leaves the reader with a balance of knowledge, ranging from the applied to the theoretical. Moreover, where possible, the use of sources of contact like web addresses means that students can engage in the task of 'finding out for themselves'. Other short cases and tips/examples augment learning with 'true to life' topics and scenarios. Tutors may also wish to write these problem-centred learning situations into their syllabuses with a view to building modules around the core ideas presented.

Our decision to write a textbook that aimed its intellectual content at the level-1 student, with little or no knowledge of deeper management issues, was a particularly difficult task. The level at which this text is written precludes a great deal of notable articles and texts, because of their rigorous and theoretical approaches. We felt such works more suitable for mid- and final-year work, and postgraduate research students. We do, however, acknowledge the influence of some of the key authors, in the UK, USA and elsewhere, who will, no doubt, recognize their subconscious influence in our writing. It is perhaps invidious to select a few in the UK, but we acknowledge the insights provided by Peter McGoldrick, John Fernie, John Dawson and Nick Alexander. We also acknowledge the work undertaken by some of the major centres for retail research in the UK, such as those at the universities of Stirling and Ulster and other centres. We do reference relevant works we feel are accessible to students, although we would have liked to have given more explicit recognition to many more authors.

Acknowledgements

We wish to express our gratitude to Thomson Learning for their support during the preparation of this book. In particular, Jennifer Pegg, our editor provided immense support and invaluable advice in the earlier stages and kept us on track. We also thank Jenny Clapham and the production team for their patience and supportive discussions. Truly they have added to what we have presented.

List of Figures

		page
3.1	The Wheel of Retailing	67
3.2	The Dialectic Model	74
4.1	The Stages of the Macroeconomic Cycle	81
5.1	The Strategic Planning Process	99
5.2	The Retailing Information System	106
5.3	A SWOT Framework	109
5.4	A Vertical Marketing System	112
5.5	Porter's Generic Strategies	115
6.1	Segmenting a Market	122
6.2	Positioning	123
6.3	The Nature of Attitudes	129
6.4	Consumer Motives Model	132
6.5	Some Major Factors Influencing Consumer Behaviour	134
6.6	The Decision-Making Process	135
6.7	Routine Decision-Making	137
7.1	An Overview of Merchandising Services	152
7.2	Steps in the Buying Process	154
8.1	Pricing Decisions	170
8.2	Demand Curve	176
8.3	Demand and Marginal Revenue	177
8.4	Marginal Analysis: Maximizing Profit	179
10.1	Catchment Area	228
10.2	Customer Spot Map	228
10.3	Contours of Customer Demand	231
10.4	Huff's Model: Calculating the Probability Contours – A Simple Example	233
10.5	A Map of Concentric Zones	234
11.1	Models of Store Layout	251
12.1	The Customer Service Flow Chart	290
12.2	Cause and Effect Diagram	292
14.1	The Retail Life Cycle	319
15.1	Basic Elements of a Supply Chain for a Product	344
17.1	The Line of Authority	403
18.1	Conventional Store versus Multiple Format Retailing	437
19.1	Classification of Retailers' International Behaviour	450
19.2	Factors Affecting International Location Decision	457

List of Tables

		page
1.1	Employment in Retailing and Wholesaling (millions)	8
1.2	Retail Industry Sales at Current Prices	8
1.3	Changes in Sales at Constant (1993) Prices	9
1.4	Retailing Sectors, 1993–97	10
1.5	Sales of Specialist Retailers as Percentage of Total Sales in Category	10
1.6	Retail Outlets by Ownership	11
1.7	Share of Sales of Independent and Multiple Retailers	11
1.8	Forms of Retailing	16
1.9	Retail Formats	18
1.10	Gearing Ratios	24
1.11	Effect on Prices and Sales When Demand or Supply Changes	28
2.1	Population of the UK	38
2.2	Household Structure in the UK	40
2.3	Index of Output (1990 = 100)	41
2.4	Employment in Britain (millions)	45
2.5	Employment Rates for Mothers by Age of Youngest Child (%)	46
3.1	Macroenvironmental Influences	53
3.2	Microenvironmental Influences	54
3.3	Retail Outlets by Ownership	55
3.4	UK Retail Businesses (VAT registered)	56
3.5	Sales of Large and Small Retail Business at Current Prices (£bn)	56
3.6	Non-specialist Food Retailers' Sales, 1993–98	59
3.7	Outlets Operated by Leading Food Retailers, 1995–97	60
3.8	Number of Businesses/Outlets, 1993–95	61
3.9	Retail Shares of Major Department Stores, 1997	62
3.10	Major Variety Stores: Market Share, 1996	63
3.11	Leading Category Killers in the UK	70
4.1	Household Final Consumption Spending (£ million at current prices)	80
4.2	Household Spending (£ million at current prices)	80
4.3	Bankruptcies and Insolvencies, 1989–94	89
6.1	Social Class Categories	124
6.2	Typical Shopping Behaviours or Habits	125

6.3	Rating Scales	130
7.1	An Example of a Merchandise Budget	149
7.2	The Merchandising Cycle of a Greeting Card Retailer	157
7.3	Fixtures and their Purpose	161
8.1	Sales and Revenue	177
8.2	Cost Terms	178
8.3	The Marginal Rules for Profit Maximization	178
9.1	Communication Effects Model	196
9.2	Developing a Retailer Advertising Strategy	207
10.1	Factors Affecting the Strength of Business Interception	220
10.2	Consumer Profile Data from Within Trading Area	220
10.3	Site Analysis for Retail Location	222
12.1	Service Quality Dimensions	282
12.2	Service Gaps	283
13.1	Tangibility and Intangibility in Services Retailing	298
13.2	Service Retailer by Category of Customer Benefit	300
14.1	Number of Firms: VAT-Registered UK Retail Businesses by Turnover	317
14.2	Sales of UK Retail Businesses at Current Prices (£000m)	318
14.3	Listed Companies in Retailing and Related Trades, November 2000	325
16.1	Some Characteristics of Category Management	374
16.2	Types of Retail Crime	384
17.1	Employment in Retailing and Wholesaling	391
17.2	Personnel Files	407
17.3	Areas of Health and Safety	410
18.1	Percentage Mail Order Sales by Leading Retailers from 1993 to 1997	428
18.2	Which Key Services Do Digital Television Subscribers Use?	432
19.1	World Products	442
19.2	Shopping at International Stores in the UK	442
19.3	International Operations of the World's Largest Retailers	452
19.4	Method of Internationalization	454
19.5	Host Country Factors Affecting Method of International Expansion	456
19.6	Macroenvironmental Influences in Internationalization	456
19.7	Evaluating Attractiveness of Potential Regions for a UK Retailer, 2001	458
20.1	Some Out-of-Town Shopping Centres in the UK	472
20.2	The Growth of Factory Outlets in the UK	479

Managing the Retailing Environment

1   Introduction to the Retailing
    Environment

2   Structural Change in the Retail
    Environment

3   Market Structure and Control: Retailing
    Structures

4   Managing in Good Times and Bad:
    Dealing with Booms and Slumps

P
A
R
T

1

Introduction to the Retailing Environment

This chapter considers the following issues:

▶ The functions of retailing.

▶ The retail industry.

▶ Retail formats.

▶ Successful retailing.

▶ The context of retail business planning.

Introduction to the Retailing Environment

Introduction and Core Concepts

Retailing is all around us. It permeates our lives. We are aware of those retailers we consider favourites – we buy products and services from their shops, their websites and their catalogues. Retailers fulfil the important economic role of making these products and services accessible to consumers and we rely on them to supply us with hundreds of products and services each year. Retailing comes from an old tradition and is rooted in the social fabric. Retailers need to understand how to read the social and economic environment.

1.1 The Functions of Retailing

Retailing in Society

The retailer is part of the *supply chain* for any product that it sells. The supply chain consists of the different stages, starting with the raw materials, that the product goes through before it reaches the *final consumer*. It links raw material producers, manufacturer, wholesalers and transport firms with the retailer and the final consumer. It includes a *distribution system* that arranges for the shipment of the product from producer to final consumer. The retailer comes at the end of the supply chain and provides the final link between producer and consumer. Much of modern retailing, however, is linked very closely to whole supply chain, and may even be the dominant part of the supply process. Major grocery retailers, such as Tesco, play a very active role in arranging distribution of products to their stores. Other retailers own production facilities and some producers of fashion items also operate stores as well as selling to other retailers.

The *economic significance* of the retail industry is shown by official statistics, where retailing is responsible for about 9 per cent of output and employment. However, as we shall see later in this chapter, retailing is an even more important activity, and goes beyond those businesses that the government officially classes as retailers.

Retailing is also an important *social institution*, because about 30 per cent of what we spend goes on products and services that we buy from retailers. Most of us have seen immense changes in the products and services we use, the way we work, in family life and in our leisure activities. Some of these changes would not have been possible without changes in retailing, such as the large supermarket or superstore, and advances in distribution that have significantly reduced the cost of shopping for groceries, electrical goods and many other items. Retailing can also be *important politically*. The large out-of-town shopping centres have developed along with the increase in car ownership. They were initially hailed as making for a better way of living, but their harmful social effects on towns and cities have become more apparent as time has gone on. They are now a real issue in public policy and an important factor in retailers' planning. At the same time, planners and politicians recognize the important role of retailing developments in the regeneration of towns, districts and regions. Retailing is also a sophisticated user of *modern technology*. For instance, electronic tills are linked to computers to help control stock and track customer spending, and various technical devices are increasingly used to combat retail crime.

Consumers and Retailers

When we go out to buy something, we are *consumers* going *shopping* for products and services. *Products* include items such as food, clothing and electrical equipment, where the main attraction for the buyer is the physical qualities of the item. *Services* include restaurant meals, insurance and repairs where something is done for a person or their property.

> ⇨ A note on terminology: *products, goods and services*. If you study economics, you will learn that firms supply products to consumers and other firms. Products include goods and services. In marketing texts, however, products are the equivalent of goods and services are still services. We use the marketing conventions here because they are the ones used in retailing studies.

1.2 The Retail Industry in the UK

Retailing and the Retail Industry

People traditionally associate retailing with the selling products to consumers. As we have already mentioned, retailers may also sell services. In fact, fast food companies such as McDonald's have long been recognized as service retailers. In the UK, public house operators and industrial caterers have declared themselves to be retailers for some time now. Medical and health services have also begun to behave as retailers, particularly with the opening up of local health centres. However, the government classifies these as belonging to the hospitality and health industries respectively. It restricts the retailing industry to product retailers. We shall keep to official conventions when talking about the *retailing industry* but, when we talk about *retailing*, we may include service retailers from other industries. We shall also include the retailing parts of other businesses.

There are many businesses that engage in some form of product retailing as part of their usual business activities. For instance, about 15 per cent of pub sales are retail sales of various kinds and most museums and visitor centres have shops. However, these are counted as part of the main business, unless a separate business unit sells them.

Measuring the Retail Industry

We can measure the economic and social importance of the retail industry in various ways. One way is to measure its share of national output. A standard measure of output in a country is *gross domestic product* (GDP), which is explained further in Case 1.1.

Case 1.1 Measuring Output

Official statistics use *gross domestic product* (GDP) as the standard measure of total output produced in the country, measured by what people spend on the output produced. It is equivalent to the income earned from employment plus the profits received by businesses and other owners of capital and property.

The government uses two main measures of GDP: GDP at market prices and GDP at basic prices. The data on spending are originally collected at *market prices*, which are the prices that the consumer pays. These data are used to calculate GDP at market prices.

However, these prices include value added tax (VAT) and other taxes on spending, which do not provide profits or wages to the retailer or its suppliers. This means that market prices overstate the amount of income earned. Similarly, when the

government pays subsidies on some products, market price understates the amount of income earned. In order to get a truer picture of the work done, statisticians remove these taxes and subsidies to calculate gross domestic product at basic prices. This figure includes only taxes, such as local authority rates, that businesses have to pay as part of their normal activity.

The Office of National Statistics (ONS) publishes these statistics in *UK National Accounts*, the *Annual Abstract of Statistics* and *Economic Trends*. It also publishes monthly and quarterly data in *Economic Trends* and the *Monthly Digest of Statistics*. Data are often subject to significant errors, in collecting data, and the ONS revises some data for up to ten years afterwards. So we should not attach much importance to small changes in published data.

The *Standard Industrial Classification* system (SIC) divides the economy into different major industry groups, one of which is retailing. A firm belongs to the retailing industry if its most important activity is retailing, measured in terms of sales. For instance, Tesco is a retailer selling groceries, clothes and other items. Its stores also run restaurants, a catering activity. However, the firm is classed as a retailer because it produces more retailing output than catering output. All its output, including its catering services, belongs to the retail industry. In the same way, firms in other industries, such as airlines, include some retailing activity in their output, but their retail sales are regarded as part of the total sales of the airline sector.

We can measure the importance of retailing by retail employment in relation to total employment. This is illustrated in Table 1.1, although the level of employment and the share of total employment have varied significantly in recent decades.

Table 1.1 Employment in Retailing and Wholesaling (millions)

Employment	2000
In Great Britain	23.69
In retailing	2.37
In wholesaling	1.09

Source: National Statistics 2000a

Another way to measure the monetary contribution of retailing is through the total *net output* or *value added* of all the firms in the industry. This represents the wages paid and profits earned in the business and is the total sales or *gross output* of retailers *minus* taxes, such as VAT, and spending on goods and services that they buy in.

However, the more usual way of describing retailing is by the level of retail activity, which is given by gross sales (or turnover) of retailers and is another indicator of the economic and social importance of the industry. This is shown in Table 1.2.

Table 1.2 Retail Industry Sales at Current Prices

	£m	% change
1993	146 303	
1997	178 303	21.9

Source: National Statistics 2000b

Table 1.2 shows how spending has increased between 1993 and 1997.

The data show the value of retail sales *at current prices*, which means the prices that customers actually paid. However, some of the change in sales occurred because consumers were paying higher prices for what they bought. This means that sales figures overstate the increase in business for retailers during this period. In order to get a better measure of the change in the volume of sales or the amount of products sold, the government recalculates what it would have cost consumers if prices had stayed at their 1993 levels. These estimates are called spending at 1993 prices. These are shown in Table 1.3.

The data show that, in effect, retailers only sold 9 per cent more in 1997 than they did in 1993. The difference of 13 per cent between the increase in sales at current prices and the increase in sales at constant prices reflects the average increase in prices charged during this period.

Table 1.3 Changes in Sales at Constant (1993) P10rices

	£m	% change
1993	146 303	
1997	159 484	9.0

Source: National Statistics 2000b

Case 1.2 A Note on Official Statistics on Retailing

The government regularly changes the method of data collection to improve the quality of their statistics. Major changes tend to occur when an industry or activity, such as retailing, receives significantly greater recognition of its importance. There have been some significant changes and improvements in retailing statistics, particularly since 1996. However, there is sufficient comparability with previous years to give a good indication of trends.

We now have a closer look at the different sectors of retailing.

Retail Industry Structure

The retail industry is made up of a variety of different businesses. Classifying the different businesses will help in studying trends and analysing competition. The Office of National Statistics uses a descriptive classification based on the different types of retailer trading in the UK at present. It uses the following categories:

▶ *Predominantly food stores*. These include retail firms where the sales of food, drink and tobacco account for more than half of total sales by value. They are divided into:
  – *Non-specialized food stores*: these include supermarkets, co-operative stores and convenience store that carry a wide range of food items and also other non-food lines.
  – *Specialized food stores*: these include bakers, butchers, dairies, fishmongers, greengrocers, healthfood shops, delicatessens, off-licences and tobacconists.

▶ *Predominantly non-food stores*. These include retailers where half or more of the total sales come from non-food items. They are divided into:
  – *Non-specialized non-food stores:* these are mixed retailers that sell a wide range of merchandise. They include department stores such as Allders, variety chains such as Woolworth and multi-sector retailers such as Boots.
  – *Textiles, clothing and leather footwear*: these include stores selling fashion, footwear and leather goods, haberdashery and household textiles. They include department stores such as Debenhams and variety chains such as Marks & Spencer, where clothing and household textiles are a dominant feature of the stores.
  – *Household goods stores*: these include china and glass stores, do-it-yourself (DIY) and hardware stores, electrical household appliances, furniture, lighting, music, radio and television.

– *Other stores*: these comprise a wide collection of stores including antique stores, bookshops and stationers, carpet and floorcovering stores, catalogue retailers, computer stores, office supplies, florists, garden centres, pharmacies and drugstores, photo/optical, sports and leisure stores, second-hand shops, toys and games stores, wallpaper shops.

▶ *Non-store retailing and repair.* This includes:
  – General mail order firms.
  – Non-store retailers, including market stalls, door-to-door retailers, vending machines and mobile shops.
  – Repair of personal and household goods.

Table 1.4 gives information on the recent state of these sectors. It shows that non-specialist stores dominate food retailing whereas in the non-food sector, specialist retailers are more important. It also shows that non-store retailing is only a small part of total retailing.

Table 1.4 Retailing Sectors, 1993–97

	Sales £m at current price		Sales £m at constant price	
	1993	**1997**	**1993**	**1997**
Total retail	146 303	178 303	146 303	159 484
Total food	*65 373*	*80 385*	*65 373*	*72 550*
Specialists	13 893	13 328	13 893	12 029
Non-specialists	51 480	67 057	51 480	60 521
Total non-food	*70 093*	*86 833*	*70 093*	*77 668*
Specialists	59 796	74 124	59 796	66 300
Non-specialists	10 297	12 709	10 297	11 368
Non-store	*10 837*	*11 085*	*10 837*	*9 266*

Source: National Statistics 2000b

Table 1.5 shows the different patterns of specialization and non-specialization in food and non-food retailing.

Table 1.5 Sales of Specialist Retailers as Percentage of Total Sales in Category

	1993	**1997**
Specialists food as % of total food	*21.2*	*16.6*
Specialists non-food as % of non-food	85.3	85.4

Source: National Statistics 2000b

These data give a picture of the UK retail industry at the end of the twentieth century. The short-term changes that occurred during the period indicate some of the longer-term more fundamental changes in retailing, but these are considered in Chapter 2. We should note that the data refer to total sales. This means that data for food retailers also includes sales of non-food products, which is an increasing amount of food retailers' sales as the large supermarkets move to a wider product range.

The non-specialist retailer dominates food retailing, whereas the specialist dominates non-food retailing. The share of specialist food retailers is declining as the large supermarkets have been developing their food departments in recent years. Local butchers have been among the worst affected among specialist food retailers. They have suffered because of general health concerns about red meat and the various food scares in recent years, as well as the trend towards eating out and the ready meals and convenience foods that the supermarkets supply. Specialist non-food retailers have benefited from the increasing complexity of consumer products together with the consumer demand for greater variety and choice. The old department store has continued to suffer decline in popularity in the face of more specialist shops that carry a greater range of products.

Retail Business Structure

In 1994 there were over 200 000 retail business firms in the UK (*Annual Abstract of Statistics*, 1997). Of these, 173 000 were small independent retailers with only one outlet or shop. Other firms ranged in size from small local retailers with two or more shops to large multiples operating hundreds of stores. The government uses two ways to define small and large retailers. One way is to class them by turnover. Small retailers are classed as those with sales of less than £4.5 million. This is an arbitrary figure, set in 1996, and it should be adjusted annually to keep pace with inflation. However, the government changes the figure in relatively large steps – the previous level was £3 million.

The government also measures size in terms of the number of stores in the business. Independents are classed as having between one and nine stores, and these would be regarded as small and medium companies; multiples are classed as having ten or more stores, and these would be regarded as large companies. We can use this definition to look at the state of the retail industry in Tables 1.6 and 1.7.

Table 1.6 Retail Outlets by Ownership

Outlets or stores (000)	1984	1994
Owned by independent (1 outlet)	202	173
Owned by large independents (2–9 outlets)	74	52
Owned by multiples (incl. co-ops)	68	65
Total	343	290

Source: National Statistics 1996

Table 1.7 Share of Sales of Independent and Multiple Retailers

Share of sales (%)	1984	1994
Independents (1–9 outlets)	42	32
Multiples (incl. co-ops)	58	68

Source: National Statistics 1996

Note the figures in these two tables do not include very small businesses that have not registered for VAT. However, the number of such retailers is probably very small and would not affect the general conclusion of the tables. The small, independent business is in decline in many part of retailing. The falling number of stores, many of them independents, and the increasing share of the multiples confirm what we have all seen happening in the high street as shops give way to estate agents, banks and insurance brokers, and people go to shop in large supermarkets and out-of-town stores. These changes reflect various economic and social changes in the country and abroad that affect the relative ability of the small retailer to deliver the retail services required.

Retailers take on different forms and sell to us in different ways. For instance, they include those businesses (or *firms*) that:

▸ sell to us through shops, such as the supermarkets and the local corner shop

▸ sell to us through mail order catalogue, such as *Freemans*

▸ sell to us through television, such as *QVC*

▸ sell to us through the Internet, such as *amazon.com*

▸ sell us services, such as *McDonald's*, the local pub and the local bank.

Definition of Retailing

At its simplest, retailing is what retailers do. So, we can define retailing by identifying those features that are common to different types of retailers and how they carry out their business. However, a definition of retailing also indicates the way we study retailing to make it more efficient and profitable, and clearly marks its contribution to our society. Bearing these points in mind, we define retailing in the following way:

> *Retailing is the set of activities that markets products or services to final consumers for their own personal or household use. It does this by organizing their availability on a relatively large scale and supplying them to consumers on a relatively small scale.*

We can note the following points about this definition:

1 Retailers sell to the *final* (non-business) *consumer.* The final consumer buys *final* products that do not undergo any further change outside the home or non-work environment. A business or non-final consumer, on the other hand, buys *intermediate* products for industrial use to produce other goods or services to sell to other people. Timber is a final product when it is sold to a householder to build a fence. On the other hand, timber is an intermediate product when it is sold to a carpenter to build a fence for a customer.

2 Retailers buy in large quantities and sell in small quantities to consumers, who buy for their own personal or household use. This differentiates retailers from *wholesalers* or other industrial suppliers

---

Case 1.3 Point to Note: Business to Business

Many retailers often sell to businesses. A taxi-driver, for instance, is a business consumer who buys petrol to use his/her taxi to provide a service (taxi-ing). However, the same taxi-driver becomes a final (non-business) consumer when he/she buys petrol from the same petrol station to use in the same taxi to take his/her family out. However, the government classes the petrol station as a petrol retailer, because its basic activity is retailing. It buys petrol in large quantities and sells it in small quantities to a very large number of consumers, non-business and business. The majority of its sales are to final consumers.

---

who also buy in very large quantities and sell in smaller quantities. Wholesalers usually sell in quantities that are too large for a buyer's own personal, household or internal business use. Their customers are retailers or other wholesalers, who resell most of what they buy; or else they are industrial firms that produce their own products or services.

3 Retailers often buy products from a wide variety of distant, even global, sources. They then resell them through a nearby store, mail order, television or the Internet and organize the required delivery and collection services.

Point to Note

Most product retailers no longer sell goods made on their premises. However, some retailers do so, for instance:

▶ Many small computer shops build or remodel computers to customer specifications using bought in components.

▶ Florists build flower collections using available stocks of flowers.

---

4 *Retailers can sell services.* Service retailers cover a very diverse range of activities, such as garages, restaurants and banks. These usually require additional manual and technical skills (as in the case of repair services and restaurant services) or knowledge (as in financial services). However, just like product retailers, they invest substantial amounts in their facilities and operating systems. These facilities are only worthwhile if the retailer uses them to deliver large quantities of services within a given period. They do so by selling relatively small amounts of the services to large number of consumers.

5 *Retailers sell to many different consumers.* Retailers are prepared to sell to whoever will buy their products. They are restricted only by legal restraint, such as alcohol to minors and by any discriminatory practices they operate. Some discriminatory practices are illegal, but any discrimination makes it more difficult to be profitable, because it excludes sales to customers and reduces chances of finding the best worker for the job.

Case 1.4 Discussion Point: Service Provider or Service Retailer?

Some activities are recognized as service retailers: for instance, travel agents, restaurants and high street banking. However, can we really say that retailing includes personal services such as hairdressing or dental services that are highly individualized to the customer? Can we really talk of a plumber or gardener as retailing services, or are they just service providers?

One response may be that it depends on whether they apply the techniques and methods of the *retailing process* to improving the delivery of these services and profitability of their businesses.

We could argue that the difference between service providers and service retailers lies in their approach to their customers. Those who sell goods to consumers have usually chosen the retail process to supply their customers. We can illustrate this with the case of the antique dealer. He or she may:

1 undertake commissions from individuals and roam the country looking for specific items. The dealer is then an *agent* for the purchaser.

2 buy items to sell to other dealers on his or her own account. The dealer is effectively a *merchant, middleman* or *wholesaler*.

3 buy items from various sources to sell in an antiques shop. The dealer is then a retailer.

Many service providers such as restaurant chains have also chosen the retail process because that is more profitable. On the other hand, a traditional restaurant owner may behave as a service provider, like the specialist antique dealer, for a small circle of high-spending clients. The relatively closed nature of the business makes it difficult for the restaurateur to respond to the needs of customers generally.

This makes the boundary between service retailers and other consumer service providers relatively fuzzy. However, economic and social pressures are leading many more service providers to see themselves as retailers and adopt the retailing process in supplying their customers.

The Functions of Retailing

Retailers meet the needs of their customers by providing the following essential services:

▶ *Accessibility of location.* Products and services have no value for consumers until they can acquire them. Successful retailers make a range of products and services, often from distant locations, accessible to the consumer. However, the trend in recent years to large out-of-town shopping centres has been seen as disadvantaging inner-city residents, most of whom are already disadvantaged in society. This has created political resistance to further developments. Retailers that support neighbourhood shopping centres create a positive image that can help them in planning applications and in promoting their stores.

▶ *Convenience of timing.* Successful retailers ensure goods and services are available when people require them. The trend in recent years to longer opening hours reflects the social and economic changes where over one in seven people work outside normal hours. They demand greater flexibility in service provision. This has also helped the small local store survive against the cheaper prices of the supermarket chains and other large stores.

▶ *Convenience of size.* Successful retailers adapt the quantities to suit their customers' needs. For instance, supermarkets can sell larger packs and quantity packs because they know shoppers may be stocking up for the week, fortnight or month.

▶ *Information.* In an increasingly complex society, the amount of information that people require to function successfully increases. This applies also to their consumption and choice of products. The government requires a range of information to be provided to the consumer, but supermarkets, for instance, have been regularly providing extra information through their codes of practice.

▶ *Lifestyle support.* Most consumers identify with a particular *lifestyle* that integrates their use of domestic equipment and appliances such as the washing machine and car into their general way of living. These integrated purchases make it difficult and relatively expensive for households and retailers to change direction. They need to guarantee the continuance of an appropriate lifestyle as, for instance, in the choice of a particular computer system. Successful retailers make their selection of appropriate goods and services to support their consumers' lifestyles. When they perform these functions effectively, they create added value for their customers, who will pay for value of the product or service provided. However, this value is *subjective* because what is valuable to one person may be of no value to another. The successful retailer focuses its activities on meeting this subjective value through effective marketing. Customers have to be won continually in the marketplace and the successful retailer builds up a regular customer base and constantly renews the relationship through a combination of service, price and accessibility.

Case 1.5 Discussion Point: Retailers, Wholesalers and Industrial Suppliers

Many businesses combine retail sales to consumers with sales to businesses. For instance, Staples supplies office products, but its selling process marks it out as a retailer. It sells in a relatively open market with no long-term tie-in with its customers, advertises as a retailer and happily sells in small quantities to final consumers. It locates its stores in retail parks to attract its customers and uses its store layout to sell to them on site. Its customers include non-business consumers who buy for their own use and many small businesses who use their products for internal organization and external communication.

Its mail order and internet competitor Viking is a little less of a retailer. Its customers are largely business customers. It does supply small orders, although its prices are usually lower when buying more than one of an item. It also quotes prices exclusive of value added tax, but provides free delivery on items over £30 – not large even for domestic customers.

However, both sellers set out their offerings very much as if they were selling to personal consumers. To a large extent they are, because of the nature of much of what is purchased. Factors such as personal convenience (rather than company value for money) often influence the behaviour of those buying for companies and is especially important for those running their own small business or home office.

Other mixed cases include 'retail banking' which refers to what people call high street banking. This includes selling banking services to personal customers and small business customers. The banks, however, behave very much as service retailers. In the same way, an enterprising supermarket manager may gain contracts to supply rolls to local restaurants from the supermarket's in-store bakery.

Social Role of Retailing

Successful retailers also recognize that people want to see improvement in the general level of consumption and social cohesion over time. Retailers that are seen to contribute to the local or national community generally receive greater political support that allows them to operate more profitably. They enhance their perceived value to the community by acting as a focal point and through effective public relations and promotions campaigns including sponsorship.

Case 1.6 Promoting Iceland through Social Commitment

Iceland, the frozen and chilled food supermarket chain has responded to current social concerns in positive ways:

▶ It commits itself to locating in inner city areas. It supports this position by a free delivery service on large orders.

▶ It was proactive in removing British beef from its products during the BSE crisis.

▶ It was the first supermarket to remove genetically modified ingredients from its own brands and then from all the products it stocked.

▶ It made a major commitment to developing organic food ranges in 2000.

Forms of Retailing

Many retailers provide these services to their customers in traditional ways that require the retail outlet or shop to be close to its customers and use the traditional methods of service, with direct interaction between the customer and the sales assistant using the sales. However, the development of modern technology is increasing the use of other forms of retailing either wholly or partly to replace the store and the sales assistant, leading to other, indirect forms of interaction, as illustrated in Table 1.8.

Table 1.8 Forms of Retailing

	Near	Far
Person to person	Store	Telephone/television
Not person to person	Vending machine	Mail order/email/Internet

1.3 Retail Formats

The category of specialist and non-specialist retailers is a relatively simple way of dividing types of stores. However, from a customer point of view, the sales appeal of a particular store is related to the way the retailer presents the store. The *retail format* is the store package that the retailer presents to the customer. The retailer uses the store to give out messages to customers about the products that will be available, the prices the customer can expect to pay and the range of additional services that the retailer may offer the customer.

Retail formats can be defined according to different attributes:

▶ *Location*. Store location significantly affects customer's expectations. Stores in out-of-town shopping centres will have to offer a superior selection to attract customers. For the factory outlet, the attraction must be a suitable range of high-class brand names at bargain price; for the store at an out-of-town retail centre such as Meadowhall, the expectation is one of quality and range.

▶ *Size*: The size of store affects customer expectations as to the range of products stocked. Small boutiques will be expected to stock an interesting variety of a limited assortment of products.

▶ *Merchandise*. This has a number of aspects that the retailer needs to take note of:
  – *product mix*: the combination of merchandise in a unit. Some stores will keep to a major category such as groceries. Other stores will scramble merchandise by mixing food and major non-food items such as electrical products
  – *merchandise assortment*: choices of merchandise within a classification
  – *breadth*: measured by the number of different merchandise brands stocked
  – *depth of merchandise*: measured by the average number of stock-keeping units (SKUs) within each brand.

▶ *Price*. A supermarket is expected to charge low prices and offer a wide range and deep assortment. Discount stores are expected to provide relatively limited ranges at lower prices. Specialist shops are expected to provide a comprehensive range of products. Specialist food shops are expected to charge relatively high prices. On the other hand, specialist non-food shops may charge high or low prices depending on the category of product that they are selling.

▶ *Atmosphere and service*. Sense of quality or low price; full service or limited service are all signals that customers pick up and use in deciding where to shop.

The limited space in the store means that the retailer has to trade off a greater offering in one sense against a reduced offering elsewhere, unless it is willing to compromise on the spaciousness of the store either through using narrow walkways or high shelving.

There are a number of different retail formats and they include the following types of store:

▶ *Neighbourhood-based stores* that relate mainly to customer convenience. These can be:
  – *General stores*: old-fashioned, with low levels of self-services. Their market is based on convenience. They are most often classified as CTN variety store – confectionery, tobacco and news.
  – *Variety stores*: these will tend to have mixed or scrambled merchandise, the range of which will vary with the size of the store.

      – *Convenience grocery stores*: open till late of an evening, these survive by offering a top-up service for shoppers over a wide range of grocery products. They will stock a wide variety of products, although the assortment will not be very deep.

▶ *One-stop shopping stores.* These stores are designed to provide a complete shopping service for a major part of consumer shopping. They include:

      – *Supermarkets*: mostly for groceries, but increasingly for certain types of clothing and some homewares.

      – *Department stores*: now relatively old-fashioned and losing market share to specialist stores, but originally able to provide a comprehensive service for quality value shopping.

      – *Hypermarkets and superstores*: French and American-based formats respectively, providing a range of shopping requirements under one umbrella.

▶ *Specialist stores.* These may be located in suburban or inner city districts to take advantage of low rents but their markets are at least the whole town. These include small computer shops, fancy dress hire and hobby shops.

▶ *Mass merchandisers.* These provide a comprehensive range within particular product areas; also known as category killers.

▶ *Discounters.* These include:

      – *Discount stores*: these sell limited lines at low prices; stock may change according to buying opportunities; these may be suburban, town centre or out of town, according to size and merchandise.

      – *Off-price stores*: such as factory outlets and retailer's secondary stores that sell overruns, seconds, discontinued lines. Again the retailer varies stock according to buying opportunities. These may be situated out of town or at edge of town to take advantage of lower rents and easier access.

      – *Warehouse clubs*: these are usually located off town centres to take advantage of lower rents, often using non-retail buildings.

Their features are illustrated in Table 1.9.

Table 1.9   Retail Formats

	Location: from customer	Size	Assortment	Price	Atmosphere
General store	Close	Small	Varied	High	Homely
Variety	Near/far	Medium	Narrow	Medium	Varied
Convenience store	Near	Medium	Wide range	High	Cluttered, compact
Supermarket	Near/far edge of town	Large	Vast range, deep and broad	Low	Busy, organized
Discount store	Near/far/town/ edge of town	Medium/large	Narrow	Low	Vastness, loftiness
Supercentre	Far	Very large	Multi-line	Low	Vastness, loftiness
Department store	Town/retail park	Large/very large	Wide range with select items	High	High status

Table 1.9 continued

	Location: from customer	Size	Assortment	Price	Atmosphere
Warehouse club	Far	Very large	Narrow and deep range	Low	Functional
Manufacturer outlet	Far	Small/medium	Narrow in specific lines	Low	Spartan, production oriented
Discount variety	Near/far	Medium/large	Narrow value range	Low	Spacious with clutter
Shopping mall	Far	Very large	Depends on retail presence	Low/ medium	High-quality sealed environment
Selling centre	Far	Medium/large	Varied with changing merchandise	Low	Rummaging and bargain hunting
Television	Far	Medium/large	Anything	Low	Impersonal, interactive, efficient
Second-hand store	Near/far	Small	Limited to appropriate lines	Low	Closed setting
Mass merchandiser	Far	Large	Narrow	Low	Volume with choice
Mail order	Far	Small/medium/ large	Varied and depends on the company	Medium/ high	Remote with personal element
Off-price	Far	Medium	Limited to appropriate lines	Low	Downbeat/ rummaging

1.4 Successful Retailing

Building Success

Retailers, like other businesses, need to make a profit to stay in business. However, making a profit today must not be at the expense of profit tomorrow. The retailer needs to plan the development of its activities to ensure continued success. Success in retailing, as in business generally, is built on success in a number of activities. The successful retailer is characterized by a number of traits, such as:

► *The retailer establishes its market position* to serve the needs of a well-defined group or groups of consumers:
  - It defines its market so it has some specific advantage to offer its customers. Smaller grocery stores operating as convenience stores counterbalance the cost advantages of the large supermarkets by positioning themselves closer to customers, with longer opening hours and more focused product lines.
  - It provides products that are appropriate to its customers' requirements.
  - It adapts to the continuing changes in the market for its products and services.

► *The retailer supports its market position*:
  - It prices the products to maintain perceived value for money relative to competitors.

- It uses appropriate layout and display to evoke the customer's hidden and perceived needs to enhance the shopping experience and so increase sales.
- It promotes the products effectively over the period to sell them according to plan.

▶ *The retailer effectively manages store operations* or mail order, television or Internet sales systems:
- It forecast sales over a period so that it can *stock the right amount.*
- It provides *good customer service* by treating customers as individuals and that the service is geared to their requirements.
- It provides *security* for customers and employees by protecting the store from theft and damage and guarding the health and safety of employees and customers.

▶ *The retailer manages behind the scenes operations effectively:*
- It has appropriate administration and personnel management procedures to ensure that supporting activities are carried out efficiently.
- It has proper financial management and control procedures to protect against fraud, ensure that it pays its bills and make sufficient profit.
- It takes advantage of developments in technology, in physical distribution and in information technology in planning *effective distribution* to ensure supplies reach the store as required and that the goods are delivered to the customer within the expected time.

▶ *The retailer maintains its business and community standing:*
- It uses appropriate publicity to show that it understands its local community and deals with consumers in a socially acceptable manner.
- Larger businesses, in particular, pay due regard to environmental concerns and contribute to the wider community by participating in various community events and by supporting community activities. These activities help retailers in dealings with local planning authorities and support their relations with central government.

Business Strategy

This success requires management at different levels, according to the structure of the business. The senior management has to develop a business plan based on the most important factors in the organization's success. It needs to:

▶ identify the strategic forces acting on the firm

▶ identify direction of change

▶ develop strategic responses

▶ ensure that there is an appropriate organizational structure through which the strategic response can be communicated and implemented.

These factors are known as strategic variables and decisions relating to them form part of the retailer's *business strategy* to achieve its profit or welfare goals. This strategy is based on an appropriate analysis of the *political*, *economic*, *social* and *technological* factors (PEST analysis) that affect the ability of the firm to successfully supply its markets. As part of the process of developing its strategy, the retailer will set out its longer-term aims and goals, sometimes incorporated into a *mission statement*. This sets out what the company aims to achieve in terms of serving particular markets and how it intends to do so. The mission statement is a means of promoting the company ethos and encapsulates the thinking of the senior management as to the strategic variables affecting future profitability.

Successful planning of the business should lead to financial success for the retailer, measured in monetary rewards for the owners of the business. Measuring this financial success does, however, need to take account of the size and legal and financial structure of the business.

Types of Business

The legal form of a business is important as it affects the size to which the business can grow, how the business can acquire and use funds, taxation, internal organization and decision-making. The major types of business in retailing are:

▶ the unincorporated business: sole proprietorship or partnership

▶ the private company

▶ the public company

▶ co-operatives.

Unincorporated Businesses

Most small retailers are unincorporated businesses. This means that there is no legal distinction between the business and its owner or owners, who are working as *self-employed* persons and who may also employ others in the business.

▶ Just one person owns a sole proprietorship (or trader). The owner invests his or her funds (*equity investment*) in the business. The owner may also borrow from banks and other finance companies, and the loans are usually secured on the assets of the business or on the owner's home or property. The owner is liable for all the debts of the business and if she or he defaults on repayment, the lender (*creditor*) can sell the assets to recover the debt. The usually limits the owner to one store, because of the effort and risks involved.

▶ A *partnership* is owned by two or more people, and the business is run according to a partnership agreement. Each partner is liable at law for the actions of the other partners in regard to the business. The risks involved and the difficulties in monitoring the partners' contributions usually limit the number of partners in a retail business to two or three, though family partnerships may be larger. They also limit the number of stores a partnership can run.

Companies

Larger retail businesses are usually corporations, that is, they have been legally incorporated and possess a separate legal identity. They were originally called joint-stock companies to distinguish them from partnerships, but they are now called simply companies. Companies are owned by *shareholders* according to the amount of shares they have in the company. A board of directors runs the company on behalf of the shareholders.

Practically all companies take advantage of *limited liability*. This means that as long as the shares are fully paid-up, shareholders cannot lose any more money. Limited liability protects investors who are unable to take an active part in the running of the company and encourages the flow of funds required for most modern businesses. In practice, limited liability for the small business does not always mean limited liability for the major shareholders, who often have to give personal guarantees of some extra security to banks that provide much of the loan capital.

Profits earned by the business can be *retained* for reinvestment (ploughed back) or *distributed* among the shareholders. Retained profits appear as the *reserves* in the accounts. Distributed profits are paid out as a *dividend* to the shareholders according to their size of their shareholding.

Case 1.7 Share Values

In the UK, each share has a *nominal* value (for instance, £1) that corresponds to the nominal share capital in the company's accounts. If the nominal value has already been paid to the business, the share is *fully paid-up*.

Shares can be traded on the market. The price at which shares sell depends on buyers' expectations about future earnings, rates of interest and other factors. The market value of the company is the total market value of the shares.

The market price of shares does not affect the actual assets of the company. Poor shares price, however, make it difficult for the company to borrow money.

Most medium-sized retailers and some large companies are private companies. They have the designation Ltd (or Limited) after their names. The directors may only raise money through personal contact and from those who would normally have a good understanding of that area of business. This often restricts the growth of the business, but does maintain a greater degree of secrecy about their operations. The larger or more rapidly growing private companies are often financed by venture capitalists. These businesses specialize in funding companies, taking a majority holding in shares and selling them on later when the company has become more established and may go public (becomes a public company).

A *public company* carries the designation plc (that is, public limited company) after its name. The directors may raise money by selling shares and loans to the general public. However, the company is subject to more stringent regulation, particularly in relation to the disclosure of information. Most UK companies raise funds by placing their shares with (selling to) financial institutions. A growing number, however, sell shares through the Alternative Investment Market (AIM), supervised by the Stock Exchange. A small number of companies have a Stock

Exchange *quotation*. Shareholders in these *quoted public companies* can sell their shares through the Stock Exchange. This gives them a wider market for their shares and ultimately for their financing.

> ⇨ Note: private and public companies are both privately owned by individuals or other companies and are different from *public corporations*, which are companies owned by the state and are usually responsible for a major part of a particular industry.

Co-operatives

The co-operative movement has been established in UK retailing for over 150 years. Originally made up of a very large number of local co-operative societies around the country, they covered everything from shops to funeral to banking and insurance. The challenges of modern retailing have seen a succession of mergers during recent decades with the Co-operative Retail Services now the dominant organization having merged with the other major group the Co-operative Wholesale Society in the late 1990s. The distinguishing element here is that the business is owned by its members, who receive a *dividend* according to the amount they have invested in the business.

The Value of the Business

The value of the business is the price it would fetch if it were sold as a going concern in the open market. It depends on how investors view the potential for future profit, taking into account the business's previous financial history, market growth and potential competition and the state of the economy. It includes the value of the property owned plus the *goodwill* of the business. Goodwill is the extra value the owners have acquired through building up customer loyalty, giving it a competitive edge in the market and therefore higher profits. The market value of a business is important because:

▶ it provides long-term wealth for its owners

▶ it provides the asset base on which loans are made

▶ it affects the price at which firms can raise new money through selling shares.

In larger organizations, modern management is driven by *shareholder value*. If management is not seen to be increasing shareholder value in line with competitors, the management risks being replaced directly or through a takeover. Small businesses also need to take account of the value of the business for resale or transfer.

Viability

Retailers are part of a supply chain. Longer-term relationships are becoming more important. However, suppliers will not commit themselves on a long-term basis unless they are satisfied about the viability of the retail business. Retailers are also concerned about the viability of their suppliers and will, as far as they can, assess their viability. This may be difficult for some areas of retailing, such as fashion. However, analysts can make some financial assessment of the company based on it *debt position*, *profitability* and *liquidity*.

Debt Position

The firm must have sufficient assets to provide security for its present and future borrowings. A firm may be able to borrow the money at a rate of interest below its expected profit rate, because a loan is less risky for the lender than taking a share in the business. This increases the net return to the owners of the business if the investment proves profitable. The original owners also retain a greater control over their business.

However, high levels of debt can cause problems:

▶ If the firm does not make sufficient profit to pay the interest on its debts, it becomes insolvent.

▶ The firm will find it difficult to raise new money from expansion and will face pressure from its bankers and financial institutions to sell off assets, or even parts of its business, to reduce its borrowing.

Firms have to keep a balance between the amount of debt and equity investment (= value of shares in the company). This is called the *gearing* ratio and is illustrated in Table 1.10.

Table 1.10 Gearing Ratios

If borrowing is	And funds provided by shares and retained profit are	Then the gearing ratio is	Then the company is
25% of total funds	75% of total funds	1:3	Low geared
50% of total funds	50% of total funds	1:1	Moderately geared
75% of total funds	25% of total funds	3:1	Highly geared

Profitability

The actual profit for the firm is the operating profit *minus* taxes, interest payments and any other special payments the retailer has to make. *Operating profit* is the profit made from the retailer's current operations. It is equal to:

Turnover (sales revenue) – Cost of sales – Administration and other costs

A retailer needs to keep a control on administration and other costs, particularly in a large group with several units. This can be particularly important during the early stages of a recession when interest rates are also high; otherwise the group may become insolvent even though individual retail outlets are operating at a profit. Good financial management is also important in keeping interest payments and taxation down.

Liquidity

The firm must have sufficient *liquid assets* (cash or credit) to pay its bills as and when required. Modern accounts now show the firm's liquid assets through its *cash flow statement*. Liquidity changes as the company's *bank* and *cash balances* change and the business must manage its cash flow profile through the appropriate timing of investment and its returns. The company must avoid tying up money in excessive amounts of stocks and debtors, as they can badly affect liquidity and may not convert into actual cash.

1.5 The Context of Retail Business Planning

The retailer needs to develop its business plans within the political, economic, social and technological context of its activities as these affect demand and supply conditions in the markets. These are grouped under five aspects here and considered in later chapters.

Structural Change

This refers to those longer-term changes that fundamentally affect demand and supply conditions in the markets. Analysing these changes should identify the basic direction in which the business should be developing and those new products and services the retailer could provide. For example, the permissive attitude of the 1970s and 1980s that encouraged large-scale out-of-town shopping developments was replaced by a much more restrictive attitude in the 1990s. These changes reflected changing perceptions of the relative costs and benefits of these types of developments and consequently have affected the longer-term plans of retailers.

Politically, the large retail firms are now much more exposed to the public gaze and government scrutiny, because of their importance in the consumption process. The movement towards wider European integration and world agreements on trade and tariffs (taxes on imports and subsidies on exports) have exposed UK markets to greater penetration by foreign retailers as well as opening up opportunities for UK retailers to expand abroad.

In social and economic terms, retailers have had to become much more customer driven and evaluate their services in relation to their role in the consumption process of households and individuals. In this way the retailer can look for those changes that are going to affect its position in the market.

Economic and technological changes have affected the value chain in retailing. Starting from the late 1970s the role of logistics and distribution in contributing to profit has become more widely appreciated. This has led to greater cooperation and partnership with suppliers. Retailers now have to make increasing use of electronic data interchange (EDI) and electronic point of sale information (EPOS) to manage their supplies to the customer.

Short-Term Fluctuations in Retail Activity

Retailers must also anticipate the fluctuations in incomes, inflation and unemployment in the national and international economy that are superimposed over the longer-term changes outlined above. These fluctuations occur over a relatively short time (up to five years) and affect the demand and the costs of supplying the market. Retailers need to assess these carefully when planning investments as well as their normal seasonal patterns of stocking.

The Market Position of the Retailer Relative to Actual and Potential Rivals

This depends on creating identifiable products with strong selling points; and on the market structure, the number and size of firms, which limit its freedom of action in setting prices or in product specification. Each retailer has to develop some form of competitive advantage, which provides it with some edge over its competitors for specific customer segments and for each of its stores in their local markets.

The retailer must position itself according to the quality range and depth of its products and associated services. The services it provides must include the basic ones of convenience and accessibility. However, it must also decide on those services that help boost sales such as after-sales services, warranties and delivery. Its stores must also position themselves in terms of accessibility and natural attraction, through layout and internal design. Shops themselves can be used to support product differentiation by supplying own-branded goods.

Retail management should provide the market with the required products at appropriate prices. The management must acquire a sound customer database that is continually updated. These customers must be provided with an adequate product range or *variety*, that is, number of different types or classes of products. Each product line should have sufficient depth or *assortment* of different styles and brands. Keeping the market supplied through good logistical management requires cooperative activity through the supply chain. This will then allow the various shops to minimize the level of *stock-outs* (items not in stock) that not only lose sales but also deter customers in the future.

Internal Management

Appropriate management structure, thinking and attitudes are important factors in driving companies forward to success. The changing economics and technology of supply and communication with customers, the increasing customer orientation of a service-driven society and the closer integration of retailing with consumer lifestyles have all made quality one of the most important factors in a company success. Communication, teamworking, training and product knowledge are all matters that the retailer must address.

Understanding the Market: Buying and Selling

The market system is a crucial economic, political and social institution in modern economies. Most modern societies rely on it to solve the problem of what to produce, how to produce and what resources to use.

Governments do not let the market system go unregulated because sometimes it can produce unsatisfactory results. A retailer needs to understand its basic operation and its lessons to understand the changes that take place and avoid unnecessary problems. It also needs to understand where and why the government may regulate the market so that it can make its business plans accordingly.

The Market Process

A *market* is any situation where general buying and selling take place. Buyers *demand* a product when they are willing to pay for it; sellers *supply* the product according to the price they can get. Buyers and sellers between them determine how much of a product is sold, of what quality and at what price according to the balance of supply and demand. Changes in market conditions affect the balance of supply and demand and cause changes in sales and prices.

The attraction of using markets to decide on outputs of different products is that they are usually self-adjusting, that is, they move fairly quickly *towards* balancing supply and demand by changing price. A shortage usually leads to a rise in price and a surplus to a fall in price, as illustrated in the 'Market Adjustment' box.

Market Adjustment

When too much is produced:

▶ there is a surplus

▶ sellers reduce price and cut output

▶ buyers buy more

▶ surplus is eliminated.

When too little is produced:

▶ there is a shortage

▶ sellers raise prices and increase output

▶ buyers want to buy less

▶ shortage is eliminated.

Changes in Demand and Supply

Changes in income, the arrival of new products and changing consumer perceptions of products all affect demand. Demand increases when people want to buy *more at the same price* or are willing to *pay a higher price for the same amount*. This happens when income increases (although people buy less of some inferior products such as bread and potatoes), or when people perceive the value for money to have gone up relative to other items of expenditure. Conversely, demand decreases when incomes fall or the perceived value for money relative to other goods has fallen.

The availability and costs of supply will also change when the underlying conditions change. Supply increases when suppliers *offer more at the same price* or *reduce the prices they require*. This happens when costs of supply have fallen, for whatever reason. Conversely, supply decreases when suppliers *offer less at the same price* or *increase the prices they require*. This happens when costs of supply have risen, for whatever reason.

The Effect of Changes in Supply and Demand Conditions

The market response to changes in demand and supply depends on two factors:

▶ The effect on profitability. Any change in prices (relative to costs) or sales causes a change in profitability for businesses in the industry. An increase in profitability attracts new investment as existing firms expand or more new firms enter the industry than leave. Conversely, a decrease in profitability causes disinvestment as existing firms contract or more leave the industry than enter it.

▶ How long it takes suppliers and consumers to adjust to the changes. Most suppliers can adjust only slowly, *in the short term*, to unexpected change in the market. Most consumers make some changes fairly easily in relation to frequent, recurrent purchases. However, some decisions involving expensive or long-lasting purchases are an investment in a way of life. In these cases, consumers adjust to changes in supply only over a period of time. This means that there can be some large initial changes in price in the short term. In the *long term*, however, as supply and demand slowly come back into balance, prices will tend to move back towards their original level. These two factors enable us to predict the direction of change according to increases or decreases in demand or supply, as shown in Table 1.11.

Table 1.11   Effect on Prices and Sales When Demand or Supply Change

	Increase in demand	Decrease in demand	Increase in supply	Decrease in supply
Short-term response	Shortage occurs	Surplus occurs	Surplus occurs	Shortage occurs
Sales	Rise	Fall	Rise	Fall
Price	Rises	Falls	Falls	Rises
Average profitability	Rises	Falls	Rises	Falls
Failure rate for businesses	Falls	Rises	Falls	Rises
Longer-term response				
Capacity	Expands	Contracts	Expands	Contracts
Sales	Rise	Fall	Rise	Fall
Price	Falls	Rises	Falls	Rises
Average profitability	Falls to normal levels	Rises to normal levels	Falls to normal levels	Rises to normal levels
Failure rate for businesses	Rises	Falls	Rises	Falls
Industry capacity	Continues to expand until profitability at normal level	Continues to contract until profitability at normal level	Continues to expand until profitability at normal level	Continues to contract until profitability at normal level

The most important implication of this analysis for retailers is that changes in demand or supply bring changes in profitability in the short term. This leads to changes in property and company values. It also leads to changes in capacity in the long term, which will tend to push profitability back towards normal levels with corresponding adjustments in property and company values. It is important not to jump on to a bandwagon of change just *after* everybody else because any investment will be overpriced and will yield falling returns as the market returns to normal.

Case 1.8 Example: Seasonal Variations in Prices

Seasonal factors often cause variations in the price of various products such as fresh goods. These variations are caused by a regular pattern of supply and demand changes that average out over the year.

We know from experience that most fresh foods have a particular season during which they are plentiful. At the beginning and the end of the season, the quantity available is low and prices are high. At the height of the season, however, the quantity available is high and the price is low. Price and output move in opposite directions and so we conclude that it is mostly the supply curve that has been shifting. This makes sense, as our tastes do not tend to change very much over the year, except perhaps for certain items such as turkeys at Christmas.

Problems in the Market

Retailers need to understand that there is always pressure on governments to intervene in the way markets work. Two important areas in relation to retailing are:

▶ The market does not work properly because of monopoly power. Some retailers have recently suffered investigation because of the feeling that they were a part of 'rip-off Britain', charging too high prices.

▶ There are external benefits or costs. For example, the government taxes road users to reduce congestion and pollution. Zoning developments and other planning controls come under this as well.

Case 1.9 Example: Changes in Price of a New Product over Time

An *innovation* occurs when a new product or process comes on stream. The innovation takes time to *diffuse* or spread through the population. Consumers take time to accept or buy a new product. Producers take time to adapt to new ways of producing a product or to switch to producing a new product instead of an older type product.

The price of a new product varies over time according to its rate of diffusion. Initially price tends to be relatively high as demand grows slowly and then takes off very rapidly, followed by a slowing down of the growth of demand. The firms who produce the product first have an advantage, but not if they produce too far in advance of the market. As the market grows the firms find that their demand is increasing rapidly so that they enjoy high rates of profit. However, the excess profits attract new entrants after a time and these will come in quite quickly. As a result, the price tends to fall fairly quickly, as does profitability.

References

National Statistics (1996) *Annual Abstract of Statistics*, London: The Stationery Office.
National Statistics (1997) *Annual Abstract of Statistics*, London: The Stationery Office.
National Statistics (2000a) *Annual Abstract of Statistics*, London: The Stationery Office.
National Statistics (2000b) *Business Monitor SDM28*, London: The Stationery Office.

Structural Change in the Retail Environment

This chapter considers the following issues:

- ► Changes in the retail environment.

- ► Sociodemographic changes.

- ► Socio-economic changes.

- ► Sociocultural forces.

Structural Change in the Retail Environment

Introduction and Core Concepts

This chapter focuses on *structural changes* in our society and their impact on retailing. These changes continue to occur over a long period of time and fundamentally change the ways in which we use retailers and the ways in which retailers supply our needs and wants.

2.1 Changes in the Retail Environment

Changes in our natural and social environment are constantly affecting what consumers want and how retailers can provide them with their requirements. Consumers are changing:

▶ what they buy as income, technology and lifestyles change

▶ who they buy from as retail formats change and supermarkets move into fashion

▶ how they are buying as the Internet brings new and better deals and to save time

▶ where they are buying as government policy affects where stores can relocate

▶ when they buy as shops open longer and new convenience formats spread.

Retailers are interested in these changes because they affect how much people want to buy and the costs of providing customers with the products and services that they want. For instance:

▶ A change in the birth rate (number of children born per 100 000 of the population per year) has an effect on consumer spending, particularly for retailers that sell babywear and related items.

▶ Changes in social attitudes to work, home and leisure affect the amount and kinds of clothing and recreational goods that people buy.

▶ Political decisions relating to the environment, shopping locations and fair trade affect where and how retailers can trade.

▶ Changes in technology bring new attitudes to buying products and services and to better organization of the supply chain.

In order to analyse the effect of these changes on retailers, we identify four types of changes: *odd events and unpredictable changes, seasonal changes, short-term changes*, and *structural changes*.

Odd Events and Unpredictable Changes

The number of customers entering the store may change every day and customer requirements may change each time they enter the store. Many of these changes balance out over a week or month so that the retailer knows fairly well how many customers will come into its store on a normal day. The retailer will also be able to supply its customers in the usual way.

However, there may be many disturbances to this pattern of trade. For instance, the demand for some products is sensitive to the weather as well as the time of year. Some products are so sensitive that larger retailers purchase detailed local weather forecasts to guard against unexpected changes in demand. The UK Meteorological Office has established a business unit called the Weather Initiative. This uses statistical analysis of weather and sales data to develop demand forecasts for various products. The privately owned Weather Action also supplies more general long-term weather forecasts (Robinson 1998). Local events, such as festivals, also affect demand and may increase security costs significantly. Retailers can make suitable preparations for these events as they get to know of them in advance.

Some events, however, are less predictable and harder to deal with. These include various disasters and strikes, at home and abroad, that can affect customer demand and interfere with the retailers' supplies as well. A strike at a major employer in a small town will have a serious effect on consumer spending power in the area during and shortly after the strike. A shutdown of a major employer, on the other hand, is a much more serious problem and may be longer lasting. It requires a significantly different approach in dealing with it. Strikes in other countries, such as those by French lorry drivers and dockers, may also cause problems for some retailers or their suppliers. Food scares are a particular problem for grocery retailers.

Most of these situations do not have a significant effect on annual trading figures, because they tend to balance one another out. However, the retailer has to be aware of those temporary situations that can occur and build enough flexibility into its plans to be able to deal with them. Otherwise it may lose out on profitable opportunities or be saddled with unexpectedly heavy costs.

Seasonal Changes

Seasonal or periodic changes are those that occur in a regular and predictable way during the year. The retailer has to change its product range (merchandise), prices and other aspects of the store to meet changing customer requirements during the year. The four natural seasons of spring, summer, autumn and winter have a significant influence on customer demand and also on the availability of some products.

However, the retailer may need to take account of other factors in consumer spending. For instance, there was a general perception of a poor summer in 2000. This had a serious effect on demand for seasonal items including summer clothing lines. The problem was compounded by the relatively harsh trading conditions with many retailers cutting prices. For example, the discount retailer Brown and Jackson, which owns Poundstretcher, What Everyone Wants and Your More Store, reported a 14 per cent drop in like-for-like sales over the period from July to mid-August (Snowdon 2000). Retailers had to determine how far trading problems were caused by the weather and how much reflected longer-term trends in the market.

Retailers may also have to be aware that it may not be appropriate to go with just the four seasons. Some fashion retailers, for instance, change their stock ten times a year in order to maintain customer interest and spending.

Short-Term Changes or Fluctuations

These are changes that occur over a longer period but are independent of the season of the year. Retailers may experience changes in demand or costs or problems in supply that last for period of a year or more. Most of these are linked to change in the level of income and consumer spending, government tax and spending policies and the level of interest rates. These are short-term changes because they follow a rough pattern and tend to balance out over a period of a few years. This means that retailers will face a different situation (better or worse) in the following year.

For instance, when the economy is in poor shape, people become less confident about the future and they cut down on consumer borrowing. However, younger people are more optimistic than older people and so the effect will be greater in those areas where older consumers spend more heavily. Retail spending as a whole will grow more slowly than in previous years and in some areas may fall. However, as economic prospects improve, consumers become more confident and retail spending grows more quickly again.

Retailers need to use forecasts of customer demand and cost levels in making their plans for the following year. Trade magazines often publish reports about demand and consumer spending, usually derived from market research reports published by market research companies such as Mintel and Key Note.

Some one-off events or a series of them may also be significant enough to have effects lasting a year or more. For instance, the conversion of some large building societies to banks between 1997 and 2000, and the conversion of some mutual insurance companies into joint-stock companies gave windfall gains of shares or cash bonuses to a large number of customers. These one-off gains helped some sectors of retailing as consumers spent part of their gains on household goods. This would have little effect over a three- or four-year period, however, because some of this spending would be spread over a period and some of it at the expense of future spending on replacing worn out goods.

Structural Changes or Trends

Structural changes are those changes that occur over a much longer period or have much more enduring effects. They have a long-term effect on the basic ways in which goods and services are provided. These changes include:

▶ *Demographic changes*, such as a change in the birth rate (number of children born per 100 000 of the population per year). A fall in the birth rate as the UK has experienced in recent years has an effect on consumer spending, particularly for retailers that sell babywear and related items. It will also have an effect over a number of years as this smaller group of children grows up.

▶ *Technological changes*, such as developments in computer technology (hardware) and in management techniques (software). These changes underlie many of the other changes because they affect the range of choices available to consumers and suppliers. The application of technological change is often inseparable from the other changes it helps to bring about.

▶ *Economic changes*, such as the long-term increases in real income. In real terms the average person in Britain is about 80 per cent better off than a similar person would have been a generation ago. However, people spend their money in different ways as they become better off, and this creates different opportunities for retailers. Economic change also brings social change.

▶ *Social changes*, such as the increase in young women in full-time employment. This has led to significant changes in attitudes to the home and leisure that have affected spending on clothing and recreational products.

▶ *Political changes*, such as the government decision in 1993 to restrict further out-of-town shopping developments. These have a significant impact on where and how people can shop and retailers can trade.

▶ *Cultural changes*, such as the role of shopping as a leisure activity. We may debate the extent to which people regard shopping as a leisure activity or even as a social activity. However, the more affluent Americans spend more time in shopping than Europeans. Retail parks, shopping centres and so on have to be attractive and filled with leisure activities to increase their customers.

These structural changes can be used to explain changes in modern retailing and also indicate where future changes may go. We can use them to explain phenomena such as:

▶ the growth of the supermarket in grocery retailing from the 1960s to their domination of the grocery trade in the 1990s

▶ the growth of out-of-town shopping centres during the 1970s and 1980s and government restrictions from 1993 that have slowed growth of such centres

▶ changes in retail formats in other areas of retailing, such as the growth of specialist fashion retail stores and the relative decline of fashion variety stores and department stores in the 1990s

▶ the growth of large firms in retailing generally

▶ the integration of supply chain activities.

Changes in the Level of Retail Activity

The four components of change work together to determine the level of demand for different products. Conceptually, we can describe the level of demand in a sector at any one time by the following equation:

Level of demand = Trend value (associated with long-term structural demand)
+ Fluctuation (caused by year-to-year changes in the economy)
+ Seasonal effect (caused by the time of year)
+ Odd event effect (caused by changes in weather, strikes and so on)

Fluctuations, seasonal effects and odd events may have a positive or negative effect on the level of demand compared with the trend value.

In practice, short-term forecasts of demand for the next 12 to 24 months use various statistical techniques to *extrapolate* or carry forward the pattern of the last few years, making any adjustment thought necessary for changes in government policy or other events.

The model above only indicates the level of sales retailers should be experiencing. It does not indicate precisely what products the retailer should be selling or, for instance, the particular designs a fashion retailer should be stocking. However, it shows the retailer has to manage short-term changes in its markets as a different problem from planning the long-term direction of the business. The retailer can only manage the longer-term direction of the business by carefully analysing the long-term trends in the industry.

There are two approaches to look at future trends. One is to understand what has been happening in the past, taking into account the factors that have been mentioned. This means going back over a number of years to understand what has been happening and see how the trends extend into the future. Retailers should also use the complementary approach of writing possible future scenarios. This approach takes account of developments in technology and relies for its effectiveness on testing ideas against current trends rather than ignoring them. It is a useful method of encouraging retailers to think creatively about the future and not become too narrow or blinkered in their thinking about the future. A number of environmental indicators help the retailer to plan for the future.

2.2 Sociodemographic Change

Population Changes

The population of a country is important to retailers because it defines the primary market for most retailers.

Case 2.1 Delimiting the Market

The retail market for a product in the UK depends mostly on the population of the UK, their spending habits and the income they have to support those habits. However, there are some customers from outside the UK, just as some people from the UK buy outside the UK. Sales to non-UK residents come from two sources: *tourists*, both business and non-business; and *mail order* and *Internet* customers.

Foreign tourists account for most sales to non-UK customers, but they still account for less than 4 per cent of total spending on all goods and services in the UK (British Tourist Authority 2000). Their impact on traditional goods retailing is significantly less, but certain retailers need to take account of the foreign element in their sales. Airports are shopping areas that will stock different assortments of products more suited to the traveller. It is important to note that airport retailing has become an increasingly profitable part of the retail sector over the last decade.

Business commuters and daytrippers as well as tourists may patronize local shopping centres and also provide demand for service retailers in the area.

As Table 2.1 shows, the population has been growing at about 3 per cent every ten years. The growth rate is similar to Western Europe as a whole, but the population in North America and the rest of the world has been growing at a much faster rate.

Table 2.1   Population of the UK

	1961	1971	1981	1991	1999
	\multicolumn{5}{c}{**Population (millions)**}				
UK	52.8	55.9	56.4	57.8	59.5
Britain	51.4	54.4	54.8	56.2	57.8

Source: National Statistics 2001

⇨ UK population data are taken from the population census carried out every ten years, the most recent one being in 2001. The Office of Population Censuses and Surveys updates the data every year based on records of births, deaths, immigration and emigration.

Official forecasts show the population trend continuing, with the population of Europe virtually stagnant. This has several implications:

▶ Retailers have to rely more on the growth in income than in population for new opportunities. This increases the competition that retailers will face from other retailers in the UK.

▶ The relative stagnation in the population in Western Europe will also encourage successful European firms to venture into Britain as a way of expanding their markets, aided, of course, by membership of the European Union.

▶ The diminishing relative importance of Western Europe will expose their retailers to greater international pressures. They will have to seek more active expansion abroad and be subject to greater pressures from foreign retailers.

Population Structure

There have been two significant changes in the population structure. One change has been the increasing number of elderly people, as people have been living longer. This is a worldwide phenomenon caused by increased standard of living and greater awareness of health issues. The second change has been the increasing average age of the population. This is partly because of the increased number of older people, but it also reflects the long-term decline in the birth rate, which has been the pattern in developed economies.

The ageing of the population brings a different pattern of demand for goods and services, as older people have different domestic and leisure requirements from younger people. Increasing longevity has been associated with higher income and this has increased the importance of the products and services for the elderly with a corresponding increase in the number of outlets required to service their needs.

Household Structure

Household structure refers to the way the population is grouped into households. A household is a group of people sharing certain domestic arrangements in common, chiefly the preparation and consumption of meals (from *Social Trends*), although households today seem to eat together less often. Table 2.2 shows how household structure has changed over the last few decades.

The large increase in one- and two-person households has come about because of the increase in pensioner households and also a large increase in non-pensioner households. The better health of older people and their increased income enables them to continue their independent lives. Non-pensioner households have increased for several reasons:

▶ There has been a massive increase in the number of dwellings available over this period. New retail developments have taken place to accommodate the location and pattern of these developments.

▶ Rising income per head has encouraged younger people to set up home on their own or to cohabit. This has driven the increase in the DIY and home improvement.

Table 2.2 Household Structure in the UK

	1961	1971	1981	1991	2000
Number of households (millions)	16.3	18.6	20.2	22.4	23.9
Household size (% in each category)					
1 person	14	18	22	27	29
2 persons	30	32	32	34	35
3 persons	23	19	17	16	16
4 or more persons	34	31	29	23	21
Household type (% in each category)					
1 person/2+ unrelated adults	16	22	27	30	32
Couple without children	26	27	26	28	29
Couple/lone parent with children/ multi-family	58	51	47	44	39

Source: National Statistics 2001

▶ The increase in economic security for women means that they become less inclined to marry or remain married and family sizes become smaller (Becker 1993). This has had a significant impact on grocery shopping and apparel retailing.

The size and structure of the household has implications for household spending patterns. For instance, the modern family household with fewer children, or none at all, has a different spending pattern from the larger household with more children.

2.3 Technology and Economic Change

The *economy* is a term used to denote the patterns of economic activity in a country, including production and employment, income, consumption and living conditions. It includes three different parts:

▶ *The formal economy*, where goods and services are produced and sold in the market or are provided by the government. It provides the largest part of a country's income, output and employment and is the easiest to measure and compare with other countries. The most useful and widely used measure of output and income is gross domestic product as explained in Chapter 1.

▶ *The informal, hidden* or *black economy*, where goods and services are bought and sold, legally or illegally, but the sale or income earned is not recorded or declared for tax purposes. It is difficult to measure the size of the informal economy, but various estimates put it at up to 10 per cent of the output of the formal economy. No retailer should be engaged in it.

▶ *The household economy*, where goods and services are produced in the home for domestic consumption or traded within a group of neighbours. It is difficult to estimate the amount produced in the household economy, but it is probably worth between a third and a half of the income produced in the formal economy.

Most adults can chose to work in the formal and in the household economy to varying degrees. Some people, however, such as women with children, may continue to work only in the household economy. They provide domestic services that have a direct money equivalent in the formal economy. They also provide other services, such as childcare, that are do not have an equivalent in the formal economy but have a clear value within their own specific household.

Increases in Output and Income

Increases in output are measured by changes in GDP. Table 2.3 illustrates the substantial increase in GDP in recent decades.

Table 2.3   Index of Output (1990 = 100)

	1969	1994	% change in GDP during period
GDP	63.0	103.5	64.3

Source: National Statistics 1995

Case 2.2 Index Numbers – a Reminder

Index numbers are widely used in comparing changes in variables such as GDP over time and between places. So here is a good place to remind ourselves how they work.

We select a base year, say 1990. Then output in 1990 is the base figure and is set equal to 100. We calculate the index for other years in relation to this base figure. For instance, the index of output in 1994 is given by the formula:

Index for 1994 = (GDP in 1994/GDP in 1990) × 100

We can also compare changes between two years by comparing their respective index numbers. So the increase in output between 1969 and 1994 is given by

Increase in output = {(1994 index – 1969 index)/1969 index} × 100%
= {(103.5 – 63.0) /63.0} × 100%
= 64.3%

The rise in output has been much greater than the increase in population, making people on average better off than 30 years ago. This increase in income has been associated with four other changes that have had a significant effect on retailing:

▶ changes in retail technology

▶ changes in time use

▶ change in the patterns of working and household activity

▶ changes in consumer technology.

Retail Technology

Technology consists of the resources and methods that are used to produce products and services. *Labour-intensive* industries use relatively small amounts of, or relatively cheap, equipment, but large amounts of labour, some of which can be highly skilled in a number of different ways. Their technology is relatively simple and the cost of their products tends to be relatively high. *Capital-intensive* industries use large amounts of equipment, but smaller amounts of labour. Their technology is complex, but the cost of their products tends to be relatively low. Much of the labour employed is not highly skilled with a smaller proportion having specialist skills only.

The traditional independent fashion shop and the multiple fashion retailer illustrate two differing technologies in retailing which may share similar product ranges. The independent store relies on a range of manufacturers or wholesalers for its supply needs. The store owner may even make trips to places such as France or Italy to pick up items available on display. He or she uses a significant amount of skill in judging the local needs and in having suitable stock available. The local chain store, however, uses sophisticated computer systems to maintain an appropriate flow of stock, has a small core of staff who make buying decisions and may also lay down specifications for manufacturers. Distribution is through their own or contracted specialist distributors. Many of their staff do not need a high level of skill, except in customer interaction.

New Technology and Economic growth

Retailing, like every other industry, is affected by changes in technology. New technology can lead to cheaper and better products or services (for example, the price of domestic televisions keep on coming down) or it can make new products (such as digital television) available. New technology has also improved the consumer supply chain by reducing distribution costs and improving the availability of products to the consumer. For instance, retailers now use computer technology to exchange information with manufacturers and distributors in order to improve the availability of products for the consumer. Grocery distribution also makes increasing use of multi-temperature trucks that can carry dry goods, chilled goods and frozen goods. These trucks have played a significant role in reducing costs and improving customer service.

New technology requires relatively expensive equipment. In retailing and distribution, this means operating larger stores, transporting larger loads in larger vehicles and operating larger depots and using more equipment to improve the operation of storage and shop units, with relatively little increase in staff required.

Increasing Use of Self-Service

Retailers face other economic pressures to reduce their workforce and increase their use of modern equipment. Low pay is associated with low efficiency and high turnover. However, the minimum wage rate makes it less economic for firms to tolerate inefficient use of their workforce. Also, higher wages in more advanced industries put pressure on retailers as they compete to retain the better workers. Retailers will also try and change working practices to increase labour flexibility as well as finding alternative ways of providing services that are labour intensive. For instance, kiosks in shops provide simple information that enables the retailer to reduce the number of staff in the store.

The design of new retail units makes them less labour intensive in general operation and in the specific services provided. The newer technologies also require staff to be re-skilled and, consequently, the proportion of managerial, administrative and technical staff increases relative to operative staff.

Increased Standardization

The availability of space on the edge of towns and in out-of-town locations with good road communications has allowed retailers to increase the size of their stores and take advantage of lower rents. It has also enabled retailers to reduce the levels of staffing required and achieve other economies that have reduced the costs per pound of sales. However, retailers need to bring their products to the customer and this limits the size of their stores to fit in with local demand. Multiple retailers have also increased the scale of their operations in recent decades by moving to centralized buying and distribution. This increases standardization of product ranges and allows better control of product quality. Centralized buying, however, can make it increasingly difficult for large retailers to be flexible in meeting demand and in responding to local markets. The Dutch retailer C&A, for instance, found that meeting the different consumer requirement of its UK market was incompatible with centralized buying for its European operations, and this was a contributory factor in its withdrawal from the UK market.

More Even Spread of Shopping

People do the major part of their shopping at the weekend, and this produces characteristic peaks and troughs in consumer spending. Most retailers are busy and their retail facilities are crowded at the weekend. However, the retailers are less busy during the week and their facilities are underutilized.

This is a relatively costly use of the large amount of capital tied up in shopping spaces, as it is only used fully at peak periods and is underutilized at other times. The increasing cost of land and building has put cost pressures on operations. Retailers have had to explore ways of increasing the utilization of their facilities through longer opening hours and more efficient use of space for storage and display. They have also had to even out demand on their facilities through various off-season discounts and other offers to encourage demand.

2.4 Socio-economic Changes

Analysing Trends in Shopping

Time has become increasingly important for people for a number of reasons. The main issues are as follows:

▶ increase in incomes

▶ change in household structure

▶ increased working hours

▶ more leisure activities available

▶ the need for extra time to consume positioning products

▶ days are crowded with tasks and social obligations which have become more complex.

Income and the Use of Time

The most important factor in changing shopping behaviour has been the increasing relative scarcity of time as income increases. People need time to spend their extra income, but there are still only 168 hours in a week. This problem is aggravated because women in many family households are now working longer hours and the many single-person non-pensioner households have no one to stay at home and do the housework.

Consumers can turn some of their extra income into time by reducing their working week or taking longer holidays. This happened during much of the twentieth century. However, in recent years, we have tended to take extra holidays rather than have a shorter working week. This still leaves us short of time in which to spend all our extra income and so we look for ways of reducing the time we spend in shopping and other essential activities. For instance:

▶ We experiment with different forms of shopping to see if they can help save us time.

▶ We gather all our core shopping needs together and at the same time. The big weekly, fortnightly or monthly shop forms the core of our shopping activity. We are prepared to travel some distance to edge of town or out-of-town locations because major roads and parking facilities reduce total access and transaction time, there is less fuss and we are more certain of getting what we want – saving us frustration.

▶ We buy products and services, such as convenience foods and ready meals, to reduce the time in domestic production. Many of us would rather be doing other things than preparing meals, cleaning and washing. We only do these at home to save money, because we cannot afford to pay someone to do them for us. However, when our income goes up, saving money becomes less important and we spend less time on these tasks. For instance, we buy or rent equipment such as washing machines and vacuum cleaners to save time. When we have this equipment, however, we spend some of the time saved on doing more housework, such as washing more clothes, curtains and so on. Sometimes, of course, we just buy expensive gadgets as a way of making our leisure time more enjoyable and less energy consuming – such as remote-controlled televisions.

▶ We take up more expensive leisure activities, so we spend our money more quickly. This increases our spending on related leisure products and services.

Household Activity: Earning and Spending

Consumers divide their time between working and staying at home depending on how attractive the work situation is. For instance, many women are happy to work during school hours or at night in the local supermarket, because the staff rosters let them be with their children out of school hours until their partner comes home. The supermarket can cope with this because it can fill gaps during the evenings and at holiday times with student workers.

Consumers also change their leisure activities according to the relative attractiveness and cost of different opportunities. For instance, a visit to a cinema or theme park costs money as well as a chunk of the consumer's valuable time. However, the major cost of watching television is the consumer's own time, since the licence fee and channel subscription costs have been paid anyway. In order to get the consumer to go to the entertainment outside the home the entertainment operator has to provide something worth the extra cost.

Another factor in changing consumer behaviour and their purchases is the amount of personal energy. As we pack more activities into our increasingly busy lives, we find that our energy runs out. So we are always looking to save energy as well as time on those tasks that do not yield direct enjoyment, such as travelling to work and the shops, and on basic grocery shopping, especially for parents with young children.

The Impact of the Changing Role of Women

The position of women in the formal economy has changed significantly during the last 30 years. A wide range of employment opportunities and rising wage rates have encouraged more women into employment. The significant improvements in domestic equipment and the development of time-saving products such as convenience foods have made it easier for family women in particular to work considerably longer hours. Table 2.4 shows how this change in employment has taken place in Britain.

Table 2.4 Employment in Britain (millions)

Age	Men (millions)				Women (millions)			
	1971	1981	1991	1999	1971	1981	1991	1999
Total all ages of which	16.0	16.0	16.4	16.2	10.0	10.8	12.4	13.0
16–24 years	3.0	3.2	3.1	2.4	2.3	2.7	2.6	2.0
25–44 years	6.5	7.1	8.1	8.3	3.5	4.6	6.1	6.6

Source: National Statistics annual

Table 2.4 shows the significant increase in the number of 25–44-year-old women who are working. The proportion of women who work full-time also increased significantly by the early 1980s and has remained fairly constant at about 55 per cent of those in work.

Traditionally, the age of her youngest child has been the most important determinant of a mother's work pattern. Table 2.5 shows how women are returning to work sooner after having children. They are also working longer hours and more of them have returned directly to full-time work.

Table 2.5 Employment Rates for Mothers by Age of Youngest Child (%)

Age of youngest child	1981			1997		
	All	Full-time	Part-time	All	Full-time	Part-time
0–4	22	6	16	51	18	33
5–10	45	17	28	66	23	43
11–15	67	30	37	74	34	40

Source: National Statistics annual

The increase in women in work has had several effects:

▶ Women spend more of their money and leisure directly in the market place. This has made leisure spending less male oriented and the style of spending has changed. For instance, family households spend more on womenswear.

▶ The total adult time available for domestic activity in family households has decreased. As women have increased their working hours, their partners have not reduced their working hours to compensate. Women still do most of the meal preparation, cleaning and washing. This is partly because of higher average wages for men, but also because focus has been on increased household spending power, not the internal redistribution of household tasks. Retailers have had to respond to this change by providing products and services that save time and reduce household work. For example, supermarkets have increased the shelf space dedicated to ready-to-eat meals and in-store restaurant facilities.

▶ There is increased pressure on family households to save on domestic time through more sharing of their other leisure activities. It has also encouraged families to combine activities such as shopping with other family leisure activities.

▶ The rising cost of time has increased the cost of child rearing. This has led to a marked decline in the proportion of families with children and a decline in the average size of the family. As result, people increase their spending on their children and family spending has become more child oriented as children have an increasing influence on what their parents buy. This has given rise to the phenomenon of *pester power.*

▶ The smaller household size also makes market consumption relatively cheaper *for the household as a group*, in relation to income per head. This reinforces the trend in convenience shopping: families are more susceptible to buy preportioned convenience food and ready meals, because the advantages of large-scale food preparation have disappeared, and family shopping can be more easily combined with other leisure spending.

Implications for Retailing

The various socio-economic changes have led to changes to the traditional opening hours and modes of operation. Advances in retailing have been driven by the idea that consumers are more and more aware of the time they spend shopping. This is for the most part because new technology and trends in shopping time have removed the need for shopping at certain times of the day. It is almost part of the social fabric for families to spend some time shopping at the retail park on a Sunday afternoon. Extended opening hours make it possible for most consumers, who have the mobility, to shop at their convenience. The arrival of newer forms of one-stop shopping such as factory outlets, warehouse clubs and catalogue stores have reduced the search time consumers have to spend. All of these factors have created a new type of consumer.

Retailing Activities and Functions: the Consumer Supply Chain

These new consumers want their products and services today, just in time. Retailers have to be highly efficient to respond effectively and tailor supplies of products and services to the demands of the consumer. The main area where this efficiency is evident is in the way retailers obtain their sources of supply.

A major change in recent years has been the increasingly greater integration between the different stages of the *consumer supply chain*, which comprises the facilities and activities in supplying goods and services to consumers. During much of the nineteenth and twentieth centuries, the process of industrialization led to the consumer supply chain becoming increasingly split into separate stages, with more of the work being done further away from the customer, as for instance, with ready-made clothes and footwear, and ready packaged groceries. Retailing developed as a distinct stage at or next to the end of a set of fairly distinct processes.

In that system, product initiatives traditionally flowed from the manufacturer to the wholesaler, then to the retailer and, finally, to the consumer. Retailers bought in markets with varying degrees of competition and battled with their suppliers for a share of the profits. In some areas of retailing, however, retailers developed a significant amount of own brands. This increased the product initiatives coming from retailers and gave them a corresponding increase in power and share of the profits.

Changes in society, particularly the development of information technology, during the last 20 years, have emphasized the need for greater consumer orientation and cooperation along the whole supply chain. The exchange of information between supplier and retailer is now vital for all large retailers, particularly in grocery retailing.

Economic, Social and Environmental Forces

The growing impact of retailing on job creation, personal income and the wider social life of communities have also firmly embedded retailing in the political life of those communities. Large retailers have to actively cooperate with planning authorities in the development of facilities and need to consider local development plans when looking for sites. For instance, the permissive attitude of the 1970s and 1980s that encouraged large-scale out-of-town shopping developments was replaced by a much more restrictive attitude in the 1990s. These changes reflected changing perceptions of the relative costs and benefits of these types of developments and consequently have affected the longer-term plans of retailers.

The activities of large retail firms are now seen to have a significant impact in many different ways. Consequently, government has begun to scrutinize their activities much more closely. This makes retailing part of a complex social and political system, where cooperation as well as competition is important.

Consumers Upgrade their Expectations of Retailing

Consumers' use of retailers' services is not really different from that of any other product. Consumers expect better services from retailers as their standard of living and lifestyle improves. However, there is a limit to how much consumers are prepared to pay for improvements to retail facilities. Consumers would rather pay for good retailing facilities that are in keeping with their lifestyle and they do not want to pay for luxurious retail settings that are seen to add unnecessarily to the cost of products. Thus, quality improvements in UK retailing facilities from the 1970s onwards have focused on improving basic facilities rather than on creating excessive luxury.

The demand for retailing services has become more dependent on particular lifestyles. Consumers are increasing the use of the car in their leisure activities, including their shopping. They now require retailers to be more flexible in their retail offerings. Retail leisure outlets need to broaden the range of services provided beyond just retailing as there is also an increasing need for family-oriented retailing. Better shopping provision is needed for single-person households, households where both partners work and for the increasing number of people who work unsocial hours.

One response has been to develop retail units into social centres. Shopping centres, such as Meadowhall, and retail parks have been in an ideal position to fill these broader needs. The edge-of-town or out-of-town location gives them the space to provide integrated retailing and leisure services for families and other groups. People use these centres as activity centres rather than using them just as shopping points. This also allows consumers to link shopping activity with social family activity and share the time costs of the various activities.

2.5 Impact on the Retail Industry

Changes in the general social and economic environment have led to significant changes in the retail industry. Many general features of the contemporary retail industry in the UK were laid down by the 1980s, but they have continued to change in response to changes in the business and social environment that have been discussed above.

▶ The number of retail businesses and the number of retail outlets have continued to decline (see Chapter 1, Tables 1.7 and 1.8). There has been a corresponding increase in the size of outlets.

▶ Food retailing had passed from the small grocery shops, general co-operative stores and specialist food shops, such as the butcher and greengrocer, into the control of the supermarket chains. The top five supermarket chains increased their share from 43 per cent to 50 per cent between 1994 and 1997 (Key Note 1995; Key Note 1998).

▶ The large food retailers have been exploiting their role in time-saving one-stop shopping by extending their product range into clothing, housewares, routine consumer electrical and sports items. Alongside other retailers, they have also been responding to the different pressures on consumer time by developing new convenience formats.

▶ As larger retail firms developed larger stores they moved increasingly to edge-of-town and out-of-town shopping centres. The changing political climate has restricted further developments and led retailers, particularly food retailers, to develop new formats as part of a broader portfolio.

▶ New technology has led to closer integration of the supply chain.

▶ The dominance of the clothing market by the old chains has been challenged by new retail formats that respond more closely to the different attitudes of a new generation.

References

Becker, G. (1993) *A Treatise on the Family*, Cambridge, MA: Harvard University Press.
British Tourist Authority (2000) *Tourism Intelligence Quarterly*, 21(4), June.
Key Note (1995) *Retailing in the UK*, Hampton: Key Note Publications.
Key Note (1998) *Retailing in the UK*, Hampton: Key Note Publications.
National Statistics (annual) *Social Trends*, London: The Stationery Office
National Statistics (1995) *Economic Trends Annual Supplement*, London: The Stationery Office.
National Statistics (2001) *Social Trends* (31), London: The Stationery Office.
Robinson, P. (1998) 'Under the weather', *The Grocer*, 29 August.
Snowdon, R. (2000) 'Retailers a bit under the weather', *Yorkshire Post*, 29 August: 15.

Market Structure and Control: Retailing Structures

This chapter:

► Explains how environmental forces have altered retailing.

► Describes how retailers operate within various market structures.

► Describes how retail institutions use their size to gain advantages.

► Identifies various theories of retail change.

Market Structure and Control: Retailing Structures

Introduction and Core Concepts

Retail firms have altered considerably over the last three decades in order to survive. The impact of changes in the general retail environment and patterns of consumer shopping have been discussed in Chapter 2. Other factors have also affected the way in which retailers have been able to compete effectively. These factors relate to the modes of competition and the relative advantages of size and location. They have made formerly competitive businesses unable to continue competing and have brought new forms of retailing to the market.

3.1 Environment and Competition

The external environment of the firm consists of those factors outside the retail firm that affect the success of the retail business. The external environment can be divided into the macroenvironment and the microenvironment. The *macroenvironment* comprises the wider political, economic, social, cultural and technical forces that affect the industry and the way people shop. These factors are summarized in Table 3.1.

Table 3.1 Macroenvironmental Influences

Factor	Includes
Political and legal	Consumer protection, equal rights, safety at work, working hours, the minimum wage
Economic	Disposable income, gross domestic product, unemployment, interest rates, inflation
Sociocultural	Social class, reference groups, culture, subculture
Technological	Products, processes, production, information handling, management
Demographic	Age, sex, marital status, household size, education, geographic location
Physical	Product availability, air and water quality, visual clutter, noise pollution

The *microenvironment* comprises those factors that originate outside the retail firm, but which the retailer can affect through its management processes. They include the actions of suppliers and other intermediaries and the location, accessibility and size of customer markets. These factors determine the number of customers in a store, but a retailer such as Tesco may attract more customers by offering a better level of service than its competitors. Table 3.2 summarizes these microenvironmental influences.

Table 3.2 Microenvironmental Influences

Factor	Includes
Markets	Segments, size, behaviours, trends, locations, level of service demand
Suppliers and intermediaries	Supply channels, availability of goods, number of alternatives, locations, geographic concentration, volume concentration
Competitors	Number, strategies, potential new entrants, rivalry

In the last three decades these macroenvironmental and microenvironmental influences have obliged most retail sectors to change their approach to selling goods and services. As a consequence, many firms have had to reshape their stores, change the range and type of merchandise, and alter the type and level of service they offer.

Adapting the Retail Offering

A *retail offering* is a bundle of benefits that the customer purchases when entering the store. The offering consists of products and services, the image and reputation of the store and other intangible benefits. A retail business can increase the value of the merchandise it sells by providing extra services as part of its overall retail offering. Customers come to view the service element, as an integral part of the retail offering and the element of service has become an important feature that distinguishes one retailer from the next.

In the 1970s retailers could simply provide an adequate range of goods for their customers, who were then enticed into stores with straightforward selling techniques. One popular method of attracting customers was to pile the goods up high and sell them as cheap as possible. In the 1980s it became clear to many retail firms that the 'cut-price' approach was not nearly enough to encourage shoppers. Consumers' expectations had changed significantly and they required something more than just cheap merchandise and conveniently located stores. Economic and social change had created a group of affluent consumers who demanded a better standard of living and a healthier lifestyle. Many customers also wanted ethically and environmentally friendly products. Younger, more discerning customers expected a total package of enhanced facilities and services. This brought fresh challenges for retailers, who were forced to compete with each other on price, quality and standard of service for a better share of the market. For many of the larger retail firms, beating the competition was all about offering the customer a better package of benefits alongside their basic shopping items. In the food sector this led to the introduction of checkout packers at one supermarket chain, while another multiple focused on helping customers to the car park.

Retail firms were thus compelled to alter the way they treated their customers in order to retain their business. For the food multiples this meant offering a better package of merchandise and services, with the guarantee of longer opening hours and conveniently placed stores in pleasing locations. Customers responded to these better levels of service and quality with loyalty and paid regular visits to the stores. In particular, customers now found that trips to the retail park made their shopping much more pleasurable and were becoming more of a day out.

Modern shopping has developed into a highly competitive leisure activity. It is now more than a trip to the corner grocer shop and has become a 'shopping expedition' that is now a regular part of our lives. There is evidence to suggest that retail parks and malls are as popular, or in some cases, more popular than major tourist attractions and destinations. For example, the Science Museum in Manchester considers retail parks in general to be one of its greatest competitors. These sorts of issues have created major changes in the industry, and have shaped the retail businesses for the new millennium.

Size of Businesses

One important way in which retailing has changed has been the relative size of businesses. This can be measured by the number of outlets or stores that a business operates, which indicates its breadth of its market presence across the country, or by the business's annual sales, which indicates its total market penetration. Table 3.3 shows clearly how these measures have moved in favour of larger retailers. The declining number of stores is also associated with an increasing share of the market going to the larger store groups, although the average number of stores per business remains roughly the same at about 1.45 stores per retailer. Table 3.4 also indicates the growing size of retail businesses, even after allowing for inflation during this period. Table 3.5 presents another indicator of the growing relative importance of larger retail businesses. The government changed the benchmark for large businesses from a turnover of £3 million to £4.5 million in this period. As the retail price

Table 3.3 Retail Outlets by Ownership

	1984		1994	
	Outlets (000)	Share of sales (%)	Outlets (000)	Share of sales (%)
Owned by independents (1–9 outlets)	275	42	225	32
Owned by multiples (incl. co-ops)	68	58	65	68
Total outlets	343		290	

Source: National Statistics annual

Table 3.4   UK Retail Businesses (VAT Registered)

Turnover £000	1990	2000
1–499	236 772	174 650
500–1999	13 158	22 120
2000–4999	1 537	2 525
5000 and over	933	1 500
Total	252 400	200 795

Source: National Statistics 2001

Table 3.5   Sales of Large and Small Retail Business at Current Prices (£bn)

	1990	1997
Large	86.6	135.6
% total	*67.7*	*76.1*
Small	41.4	42.6
% total	*32.3*	*23.9*
Total	128.0	178.2
Retail price index – all items 1990 = 100	*100.0*	*126.0*

Source: National Statistics 2000; Key Note 1998

index increased by about 26 per cent over this period, it biased the statistics in favour of small businesses but, as Table 3.5 shows, large retailers have been increasing their share of sales.

The rapid decline of small independents and the increasing relative size of businesses during recent decades have shown that size has a major influence on the ability of retailers to compete in the market. Large firms may have an advantage over smaller firms for several reasons and changes in recent decades have tended to enhance these advantages.

1 *Larger retail businesses may deliver greater value to the customer.* Stores have learnt how to reach (or target) their customers more effectively and sell the right assortment of merchandise. This is particularly true in traditional store retailing, as large retailers tend to operate larger stores, which carry a greater assortment. This gives customers greater choice, which has become more highly valued as consumers have become more affluent, knowledgeable and sophisticated. Time-pressured consumers also value the greater assortment of larger stores because it reduces the time spent in searching for products and increases the effective shopping time.

2 *Larger firms may have a cost advantage over smaller firms.* Operating on a large scale may allow the retailer to cut costs in a number of ways and these costs savings can be passed on to the customer. These cost advantages are called *economies of scale.* Larger retailers may also enjoy *economies of scope* where broadening the range of products, such as selling food and clothing, provides similar cost advantages. The large retailer can obtain these cost advantages in several ways: purchasing and distribution, management and personnel, marketing, finance and risk.
   (a) *Purchasing and distribution.* Large purchases reduce costs for suppliers and enable them to reduce prices. The larger companies can take advantage of their market power as important buyers

and can insist on quantity discounts. Independent retail businesses avoid the costs of managing large complex operations. However, they lack the market power of large retailers and are forced to take advantage of seasonal and periodic offers as available to reduce costs.

Large retailers can also organize the distribution of products more effectively: centralized warehousing and distribution networks enable them to make more efficient use of vehicles, storage and ordering processes. In contrast, the smaller retailer may visit their local cash and carry stores, perhaps weekly or twice weekly, or else have to rely on small-scale distribution from wholesalers.

(b) *Management and personnel.* In human resources, for instance, the large chain multiples have highly skilled personnel divisions to handle all their training and employee relations. They can standardize their operating procedures and thereby reduce the costs of training their staff. The smaller independent on the other hand assigns these types of duties to store managers, or senior staff members. Larger retailers can also transfer managers more easily between different units in the organization, which reduces disruption when managers leave. Large stores can also use their sales staff more effectively.

(c) *Marketing.* Large retailers can advertise and promote their products more cheaply because they can spread the costs over a greater amount of products. They can afford to advertise nationally to customer groups and significantly increase their sales. The big retailers have built up a following of loyal customers who are attracted by the range and quality of the goods sold. Multiples like Tesco and Safeway are thus able to pass on these advantages to their customers in the form of keener prices, the availability of luxury items at an affordable shelf price, and an ever-increasing range of merchandise. Big retailers can thus use their economies of scale to influence the scope of their businesses.

By increasing the range of goods they sell retail multiples can increase the size and scope of their operations generally. One example of this is Sainsbury's expansion into petrol filling stations and pharmacies in their supermarket chains. Customers are free to buy groceries, fill their prescriptions, and fill up with petrol at the one location. Other in-store facilities such as photocopying, coffee shop, and kiosk operations like passport photographs, add popular services to the range. When the convenience of off-road parking and a pleasant and customer-oriented atmosphere is added, this presents a powerfully attractive package of goods and services for the customer. At one time stores only provided the basics for the weekly shop. But now most food multiples provide self-service restaurants offering reasonably priced high-quality food, where customers can buy an affordable meal after they have finished shopping. Such incentives have redefined the family trip to the supermarket and changed the way stores think about their facilities.

(d) *Finance.* Raising large sums of money is usually cheaper because of the relatively lower processing costs. This is certainly true in the UK where a significant number of smaller public companies have found it difficult to raise money and where their shares have been undervalued in the market.

(e) *Risk.* Even small changes in consumer demand for the retailer can make very significant difference to retailers' profits. Smaller retailers are more vulnerable to changes in shopping patterns and are less likely to have accumulated sufficient financial reserves to tide them over bad years or invest in the changes that are necessary to maintain profitability. Larger firms are often able to survive periods of poor results because they can often satisfy their shareholders and lenders by changing their management.

3 *A larger firm may use its financial and market power to restrict the ability of competitors to compete effectively.* There are several ways in which large firms can prevent competitors from being able to compete for customers on an equal basis. This jeopardizes the long-term interests of consumers. The government and, importantly, the European Union take a dim view of such activities and where discovered they can banned. However, as recent investigations have shown, anti-competitive practices occur and smaller firms tend to get squeezed out. Larger retailers need to maximize those advantages without engaging in illegal practices or those that are likely to provoke government reaction and further regulation.

Competition and the Small Retailer

Smaller retailers can take steps to combat some of the advantages large retailers possess and compete effectively in the market. They can, for instance, join co-operative chains that can use their buying power to negotiate better prices and also distribute the products more cheaply to their members. Small retailers can also operate in small well-defined niche markets where larger retailers cannot take advantage of economies of scale.

Large size is not itself a guarantee of success. Some large retail firms have fallen by the wayside and others have evolved into new sorts of outlets. The changing economic and social environment brings new consumer demands and shopping habits. These may favour some large grocery multiples such as Tesco and Sainsbury. These chains have capitalized on their convenience factor to expand their range of food items at the expense of specialist food retailers (which are naturally smaller businesses). They have also moved into non-food products, which affected the market share of other retailers.

However, economic and social change may also cause the decline of existing large firms and the rise of new firms. Where a retailer has acquired a range of businesses that do not fit easily together, changing circumstances may force the company to refocus its business. For instance, the British Shoe Corporation (BSC) had built up a dominance of the high street footwear market through its various store brands. However, the group was broken up and sold in bits when its owners, Sears, decided to withdraw from the market in 1997 to concentrate on its Selfridge's department store.

The Arcadia group in the late 1990s had a diverse portfolio of men's and women's clothing stores. It was forced to reappraise and downsize its operations to eliminate some of the less successful operations.

Small businesses can grow quite rapidly if they can devise new formats for the presentation that are more suited to the changed consumer environment, as illustrated by the international growth of the American GAP company and the discount clothing retailer Matalan. These have been successful because they have grasped the opportunities offered by the changing patterns of retail development, which are considered in sections 3.4 and 3.5.

3.2 The Competitive Environment in Different Retail Sectors

One way of viewing the competitive position of firms is to look at the changes that have been taking place in the different sectors of retailing. Government statistics in the UK are the major source of information on the changing structure of retailing in the UK and form the basis for much of the discussion and analysis of UK retailing. The major market research organizations, such as Mintel and Key Note, use this classification as the basis for their reports, and supplement the data with their own market research. The classification of the retail sectors was discussed in Chapter 1. These statistics were overhauled significantly during the early 1990s so we must exercise caution in viewing changes before then.

Food Retailing

Food retailing comprises the largest sector of retailing. It is divided into specialist retailers such as greengrocers and non-specialist retailers. Non-specialist food retailers now account for about 85 per cent of food sales and include large food retailers such as Tesco that have developed non-food lines. As explained in Chapter 1, data for this sector includes food retailers' non-food sales. Consumer spending on food does not increase proportionately so the sector would decline in relative terms as income grows. This reinforces the economies of scale in distribution and sourcing of products and encourages consolidation of the sector into fewer larger firms. It will also move the flow of investment towards other areas. Thus the large multiples have been increasing their share of the market from about 45 per cent of total food sector sales in the early 1990s to over 50 per cent currently. Table 3.6 illustrates the dominance of the non-specialist food sector.

Table 3.6 Non-specialist Food Retailers' Sales, 1993–98

	1993 £m	1998 £m
Tesco	7 581.0	14 460.0
J Sainsbury	8 886.0	11 629.0
Asda	4 396.0	7 600.8
Safeway	5 196.0	6 978.7
Total	43 423.9	52 575.5

Source: Mintel 1999

Non-specialist food retailers are increasing their domination of the food sector, with some specialists such as butchers being squeezed very heavily. However Marks & Spencer is still a significant supplier of food. The grocery sector has seen major changes as the major food retailers vie for position. Earlier competition between them created a great deal of growth in large store outlets in this sector and led to a copycat store location policy. Where one multiple built another would follow, and so on. Table 3.7 shows the number of stores operated by the top four food retailers between 1995 and 1997.

Table 3.7   Outlets Operated by Leading Food Retailers, 1995–97

	1995	1997
Tesco	519	568
Safeway group	547	490
J Sainsbury group	365	390
Marks & Spencer	283	286
Asda	203	213
Total food outlets	8 002	8 188

Source: Mintel: 1999

The food giants have a considerable advantage over smaller food chains such as Somerfield Plc and the Co-operative. This is mainly because of their ability to buy in large quantities and demand a high level of both commitment and service from their suppliers. This buying 'clout' has meant that they have been able to squeeze out the competition that could not compete on price and range, etc. Smaller food retailers have been reduced in numbers as a result of the increasing power of the giants. This dominant force in the marketplace has been the demise of the smaller independent retailer. More and more the individual shopkeepers have disappeared from the market to be replaced by a few super-retailers.

Many of the smaller non-specialists have converted themselves into convenience stores. Budgen's for instance is also developing petrol station forecourt retailing in conjunction with a petrol supplier. These innovations are now being copied by large multiples with their own facilities. Specialist food retailers are also in long-term decline. Most sales in this sector are from small multiples and independent retailers. However, there is now a greater use of specialist food retailers for *top-up shopping*.

> ⇨ Top-up shopping is the practice of shopping around for certain products, such as fresh fruit and vegetables, in between shopping trips to the super-market. For example, supermarket customers may augment their weekly shop with a visit to the greengrocers and butchers. This practice reduced in the 1990s because the major supermarkets increased the range and quality of their fresh food lines.

Clothing Sector

Other sectors such as fashion present a similar picture. In the fashion market, stores such as Next, Miss Selfridge and River Island have come to dominate high street sales. Despite the market domination by the major multiples, the clothing retail sector is generally fragmented with many small businesses. For example, in the specialist women's wear sector there are around 15 000 retailers in the UK, and women's clothing is also sold by around 43 000 non-specialist retailers, including super-markets, market stalls, department stores and variety stores. Table 3.8 shows the number of women's clothing businesses in the UK and the number of outlets per business. We can see from the table that the average number of outlets per business between 1993 and 1995 was only 2.5. These figures show a decline in the number of businesses between 1993 and 1994 reflecting business closures as a result of the economic recession over this period.

Table 3.8 Number of Businesses/Outlets, 1993–95

Clothing businesses and outlets	1993	1995
Outlets (000)	29.9	32.9
Businesses (000)	13.6	13.4
Outlets per business	2.2	2.5

Source: Mintel 1998

Department store chains such as Debenhams and Allders have always been big sellers of fashion garments. Up to the 1960s, department stores were generally considered more attractive than specialist fashion outlets, as they sold a wide variety of other lines. However, things changed when variety stores such as Marks & Spencer, British Home Stores (Bhs), C&A and Woolworth began to seriously chal-lenge them. These stores offered a very competitive range of goods, which ranged from high-quality garments to low price value-for-money items. From the 1970s, specialist multiple groups in fashion (Debenhams), electrical (Comet), audio-visual (Dixons), furniture (MFI) and other goods began to evolve into national chains, providing a wider choice and more competitive pricing than the conventional department store. When the 1980s explosion of out-of-town shopping created malls and retail parks, which brought together a wide range of specialist retailers under one roof, offering diversity and convenience, this posed a further threat to the department store.

Ten years ago the outlook for department stores was very gloomy. In towns and cities all over the country, department stores were closing and being converted into fast food and grocery outlets, variety stores, and multi-store shopping centres. In the late 1990s the department store is having a 'renaissance' with new upgraded stores, supplying a wide range of quality merchandise and higher levels of service and expertise. This has made department store groups such as John Lewis and Debenhams profitable national chains, while smaller regional groups such as Hoopers (which opened its first store only in 1982), James Beattie and Beales are also flourishing. Harvey Nichols is the department store success story of the decade, while the giant House of Fraser group is number two in the league. Table 3.9 shows the percentage share of the market enjoyed by the major department stores, and the value of this share.

Table 3.9 Retail Shares of Major Department Stores, 1997

Store	£m	%
John Lewis Partnership	1 621	22
Debenhams	1 130	15
House of Fraser	781	11
Allders	491	7
Harrods	437	6
Selfridges	299	4
Fenwick	231	3
Harvey Nichols	110	1
Other	2 300	31
Total	7 400	100

Source: Mintel 1998

Another segment of the non-food market, which represents a huge force in retailing generally, falls under the heading of variety stores. These stores can be conveniently grouped into various non-food bands and linked to some of the major and well-known names in retailing. The categories are as follows:

▶ retail sale of clothing (Marks & Spencer, Bhs and Littlewoods)

▶ non-specialized stores (Boots, Woolworth and TJ Hughes)

▶ books, newspapers and stationery (WH Smith)

▶ other retail stores (Index, Argos).

Government figures show that the major multiples increased their share of this market by 1.5 per cent during the period from 1992 to 1996. Some of the largest of these have a considerable foothold in the retail market; the following short profiles look at some of these stores describing their general activities.

Under the heading of 'other stores' Argos and Index are catalogue retailers offering a comprehensive range of products at mark-down prices. These stores provide a service, which is a cross between home catalogue shopping and a high street department store. Their unique service offers the best of both worlds, discounted goods and a warm pleasant environment in which to shop. Argos is the largest catalogue showroom retailer in the UK, and sells a wide range of predominantly household products like electrical goods, furniture, kitchenware, linens, jewellery and toys. The products are all displayed in the Argos catalogue, allowing customers to browse and select at home and then go shopping with the convenience of a high street location nearby. Index is the catalogue retailing division of the organization, which owns and operates the large variety chain, Littlewoods.

Variety stores are classified by the UK government's departments as 'predominantly non-food businesses'. The number of these stores generally make them a significant force in retailing. As consumers we are aware of these retailers instinctively due to the part they play in our everyday lives, and their familiar presence on the high street. Without these stores shopping would be less enjoyable and the range of merchandise available less easy to locate. Table 3.10 shows the market share enjoyed by the larger of these stores in the non-food sector.

Table 3.10 Major Variety Stores – Market Share, 1996

Store	£m	%
M&S (UK, non-food)	4 286	32.1
Boots the Chemist	3 314	24.8
Argos	1 660	12.4
Woolworth	1 535	11.5
Bhs	806	6.0
WH Smith Retail	788	5.9
Littlewoods Stores	483	3.6
Index	429	3.2
TJ Hughes	63	0.5
Total	13 364	100.0

Source: Mintel 1998

Case 3.1 Profile: Marks & Spencer

Marks & Spencer (M&S) is one of the largest of these retailers with 286 UK stores and 35 European stores (in 1998). The store's main lines are clothing and footwear, accessories, housewares including furnishings, kitchenware and home decorating. M&S has retained its presence in the high street although it has been driven by the UK market and opened in out-of-town locations. The chain has also developed a food-based store format for smaller neighbourhood sites. In addition to its main lines, M&S has moved into areas such as wedding list services and financial services. The company has its own store credit card. M&S has become very popular in the UK largely due to the company's focus on high-quality products. The company maintains very high standards of housekeeping and organization. Price labelling is clear and always on show so reducing the need for customer service and queries. Customers are loyal and generally purchase all their shopping needs from within the M&S range. Most of the goods sold by M&S are of the type normally stocked by department stores.

The figures give an indication of how the non-food variety store sector has performed, and demonstrates how this sector has been at the heart of the change that has taken place in the industry. This is because variety stores cover such a broad range of products, and the demand for these products is affected by a variety of demographic, social and economic indicators. These include the age of the population, levels of disposable income, the housing market, trends in female employment and marriage rates. One way to illustrate how these factors influenced the sector is to reflect for a moment on the UK's entry into the 1990s, and when the boom of the late 1980s had given way to recession. During this period consumers began to behave in a more cautious manner, putting more of their disposable income into savings and reducing their personal debt (loans). Uncertainty about the economy, particularly during the house price slump, meant that retailers experienced only modest rises in their sales.

Clearly as the population's personal disposable income increases, levels of personal expenditure on goods and lifestyles will also grow. This will positively influence all retailers, but in particular the variety store retailers who serve those consumers who want to spend more on themselves and their homes. Variety retailers have demonstrated that they will remain a significant force in the UK high street, and are likely to continue to grow in size. In variety store retailing the major players dominate, with very few independents or minor chains in the sector.

3.3 Government Policy, Competition and Consumer Demand

The demise of the smaller retailer has to some degree been widely accepted as a necessary part of the change, which has taken place in the UK marketplace. A key indicator of this change is the manner in which consumers spend their money, and what factors influence this outlay. Over the last two decades consumer expenditure has been less positive due mainly to the pressure on consumers' disposable income in the recession of the 1980s and 1990s. A downturn in both the world and the British economies over this period was largely responsible for this decline in growth and consumer spending generally. This has meant that consumers were more conscious of value for money and less likely to pay the premium asked by the smaller retail business. Also, there has been a fundamental shift in consumer expenditure from goods to services. While many services are provided by the small retail business (like the taxi firm) the larger companies dominate the market. Because of their economies of scale and scope, the major operators are more able to deliver the standard and volume of service required. Consumers expect much more than just a basic service they want a range of other supplementary benefits alongside.

Consumers have a more sophisticated set of needs that have developed over time, and as a result of social, economic, technological, and political changes. As changes in government take place and new policies are adopted and accepted society-wide attitudes are created. For instance, in the 1990s it is an accepted practice that if a company is in financial trouble it has to bail itself out of difficulties. Not so in the 1970s under a different political way of thinking. Then it was the role of a maternal state to help when companies like British Rail and British Steel needed funds. Today companies are expected to compete effectively and make money regardless of the business they are in. Even government enterprises are expected to maximize their operational effectiveness (reducing costs) and policy is designed to help this along.

There are five main roles of government in relation to business; these are as a policy maker, a sponsor, a regulator, a customer and owner, although very rarely all at once for the same industry (Grant 1987). But most importantly, government acts as policy-maker, affecting all businesses in one way or another. The design of policy is closely connected with government's role as the sponsor of the different industries. Due to the privatization of various nationalized industries, government's role as owner has been constantly declining over the last 15 years, whilst its role as regulator for those industries has dramatically increased. However, privatized industries are still under indirect government control as they are frequently represented by regulatory bodies that set and review prices and quality standards for the products and services. The retail industry is no exception to this general rule.

In the design of policy, the sponsoring role of government depart-ments provides a valuable channel for contact and input from the retail industry. Inputs do help as the full consequence of a proposed piece of legislation cannot always be recognized by governments. Retail institu-tions have a mass of information at their disposal, which may brief and even forewarn government of impending political problems. Thus input plays an important role. Business representatives develop a working relationship with civil servants while putting the retailers' views across, even trying to slightly change policy.

Large multiple chains might be approached for cooperation with initiatives, such as training for the young unemployed, and business associations can assist by providing information about new legislation and its applicability to members. With the state seeking to reduce the scale of its directly managed functions, implementing public policy has increasingly been delegated to business associations. For example, in the toiletries sector, the British Aerosol Manufacturers' Association (BAMA) was asked to act as government agent to ensure the reduction of chloro-fluorocarbons (CFC) propellants used in aerosols by member and non-member companies by 30 per cent as required by European Union policy for the protection of the ozone layer. Such action is beneficial for business as well, by providing opportunities to be proactive and self regulate oneself before legislation is considered and possibly imposed (Grant 1987).

This privatization of public policy is however not generally welcomed, especially where consumers are concerned. For example, the regulatory framework, which grants the financial services industry its self-regu-lation has been heavily criticized. This was because of a concern for investor protection was thought to be overridden by sensitivity to the views of the financial sector. Although as a result of continuing pressure from the onlookers the consumer is now beginning to gain more protection. Elsewhere consumers have had the benefit of maximum protection for some time, in foodstuffs for instance. Here the gradual expansion of government policy and legislation to cover environmental issues, reflect the concerns of a more health conscious society. The impact of global warming, and the need for a reduction in the use of fossil fuels, has had a far-reaching impact. Retailers have had to deal with more and more legislation governing the supply and delivery of goods to their stores.

Consumer beliefs about the ingredients of grocery items forced producers to exercise more control over the sorts of additives they placed in their products. Realizing that they had to change if they wanted to survive, retailers became far more responsible about the content and nature of the products they sold to their customers. On the whole the new set of ethical values held by society changed the way the retail industry thought and operated. Retail businesses were obliged to develop much better relationships with their suppliers to ensure the integrity of the merchandise they sold. These new policies created a far more inte-grated retail industry.

Many of the larger retail institutions formed fully self-contained oper-ations to exercise greater control over their costs. These lines of supply in some cases stretched from manufacture to sales counter so cutting out many of their intermediaries like wholesalers or distributors. The big food chains like Tesco have their own exclusive farms and suppliers of produce or raw materials for their stores. This is called *vertical integration* and refers to a firm's expansion either backwards, into the actual manufacture of the resources, or forwards by selling the finished products to the final consumer. With Tesco, already a retailer and selling the finished products to consumers, it benefits the company to undertake *backward vertical integration*. As a result it is able to reduce costs, maintain control over the quality and delivery of the raw materials (in this case produce), and restrict the competition. Tesco is able to exercise a good deal of control over the marketplace generally as it is itself a supplier.

3.4 Retail Development and Competition

Changing Spatial and Product Structures

We have discussed how the retail marketplace is continuously changing as a result of the various forces at work. Among these influences, the nature and actions of a firm's main competitors are major factors affecting the way retail organizations develop. For example, new innovations such as fresh store designs and merchandise ranges can create a distinct competitive advantage by attracting shoppers away from the competition. Here the attraction to the retailer is that they will enjoy a greater market share and may become market leader. Such advantages are sustained for a limited amount of time, however. Competitors, anxious not to lose their place in the market, must now think of new and innovative strategies. At the very least they must retaliate with matching tactics; this may take the form of a copycat policy with a similar store format and range of merchandise. Such movement in the sector means that the scope of retailing is constantly widening and retailers are often obliged frequently to alter their organizations in order to compete. This can be linked to the social behaviour of rival groups in the animal kingdom, and their tendency to compete for pecking order.

Examples of this type of competitive behaviour are evident in the apparent expansion of stores such as Argos and Index. These high street retailers started life as relatively basic discount stores (see classification list in Chapter 1, section 1.2), but have now evolved into fairly sophisticated and customer-service oriented outlets. Comet is another example of a low priced discount warehouse, with a trade counter service, which has traded up to become a value electrical outlet with a wide merchandise range. Competitive strategies have driven such stores to change the very nature of their operation and even the type of customer they target.

The Wheel of Retailing

There are a number of theories which attempt to explain the evolution of retail enterprises, and the *wheel of retailing* is probably the most well known of these. Wheel theory is one of the oldest methods for explaining the patterns of competitive development and change in retailing (McNair 1958). Developed by Malcolm McNair at Harvard University, the theory attempts to describe the competitive nature of the retail sector. It is important to note that it was designed to describe a post-war US retail sector.

Using the model in Figure 3.1, we can see how new businesses tend to enter the market as fairly low status, low margin, and low price operators. This limited positioning and strategy permits them to compete quite successfully with the larger and well-established rivals. Over time, the new arrivals gradually meet with some success and acquire more sophisticated and elaborate facilities. Clearly, this requires a greater investment and leads to a subsequent rise in the individual retailer's operating costs. The more established business is thus forced to raise its prices and operating margins. Actions such as these make the firm vulnerable to a new entrant, and low margin retailers, who then compete and progress through the same or similar pattern.

This pattern can be seen at work in many types of UK high street retailer. In illustration, firms such as River Island, Dorothy Perkins and even Marks & Spencer have started life in a modest fashion if compared to their current operation. They have generally evolved in the way described in Figure 3.1. Another company which appears to follow the direction indicated in the wheel theory is Johnsons the Cleaners, a service retailer. They have grown from what was a purely functional operation to a completely new type of dry-cleaning store format and product type. Now the emphasis is placed on the time taken to fulfil the service, and the additional benefits such as customer service and packaging. Johnsons set out to provide a new style drive-through operation which prides itself on short lead times, and a high-quality service straight to the customer's vehicle.

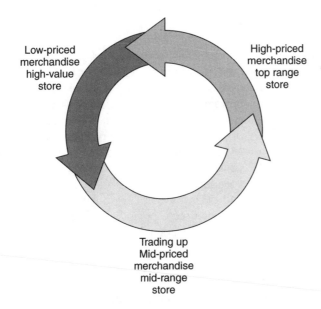

Figure 3.1   The wheel of retailing

In the fast food sector the accent is on improving the product range and less and less on diversification of store formats. But this was not always the case, and before the advent of the McDonald's, Burger King and KFC-type formats in the UK, consumers had little or no choice. Whoever was located in the high street (it was rare to see more than one or two outlets) got the business. The general offering, however, was very basic and of low quality. Competition, and of course consumer expectations, have progressively driven the market to its present position. Out of the simple Wimpy outlets of the 1960s and 1970s we have seen how the US fast food chains have considerably altered the general criteria for this style of restaurant. Today the emphasis is on product standardization with a high-quality customer service dimension. All burger-type food chains are now obliged to conform to this general model in order to compete. The way this sector has evolved helps to illustrate some inconsistency in the wheel theory.

Conflicting evidence has led to questions being asked about the usefulness of wheel theory. The Bon Marche low priced fashion store, for example, is a case in point where merchandise quality and price have remained unchanged, and only the format has altered since the store's conception. Traditionally, Bon Marche targets the mature female and price conscious shopper. Recently, the customer base has become increasingly younger and different socio-economic profiles now frequent the chain. Has this low-priced fashion store evolved, or does it just target different customers since it altered its format? Some explanation for the new types of customer groups in-store can be attributed to location policy. The management is keen to locate its outlets close to key multiples like Marks & Spencer. Is this perhaps the reason why new groups are attracted? Are consumers more prepared to shop around (mix and match) for fashion items in the 1990s? The short case study outlines the Bon Marche experience.

Case 3.2 The Bon Marche Experience

The UK-based store Bon Marche is a fashion retailer based in Leeds who mainly aim their merchandise at the mature female consumer. Their whole approach to the customer and the design and layout of their stores reflected this aim. The prices of Bon Marche garments were and still are the major attraction of this high street retailer. They focus on low prices and good value for money. Styles and fashions in their stores tend to reflect, not surprisingly, the sort of consumer they wished to attract. In the 1990s things started to change and they found that different types of customer were using their stores. A younger, and sometimes much more affluent, female group appeared to find some of their goods attractive. After carrying out some research the chain decided that this new group of customer only purchased single lines. More research suggested that the younger customer appeared to be shopping in nearby stores like Marks & Spencer and using Bon Marche to complete the fashion look. Rarely if at all would the younger customer purchase a complete blouse and skirt outfit. Instead they took advantage of special lines and some of the Bon Marche fashion items to supplement their mix and match selection.

Certain high street businesses do provide evidence of the changes described in McNair's (1958) wheel theory. Specsavers, for example, have altered the face of optician retailing, with their integrated sales and production style operation. They have evolved, or perhaps the word is 'matured' as their operation is far simpler than it used to be, into a specialist chain offering a number of in-store services and products. Other traders offer little or no evidence of this maturing process suggested by the wheel theories. The Kwik Save format, for example, has barely altered since it began trading and it is still a low cost food multiple offering a limited range of goods and service. It is currently positioned somewhere between a traditional supermarket and a discounter. While it can be said that the Kwik Save brand has undergone some realignment (having merged with Somerfield), the stores offer the consumer a very similar selection and standard. Any changes can be attributed to the emergence of continental discounters in the UK market, such as Aldi the German discount grocery retailer (Wileman and Jary 1997:105), rather than any explanation based on wheel theory.

The Retail Accordion

Another theory which helps to explain the way retailers change their operations over time is *retail accordion theory*. Hower (1943) describes this as an alternating movement from side to side, a movement which resembles the actions of a musical accordion. Hower noted that retail firms, when conducting their operations, appear to swing towards specialization and then away towards diversification. To apply this model to the UK we will first discuss some of the forces that have altered the retailing scene since the post-war years, at the time of Hower's initial observations.

As in the USA, in post-war Britain the general grocery store format was a popular feature in both towns and villages, where consumers needed the convenience of shopping on their own doorsteps. This was before motorways and at a time when there were fewer vehicles on the road. In addition to the grocery store, a range of specialist shops such as the bakery, butcher shop and fishmonger supported virtually every community both large and small. In the more populated areas, the issue of accessibility was less of a problem due to the availability of better infrastructure and a public transport system. Here, in addition to the neighbourhood shops, more comprehensive and upmarket stores served the surrounding communities. These were the multi-line department stores, which sold clothing, furnishings, electrical goods and foodstuffs all under one roof. Department stores were few in number and located in major cities. Increased accessibility, due to the better road and transport system, produced a gradual increase in the popularity of city department stores. These chains prospered right up to the 1970s when supermarkets began to move towards generalization.

More recently in the UK multi-line department stores have been in decline. This is due to pressure from supermarket giants like Tesco and Sainsbury who have successively added non-food items to their ranges (Cox and Brittain 1996: 13). Grocery superstores and hypermarkets have been incorporating many product categories into the traditional weekly shopping trip. Apart from the now customary range of alcohol and tobacco, superstores are home to a value coffee shop, newsagents, petrol station, health store and other services. This venture into general-ization, coupled with the convenient location with adequate parking, adds up to a considerable pull factor. It is this and the other out-of-town locations that have eroded the attraction of shopping in the city centre and the department store.

Another factor in the general decline in popularity of the department store, is the increasing number of specialized outlets or single-line stores located in the high street. These newcomers have targeted merchandise such as socks and ties normally sold by department stores who, due to their size, could accommodate the traditionally small level of sales. Stores such as Tie Rack and Sock Shop have changed customers' percep-tions over the purchase of such items. The resulting popularity of the single-line concept has swelled the numbers of these high street oper-ators. Body Shop's immense success characterizes how specialization stores have succeeded in high street locations, which is the traditional domain of the department store.

From the high street to the out-of-town locations favoured by the large supermarket chains another type of retail specialist has started to dominate the scene. First introduced in the USA, the so-called *category killer* has emerged as a very successful and serious competitor in the retail sector. In the North American and European marketplace, category killers have been the source of the largest growth over the last decade or so (Wileman and Jary 1997: 78). Their formula for success hinges on their ability to focus on a product category (for example, toys, furniture), offer the widest possible range, and undercut their competitors. The sheer size of these retail giants provide them with a significant competitive advantage over other mixed retailers. Stores such as Toys 'Я' Us are able to offer very keen prices due to their bulk buying expertise. As a result of these economies of scale category killers are able to 'kill off the competition'. Hence, the term 'category killer' (see Table 3.11 for examples of UK category killers).

Table 3.11   Leading Category Killers in the UK

Trader	Type of business	Number of outlets (1997)
B&Q	DIY	280
Ikea	Home and office furniture	8
Toys 'Я' Us	Toy retailer	56
Allied Carpets	Carpet discounter	238
MFI	Flatpack home furniture	186
PC World	Computer retailer	36

Source: Mintel 1999

New types of category killers are frequently being considered and this type of retail outlet has in no way reached its maximum. For example, a US company has recently launched a used car category killer. Other areas where the category killer has taken hold is the service industry. Some tourist destinations in Spain have literally killed off the compe-tition, and in the theme park business the name Disney in Florida conjures up a similar picture. Closer to home large shopping malls like Meadowhall have in their own way tempted trade away from the high street and other retail sites. Malls offer a broad range of activities such as cinemas, nightclubs and restaurants alongside the more traditional retail settings. In this manner, malls cater for shopping and recreational needs and have almost everything for the modern consumer. It is this point which best illustrates the harmful influence a category killer can have on local independent and mixed retailers. Their very survival hangs in the balance and only the strong will survive.

3.5 Additional Theories of Conflict and Development

Darwinism

The next theory provides the clearest and most obvious explanation for the reasons retail organizations change over time. It stems from the work of Charles Darwin (1809–82) the great British naturalist who sailed the world observing and investigating life on earth. His theory of evolution and natural selection which he describes in his book the 'origin of the species' revealed that organisms evolve and adapt in order to survive. This has given rise to the term *survival of the fittest*. If we apply this notion of Darwin's to the modern-day retail sector it gives us a convincing way of explaining structural change. For it is clear that firms who are best able to change and adapt to the actions of their competitors tend to remain in business the longest. For proof of this we simply need to reflect on some of the past retail wars. A good example is the food multiples battle for supremacy with store cards, or the way out-of-town retail parks have forced some town centres out of business. For many of the more successful retailers this frequent shift in the sector is a feature, which they have turned to their permanent advantage.

To fully understand how *natural selection* can work in retailing the terms that Darwin used can be directly related to the trading situation. The sometimes hostile environment, for example, is the marketplace which consists of consumers, competitors, supply channel and the surrounding legislation. In this retail jungle the predators are other retailers who naturally wish to maintain or even advance their position relative to each other. They respond to any threat to undermine that position by matching what the competition is offering, and so they adapt themselves to the marketplace. The prize they are after of course is a greater and greater share of the prey, that is, regular customers patronizing their stores who spend lots of money.

Unmistakable examples of this predatory behaviour are evident in the UK marketplace and stem from the key changes that have taken place. The market has become far more segmented over the last 20 years and some retailers have failed miserably to respond to this. Department stores, for example, until recently have continued to uphold their rather staid and at times unexciting image. This has led to a period of decline for them, although not to the point of extinction. In contrast, many new speciality stores have emerged in the wake of departing high street traders, such as independent opticians and tailor shops making made-to-measure clothing. In contrast, new speciality and single-line stores have experienced rapid growth. This is largely due to the very strong positions they have developed for themselves by tapping into the desires of the modern consumer. Success is about creating a strong image and appeal to specific types of customers, and lifestyles groups. Gap and some of the large sportswear retailers like JJB Sport are examples of this highly successful strategy.

Department stores have recently hit back with their own brand of tactics, such as creating specialized departments in-store for individual customer groups. This comeback has had a mixed response from customers and some retail critics, who think that this image presents an uncoordinated and odd use of floor space. Space utilization is important for department stores that are obliged to circulate customers round their stores to encourage them to spend money. Creating a collection of speciality stores within the store conflicts with the general aim of attracting 'multiple purchases across departments' (Lusch, Dunne and Gebhardt 1993: 115). Other high street multi-line stores have faired better by adapting to changing customer needs and expectations.

Some retailers like Woolworth have significantly changed the layout of their stores and the type and quality of the merchandise they offer. The following case shows how this well-known high street chain has significantly altered its image and reputation.

Case 3.3 The Changing Face of Woolworth

Woolworth is probably one of the most famous of all the low price multi-line stores, and is a familiar sight in any town centre throughout the UK. In recent years the Woolworth Company has undergone a great deal of change in an attempt to woo back the customers it lost to the category killers and supermarket chains. A Woolworth store now stands for value for money and quality, with central customer payment desks and smartly uniformed assistants. This is a distinct departure from the old Woolworth's image, which had a fairly 'cheap and nasty' reputation pre-1980. Woolworth adapted to the environment and has thus survived to present a fresh challenge for other retailers, and not just those in the high street. Big name category killers like Toys 'Я' Us have had some of their trade skimmed due to the new merchandizing policies. Perhaps consumers see that there are some benefits to be had from choosing to shop in their local high street. There are, after all, lots of new and interesting specialist retailers there now.

In response to a changing social, economic and technological environment, and in the wake of departing traders, a fresh wave of specialist retailers has emerged in the last decade or so. These new businesses have focused on very clear areas or niches in the market created by the forces of new technology. One area that has enjoyed considerable success is the music entertainment and electronic games sector. Popular names such as Virgin Records, HMV and GAME have led this venture into bespoke music shops and computer game boutiques, which cater for the younger collector and enthusiast.

One specialist retailer who has added an interesting and distinct range of merchandise is the games retailer Electronics Boutique. What makes this retailer so different is the mix of both new and part-used merchandise, and the positioning of their shops in top high street locations. Such ideas would have been unthinkable a few decades ago as second-hand shops belonged exclusively to the poorer districts of cities, where they were more accessible to lower income groups. The Electronics Boutique has capitalized on the high cost CD-ROM game market, which is popular with both younger and older people. This mounting consumer interest in the electronic interactive game market has helped to boost sales of multi-level board games generally. This has made way for another high street retailer Games Workshop, who offer the more traditional non-electronic versions which are modelled on the toy soldier of yesteryear.

The rising number of new-style specialist retailer has made up for the decline in more traditional specialists in our high streets. Of course, some of the more familiar retail institutions have adapted and survived as a result. To do this they have been forced to consider carefully their customers' needs, and possibly change their merchandise ranges from wide assortments to specialized stores, which offer narrow assortments. Retailers who read the market and are prepared to meet the challenges presented by the competition have faired well in the marketplace.

The Dialectic Process

At times, the upgrading of retail products and facilities by one retailer, in response to the actions of its competitor, produces two retailers that are very similar to each other. This has given rise to another framework, which demonstrates the evolution of retail firms. We call this the *dialectic process*. Some North American authors also use the term 'melting pot theory' as this suggests the type of synthesizing process that the theory attempts to describe. The crux of this is that retail firms mutually adapt in the face of rival competition, and so tend to adopt the plans and strategies of the opposition (Lusch, Dunne and Gebhardt 1993: 115). In the food sector, for instance, the policies of the two market leaders, Tesco and Sainsbury, have almost converged. Customers in both stores earn rewards with bonus points and loyalty cards for their continued custom. Each store has moved closer and closer to one another in their attempt to match the other's customer service policy. In fact, it can be said that each store has similar facilities, offerings, supplementary services, and of course prices. This new concentrated force in the market is now vulnerable from other predators who would neutralize or *negate* their competitive advantage.

Retailers outside the food sector are prone to mimic one another to the extent that they often become almost indistinguishable. In the electrical white goods sector firms like Comet and Currys have constantly matched each other's merchandise selection, store designs and pricing policies. Since Comet first took on a new look and designed for customer comfort, rather than its cash and carry style shopping image of the 1970s, it has moved closer to rivals like Currys. In the 1990s both these stores offer fairly similar ranges of merchandise, and use almost identical in-store architecture.

The dialectic model (see Figure 3.2) can also apply to catalogue shops like Argos and Index, who reside in the high street and most shopping

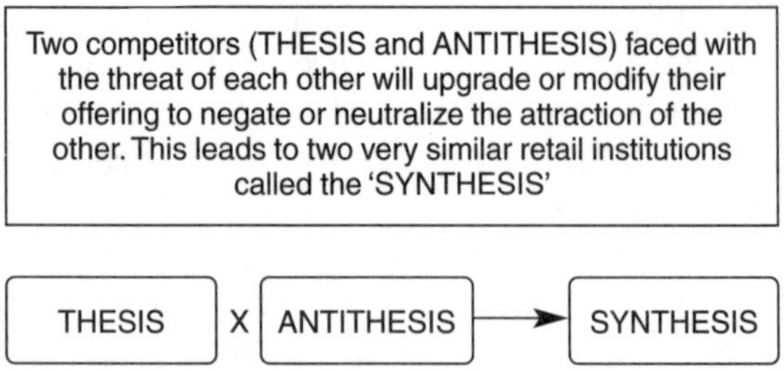

> Two competitors (THESIS and ANTITHESIS) faced with the threat of each other will upgrade or modify their offering to negate or neutralize the attraction of the other. This leads to two very similar retail institutions called the 'SYNTHESIS'

THESIS X ANTITHESIS ⟶ SYNTHESIS

Figure 3.2   The Dialectic Model

malls. Both stores offer a very similar range of goods, they both process their customers in the same way and their interior designs suggest the same type of offering. In an attempt to differentiate itself from its main rival Index, the Argos store introduced a home delivery service to enhance its customer appeal. This initiative prompted a similar response from Index who matched the strategy with the launch of their own home shopping service. The dialectic mechanism ensures that both Index and Argos continue to move closer and closer to each other and are therefore vulnerable to their competitors.

One sector that presents us with a clear picture of the classic thesis–antithesis–synthesis process is in petrol station retailing. We must however stress that many forces drive this industry and that the following example only considers price competitiveness. Market leaders like Esso, Shell and BP are frequently restructuring their prices and altering their products in response to the actions of one another. For example, Esso launched its 'price watch' campaign with the character-istic 'eyes of the tiger' pictures on their forecourts. The campaign guar-anteed the lowest priced petrol in the locality. But this move created a competitive advantage, which encouraged retaliatory measures from Shell and BP who also lowered their prices to compete. In addition, they raised the apparent standards of their products. Low emission petroleum fuels and low sulphur diesel products gave these companies the edge at a time when environmental issues mattered the most. This redressed the balance and reversed any advantage.

If we were to attribute the changes that have taken place in the petrol industry solely to competitive price matching we would be guilty of forming inaccurate conclusions. Other forces at work are equally respon-sible for the way petrol retailing has progressed and altered, and also help to explain the steps of the dialectic process. One shift is particularly useful to mention as it shows how new retail institutions entering the market can affect the current conditions. This major change for the industry took place during the 1960s when two new types of firm emerged in the UK. These were the independent integrated oil companies and cut-price wholesalers. Their very presence greatly reduced the possibility of price stability (Cook 1997) and so changed an industry based on pegged price levels. The forecourt war that followed resembles the processes of dialectic model. As petrol retailers faced the threat of each other they modified their offering to negate or neutralize the competitor's attrac-tiveness. This was an ongoing process throughout the 1990s.

What has taken place in the petrol market is very similar to the type of restructuring evident in most sectors of retailing. A highly mobile UK population with more money in their pockets have demanded a different sort of retailing, and retailers have had to respond accordingly. The out-of-town superstores and retail parks are the response to this demand. Many retailers, in particular the independents, have been unable to compete on this scale, unlike the larger chain multiples who had the financial size and could compete. The result was a gradual erosion of many retail businesses that have been unable to compete on price, retail sites and range of goods offered. In the smaller and low-value end of the market the small independent corner shop has survived quite well over time.

Polarization

The retail industry has seen a fall in the number of retail outlets to just above half the 1980 figure of 1971. The reasons for decline are mostly due to competition from multiples who have the buying power and economies of scale. This is called *polarization* and is all about the shift towards larger and smaller retailers with medium-sized businesses encountering the most difficulties. Often these small businesses have been forced into bankruptcy as a result of sheer scale and efficiency of the superstore competition. Independent traders have found it increasingly difficult to stay in business and compete with the multiples and co-operatives who can offer better ranges at lower prices.

The availability of large supermarkets and superstores with a wide range of goods has led to a greater quantity of merchandise handled by a smaller number of outlets. The larger stores offer the one-stop shopping experience that gives rise to prosperity in many sectors of the market. In the domestic appliance sector Dixons bought out Currys and Boots in order to improve their efficiencies. Over the last ten years stores such as Argos, Index, Next, Halfords and Tesco have adopted similar expansion plans. Thus the larger chains have combined to form even larger groups with the greatest evidence of this in food retailing.

Such rationalization in the retail industry has driven many independents to close their smaller shops and open fewer new ones. Others have prospered for the very reason that they are small and have limited ranges. Smaller independents can offer a very specialized retailing, which appeals to many groups of the population. For some the specialized retailer is a source of merchandise that is ordinarily difficult to find. The hardware store or ironmongers is a typical example of this type of service. Stores such as these are sought after by the 'do it yourself' enthusiast who is in search of the unusual bathroom fitting or shade of paint. Large operators like B&Q and Homebase, are unable to stock such items due to a number of reasons. To begin with they only sell fast-moving goods which they can turnover in volume. Their merchandise must therefore be highly saleable and popular in order to maximize on storage space. Individual and specialized items are difficult to move and so take up valuable space. In addition, the cost of these sorts of items is usually high and discounting is impossible.

In other parts of the homecare market the small independent provides the only real source of supply for the customer. With the sale of cut flowers and floral arrangements, for example, supply is monopolized by the smaller operator. Often operated on a franchise basis, florists like Interflora are able to expend both time and resources to provide a specialized service for the customer. Flower arrangements are gift-wrapped to the customer's own specifications while they wait. In kitchen design, and usually with special imported and expensive brands, the same emphasis on personal service brings the customers into the store. Similar trends are found in fashion and fashion items where high-class retail businesses cater for the more affluent consumer. Retailers in this sector purchase a few exclusive fashion lines at a relatively high cost and sell them on in small numbers. Small retail businesses are thus able to provide their customers with both the merchandise and service that big operators are unable to do.

There is plenty of evidence to suggest that small independent retailers have been severely affected by the influx of the multiples over the last two decades. However as specialized businesses increase in number, and size, many of these firms will evolve into medium-sized businesses. This may well plug the gap in the structure of the UK retail sector. Movement of this kind is not confined to the UK and similar tendencies are apparent in the US market and in Western Europe.

References

Anderson, C. H. (1993) *Retailing: Concepts, Strategy and Information*, St Paul, MN: West Publishing.

Cook, G. (1997) 'A comparative analysis of vertical integration in the UK brewing and petrol industries' *Journal of Economic Studies* 24(3): 152–66.

Cox, R. and Brittain, P. (1996) *Retail Management*, London: Pitman Publishing, p. 13.

Grant, W. (1987) *Business and Politics in Britain*, London: Macmillan Education.

Hower, R. (1943) 'History of Macy's of New York 1858–1919', in R. Lusch, P. Dunne and R. Gebhardt (1993) *Retail Marketing*, Cincinnati, OH: South-Western Publishing, pp. 113–14.

Lusch, R. F., Dunne, P. and Gebhardt, R. (1993) *Retail Marketing*, Cincinnati, OH: South-Western Publishing, p. 115.

Marketing Business (1994) Killing off the Competition, pp. 10–14.

McNair, M. P. (1958) 'Significant trends and development in the postwar period', in A. B. Smith (ed.) *Competitive Distribution in a Free High-Level Economy and its Implication for the University*, Pittsburgh, PA: University of Pittsburgh Press.

Mintel (1998) *Variety Stores Retailing* (April), London: Mintel International Group Ltd.

Mintel (1999) *Retail Review 1999*, London: Mintel International Group Ltd.

National Statistics (annual) *Annual Abstract of Statistics*, London: The Stationery Office.

National Statistics (2000) *Business Monitor SDM28*, London: The Stationery Office.

National Statistics (2001) *Business Monitor PA1003* (monthly), London: The Stationery Office.

Wileman, A. and Jary, M. (1997) *Retail Power Plays*, London: Macmillan Business, pp. 78, 105.

Managing in Good Times and Bad: Dealing with Booms and Slumps

CHAPTER 4

This chapter explains:

▶ How and why fluctuations occur.

▶ The features of government macroeconomic policy.

▶ How macroeconomic activity and policy affect the retailing industry.

▶ How firms may anticipate and deal with fluctuations in the economy.

Managing in Good Times and Bad: Dealing with Booms and Slumps

Introduction and Core Concepts

This chapter helps the student to understand the complexities of the economy within the context of managing the retail business. It starts with those aspects of the macroeconomy that a retailer would come across in reports (such as Mintel or Key Note) relating to the current retail environment. The more important factors affecting consumer spending, interest rates, taxes and investments are briefly discussed. This leads on to the practical issues in maintaining profitability and liquidity as economic circumstances change.

4.1 The Mood of the Nation

Changes in Consumer Spending

Most retailers experience changes in the level of customer spending. Some of these changes reflect changes in the competitive position of the retailer and may occur gradually over a longer period or they can happen within a short period of time as a new retailer or shopping centre opens up nearby. These have been discussed in Chapter 3. However, some of the change in customer spending reflects changes in the general level of consumer spending. Table 4.1 shows the pattern of consumer spending over a recent ten-year period, including details for some categories of products. (The data refer to consumption spending and exclude investment in property.)

Table 4.1 shows how household spending has been growing over a number of years. The data are at current prices and so they overstate the increase in real consumption. However, they show that consumer spending has been increasing, but not at a steady pace. Some of the changes in the general level of consumer spending reflect longer-term

Table 4.1 Household Final Consumption Spending (£ million at current prices)

	Total spending	Food, alcohol and tobacco	Clothing and footwear	Durable goods (not vehicles)	Other goods
1990	336 492	71 826	21 212	15 483	39 659
1991	357 785	76 722	22 209	15 890	42 171
1992	377 147	78 746	23 404	17 044	44 461
1993	399 108	81 999	24 777	17 311	46 738
1994	419 262	83 746	26 893	18 102	48 935
1995	438 453	86 730	28 347	18 747	51 947
1996	467 841	92 131	29 564	20 212	57 094
1997	498 307	94 046	31 115	23 194	61 921
1998	530 851	95 722	32 376	25 283	67 533
1999	564 369	99 473	33 530	27 218	72 867

Source: National Statistics 2000

changes in income and economic structure and these were discussed in Chapter 2. However, the retailer is often immediately concerned with consumer spending during the coming 12 months in order to make its seasonal merchandise plans. Being able to foresee fluctuations in the growth of consumer spending improves its planning for the coming year. Increases in consumer income during this period will lead to increased consumer spending, but pessimistic expectations about unemployment and higher interest rates will discourage consumer spending.

Consumer spending can also change for other reasons, such as seasonal factors. This is illustrated in Table 4.2, which shows that consumer spending is consistently higher in the final quarter of the year, October, November and December, leading up to the Christmas period.

Table 4.2 Household Spending (£ million at current prices)

	Total	1st quarter	2nd quarter	3rd quarter	4th quarter
1996	467 841	110 023	113 048	120 548	124 224
1997	498 307	116 475	120 848	128 738	132 246
1998	530 851	124 171	129 487	136 429	140 764
1999	564 369	132 785	138 512	143 213	149 859

Source: National Statistics 2000

The change in demand facing the retailer results from a mixture of all the factors that have been mentioned. However, a dominant factor in short-term retail planning will be the state of the economy in terms of consumer income, unemployment, interest rates and the level of wage and price increases. Variations in these are called macroeconomic fluctuations, which occur about the long-term trend in activity (see Chapter 2). Figure 4.1 illustrates this pattern. The repetitive nature of the fluctuations gives rise to the term *economic cycle, business cycle* or *trade cycle*.

The long-term growth that we have been experiencing means that the UK has suffered only mild and very short-lived drops in output since 1960. However, there have been periods where rising output has been followed by a period of very low or no growth and severe unemployment. We identify these periods as either a recession or depression. For

For business and pleasure.
Whitbread use a spacious car park to link its TGI franchise and Travel Inn outlets. This allows the retailer to meet the needs of local and travellers.

Tradition on the motorway.
Following customers' lifestyles, Thornton's elegant store makes it easier to buy that special gift.

Eat and go.
The clean uncluttered lines assure the traveller of a quality and value food service.

Make your choice.
The layout of this catalogue store guides the customer through all the stages of purchase.

The promise to come.
Rich, luxurious hues for excitement. Large displays for more next time. Floor bins for value. Luxury and value at Wine Rack.

Competitive value.
Soft colours for quality, well stacked displays for value and a counter for old-fashioned service create a unique appeal for this (Oxfam/charity?) shop.

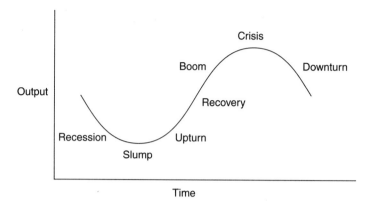

Figure 4.1   The Stages of the Macroeconomic Cycle

instance, the *unemployment level* reached over 3 million people (over 11 per cent of the workforce) at the worst points of the cycle in 1986 and in 1993. However, this high level of unemployment reflected the low point of another very long-term, 50- to 60-year, cycle. We are now on the upswing of this very long-term cycle, which means that unemployment even during the low points of short-term business cycles should be much lower in the first decades of the 2000s.

Demand and Supply in the Economy

The level of economic activity depends on the *demand* for and *supply* of *final* goods and services. (These are sometimes called *aggregate* demand and supply, to refer to the economy as a whole.)

> ⇨ Final goods and services in national accounting statistics means those goods and services which have no further work done on them. This distinguishes them from intermediate goods and services, which are used in further production. We can only count final goods and services in calculating output. If we include intermediate goods we would be double counting some output.

The level of demand in the economy reflects the amount of money that people and organizations are willing to pay to businesses in the UK. It consists of:

▶ *Consumer spending on goods and services*. This varies with the level of income, but is the actual proportion of income spent over the economic cycle. (Consumer spending in government statistics includes spending by non-profit institutions. Spending on house purchases [net of sales] is part of investment, in the next category.)

▶ *Investment spending*. This includes investment in fixed assets (plant, machinery and vehicles) and inventory investment in stocks and work in progress.

▶ *Government spending on goods and services.*

▶ *Exports of goods and services.*

The different components of demand mean that demand increases when:

▶ People expect income and employment to increase. They feel better off and more optimistic about the future and they are then willing to spend more.

▶ The value of the pound falls against foreign currencies. This reduces the prices of domestic (UK) products relative to imports and consumers and businesses spend on home produced goods and services and less on imports.

▶ The rate of interest falls. This makes it cheaper for firms and consumers to borrow money. They will then increase the level of investment and consumer spending.

The supply in the economy is the amount of goods and services available to satisfy demand. It includes the goods and services produced by UK firms plus imports from other countries.

The Balance in the Economy

When the goods and services that people want to buy match the goods and services available, demand and supply in the economy are in balance. However, growth in the economy has seen a shift to services, which are labour intensive and relatively costly to provide. This tends to push prices up even when the economy is in balance.

When demand is greater than supply, businesses feel optimistic about expanding their operations. Retailers experience increased sales and so they increase their orders from their suppliers. Manufacturers see orders increasing and they try to increase the output accordingly. However, shortages and bottlenecks in production or delivery occur and push up prices. Retailers may also experience difficulties in recruiting staff of the right calibre or may have to resort to overtime payments. Either way, costs increase disproportionately to sales and so price has to rise. The net effect is that there is pressure on prices to rise even faster than before.

Conversely, when demand is less than supply, retailers experience falling sales. This makes them pessimistic about the future and they cut back on their orders and resort to price cutting to clear unwanted stock. This has a knock-on effect back up the supply chain. Employment tends to fall and prices rise more slowly. There are always seasonal reductions in prices. However, when the situation is very severe, prices may even fall significantly below the normal seasonal level.

4.2 Maintaining the Balance in the Economy

The government is expected to maintain a balance in the economy in order to protect people from unemployment and high prices and also to help people become better off in the future. However, there are a number of problems in achieving this.

▶ *The level of demand is affected by the amount of money and credit consumers and businesses have to spend.* The financial sector (which includes banks, building societies, pension funds and insurance companies) converts savings into funds for investment as well as supply consumer credit. However, financial institutions may lend or invest money overseas or not invest at all. This means that the level of investment or consumer spending can increase without a corresponding change in the level of saving.

▶ *Taxes reduce demand and government spending increases demand in the system.* If the government balances its budget, the economy should be in balance. However, *taxes and government spending can affect saving and investment in the economy.* For instance, people tend to save out of disposable, after-tax income. So increasing income taxes reduces people's savings and increases the level of demand. *Government borrowing usually increases the amount of money in the economy.* A growing economy needs extra money to finance the increase in everyday transactions, but if the government increases the amount of money too much, the level of demand will increase further.

▶ *Exports increase demand but imports reduce demand by providing alternative supply.* Outflows of money have to balance inflows over time, but *exports may not balance imports in the short term.*

Interest Rates and Economic Activity

Changes in the rate of interest also affect economic activity. The rate of interest varies according to the demand or supply of money and credit. However, the government manipulates the rate of interest in order to control the level of money and spending in the economy.

Balance of Payments and the Economy

The balance of payments is the difference between the spending by non-residents on goods and services produced in the UK (exports) and the spending by UK residents on goods and services produced abroad (imports). When the level of exports is less than the level of imports, the value of the pound tends to fall against foreign currencies. This is known as a *fall in the exchange rate* or *depreciation of the pound.* The result is an increase in the cost of imports and a fall in the price of UK exports. Imports are reduced as a result of this and as people buy more home produced goods. This increases total demand in the economy.

For various reasons, however, the government may not wish the value of the pound to fall. It may instead increase interest rates to attract foreign lenders into the country.

Why Fluctuations in Output Occur

One reason for fluctuations is that investments actually depend on the level of output expected. When investment, government spending or exports increase, demand in the economy also increases. In general, firms do not have the appropriate amount of equipment to produce the extra output efficiently, so they begin to increase their investment.

As firms increase their investment, output and income rise still further and this encourages more investment. However, factors such as a shortage of investment funds or bottlenecks in production eventually reduce the rate of investment. In practice, the UK growth rate is about 2 per cent per annum on average. It cannot sustain an annual growth rate of 3–4 per cent for more than a couple of years. The rate of growth slows down and so reduces the need for more investment. The economy may then stop growing and, as investment starts falling, reverse into decline.

4.3 Government Macroeconomic Policy

Macroeconomic Policy Objectives

The government uses various *macroeconomic policies* to control the fluctuations in economic activity. Underlying these policies are various objectives that are based on a mixture of ideology, electoral considerations and outside pressures such as those from the European Union (EU) on movement towards a single European currency. These objectives can be generally stated as:

1 Control inflation (the target is usually around 3 per cent or less).

2 Control unemployment.

3 Improve the rate of growth.

4 Control the balance of payments.

5 Limit public sector borrowing to 3 per cent of GDP.

6 Limit the national debt (total accumulated government borrowing) to 60 per cent GDP.

The control of inflation and unemployment are the two major goals. Controlling the balance of payments is important because balance of payments problems have in the past been a major obstacle to economic growth. The balance between unemployment and inflation is one that varies between political parties. Objectives 5 and 6 are additional EU criteria for implementing the single currency.

Inflation

Inflation is defined as a continuing rise in prices. In the UK, the Retail Price Index measures these price changes. This is based on the cost of the average shopping basket. There are three reasons why prices continue to rise:

1 *Excess demand in the economy.* This causes prices to rise until the excess demand is eliminated.

2 *Cost increases occurring independently of demand.* Increases in the prices of imported goods and services, and trade union pressure on wages, can cause prices to rise without any increase in consumer demand.

3 *Structural change in the economy.* Excess demand in some areas leads to a rise in prices, but excess supply in other areas causes unemployment. As a result, average prices continue to rise.

Unemployment

The UK has a population of over 59 million. According to official government statistics about 28 million are economically active, that is, in employment or actively seeking employment. About 27 million people are employed and 1 million are actively seeking work. Those in employment may be fully employed (with or without overtime working) or underemployed, on short-time working. Unemployment is caused by the following:

▶ *Seasonal factors.* For instance, some retailing workers are only in employment for part of the year. Other workers are laid off temporarily because of bad weather. Unemployment data are *seasonally adjusted* to eliminate this element.

▶ *Supply-side factors.* These are caused by difficulties in people adjusting to changed employment and industrial conditions. They include:
  - *Frictional unemployment.* This includes people temporarily out of work or between jobs. Improving communication flows in the labour market can reduce this situation.
  - *Structural unemployment.* This includes workers who have the wrong skills or are in the wrong area because changes in the economic structure have led to the loss or decline of traditional industries. The government needs to help such people with retraining or relocation. Local authorities can tackle depressed areas through new developments in conjunction with large retailers and distribution firms. Structural unemployment often leads to:
  - *Long-term unemployment.* This includes people who have been out of work for a long time. It is difficult for such people to get into the labour market. The government needs to reduce these numbers through retraining programmes.

▶ *Demand factors.* When the economy goes into a downturn, firms reduce employment. The government can improve the situation by stimulating demand in the economy.

Constraints on Macroeconomic Policy

There are a number of constraints on government economic policy that prevent it managing the economy as easily as it would like. The UK economy is not independent of other economies, particularly as regards interest rates and the level of exports which both affect the level of demand in the country. Membership of the European Union, for example, creates considerable constraints. A substantial part of UK output and consumption depends on international trade. This represents about 30 per cent of its output.

This links economic growth and cycles to world levels of economic activity and reduces the ability of the government to control its own economy. International capital mobility makes it difficult for the real rate of interest in the UK to differ much from the real interest rate in world financial markets. The real rate of interest is the actual rate of interest adjusted for inflation. In practice, this does not mean that changes in the rate of interest in other countries particularly the USA and the EU will have an immediate impact on UK interest rates, but it puts the government under increasing pressure to follow suit. Large amounts of funds move quickly round the world in response to changes in interest rates, which are used as part of the measures to balance the movement of funds into and out of a country.

Any change in government policy generates signals to consumers and businesses. The way these signals are received and interpreted affects business and consumer confidence. This in turn affects their investment and consumption behaviour. The problem for the government is that the same measure could be interpreted differently on different occasions. Making sure that business and consumers interpret the signals correctly is more a political than an economic problem. The policy measures have some economic effects, but these could be swamped by the confidence factor.

Implementing Macroeconomic Objectives

Macroeconomic policy regulates the level of demand and supply of goods and services in the economy. Hence, there are two basic policy programmes: demand management and supply management. Demand management regulates the level of demand in the economy by controlling the various elements of demand. Supply management means improving the supply in the economy so that greater amounts are supplied at lower prices by improving productivity and labour supply – reducing the rate of increase in labour costs – and also by reducing other costs.

In practice demand responds quicker to current income flows and expectations about the immediate future. Supply, however, is more affected than demand by past decisions about investment in physical and human capital. Hence, demand problems can be dealt with more quickly, while supply-side problems take longer to deal with. So macroeconomic policy is more concerned with controlling the level of demand in the economy.

Monetary Policy

This controls the amount of money and credit, including the rate of interest and bank lending, in the economy. The essential feature of money is that it is a highly liquid asset, that is, it can be easily and quickly exchanged for goods or services of the same nominal value. All assets can be classed according to their liquidity. There are, however, many financial assets that are very liquid and often perform the functions of money and this makes monetary control more difficult. Consequently, the government employs two concepts of money: narrow money and broad money. Narrow money is close to what we would call money, while broad money includes a range of bank deposits and easily utilized credits. Expansionary monetary policy occurs when the government expands money supply faster than before. Interest rates then begin to fall and so may the exchange rate.

However, the UK government has pursued an anti-inflationary strategy based on the long-run control of the growth of the money supply. Crudely put, the long-term growth rate of the UK economy is about 2 per cent per annum. This means that on average for every £100 of goods and services produced last year the economy now produces £102 at last year's prices. If the money in the system has also grown by 2 per cent, then for every pound of purchasing power last year there is now £102. Hence there is £102 of money demand for every £102 of goods and services available. This means that supply and demand balance and there is no need for price to rise.

However, if the government increases the money supply by 5 per cent, there is now £105 of money for every £102 worth of goods and services available. Demand exceeds supply and so prices rise. The approximate rise in prices is given by the equation:

% rate of inflation = % increase in money supply – % increase in
$$\text{productivity}$$
$$= 5\% - 2\%$$
$$= 3\%.$$

In practice, there is a time lag of about a year and the relationship does not strictly hold in the short term and when unemployment may be significant. However, it gives some idea of how costs and price may behave in a year's time.

Fiscal Policy

This uses government spending and taxation to control the economy. The main instruments of fiscal policy are:

► direct taxation on income and wealth, including corporation tax

► indirect taxation on spending and production

► spending on investment and consumer goods and services

► grants (including pensions and other direct subsidies) to consumers

► grants and allowances to investors.

If the government balances its budget, so that spending is the same as taxation, it returns the same amount of money into the system as it took away in taxes. However, the level of demand may still increase, depending on the way the government gets its taxes. This is because consumers plan their spending and savings according to their *disposable income* (which in this context means income after income tax and other deductions). A major consideration in policy is the need to control the public sector borrowing requirement or the annual increase in government debt. This is because increased borrowing either raises interest rates or increases the money supply, which affects the rate of inflation in about one to two years.

4.4 The Impact of Economic Fluctuations on the Retailing Industry

Fluctuations in income, employment, and interest rates affect demand and supply conditions in the retailing industry. For example, a large pool of potential employees makes it easier for the retail manager to recruit. Low interest rates can induce purchases of durable goods and some services like holidays. Fluctuations make investment planning such as buying property or investing in stock more difficult because it makes the returns less certain. An investment may be appropriate for the long-term trends in the market, but the timing may be wrong. Investments such as building a retail outlet take time to earn revenue, that is, bring in customers and cash. If a retailer brings an investment on stream when the economy is going into a recession, it may have to pay for equipment that is not being utilized because demand is low. This may jeopardize the profitability of the investment and the ability of the company to meets its obligations in the long term.

Businesses experience a direct impact of economic policy when the government uses the industry or a closely related industry as an instrument of policy. For instance, the government may decide to increase its hospital or road-building programme to increase the general level of spending in the economy. This would have an immediate impact on the construction and civil engineering industries. However, this is rarely the case with the retailing industry.

Retailers do, however, experience an indirect impact of government macroeconomic policy when the direct effect of policy decisions has a knock-on effect on the retailing industry. For instance, if a change in government policy brings an increase in consumer disposable income, this leads to an increase in demand in various sectors of the retailing industry. Retailers can expect demand in the shops to follow the pattern of consumer spending over the economic cycle. However, some sections such as the DIY and home improvement market reflect general changes in the housing market, which tend to overreact to changes in the level of economic activity.

The costs of operation and product prices are affected by the rate of inflation, taxation levels and to some extent by variations in the exchange rate. The cost and availability of finance should be considered separately, since they may be affected differently by changes in the general level of activity. Table 4.3 shows how the recession affected the level of individual bankruptcies and company insolvencies in the industry during the last major recession. It shows that the worst time tends to come as the economy is moving out of recession. There are several explanations for this:

▶ The greater the length and severity of the recession the greater financial strain on firms, so that more firms are likely to be vulnerable at the end of the recession.

▶ Firms expand activities too fast for their depleted funds during the upturn in the market.

▶ The reviving markets allow creditors to recoup more of their money from ailing businesses by selling off assets.

Table 4.3 Bankruptcies and Insolvencies, 1989–96

	1989	1990	1991	1992	1993	1994	1995	1996
Bankruptcies of all self-employed	5 860	8 489	14 609	19 525	18 561	15 114	13 282	12 667
of which retail	1 022	1 557	2 699	3 559	3 606	2 939	2 664	2 257
Company insolvencies	10 456	15 051	21 827	24 425	20 708	16 728	14 536	13 461
of which retail	1 039	1 559	2 114	2 477	2 005	1 711	1 568	1 419

Source: National Statistics 2001

4.5 Managing Fluctuations

Predicting Macroeconomic Changes

Retailing firms can use various sources of economic information to reduce risks, avoid pitfalls and cope successfully with fluctuations in activity. The most convenient to use are the economic activity indicators published by the government. An economic activity indicator is an index number for a particular variable whose behaviour is similar to that of the economy as a whole.

Consumer credit is a good example of a *leading indicator* or variable that changes ahead of economic activity as a whole. An increase in credit means that consumers want to spend more money. When producers perceive this increase to be continuing, they increase output and so employ more people.

In fact, the Office of National Statistics (ONS) publishes four sets of indicators:

1 *Longer leading*, where changes takes place about six months ahead of the economy.

2 *Shorter leading*, where changes take place about three months ahead of the economy.

3 *Coincident*, where changes take place about the same time as broader economic activity.

4 *Lagging*, where changes tend to take place after changes in the economy as a whole.

The ONS decides where data series fit best. Each series is converted into real values (eliminating the effects of inflation), smoothed and detrended using time-series analysis techniques. The standardized series are amalgamated with others in the same category to give the four composite indicators. Notice that the series have been detrended, that is, the long-term growth has been removed. This allows us to see the short-term cyclical pattern more clearly so that we can judge whereabouts on the short-term cycle the economy is. You should also note that the series do not all tell the same story all of the time so there is still some art left in interpreting them.

Managers can assess the impact of macroeconomic change by using the following approach.

1 *Look at forecasts published by different institutions.* The Treasury, the National Institute for Economic and Social Research, and various university business schools all publish surveys, and summaries of them are published in newspapers. The forecasts differ, because they reflect different assumptions about how the economy works. These differences often reflect political ideologies, so that it is useful to know something about the background of the forecasters, which affects their views on whether fiscal or monetary means are best for managing the economy. Retail associations also provide their own forecasts to help retailers.

2 *Look at economic activity indicators.* These will give some indication of which way the economy seems to be going. Remember that international constraints are important in open economies and that boom follows slump follows boom.

3 *Be sensitive to political factors.* Be aware of which indicators the government pay particular regard to, as these may change if the government changes and even during the existing government's period of office. Important indicators that affect government policy are:
   (a) *The rate of inflation.* If it goes up (down), the government may implement contractionary (expansionary) policies such as higher (lower) interest rates or higher (lower) taxes.
   (b) *Retail sales.* Rapidly rising (falling) sales may lead to contractionary (expansionary) policies.
   (c) *Balance of payments (= export – imports).* If the deficit is rising, there will be pressure on the pound. This will lead to increases in interest rates or expenditure or credit controls.
   (d) *Government borrowing (public sector borrowing requirement).* If this becomes too high a proportion of GDP, the government will raise taxes or cut spending.
   (e) *Growth of the money supply.* The government sets a target band rate of growth (say 2–4 per cent a year). If the money supply increases faster than this, the government will act to reduce the rate of growth of the money supply. For instance, increase in the amount of *broad money* equals increase in government borrowing

plus the increase in bank lending to the private sector *minus* the increase in private lending to the government.

The government can act to change any of these variables and this will have a knock-on effect on firms.

Dealing with a Recession

Retailers should take the regularity of the recessions into their long- and medium-term planning so that they avoid unnecessary problems. They should:

▶ Forecast the time path of the recession using the cyclical indicators described above. Identify the cyclical hazards to the business, and prepare preventive action to deal with them.

▶ Plan product lines and rebranding so that the growth of the market is relatively high during the downturn period so that there is a buffer against the general fall in demand. This allows further capital expansion to occur when property prices and interest costs are lowest at the end of the recession.

▶ Keep assets flexible. Avoid unnecessary diversification of activities. Many large and small retailers have to undergo a period of restructuring to divest themselves of peripheral business caught up in the periods of expansion.

▶ Control liquidity so that the core business can survive without requiring large cash injections during any recession. Controlled borrowing during good times is important so that large increases in interest rates and sharp downturns in consumer spending will still leave the retailer with sufficient funds to cover the interest charges and any capital repayments. This leaves a clear margin that allows for a fall in property and other values, which affect the security offered to lenders.

References

National Statistics (2000) *Monthly Digest of Statistics*, December (660).
National Statistics (2001) *Annual Abstract of Statistics*, London: The Stationery Office.

Retail Marketing: Planning and Development

5   Strategic Marketing Planning for
    Retailing: Setting up the Business

6   The Customer and the Retail Business:
    Knowing your Customers

7   The Fundamentals of Merchandising:
    Product

8   Establishing a Pricing Strategy

9   Promoting the Store: Sending Out the
    Correct Sort of Messages

10 Locating the Store in the Retail
    Environment

PART

2

Strategic Marketing Planning for Retailing: Setting up the Business

CHAPTER

5

This chapter:

- ▶ Explains the strategic planning process.

- ▶ Shows how retailers use integrated marketing systems.

- ▶ Links supply chain relationships to competitive advantages.

- ▶ Identifies the role of retail formats and merchandise in the strategic plan.

Strategic Marketing Planning for Retailing: Setting up the Business

Introduction and Core Concepts

Planning is about making sure that the future turns out the way you want it to. Planning is about anticipating and organizing the various parts of the business to reach a predetermined objective. Making plans is an essential part of the retail management function and good planning helps to create successful businesses. It is vital for students of retailing to understand how the strategic planning process works, and why a carefully constructed plan can mean the difference between success and failure for a retailer. However, before describing the strategic planning process we will first define the terms planning, strategy and strategic planning.

5.1 The Strategic Planning Process: A Framework

It is not just retailers that become involved in planning but all manner of entities and organizations like people, institutions and even nations. Planning for the future is a necessary task of government and good economic planning may, for example, help to create the right climate for low inflation over a period of years. Individual people make plans also. This may involve the holiday of a lifetime or the purchase of a new home, or even a trip to the local supermarket.

Of course there is another approach we could use which is not to make any plans but simply to let the future take its course. This however is a high-risk strategy and may lead to undesirable outcomes. For example, a nation could end up in recession because interest rates are too high. The holiday of a lifetime may turn into a disaster because it was the wrong time of the year and the weather was awful. A trip to the supermarket may be a waste of time if the store closes before you get there (unlikely to happen as most supermarkets have extended opening hours). It is far more satisfactory to find out the opening times before visiting the store, and then map out your visit and compile a list of items to buy. Then things will turn out the way you want.

For retailers planning is also concerned with trying to prepare for what the future holds, such as what sorts of styles, ranges, quantities and sizes customers will want in the coming year. This sounds easy but it is difficult to judge in advance exactly what ranges customers will want in the forthcoming season. The short case study that follows considers the problems of the highly successful chain multiple Marks & Spencer, and their inability to predict demands for the first time in their spectacular history.

Case 5.1 Marks & Spencer: Even They Can Get It Wrong!

The new chairman of M&S, Luc Vandevelde, believes that the retailer needs to offer new and better clothing ranges. Customers have been telling M&S this since 1998. But despite repeated promises M&S has resisted temptation to ditch its old strategy. Plans to switch more buying overseas, revamp stores, cut head office bureaucracy and improve the supply chain may help. However, the retailer has yet to convince the British public that it has a recovery plan.

Source: Barker 1998: 7, 9, 11–12

So while planning does not always guarantee success it will help to ensure that management is more effective, and careful planning can increase the likelihood of achieving the financial and other objectives. This applies to all types of retailing regardless of the size of the business. Many of the smaller retailers have floated successful enterprises by anticipating change and planning accordingly. Often they have beaten off the larger multiples and stolen some of their customers by the process of careful planning.

> ⇨ Planning is therefore an activity, a process in business that provides a systematic structure and framework for considering the future, appraising options and opportunities, and then selecting and implementing the necessary activities for achieving the stated objectives efficiently and effectively (Brassington and Pettitt 1997: 876).

Strategy is also a type of plan but much more comprehensive covering all parts or functions of the organization. Frequently called a 'game plan', strategy provides a collective direction for the organization as a whole. Retail strategy is thus a broad plan of action, which identifies for the retailer the necessary changes they must make to adapt to the dynamic marketplace.

For example, a retailer may decide that it intends to become a leading brand name in the grocery sector, much like Tesco did when it turned away from its old 1970s image. The sorts of tactics the retailer might employ to achieve the strategic goal may be to substantially improve both quality and range to a level beyond that of the major competitor (in our example Sainsbury). Tactics are therefore the individual measures undertaken to make the strategy work. For example, Tesco introduced a store loyalty scheme to attract and retain more customers as part of its tactical manoeuvres. This had the effect of improving its overall share of the market in line with its strategic objective.

A strategy will consequently envelop a retailer's basic reason for being in business, which may be:

▶ to increase profitability

▶ to reach more customers

▶ to be the market leader.

Typically, strategy will cover corporate policies, the allocation of resources, customer markets and the competitive environment in which a retailer operates. *Strategic planning* combines both planning and strategy to provide the key ingredients of the retail management process (Anderson 1993: 39). This process is best explained as a series of basic steps or stages, which are important milestones in the strategic planning process (Figure 5.1).

The strategic planning process consists of the six components illustrated in the model in Figure 5.1. In this section we will look in detail at the first four of these stages to examine how the results of one decision can provide data for the next. The following list expands the stages with emphasis placed on the need to analyse the marketplace. This analysis permits management to adapt and change the business in line with their defined objectives.

1 The development of a statement defining the mission of the business.

2 A definition of the specific objectives of the business.

3 Statement of the desired market position of the business.

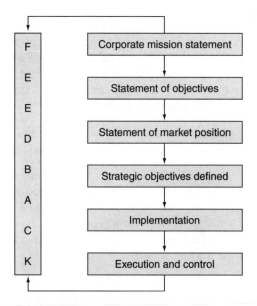

Figure 5.1   The Strategic Planning Process

4 An analysis of the various opportunities in the retail marketplace.

5 The development of the basic strategies (there may be several) that will enable the business to reach its objectives.

6 Implementation or commitment of resources to accomplish the strategic intent.

7 Execution or activation of the strategic plan and control systems.

Usually, the evolution of a strategy will follow a particular pattern; in the case of a small retailer this may be as straightforward as maintaining cash flow for survival. Larger businesses will create more complex strategies that will change in a continuing process, with one decision affecting the next. To simplify the problem of explaining this process we will start with the mission statement, which states the purpose of the business.

Case 5.2 Definition: Mission Statement

A mission statement represents a vision of where the organization is today and where it wants to be in the future. It expresses the core values of the organization and is intended to guide functional and business unit areas in their strategic development. It should encompass segments served, the needs to be fulfilled in the market, and the technological or service character of the organization.

Source: Abell 1984

Mission statements vary in length and complexity but invariably offer a vision of where the business is today and where it intends to be in the future. This may consist of a *philosophical target* which simply means a statement reflecting the deep-rooted values and beliefs of the organization from which it stems. Also, there are likely to be some guidelines for the development of the retailer's goals and objectives, and the policies and strategies needed to achieve them. The effective mission statement is above all customer oriented and will motivate or inspire the employees. Besides this, specific comment will provide the necessary guidelines for operating the business. Here are some examples of statements drawn from two very popular fast food retailers:

▶ KFC aims to 'provide families with affordable, delicious chicken-dominated meals'.

With KFC the emphasis is placed on the customer, in particular families, and the provision of value-for-money products. There is an implicit assumption that chicken is not only liked universally by customers with families, but that it is acceptable not to serve meats other than chicken. The next mission statement is also from a famous fast food retailer but this time it's McDonald's.

▶ McDonald's 'will provide great tasting food backed up by excellent operations and friendly service in a relaxed, safe, and consistent restaurant environment'.

There are many more factors considered in this McDonald's mission statement. For example, the element and standard of service is guaranteed, as is the consistency of the overall product. Customers are therefore reassured about the nature, quality and standards of the retailer. The following mission also focuses on the needs of customers with promises of service and commitment to quality. This time, however, the company mission acknowledges the importance of meeting the changing needs of customers.

▶ Tesco 'is one of Britain's leading food retailers. The company owes its success to its emphasis on meeting changing customer needs through service and innovation, while maintaining its commitment to value and quality'.

More complex and detailed than the earlier examples, Tesco's mission takes a clear position on the importance of customers. So much so that it expects customer needs to change and will adapt accordingly. The mention of innovation takes this idea one step further by saying that the company endeavours to anticipate customer needs beforehand. An illustration of this is Tesco's venture with the Royal Bank of Scotland, launched in November 1997, which offered customers competitive financial services through its stores.

Most retail markets are intensely competitive and no serious contender can afford to rely on its achievements. This fact has encouraged retailers to pioneer many new ideas by listening and responding to customer needs. Clearly, these will change over time as will the general environment in which the business operates. The mission statement will undergo alterations in line with these changes. Thus the mission statement provides the retailer with a 'guiding force' for all their strategic plans (Lusch, Dunne and Gebhardt 1993: 34). In the next stage of the strategic planning process specific objectives are defined to provide direction and accuracy to the business. The following is an example of the sorts of objectives a retailer might aim for:

'Our core purpose is to continually increase value for customers, and to earn their lifetime loyalty.'
Source: http://www.tesco.co.uk/indexn.htm

In the above statement we can see that the objectives provide a visible direction for the business, and from which it can draw up its strategies. The statement also provides a clear standard against which the company, in this case Tesco, can measure and evaluate its performance. For example, the loyalty card scheme would furnish one method of testing the effectiveness of customer loyalty. Other factors such as the share of the market and sales will show whether the company is meeting its targets.

5.2 Objectives to Position the Business

The objectives that companies set are linked to carefully considered targets that, providing the objectives are met, will strengthen the retailer's position in the marketplace. Most objectives have clear and well-defined areas specified in them, which target specific aspects of the operation generally. In the following example, which is drawn from the Debenhams group company statement, focusing on customers is at the heart of their strategy and places the emphasis squarely on merchandise, relationships, staff motivation and store layouts:

▶ Building strong merchandise and brands.

▶ Enhancing relationships with customers and suppliers.

▶ Developing, motivating and retaining key staff.

▶ Effectively managing and expanding retail space.

Source: Debenhams website http://www.debenhams.co.uk/corporateservice/information/index.htm

---

⇨ You may wish to visit the Debenhams website and check out the breadth of its strategy, and the way in which it focuses the retail business.

We can see that Debenhams has drawn up four main objectives which it feels are key to building and maintaining its position in the market. The first of their objectives is to focus on building strong merchandise and brands, that is, selling only those brands and merchandise that are most successful. In fact Debenhams concentrates on the higher margin products where it has a competitive advantage, and has stopped selling some of the traditional department store categories like furniture and electrical products. This shift is the result of changes in the demand for these types of goods and is consistent with the market-wide review of department store trading.

Next, by enhancing relationships with customers and suppliers Debenhams seeks to build both customer loyalty and loyalty from its suppliers. With this objective they acknowledge the importance of both customer and supplier relationships. It is easy to see why they should wish to constantly improve customer relationships, as this will enable the company to provide the right goods and services at the right time. For example, regular product updates will not only ensure the right products are available on the shelves but will also create a feeling of 'newness' (as Debenhams put it) in their stores. In the long run this strategy can lead to an expansion of the customer base by improving customer choice through the development of brands, ranges and customer service initiatives (such as the Debenhams gold card). In other words they can offer the type of service (merchandise range and the various facilities) that their customers expect. Indeed, if they fail to achieve this objective they may find themselves losing customers at a fast rate, and in a very short time.

In the second part of the objective Debenhams talk about enhancing relationships with its suppliers. Let us look at what it generally hopes to achieve with this element of strategy.

By enhancing relationships with suppliers a retailer can expect to accomplish two main goals. First, as with any relationship, the closer you are to one another the better the understanding of each other's needs. For the retailer this may translate into holding the necessary stock, short delivery times and making every effort to provide a flexible and friendly service. It also reduces the administration costs associated with Debenhams' supply chain, which is an important element of the business as we explained in Chapter 1. This policy will allow Debenhams to respond rapidly to changes in the retailing environment and is critical to the success of the company. So, for example, when fashions and trends change, or when consumer spending is tight, Debenhams can adjust the nature and volume of its merchandise. For suppliers this means guaranteed business in the medium or long term, and increased business in the future. It can also mean greater prosperity due to their association with such a strong company name.

The second goal, that of working closer with suppliers, is all about building partnerships for success. By getting to know their suppliers' strengths and weaknesses, Debenhams can work within these limitations. Ultimately this will help to eliminate broken promises and misunderstandings. These might arise from a simple issue like not knowing what the minimum time (or lead time) the supplier needs to deliver merchandise, or the quantity of stock the supplier holds at any one time. With this type of information readily available Debenhams can plan ahead and make realistic promises to its customers. The result benefits both retailer and supplier and joins them in a long and rewarding and mutually advantageous business partnership.

In their third objective Debenhams say they want to motivate and retain key staff. So why should they want to do this? Clearly the obvious reason for this lies in their main purpose for being in business, which is to satisfy and retain their customers. To do so they need high quality and loyal staff who are pleased and able to respond to customers' needs. Once the right type of staff is in place they must receive suitable training and gain experience to provide this level of support. Given this investment (both in people and in training) it is vital for the company to retain these people, as losing them means starting over again with new inexperienced staff. Good sales staff hold the key to high-quality customer contact and service, as they are experienced and know most about how the business runs.

> ⇨ This process of attracting and retaining people starts with a capable management team who have the foresight to encourage 'quality' training and install retention systems. Such initiatives must always start at the top of an organization with those who have the power to make policy decisions. Failure to introduce good training schemes and (pay-related) incentives can lead to a frustrated workforce and high staff turnover.

As we can see from their statement of objectives, the Debenhams Company has managed to achieve both these targets for success. They have put together an experienced and successful senior management team and a motivated workforce. This is a direct result of the influence of the directors (at the top of the organization) who strongly believe that good staff build customer loyalty. The number of incentive schemes and training and development programmes in place demonstrate the management's commitment to this belief. These development programmes help to maintain the continued commitment of all staff to improving the business. Other indicators of success are the high level of internal promotion and a relatively low level of staff turnover – a key issue in the retail sector.

We learnt in Chapter 3 that space and the allocation of it are important issues for retailers. These issues are so important that the allocation of space is usually mentioned in the objectives of a retail organization. Management often use space to establish a particular type of merchandise that then becomes synonymous with the image of the company. Sometimes this technique is used to focus or refocus the company or brand in the mind of the customer (Hasty and Reardon 1997: 271). Space can thus assist managers to build up images of product lines and so influence shoppers' ideas about the store.

From the objectives that Debenhams have written into their strategy we can see that they use retail space effectively to enhance the visual appeal of their stores. Ultimately, this leads to an increase in financial returns from the strategic use of sales space. Other factors such as the modernization of the stores, new store openings and the use of the latest visual concepts augment this strategy.

In general, when retailers improve their space utilization it can lead to significant growth in the operating performance of their businesses. Good planning provides the flexibility needed to allow for any fluctuations in the day-to-day running of the operation. For the retailer this is crucial because the marketplace is so dynamic, and it is very difficult to forecast any down or upturn in trading. Retailers are thus obliged to constantly monitor key product categories and the amount of retail space allocated between ranges. By achieving the optimum product offering retailers can be sure of their position in the market relative to their major competitors.

▶ Being one step in front of the competition is about 'providing the right products in the right place at the right time'.

Case 5.3 HMV Faces the Music

How easy is it to be different from the competition? Well sometimes this objective is very difficult to accomplish due to pressures from the marketplace. For the music store HMV the decision was whether to guarantee the customer the music recordings they wanted or diversify into computer games and videos. Other high street music stores had taken a bite of the 'Playstation' and 'Nintendo' cherry and were growing steadily in the wake of customer sales. Some chains had stuck to music but offered narrower ranges focusing on particular styles. Faced with this dilemma HMV decided to maintain a focus on music but offer a wide selection. With the help of a computerized stock control system, they assessed demand and tracked the availability of 270 000 releases – the number of current releases in the UK at any time. HMV customers could find any current recording they wanted, or as the HMV chairman put it: we offer customers 'the right stock in the right place at the right time' (Fraser 1995: 36).

We can see from the above case study that the success of a retail business (or any business for that matter) usually hinges on the management's ability to offer exactly what the customer wants. Markets and customer needs change over time which is why retail management must plan to survive. However, the best laid plans can at times be thwarted by the lack of accurate information about the market, the competitors and of course the customers. To ensure that up-to-date market data are collected and available for the planning process, detailed audits must be carried out. An audit is a data gathering exercise, which is designed to investigate the retail marketplace. Audits are sometimes referred to as market opportunity analyses and are a vital part of the management function.

Audits and SWOT Analyses

It is more common to use audits to examine the financial aspects of businesses, describing the quantitative elements of a firm's assets and liabilities. In marketing, audits have a much wider interpretation and refer to the systematic collection of both figures (data) and information. Information may be qualitative, that is to say not just comprising of numbers but containing written facts or issues.

> ⇨ Example: consumer reports contain both tables of figures and written sections to explain trends in consumer spending.

For retail management vital data and information come from both the external and internal environments. Management then uses this knowledge to make the necessary changes to their plans and strategies, which may then cater for shifts in customer attitudes and market forces. Earlier on we saw how the music store HMV focused on a wide music selection to enhance their position in the market. The decision to use this strategy was not a simple one but based on extensive internal and external research. Much of this investigation focused on the type of service their customers wanted. Internally, the company had to consider whether they were able to handle the 270 000 titles and what systems they needed to deal with this effectively. To plan, the retailer HMV needed to collect a great deal of research about their existing customers, potential customers and their major competitors. A full audit, however, is a major activity and involves collecting data and information across the range of marketing's activities.

Data and information collected specifically to analyse a business soon become out of date. Customer buying habits change as do the social forces that guide them. Equally, macroenvironmental and microenvironmental forces (described in Chapter 3) alter over time. Audits must therefore be routine and above all continuous.

▶ A constant and consistent flow of data and information is needed to inform the planning and strategy process.

Part of the task of building a sound business involves the efficient handling of data and information. The arrival of the personal computer and server-based system has meant that retailers can make full use of the data they collect. Even small retail businesses benefit from the use of computer-based applications like word processors that produce high-quality business letters. Spreadsheets make calculating day-to-day sales and purchases straightforward. Larger companies have more complex needs, however, and tend to take a more integrated approach to the use of retailing information systems (RIS). For them computer technology is a crucial part of the operation and links each part of their business. Let us now look at the definition of an RIS and see how it fits into the strategy and planning process.

> ⇨ Definition: the RIS is a blueprint for the systematic gathering and structuring of management data and information, from sources inside and outside the retail organization.

Figure 5.2 contains an illustration of the RIS commonly found in major retail businesses. From this we can see that there are various external and internal inputs to the system. These originate from data and information accumulated by the retailer and then classified, indexed and stored in the system. For example, important PEST data and information are held in the RIS and used to predict future customer trends so retailers may respond more effectively. In the case of the HMV store mentioned earlier, data held on the RIS showed exactly what the opposition was offering. Later it also made the tracking of 270 000 music titles possible which enabled HMV to offer a better service than their competitors.

> ⇨ Key point: in modern times no business can afford to ignore the importance of technology and in particular the personal computer and server-based systems.

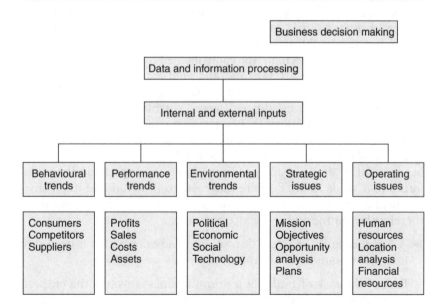

Figure 5.2   The Retailing Information System

Computers are the most efficient means of handling and analysing large quantities of information and data for business purposes. With the help of the RIS data and information can be processed with regularity and day-to-day adjustments made to plans. Sometimes plans go wrong or strategy is altered as a result of unexpected changes in the behaviour of customers or competitors. New opportunities are created which, if exploited, can propel those retailers who grasp the chance to get ahead of the competition. These situations are called market opportunities. Before examining this question, however, we should first consider the role of the RIS in problem-solving activities.

There are of course many types of problems, which can occur during the course of the business cycle. For the time being we will focus on the strategy and planning side of the management function. Here important policy statements like the mission statement may become totally irrelevant or even obsolete when big changes take place in the retail environment. One example of this is when consumers elected to have their motor cars serviced and repaired by Halfords, a relative newcomer to car maintenance, rather than the main motor-car dealers like Ford and Toyota.

Case 5.4 Halfords Greases up its Strategy

Why did UK motor car accessory and cycle retailer Halfords diversify into car servicing and maintenance? Car maintenance, and in particular periodic servicing, was an area that was traditionally a job for the big name motor-car manufacturers cum dealerships. Main dealers have successfully 'tied in' the customers of new motor cars for many years using the *small print* found in new car warranties and guarantees. These clauses point out that warranty validation is contingent on periodic maintenance being carried out at the regular intervals specified in the service handbooks. More importantly, however, this work has to take place at main dealerships. While this type of stipulation may seem unfair it did carry a 'money back' assurance for the motorist, who took comfort in the fact that any maintenance undertaken had the seal of the manufacturer. Often it was impracticable for other motor mechanics to carry out the work anyway as it required special tools and equipment carried only by the main dealerships.

Then Halfords came on the scene and offered cut-price servicing across all makes of vehicles. This had a drastic impact on major car dealerships like Ford and Rover, who had previously enjoyed a virtual monopoly in the car maintenance sector. There had, of course, always been a cheap car maintenance market but this catered for the lower end of the car ownership spectrum. Discount servicing was usually confined to small 'back street' garages and workshops. The Halfords service product provided high-quality and reasonably priced maintenance and servicing for a range of customers. This effectively priced the main dealerships out of the market and heralded the beginning of a servicing price war in the early 1990s.

The Halfords case study illustrates the importance of monitoring the retail environment to take into account fluctuations. For big dealerships like Ford and Rover who were and still are retailers of car maintenance and servicing, the arrival of low-cost players like Halfords has meant a drastic change. Since Halfords first ventured into servicing other firms like Apple and Smileys have arrived on the scene. This resulted in increased competition and keener prices for the motorist, who has benefited greatly from the price war. Fixed price offers on items like oil changes and tune-ups brought increasing product and price flexibility. Customers immediately saw the benefits of 'shopping around' for individual services rather than obtaining their car maintenance from one firm. For the major retailers of car maintenance this was a significant departure from the status quo and change was therefore inevitable. However, the main dealerships were particularly slow to respond and lost business as a result.

Big garages like Ford and Rover finally hit back with new fixed-price deals and 'off-the-shelf' packages aimed at the cost-conscious motorist. This was a time when motorists had already suffered at the hand of the Chancellor of the Exchequer and, as such, were looking for low-cost deals to help them through the monetary squeeze. Vehicle owners were prepared to forestall or even miss out a service to save money. Halfords came to their rescue and provided a low-cost value-for-money option. This is a typical example of a *marketing opportunity* and shows the importance of constantly monitoring the competition and analysing the results. The means to undertake this type of analysis is provided by the RIS, however, there are other more fundamental ways of analysing the business environment. Performing a SWOT analysis can provide a quick method for evaluating a range of situations, large or small, inside or outside the retail organization.

> ⇨ Definition: SWOT is an acronym, which stands for Strengths, Weaknesses, Opportunities and Threats. The SWOT technique has become the basic tool of analysis and provides management with a useful framework with which to examine the internal and external parts of an organization.

Managers can use SWOT to analyse and plan for many situations and long-term business decisions. SWOT can also help when sudden changes to the operating environment (both inside and outside the firm) occur. In general, a SWOT analysis will provide:

► a snapshot of the situation in hand

► a summary of the key issues

► some idea of what issues to focus on

► an understanding of the relationships involved.

Let us look at each of these points and discuss them within the context of a typical retail firm. On this occasion we will consider the fashion sector where, like grocery retailing, the competition is fierce. A high-class fashion retailer such as Jaeger may find that as a result of the rapid growth in popularity of the out-of-town factory outlets their business is suffering. While the factory outlet concept does provide high-quality brands like Jaeger with a first-class method of reducing end-of-line products, slow-selling items, cancelled orders, seconds and returned purchases, there are considerable risks involved. For example, customers can be tempted by the low prices away from Jaeger's prime town centre locations.

> ⇨ Just to recap: factory shopping villages will generally save customers around 30 per cent on high street prices. This figure rises up to 70 per cent at sale time (Stuart 1998: 2). For consumers who would like to buy designer clothes but cannot afford the prices these outlets are a great way of slashing the price tag on high fashion clothing. Moreover, buying goods in a factory shop does not alter a consumer's rights. So customers who unwittingly buy faulty goods may obtain refunds. Around 3 million people visit the factory outlets every year.

Using an initial SWOT analysis Jaeger management are able to judge what actions should best address the current situation. As we considered above, the main purposes of undertaking SWOT analysis is to obtain a snapshot of the situation in hand. This helps management to identify important issues affecting their business *today*. Second, by obtaining a summary of the key issues management can set aside the lesser issues in favour of the more immediate and vital factors influencing the business. This enables management to determine what issues to focus on, and how one issue can affect another. In other words the relationships involved. All these factors help to bring together a coherent and integrated strategy incorporating markets, products and other areas. The fashion retailer in our example is far more prepared as a result of undertaking a SWOT analysis to make informed decisions. These decisions may relate to the markets they are targeting (both now and in the future) and the suitability of their products for these markets.

You will find one example applicable to Jaeger across each category in the SWOT framework drawn in Figure 5.3.

SWOT is an excellent and relatively simple tool for understanding all manner of situations. The example in Figure 5.3 relates to the macroenvironment and considers the external situation. In real life this would have uncovered consumer-related issues such as which customers are most likely to buy from factory outlets. Recent market research suggests that two out of five shoppers at factory outlets said they would not have bought the goods at full price (Stuart 1998: 2). Hence the threat to

STRENGTHS	WEAKNESSES
22. High-quality brand name	15. High cost of merchandise
23. –	16. –
24. –	17. –
25. –	18. –
26. –	19. –
27. –	20. –

OPPORTUNITIES	THREATS
8. Seek new markets	1. Low-price factory outlets
9. –	2. –
10. –	3. –
11. –	4. –
12. –	5. –
13. –	6. –

Figure 5.3   A SWOT Framework

Jaeger's business may not be quite so serious as originally thought. The SWOT technique could be equally successful at identifying internal organizational issues.

5.3 The Integrated Marketing System

After undertaking a survey of the business environment using PEST and SWOT analyses, a retailer is able to identify their markets and customer needs. Retailers employ fairly sophisticated systems to ensure they can sell the products and services their customers expect. These systems are integrated to provide a tight and cost-effective way of delivering the product (and or service) to the customer.

> ⇨ Definition: integration is the act of bringing together different groups or the coordination of different processes into one, in this case the various functions in the marketing system.

Integrated marketing systems bring together many functions, which include: buying, selling, storing, sorting and transporting items. We will start by considering the buying process, as this is the point at which the merchandise first enters the retail system. In this section we will not consider the merchandise strategy but focus instead on the buying function itself. The nature of the merchandise and service offering is an extension of the retailer's business philosophy. Merchandise assortments are frequently mentioned in the mission statements of retail organizations. For example, with the Debenhams example we saw reference made to brands in their mission statement. Merchandise strategy is thus determined in advance and forms a vital part of the overall retail strategy.

After selecting the right type of merchandise, the retail organization must seek out suppliers. Before this takes place, however, someone in the organization takes on the responsibility for organizing the buying function. In large retail institutions buyers hold very important positions charged with the task of maintaining the retail organization's profitability. The buying function in the small retail firm is usually the task of the owner or manager who places orders with representatives or wholesalers.

The timely transportation of merchandise to the retailer is a critical part of the integrated marketing system, and enables the retailer to function in the way their customers expect them to. An efficient delivery system brings to the store the range of products the customer wants, when they want them, and in sufficient quantity or frequency to meet customer expectations. In some retail sectors, like mail order for example, the transportation system is also the main interface with the customer. Without this close link and method delivery, the mail order customer or agent is isolated. Mail order retailing relies heavily, therefore, on reliable delivery systems to maintain customer service and contact. The Next Directory is an example of this with a difference, as its mail order success stems from its fame in the high street.

Case 5.5 Next Directory

Next merged with Gratton the mail order retailer in 1986 and became Next Plc. Two years later Next launched Next Directory a mail order company. This new business approach provided Next with a differential advantage over competitors.

Fast and efficient delivery systems are an important feature of the retailing industry as a whole. Managing the stock, or inventory as it is commonly called, is paramount and affects the bottom line. Retail management must minimize their investment in inventory (stock) without endangering sales, and possibly alienating customers. A system of 'just-in-time' delivery has been adopted in many sectors such as fashion retailing to ensure customer satisfaction. This type of stock delivery provides the exact amount of inventory (however small) the retailer wants, when they want it, and to suit their current demand. While the benefits of this are considerable the main advantage is reduced storage and therefore *cost*.

Financing the cost of inventory is a major undertaking for the retailer, as the demand for merchandise often occurs at a different time than the creation of the merchandise, for example, before new clothing fashions are launched or when a new trend in children's collectibles is created.

> ⇨ The Beanie Baby craze in Britain and the USA caused a huge demand for soft toy products produced by the TY™ Company. Retailers were obliged to purchase large consignments of assorted Beanie Babies or lose customers rapidly. Their customers, however, craved for the latest Bear or a particular one to add to their collection. This resulted in a great deal of overstocking and investment on the part of retailers.

In these circumstances someone needs to pay for holding the inventory, and sometimes this is the final consumer. Orders are sometimes taken in advance of launches to reduce the cost or level financing for the retailer. Generally, this does not happen and inventory is paid for ahead of event such as Christmas and Easter, which is the traditional time for weddings in the UK.

Taking risks is part of the retail management function and careful customer research and merchandise planning can reduce the overall level of risk. The selection of lines for seasonal events, and the quantities ordered, is a matter of knowing your customers and bringing together the many functions of the integrated marketing system. This includes buying, selling, storing, sorting and transporting items and, above all, information gathering and exchange. It is the exchange of information between the sellers and the suppliers, about the levels of demand and the needs of each other that create success exchanges. The aim is to match the supply to demand and this often relies on close relationships between suppliers and retailers.

Vertical Marketing Systems

In the last section we discovered the importance of creating relationships for success. Here we consider the use of vertical marketing systems (VMS) to coordinate the various functions of the producers, wholesalers and retailers. Figure 5.4 suggests the alternative to the conventional marketing channels, where the producer, wholesaler and retailer are operated as separate firms. The move to vertical marketing systems creates an entirely different way of thinking where the emphasis is placed on the coordination of activities.

> ⇨ Definition: vertical marketing systems are a means of unifying the functions of producers, wholesalers and retailers. The system coordinates the production, distribution and selling of goods and services under one common ownership or sphere of control.

Vertical marketing systems exist where a producer, retailer or wholesaler owns two or more stages of production or distribution. For example, a supermarket chain may control or own the distribution network that supplies its stores. Where the entire channel is owned or controlled by one entity or owner the channel is said to be *totally* integrated. The fast food retail sector is particularly attracted to this sort of channel because they need to guarantee regular supplies in short time frames.

A VMS produces better economies of scale, greater bargaining power in negotiations with other firms, and the guarantee of a constant supply of merchandise. Firms are free from the intercompany conflicts that exist in conventional marketing channels. The apparel retailer Cotton Traders, for example, produces, distributes and sells its own fashion products. Its constant supplies are maintained through the firm's factories and distribution system. Sales are maintained via the company's mail order catalogue and to a lesser degree from the Cotton Trader branded retail outlets dotted around the UK. A VMS assists the Cotton Trader firm to develop new retail formats, launch innovative products and unique merchandise ranges. This is called a *corporate* VMS and refers to a manufacturer who has integrated vertically to reach the consumer, or a retailer that has integrated vertically to create a network of supplies.

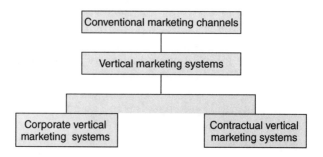

Figure 5.4   A Vertical Marketing System, adapted from Anderson 1993

> ⇨ Explanation: in practice, retailers or manufacturers may integrate either backwards or forwards to combine various levels of production and distribution, under single ownership.

In the grocery sector, it is common for supermarket chains like Tesco and Sainsbury to own or have controlling interests in production processing and distribution facilities. This may involve transporting fresh produce from the company-owned farms in UK and other parts of Europe. The discount furniture retailer MFI own the Hygena Kitchens and Bedrooms manufacturer, and also operates its own distribution network. Many fashion apparel retailers create carefully engineered distribution and production systems to maintain a foothold in the highly competitive fashion market. These are all examples of corporate backward integration.

There are two other types of VMS and these are contractual and co-operative systems. The first of these, *contractual* VMS, is of great benefit for the smaller retailer who seeks economical and efficient expansion programmes. The contractual VMS generally facilitates wholesaler sponsored groups and retailer-sponsored co-operative groups. The former provides an excellent strategy to combat the large retail chains with their considerable buying power. It is a wholesaler initiative, which organizes independent retailers into groups. This is very attractive for the small retailer who benefits from the economies and merchandising opportunities. Retailer-sponsored *co-operatives* are similar but it is the retailer who provides the impetus for organization and group advantages. The retailers form their own wholesale company, which services the member retailers. Buying in this way means that the smaller retailer can receive the discounts associated with bulk buying and so reduce the unit costs. Another form of contractual arrangement is the franchise that operates on a similar basis.

> ⇨ Definition: a franchise is where the franchisor (the owner of the brand) gives the franchisee (an independent operator) the exclusive right to distribute its products and/or services within a specified area for a specified period of time. It is customary for the franchisee to agree to sell only the franchiser's products during the agreement period.

The franchise allows the smaller operator to 'buy into' an established brand (Holland & Barrett in the UK) and therefore improve their chances of success. In some sectors, such as health foods this is especially important. The nature of the health food market makes it difficult for small operators to obtain the information and the supply system necessary for success. Health food shops carry a large range of products and only attract a relatively small turnover. Body Shop is another franchised operation that provides an opportunity for the small independent to sell a range of well-established products.

5.4 Forging Relationships for Success

All VMS integrate the retail business through the development of a supply chain relationship. This is crucial to the success of any large retail business. The smaller retailer can also gain from a standardized system of supply. Retail businesses, both large and small, must be able to rely on their suppliers. It is acutely important that products are delivered on time, in a consistent manner and in the quantities necessary for the retailer's needs in order to meet the demands of the market as efficiently as possible. Suppliers and retailers can cooperate to achieve considerable benefits:

▶ Electronic point of sale (EPOS) information can easily transmitted back to suppliers. Thus they can forecast probable demand from retailers and organize production accordingly. This reduces costs and increases promptness in delivery.

▶ Cooperation improves quality of the product because it allows retailers flexibility to programme the quality into production through tighter specification to their own requirements.

▶ Cooperation encourages suppliers to invest in quality and innovation as their success becomes more visibly tied to that of the retailer.

▶ Where health or environmental concerns are important it protects the retailer because it allows greater traceability of products.

Difficulties can, however, arise in such longer-term relationships and these have to be appropriately managed by the retailer. One of the problems that can arise is the excessive power of retailers. The manufacturer may become too dependent on the retailer and large retailers may require too large a commitment of its supplier's capacity. The retailer cannot expect such commitment without a corresponding commitment on its part to maintain the level of demand. This causes problems if the quality of the products received declines temporarily. Switching suppliers would then be interpreted badly within the market and deter other firms from entering into long-term contracts.

A similar problem can also arise when the retailer changes product lines or switches to sourcing outside the chain. This problem is aggravated when, for instance, a clothing store chain switches to offshore sourcing and the resulting publicity can be damaging to the status and image of the retailer.

Another difficulty can arise where retailers wish to supply own brand goods. A supermarket places contracts for different frozen products with a range of food manufacturers. This tends to give the supermarket excessive power with relatively small manufacturers. However, there may be insufficient order quantities so that those manufacturers have to commit factory time to supplying other retailers. This can increase problems in assuring quality and reliability of supply. Also, the supplier's dependency on the supermarket chain, and the power wielded by the supermarket itself, can give rise to conflicts. In some circumstances this can have a damaging effect on the long-term interests of the chain in delivering its own brand of products.

Case 5.6 Timberland: Supply Chain Cooperation

Timberland the manufacturer of upmarket rugged outdoor wear and accessories grew rapidly in the 1990s with its products and operations extending to 90 countries. It also developed a chain of 74 of its own stores in the USA and Europe, which by 1998 accounted for over a fifth of its revenues.

The rapid growth of the company meant that supply operations were having difficulty keeping up with its retail successes. Timberland needed to completely overhaul its retail, distribution and warehousing operations, which were fragmented, in order to maintain its customer service.

Its warehousing reflected its sourcing and production operations, and this led to different products being shipped from different facilities. The company reorganized its warehousing by region, with one in Holland to supply Europe and two in the USA to supply the geographically larger market there.

Timberland considers strong relationships with its retailers to be important. It chose a warehouse management system that allowed it to respond to the varied demand of their retailers. This included sorting, packaging and labelling so that product arrived ready for shelving. It also allowed Timberland to support retailers in responding to changing fashion and consumer demands.

Source: Drapers Record 2000: 50

5.5 The Role of Retail Formats and Merchandise

Any strategy for maintaining long-term profitability must be focused on the consumer. This is because of the increasing amount of power being transferred to the consumer through the greater availability of information, for example, the Internet and the media generally. One of the approaches available to retailers can be exemplified by an adaptation of Porter's generic strategy model illustrated in Figure 5.5. We have used this model because it can be adapted readily to the retail situation, and competitive advantages that may be achieved through retail formats and merchandise. Students of retailing can if they wish use Porter's model to work out a retail strategy based on the variables or dimensions.

In the model we can identify three key decision variables: the retailer's cost leadership, the type of differentiation they adopt and their market focus. For example, a retailer may wish to focus on cost leadership, which requires the business to establish lower costs than those of their competitors.

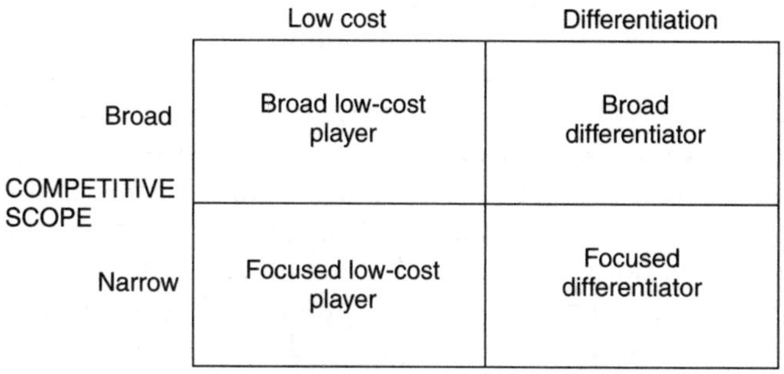

	Low cost	Differentiation
Broad	Broad low-cost player	Broad differentiator
Narrow	Focused low-cost player	Focused differentiator

COMPETITIVE SCOPE

Figure 5.5 Porter's Generic Strategies

> ⇨ In Figure 5.5 the left-hand vertical column relates to low cost.

Differentiation is also an option and by emphasizing particular benefits such as store loyalty schemes and discounts for regular shoppers, a retailer may stand out from their competitors. A store's format and the merchandise it sells create an important means of differentiation, which may also be linked to costs. So a retail business may differentiate itself on the type and price tag of the merchandise it sells, which stems from a low-cost base.

> ⇨ The right-hand vertical column in Figure 5.5 refers to differentiation.

On the left-hand horizontal rows of the model we can see that the scope of the retailer's competitiveness can be either broad or narrow. This relates to both the needs of the consumer at the time of purchase, and the retailer's ability to supply the merchandise. The competitive scope in this example is therefore about what the retailer sells, and what position in the market this creates. For example, a narrow segment of the market with specialist knowledge or alternatively a broad approach that sweeps up the competition (for instance, the category killer Toys 'Я' Us). For the consumer this can mean does the retailer stock a wide range of products or a small range of products? Again variables can be linked to other variables. For instance, is the merchandise range limited, cheap to buy, value for money and better than that offered by the competition?

> ⇨ The far left competitive scope in Figure 5.5 refers to the market focus: broad or narrow.

As a strategic tool Porter's model is useful but does not offer a definite solution, and any strategic decisions regarding merchandise and formats must be based on a wider number of criteria. In our examples all three variables suggest the choice of a retail format (supermarket, convenience store), the selection of merchandise (wide or narrow range) and the market scope (specialist or variety). This has the potential to help the retailer to position themselves in the marketplace in relation to their competitors. However, using these three variables by themselves can be limiting and neglects other factors that may be of greater importance.

In fashion retailing, for example, a retailer can be both a broad low-cost player and a focused differentiator at the same time and in the same location. This may be necessary to satisfy the needs of the retailer's target market. For example, the discount or value retailer Matalan sells high-quality fashion brands at affordable prices, alongside a wide and relatively cheap range of general clothing and household textiles. They are both a fashion forward retailer (that is, selling designer clothing) and a broad discounter, trading out of sheds located in retail parks. This is best for their particular business needs and helps them to attract a loyal customer base that is tied into the company's membership scheme. This example demonstrates that whilst Porter's model can be used to help with the formulation of strategy, it is not intended to provide an exact answer.

Ultimately, the aim of any retail strategy is to focus on the customer when making decisions about the location of the store, the construction of the brand, format, and the range and depth of merchandise. In the development of strategy a whole range of microenvironmental and macroenvironmental forces must be considered to ensure the success of the business. By focusing on the customer continually when developing retail strategy the retailer is likely to produce the right offering, which will ensure success.

References

Abell, D. F. (1984) 'Metamorphosis in market planning', in K. K. Cox and V. J. McGinnis (eds) *Strategic Market Decisions*, London: Prentice Hall.

Anderson, C. H. (1993) *Retailing: Concepts, Strategy and Information*, St Paul, MN: West Publishing, p. 39.

Barker, P. (1998) 'Malls are wonderful', *Independent on Sunday*, 25 October: 7, 9, 11–12.

Brassington, F. and Pettitt, S. (1997) *Principles of Marketing*, London: Pitman Publishing, p. 876.

Drapers Record (2000) 'Stabilizing roots for future growth', 19 February: p. 50.

Fraser, I. (1995) 'Sight and sound', *Marketing Business*, October: 36.

Hasty, R. and Reardon, J. (1997) *Retail Management*, New York: McGraw-Hill, p. 271.

Lusch, R. F., Dunne, P. and Gebhardt, R. (1993) *Retail Marketing*, Cincinnati, OH: South-Western Publishing, p. 34.

Stuart, L. (1998) 'Up front: high fashion and low prices in the village', *Guardian* (Features), weekend 26 September: 2.

The Customer and the Retail Business: Knowing your Customers

CHAPTER

6

This chapter:

▶ Considers the use of marketing methods in classifying customers.

▶ Introduces various techniques to categorize customers.

▶ Considers the use of postmodern perspectives in understanding customers.

▶ Considers reasons why and where customers shop.

▶ Introduces models of customer behaviour.

The Customer and the Retail Business: Knowing your Customers

Introduction and Core Concepts

In retailing customers (or consumers) are the most important aspect of the business. If you are unable to define who your customers are, or what they are likely to buy, the business is unlikely to survive. Consumer behaviour is a complex area that draws many of its concepts and theories from general psychology and sociology. In this chapter we focus on the more fundamental of these models that show how customers' minds work.

6.1 Focusing on the Consumer

The first step a retailer needs to take is to identify their customers. This enables them to plan their market strategy using concepts such as the Porter model (see Chapter 5). As customers come in all shapes and sizes (they are heterogeneous) it is necessary to break them down into meaningful groups.

A meaningful group is one that is sufficiently large and willing to spend sufficient money to make it worthwhile differentiating them from other groups. For instance, a high-class fashion retailer knows that it needs to sell to women who are willing and able to buy its products. It also knows that certain factors affect their willingness to buy such as:

▶ age – because clothing styles differ with age

▶ income – because they need to be able to afford the clothes

▶ geographical location – because the nearer they are the more likely they are to visit the shop

▶ lifestyle – identified by, for instance, occupation or marital status, because this will affect their desire to buy these clothes.

Consequently, when identifying potential customers, the retailer would break the population down into groups by such characteristics as gender, age, income, geographical location and lifestyle.

However, each group must be sufficiently large to make it worthwhile catering for them. So the retailer must choose broad categories for each characteristic so that it has reasonably sized groups. For instance, while there is probably a big difference in attitudes between say a 25-year-old and a 35-year-old, there is probably not much difference between a 25-year-old and a 26-year-old. Thus age is usually defined in terms of broad bands such as 16–24, 25–34 and so on. Similarly, women in professional occupations are going to be affected more by income differences than the particular profession they are in. So, the retailer might then classify women by general type of occupation, such as professional or managerial, but only in as far as it expected the different categories to have a significant impact on buying behaviour.

Where people are located in the region is another factor influencing decisions about potential customers. The type of customer will vary between geographical locations, and the retailer will have to consider the store location carefully beforehand. Market research will reveal where the targeted customers live, or the catchment area, and this will guide location decision-making. In the fashion clothing sector, a retailer such as Matalan is likely to attract very different consumer groups than a high-class clothing retailer like Harvey Nichols. Similarly, in the food sector, supermarkets like Sainsbury and Tesco want to target the prosperous family unit. Retail management must therefore consider what business they are in, and how they can best target specific groups of customers.

This process of grouping customers is known as market segmentation, and is illustrated in Figure 6.1. Most markets can be segmented to identify suitable customers, and in sufficient quantities to make them of interest to retailers. Research is undertaken to identify uniform (or homogeneous) clusters of customers from what is initially a heterogeneous market. There are some basic steps in identifying market segments, the first of which is to search, using demographic and other suitable variables, for common groups.

⇨ Definition: demography is the study of human population including age distribution, gender, ethnicity, income, education, family unit characteristics, occupation and social class.

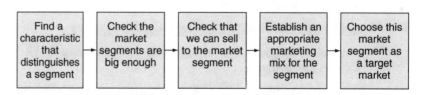

Figure 6.1   Segmenting a Market

These important variables provide a suitable set of characteristics to classify groups whose purchasing behaviours are all similar. Such behaviours reflect the customers' views about the retailer.

How the customer views the retailer is very important. Even more important is how the customer views the retailer in relation to the retailer's competitors. This is often called the consumer's image of the retailer. Customers make judgements based on their experiences gathered over time, and based on advertising sources and visits to the store. This is a process of internalization that gives the customer a database of imagery for decision-making. Ultimately, the process determines which store the customer will frequent. Retailers use this process as means of positioning themselves in the marketplace, by tailoring their offering (see Chapter 5) to the customers they wish to target. Simply put, market positioning is how the retailer seeks to place itself in the consumer's mind in relation to its competitors. Positioning involves many factors such as:

► the type of merchandise sold

► the store format

► the marketing system adopted.

A good way to illustrate market positioning is to construct a market-positioning map, which helps the retailer visualize their place in the market. In Figure 6.2, the simple map shows just two dimensions. This explains the nature of the store's operations: the vertical axis illustrates the retailer's position in relation to high- and low-priced products, and the horizontal axis shows its position on a scale of functional (everyday use) and symbolic (special occasions).

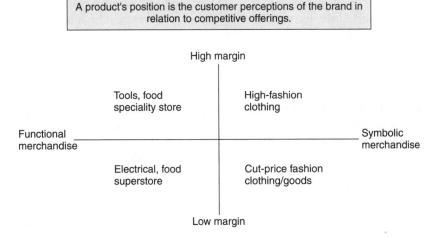

Figure 6.2   Positioning

6.2 Mapping Out Society: Psychographics

As discussed, it is important for retailers to be able to break the market down into clearly defined segments they can target. The retail marketer defines these segments using appropriate measures. These enable the market researcher to group the customer population conveniently, and exclusively.

> ⇨ Exclusively: we need to split the population into completely separate groups, which make up the entire population, for example, age and gender.

People are classified using standardized classification indices. One set of indices that is used in the UK is the Registrar General's Social Classification Index as shown in Table 6.1.

Table 6.1   Social Class Categories

Social class A	Higher managerial, administrative or professional
Social class B	Intermediate managerial, administrative or professional
Social class C^1	Supervisory or clerical and junior managerial, administrative or professional
Social class C^2	Skilled manual workers
Social class D	State pensioners, widowers (no other earners), casual lowest grade workers or long-term unemployed
Social class E	Unwaged, pensioner

This is a valuable indicator of these customer groups, based on income and social behaviour. However, sometimes it is possible for people to be either members of more than one group or wrongly classified. This happens, for example, when retired professionals are classified as pensioners as in the case of category E. This has the effect of distorting the outcomes and, so, the usefulness of the data. This is because the retired professional may have income as great as or even more than skilled workers. Also, this does not take into account the lifestyles of customers, which can reflect more important indicators of purchasing behaviour. These may be culture, family unit, place of residence, social reference groups and aspirations.

Lifestyles

Lifestyles are another way of splitting the population into segments and also provide a good reference for advertisers. Lifestyles can be defined using different variables such as family size and place of residence. However, the way the market research companies incorporate the variables can be very complex. For instance, CNN produces the Mosaic system that uses a combination of economic, social and geographical factors when constructing consumer lifestyle profiles. These data allow Mosaic users to classify each household in a postcode area as belonging to specific groups. This allows all types of retail businesses to target specific customers within streets, districts and other defined locations.

Case 6.1 Anglia Double Glazing

Have you wondered why firms like Anglia target homes in a specific area? What are the factors that guide them when they choose to post leaflets through household doors? Firms such as these make great use of lifestyle profiling data to target the sorts of customers they think are likely to buy their products. Retailers who sell directly to the public have to target their customers more carefully as they do not have the advantage of passing trade. Firms like Anglia use a number of promotional tools to reach their customers. The mailshot (advertising leaflets) allows them to cover specific areas and encourage immediate responses. Without the accurate customer profile information provided by lifestyle indicators it would be difficult for such retailers to target their customers effectively.

Another type of lifestyle classification is to group people into categories that attract some kind of label, such as 'achievers', 'strivers' and 'strugglers'. One such grouping is called the VALS™ 2, which is a copyrighted framework designed by SRI International to segment consumers into one of eight basic classifications. These classifications provide an interpretative view of people based on general characteristics rather than relying solely on economic and social variables. For example, 'achievers' tend to be 'successful career people' who 'feel in control of their lives'. 'Strivers tend to seek motivation, self-definition and approval from the world around them' (VALS™).

Research is continually being undertaken to find new ways of understanding and analysing customer behaviour. For instance, lifestyle classifications may be used in conjunction with customer behaviour to cluster consumers into groups. These are called behavioural variables and represent the various criteria for clustering customers. This process helps the retailer to segment the target market more effectively.

> ⇨ A behavioural variable can be any behaviour that influences other things, such as a general increase in the number of family shopping trips. It may also be a unit of measurement like the distance a customer group is prepared to travel to shop at their favourite store.

A typical list of shopping behaviours or habits is shown in Table 6.2. These represent real-world issues that retailers have to account for when they calculate their customer bases and target markets. It is important to remember, however, that whilst these represent large sections of the population they do not account for everyone. Some people, for example those without personal transport, are not properly represented, although public transport access to some areas is available.

Table 6.2 Typical Shopping Behaviours or Habits

Behaviour 1. Distance travelled to shop	More distant locations such as city centres and other major towns attract high numbers of occasional shoppers.
Behaviour 2. Shopping in retail parks	Conveniences of access, parking and opening hours are the main attraction of retail parks. These factors make it difficult for town centre retailers to compete.

Table 6.2 continued

Behaviour 3. Sunday family day out	Sunday trading laws and a general lack of time has meant that families are more likely to shop on Sundays. The Sunday shopping trip or day out has become a leisure-influenced activity.
Behaviour 4. Alternative shopping sources	Newer types of shopping such as factory outlet villages or warehouse shops are attracting most family groups.
Behaviour 5. Shopping at local retailers	Local shopping still has a role to play and retailers attract customers with appeals such as convenience and specialist product ranges and service.

Source: derived from Mintel 1998

6.3 Postmodern Consumers

Over the last two decades society has altered its views regarding the role of retailing in everyday life. In the 1950s and 1960s general household shopping was a functional activity mainly carried out by one member of a large family unit. The task of bringing in the weekly shop was accepted by most groups as part of the female role. Other shopping, such as the purchase of expensive items like furniture and durables, represented large-scale investment by the household in its lifestyle. As such, it was a male or joint male–female decision. Today the trip to the shops has become an important feature and event in family life.

This change in the role of retailing reflects the altered state of family life and the integration of leisure, work and domestic activity. The desire (mostly socially driven) to improve our position in society has become the dominant goal for most people. Despite increasing prosperity and labour-saving devices a lack of time has become the major problem in family and social life. Retailing has responded to these changes by providing services that ease the pressure on time. These include longer opening hours, a more convenient range of products, one-stop shopping in one location. In addition, retailers have provided exceptionally interesting and pleasing environments for consumers to shop. Shopping malls and centres have become part of the leisure experience and rooted in the social and cultural fabric of society.

Culturally we are acclimatized to accepting the retail revolution and the integration of retailing with domestic activities generally. This has meant a fundamental change in values and beliefs about the nature of consumption. All manner of shopping is used for self-expression. This is termed by some as a means of constructing identities – that is, creating 'who we are'. In many ways when we show who we are this also states where we are in the social order. Buying is now more important for most people as it acts as a positioning device and creator of identity. People consume to demonstrate their position in society which itself is oriented towards the consumption of lifestyle symbols. Changes such as these describe, although not completely, a postmodernist view. All consumption is the vehicle for creating identity and positioning oneself in society. This has several implications for retailers. In the past, for instance, people would tend to buy clothes that related more to their income and position in society. Nowadays, it is quite acceptable (by the majority) for all socio-economic groups to mix expensive designer wear with low-priced garments. This mixture cuts across traditional economic beliefs and values (Bocock 1993).

Case 6.2 Values, Attitudes and Charity Shops

Most of us are aware of charity shops and their locations in our towns and cities. How many of us, however, are aware of the underlying values and attitudes that help to support these businesses. Charity shops are retailers who trade on behalf of their sponsors and beneficiaries. By and large, the retail stores they operate are similar in layout to the second-hand stores that were once (and probably still are) a regular feature in heavily student-populated areas of our cities.

The charity shop serves an important need that crosses three or more boundaries. First, they generate income for underprivileged groups and Third World countries. They do this by obtaining free donations of goods and clothing, which they sell on at a profit. Their second stakeholder group are those who feel benevolent because of the contribution they make by working voluntarily for the charity organization. These are the people who work for the charity and, in particular, those who serve customers in the store. By working for low pay, or no pay at all,

they feel altruistic and supportive for the contribution they make to a worthy charity. Finally, there are the regular customers who also experience a great deal of pleasure from buying second-hand goods whilst contributing to a needy cause. It is this same attitude or set of values that encourage high-status groups in the population (A, B and C[1]) to buy second-hand items from a charity shop. In different circumstances these socio-economic groups may well feel far too embarrassed to buy second-hand goods.

Values are important feelings that are influenced by our culture, family and day-to-day contact with other individuals. Exposure to the media, such as television advertisements and publicity, can manipulate values and distort issues. An example of this is the seesaw motion of political campaigns during a general election. However, one enduring and commonly held value is the importance of feeding, clothing and supporting Third World countries. Buying an overpriced item in a charity shop reinforces this ideal.

Another issue that stems from the postmodern view of consumption is the idea that leisure time has merged into shopping time for most households. This factor has affected the proliferation of retailing, especially of services. The trip to the shopping mall or retail park is now mixed with other forms of leisure activities such as meeting friends, days out and family trips. This has led to shopping becoming an important feature of everyday life. Because shopping has become so important, retailers have had to become more sophisticated in their approach to engaging the consumer. One way is to focus on gendering consumption.

An important aspect of the postmodern consumer is the move away from traditional behaviours, such as the role of female purchasing habits. Although women are more enthusiastic shoppers than are men, the latter have tended to take the lead with some goods over the last decade or so. Retailers have capitalized on this by focusing on goods that have more appeal for male consumers. Stores have widened their merchandise ranges and redesigned their layouts to focus on contemporary male consumers. Selfridges in Manchester, for example, have several departments dedicated to the male persona. This rise in the importance of male consumption is matched by the increase in advertising that send out messages to reinforce male consumption.

As modern consumers try to create differences with the products they buy, the presence of other people or reference groups are important. Consumers feel the need 'to have been seen to have been there', and shopping is an event that signifies meaning to the individual and to other shoppers. People have lots of tasks and social obligations that become more complex and require more frequent servicing. To help with this consumers search for better methods of shopping in order to save time, which is always in short supply. New buying methods such as home catalogue shopping and Internet websites bring new and better ways to deal with this shortage of time. Many supermarkets multiples, for example, have moved into other products, such as fashion and white goods, to accommodate customers. New convenience-style retail formats sell products and services that save time and reduce household work.

Consumers are today much more aware of price variations and search for 'value retailing', especially in the food retail sector. Retailers have to respond to any changes in consumer expectations. Food supermarket Sainsbury, for example, has built on customer perception of quality. Tesco on the other hand sees its mission as 'one of Britain's leading food retailers'. The company owes its success to its emphasis on meeting changing customer needs through service and innovation, while maintaining its commitment to value and quality. As we discussed in Chapter 5, Tesco has also successfully introduced a store loyalty scheme to attract and retain more customers as part of its tactical manoeuvres.

Modern consumers are better informed about product quality, prices and availability. Rising expectations about retailing have increased selectivity, reduced store loyalty and diminished the effectiveness of traditional modes of shopping. The tendency, therefore, is for consumers to switch stores or shop in multiple locations (Doyle and Broadbridge 1999). These new attitudes to food shopping have led to changes in retail formats, including the development of the new convenience formats. We can see from this that consumers' attitudes are an important consideration and indicator of future developments in retailing.

6.4 Learning Attitudes, Motivation and Perception

Consumers' likes and dislikes are called attitudes. Attitudes or ratings are valuable indicators of marketing and advertising effectiveness, or how well the advert has worked. Likes and dislikes about a product brand or the retailer who sells it can be measured using rating scales in questionnaires. For retailers, consumer attitudes hold the key to whether or not customers will enter and purchase goods in their stores. For example, the customers targeted by a retail grocery chain will have similar likes and dislikes, and a predisposition towards the retailer. To customers, this will seem like a simple matter of liking Sainsbury more than Tesco, or vice versa. For the individual consumer this liking or attitude towards or otherwise is something that is learnt over time.

People do not know instinctively which stores to use and what goods to buy in them, they learn this information incrementally over time. Time therefore plays an important part in establishing the retail business, and its marketing efforts are used to teach the consumer about the store and its products. Attitudes are generally enduring and built up over a period of time. They may change as a result of new opportunities such as better value elsewhere, or unfavourable experiences like poor customer service. We will turn to the way that attitudes are formed and use the diagram in Figure 6.3 to demonstrate the stages of attitude formation.

In the first stage of development of the customer's attitude there is usually some information that informs judgement. This assessment data is gathered by the human senses: visual, olfactory, aural and tactile (the sense of sight, smell, hearing and touch). These data help people to make sense of the mass of information or cues present in their immediate surroundings, and inform judgement. This process may start with something as straightforward as a friend recommending the store, or as complex as an unconscious response to seeing a persuasive advertisement or message. Consumers are sometimes unaware of the messages they receive and process. These early beliefs are the beginnings of an attitude (or conviction) that people develop about all manner of things including retailers and of course life in general. In the retailer–customer situation, these first stages are important, as they are likely to mean that customers will be loyal over time. This process may also apply to customers who are switching retailers and have been loyal shoppers in other competitors' stores. So the first stage in the model in Figure 6.3 represents the mental beliefs consumers possess about a retailer and their brand.

Next we consider the *affect* or evaluation, which normally takes place after the customer has entered the store. On occasions, however, evaluations of the retailer brand may take place away from the store, as in the case of Argos and their home shopping catalogue. Take, for example, a regular customer who obtains very poor service or low standard of goods. They may develop negative attitudes towards Argos in general as a result. This shows how fragile the retail image and reputation can be and how important it is to maintain the standards throughout the business.

The final stage in the model, behavioural intentions, are about what the consumer actually does. For example, when attitudes towards a supermarket chain are positive, customers are likely to regularly visit the store and buy their weekly shopping. So the final stage describes what

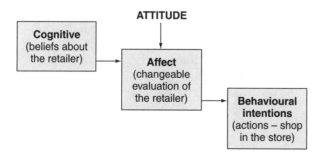

Figure 6.3   The Nature of Attitudes

consumers intend to do. These intentions that enter the consumer's mind usually take place while they are in contact with the retailer. Many retailers use this opportunity to gather customers' attitudes towards their goods and services while they are in the store. Ratings can be then be measured (see Table 6.3) with questionnaires and analysed using statistical techniques. Smaller retail businesses are unable to afford or consider such techniques unnecessary, and because of their smallness tend to reply on word of mouth. Market research firms are generally called in to carry out these research methods and provide the larger retailer with data about their customers' attitudes. This helps retailers to alter where necessary aspects of the offering that customers dislike.

> ⇨ Attitude measurement: customer attitudes may be measured with questionnaires using rating scales. This is known as the *semantic differential* and uses a number of statements or questions, placed in a scale of 5 or 7 points. This is then used to measure customers' attitudes towards the retailer's various services and offering.

Table 6.3   Rating Scales

Please circle *one* number on the following scale: 1 = poor and 7 = excellent.								
Q1. How did you like shopping in the store?								
Poor	1	2	3	4	5	6	7	Excellent

Analysis of these questionnaires, and the relationships between attitudes and actual behaviour, involves the use of statistical models. One such model is Fishbein's multiattribute model and students may wish to consider using this and further reading (see Assael 1998: 303).

Personality Measurement

People have different personalities and this can influence how they shop, and influences their emotion and behaviour generally. The popular approach to understand and interpret personality uses trait theory to interpret behaviour. This behaviour can be measured using rating scales to gauge how socially outgoing people are and whether they are more inclined towards extrovert or introvert behaviour. However, this is of limited use to retailers, and standard personality traits are not reliable enough to predict choice or intent to purchase. However, personality data may be incorporated with other lifestyle information and used in merchandising displays.

A major factor that will dictate whether or not a customer will shop in a store may well be determined by a need. They may, for example, be very short of milk or bread and have a large family to feed. Hunger is therefore the major drive or motivation to go shopping. Human motives are very important and create reasons for us to undertake various tasks, like shopping. There are several theories of motivation but in this retailing textbook we feel it is more useful to explain consumers' actions using retail situations. For example, the need for food and drink may be activated, as it was above, by simple factors such as pictures on the side of a McDonald's distribution vehicle. Needs or motives may *not* be activated due to other factors like the situation that the consumer is in at the time. For example, when we are not hungry the need to eat is not activated. However, if the smell of fresh baked bread and brewed coffee are introduced into the situation the need may well be activated. An external stimulus such as an advertisement may arouse motives into actions.

There are two distinct types of motives: psychological and social. Psychological needs arise from our natural biological mechanisms. We may, for instance, be mentally aroused by hunger and respond as a result. Social needs are the result of contact or interaction (because it is two-way) with our social environment, or the other people around us. Shoppers, for example, in an expensive fashion retail store will tend to motivate us to act. In Selfridges in Oxford Street, London, we may buy ourselves a gift in order to feel special, and akin to the customers around us. This means that consumers are not always motivated by rational and practical things, but often by emotional and irrational drives.

> ⇨ Motivation: a state that causes consumers to start behaving in a certain way.

> ⇨ Need: humans needs are not always activated. Stimulated needs are called motives.

People may be motivated to go shopping just because they are bored or because they like shopping. They may also be motivated to buy certain products like holidays just to have fun. Motives are therefore difficult to classify, but for convenience we can split them into two distinct groups: rational and emotional. By doing this we can explain how the retailer appeals to the targeted customers and reaches into their minds. Both rational and emotional appeals are used to motivate customers to enter a store and purchase products. For example, a simple rational appeal may be illustrated by the promotional offers two-for-one or three-for-two in the local supermarket. Here the customer is drawn in by the lure of value for money, which is a functional part of the shopping experience. In contrast, there may be a very nice looking CD radio cassette in the non-food section that the customer falls in love with. In this case the appeal may be purely the desire to possess the item, and the social positioning it brings. Many purchases are driven by emotional appeals and the desire to own something new and shiny like the latest motor car in the showroom.

Motives are stimulated through advertising and linked to both the store and the products and brands that the retailer stocks. This is similar in method to the formation of attitudes. For instance, a particular toothpaste advertisement may make reference to the social implications of not using it (emotional), and at the same time demonstrate value for money (rational). In Figure 6.4 we can see this flow of information or stimuli as it acts on the consumer's motives. Using the toothpaste example above, we can see how the consumer is drawn into the

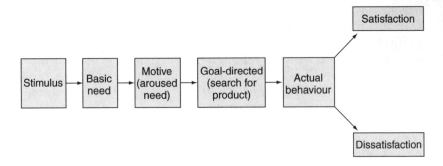

Figure 6.4   Consumer Motives Model

purchase phase. In the first stage a stimulus, in this case the advertising message, acts upon the customer creating a basic need. Motives (there may be more than one) are aroused followed by a search in the store for the chosen product. This assumes that the goal of finding the product is of major importance. Finally, the customer buys the product and the whole process starts again.

At the end of the process shown in Figure 6.4 we can see that, ultimately, consumers will feel either satisfied or dissatisfied with their products or shopping visit. The significance of this for the retailer is that if advertising boasts a high-quality service, or extended merchandise range, the customer must experience this and see it to be true during their store visit. If not, customers are likely to shop elsewhere. Issues such as the unavailability of stock, or shortages of staff, will therefore impact on the retailer's brand name and reputation. As we considered in Chapter 5, this will have a significant impact on the retailer's goals.

It is very important to retail businesses, and for that matter any business, to be viewed or perceived in a certain way. For retailers, how they are portrayed in advertising and other promotional efforts can be tested by their customers almost instantaneously. Customers just need to enter the store. They therefore need to be particularly vigilant and maintain high standards consistent with their perceived image. This perceived image is what the consumer uses as a mental guide when choosing in which store to shop. Perception plays an important part in creating this (brand) image. For instance, the perception of quality is more important than the true reality.

Like attitudes, perceived image is built up over time. Advertising plays a key role in establishing consumers' perceptions of things like retail stores, brands, products and all types of everyday issues. For example, when the country nears a general election the various political parties use advertising extensively to alter people's perceptions. Perception is part of the mental or cognitive process which people use to make sense of the world.

> ⇨ Cognitive process: refers to the human internal mental processes. The term comes from general psychology where it is used to describe areas such as learning, attitudes and perceptions.

Human perception is a complex area to discuss so we will use examples from retail situations to help develop our understanding. Students of consumer behaviour who may wish to read in greater detail about perceptual process should refer to texts dedicated to consumer behaviour (for example, Solomon 1996: 55–87).

> ⇨ Perception is the process of interpreting sensations and giving meaning to stimuli.

We all see things very differently and often this is due to our particular role or position relative to the stimulus. For example, a new house is seen differently from the point of view of the purchaser, the agent selling it and the individual members of the family who will live there. This same rule applies to the retailer, who will have a different view of a store than the customers who shop there. Perception therefore provides meaning as people try to make sense of the world around them. Advertising agencies use this to great effect and create powerful messages, which convey meanings relating to products and retail stores. This process works by producing stimuli that are designed to appeal to the retailer's target market, and necessitates careful research of the target audience and their preferences. For example, a storyline may follow the exploits of a shopper as they apparently enjoy the many features of a supermarket. People watching the advert are likely to place themselves in the shoes of the shopper and respond favourably to this stimulus. Overall, this reinforces the audience's perception of the retail brand. Some exceptions to this are considered in the 'Perceptual selectivity' box

---

Perceptual Selectivity

People have a tendency to screen out certain stimuli or to apply certain meanings to other stimuli as a result of their personal backgrounds.

This is called *selective perception*. A similar thing can happen when students attend the same lecture and often have differing interpretations.

We cannot escape our past experiences or prejudices which are the result of learning over time. Adverts sometimes use this by only showing part of a product or its shadow. Relying on the consumer's knowledge and experience to finish things off.

6.5 Modelling Consumer Behaviour

It is very useful for retailers to understand how their customers' minds work so they may provide them with the sorts of products they want. Also, the retailer may wish to work out patterns of buying behaviour, for example how many times and when customers shop in the store. Data on customer shopping habits may be collected from sales and loyalty information, which provides a reliable source of customers' actions. For the small independent retailer collecting these data may be just a matter of recalling when your regular customers last came in. This is called

Development

store patronage and larger multiples or department stores regularly record this information so they always know who their customers are. However, as we identified in Chapter 5, knowing who your customers are is not enough; you have to understand how they tick.

We will now look at a basic model of consumer behaviour, which contains many of the factors so far considered in this chapter. Organizing these factors in a model or flow diagram helps us to remember the processes involved. It also groups the different factors from this chapter into stages. This makes sense of the complex processes that underlie human behaviour.

Behaviour of any type, including customer behaviour, is a function of the interaction between the person and the environment around them. This, however, is a very simple way of explaining human behaviour, which is in reality a highly complex process. There are numerous forces that can affect the purchasing decision. For example, we have already considered earlier in this chapter that issues such as mental processes, lifestyles and age all influence behaviour. There are many other forces at work, some of which are illustrated in Figure 6.5. The model contains the most common variables influencing consumer behaviour. It is, however, by no means inclusive.

As Figure 6.5 shows, the flows of influence start in the first stage with the consumer's individual background. Issues like culture, family and social class shape the way people behave, and determine their preferences. For instance, when we go shopping at the retail mall with our family, we are greatly influenced by their presence and the part they play in the decision-making.

> ⇨ Decision-making is a set of cognitive processes, which interprets stimuli
> and organizes thoughts and ideas. Sometimes this process is so rapid we
> do not notice it happening.

Issues such as where to eat at lunch time and which shops we go and see are usually consensus decisions. Individual decisions are also undertaken in these situations but these may be subject to group pressure.

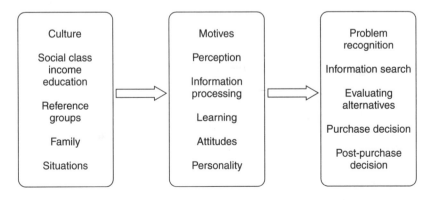

Figure 6.5   Some Major Factors Influencing Consumer Behaviour

⇨ Group pressure – other people, even family, influence our behaviour and ultimately our decision-making. Most decisions consumers make are made with the help of other people, and sometimes strangers waiting in the queue next to them.

Consumers each possess a set of mental constructs or categories such as learning history, attitudes and perception. These determine individual preferences and inform the consumer's final choice, such as store or product type. In stage two of the model above we can see the range of constructs that shape decision-making. For example, a customer will use their learning history, perceptions and attitudes to choose which retail store to visit. First, they will recall past visits when they formed attitudes and perceptions about the service or general product. The result of this internal scan will determine whether or not they wish to revisit the store today.

The last stage shown in Figure 6.5 is the decision-making process. This is usually the final stage of the buying process, and occurs after the other influences have taken affect. However, human behaviour is not so exact and we often enter the decision-making phase at different times in the buying process. Sometimes, for example, we seem not to need any thought at all before making a decision to buy something.

Reflect on your own experiences and try to think of a situation where you recall spending little or no time deciding about a purchase.

Once again it is useful to place the various events into a model or flow diagram. Figure 6.6 shows the sequences of the internal decision-making processes. This will help us to understand in more detail how the customer makes decisions.

The model in Figure 6.6 describes a buying situation where extensive problem-solving is required and *high involvement*. This means that the customer will spend longer making up his or her mind about a purchase and probably spend longer searching around for alternative products or services.

⇨ High involvement refers to the degree to which a consumer becomes involved (often emotionally) with the purchase, for example, when buying an expensive camera. High-involvement products are usually status items and expensive to purchase. The once in a lifetime gift falls into this category.

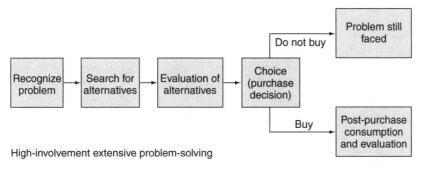

High-involvement extensive problem-solving

Figure 6.6   The Decision-Making Process

When the risk associated with the purchase is high, for example, where money and status are involved, the consumer will usually search for longer. The consumer search provides the retailer with an opportunity to reduce prices, extend guarantees and emphasize brands. It is also useful for retailers to be aware of the probable duration of the search process. A customer is likely to spend longer over buying a new personal computer from PC World than they would when buying a tin of baked beans in the supermarket. One method of explaining how the decision-making process functions is therefore linked to the product or service, and the extent of the purchasing process.

Case 6.3 Risk

In most situations the availability of alternatives, such as greater selection, will usually increase search and may even increase risk. The search process is both internal (retrieval from memory) and external (scan the store for products). Risk is increased when the items being purchased are more expensive, or critical to the purchaser in the particular *situation* they find themselves in. Realizing your motor car is running out of petrol, and the risks this presents, can create its own set of special circumstances. For example, if you are running short of petrol on the motorway or freeway the nearest petrol station is more important than the price of the fuel. In general, status goods such as expensive watches carry a greater level of risk than utilitarian products like the Christmas paper to wrap them in.

For example, a consumer needs a new computer because the old one has broken down or is unable to process data fast enough. A problem is therefore recognized and the search stage of the process is entered. Performing a scan of the internal memory identifies prior experience and external searches provide information to help the decision-making process. In the next stage, product evaluation, customers' weigh up the best products to buy based on the available information. A higher degree of involvement with products will influence the decision at the evaluation stage. In the final stage the decision to buy is made and either post-purchase consumption or renewed problems are faced.

Other purchasing decisions require much less thought and involve the customer in fewer decisions. Let us consider, for example, the decisions necessary when choosing which dry-cleaning shop to use and the type of service to opt for. In this situation the customer is obviously limited by the availability of dry-cleaning stores in the locality. Other considerations include the type of service available and any special offers which may reduce the cost of the service. Customers are thus more likely to move more quickly through the decision-making process, or skip some stages of the process entirely.

Some decisions therefore require a shorter period of time to make. This is called routine problem-solving and is characterized by *low involvement*. Figure 6.7 illustrates the reduced number of stages and therefore effort that the customer is obliged to undertake.

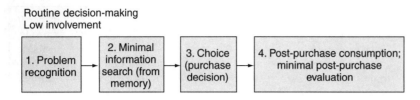

Figure 6.7   Routine Decision-Making

⇨ Low involvement is when the product or service the consumer intends to purchase is unlikely to evoke any emotional intensity. Such purchase decisions are relatively routine (habitual) like buying the daily newspaper from the newsagents. Low-involvement products are usually utilitarian items and inexpensive to purchase.

Case 6.4 Cheap Mobile Phones at Tesco

From the discussion of various types of products and the associated decision-making, we can see that things are not always straightforward. Take, for example, the buying situation where the costs and advantages of identical products offer very different benefits. This usually arises because both manufacturers and retailers aim to provide as many enticements to purchase as possible, and the associated benefits are the best way to extend the product. The mobile phone package on special offer at Tesco during Christmas 2000 is a case in point, and illustrates differences in decision-making. Leading up to Christmas, which is a traditional time for special offers and sale items, Tesco offered £20 reductions on pay-as-you-go phones (no tied network contracts) when purchased with more than £50 worth of shopping. This presents some interesting ideas about decision-making and risk. For instance, buying a mobile phone package with a one-year network contract may require considerable thought. Customers are likely to weigh up the advantages and disadvantages very carefully. However, purchasing the same phone on a pay-as-you-go package, with no binding contract is a much simpler choice to make. This is especially so when the cost of the handset is greatly reduced.

High-Involvement versus Low-Involvement Goods

The problem-solving models have helped us to understand the process that consumers go through when purchasing products and services. Students should now be aware that when consumers buy things the amount of time they spend on decision-making varies. The allocation of time will usually depend on the buying situation and the level of involvement. As we discussed, this will usually depend on the nature of the product and the particular situation. For example, finding the ingredients for a meal will evoke more involvement than the purchase of a ready meal. This has important implications for retailers and the way they present merchandise and locate it in their stores. Also, the degree of space allocated to low-involvement products should arguably be less than for high-involvement goods. However, things are not that simple and retailers tend to *expand* displays selling fast-moving utility products, to increase sales and, consequently, their profits.

> ⇨ Consumer involvement is a complex area and students may consider it necessary to read this subject in more detail. There are, for example, several forms of involvement some of which are related to the advertising process. When shoppers are uncertain about brands they seek out information to reduce uncertainty before deciding which brand to buy, or whether to make a purchase at all. For further readings on consumer involvement see Solomon (1996: 146).

The majority of the models used in this chapter assume that consumers are problem solvers, weighing up alternatives and seeking and processing information. It is not always possible to determine how consumers think. Human beings frequently do unexpected things, like failing to buy the big value items located in the rear of the retail store. We use models to make sense of our customers' behaviour, and in an attempt to understand a highly complex process.

Case 6.5 The Many Aspects of Decision-Making at an Argos Superstore

When shopping there are numerous occasions when consumers make complex decisions because they need to constantly evaluate and re-evaluate their situation. As customers walk through a retail store, choosing direction, walking speed, which way to look and whether to buy or not are just some of the many decisions to be made. We are accustomed to decision-making and routinely carry out these mental evaluations each day of our lives. When shopping the task can at times become highly taxing.

Since their inception, Argos the catalogue and high street retailer have extended their operations to out-of-town retail sites, and a superstore-type format. Their superstores provide consumers with many conveniences and the promise of a much wider variety of in-stock items. The larger floor area makes it possible for Argos to display products and segment the stores into several functional areas: customer waiting, cash points, collection points, product selection and customer service. The latter area enables customers to order by phone, with delivery to home.

For the customer this creates many situations within the store where different types of decisions are required, and where some decisions are more difficult to make than others. Product selection may require extensive thought, but at collection points little involvement is needed. Customers may seek help at the customer services counter and perhaps need to decide whether or not to take a cash refund or buy an alternative product. In customer waiting areas, customers are involved in decisions about where they are going to sit, and how long they are prepared to wait.

References

Assael, H. (1998) *Consumer Behavior and Marketing Action*, London: Thomson Learning.

Bocock, R. (1993), *Consumption*, London: Routledge.

Doyle, S.A. and Broadbridge, A. (1999) 'Differentiation by design: the importance of design in retailer repositioning and differentiation', *International Journal of Retail and Distribution Management* 27(2): 72–82.

Mintel (1998) *Consumer Shopping Habits*, April, London: Mintel International Group Ltd.

Solomon, M.R. (1996) *Consumer Behaviour*. London: Prentice Hall, pp. 55–87, 146.

The Fundamentals of Merchandising: Product

This chapter considers the following issues:

- ▶ Planning for merchandising.

- ▶ The aims of merchandising.

- ▶ Various forms of merchandising.

- ▶ The merchandising process.

The Fundamentals of Merchandising: Product

Introduction and Core Concepts

For any retailer selling the right merchandise is crucial to the success of the business. How that merchandise is displayed is just as important as the goods are part of the layout of the store or shop front display. This tells the customer what to expect and sends out numerous other messages. Merchandising is a key factor in attracting the customer and encouraging repeat business. Whether goods or services a retailer's future will hinge on their ability to develop the best retail offering. Getting the merchandise right for the store's image involves careful planning which must be related to the direction that the retailer wishes to follow. Questions like 'do we wish to offer discounts and, if so, how will this affect our image', and 'are we a wide and deep range retailer', need to be asked beforehand. The type of customers (discussed in Chapter 6) will help to answer these questions and formulate a merchandising strategy. This strategy will emerge from the retailer's strategic plan – or making sure that the future turns out the way you want it to!

7.1 Merchandise Strategies

We saw in Chapter 5 the strategic goal of the organization determines the direction and the formulation of the 'game plan'. For retailers, like most organizations, this game plan is closely guarded, as it will determine the success or failure of the business. The planning, locating, buying and displaying of merchandise are fundamental to the direction of the business.

A merchandise strategy is all about targeting the right people, with the right merchandise at the right time in the right place. In this case the right people will be the retail customers you wish to target. For example, a catalogue retailer like Next Direction must plan their collection (merchandise offering) in advance of the coming year. This means they have to know the likely trends in fashion before sourcing the merchandise. Forecasting makes this type of advantage possible. Suitable manufacturers are located and the range of garments and sizes ordered. Providing a well-balanced assortment for consumer types ensures customer satisfaction and repeat business. This is especially important for the catalogue retailers who sell their products remotely.

A *balanced assortment* is a well-planned variety of merchandise. In the case of an apparel retailer this means ordering a suitable range of styles, sizes and colours for the target market. The high street florist will provide for coming occasions such as Valentine's Day by ensuring there are adequate quantities of red, pink and white roses and carnations in the store.

The right place means that the store must have a suitable quantity of floor space and appropriate merchandise for the area it is located in. Location is important when we plan merchandising strategies because the local environment signals what type of goods we should sell. For instance, some discount apparel retailers use out-of-town sites, which imply value for money.

High street retailers tend to copy each other and produce similar ranges within product classes. Children's clothing is a case in point with most clothing stores offering similar product ranges, colours and even similar styles.

Each retailer has a different merchandising strategy determined by the sector they operate in. Electrical discount retailers, for example, follow a similar pattern and tend to offer a low-priced, wide range of merchandise. Most discounters operate out of sheds in retail parks. Their competitors are other discount retailers in similar locations. High street independent hardware stores do not really pose a threat as their location, range, price structure and purchase situations are different. The small independent attracts opportunistic sales and customers who have limited access to transport.

Large discount stores such as B&Q source and buy their merchandise centrally and distribute using their own logistics system. This allows them to sell on at a discount and compete successfully with other similar outlets. Their buying power means that they can afford to offer large ranges. The appeal of one-stop shopping is one of the main features that attract customers to this type of outlet. Another factor is in-store arrangement and displays, which allow customers to browse through large stock ranges. Bedroom and kitchen discount retailers are able to display suggested interior designs, which allow the customer to visualize more readily. This also promotes sales of full kitchens and bedrooms rather than selling items piecemeal. In this way the retailer corners the market in all the products and items displayed in the mock up. There is literally no need for the customer to shop elsewhere.

High street retailers and small local stores tend to offer more customer service as part of their strategy. In part this makes up for the lack of assortment depth and width. Service is an important part of the merchandise strategy because the two are in many ways intertwined. As we discussed in Chapter 5, the customer service element is built into the retail marketing strategy. The nature of the merchandise is also part of this strategy. Retailers display their merchandise according to the image they wish to impart. Customers are guided by the extent of the assortments and the type of layouts, and make assessments about the availability of customer service. Retailers also make this type of assessment, and large assortments such as those available in retail sheds are unlikely to offer much service availability. Mainly this is because the cost of providing service personnel throughout the store would be far too high. Customers have learnt to expect less service when shopping in discount stores.

The merchandise on offer is tied in with the location of the store, the logistics of delivering the goods, and in-store arrangements and displays, and the way the customer is served. Type of merchandise also affects stockroom management and the service employees who work to accomplish stock replenishment. Merchandising technology in some sectors may drive the range planning and replenishment systems. In the fashion sector, for example, technology is a key driver and vehicle for business success.

Stages of Merchandising

When we think about the task of merchandising a retail store we tend to forget about all the effort required in choosing and sourcing the products and services displayed. Merchandising is not just about laying out items on shelves; it is also concerned with the planning, sourcing, buying and arranging of these products and services. It is the coordination of these and other functions that make for a successful retail business. Merchandising is necessary for most types of products and services.

The term 'merchandising' is used to describe many aspects of the planning and presenting of stock. It also refers to the intermediate stages, which the products pass through from the original source to the end consumer. These stages are: *planning, sourcing, buying, arranging, displaying* and *space management* of products or services.

▶ *Planning* retail ranges involves careful consideration of the customer, competitors and the type of retail business, that is, discount/upscale, high priced/low priced.

▶ *Sourcing* is the locating and purchasing of merchandise to sell in the store. An apparel retailer will source catwalk fashions from low-cost sources to enable them to sell at high street prices.

▶ *Buying* involves negotiation and the step-by-step process illustrated in Chapter 5.

▶ *Arranging* and *displays* can have a major affect on sales. Customers reasonably expect displays of merchandise to be exciting and enticing. At certain times of the year display is more critical than others, for example, Christmas and sale time. The way the merchandise is laid out in a store is critical, for example, the perishable foods in a supermarket, the placing of likely accessories next to clothing items in a women's fashion store.

▶ *Space management* is planning for space allocation and may require the use of computer-based planning models.

From this discussion we can see that buying merchandise involves many decisions. Regardless of the type of retail business, or the nature of the merchandise, a successful buyer will consider how and to whom the products are going to be sold before searching for the merchandise.

7.2 Planning

Retailers plan for the types of goods they wish sell to their customers. This necessitates thinking about the image of the retail business and the requirements of the customer. These two objectives in fact run in tandem with each other. For example, we need to keep the customer happy by selling the right merchandise. However, before we can attract the customer in the first place we need to display the type of retailer image that attracts the customer into the store. As we considered in Chapter 5, this will depend on the objectives of the retailer and the type of image they wish to project. To help us understand the extent of merchandise planning it is useful to think of merchandise fitting into four groups or categories. Merchandise characteristics can be classified into: impulse, convenience, shopping and speciality. The box below explains each category in the context of the buying process.

Merchandise Characteristics

Impulse goods: these are products that customers may well buy in an unplanned manner, the impulse to purchase will often involve an emotional feeling or component. For example, buying a magazine at a supermarket checkout or an expensive watch in an airport retail outlet. Impulse goods can be high- or low-involvement goods.

Convenience goods: these are every day items such as a newspaper or disposable batteries. They are the type of goods which are *purchased with little thought* and tend to be a well-known brand or whatever is available at the time. Convenience goods are generally low-involvement goods.

Shopping goods: regularly purchased items, which are probably important to the customer and have a significant impact on store choice. The customer is therefore willing to search for and compare ranges from store to store. With these goods customers are prepared to spend longer to find the right goods or the goods they are looking for. Shopping goods can be mid- to high-involvement goods.

Speciality goods: customer may be prepared to spend a great deal of time and effort researching and locating these types of goods. They are high involvement articles and form an important part of the customer's lifestyle and self-image. They may be as simple as the correct brand of wine or as complex in information gathering as specialized hi-fi equipment. The customer will not normally accept a substitute and may insist on the genuine article even to the point of switching stores.

The sale of one item can often promote the sale of impulse and convenience merchandise. So these benefit by being located in high-traffic areas where customers are likely to pick up an item. For example, in many supermarkets the checkout will be packed with impulse goods such as sweets and chocolates.

There is, however, a more functional side of planning, which involves obtaining regular supplies of merchandise from suppliers. This involves making decisions about selection, turnover, replenishment of stock and relationships with suppliers. The following are key questions a retailer will have to consider when writing a merchandising plan:

▶ What do our customers expect? Where can we obtain it? What price will we have to pay for it?

▶ Stock turnover: how often will we have to replace the stock and replenish the store(s)?

▶ How can we provide for changes in the market? Can we accommodate change through our sources of supply? Are there substitutes available?

Replenishment and Stock Rotation

Part of the retailer's function is taken up with sorting the merchandise into manageable quantities. Often the producer or supplier will dispatch bulk quantities of different or heterogeneous items. Before this merchandise can be placed on the shop floor it must first be sorted or subdivided into similar categories. In fashion retailing, for example, this is essential so that displays can be arranged with complementary items to maximize customer sales. Food supermarkets spend considerable amounts of time breaking down large bulk deliveries into smaller quantities so staff can restock shelves quickly. This not only ensures continuous sales but also guards against stock wastage due to out-of-date items. Stock rotation is one of the most important functions in the stock room and has a significant effect on the bottom line. As we might expect, wastage in the grocery sector is high and is often a trade-off between providing what the customer expects and accepting losses. The speed of the delivery system from the producer to the supermarket shelves can make the difference between profit and loss.

We will now discuss how retailers plan their merchandise from the decisions they make about the choice of assortments, to the budgeting and ultimate evaluation of stock.

Customer' expectations lead the way in any decision-making regarding merchandise selection. The hotel chain will, for example, plan for the occupancy or number of guestrooms it intends to sell. To arrange the rooms in the manner in which their guests expect involves the sourcing of soap, free shampoo, laundry services and other guest-related items. These items are an important part of the service product the hotel is trying to sell. When guests come to stay the reception and rooms are arranged in the corporate or (in the case of an independent hotelier) familiar and possibly homely style format.

Assortments and Mix

For most retail merchandiser's variety is their stock-in-trade. Constructing the right mix of products or services to satisfy the target customer at the same time as producing the projected sales and profit levels is a science. Most retailers manage to do this effectively by using an assortment plan. An assortment plan is a tool that helps the retailer in any sector make wholesale purchasing decisions and coordinate different areas of the business to meet shared sales objectives. It also helps ensure that the available finances will adequately support the merchandise categories. A seller uses an assortment plan to work out their seasonal financial plan (called the merchandise plan) into product styles or models by merchandise category, before any orders are placed with suppliers. For example, the financial plan of a home improvement retailer such as MFI might allocate finance for kitchen and bath fixtures. The assortment plan would detail how many and which types of fixtures to purchase in order to generate sales for the summer season.

Assortment plans include the number of SKUs, projected quantities to be delivered and the costs of all merchandise destined for the store over a particular time period. An assortment plan can also provide information about the type and number of styles or models (in the case of motor cars), and the delivery flow of that merchandise.

> ⇨ SKU is an abbreviation for stock-keeping unit and is distinct from other similar merchandise because of its assortment factors. For example, in a clothing store, the small size men's shirts in white have a different SKU than men's shirts large in blue.

Assortment Plans and Retail Strategy

It is important to understand that the assortment plan follows, rather than directs, the overall retail business strategy. As with most planning, developing an assortment plan is not a one-off activity. Ideally, they should updated periodically from the point where a plan is conceived to the orders actually being placed. Revising and adding merchandising details is necessary to reflect business trends, product-sourcing problems and changes in customer preferences, all help retailers tailor their offering to meet customer needs, tastes, and expectations. This improves profitability.

The sorts of factors driving the assortment plan include:

▶ Pricing strategy – will merchandise be marketed at special offer or everyday low prices? Are there key price issues that are important to customers? For example, in a restaurant the house wine sells at £5 per bottle and the well-known labels sell at over £10 per bottle. How do prices compare with competitors' merchandise? Is there a need for several prices within a category to attract customers willing to spend different amounts of money for the same type of item?

▶ What is the desired mix of novel versus basic product lines? Where are the growth opportunities?

▶ What is the projected style or model trend? How much variety in style or model should be offered? How many SKUs should be created for each? How did the previous season's styles or models perform? Based on last year's sales, was there enough, too little, or too much variety offered?

All retailers must assess the risk of the assortment plan and develop ways to minimize that risk. For example, if sales fall below the target the retailer may be able to negotiate with the supplier to postpone or cancel additional shipments. It may be possible to arrange a sale-or-return agreement.

> ⇨ Sale or return refers to the return of unsold merchandise at the end of the selling season. Confectionery, tobacco and newsagent (CTN) retailers operate this system with newspapers due to the high volume and wide range of merchandise they handle.

Having the right type of items or merchandise for your customers is not enough; they also need to turn up in the right quantity and at the right frequency. The issue of stock turnover is very important for the grocery retailer who also sources the food and non-food items for specific customers. In this sector the high rate of product change means that for this type of business a much faster response is required. As products move off the shelf they must be replaced immediately or short-term and long-term sales are lost. Any breakdown in this supply, for example when the supplier is unable to provide the same merchandise, may cause a considerable loss of business. This is because shoppers can be very fickle when purchasing some products and services, and may switch to other retailers. This is specially the case when brand loyalty is at stake. So customers will switch to other stores to obtain their preferred brands if their favourite supermarket or store is out of stock (Verbeke, Farris and Thurik 1997).

Most retailers develop a seasonal merchandise plan, ranging from one to three months, when purchasing from an outside supplier. The plan usually covers a six-month financial season, depending on the selling period of the merchandise. Plans will not only determine the selling period of the merchandise but also the lines the retailer wishes to stock. This is called *line planning*.

> ⇨ Line planning is simply deciding exactly what items you wish to have on your shelves, and the extent of the range. This may vary with the seasons and be adjusted throughout a sales year. Assortments or the range of choices offered may also be adjusted over time.

The complexity of line planning will vary with retail sector, as some sectors will have the need to change product lines more often than others will. Satisfying the customer is key and lines may be changed frequently to ensure customer satisfaction. For example, a video rental business would require constant updating of stock. Periods of re-planning may be also necessary to compete with other similar stores and provide the assortment customers require. In fashion retailing, planning will take place more frequently than in the local NTS (newsagents), where ranges of newspapers, sweets and cigarettes are unlikely to change too often.

Use of an assortment plan gives the retailer an opportunity to place on the shelves a good mix of merchandise across the desired categories. In a clothing store, for example, the assortment plan would address the need to coordinate the colour, fabric, size and body shape of available lines so that individual components could be placed together as ensembles. It also helps to confirm that different fashion coordinates are available in the fabrics and colours that customers are likely to wear.

The same planning process is used in non-fashion areas. In the garden centre, for instance, an assortment plan can determine the right mix of barbecue equipment and supplies (including grills, charcoal and utensils) to stock at the start of the summer selling season to offer a cohesive package to customers and thereby boost sales potential.

Merchandising Budgets

Merchandising budgets are tied to the retailer's planned assortment and therefore the individual retailer's strategic goals. These data will also include estimates of the quantity of merchandise from the prior season that will be carried over to the next season. Budget information is a wide range of financial data, which gives details on future or projected sales and actual sales. Depending on the retail sector, budget planning will consider the possible damage caused by stock outs, and build in contingency plans for this.

Case 7.1 Stock Outs

Stock outs are when no stock is available for customers to buy. This is undesirable in most sectors but critical in some like fashion retailing and grocery. Imagine the reaction from customers when the supermarket is unable to supply a turkey on the run up to Christmas. Time utility (freezing) allows supermarkets to store food products such as these but stock can be depleted quickly when demands are incorrectly calculated. Careful planning and special relationships with suppliers guards against this sort of incident. The independent grocery retailer, however, must rely on a sound knowledge of customer requirements. Small businesses do not normally have the resources and buying power.

The budget will also contain information on stock levels, initial and maintained mark-ups, and projected markdowns.

⇨ Mark-ups - not to be confused with markdowns, this is the difference between the wholesale price and the original selling price. In other words the amount of profit.

⇨ Markdowns - this is the difference between the original selling price established by the retailer and the final clearance price. Sales and promotions are used to clear out-of-season lines, which are usually made up of markdowns.

An example of a merchandising budget is presented in Table 7.1. This is laid out to illustrate a 12-month period and assumes only five categories. Other factors may be introduced into the budget or spreadsheet and the calculations from this used to work out the purchase of merchandise.

Table 7.1   An Example of a Merchandise Budget

	Jan	Feb	Mar	Apr	May	Jne	Jly	Aug	Sep	Oct	Nov	Dec	Total
Store or line													
Sales													
SKUs													
Markdowns													
Purchases at cost													
Mark-ups													
Stock to sales ratios													

Planning a typical budget is likely to involve:

▶ strategic goals – identify which merchandise the business is to be identified with

▶ line planning – identify products and the extent of the range to be purchased

▶ evaluating past performance (where applicable) – estimate sales for the coming year

▶ classifying priorities – stock for sales or promotions, sizes, stock outs, models, assortments, accessories, space allocation

▶ identifying investment – this may be by category, range or other suitable variable

▶ evaluating the competition – are new lines needed to compete?

▶ research into trends – buying patterns and consumer lifestyles.

Try to plan your own merchandising budget using imagined data and a suitable retail sector. It is useful to work in groups to simulate the merchandising team effort. Case 7.1 provides an example, which you could use to develop a merchandising budget.

Merchandising budgets may be very simple affairs or very complex calculations. The degree of investment will depend on the type of retail business. For instance, an independent retailer is likely to think in much smaller quantities than a multiple such as Carpet World. Advantages of size mean that greater discounts are possible and even an improved range of merchandise, or items at *no cost*. This is because suppliers are naturally anxious to please the high-volume customer and offer incentives (frequently to buyers) to purchase. The retailer's plans and goals will determine the levels of both merchandise spend and mark-up. These are important issues in the retailer's efforts to achieve desired profitability goals.

Case 7.2 Pete's Pets

Pete's Pets is an independent retail business located in a quieter part of a high street in a busy town centre. Business is brisk with a good outlook for the future and little competition from out-of-town retailers. Sales have increased by 5 per cent year on year and regular contact with customers has led to repeat business. The merchandise mix is varied, with dogs, cats, hamsters and rabbits being the most sought after. These account for 70% of sales. Other stock items include cages, food and accessories accounting for the remaining 30% of sales. Mark up on pets is 35–40% and on accessories 20%. Markdowns on pets are infrequent as there is little wastage (Pete's pets rarely die) and great demand. In fact, demand invariably outweighs supply. It is often necessary to mark down accessories as demand is uncertain and merchandise deteriorates in the dusty conditions of a pet store. Pete is thinking of making some alterations to his merchandising plan and budget. Have you any suggestions?

Merchandise Planning and Control

A department store, for example, may establish a 60 per cent initial mark-up for the year. Using an assortment plan, they can adjust the mark-up by changing either the cost (the price paid to the supplier) of various SKUs, or the selling price to the customer of some or all of the products to achieve or exceed 60 per cent in the merchandise category.

The Importance of Planning and Control

Planning and control optimizes the performance of the retail business. Good planning and control helps the retailer to:

▶ balance customer expectations and the business's financial objectives

▶ manage changes in consumer tastes, preferences and demographics

▶ manage the variety of merchandise (number of different lines)

▶ manage the assortment of merchandise: width, depth, consistency as determined by customer expectations

▶ allow for the flood of new products and more intense competition

▶ account for changes in the consistency and maturity of the market(s)

▶ respond to merchandise life cycle and sales variability (styles, trends and fashions)

▶ expand their stores across geographic areas

▶ expand into international markets.

Evaluating Merchandise Performance

Retailers use methods for monitoring the performance of merchandise so that any changes to the range may be carried out quickly. Changes may be necessary to improve return on sales space, or after a revaluation of the assortment mix. Evaluations may be undertaken internally by sales staff who are in a position to observe customers purchases. Further data is available though past sales data and customer surveys, diary panels and focus groups. Externally, the retailer can use trade publications, advertising media research and, of course, competition as a guide to the success of their merchandise strategy.

7.3 Sourcing

Sourcing is all about obtaining the merchandise we wish to sell at the right price, quantity, and quality in a timely manner. We may be looking for a product or service, tangible or intangible goods, raw materials or even parts of an overall range of merchandise. The process involves searching the country, and often the world, to find the best product for the best price and the most receptive supplier(s). We will first consider the sourcing process, which may be broken down into a number of steps. It is important to remember that these will vary considerably according to the sector type and retailer agreements in place.

The Sourcing Process

The sourcing process is normally undertaken in four stages but in some of the retail sectors there may be more or less stages in the process.

Stages in the sourcing process:

▶ The retailer has a need for a product.

▶ The need is clearly defined.

▶ The product specifications are agreed.

▶ A suitable supplier is found (sometimes with outside help).

The retailer then agrees:

▶ quantity

▶ date of delivery

▶ target price

▶ packaging weight and volume

▶ mode of transportation

▶ payment terms.

Once all the terms and agreements are clearly established, the retailer is then able to find the best product at the most competitive price. Depending on the type of merchandise, a sourcing agreement may be given to a third party who has the resources to solve the purchasing and logistics problems. This is called a full sourcing package or FSP agreement (Figure 7.1). Such agreements include the details of delivery such as the timing and frequency. Large retailers sometimes use agents to contact suppliers and manufacturers via telephone, fax, email or whatever means necessary.

The company that handles the FSP will arrange and schedule the transportation details (whether by air or sea, and the cost including insurance) and date of delivery. Using an agent costs more but helps to smooth over

These are the various services that a FSP company will offer a retailer who wishes to take advantage of an outsourcing package. Companies such as Globe-Tex of New York provide clothing retailers with a full sourcing package. Try logging on to their Internet site and browsing through their services: http://www.globe-tex.com/index.html

FSP may include:
- stock assortment plans
- buying plans
- merchandising development
- inventory control
- product logo and licensing strategies
- fresh and proven new approaches to visual merchandising
- sourcing and buying
- supplier relationships
- EDI programs, including automatic sales and inventory reporting, repeat ordering and electronic payment
- training and implementation programmes.

Figure 7.1   An Overview of Merchandising Services

any problems that may appear any time during the sourcing and purchasing process. The *benefits* of outsourcing (as opposed to insourcing) may be summarized as follows:

▶ More efficient sourcing of a broad range of products.

▶ Streamlined transactions.

▶ Access to more trading partners.

▶ Direct and continuous communication.

▶ Potential for enhanced profit margin reductions in sourcing costs.

These benefits must outweigh the extra costs of using this type of service and it is not usually an option for smaller independent retailers. Major retailers are able to gain significant advantages from sourcing.

Competitive Advantages

Retailers are able to achieve competitive advantages from the way they source their merchandise. For example, a retailer may encourage a direct involvement and interaction with suppliers. This direct talking helps them to select the right sort of suppliers and satisfy the retailer's demands on quality, cost, delivery and general requirements. Marks & Spencer are well known for this type of approach and have long-standing relationships with a range of suppliers. For them and other large retailers, relationships with suppliers create the foundation for improvements in future performance. This may mean shorter delivery times, higher-quality products and better terms and conditions. Retailers that improve supplier quality by this method may also create advantages that are not available to other competitors. Where necessary, retailers may be forced to source their ranges overseas. This is called global sourcing, and is where a business searches worldwide for the best sources of supply.

Global Sourcing

It may be necessary to obtain sources from a number of countries to satisfy the quantity or range of a particular merchandise group. Sourcing companies provide agents in other countries who will handle all sourcing arrangements. There may, for example, be a necessity to order items from several different countries to ensure the extent of the product range. Some countries are more experienced than others in manufacturing products. This is particularly so in the clothing sector where some fabrics may only be sourced in certain countries. For overseas sourcing the same sorts of techniques apply. Retailers can reduce costs, time and improve delivery performance and quality from strong relationships with suppliers. There are some problems associated with the selection of sources of supply in developing nations.

Exploitation and Social Responsibility

The press has made examples, with good reason, of those companies who decide to source their merchandise in poor countries with low wages. Exploitation has been widely demonstrated in the clothing industry with apparel 'sweat shops'. Workers (mostly women) are employed to machine branded goods on subsistence wages. This sort of unethical behaviour is not confined to developing countries (Headden 1993). For the retailer this is a key factor in its sourcing decision-making as it raises issues for their buying policy. The image of a retailer can suffer great damage as a result of unethical buying strategies. When the retailer sources merchandise it must be carefully planned beforehand to ensure the strategic direction of the retailer is maintained. This is because purchasing stock is not just about the strategic impact of quality, cost and delivery, and having the right products on the shelves. It is also about being responsive to the needs of customers and maintaining the right sort of image. As we discussed in Chapter 5, buying merchandise must become more than a reactive order and the retailer's approaches should be the result of a rigorous strategic planning process.

Buying

Every retailer has to buy stock in a managed and cost-effective manner. Most large retail firms have dedicated buying departments or systems. Small independent retailers are unable to afford the luxury of this type of function. The owner of a small independent retail business often takes on the role of buyer. Many independents rely on wholesalers or buying co-operatives to provide a suitable selection of merchandise. Buyers have to undertake a number of activities.

> ⇨ Buyers select the merchandise and negotiate the terms with suppliers. These duties include following up orders and shipments to ensure they arrive as and when specified.

There are a number of identifiable steps in the buying process and it is through this route that the buyer must travel to ensure success. Buyers have significant influence over the following factors:

▶ Sales volume – merchandise in the right quantity and at the right time in the right place.

▶ Gross margins – the cost of the merchandise, the extent of the mark-up, and the price paid by the consumer.

▶ Markdowns – buyers influence markdowns as they regulate the quantity, price, purchase period and the type of merchandise ordered.

▶ Stock levels – buyers balance stock levels to achieve high sales with low inventory.

The steps in the buying process, listed in Figure 7.2, show the importance of research, and the acquisition of data about the suppliers, products and sources. Passing through each of the steps requires expertise in a number of areas, and previous knowledge of the retail sector is important. Many issues can arise and good leads and contacts with opposite numbers in suppliers and manufacturers can impact on profits. The formal contracting process creates the framework for conducting business between two or more firms.

A buyer will first attempt to locate the right sort of product information, which requires knowledge of potential suppliers and good contacts in the industry. Other sources of information inside the retail organization are sales histories, customer comments and returns, and store market research. External sources are probably more important and include trade shows, trade publications, market reports, vendors, professional reports, and mystery shopping reports. The purpose of this scan is to identify the most suitable product and supplier from a variety of possible sources. Just like consumers, buyers shop for the best deal and the most desired lines. This process of evaluation can involve a number of methods including running

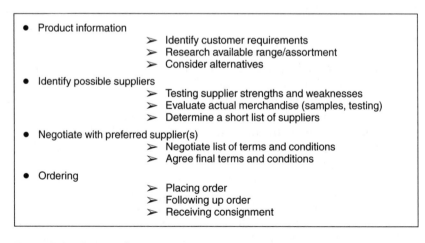

Figure 7.2   Steps in the Buying Process

computer simulations and analysis. Other key points such as the ability to deliver at certain periods, the amount of mark-up associated with the order and the quality of service offered can determine the choice of supplier. Once selected contact is made with a likely supplier and negotiation begins.

> ⇨ Tip – negotiation with suppliers is crucial as it establishes the cost price a retailer pays for the merchandise. By negotiating the best possible cost price a retailer can reduce the price of the goods to the customer.

Each player in a negotiation will try to move costs away from their side of the deal. This may lead to conflict but the most successful negotiation takes place when buyers realize that vendors are really their partners. The buyer and seller should try to make the negotiation a 'win-win' situation, which is when a mutual benefit is reached. Ultimately this can lead to long-term relationships developing between firms. During the period of negotiation a retail buyer will discuss a range of factors that influence the final cost of the purchase. The sorts of issues that may arise out of negotiations with the vendor (as suppliers are sometimes called) are the price of the merchandise, delivery dates, carriage terms and the levels of discount. These discounts will all affect the retailer's level of profitability and cash flow.

> ⇨ Definition: discounts are a form of compensation a buyer may receive from a supplier for performing certain services. The size of the discount will vary with the extent of the services provided.

> ⇨ Independent retailers run a much smaller operation, with basic accounting systems, and so are more likely to pay cash for their merchandise anyway.

We can see that discounts are very important for retailers, as the level of discount will ultimately affect the 'bottom line'. This refers to the profitability of the retail firm, which relies on the cost of the merchandise. In some circumstances the price paid for the merchandise can greatly affect a retailer's market share. This happened in the supermarket price wars described in Chapter 3.

Types of Buying

The timing of stock purchases is more critical in some sectors than others. This is particularly the case with products that have a limited shelf life such as clothing fashions. Computers and computer accessories also enjoy a short life cycle. As these products change regularly, and often overnight, the timely purchasing of stock avoids overbuying or wastage. In fashion retailing stock changes take place throughout the year in order to maintain customer interest and loyalty. Buyers have to be responsive to these changes and plan accordingly.

Case 7.3 Five Types of Discounting

There are five different sorts of discounts, all of which may form part of the negotiation:

1 Trade discount

2 Quantity discount

3 Cash discount

4 Promotional discount

5 Seasonal discount.

Let us now discuss two of these forms of compensation: quantity discount and cash discount.

Quantity discount is certainly one of the most widely used forms of discounting. It is a price reduction offered by the vendor (or supplier) in exchange for, and as an inducement to purchase large quantities of merchandise. This type of discount comes in three forms:

▶ *Non-cumulative quantity discount*, which is a discount based on a single purchase.

▶ *Cumulative quantity discount*, a discount based on total amount purchased over a given time.

▶ *Free merchandise*, where merchandise is given free instead of price reductions.

The following is an example of non-cumulative quantity discount:

Example: When 1000 items are purchased the retailer receives a 10% discount on the total cost of the order.
1000 × £1.00 = £1000.00 − 10% Discount = £900.00*
* This is what the retailer pays

Cash discount is a discount offered for prompt payment of bills and is a useful tool in the negotiation stage. For example, during negotiation retailers may offer suppliers a cash payment (or an immediate payment) to settle their account in exchange for a lower cost price or other benefits. The reverse is true of suppliers who try to obtain quick payment by extending attractive discount offers. Small retailers can also take advantage of this type of discounting and do so when they buy from wholesalers. Usually this is because they are obliged to pay cash for the goods they purchase (you may remember the term 'cash and carry') and wholesalers encourage bulk purchasing with tempting discounts.

The Buying Cycle

Most retailers regardless of their size develop their own ways of classifying the buying cycle. This refers to a number of selling and transition periods that reflect the buying cycles of customers (Kunz 1998). To determine when the cycle starts and finishes the following criteria should be identified:

▶ the start of the selling period

▶ the end of the selling period

▶ the number of peaks (high sales points) there are

▶ the weeks that peaks occur.

We will consider the buying cycle of a greeting card retail chain such as Birthdays to see how the merchandising cycle functions. We all buy greeting cards of some kind and at differing times throughout the year. Some greeting cards, such as for birthdays, are purchased all year round. Others like those for Christmas and Mother's Day must be in the shops only during certain weeks. This means that sales for these special occasions will *peak* during these months. Birthday cards, however, are likely to sustain fairly regular sales throughout the year. There are therefore some obvious points in the selling periods (see Table 7.2) when some cards are likely to be in demand more than others. Mapping this data with computing forecast software permits the merchandiser to plan more accurately.

Table 7.2 The Merchandising Cycle of a Greeting Card Retailer

Month	Week	Event	Selling cycle
January			
February	3	Valentine's Day	Peak
March	7	St Patrick's Day	Peak
April	11, 12	Easter Sunday	Peak
May	16	Mother's Day	Peak
June	20	Father's Day	Peak
July			
August			
September			
October			
November	40	Halloween	Peak
December	45, 6, 7	Christmas/New Year	Peak

A good merchandising system is essential to the success of any retail business. For larger concerns, computerized classification systems with forecasting capabilities ensure a highly efficient stockholding.

7.4 Arranging and Displays

Apart from stock replenishment, the manner in which merchandise is arranged will have a great impact on sales and customer perceptions. As an example let us consider outdoor clothing, which has become increasingly popular for day-to-day dress, although originally designed for hardy hikers and rock climbers. People, as an antidote to the stresses of working life, often take up outdoor pursuits. The feel of the great outdoors has moved indoors as outdoor wear has become sought after by high street shoppers who are brand aware. This has posed an interesting question for retailers who wish to display merchandise and specialist equipment in a way that combines both function and fashion. Retail outlets selling outdoor wear look more like fashion stores, with wider entrances and displays of brightly coloured merchandise for customers to gaze at. Labels such as Timberland, Berghaus and Rockport must now appeal to a new audience as well as established customers. This is accomplished using in-store displays and merchandising techniques.

The market trader may prefer to use a random arrangement of products to infer the 'bargain offer' nature of this type of selling format. High-class fashion retailer Selfridges will determine the format of each in-store selling space by the brand name sold there. High-class 'designer labels' brands such as Versace Sport command lots of space and important locations in the store. The motor-car retailer will allocate space and prominence to the more expensive cars in their range. The lower-budget models are relegated to the rear of the showroom or less visible positions.

Among the tricks employed by retail merchandising teams to attract the attention and appeal of their customers is to use 'open merchandising'. Customers have an expectation of being able to examine expensive products.

> ⇨ Open merchandising allows the customer to interface with displays and physically touch the products they may wish to purchase. More traditional methods of merchandising do not encourage customer contact with displays.

The merchandiser attempts to fine tune merchandise to fit individual stores. For example, mountain bike shops may adopt a clean, open interior designed to help customers view and touch the product in the space that sells a lot of complex equipment. In-store visual displays are used to attract the customer. Stained softwood, white oak and a mix of hessian and wooden flooring capture images of conservation while sparkly lighting gives a more high-tech atmosphere. This is all designed to make outdoor pursuits merchandise look attractive and encourage customers to impulse purchase. For example, a merchandising initiatives used to sell outdoor clothing at Liverpool-based Wade Smith is a 42-foot climbing wall, which runs through the middle of their store. Timberland merchandise is sometimes sold in a 'cabin-style' setting including a cosy fire with chimneybreast, leather chairs, brick walls and wooden floors. In other settings a wall of water is used as a backdrop to selling outdoor shoes and other accessories.

Case 7.4 Themed Displays

Most retail stores use themes of some sort when displaying their merchandise. Themed displays are stacks or arrangements of goods, which have been placed on special offer, or part of a promotion. For instance, during the Christmas period the greeting card specialist retailers reorganize their stores to reflect the seasonal lines. Such items as Christmas cards wrapping paper and other festive items are given priority over the regular birthday and special occasions stock. Consumers *expect* this and retailers that fail to promote or show off their merchandise in this way lose out to the competition. Other types of themes may focus on the holiday atmosphere, foreign merchandise and cultures, and lifestyles. This is not a complete list and the purpose of displays will vary with the sector (for example, electrical or fashion clothing) and store type.

Displays vary considerably and may revolve round themes. For example, in the fashion world retailers may wish to emphasize an international flavour with colours and national emblems from distant places. Far Eastern displays have been used with great success to sell certain product types such as rugs and ceramics in department stores. Product types are generally grouped together, as in the case of washing machines and similar white goods, and then grouped by manufacturer. Discount electrical stores such as Comet and Courts usually adopt this type of layout. It benefits the consumer by making it a lot easier to find all the available (in-store) alternatives. There is, however, another reason linked to customer buying motives for this type of arrangement. The strategy is called complementary merchandise. This is when the sale of one item promotes the sale of another. We see this in video rental stores where high-quality ice cream and popcorn is sold alongside the latest blockbuster.

The Effective Use of Displays

As we learned from our greeting card retail example some departments need considerable space at certain times of the year. These are called seasonal departments. Toys at Christmas and gardening items in the spring mean that layouts must accommodate seasonal changes. Displays play an important role in a retail store and attractive and informative displays can help to sell goods. Poorly designed displays can reduce the chance of success and, most importantly, ruin the store's atmosphere and create an uncomfortable setting. Here are some guiding principles that help to ensure the effectiveness of displays:

▶ When building a display it is important to maintain a balance for the viewer.

▶ Where possible, displays should be designed with a central point that attracts the spectator.

▶ Displays should direct the eyes away from the dominant feature and encourage spectators to scan the remainder of the display.

▶ Merchandise should be arranged so that small items are placed at the front with large items at the rear.

▶ The height of merchandise is critical and creates the best effect when placed at eye level, as spectators tend to look straight ahead.

▶ It is better to group merchandise together rather than present them in long lines that take up space.

▶ Displays should always show the very best merchandise that the retailer has to offer.

▶ Simple displays are best as too many items in a display will confuse the customer and tend to create a bad atmosphere.

▶ Top shelves are usually reserved for quality items and as the human eye scans from left to right retailers usually place less important merchandise on the left.

The need for product focus displays varies with the retail sector (for example, electrical or fashion clothing) and the retail store format. In some sectors like grocery displays may utilize a variety of formats, which may be random, product focused, special offer (two for one) and brand specific. There is a hierarchy in the stock arrangement display, which is usually based on the value or price of an item. So the higher the product cost to the customer, the more prominent the product in the display. The idea behind this strategy is that the customer will immediately identify with the best quality merchandise or brand, because it receives pride of place. As quality is usually linked to price and brand the customer will assume that the most prominent item in the display is the best money can buy. Similarly, the customer can identify with the lower-priced or budget items. Colours also play a part in this strategy and help to stress particular features or brands in a display.

Store Design and Displays

The psychological effect of colour is important to retailers and used to draw attention to displays. For example, yellow is used to emphasize Easter and Mother's Day, and creates a warm and familiar holiday atmosphere. Although evidence to support the psychological effect of colours on buying behaviour is limited, there is some benefit in the use of colours to motivate customers. In general, warm colours like red and yellow help to draw customers into the store and cool colours have been shown to create calm moods. Blues and greens tend to make people feel calm and are useful in areas where decisions are being made. In-store lighting is used with colour schemes to extract the maximum effect from displays and visual merchandising.

Store lighting is expensive and consumes 60 per cent of the utilities used by a retail store. Lighting is, however, crucial in retail design and is an integral part of the store's interior. It should complement rather than detract from the merchandise. Exterior lighting should match the mood the retailer is attempting to create and complement the rest of the store's design features. Areas of the store's interior can be lit with strategically placed lighting that highlight racks of goods and tempt customers with attractive offers, leading to impulse purchasing. Lighting also performs a security function by providing illumination in the store at night. This also has the effect of identifying the store and its merchandise to people passing the shop windows.

Ceilings perform a number of functions the first of which is to provide a fixing for lighting booms. Networks of ceiling light clusters are used to identify goods and specific areas within most stores (for example super-markets, department stores). In older more traditional buildings the internal ceilings are important features and add to the personality and ambience of the store. Ceilings found in older stores are generally much higher than those found in discount stores (sheds) where shoppers are willing to give up ambience for greater selection. A high open-girder construction is quite common in discount warehouses like Toys' Я'Us. Structures with high ceilings cost more to heat or cool.

Floor coverings suggest the nature of the offering, and deep pile carpets feel warmer and generally suggest higher-priced merchandise. The range of choices is endless: carpets, wood, terrazzo, quarry tile and vinyl floor covering. Colour-coded floor designs and shelving are useful on multi-level stores to demarcate product areas. Shelving must be compatible with the merchandise strategy and the overall image of the store. For example, stainless steel shelving creates an entirely different image than natural wood effect. Glass shelving creates an element of elegance and places total emphasis on the merchandise it displays. This is ideal in situations where stock must be displayed to maximum effect, such as expensive fashion items.

For the retailer the arrangement of stock has another important function linked to the replenishment system, or re-stocking of shelves. The type of in-store fixtures or shelving must be easy for the customers to access, and for the staff to replenish. Types of fixture vary with purpose.

In-store Fixtures

We will focus on ten main types of fixture that are used in retailing to contain and display stock to the customer. The use of these fixtures will vary considerably with the nature of the offering and the profile of the retailer (whether they are high-quality and expensive or value retailing). Also the type of retail business usually dictates the forms of shelving and fixtures required. An example of this is the electrical discount retailer that regularly uses stacking fixtures from ceiling to floor. This promotes ease of storage and access for the customer with the value-for-money image. To make it easier to identify the different types of fixture available, we have placed them in a table (Table 7.3) with linkages to other factors like location in the store and purpose.

Table 7.3 Fixtures and their Purpose

Fixture	Location in-store	Purpose
Gondola shelving or bins	Commonly in the centre of aisles and walkways	To attract the customers' attention to sale items and promotional offers
Racks	Generally on back walls and divisions between themes or product areas	To hold and display stock and to provide efficient storage space
Hangers	Racks and against wall mounted displays	To display clothing items effectively and protect them
Glass	Acts as shelf in showcase or wall-mounted shelves	Creates a sense of depth and focus on the merchandise
Pegboard	Wall or fixture mounted	Used for mounting displays and featuring products
Counters	Check out and customer service points	Spacious flat surfaces for wrapping and till points
Mannequins	Window displays, lifestyle themes and next to racks and mirrors	Dummies provide a lifelike way of displaying clothing and associated products
Mirrors	Against walls and dividers. Behind displays	Used by customers in clothing stores. Give a sense of depth for displays
Custom fixtures	Anywhere in the store – made to fit	Themed (lifestyle) displays and special promotions

The list in Table 7.3 is not intended to be comprehensive as each retailer will employ his or her own designs and specifications. Retailers need to choose the in-store fixtures carefully as they form part of the design and overall retail or store image. It is important, therefore, to carefully construct the interiors to fit in with the desired store image. For example, the French sporting goods retailer Decathlon utilize a discount-style format, which enables them to display the merchandise for volume sales. This format also appeals to their target market and, above all, is what their target market *expects*. In this instance the layout denotes value for money, the availability of a wide range of products and speedy service with low staff contact. The racks and fitting in the Decathlon stores make this possible by creating the floor space, storage space and free space necessary. Displays and storage vary with product types.

Types of Products and their Fixtures

We have already discussed how merchandise can be grouped into impulse goods, convenience goods, shopping goods, etc. This also provides a reasonable guide to designing the layouts and fixtures in the store, based on buying behaviour. For example, impulse goods are products that customers buy as unplanned purchases. Their purchase may be prompted by in-store cues such as smells or catching the eye of the customer at the checkout. Products displayed at the checkout with the intention of capturing this market are called *point of purchase displays* or POP. Sweets and chocolates fall into this category, as most parents will testify. Convenience goods, which are goods that customers put a minimum amount of thought into, are generally stored in functional racks and fixtures that promote ease and speed of purchasing. However, specialty goods, which customers make a specific effort to purchase, are usually allocated more space and prominent display fixtures and floor area. An example of this is high-status fashion brands such as Hugo Boss. Fashion retailers will give more space and thought to the location of high-status products because of their relative importance and high margins of profit.

The nature of the retail sector will influence what fixtures the retailer will use. In the grocery sector product class is used to arrange goods. This keeps the arrangement of the products consistent for the customer and easy to service for the staff. It is also important for the customers to be able to find their shopping items easily, and on a regular basis. So fresh food is typically presented in the grocery supermarket at the entrance of the store. This makes it easy for customers to locate and encourages a greater turnover of stock.

> ⇨ *Stock turnover* is crucial to retailers and especially where perishable goods are sold. Stock turnover refers to the number of times average stock is sold over a given time period. For fashion retailers moving stock is equally vital as fashions and trends have a limited life, and stock has a limited shelf life. All stock has a maximum shelf life.

In other forms of retailing the trend is towards more efficient rack systems for arranging and displaying stock. Competitive forces in the industry have driven many retail businesses to target merchandising as a way of gaining significant competitive advantages. For example, in the DIY sector megastores like B&Q lead on range and the accessibility of stock (due to the linear footage of storage space) for the customer. Most large garden centres provide model gardens and examples of layouts, and stock the goods to create them. Travel agents have altered their formats to bring customers further into the store, and surround them with travel information. This is a break from the traditional travel agent, which offered little space for the customer, and fewer displays for merchandise. The trend is towards a greater number of display boards, which advertise a wider variety of holidays and flights. Independent retailers are unable to compete with these formats and tend to rely on location and speciality to attract customers.

The merchandising efforts of an independent retailer are lessened by the lack of resources and buying power. Customers tend not to expect the local independent store to obtain, stock and present merchandise in the same manner as the one-stop retailers. Small stores are valued for their convenience and friendly atmosphere. Independent retailers are restrained by a distinct lack of resources and in-store space, which limits their choice of layout and fixtures.

7.5 Space Management

If a retail business is to provide the merchandise its customers want it is obliged to carry stock levels of sufficient quantity. Storage, and above all space, is for most retailers crucial. In some sectors, such as grocery retailing, space is probably the single most important aspect of chain store or supermarket design. Accommodating the large volume of items (between 25 000 to 30 000) requires significant amounts of space in-store. The majority of food and non-food items are stored *in situ* with some centralized storage space outside the selling areas. This allows the chain retailer to order goods in advance or when high customer demand (for example, Christmas holidays) occurs. In practice, storage space is always in short supply and most retailers will shift the warehousing function on to the supplier or distributor where possible. This makes good sense, especially when the demand for certain merchandise is likely, due to peaks in the buying cycle for example. Apparel and grocery retailers are particularly good at designing efficient storage and ordering systems.

Space management is concerned with placing merchandise within the store in the most profitable manner. The most significant factor in planning merchandise layout is that space varies in value. Some parts of the store are more valuable because customers visit them more frequently. It is easier to make sales along these routes than other less travelled routes. Space closest to the entrances and exits is the most valuable and values decrease further into the store. Height from the ground also affects value, hence space on the upper floors or in the basement have less value that the main floors; the most valuable in terms of profits per square metre are at the entrance location. As a general rule, then, it is best to locate the highest profit generator in prime locations in order to maximize space productivity.

There are four ways to express space within stores and its value depends on the location in the store. These are as follows:

▶ Sales per square foot is the typical measure for a store department or free-standing display.

▶ Sales per linear foot is the common measure of shelf space for items like grocery, health foods and cosmetics.

▶ Sales space is sales per square foot of exposure space.

▶ Sales per cubic foot is relevant to refrigeration and freezer units.

> ⇨ The word 'linear' refers to the measurement 'in a straight line' of sales footage. Exposure space is calculated by the length times the height measure of vertical space – here space has a height value in addition to linear value

Planning the Layout of Merchandise

When considering the layout of stock, retailers have to take into account the available space and the best location for their stock. For example, people scan objects from left to right, and the mind tends to retain the last object seen by the eye. Therefore, retailers place less important merchandise on the left. This process is of greatest importance in grocery retailing where the allocation of merchandise and space follows a rigorous plan.

There are several methods of planning the amount of space a store, department or product range requires. Making a rough plan of the store helps to allocate appropriate amounts of space for each category. These may be by one or a mixture of the following:

▶ *Historical sales*. If sales of women's wear equal 50 per cent of total store sales, then half the floor space will be allocated to women's wear. This, however, can cause a problem when sales are fluctuating over time and do not take account of the relative importance in generating profit.

▶ *Contribution to profit*. This emphasizes the need for using space profitably, because space costs money. There are a number of variants on this with different degrees of sophistication:

▶ *Gross margin*. This is a sale less cost of goods. It is a fairly simple system to implement, but does not take into account the differences in display and replenishment costs. Allocating according to net margin can rectify this. Such systems must be used with caution, because they do not take account of general demand conditions. As we know from Chapter 1, generally speaking, lowering the price will tend to sell more items. Allowing for the effect of searching on customer demand, we can expect sales at a price to vary within broader or narrower limits. This accounts for the traditional control used that sets limits to the space allocated, according to the manager's discretion within the overall space of the store.

▶ *Industry average.* Stores often use industry averages to allocate space and provide the same proportions of space as the competitor. This creates a safety factor according to group experience. However, it creates a 'me too' atmosphere that does not differentiate the store from competitors.

> ⇨ Often a store will wish to build up stock in a particular line or product line. This is sometimes used in short-term promotions.

In grocery stores space may be allocated on the basis of the speed at which the items are sold. The arrangement of merchandise can follow a number of schemes such as by brand, size, product or, in some cases all three of these criteria. Shelves are normally divided by product type (for example, tinned food, dairy products). Bottom shelves can be allocated to high-volume items and the easier to reach shelves to high-margin items. Top shelves are usually reserved for speciality items.

The strategic aims of the retailer will naturally play a role in the display and location of merchandise throughout the store. These tactics can range from placing items that consumers expect to see in the store to the most frequently purchased products. Knowing which are bestselling lines and the best locations enables the retailer to map departments or sections within the store. The block plan should be adjusted to take account of adjacencies in the goods.

Adjacencies are linkages that retailers create that correspond to types of merchandise, which according to consumers' perceptions, are connected but different. For example, a customer may wish to buy formal wear. The retailer therefore provides the customer with cues to buy leisurewear. This may take the form of visual merchandising such as displays illustrating the outdoor situations where this type of clothing can be worn.

In keeping with the store image the retailer may decide to place departments containing select goods close to each other to generate additional sales. This action creates what is called *associated sales* such as fashion clothing and jewellery, or sportswear and sporting goods. Some departments, for example, toys at Christmas and gardening items in the spring, need considerable space at certain times of the year and layouts must accommodate these seasonal changes. This departmental plan is then checked against the footprint for the different departments. To produce something that is consistent overall with customer flow and image of the store.

There are a number of commercial computer programs that enable retail management to position and track their stock accurately. The high cost of these systems, running into several thousand pounds, means that large retail chains are more likely to use them rather than the smaller independent retailer.

Case 7.5 Computer-Based Space Management

The use of technology in space planning means that product and line assortments can be managed more effectively. Some merchandising software systems include an assortment–planning module or Planogram, which helps the retailer allocate merchandise throughout the store. A Planogram is a graphical representation that shows the space to be allocated and the full description of the stock-keeping unit (SKU). Planograms provide a map of the length, height, depth of shelves with the number and location of the SKU. This is used by the staff to stock the shelves effectively. Independent retailers may not be able to afford this type of sophisticated system but the same type of plan can be built into a spreadsheet or even sketched by hand.

Source: http://www.shelflogic.com

References

Headden, S. (1993) 'Made in USA', *US News and World Report*, November: 48–55.
http://www.shelflogic.com
Kunz, G.I. (1998) *Merchandising: Theory, Principles and Practice*, New York: Fairchild Books.
Verbeke, W., Farris, P., and Thurik, R. (1997) 'Consumer response to the preferred brand out-of-stock situation' *European Journal of Marketing*, 32(11/12): 1008–28.

Establishing a Pricing Strategy

This chapter considers the following issues:

► The link between the price of merchandise and the retailer goals.

► The importance of calculating the right prices for various customer segments.

► The hidden aspects of pricing

CHAPTER

8

Establishing a Pricing Strategy

Introduction and Core Concepts

Price is one of the most important variables in retail decision-making. It is also the easiest and quickest variable to change. Retailers must make the correct decisions about the price of the merchandise and services they sell, or face the possibility of falling sales or even loss of business. For the customer, price is frequently a major reason for shopping in a particular store. However, in some situations price may suggest low- or even poor-quality merchandise. Therefore it is essential for the retailer to know the implications of its pricing decisions.

8.1 Pricing Objectives

'What should I charge for this product?' is a fundamental question that is posed countless times a day in retailing. The retailer has to answer this question for each product in store. However, fixing prices should not be conducted in an arbitrary manner as this can lead to numerous problems that impact on the image of the retailer. A successful retailer sets the prices of the various products in line with clear pricing objectives.

> ⇨ Pricing objectives are the goals that the company wishes to achieve through its pricing.

The retailer's pricing objectives take account of the important factors that make its products attractive and the retailer competitive: the retailer's mission statement, its goals and objectives, types of customers and the location of store. Retailers usually disclose their mission statements and goals in their annual reports and these tend to directly and indirectly guide their pricing strategy. We discussed mission statements and strategy earlier, in Chapter 5, with retail planning and strategy.

Small independent retailers usually have more constraints on their pricing strategy than larger concerns. They lack buying power and are often obliged to aim for higher margins. Nevertheless, like large multiples, the corner shop must compete effectively where possible. Pricing is one area where smaller retailers are less likely to succeed, so they trade on their specialisms or convenience as an alternative.

For major retailers the task of setting prices or price structures may be compared to a scientific process with cause and effect relationships. For example, lowering prices in some sectors may lead to price wars (for instance, grocery, newsagent) and thus price can be a major factor in differentiation. At its simplest, price determines who will buy the product, or who can afford to buy the product or service. Price also tells the consumer a great deal of information about the nature of the retail business and the sort of products it sells. Figure 8.1 illustrates the stages that a retailer should follow in order to make pricing decisions.

We can see from Figure 8.1 that the first stage is to formulate objectives regarding pricing. This means that a retailer must first consider carefully its position relative to the market. The market consists of competitors, customers and other interested parties. This means that the retailer may require more than one set of pricing objectives. There may be, for example, a need for short-term and long-term pricing objectives. This is particularly useful for new market entrants that need to first establish a brand, and then enjoy increasing profits as the brand takes off. An example of this is the sporting goods discount and France-based retailer, Decathlon, which faced quite a challenge in making its mark in the competitive world of UK sports retailing.

Underpinning Decathlon's objectives were the fundamental issues of branding and positioning. The company's first task in entering the market was to establish a name for a quality end product range while differentiating itself from established competitors such as JJB Sports and Allsports. To achieve this, it used selected discounts to provide value for money without damaging the high-quality image of the organization.

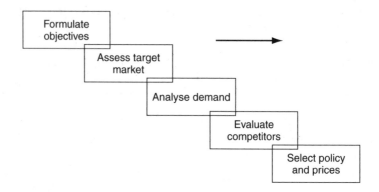

Figure 8.1   Pricing Decisions

Case 8.1 Decathlon: The Price of Success

The operation of Decathlon the sports retailer spans many countries, including France, Belgium and Germany, with some 200 stores in France alone. In general, the stores cater for 60 different areas of sport with a huge assortment of merchandise. In the UK there are just three large-capacity (45 000 sq ft plus) stores located in out-of-town sites in accessible locations near to main road access points. However, the relatively unfamiliar name of Decathlon in the UK, and the strong competition from the major sports retailers, mean that the company is forced to take measures to establish market position. Pricing is major part of this strategy.

Decathlon sells a limited amount of branded lines such as Nike and Adidas. The large majority of their stock consists of Decathlon *own-brand* goods, which are recognized in Europe as high-quality merchandise. Since entering the UK market,

Decathlon has offered its British customers this range of *own-brand* high-quality goods at 30 per cent below competitors' prices for similar items. Their branded goods are sold at more or less the same price as those of their high street competition. In the medium and long term Decathlon wishes to win the loyalty of varying customer groups who are normally forced to buy from a variety of sports retailers. The chief attraction for customers is high-quality merchandise under one roof, with brands that customers are familiar with and the Decathlon brand available at knockdown prices. For Decathlon, the main objective is to build up a base of loyal customers who recognize the Decathlon brand, and in doing so extend its operation to the UK market. Decathlon's pricing objectives are to make it the most competitive sports retailer in the world.

Pricing objectives are specific to the retailer and the sector and environment in which the firm operates. There are, however, some general motives that guide retailers and other businesses when they formulate pricing objectives. Survival, for example, is a key reason for altering prices (these may be specific or across the board), which we have already determined is the simpler variable to adjust. Maximizing profits can be difficult to achieve due to uncertain costs, and raising prices will address shortfalls. For the smaller independent retailer raising or lowering prices (to rapidly increase sales) may help to generate badly needed cash flow. In general, retailers will alter their pricing objectives to obtain or retain market share (Dibb *et al.* 1997). The battle of the grocery supermarkets is testimony to this.

Case 8.2 High-Priced Supermarkets

Grocery retailing has always been highly competitive. Towards the end of the 1990s UK supermarkets found themselves in the position of having justify their pricing strategies due to pressures from external markets. Unfavourable comparisons were drawn between the prices in UK supermarkets and the supposedly expensive French counterparts. Daily newspapers at the time published regular shopping basket comparisons that focused

consumer attention on the variability of prices across markets. More important for consumers were the comparisons of profit margins from country to country. Even high-wage economies such as the USA were able to offer more competitive prices due to the lower margins adopted by retailers. The UK was identified as a 'high-profit' market to enter.

8.2 Pricing for Markets

In the Decathlon case, the sports retailer targeted varying customer groups as part of their strategy. Identifying these groups is an important stage in the steps of pricing decision-making. It easy to see that different markets will warrant different pricing strategies. However, the overall objectives (both pricing and strategic) of the retailer will influence this decision. To understand this fully, we will now consider several large and small retail businesses in the context of pricing for markets.

Using Price to Define a Market

Fashion retailers such as Selfridges and Harvey Nichols use price as a lever to encourage market segments to shop. High prices and expensive brands encourage higher socio-economic groupings into their stores. The Next brand targets the higher end of the mass market.

> ⇨ Mass market refers to the large majority of consumers who in general have the means to shop for consumer goods. Markets are stratified into segments, the higher end being the most lucrative as consumer spend is higher.

Next claims that it has established a market position based on individual style, quality and value for money. This means that the potential market for the products will be based or referenced round other similar retailers who target the same segment of the market. Next is also able to target other less affluent segments of the mass market with their 'Next to Nothing' brand, via factory outlet sites. In these locations Next and other high-status brands such as Thorntons, the luxury chocolate retailer, reach a broad mix of customer groups. Prices in these outlets are 50 per cent (or more) below their equivalent high street operations.

Case 8.3 Thorntons: Quality Sweets?

Thorntons intends to remain the most popular confectionary shop in the high street and shopping centres by focusing on *high-quality* products. Its point of difference is the quality and expertise with which its products are designed and made. It invests a lot of time and effort to serve particular market segments with products that meet the needs of customers within those segments. Its customers can afford, and are prepared, to spend quite a bit more to enjoy the luxury Thorntons brand. But what of the Cadbury brand? Cadbury has a tiny retailing operation and sells most of its products through other retailers. The Cadbury range sells for much less and appeals to *all* groups in the market. We buy Cadbury chocolate to eat anytime, but Thorntons are special, and priced accordingly.

The Effect of Location on Price

The geographic location of the retailer has a strong influence on pricing. In some circumstances it may be the major determinant. For instance, in a depressed area with high unemployment a store may be forced to stock only certain types of merchandise, charge lower prices and adopt a particular store layout and design. In other situations the retailer may be inclined to raise prices of similar merchandise to meet fully the expectations of customers residing in the area. Examples of this are evident in areas where urban development or gentrification creates pockets of high-quality retailing. Owners of antique shops and craft boutiques in areas where demand for expensive merchandise is high, adjust prices to match. Increased profit margins in these circumstances would be required to meet the higher rents and other property costs in these areas.

The lack of competition in an area may also allow retailers to increase prices. This happens frequently in rural and farm communities where one general store serves the whole community. Distribution costs may also be a cause of higher prices in remote regions.

Niche Markets

Niche markets are areas where pricing may vary considerably because of the location, merchandise and type of customer they serve. Even the store's format influences the pricing in this sector. Retailers such as Tie Rack, offer a single-line range of merchandise, which is priced according to the market they wish to target. Their customers are usually seeking a special purchase such as a gift from stores that are accessible and convenient. Alternatively, they are impulse buyers from airports or railway stations. Impulse buyers tend to have a relatively low sensitivity to price. This is reinforced by the sense of exclusivity that the store format induces.

Body Shop is a case in point of a niche retailer that has a special appeal because of its overt ethical policy. This ethical stance comes from its no animal testing policy, appeal to nature and responsible supply chain policy. Body Shop's emphasis on its ethical position allows it to charge premium prices without alienating its customers. Its customers become real stakeholders in the success of the business, and this in turn generates loyalty. Also, the firm's relationships with its customers help create the image of the business. For example, Anita Roddick made a commitment to environmental issues the cornerstone of Body Shop. This image directly affects consumer attitudes and the place the retail business takes in relation to society. For their customer groups this ethical stance is an important reason for buying from the retailer, and returning to shop again.

Ethical Considerations

Ethical issues are strong determinants of store patronage. That is to say, customers shop where they feel comfortable with the policies and ideals held by a particular retail organization. Ethical issues are also an important feature of pricing strategy in most retail sectors. There are many customers who are willing to pay extra for products that are perceived to be healthier or in accordance with environmental principles, or are considered fair to suppliers or workers further back up the supply chain.

In the late 1990s, for example, various pressure groups raised consumers' awareness of genetically modified (GM) food and made them much less willing to accept products derived from genetically modified ingredients. This has had a major influence on where people shopped for their groceries. Iceland the frozen food chain decided to ban completely products that had a GM food content. Other retailers such as Tesco, Sainsburys and Marks & Spencer had already taken steps to restrict the sales of such products. The key issue here is that a change in consumer views changed the plans of major retailers. Companies such as Ben & Jerry's ice cream, Benetton, Body Shop and Boots have implemented specific policies that their major customer groups have perceived to be beneficial to society as a whole, even though this may have raised direct prices to the consumer. A good reputation translates into long-term improvements in profitability. Positioning a retailer as a socially responsible organization raises customers' expectations (Piacentini, MacFadyen and Eadie 2000). Providing a retailer is able to meet these new expectations, it will encourage loyal groups of customers who will be prepared to buy (at a price) in accordance with such principles.

The Influence of Changing Price Levels

Retailers realize that their particular price position in the market depends on the general level of prices for the products they sell and the degree of customer acceptability and price sensitivity under different situations. Retailers also have to take account of various price movements that occur over periods of time in the market. These price movements reflect changes in the underlying supply and demand conditions and include the effects of technical innovation, social change and customer attitudes, and the diffusion of a product or lifestyle among consumers. Personal computers and mobile phones are good examples of these changes.

The personal computer market provides a range of products from low-specification entry-level products to powerful high-end professional computers with a consequent price range. Computers undergo constant technical development that lead to more powerful and sophisticated computers, reducing the cost of making them. However, during the 1990s, entry-level computers hovered around the £1000 mark as suppliers maintained prices while raising the specification. Then in 1999, many brands became significantly lower priced as consumers began to reduce their target price.

The mobile phone has also undergone major technical development and widespread diffusion since the early 1990s. Until then it was a rather costly product to make and expensive to buy and run. The market was limited to comparatively well-off, optimistic or innovative consumers, such as the 1980s yuppie (young upwardly mobile) who bought from a limited number of dealers. Since then technology has moved quickly, reducing the cost of owning and using a mobile phone. The market for mobile phones has moved through the typical stages of a technologically new product (see Chapter 1, section 5). It has gone from a high-cost, low-volume, high-price product to a low-cost, high-volume, low-price product, which can now even be bought in the local supermarket. As the market grew suppliers and retailers enjoyed high rates of profit that attracted new entrants and crowded the market. Now retailers use special discounts to compete and also have to provide a range of products with different features to maintain average prices and market share.

Macroeconomic Influences on Price Trends

Long-term price deflation or inflation can exist and affect the general level of prices. Consumers and businesses have become accustomed to continuing changes in the price level. Generally these have been upwards. However, the experience of the recession in the 1990s, and the widespread diffusion of information about alternative sources of supply, has created a climate of low price expectations. Prices, as measured by the Retail Price Index, have continued to rise in the UK by about 3 per cent per year. However, this reflects the rising cost of services, such as personal services and eating out. Product retailers generally face consumers who are demanding lower prices. Thus while consumers have been increasing their consumption in real terms, many retailers have only seen growth in value of their sales by getting consumers to trade up to perceived higher-quality brands. The greater sophistication of the consumer will continue to exert downward pressure on retail prices. During the downturn in the economic cycle when the economy grows more slowly, consumer caution will move consumers towards the cheaper end of the market. However, as consumer confidence improves, they will move back towards the higher end of the market and be more relaxed about paying higher prices for higher-quality goods.

8.3 Pricing Calculations

The next stage of the process is to determine the demand for the merchandise or services. This refers to the degree to which the products or services will be sought after by the target market. We first look at the concept of demand and then how retailers can use this in practical pricing decisions. This is best illustrated by a model which shows the *demand curve* of price versus quantity.

> ⇨ The demand curve shows the relationship between price and quantity in a graphical form.

Like most graphs of this type Figure 8.2 is just a universal example and does not refer to a particular retailer or situation. Retailers sell many different products, some of which are very similar. So the graph should only be taken to illustrate the market for a product range. For instance, a retailer may sell a range of suits with a range of prices to match. The demand curve then illustrates the market for *average suits*. The price of a particular suit has some relationship to an average suit depending on the

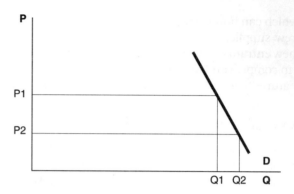

Figure 8.2 Demand Curve

quality. This allows us to explore the relationship between the price of suits and consumer demand. The graph shows the case we normally experience – that consumers will buy more the lower the price of the product. So how much will they buy at different prices? That depends on a number of variables, such as income, expectations about the future and the cost of other products, such as food and housing, which tend to take priority.

But what about luxury goods? Some retailers depend for their business on the exclusivity of their products – they sell because the price is high and high prices are used as a sign of quality. This is true, but it does not mean that people buy more the higher the (average) price. Products are exclusive because ordinary people cannot afford them. Retailers who stock high-value goods are clearly differentiated in the market. Lowering prices will not spoil their market, because their prices will still be high. They know that lowering prices will increase sales, but the real question is whether it would be worth it. This question is the same for any retailer and in order to answer it we need to consider relative profitability at different prices to determine the best price levels for a particular product line.

Demand and Revenue

We need to introduce the following terms relating to revenue and cost:

> ⇨ The total revenue or sales revenue from a product is the income received from the sale of the product. If the retailer charges each customer the same price, then revenue is the price times the number of items sold.

> ⇨ Average revenue is the average price of the goods sold. It equals the total sales revenue divided by the number of items sold.

> ⇨ Marginal revenue is the increase in total revenue as one more item of the product is sold.

Table 8.1 uses a simple example to illustrate the meaning of these terms.

Table 8.1 Sales and Revenue

When the price is	The retailer sells	Its sales revenue is	Its average revenue is	Its marginal revenue is
£21	0 items			
£20	1 item	£20	£20	£20
£19	2 items	£38	£19	£18
£18	3 items	£54	£18	£16

> ⇨ For instance, the marginal revenue from selling one item would be £20. This is the revenue from selling one item minus the revenue if it sold nil items.

We can see that the marginal revenue becomes less than the price when the retailer has to lower price in order to sell more items. The retailer is then a price searcher. If, however, market conditions mean that the going price is fixed, the retailer faces a flat demand curve and marginal revenue is the same as the price. This is shown in Figure 8.3.

In order to determine its appropriate level of sales and the prices it should charge, the retailer needs to know when it would make the most profit. This requires information on costs. There are some important cost concepts that the retailer needs to use. The principle of opportunity (or alternative, or avoidable) cost states that the only costs that are relevant to a decision are those costs directly associated with the decision, in this case how much to stock and sell. We introduce the following terms:

> ⇨ Total cost of sales is all the expenditure incurred in selling the product.

> ⇨ Average cost of the product is the total cost divided by the number of items sold.

> ⇨ Marginal cost is the extra costs incurred in selling an extra item of the product.

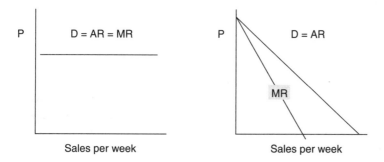

Figure 8.3   Demand and Marginal Revenue

Table 8.2 illustrates the meaning of these terms:

Table 8.2 Cost Terms

Sales	Total cost of sales	Average cost	Marginal cost
1 item	£16	£16	£16
2 items	£30	£15	£14
3 items	£42	£14	£12

> ⇨ In practice, a firm knows how its total costs (in the second column) vary with output and it can calculate its average and marginal costs from these data.

Profit Maximization

In order to maximize its profits, the retailer should set its price and target output according to the following rules:

> ⇨ The firm should set its level of sales so that *marginal cost = marginal revenue*. This means that it should try to increase its sales as long as the extra costs are less than the extra income received. However, this condition is also consistent with making minimum profit (or maximum loss), so we have to add a second condition, namely: *marginal cost is increasing above marginal revenue*.

Table 8.3 explains and illustrates these conditions. In this case we shall assume that the retailer can sell any quantity of items at a fixed price of £5.

Table 8.3 The Marginal Rules for Profit Maximization

Sales items	Price	Sales revenue	Marginal revenue	Cost of sales	Average cost	Marginal cost	Profit	Marginal profit
1	5	5	5	6	6.0	6	−1	−1
2	5	10	5	11	5.5	5	−1	0
3	5	15	5	15	5.0	4	0	+1
4	5	20	5	18	4.5	3	2	+2
5	5	25	5	22	4.4	4	3	+1
6	5	30	5	27	4.5	5	3	0
7	5	35	5	33	4.7	6	2	−1

This simple case shows that *marginal cost = marginal revenue* when sales are two items and five items. However, when sales are two items, profits are at a minimum because marginal cost is falling below marginal revenue. On the other hand, when sales are five items, profits are at a maximum because marginal cost is going above marginal revenue at any higher level of sales. Figure 8.4 illustrates these rules graphically.

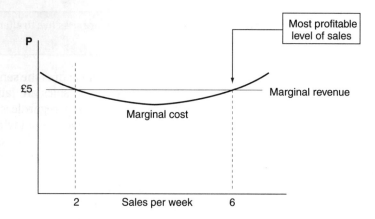

Figure 8.4   Marginal Analysis: Maximizing Profit

Pricing and Potential Competitors

Firms with large shares of market sales have market power and can exercise monopolistic or oligopolistic control over the market. This means that they can sell their products for higher prices than they would otherwise be able to. The higher profitability of monopolistic markets sooner or later attracts new retailers into the market. Existing retailers can try to deter potential rivals from entering the industry by reducing the prospect of profit. One way is to keep prices low enough that customer loyalty is built up and the prospect of profit for the new retailer becomes less. Retailers can still maintain higher profits because they can keep prices higher than they would otherwise be.

Demand Fluctuations

In hard times retailers tend to sell fewer luxury products and there is a relationship between environmental factors and demand. For example, in the retailing of services, such as food and hospitality, demand is variable and may depend on seasonal factors. The following example explains this concept within the context of eating out and overnight accommodation:

Travel Inn, part of Whitbread PLC, is a mid-priced hotel chain which offers motel-style value-for-money accommodation, alongside premium-priced chain dining facilities. Their American-style restaurant chain TGI Friday's is usually located close to the hotel for the convenience of guests. Demand for room bookings vary with seasonal variations at Christmas, for weddings in the summer and when local events warrant. Restaurant sales (demand) are kept buoyant and reasonably level with a combination of hotel guests and passing trade. This arrangement helps to smooth demand for the entire business. In this instance, small alterations in price are unlikely to appreciably affect demand. However, large increases may reduce hotel bookings but not necessarily the demand for restaurant sales, which are less *elastic*.

> ⇨ Elasticity of demand measures to what extent prices are sensitive to alterations before demand changes.

Elasticity of demand is an important concept and measures the sensitivity of demand to price increases. For example, petrol sales are fairly *inelastic* as the demand for petrol is reasonably constant regardless of price changes. The decline in demand for petrol is relatively small when prices rise. On the other hand, when the price of new motor cars increases the demand falls and there is a decline in the number of cars sold in the market.

Calculating the elasticity of demand is useful for retail management as these data help to make pricing decisions. It is important to know exactly what to charge for goods or services to maximize profits and retain customers. Two measurements are required to calculate whether merchandise is 'price elastic' or 'inelastic'. These are quantity of sales and the price of merchandise. For example, a retailer may sell 600 electric drills in one year at a price of £40 each. Here the total sales revenue is sales times price which comes to £24 000. The formula for calculating price elasticity is:

> ⇨ $$\text{Price elasticity} = \frac{\%\ \text{change in the demand}}{\%\ \text{change in price}}$$

The demand can be termed *elastic* when an increase in the price of electric drills will decrease revenue as demand falls. An *inelastic* demand will result in increased price and increased revenue, because the increase in price more than makes up for the reduction in quantity. Beer has an inelastic demand, which is why the government likes to put taxes on it – people will still consume nearly as much beer, even with the added taxes. If the retailer decreases the price of electric drills this will result in a decrease in total revenue. Calculating this information is important as it impacts on profit projections.

When setting prices the relationships between demand, cost and profit need to be considered. The previous demand analysis is useful in guiding decisions about the market, but often the demand for a product is difficult to estimate. However, once those decisions are made about lines to be stocked, the retailer needs to make a more detailed study of price and cost and the sales requires. The retailer can then make use of another useful technique, called break-even analysis.

> ⇨ Break-even analysis refers to the point at which the sales revenue covers the cost of the fixed investment. To calculate this we need to know our fixed costs, unit variable costs and selling price.

Consider a small independent retailer who wishes to calculate the point at which he or she breaks even with a new line of merchandise. For this example let us imagine the merchandise is a range of greeting cards. To make our example easier let us also imagine that, according to the wholesaler, the cards normally sell for the same price regardless of title or size. However, before setting the price, the retailer firsts needs to work out the break-even point.

As discussed, to work out the break-even for the merchandise we need information about fixed costs and unit variable costs.

> ⇨ *Fixed costs* refers to the amount that the retailer must invest to stock a line of merchandise. As the term 'fixed' implies, fixed costs are always present and refer to rents, salaries, fixtures and fittings, taxes and liability insurance.

> ⇨ Variable costs – unlike fixed costs variable costs will change with the volume of merchandise purchased by the retailer. Other costs may apply such as increasing the number of sales assistants (wages) to sell the additional merchandise.

By calculating the break-even point our independent retailer will be able to work out how many greeting cards need to be sold to recover the cost of his or her expenses. The following example using greeting card merchandise helps to explain this:

Case 8.4 Break-even Point for Greeting Card Merchandise

Fixed costs   –   £350 [total cost of stock]
Variable costs   –   £50   [visual merchandising]
Selling price   –   ?

$$\text{Break-even point} = \frac{\text{Fixed costs}}{\text{Selling price} - \text{Variable costs}}$$

$$\text{Greeting cards} = \frac{£350}{\text{Selling price} - £50}$$

Working in groups, use your knowledge of prices and the above formula to work out a suitable selling price for the greeting cards.

Selling price is missing from the example above, as this will depend on the retailer's individual mark-up. We discussed mark-up in Chapter 7, with merchandising strategy. A small independent may have to obtain higher mark-up because they achieve a smaller volume of sales and lack buying power. Customers normally accept this as part of convenience shopping; buying locally rather than in a town centre or retail park. Wherever the retailer is located, however, the ultimate goal is to make a profit. The next section considers the relationships between demand, cost and profit.

There is constant pressure on retailers to reduce prices and remain competitive. The point at which they can no longer reduce the price of merchandise before sustaining a loss is therefore an important factor. Many retail businesses, and especially those in highly competitive sectors, stake their image and reputation on providing value for money. For example, some supermarket chains advertise the cost of a weekly shopping basket and use this to gain advantage over competitor prices. Petrol retailers such as Esso employ a 'price watch' to ensure the lowest petrol prices in the locality. Electrical and DIY retailers like Comet and B&Q both run a price guarantee service that ensures the customer pays no more for items stocked than at any other retailer. All these policies require a sound knowledge and understanding of the relationships between costs and demand.

Case 8.5 The Cost of 'Fine Wine'

'Fine Wine' is small independent licensed retailer that trades on a busy modern housing estate. The owner rents the property and fixtures for a fixed cost of £30 000 per annum. Other fixed costs include items such as the specialized refrigerator and cash register amount to a further £2500 per annum. Variable costs, that is to say those costs that alter with the amount of business, include a part-time sales assistant on Saturdays and expenses for trips to the cash and carry. When averaged out these variable costs amount to a further £11 000 per annum. To calculate average fixed cost the retailer divided the fixed costs by the number of bottles of wine sold. Average variable costs are also calculated by dividing the total variable costs by the number of items sold.

When applying these financial rules students must remember that for some retailers other non-financial factors may take priority. For example, when a retailer lowers the price of merchandise to conform to customer expectations and ensure repeat business. The actions of the competition will also fuel pricing decisions. On other occasions management may decide to continue to sell unprofitable merchandise as part of their competitive strategy. For example, a reduction in prices, and therefore increased sales volume, may be part of a promotional event to encourage new business.

Non-Profit Related Decisions

At certain times of the year merchandise may be purchased with the intention of making large markdowns to encourage customer loyalty. Reductions in prices can be used to clear out-of-season goods and loss-making lines. When these items are sold off they can offer great advantages for customers who may pick up bargains at offer prices. Merchandise may be promoted with an emphasis on price. As an important part of the retail mix, price can encourage greater throughput on certain types of offers. For example, the two for one offer is commonly used in grocery retailing to encourage *knock-on* sales. Price is a great attraction and retailers use this to pull customers into new stores on rollouts and to reinforce repeat business.

8.4 Pricing Policies

Each retailer has an individual approach to pricing, which is determined by factors such as the market, the consumer, cost structure and the positioning in the marketplace. The relative importance of these factors to the specific retailer can change over time, and a pricing policy and strategy needs to be adaptable to account for this.

> ⇨ Pricing policy is a company-wide understanding and view about the level of pricing that the retailer chooses to follow. For example, a value-for-money variety store such as Poundstretcher will follow a policy of obtaining stock and selling on at the lowest possible price. This ethic will be understood by all the company's staff and will inform customers' expectations.

It is absolutely vital that pricing strategy reflects the pricing policy, otherwise customers are likely to become confused. This can lead to loss of sales and at worst a decline in the business generally. For instance, when a retailer establishes a high-quality image with prices to match, continuous sales and markdowns in store make the customer think standards have altered. Regular customers may thus become reluctant to use the stores due to the ambiguous nature of the offering. This demonstrates the importance of establishing a clear pricing policy and sticking to its framework.

When determining pricing, retailers must also take into consideration the legal and regulatory constraints that the government imposes. Such considerations are interwoven into the strategic goals of the retailer. There is a general presumption that any form of collusion between retailers and their suppliers to limit supply, or fix prices, are against public interest. For example, from 1998 to 2000, various groups of UK motorcar retailers have been obliged either to justify or reduce prices and margins in response to consumer groups and media pressure. These pressures have resulted in government investigations, which in turn have reinforced the need to be seen to be competitive. They have also heightened customer awareness of alternative sources of supply such as motor vehicles from mainland Europe.

To develop a pricing policy retail management need to make careful decisions about the company's strategic direction, in the following areas:

► which market segments to target

► which merchandise to sell

► what type of promotions to employ

► which geographic locations to focus on.

Market Segments

Often retailers in the same sector have very different pricing policies that are suited to their particular markets and target groups. For example, two discount fashion retailers may approach their market in diverse ways. Our first retailer may be selling seconds, overruns and special purchases of designer wear to young female consumers. These types of customer have a good idea of the price of these products in the high street and are likely to be tempted by the percentage comparisons with high street prices. A good example of this is the factory outlet that has gained in popularity among less well-off families. Our second retailer may be targeting its merchandise specifically at young families. These customers will be more income constrained and may buy within particular price ranges.

Merchandise

Some markets will determine the level of pricing a retailer can charge and remain competitive. However, it is the customers in the marketplace who determine the price that retailers can charge for their merchandise. Sometimes the merchandise itself can be a major determinant of pricing. For example, branded jeans will not stand too much discounting. The customer may think that the garments are either faulty or not the 'real thing'. Another possibility is that the suppliers may stipulate the pricing structure for the merchandise, which may preclude any reductions in selling price.

As we have already stated in Chapter 7, the price of an item or range of merchandise is geared to many factors. These can be reputation or image of the store, the sort of market it serves, the retail mix and the buying power or cost price to the retailer. Merchandise selection is also based on the goals of the retail firm. Some retailers are specialists and are therefore obliged to sell certain types of merchandise. This may also restrict the price that goods may be purchased for and sold for, to maintain exclusivity. Pricing also has a role to play in the merchandising of the retail store as it establishes areas or regions that make the layout more attractive to the buyer. Fashion stores like Selfridges use merchandising plans to allocate higher priced brands to better selling areas in the store. These 'hot spots' produce much higher sales per square foot than other parts of the store.

Promotions

In-store promotion is probably one of the most important ways in which the retailer can use prices to influence sales. Special offers and seasonal promotions are effective ways of generating additional sales. These also create an image of value without sacrificing the image of quality. For example, an upscale department store like Allders can offer bargains throughout the year boosting trade without sacrificing retail image. Even multi-save items (for instance, two for the price of one) can be sold in upmarket stores with no loss to retail image. This practice is increasingly evident in most sectors and emphasis for the customer is on value retailing. For the retailer this increases the degree of flexibility they have when setting prices. The reason for this is that any price reduction is viewed as customer friendly and withdrawal of offers is never seen as customer unfriendly.

Regular in-store promotions may be a part of the pricing policy, for instance 'two for the price of one' offers. Furniture discount store may wish to adopt a permanent policy of cutting prices to increase their volume of sales. Flat-pack manufacturers like MFI run regular but varied sales which typically offer as much as 50 per cent mark-downs to stimulate demand. These types of strategy increase customer spend and also help to stimulate repeat business. This is essential for discounters as customers may be satisfied but not necessary loyal. The prospect of further bargains captures their time, which would be spent looking elsewhere.

For example, if a competitor charges a lower price for an item or items carried by one store this may compel the store to undercut the competitor.

Case 8.6 The Carphone Warehouse

The Carphone Warehouse is an independent mobile phone retailer. It positions itself in the market by offering the best priced deal combined with impartial advice and clear comparisons of alternative tariffs according to usage. One of the advantages of this strategy is that it is able to utilize the brand image of the mobile phone provider whilst offering discounted pricing to the customer. The customer, meanwhile, is safe in the knowledge that they are purchasing a high-quality brand item, at a competitive price. When buying a product the customer is guided by the image of the individual mobile phone company, as well as the Carphone Warehouse promise and guarantee. This adds to the value of the purchase without cost to the consumer.

Geographic Locations

Location of the retail store can determine the pricing strategy. The type of location (such as high street or retail park) will attract different customer profiles and perceptions of price/quality. This will affect the quantity of special offers and promotions. Even large multiples that adopt a company-wide price structure may vary promotions according to locations. Grocery supermarkets, for example, may run promotions in more price sensitive areas (those with lower socio-economic profiles) than in other regions of the country.

8.5 Pricing Strategies

In this section we explain various types of pricing strategy and provide examples of pricing strategies, and uncover what is meant by a retail pricing policy.

Most retailers identify with a specific market or markets and focus their efforts on maximizing market share. Pricing for certain types of markets mean that market entry is reliant not only on the types of merchandise sold, but the price it sells for. The location, store format and merchandise dictate the most appropriate price position for a retailer. There are three basic price positions:

▶ above the market

▶ at the market

▶ below the market.

Above the market pricing means that a retailer can safely sell their merchandise at a price or prices greater than their competitors. In the case of a convenience store, the location and hours of opening allows the retailer to price their goods at a premium. However, when competitors are located next door a retailer must rely on the perceived quality of their offering (format, merchandise and image) to maintain sales.

At the market pricing is the most common policy as the retailer lowers risk by selling at the same price as surrounding stores. The competition, however, can be fierce and this may push the retailer into adopting a different approach. This may take the form of price-cutting such as the 'two for one' offers, or value creation through added benefits like gifts and services. For example, 0 per cent finance for cars, furniture and electrical goods. Banks and financial institutions also adopt this type of strategy.

Below the market pricing means that a retailer is prepared to sell merchandise at less than the average price. This is a popular strategy for discount multiples and 'cut-price' firms that usually operate at the lower end of the market. However, below the market pricing is not confined to these retail businesses alone. It is also popular amongst leading retailers as a means of pulling into the store the price conscious consumer on the basis of 'selected lines'.

Once the market position has been chosen a retailer needs to set the band or range in which they wish to set prices. There are a number of factors influencing the final price of merchandise. As we continually point out, retail management decision-making must take into account the nature of the business, the image of the store and the type of customer. A designer factory outlet, for example, might sell products at a lower price than their high street equivalent without damaging the value of the brand to the customer. This is because customers in factory outlets *expect* high-priced bands at below the line prices. However, they will use the equivalent products from standard high street stores as a reference point for determining the price they could pay. At the other end of the spectrum a deep discount store like Wilkinsons will sell selected lines at a low price to draw customers away from the competition. Customers expect to find prices to be 10–50 per cent cheaper than competitors.

As a rule, retailers will have guidelines for their pricing strategy embedded in their corporate strategy. Earlier in this chapter we considered how Next, the fashion retailer, attracted different market segments. The Next brand is targeted at the higher end of the mass market. The company claims that it has established a market position based on individual style, quality and value for money. Next sells their products through the high street stores and home shopping. Most of the stores offer womenswear, menswear and childrenswear, and the home product range (that is, household items) is offered in 78 of the larger stores. From Next's corporate statement we can infer what the company pricing strategy and policy is likely to be based on the main goals. These are:

▶ Next serve a mass audience or broad segment of the market.

▶ Next are fashion retailers who reach all age ranges.

▶ Next target the higher end of the consumer categories.

▶ Next offers stylish and distinctive ranges.

▶ Next offers value for money.

> ⇨ Log on to the Next website at www.next.co.uk/corporate/about/results and find out about the company. Try to locate their annual report and mission statement.

From the above statements it is possible to develop a pricing profile for Next, which will help us to understand and evaluate their pricing strategy. It will also help us to uncover their pricing policy. Our task will be made much easier if we focus on a particular merchandise range sold in Next stores, and use the above bullet-pointed criteria. For instance, in order for a range of men's formal ties to appeal to a mass audience and broad market segment they would have to have certain characteristics. The material, texture, style and finish will all alter the cost to the retailer and the price people expect to pay.

▶ Silk will reflect a high-quality image. These will be premium priced.

▶ A fine-textured product is required. This justifies a higher price.

▶ Styles must range from the traditional to fashion. Priced accordingly.

▶ The product needs to be well finished. It will therefore command a high price due to its high quality appearance.

In line with the Next strategy ties would have to appeal to all age ranges, and a range of designs would be needed from the young would be 'professional' to the older and mature wearer. The material, texture and style of the product are likely to appeal to the higher end of the market or consumer groupings. Above all, the ties should be perceived, as value for money so pricing is likely to be above the market price charged by general retailers in that category.

Psychological Pricing

From the above discussion we can see that product design and the materials used in the manufacture, will all influence what the customer perceives to be an expensive or cheap purchase. This fact is widely used in retailing to influence the price the retailer can charge, and the image of the business (store image) and products or services it sells. In this sense price is a very important variable and allows retailers to position or reposition themselves time and time again. Here are some general guidelines that can be used to determine the price of merchandise:

▶ High prices tend to suggest high quality. Branded products in supermarkets are usually more expensive than non-branded or own label goods.

▶ High prices tend to suggest exclusivity. This can be seen in boutiques and fashion followers (retailers who stock the latest fashion items).

▶ Price can be used to reinforce the image of the store. The layout of discount stores give the impression of low prices.

▶ Price can be used to increase the customer base. By attracting extra customers at sale time you can encourage new customers to sample the store.

▶ Price is a very useful way of moving discontinued lines. For example, the specialist store sells overruns or surplus stocks and some stores have secondary (factory) outlets to sell off excess stock.

Customer Service and Pricing

Price and customer service is inter-linked but the linkages are often difficult to determine. Generally, customers expect lower prices to yield lower levels of customer service. However, this is because people who search out low prices are less interested in additional service and more interested in reduction in price. They expect to pay extra for additional services.

Case 8.7 The Electrical Retailer Comet

Comet has a policy of selling goods at prices much lower than the competition. In fact they guarantee their prices are the lowest around and match any competitor price. They also operate a 28-day refund or exchange for unsatisfactory items and a no-lemon policy of replacing a product if two or more faults occur within 12 months. However, Comet customers do not expect to enjoy free delivery of their products or very high levels of customer service. Sales personnel tend not to possess a detailed knowledge of products on the shelves. Consumers are prepared to accept this and the reduced element of service in exchange for value for money products.

Customer service is an important and integral part of the customer experience and high-priced retailers use this as a way of adding a degree of status to customer purchases. For the premium they pay consumers expect a balance of pre-purchase advice and product knowledge, empathy during the purchase process and consideration after the purchase phase. In conclusion, whilst service is generally associated with premium or regular pricing, the trend is to increase levels of service in retailing.

Leader Pricing

Most common in the electrical and furniture sectors, leader pricing is the practice of offering high-demand items at a low price. These are then advertised heavily to stimulate demand. A good example of this is the home and garden appliance market and items such as lawn mowers, electric drills and vacuum cleaners. Retailers like Comet and B&Q use this type of strategy to draw customers into the store and encourage associated sales.

Bait Pricing

Used widely during the sales and holiday periods 'bait pricing' is a technique retailers employ to lure customers into the store. The bait is usually an item such as a sofa (for example, a leather settee), video recorder or television, which is widely advertised at a special low price or discount. Once in the store customers may find the items are unavailable. This may be because stock is depleted due to high demand, or limited numbers were available in the first place. Sometimes disappointed customers will switch stores to obtain the nearest equivalent model, especially when numbers are restricted in the marketplace. Alternatively, customers may be encouraged by sales staff to make 'on-the-spot' judgements and choose alternative items at higher prices. This may not always be a good idea for the retailer's image and reputation. Retailers must display a social responsibility and demonstrate an ethical stance when dealing with the public. Ultimately, using dubious price tactics is likely to lead to loss of business as customers lose faith and shop elsewhere.

Price Lining

Price lining is the practice of creating lines or points for each group of merchandise, so that customers can purchase goods within a particular price bracket. This is widely used in clothing retailing and helps customer to make informed comparisons between merchandise based on the different price category. For example, a shoe retailer may sell casual walking shoes in the following categories: £29.99, £39.99 and £49.99. In general, retailers will opt for lines that have the greatest customer demand and display a meaningful difference between lines (Lusch, Dunne and Gebhardt 1993). Often retailers will specialize in a particular line or lines to focus their efforts on a specific target market. Taking this approach helps to stabilize the buying function, and other areas such as stock turnover, promotion and retail image.

Multiple Unit Pricing

Of great benefit to both the customer and the retailer, multiple unit pricing is the practice of bundling items in packs at a markdown price. For example, in supermarkets foodstuffs such as beverages and dairy products like cheese and milk are commonly sold in multi-packs. A pack of four costs the customer the price of a pack of three. As this method of selling encourages the customer to purchase a greater quantity of goods, it is also beneficial to the retailer who profits from increased sales.

Pricing Ethics

At store level, there are various constraints on pricing and price displays. When goods are advertised at sale prices the normal or higher price must also to be displayed. The retailers must also state when those higher prices were charged, which must be for a minimum of 28 days, and at which stores. Existing stock cannot be re-labelled at a higher price unless the lower price was specifically advertised for a limited period (that is, a special offer). Where credit arrangements are offered the retailer must supply full details of the transaction. The annual percentage rate (APR) must be displayed alongside the cash price and total credit price. Retailers must therefore be prepared for any changes in government regulations as well as customer and media sources.

> ⇨ Students of retailing may wish to read more about pricing strategy in Lusch, Dunne and Gebhardt (1993), *Retail Marketing.*

Case 8.8 The Invasion of Discount Retailers from the Continent

In the early 1990s the grocery sector could be divided into three broad categories. These were the convenience stores, represented by Spar and similar types of chains. The second type was the supermarket represented by Tesco and Sainsbury. The third type was the discount store represented by Kwik Save. These offered three broad pricing levels. However, the lowest price level, the discount store, tended to shadow supermarket prices rather than cutting prices deeply. This opened the way for the real discounters, such as Netto and Aldi, from mainland Europe. The limited range of goods in these stores did not affect supermarkets as much as the existing discounters like Kwik Save who had to re-evaluate its pricing policy.

References

Dibb, S., Simkin, L., Pride, W.M. and Ferrell, O.C. (1997) *Marketing Concepts and Strategies*, New York: Houghton Mifflin.

Lusch, R.F., Dunne, P. and Gebhardt, R. (1993) *Retail Marketing*, Cincinnati, OH: South-Western Publishing Company.

Piacentini, M., MacFadyen, L. and Eadie, D. (2000) 'Corporate social responsibility in food retailing', *International Journal of Retail and Distribution Management*, 28(11): 459–69.

Promoting the Store: Sending Out the Correct Sort of Messages

This chapter considers the following issues:

► Communicating the image.

► Promoting the retailer brand.

► The promotional mix.

► Advertising and sales promotions.

► The role of publicity.

CHAPTER

9

Promoting the Store: Sending Out the Correct Sort of Messages

Introduction and Core Concepts

This chapter examines the range of methods available and some of the means used by retailers to promote their offering. It examines factors determining the effectiveness of the retailer's communications and the choice of appropriate promotional goals. These goals help to identify suitable messages to communicate to the consumer. The retailer needs to evaluate methods for using effectively its advertising budgets.

9.1 Communicating the Image

Promoting the Store through Communication

Finding and converting consumers into customers require a selection of methods to promote the retailer and its stores. Promotion is one of the main instruments of retail marketing. It comprises those communication activities that the retailer undertakes to improve its image and that of its stores in order to increase shopping activity and, above all, spend. This in turn leads to greater profitability. The retailer communicates its messages to customers and other interested parties (stakeholders) that affect consumer buying through *advertising*, *publicity*, *sales promotions* and *personal selling*. These are called the promotional mix.

The retailer aims its promotional mix at *consumers* in its target markets:

▶ to improve their perceptions of the retailer in order to increase store loyalty (for example, 'they sell high quality at good prices/you get some good bargains there')

▶ to improve their attitudes to the store in order to increase store visits (for instance, 'it's worth making the journey just to visit the store')

▶ to orient their behaviour in order to increase product purchase ('we are here to buy and we will look for extra things to buy')

▶ to position the retailer favourably on such ethical concerns as child labour, animal testing and environmental issues, that have a direct impact on many potential customers' behaviour.

Promotional activity also takes account of other important groups that have a significant effect on consumer shopping behaviour: manufacturers, suppliers, the community and staff. The retailer uses promotional activity to generate a favourable public image among *suppliers*. Suppliers' attitudes are important in developing supply relationships, particularly where the product brands are important, which can help to lower costs in the long run. Promotion is used to create impressions such as:

▶ The retailer is close to its customers so it can sell our products better.

▶ They have strong brand image, so it's worth supplying them on a long-term basis.

▶ They support our brands so we will support them through cooperative promotions.

The retailer promotes itself to the *community* to generate public esteem across a range of issues such as product pricing and retail development. The retailer promotes itself to the *media* and *public bodies* to create images such as:

▶ The store supports us through its community programme – so this is *our* store.

▶ The store follows ethical and environmentally friendly policies – so we will support it rather than the competition.

The retailer also promotes itself among its *staff* to enhance their roles and their pride in the jobs they do. This has a positive effect on their selling activity:

▶ B&Q employees appear in adverts to emphasize that they, the staff, believe in the products they are selling. Staff members watch the adverts and are more oriented towards customer service as a result.

These messages have to be appropriate to the social and cultural context of the intended audience. *Messages must therefore be tailored to the audience.* The retailer also needs to be clear as to what the target customer segments believe about the store and what it wants them to believe. It can then select the appropriate messages to send to these groups of consumers.

The retailer needs to choose the appropriate mix of methods to promote the store in the best possible way. Advertising, publicity and sales promotions can all generate external appreciation of the retailer's offering. The retailer can then back these external promotions with various forms of in-store sales promotion, the most important of which is usually personal selling. The retailer can also support its promotional efforts by various links with producers and wholesalers.

The Communication Process

Retail promotion is about communicating with customers in such a way that they will form a particular view of the retailer. Communication is about ensuring that the customer receives the correct message. In order to achieve this the retailer needs to understand how people receive (*receptivity*) and interpret messages (*interpretation*), particularly in relation to retail purchases.

Many promotional messages are highly contextualized. They are usually brief in terms of words and also in terms of the time the customer has available to digest the message. The message therefore has to convey the appropriate meaning by setting it within the correct frame of reference for the consumer. The message does this through the use of various codes and signals that the consumer recognizes and will use to interpret the message correctly.

All communication, however, has to deal with 'noise' that interferes with the clear transmission and reception of the message. In order to avoid problems, the retailer should:

▶ Be clear about the message it wants to communicate: 'What type of store we are and what type of products we sell'.

▶ Codify the message appropriately by using signs, symbols, words and actions that the consumer recognizes. These are socially and culturally determined.

▶ Ensure through market research that it knows how the consumer will interpret these codes. Good retailers know their customers' behaviour well and build up a profile of their customers through sales data.

▶ Choose channels of communication (for instance, television, newspapers) that the customer trusts. The type of medium usually indicates the standing of the retailer.

▶ Ensure the channel conveys the message appropriately, such as timing television adverts sensitively and to the right audience and ensuring leaflet and flyers appeal to their audience (colours and quality).

The retailer needs to send messages that are appropriate to the intended audience. There are a number of influences that affect how consumers receive messages and how they interpret them:

▶ Retailing is a social and cultural institution as well as an economic activity. Potential customers operate within their own social context and are affected by their social position. Their interpretation of social norms influences the type of message retailers should give.

▶ Differences in their economic situation affect the kinds of messages consumers are receptive to and how they interpret those messages.

▶ Existing beliefs about the store influence receptivity and interpretation of messages. The retailer needs to be clear as to what customers believe about the store.

▶ The current situation of the retailer will influence the way messages should be constructed and how the consumer will interpret them. The position of the retailer on the retail life cycle, the economic climate and the season of the year will all have an impact on the appropriateness of particular messages.

Any good communication system will also contain appropriate feedback mechanisms so that deficiencies can be corrected. A feedback loop is often provided through customer in-store surveys and comment cards.

Making Communication Effective

In order to evaluate the probable effectiveness of different messages, we need to understand the communication process in the context of the consumer purchase decision. The producer or retailer's promotional efforts have to take the consumer from ignorance of a product or offering to purchase. One model of this process is the communication effects model (Zikmund and d'Amico 1993). This models the process as a hierarchy of steps or stages that the customer goes through, namely: *brand ignorance, awareness, knowledge, liking, preference, conviction* and *purchase* (Table 9.1).

The model suggests that the retailer should use different promotional methods at different stages. Although the model can be used in terms of a single purchase, we can apply it to the process of confirming a customer (or group of customers) as a convinced and enthusiastic buyer who will spontaneously promote the store through word of mouth. To help students use this model more effectively we have inserted the different stages into a framework for ease of use. The model is applied to retailer as a brand (with its application to a product in brackets).

Table 9.1   Communication Effects Model

Stage	Retailer (product) situation	What to do	How to do it
Brand ignorance	The retailer (product) is unknown. Potential consumers may be aware of the retailer (brand) but have yet to try it	Inform customers by advertising and store promotions. They enter the store with a certain level of expectation	Use various methods such as word-of-mouth, newspapers, television advertising, mail shots and press publicity
Awareness	Customers are more able to identity what brands the retailer stocks (which store(s) stock the brand). Customers are also more conscious of the retailer (product) and its importance.	Promotion levels become more important to encourage more than an occasional purchase or visit. Constantly remind consumers of retailer's (product's) presence	Extend the initial four elements of promotion; but now place more emphasis on particular targeted group
Knowledge	Location and market positioning of the retailer (product) are more clearly established in the mind of the consumer. Customers visit the store more frequently. They position the retailer (product) according to its symbolic and functional values: for example, do these jeans have the right image? Do they wear well?	Emphasis must be on establishing the right image, which will be a mix of symbolic and functional values. Match the message to the service offering/ product. Targeted and potential customers must be tuned in to the mix of functional and symbolic	Personal selling and in-store merchandising. State the right sorts of messages at the right time (Christmas = turkeys and a festive occasion). At a basic level the items the consumer expects to be in stock must be available

Table 9.1 continued

Stage	Retailer (product) situation	What to do	How to do it
Liking	Customers develop a liking for the particular product (store), usually after using it (visiting the store). This liking may be the result of the right sort of promotion without any further reinforcement from a store visit, or by word of mouth	Retailer (producer) must meet customer expectations to obtain repeat business. Anticipate customer needs by ordering in advance. Maintain the standards of service through continuing customer feedback	Use store card information and other means to show customer purchasing patterns Use information to provide the right products in advance (for instance, during hot spells)
Preference	This becomes established over time and may be changed with persuasive store's image (in-store communications, such as the displays). Other forms of communication take place such as customer–customer and staff–customer interaction	Recognize the consumer through appropriate and consistent displays, in-store promotion and customer service	Train staff to retain customers by extending high-quality service. Update product ranges in line with changing customer preferences. Ensure relationships with suppliers are maintained and improved
Conviction	Place, time, situation and social group establish conviction. Beliefs and norms about fashion and the times we live in drive us	Show retailer commitment to products or services and align with the customers	Ensure appropriate product ranges and visual merchandising consistent with customers' expectations
Purchase	All the above culminate in the purchase decision/high degree of customer loyalty	Use in-store communication provided by the retailer (producer) to persuade customer to buy	Use all these promotion types to convince the customer. Advertising confirms product choice

9.2 Promoting the Retailer as a Brand

The Nature of a Brand

At its simplest level, a brand is any name, term or sign that identifies a product or group of products as being produced or supplied by a particular firm. Kit Kat is an example of a well-known single product. Other top brands in the UK include multiple product brands such as Coca-Cola (Coke, Diet Coke, Cherry Coke) and Ariel (Ariel, Ariel Future, Ariel Colour).

These brands have certain recognizable elements that may include:

▶ *The brand name.* This is the verbal part that people tend to remember and is used to promote the brand.

▶ *The logo.* This is a brand name or company name written in a distinctive way.

▶ *The trademark.* This is a legally protected brand name or brand mark. The producer registers a symbol or name to give it exclusive rights to its use, such as Microsoft Windows. Service providers may similarly register a service mark.

▶ *Distinctive packaging*, as with Kit Kat or Coca-Cola, that becomes part of the product identity. The equivalent in service provision may be the service setting such as a restaurant decor, furnishing and menu design.

Packaging and the logo are extremely important in maintaining brand identity. They provide the visible clues and signposts that guide consumers in their buying decisions. Competitors can position their products in consumers' minds as being similar simply by packaging the product in closely similar fashion (Yeshin 1998: 62).

The influence of visual and tactile aspects in the market positioning of a product provides support for the view that a brand is more than just a name. Instead, the brand becomes a complex of ideas that encompass attributes such as quality, price and location that enable consumers to differentiate the product from all other products. Through knowledge of the product, consumers associate a set of characteristics with the product. These endow the product with symbolic qualities that reflect and in part determine people's perceptions of the physical attributes of the product. This is why copycat branding becomes a problem for the original brand producer.

The Added Value of a Brand

A good brand adds value to the business. Consumers are prepared to pay significantly more for these product brands relative to cost. This *price premium* generates extra profits for the supplier. The value of the brand can be roughly estimated as the difference between the market value of the company and the underlying value of the assets used to produce these products. This can be very substantial in some cases (Wileman and Jary 1997).

The brand can deliver extra profit because:

▶ The producer can use it to segment the market more effectively, when this is required.

▶ More importantly, it differentiates the product from competitors in a way that creates value for the consumer (Wileman and Jary 1997).

Consumers value brands because they represent a guarantee of quality and other benefits. For instance, a consumer may go to an open-air market and buy an apple. The consumer can judge the physical and eating quality of the product. However, the consumer will no longer be able to determine the quality of the product if he or she becomes concerned about the use of pesticides or genetically modified food. A branded product could assure the traceability of the product and by removing uncertainty from the consumer, increase the value of the product. This simple illustration can be applied across the whole range of consumer products. The consumer today is increasingly knowledgeable and sophisticated. This does not mean that they can judge better the value in use of a product, but they do get to know which brands have been known to provide quality and reliability in use. The complexity of modern living, the pressure of time and the interlinking of so much consumption mean that branded products have become more important.

The consumer may also receive psychic benefits from the purchase of a brand. Buying a well-known branded product gives a sense of having made the right choice, particularly in the eyes of the customer's peers.

Most of the brand names that people recall easily are producer brands, such as Coca-Cola, Sony, Mars, Levi and Hoover. These brands have become well established for several reasons:

▶ *Presence*. Consumers readily recognize and recall the brand because the producer has consistently maintained the brand over a long period.

▶ *Quality*. Consumers perceive the product to satisfy a particular requirement because of its high quality and reliability.

▶ *Availability*. The product is readily available because producers have supported the large-scale supply of the product through long-term relationships with their suppliers and distributors.

▶ *Customer interaction*. The producers have maintained continuing customer contact through market research and promotion.

▶ *Investment in the brand*. The producers have constantly rebuilt and renewed the brand through product development, where appropriate, quality management and personnel training.

Developing a Retailer Brand

These producer brands made the transition to well-known and leading brands at various stages in the twentieth century. This was at a time when mass production and mass marketing were dominant in the consumer supply chain and when retailer power was quite weak. However, some industries such as the clothing industries were fragmented without dominant manufacturers. This enabled retailers such as Marks & Spencer to really put their stamp on products and in effect develop their own brands. The balance of power has now shifted from producer to retailer in many areas. This has created favourable conditions for long-established and newer retailers to develop their own retailer brands.

The experience of different retailers has shown that a retailer can build its *store as a brand* using the five principles above. However, the retailer can build its brand in three different ways:

1 *It develops a reputation for stocking quality branded products*. The retailer may develop its store as a major stockist of quality brands. It will stock several brands to ensure customer choice and will support its position through the depth of its assortment. It may also offer in-store concessions, where appropriate, to brand owners. This approach is popular in fashion retailing and other areas where the market segments clearly do not overlap greatly. The retailer may also have exclusive dealing rights, such as those signed by electrical retailer Dixons with computer manufacturers Compaq and Packard-Bell in 1999.

2 *It brands its stores on their comprehensiveness and price*. This approach is suitable when customer segments overlap and where technological change or the need for reliability with choice increases the perceived

value of familiar brand names. Category killers such as Toys 'Я' Us and electrical retailers Currys and Comet use this approach. They cater for a wide range of needs and different customers, by building their assortment around a core of nationally recognized brands. Price will then be a very clear way of differentiating one store brand from another.

3 *It develops a range of own branded products.* Many retailers now stock their own store brands, although the role of own branding tends to vary across retail sectors. Supermarket chains now have extensive ranges of own branded products and own branding has now reached 50 per cent of grocery sales. Consumers now trust the brands of some leading firms to such an extent that the trust has transferred to the supermarket itself. Most people now take the supermarket as a brand in its own right that guarantees the quality of the products it stocks.

Some fashion retailers such as Marks & Spencer and Gap stock only their own brands. These retailers can take on different market positions according to factors such as age group, price, service and quality. Some aspects of clothing quality are relatively easy to determine, such as material, cut and finish. However, style is also an important quality factor, but it is hard to evaluate. The style or cut of a garment may give the appearance of high quality. Young consumers are the group most willing to pay a higher price for perceived quality (Mintel 1999) and are an important factor in establishing retailers such as Gap. This retailer targets young people but we know from its brand messages that the price is quite high and items are exclusive.

Some stores that stock all or mainly their own brand may use a different label to indicate more upmarket products or even to target a particular group. Boots for instance uses the Boots brand to signal quality and value over a wide range of products alongside other brands. However, it also uses distinctive brands like Boots No. 7 to establish itself within the market for mid-quality value. Retailers who have managed to establish these store powerbrands have begun to sell them through other retailers, particularly internationally.

Developing own-brand product ranges helps stores develop themselves as brands. However, developing the store as a brand is different from and goes beyond using own-label products. It requires a change in outlook from traditional retailing management, which tends to deal with the various components of the retail format, such as product range and store design, on a non-integrated basis. It requires the long-term approach of some major retailers such as Marks & Spencer and IKEA (Wileman and Jary 1997) that invest in the brand as an integrated whole. This is a costly and difficult process and requires investment in people, product quality, supplier relationships and in-store brand development.

Fashion brands, for instance, are highly volatile and both businesses and brands can emerge, peak, decline and disappear in ten to 20 years. However, the retailer can commit itself to developing a brand that will maintain a distinctive place in the market that will continue to attract customer loyalty.

Segmentation by Branding

The retailer can develop its brand, depending on the retail format used, to deliver market segmentation and differentiation that can create added value. For retailers, segmentation may be of limited relevance (Wileman and Jary 1997). However, some retailers have developed brands in response to the demands of different market segments:

▶ Tesco has developed its Tesco Metro to cater for the convenience store market segment.

▶ Allders has a department store in the centre of Leeds and another outlet away from the centre selling discounted, end of season and special lines that appeals to a different market segment. The layout and atmosphere of the two stores are distinctly different.

▶ Next has factory outlets to dispose of previous season's fashion – but these are successful because they are still distinctively Next. Other fashion retailers do the same.

Differentiation through Branding

Store brands have become dominant in the fashion market, with leaders like Marks & Spencer, Gap and Next. There are some areas, however, such as jeans and footwear, where producer brands still dominate and there has been a resurgence of distinctive upmarket brands. Some retailers position themselves as fashion-forward or as fashion-follower. Club wear for 16–24-year-old women has to be fashion-forward but held at affordable prices. Fashion chains often have their own in-house teams for product design and development:

▶ Gap uses a distinctive and recognizable house style that is consistent from one season to the next to position itself.

▶ Top Shop is usually targeted at very specific customer groups, whereas Tie Rack is targeted at specific product groups.

Overfocusing on the brand image rather than the customer can cause problems, however. Marks & Spencer are a good example of a retailer that was forced to rediscover its customers. It had originally built its customer base round the middle-aged, middle-class woman, but its strong brand image has been used to provide products for a wide range of customers. Unfortunately, a successive lacklustre range of products alienated this customer base, and appealed little to other customer groups. The subsequent readjustments have led to a down-grading of the retailer's traditional logos. In addition, the recent intro-duction of the Autograph range refocuses customers away from the solidity and dowdiness of the past. This suggests more flexibility and greater responsiveness to the consumer. However, the store continues to support the traditional quality image. Image is important and retailers are conscious of their store brand as it determines how the customer views them.

Extending the Brand

Retailers can use a brand to develop other activities. A retailer may have an *umbrella brand*, such as Boots No. 7 range of cosmetics. The retailer needs to maintain investment in the brand to build a high level of consumer trust in the brand. Once the retailer has achieved a high level of trust in the brand, it can exploit the opportunities provided. It can then extend the *branch franchise* to support a minor product or to widen the range of products covered. This reduces the cost of market communication by more quickly achieving customer *knowledge* and *liking*. The retailer can also extend the brand into other areas.

Case 9.1 Boots Powerbrand Going Global

Health and beauty retailer Boots has set up a special marketing unit to develop the brand portfolio internationally. It will further develop its powerbrands such as Natural Collection, No. 7 and New Botanics, and aims to increase international distribution. It will sell them through its own stores abroad, but will also look to place them with other large retailers internationally, as it has done with its No. 7 make-up range with Swiss retailer Migros.

Source: Morrell 2000: 3

9.3 Selecting the Promotional Mix

The Various Types of Promotion

Promotion depends on communicating messages to customers (and other interested parties). These messages are appropriate to the target markets when they:

▶ take account of the social and cultural context of the intended audience

▶ take account of what target customer segments believe about the store

▶ convey what the retailer wants them to believe about the store.

There are four methods of promotion:

1 *Advertising.* Non-personal communication using any form of paid space or time to directly influence customer spending.

2 *Publicity.* Any communication using an unpaid third party to positively influence perceptions about the retailer. Publicity may involve the retailer in costs not directly associated with any particular product.

3 *Sales promotions.* Specific, time-limited activity designed to increase consumer demand for specific products or for store items in general.

4 *Personal selling.* Direct interaction by retail staff with a customer. This may be face to face, by telephone or through personal correspondence.

The retailer needs to choose the appropriate mix of methods to promote the store in the best possible way. Advertising, publicity and promotions can all generate external appreciation of the retailer's offering. The retailer can then back these external promotions with various forms of in-store promotion, the most important of which is usually personal selling. The retailer can also support its promotional efforts by various links with producers and wholesalers. There are four factors the retailer needs to take into account in planning the mix of promotional activities:

1 The retailer's goals, which in turn affect promotional goals.

2 Other channel promotional activity, including in-channel promotion.

3 The relative cost-effectiveness of the different methods.

4 The budget available.

Retailer Goals

A retailer's successes depend on how well it knows and targets its customers. Understanding its customers enables the retailer to answer such strategic questions as:

▶ Where do we want to go as a firm?

▶ What is our market and type of customer?

▶ How do we get there?

Answering these questions enables the retailer to set out its vision for the company and its customers and to set objectives for the business. Corporate objectives are then translated into marketing objectives that the retailer can use to direct its communication strategy. This in turn will lead to effective targeting of its customers and provides a framework within which the retailer can decide on its promotional mix.

The retailer can communicate its corporate goals to the consumer to boost confidence in the company. For instance, the conglomerate UK retailer Kingfisher owns electrical retailer Comet and Darty in Europe. It also owns DIY store B&Q and has a controlling interest in Castorama in continental Europe. It uses the company website to set out its objectives or vision (*http://www.kingfisher.co.uk/english/index2.htm*).

Case 9.2 Renewing Promotion

Successful promotion does not have a permanent effect, because market segments change as customers grow older. It requires constant effort to appeal to the new generation. Some retailers, such as Marks & Spencer and C&A (in the UK), have promoted themselves successfully in the past but lost touch with what their customers wanted. Marks & Spencer had to re-think their whole product and promotion strategy in 1999, while C&A decided in 2000 to withdraw from the UK in large part because it failed to communicate in an attractive way with the new generation of customers in the late 1990s.

From its early successes in the 1970s, with its 'man at C&A' promotional image it failed to capture the imagination of the new generation in the 1990s. The recent campaign entitled "C&A Today" positioning it as a high-street value retailer did not revitalize their fortunes. This together with its changing European focus led to its decision to withdraw from UK retailing in the early part of 2001.

The remarkable thing about this example is that through the power of communication and promotion C&A had become embedded in people's minds. The older customer base, who remembered the 1970s image flocked to C&A to buy souvenirs of the store, when it announced in June 2000 that it was closing down its UK operations.

▶ *Our vision* – to enable people to enjoy their home and lifestyle better than any other retailer.

▶ *Our aim* – to provide an unbeatable shopping experience built on great value, service and choice, whilst rapidly identifying and serving the ever-changing needs of our customers.

▶ *Our focus* – to grow and develop a great business, deliver superior returns to our shareholders and provide unique and satisfying opportunities for our people.

The vision and aim here provide a clear customer orientation to the business. It targets the provision of products and services to support the home through a first class shopping experience. When the organization is being consistent with its vision, it will ensure that promotional activity will clearly relate to the homes and lifestyles of its customers. In addition, it will create levels of expectations about shopping that will be geared to what the stores can deliver.

Promotional Goals

The retailer needs to set its promotional goals in order to support the goals of the business as a whole. When planning promotional activity, retailers need to recognize that different promotional efforts tend to take effect over different time periods. Creating a particular store image requires a longer-term developmental process whereby customers receive continuing confirmation of the promotional images. This requires longer-term promotional activity to support the brand image of a store or its products and build relationships with customers. Advertising may help in confirming people's behaviour but other forms of promotion will be important. For instance, own-brand food increased their share of the market from about one-fifth in the mid-1980s to nearly one-half by the late 1990s. This would not have been possible without promotion efforts calculated to develop long-term customer relationships.

Building long-term relationships with customers and the community provides the basis for long-term shareholder value, although the quality image can be used to support short-term promotional efforts. On the other hand, specific short-term promotional efforts are needed at particular periods or for particular products to increase the intensity with which existing customers use the store. They can also be useful in attracting new customers to the store. However, the retailer needs to help new customers into becoming longer-term customers through positive exposure to longer-term promotion efforts.

The retailer must also set comparable goals for each promotion method so as to ensure consistency between the different elements used. Thus if a discounter wishes to emphasize low prices on well-known brands, advertising and in-store promotion should both convey that message.

Promotions by Other Channel Members

The retailer is a part of a distribution channel for the products it sells. The other members of the channel are the manufacturer and (if present)

Checked out item summary for
Hood, Derrick H.
Wed Feb 12 17:33:36 CST 2003

RCODE: 31405034391288 LOCATION: smavi
TLE: Wonders of the African world [vid
DATE: 02-19-2003

CODE: 31405034391270 LOCATION: smavi
LE: Wonders of the African world [vid
DATE: 02-19-2003

#44 Wed Feb 12 2003 05:18PM
em(s) checked out to Hood, Derrick H..

LE: Random family : love, drugs, trou
CODE: 31405038570457
DATE: Mar 05 2003

LE: Retailing : environment & operati
CODE: 31405037066721
DATE: Mar 05 2003

ebrate African-American History #2/12
:00 noon*** African-American Genealogy

the wholesaler. There may be other intermediaries when the product is imported. The retailer needs to take account of other channel members in developing its promotion strategy, because of the different objectives of the other channel members. A manufacturer wants to promote its product over its rivals by focusing on its customer benefits. A manufacturer may also want target customers who accept different price–benefit combinations by providing customers a choice from a range of alternatives, such as similar models of vacuum cleaner, different sizes of televisions and ranges of differently specified computers However, the retailer may have different objectives. The retailer may be branding itself as the place to buy a quality product. It may also offer the customer different price–benefit packages, but it can do so by combining selections from different manufacturers' ranges. This is the practice with some electrical retailers, particularly within their smaller stores.

In-channel Promotion

There is also the conventional distinction between manufacturer's *push* and *pull* strategies in the market. In a *push strategy*, the supplier promotes the product to the marketing intermediaries who would then push it through the channel of distribution. A manufacturer of an unbranded product would need to use a push strategy and use all forms of promotion to sell to the intermediary. It also represents the traditional approach in a fragmented retail market, even for products with national recognition. The sales effort is oriented much more towards the retailer. Modern push strategies however, now take the form of joint marketing activity. This could include special producer-retailer promotions of products, often used in supermarkets and special display features in local CTN shops and pharmacies.

The converse approach is a *pull strategy*. In this case a producer promotes the product to the ultimate consumer in order to stimulate final demand and so pull the product through the channel of distribution by encouraging the retailer to stock the product. The producer uses national advertising and promotions, which may be supplemented by in-store demonstrations. For example, mobile phones are marketed to the consumer using adverts, particularly on radio and television, which create demand and thus *pull* the products through the chain.

The Relative Cost-Effectiveness of Promotional Methods

A retailer will usually use all four promotional methods to some extent, although there are noticeable exceptions. The choice of promotional methods depends on their relative cost-effectiveness in getting the retailer's message across and the size of the promotional budget. The retailer needs to consider each method carefully to make best use of the promotional budget it wishes to or can use. Evaluating the different promotional methods is complicated by the fact that they comprise a collection of dissimilar techniques that have relatively different impacts on consumers in different circumstances. For instance television advertising can convey certain messages more effectively than newspaper advertising and conversely.

Case 9.3 Different Strokes: Different Promotional Mixes for Different Objectives

Publicity better than advertising?

Body Shop use publicity rather than advertising by publicly espousing the company's green marketing policy. The early successes of the store and the personal philosophy of its founder Anita Roddick created a fund of publicity that has become self-generating. Now hundreds of young, educated and socially aware, female business strategy, marketing and retail students have read minicases on the company and accessed information packs!

Personal selling alongside TV advertising

The Carphone Warehouse uses and places importance on their personal selling. They succeed in this by calling their personal selling 'impartial advice'.

Sales promotions with television advertising

Furniture retailer MFI has *constant sales promotions with television advertising*. Their strategy is to extend the sales deadline, offer all-inclusive packages, tied discounts, and seasonal sales across all product ranges.

Four elements + the Internet

Some travel companies use less well-known subsidiaries to sell off their surplus seating or spare capacity via the Internet. This utilizes the four elements of the promotional mix:

▶ The on-screen display of text and images is a form of direct advertising.

▶ Using a well-known logo or travel brand on the offers sells and publicizes the brand.

▶ The offers are a sales promotion as they are discounted well below the normal price.

▶ The freephone 0800 number encourages contact and interaction with sales personnel.

9.4 Advertising and Sales Promotions

Advertising and sales promotions are fundamentally different although they have aspects in common. A retailer pays a third party for time and space in which to put its message across in such a way as to persuade customers to spend more in the store. Sales promotion on the other hand uses various forms of inducement to the customer to visit the store more and buy more products. Where advertising is pushing customers into the store, sales promotions are pulling the customer into the store. However, there are some similarities. In particular, some sales promotions necessarily use advertising to get their message across.

Advertising Formats

The impact of advertising depends on the message it gives and medium, such as television, that it uses. The retailer's promotional strategy will determine advertising objectives. The retailer can develop its advertising strategy through a number of steps that make use of the standard basic questions of any enterprise, as illustrated in Table 9.2.

Table 9.2 Developing a Retailer Advertising Strategy

Ask	Do	Consider following factors
Why do we want to advertise?	Set objectives for advertising that match up with company goals	1. *Price advertising* – appropriate for discounters 2. *Assortment advertising* – suitable for category killers, specialist and designer range retailers 3. *Repositioning* – showing the new face after realignment or restructuring 4. *Customer focusing*: to recruit new customers, retain old customers, remind customers 5. *Stock turning* – promoting sales, stock clearances or roll outs
Who are we aiming our adverts at?	1. Decide target customers 2. Determine beliefs and attitudes we expect to tune into	1. Are we reaching sales staff? 2. If so, what is the message we are conveying?
What do we want the customers to believe about the store	Be clear about the attitude to the store it expects its customers to acquire	1. Are these reasonable to expect?
How are we going to present our message?	Express clearly the message it wishes to send Make sure customers are comfortable about the context of message	1. Based on what it knows target customers are looking for and 2. What is acceptable to them
How much advertising do we do?	Relate the level of advertising to the store's positioning policy	1. Current position 2. Merchandise 3. Competition
When is the best time to send out these messages?	Be clear about the intended benefits of media scheduling	1. Is prime time on radio/television necessary? 2. Should we advertise in the Monday or Friday paper?
Where are the adverts to be placed?	Specify where the messages should be placed, such as on television or on hoardings	1. The larger the market the more general and wide spread the advertising and the greater supporting promotional activity required

Media Selection

The different media used in advertising can be split into two types: mass media and specific market media. Mass media is aimed at a total market, where the audience runs to millions. These media include television and newspapers because of the size of their audiences or readership. Radio, magazines, the Internet and direct mailings are more targeted, although some larger radio stations may access substantial audiences. The quantitative impact of advertising is a function of the reach and frequency of an advert. Reach is the actual number of customers who come into contact with the advert, while frequency is the average number of times those reached are exposed to the advert.

The retailer can compare media on the basis of cost per thousand reached method (CPM). However, this is useful only when comparing similar media adverts, since different media can provoke different reactions. Different media have different qualitative impacts. This can also be affected by the timing of advertising in a particular medium.

Advertising Budgeting

Setting the budget for advertising is rather a tricky problem. One reasonable approach is the objective and task method (Lusch, Dunne and Gebhardt, 1993). This identifies a number of advertising objectives that need to be achieved. Each objective can be met using a particular activity or instrument such as direct mailing or television advertising slots. These are then costed out and totalled and that sets the budget required. Conceptually, this is appropriate if the technical and financial problems can be dealt with.

Technically, the retailer needs to first determine the appropriate level, timing and placing of these activities. This is, of course, difficult to achieve. Often the tasks to be done are dictated by competitor's behaviour. Financially, the required budget may be more than the retailer wishes or can afford and it may fall back on to a more frequently used approach such as percentage of sales. Often this will be determined by keeping a level similar to those of competitors.

Sales Promotions

Sales promotions are specific, time-limited activities designed to increase consumer demand for specific products or for store items in general. Retailers often use external advertising to publicize the promotions to their customers. However, the distinguishing feature of the promotion is that there always some extra incentives for customers to visit the store or buy certain specific products or services when they get there.

Sales promotions can be of various kinds:

▶ price reductions, including:
  - general offers such as reduced prices at sale time, which tie in with cycles of consumer spending
  - money-off items – specific offers at certain times
  - coupon or linked price reductions; stores may offer vouchers redeemable against next purchases when the customer has spent a certain amount
  - multi-pack and bonus pack offers such as 'buy one, get one free'
  - additional price reductions for store card or loyalty card holders.

▶ free gifts

▶ contest and competitions

▶ in-store sampling.

Effectiveness of Sales Promotions

The role of sales promotions is important in stimulating sales and recognition of the retailer. However, the short-term nature of sales promotions means that they are more useful for short-term promotion rather than longer-term development of the retailer brand. Based on common experience and the results of various researches (Yeshin 1998), we can note the following:

▶ Sales promotions are by their nature short-lived. The effects of one-off promotions will therefore be short-lived. This is satisfactory to the retailers when the purpose is to offload end-of-line merchandise and similar unwanted or short-lived stock.

▶ Promotions can also be used to reward existing customers. Loyalty bonuses can reflect use of loyalty cards, or using store cards with which to make purchases. Most consumers, even for grocery items will shop at more than one store for a similar range of items. These offers encourage them to increase the intensity of their spending and spend more of their money at a particular store. Promotions can also be a means of attracting other customers to the store. However, sales promotions will not be sufficient to keep them there and the retailer must build a longer-term relationship with the customer.

▶ A large number of consumers are promotion oriented. Looking for special offers is part of their shopping activity. The increasing use of promotions can have a long-term impact on customers who are being encouraged to reduce their brand. However, stores can use changing promotions to create an image of customer-oriented pricing and attract and retain promotion-oriented customers.

▶ Promotions can be an effective means of price discrimination. The 'must have' customers will buy at any time. The more price-sensitive customer will wait until promotion periods to buy. Using promotions sensitively in this way enables the retailer to enlarge its market.

9.5 Publicity, Personal Selling and Relationship Marketing

Publicity

Publicity may be either *proactive* or *reactive*. Proactive publicity occurs when the retailer undertakes any *planned* activity designed to improve public perception of the retailer. This includes activities such as sponsorship of events or passing news to the media. Proactive publicity should be highly controllable.

Reactive publicity occurs when the retailer has to respond to any *unplanned* event or story that affects the reputation of the organization. This includes events such as food scares or stories about child labour being used to make clothes sold in the retailer's stores or the degradation of poor farming communities in Africa to produce vegetables for the retailers. The retailer must have a system that enables it to react quickly to any event or story that may affect the reputation of the organization.

In planning its publicity the retailer needs to determine its publicity budget. This should, ideally, be part of the general promotional budget and money allocated to different promotional activity on a strict cost-benefit basis. The difficulties involved make this impractical on a day-to-day basis but the global sum allocated to such activities should be reviewed annually. These annual reviews should attempt a proper evaluation of costs and benefits, as part of a rolling longer-term promotional plan that fits in with the retailer's mission or goals. Estimating the benefits is difficult. If the retailer cannot determine the effects in terms of increased consumer spending over a long period, it should at least set targets for the promotional activity to achieve.

Sponsorship is an increasingly important form of publicity, though it does not strictly fall completely within the area of publicity as it does require payment of some kind to the sponsored group or person. Retailers can now access professional organizations to help with sponsorship. National supermarket chains in recent years have been sponsoring school equipment programmes. This is a detached form of promotion as the money is paid to a third party but linked to customer spending. It helps promote the retailer but costs are reduced by slippage between the number of coupons given out and the number redeemed.

Smaller retailers can undertake local sponsorship but need to take simple measures to check the effectiveness of their programme. For instance, a local sports retailer may set targets in terms of local sponsorship of sporting or outdoor activity. The effects can be measured by the number of people directly and indirectly affected and the level of press coverage obtained.

Publicity and personal selling are two quite different promotional activities. However, they are both important means in developing longer-term relationships with customers through generating commitment from retail staff and in displaying the retailer's commitment to customers and their community.

The retailer has also to guard against unplanned events that could damage its reputation. The best protection against this is preparedness on the part of the marketing department. This means that the person responsible for dealing with publicity undertakes as much preventive work as possible, based on knowledge of the firm's operations and its supply chain. The firm can identify monitoring areas. These can be according to issues such as environment, Third World exploitation, sweated labour, safety, public responsibility and customer relations. A database of activities can be set up. This is easier in larger organizations that have now begun to develop traceability of products from source to the retailer.

Finally, education of staff is important so that they react positively to any bad publicity, to not make public comment but leave that to designated personnel within the organization.

Personal Selling

Personal selling occurs in any direct personal contact between a member of staff and a customer. It can be face-to-face, as in a store, by telephone or by fax or email if it is to a specific person in the organization. The purpose of personal selling is to track the customer from entering the store or initiating enquiries in order to complete a sale and make a return visit. Sales staff must:

▶ Identify customer requirements when they enter the store.

▶ Advise the customer on suitable product.

▶ Secure the sale of the requisite item.

▶ Stimulate impulse purchase by identifying extra suitable products.

▶ Complete the transaction to the customer's satisfaction and encourage return visits.

The effectiveness of staff depends on whether they are order getters rather than order takers. Order getters are required when there is a significant non-routine element to customer purchasing activity and the order promoting function is difficult to achieve through other means such as display information. Non-routine purchases present a hazard to consumers. The hazard is a function of the risk of inappropriate purchase and of the consequences of mistaken purchase. Order getters work for the retailer's longer-term benefit when they interact positively with the customer to reduce the risk of inappropriate purchase. They also help by showing the customer how to make the best of their purchase so that what is an appropriate purchase becomes an effective one. This means that sales have an important role to play when:

▶ The potential purchase is high cost.

▶ The product is technically complex and there is a wide range for the consumer to choose from.

▶ The product can be tailored to the customer's requirements.

▶ The price has to be negotiated.

Case 9.4 Going to the Customer

The new wave of dressing down at the office has reached foreign banks and financial institutions in the City of London.

Harvey Nicholls, the high fashion retailer, has taken the opportunity to get its message home where it counts. Personal shoppers from Harvey Nicholls (its advisers on how to dress) have been promoting its range of smart casual wear. They have providing in-office demonstrations to show staff how to dress down appropriately.

Source: Retail Week 2000: 3

Staff should be trained and developed to become order getters rather than order takers. However, there needs to be proper incentives for them to be active on behalf of the retailer, not least to be treated with respect and appreciation.

References

Lusch, R.F., Dunne, P. and Gebhardt, R. (1993) *Retail Marketing*, Cincinnati, OH: South-Western Publishing, pp. 497–8.

Mintel (1999) *Retailing*. London: Mintel International Group Ltd.

Morrell, L. (2000) 'Boots Powerbrands extend global reach', *Retail Week*, 9 June: 3.

Retail Week (2000) 'Harvey Nicks give City a lesson in dressing down', 23 June: 3.

Wileman, A. and Jary, M. (1997) *Retail Power Plays: From Trading to Brand Leadership*, Basingstoke: Macmillan.

Yeshin, T. (1998) *Marketing Communication: The Holistic Approach*, Oxford: Butterworth-Heinemann.

Zikmund, W.G. and d'Amico, M. (1993) *Marketing*, 4th edn., St Paul, MN: West Publishing.

Locating the Store in the Retail Environment

This chapter covers the following topics:

▶ Why location is so important to the retailer.

▶ The hidden side of locating the retail business.

▶ Models of location and how to make the right decisions.

CHAPTER

10

Locating the Store in the Retail Environment

Introduction and Core Concepts

Location is the most important ingredient for any business that relies on customers.It is also one of the most difficult to plan for completely. What is absolutely certain is that all retailers, regardless of size, must make the correct decisions when locating the store in the retail environment. By definition, the retail environment is in a state of flux, and what bides well today may not be accepted tomorrow. Where a retailer locates tells the customer what sort of retailer it is. Throughout this chapter we offer methods of analysing the potential of a site, but these measurements do not provide all the answers. Location is about positioning, target market, image, pricing strategy and access. For the large chain multiples it can be more about government planning, sustainable development, property acquisition and political decisions.

10.1 Developing a Location Strategy

Whether you are searching for a new retail site or relocating an existing business, retail management has the power to dramatically increase profits by choosing the right location. If management get it wrong the result can be as equally dramatic. Choosing the wrong site can lead to poor results and, in some cases, insolvency and closure. But how can retail management tell which is the best location for their business? In this chapter we will cover a range of important issues and measurements that retailers must prepare before committing themselves to a particular location.

When formulating decisions about where to locate, retail management must refer to the retail strategic plan. This should contain all the strategic goals that the organization hopes to achieve in the future. It may be, for example, that the retailer's mission statement contains the desire to increase profitability, and to become a leading brand name and market leader. These goals will impact considerably on the retail location strategy, and probably determine where, when and how the retailer locates. For instance, the retailer may be obliged to choose locations that compete directly with the market leader. This strategy calls for careful decision-making as this may necessitate a complete repositioning, to reach the new customers.

Repositioning is expensive and requires changes to such areas as merchandise, store format, pricing strategy and customer service. New town-centre locations, for example, would perhaps require a much more service-oriented approach, as customers in towns may be used to higher levels of service. Moving out of the town into a retail park may be different again, with large-discount type formats, value merchandise and self-service. Making changes will influence the image of the retailer relative to the competition. By moving to new locations, therefore, the retailer can alter its position in the marketplace, and the way customers feel about it.

Smaller independent retailers will take a much more informal approach to location decision-making. But, nevertheless, they too must plan carefully to fit in with the customers' needs. Like the big multiples, independents must also consider issues like trends in retail location, planning restrictions, infrastructure and competitive positioning. However, for the smaller business there are likely to be numerous restrictions in place, which limit the options available. For instance, the cost of either renting or buying premises will be higher in districts that attract the more affluent consumer groups. It may be that the retailer wishes to sell a particular type of merchandise and this requires a certain location. An example of this might be antique shops that usually congregate around certain areas, and would look out of place elsewhere. Above all, retailers must plan strategically for their target market, and this means carefully assessing the area in which they wish to locate.

Know your Market Position

Large supermarket chains and other major retailers use highly developed methods to help them make location decisions. At the heart of their strategy is a good understanding of their market position, and who their customers are. In Chapter 6 we discussed the process of market segmentation and how to target the customer effectively. Retailers should first undertake this research before formulating a location strategy. Failure to do so is likely to lead to poor location decisions and even the closure of stores, as the area may be unsuitable for their merchandise or type of business. There are exceptions, however, where a retailer is too small an operation to undertake formal research, or has no previous data or experience to draw on. Independents very often locate in an area because they like the 'feel of the place'. This may follow a period of time walking around the area of location, chatting to local people and watching the patterns of daily life. This method is also used by the big chain multiples, or by market research companies on their behalf.

Market research is undertaken to establish the profiles of customers in the retailer's proposed location. This may involve gathering census data from government sources and surveys of the local population. Following the survey, the survey data would be analysed to establish the customer profiles. This information could then be used to establish the potential customer base. Ideally, there should be a perfect match between the types of customers in the area, their likes and dislikes, and the merchandise on offer. Price is also important and the retailer's pricing strategy will help to determine whether the location is suitable or not. For example, a value clothing retailer like Matalan is unlikely to do well in an affluent district that comprises stockbrokers and merchant bankers.

Every retail store has a following of loyal customers or clientele. The large chain multiples develop their brand loyalty over a period of time, and at great cost in promotional campaigns and effort. Loyalty schemes and bonus point systems help to maintain this following and encourage repeat business. Smaller independent retailers are just as likely if not more so to have a loyal customer base. Local neighbourhood stores are popular places to meet and the owners often have informal contracts about which merchandise to stock for regular customers. These attributes form part of the brand image that customers identify with. The location of the store is just as important and must fit into the customer's mental image of the retailer. Store image was first discussed in Chapter 7, and here we wish to stress that the typical location of the store is every bit as important as attributes like price, merchandise and service.

Price Wars and Location

The retailer must match itself to the location it wishes to acquire and, usually, the need to locate is driven by expansion plans. In the case of the supermarket chain or discounter, this may be competitor driven and part of an overall strategy to thwart the competition. For example, we invariably see Tesco and Sainsbury within easy reach of each other. In electrical retailing, Comet and Currys tend to be close neighbours and compete fiercely on merchandise and price. It is this strategic element that makes the careful planning of location so important, and key to the success of a retail business. Locating the store is like planning an important league game or soccer match. From the start of the game, the team places itself in strategically important positions (or locations) that can offer tactical advantages. The goal for retailers is increased market share.

Independents are just as likely to compete in this way and frequently locate in close proximity to each other. Often the impact of competition on a small corner shop can be more devastating than the corresponding action between multiples. This is because the smaller retailer has less available resources to fend off the competition. For example, two or even three retailers may clash over merchandise assortment, with one offering more than the others. Another tactic is expanding into new product areas such as the newsagent moving into grocery retailing. Here the retailer analyses and learns from the opposition to make their store a better shopping option. In areas where there is little choice, or where customers are less price-conscious, a retailer may find opportunities to diversify.

Case 10.1 Co-op Village Store Threatened by Nisa

Co-op village stores are a relatively new retail brand and introduced by the Co-op in its attempt to address its declining market share. The new outlets used mainly existing locations, which were extensively refitted, focusing more on the modern consumers' needs. The merchandise offered reflected new tastes with freshly baked bread and ready-to-go Asian dishes. Pricing levels were higher than those charged by large multiples like Tesco, and typical of the Co-op's strategy of charging slightly higher prices. In exchange for these higher prices, customers enjoyed opening hours of 0800 to 2300 seven days a week.

Nisa is a small franchised grocery chain that can pose a real threat to well established grocery retailers. Nisa attracts existing retail businesses, such as newsagents, by offering to convert their premises to accommodate additional grocery lines, which are competitive and offer better value for money. Key benefits for customers are lower prices with the longer opening hours. Newsagents open early and close late.

Rather than causing a threat, some retailers place themselves strategically close to high-performing stores so they may feed off their success. Retailers can sometimes complement each other and locate closely to encourage increased business. For example, fast food outlets like McDonald's and Pizza Hut tend to locate next door to the large grocery multiples. This is an intentional part of their strategy and allows them to capitalize on the passing trade. We are more likely to see this in retail parks, but it is also apparent in town-centre developments.

Large variety retailer Marks & Spencer and the grocery chain Sainsbury act as anchor stores and provide the 'pull' to bring in the customers for other lesser retailers. These pull factors are very important aspects of retail location and retail location strategy.

> ⇨ Anchor stores are the high-status and very successful multiples that encourage large numbers of customers to patronize the site. This, is turn, creates a draw or pull that other retailers on the site can use to increase their trade.

For the small grocery retailer, the large supermarket and anchor store can pose a real threat. However, there may be some benefit and this will depend on the type of outlet and the merchandise range and assortment. For instance, when consumers encounter stockouts they frequently switch to other retailers. Independent grocery stores that locate fairly close to large chain multiples are likely to capture this additional trade. However, this may not always be the case. When purchasing clothing and electrical goods, for example, consumers are more price and brand sensitive, and much less likely to trade down. This is also true for some grocery items, however, most consumers will buy similar items from the local store when the supermarket has run out.

10.2 Evaluating the Trading Area

For all types of retailers, evaluating the profitability of a proposed site is very important and converts to the 'bottom line', or how much business can be generated. Making a profit is, after all, the principal reason for opening a retail business in the first place. A clear and well-developed location strategy ensures that the retail business is in the right place, with the right merchandise at the right time. Location strategy is about making sure that:

▶ customers are close to the store or at least can access the store in some convenient way

▶ the store 'feels' right for the customer and the retailer

▶ the store fits in with the local environment and does not clash

▶ the site is able to provide a competitive and profitable position for the retailer.

Selecting the location of a retail site commences with the process of first defining and then evaluating the trading area. This is the area of the market drawn upon by an individual shop, store or shopping centre. It is vital that this part of the location strategy is carefully considered and its success will depend on a number of factors. The first is the relationship, if any, of the site to the main shopping centre or local town. This may be a retail park or other cluster of shopping facilities that is a draw of the potential customers in the location. If there is a town, for example, next door to the proposed site, this is likely to draw people away from the site.

Accessibility

Accessibility is crucial, as there is no point in locating in a region where consumers find it hard to reach the store. Some basic questions can be asked such as: is the site accessible to the target market? Can they reach the store? For example, are there any buses, car parks, motorway systems, trains, etc? Other considerations are whether or not the site is located on main pedestrian routes, or whether it is hidden away from view. Poor access, confused signage, and complex pathways are all reasons for questioning whether the site is a suitable store location. Ultimately, the degree of *pull* the store has will depend on these and other

---

Case 10.2 Oxford City Centre 'Park and Ride'

The city of Oxford has a great deal to offer tourists and shoppers. The city is a historic place to visit but also has an excellent shopping centre. In an attempt to reduce noise and carbon monoxide pollution, the planners built a 'park and ride' facility outside the city centre. Extensive car parking is provided, with moderately priced bus services to the town centre running continuously. For Oxford, this is an ideal method for retaining local custom, and pulling in additional custom from outlying areas. Consumers benefit from easy motorway access to car parks, low-priced transport and a stress-free ride to the shopping areas. Local retailers benefit from the pull created by the easy access to the shopping areas.

factors, such as whether or not the nearest centre has considerable pull. Facilities and attractions such as cinemas and good car parking may create additional pull factors.

The effectiveness of a location to intercept business for the retailer is an important feature of a location. Retailers call this 'the strength of business interception' which is the measure used to judge the effectiveness of a trading area. Pinpointing the right site is likely to mean investigating some or all the factors illustrated in Table 10.1.

Table 10.1 Factors Affecting the Strength of Business Interception

1. Size of the town or city's trading area
2. Population and population trends in the trading area
3. Total purchasing power and the distribution of the purchasing power
4. Total retail trade potential for different sectors
5. Number, size, and quality of the competition
6. Progressiveness of the competition
7. Adequacy and potential of traffic passing the site
8. Ability of the site to intercept traffic en route from one place to another
9. Complementary nature of the adjacent stores
10. Adequacy of parking
11. Vulnerability of the site to unfriendly competition

It stands to reason that pedestrian and motorized traffic are an important consideration, as without them a retailer is unlikely to attract much business. Small retail stores depend upon the traffic created by large stores. Large multiples in turn depend on attracting customers from the existing traffic. However, where sales depend on nearby residents, selecting the trading area is more important than picking the specific site. When choosing a site, retailers must be able to predict the potential business generated by a site. To do this, retail management calculates the demand customers are likely to place on the retail location.

Demand and the Population

Retailers need to look for market areas that have generally desirable characteristics, and where the population is likely to spend money in their stores. This means researching generally published data on household income, consumer expenditures, business growth, or population growth by geographical (or city/town) area. Regardless of the type of retail offering, high-income and growing regions are generally better prospects for new retail operations. However, desirability will depend on the retailer's budget and retail marketing strategy. For larger-scale developments retail management would need to build a profile of these market areas using types of data listed in Table 10.2.

Table 10.2 Consumer Profile Data from Within Trading Area

Geodemographic data	Data on the average economic and demographic characteristics of inhabitants within small geographic areas
Lifestyle data	Data on the location and buying habits of consumers
Geo-lifestyle data	Data that draws inference about the buying habits of consumers that live in small geographic areas

Management can buy in this information from retail location services but this is an expensive way of gathering population data. Small independent retailers, and businesses that have in-house market research teams, would rely on their own research using government sources and market intelligence reports. For both large and small retailers a certain amount of intuitive evidence will support the hard data. This may take the form of a 'gut feeling' or 'environmental observation' and may be an imitation of nearby competitors.

Buying Power and Demand

As well as examining the profile of the population in the areas of interest, it is important to establish the ability of the population to buy merchandise. There is little point locating a store in an area where local customers or passing trade are unable to afford the goods. A fairly simple calculation can be used to establish the buying power of the population, using the buying power index or BPI.

> ⇨ Buying power index or BPI is a measure that calculates the buying power of the population, or the ability of customers to purchase (Hasty and Reardon 1997). The calculation considers retail sales, population and effective buying income:
>
> BPI = 0.5 (percentage of effective buying income)
> + 0.3 (percentage of retail sales)
> + 0.2 (percentage of population)

Using the BPI calculation helps retailers to make a more complete evaluation of the trading area, and considerably reduces the chances of business failure. For instance, a medium-sized retail chain may wish to locate in a particular region. After undertaking a trading area analysis, the retailer may find that the local customers are unlikely to afford their merchandise. The decision then hinges on whether the retail brand will be enough to draw or 'pull' customers from outlying areas into the store. Some larger multiples such as B&Q and Toys 'Я' Us fully expect to attract local trade as well as the custom from other areas. However, retailers like Homebase, formerly owned by Sainsbury, tend to rely on the *pull* and prominence of their brand to attract customers from outside the locality.

10.3 Locating: A Practical Guide for All Retailers

Many factors that influence decision-making are tied to the economic benefits of locating on a particular site. For example, the decision may be taken about the rents and leases that a particular site has to offer. Town and city centres are expensive to locate in but may be necessary if the retailer's image is to be maintained. The big well-known retailers like Debenhams and John Lewis are obliged to locate in places where their target market *expects* them to be. However, some value-for-money stores are able to locate more or less anywhere and rely on promotion to draw in the customers. Table 10.3 presents a number of factors that retailers may wish to consider when making location decisions.

Table 10.3 Site Analysis for Retail Location

Social and amusement attractions	Are these nearby or on site?
Population of area	This is critical and will determine site attractiveness
Density of population	This may effect frequency of visit, car parking, etc.
Type of consumer	Is the consumer profile right for our sort of business?
Distance to travel	We need to consider how far they will they travel
Lines of communication and transport	Is there a suitable infrastructure for customers and deliveries?
Car ownership	Can customers reach our store? Do they have the means?
Nature of the competition	Can we compete? Is Marks & Spencer or Sainsbury nearby? Do we need to locate near to an anchor store?
Direction of the area expansion	Are there any plans for motorways or shopping centre developments?
Nature of planning regulations	Are there any special planning regulations? Is the region known for its planning restrictions?

Planning Issues

Government planning authorities plan economic and regional developments several years in advance. This is a good source of information about what may happen in the future, and can probably provide valuable insights to help with potential retail locations. City and town centres map out their strategies for retailing and recreational areas, and will provide an idea of the proposed retail location and surrounding areas. Here are some questions that retailers need to consider:

▶ Are there restrictions that will limit or hamper the business?

▶ Will future construction or changes in road use present barriers to the store?

▶ Will any competitive advantages currently at the location be diminished by future planning changes? Will these changes be advantageous for competitors or even allow new competitors to the trading area?

Grocery multiples and discount retailers in particular are hampered by planning regulations that restrict the building of large sheds. Supermarkets like Sainsbury and Tesco compete vigorously for locations large enough to accommodate stores in excess of 50 000 square feet. Land is a major problem in the UK because of its scarcity. Greenfield sites are rare and most retail parks are relegated to brownfield locations.

⇨ Greenfield versus brownfield locations – the diminishing countryside and acute shortage of building land in the UK has created a conflict between the need for facilities, and the environmental impact of those facilities. In retailing, the use of greenfield sites has become increasingly difficult to justify, and reclaimed land or brownfield sites are a good alternative. Government planning regulations restrict the purpose that land may be used for.

Large property acquisition companies tend to control inner-city and out-of-town land sites used for retail facilities. Factory outlet and retail parks operate under a similar arrangement and tend to be owned and managed by property companies rather than retailers. Rents and agreements in these locations are controlled by the owner managers.

Leasing Property

When a retailer decides to locate in a region, decisions have to be made regarding the rental or purchase of premises. For the independent retailer, a major factor in this decision may be whether or not the business is to operate in the location indefinitely, or whether to try the location out for a set number of years. Another factor influencing this decision is whether the retailer wishes to expand at the location in the event of the business being successful. A major reason for renting premises is property prices, which may be so high that buying the premises is beyond the means of the retailer. Conversely, buying may be the cheapest and best option in the long term, providing protection against inflation and the restrictive practices of landlords. Many retailers lease rather than buy their property.

Before a retailer enters into any rigid lease agreement he or she must consider several issues. For example, as we have already said, a decision needs to be made about the length of time the retailer wishes to remain at the location under consideration. This will affect the attractiveness of the leasing arrangement. For instance, a five-year lease that ties the retailer to a location is both desirable and undesirable. A flexible lease may provide the option to renew after a specified number of years, and this may be preferable to more rigid terms that do not take into account the business cycle or economic change. Another area where the lease must be explicit is with regard to planning. The particulars of a lease must be directly related to any current or future planning restrictions and the intended length of stay.

The smaller retailer must study the proposed lease agreement carefully and obtain advice from a legal expert. Larger retailers usually have their own in-house legal departments that arrange property acquisition. Retailers should use the following tips before entering into any agreements.

> ⇨ Does the leasing agreement:
>
> ▶ fix rent to sales volume (is there a ceiling?) or is the rent merely set?
>
> ▶ protect you as well as the property owner?
>
> ▶ place in writing agreements the property owner has made about repairs, construction and reconstruction, decoration, alteration and maintenance?
>
> ▶ contain limitations about subleasing?

The arrangements surrounding the buying or leasing of the retail premises are critical to the success of the business. For instance, the responsiveness of a landlord (this may be a large metropolitan council) is directly related to the appearance of a retail location and the individual retailer's needs. Regrettably, some property owners actually hinder the operation of their tenants' businesses. In fact, they are frequently responsible for the failure of their properties. For example, landlords may restrict the placement and size of signs, or ignore badly needed maintenance and repairs. Worse still for the retailer, a landlord may rent adjacent spaces to incompatible or directly competing retail businesses. This will have the effect of crippling a retailer's attempts to make the business work.

The best way to find out about a landlord is by talking with current tenants. Before locating, retailers need to find out:

▶ the nature of the former tenants' business.

▶ why they left, and did they fail or just move?

▶ what support or hindrances did the landlord provide?

▶ would they be retail tenants of this landlord again?

Concessions and Incentives

New developments in town centres and cities sometimes offer short-term incentives for retailers to locate. The reason for this is that they prefer newly refurbished property to have a full tenancy rather than lie empty for years due to a high-rent structure. This is an opportunity for small and medium-sized retail businesses that would not ordinarily have access to this type of location. However, leasing agreements of this nature are likely to require a minimum occupancy, and this may seriously reduce the benefits to the retailer when the high rents are applied at the end of the concession period.

Case 10.3 Check Out the Service Charges

Locating inside a shopping mall, or multi-let building, is within the means of most retail businesses. For fashion retailers, for example, the type of trade generated in shopping malls and arcades that offer an enhanced shopping experience under one roof is particularly attractive. A high volume of customers concentrated in the one location improves the chances of increasing sales. However, unfair service charges levied by landlords may cause pitfalls for retailers.

Service charge arrangements are designed to cover the cost of maintaining the site facilities, such as the building fabric, walkways, lifts, interior and exterior decorations, car parks, promotion, etc. Retailers must ascertain before entering into any agreements that the apportioned costs of this maintenance are fairly distributed. For short-term leasing, retailers should limit their liability for major items like roof repairs. Contributions should reflect the arrangements made by similar tenants in the local area.

Source: Morris 2000: 26

Some town and city centres offer short-term leases to opportunistic retailers during the Christmas period. Typically, a retailer might sell a wide range of Christmas decorations, cards, toys, confectionery and cut-price items. Rents are lower than usual, arranged on a short-term lease basis for around three to six weeks, and take into account the type of retail business. For the retailer this provides an opportunity to sell merchandise in reasonably high-profile locations, with the clientele to match. In general, the merchandise on offer in these circumstances must be value for money and the retailer should be geared to high volumes of sales. Margins may be low with a dependency on turnover to recoup the cost of rent and overheads.

10.4 Researching the Proposed Trading Area

Many factors influence where stores can locate. Getting it right is vital and can make the difference between success and failure for the modern retailer. To ensure a high level of certainty, retailers need to think about the type of merchandise sold in the area and whether or not the location has the capacity for the retailer's particular product area. For example, a second flower shop in a sprawling (urban) trading area will generally do well, providing there are sufficient potential customers living in the area. Thus, the nature of the competition and spread of the population is just as important as the cost of leasing or purchasing premises.

There is no substitute for exhaustive research, and there is a range of methods available to uncover significant amounts of information before the final decision is made. For the small independent the nature and relative position of the competition is highly significant. Trading areas are chosen carefully for their compatibility and yield; in this respect even the large multiple is vulnerable if the wrong site is chosen. Careful data collection can provide knowledge about the customer base and concentration of competition in the proposed location. Generally, it is the size and type of retail business that determines the sort of location needed. A location that is right for one retailer is not necessarily right for another

Concentration

The number of stores in an area that offer similar merchandise is an important variable in location decision-making. It is easy to see that that the number and type of the competitor stores in an area will influence location decisions. For instance, a market area with a wide dispersal of stores is likely to offer a very different retail opportunity than one with many competitors cramped into a small trading area. Larger multiples such as B&Q and Comet carefully consider this accumulation or *concentration* of competitors. Smaller independent retailers are just as likely to evaluate the degree of competition, but tend to use informal methods such as walking round the area. A rule of thumb measure of concentration is the distance that customers are prepared to travel to a retail store. Naturally, this can vary with the type of location, the economic climate, the type of retail business and the customers' degree of mobility. The significance of concentration is that it provides a guide to the profitability of a retail site.

Not all competition limits trading. In fact, as we have already explained, some forms of competition enhance the retailer's chances of success. The anchor store, for example, will encourage passing trade and draw customers into the area. However, this may be a disadvantage if they are the wrong type of customers. Smaller retailers can usually function quite well near to larger multiples, providing they sell merchandise that complements rather than attempts to compete. Multiples on the other hand need to carefully calculate the number of competitors offering similar merchandise, or merchandise that customers tend to compare the most. The impact of retail competition can be reproduced on a local map that shows the trading area or areas. A more exact method of measuring the degree of competition in a location is the index of *retail saturation*.

⇨ Index of retail saturation (IRS) measures the level of demand in a market based on the population, consumer expenditure, competing retail space and a particular product or product area (adapted from Anderson 1993: 328).

⇨ The index of retail saturation is calculated using the following factors that can be reduced to a mathematical equation:

Index of retail saturation in area for products	=	IRS
Population in area who are likely to buy products	=	POP
Per capita retail expenditure in area on products	=	EXP
Current retail space (sq ft) in area selling products	=	CRS

This is expressed as the following equation:

$$IRS = \frac{POP \times EXP}{CRS} = \frac{Demand}{Current\ retail\ selling\ space}$$

The IRS measures the level of demand in a market that the retailer is hoping to break into, or is perhaps already committed to. When the above calculation has been performed, it provides some measure or index of the attractiveness of the trading area for a particular product line or product area. The higher the index the better the chances are for the retailer, and a low index suggests that the area is *saturated* with similar competitors. Trading areas or markets may be classified as *over-stored*, *understored* or *saturated*. In a saturated market the volume of retail equals the amount that is being consumed by the population. Overstored markets exceed the volume required by the population, whereas in understored markets there is insufficient volume for the potential customers. Decisions about the suitability of a trading area will also take into account the number of customers that may be drawn in from the surrounding geographical areas.

Case 10.4 A Bed of Roses?

A medium-sized retail garden centre decided to measure the attractiveness of a particular trading area using the IRS method. The following figures were obtained from local government statistics and market research sources:

Number of potential
consumers in area   150 000

Consumer expenditure
on gardening products   £2.00 per week

Current selling space in
area (sq metres)   18 000

$$IRS = \frac{POP \times EXP}{CRS} =$$ £16. 67 (rounded up)

This was a useful way of evaluating the relative opportunities offered by the site, and also provided a good guide to the likely margins of other garden centres in the location.

Students may wish to form their own conclusions regarding the IRS for this particular business, and draw some conclusions about the viability of the location for the retailer.

During the location process, retailers are usually faced with the problem of defining the area they wish to move into. This is called the catchment area. The term, catchment area, is borrowed from geography and describes the sphere of influence around an area of interest or importance. For retail location strategy, the retail catchment area is the geographical area from which a store draws its customers. It can also refer to the shopping area of any retail outlet such as shopping malls, factory outlets or shopping centres.

> ⇨ A retail catchment area is the sphere of influence around a retail attraction from which the retailer is likely to draw customers.

In general, catchment areas are illustrated using maps which may be to scale or simply drawn as a representation of the actual area (as in Figure 10.1). A typical catchment area map will show a main shopping centre or store at the focus of the map, with other centres pinpointed to illustrate the pull of these attractions. The reason why other centres are shown is that these create a draw and can distort the potential of the main centre as customers may go elsewhere.

The map in Figure 10.2 demonstrates the process of defining the catchment area using a map for a given location. The information held in store databases can furnish data specifying the location of target groups within the areas surrounding the centres. Individual customer data is converted to specific points on the map of the area. These are then used to show the clustering of the target population in regions around the store. The dotted line represents the borders of the catchment area, which are defined by the heavy clustering of potential consumers.

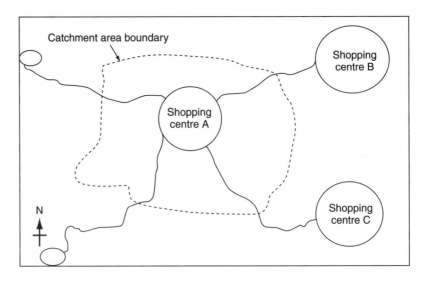

Figure 10.1   Catchment Area

The method of identifying potential customers is called *customer spotting*. This is based on a shopper questionnaire or an analysis of customer credit facilities that may be accessed through confidential sources.

> ⇨ A customer spot map (Figure 10.2) is an accumulation of dots placed on a map of the catchment area, and based on the number of customers in a given geographic location. Data for this can be obtained via survey questionnaires and/or data kept on record such as loyalty card data, credit purchases and general customer information.

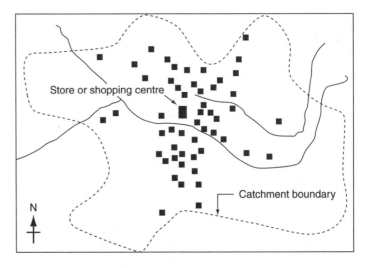

Figure 10.2   Customer Spot Map

Catchment areas can be researched in a number of ways. To establish the profiles of the population in the catchment area necessitates comparable methods to those employed in other parts of retailing, such as consumer research. For instance, a survey questionnaire could be distributed to capture data on customers' lifestyles, shopping behaviour and demographic information like age and gender. This will provide the segmentation data, which forms the basis for clustering in geographic locations.

> ⇒ A survey questionnaire is a structured document that is marked off in sections that contain questions and scales to answer them. Questionnaires may be self-administered, that is to say, filled in by the customer, or completed by the interviewer. Surveys may also be administered by telephone or through the mail.

Research may also draw on information obtained from the government census database, which categorizes the population into profiles. Observational methods can also provide support for such things as natural boundaries like rivers and railway lines, that cross and therefore segment the geographic area. Independent retailers will benefit from simply driving round the area to identify boundaries such as motorways. The degree to which customers will patronize shopping areas will depend on the *pull* of those centres.

10.5 Defining the Catchment Area

There are a number of ways to measure the tendency for customers to use a specific location using gravity or spatial interaction models. These models presume that customers will travel a distance to shop based on the population of the shopping area and the distance between the areas.

> ⇒ Gravity models measure the pulling power of competing locations, whether cities, shopping centres or towns, and the influence this has on the customers that reside within the boundaries. Models identify a boundary line, called the *breakpoint*, at which customers will be attracted to either one side or the other of the line.

Calculations can specify a particular breakpoint, or point of maximum pull, between two population (that is, shopping) centres. The first of these models is called Reilly's law, after William Reilly who originated the theory in 1925. Reilly called his approach 'The Law of Retail Gravitation'. Later research introduced a 'breaking point' technique (Ghosh and McLafferty 1987). This is a very useful feature of the gravity model as it permits retailers to calculate the point at which consumers will be attracted to one side or the other of the imaginary line or breakpoint.

Gravity Models: Reilly's Law

Reilly's law is useful for calculating the trade boundaries between two shopping areas. Using the simple rule that population centres attract retail it is possible to calculate the major breakpoints between Centre A and Centre B featured in Figure 10.1. Let us remember that the breakpoint is the point at which customers are no longer likely to be attracted to the centre in question. The following illustrates how the formula for calculating the breakpoint is applied:

⇨ The breaking point formula:

$$\text{The breakpoint from A} = \frac{\text{Distance from Centre A to Centre B}}{1 + \sqrt{(\text{population B/population A})}}$$

Case 10.5 A Breakpoint Serving Business Strategy

A medium-sized estate agent selling domestic and commercial properties wants to calculate the breakpoint in the catchment area surrounding two of the firm's major locations. The idea is to have a different promotional offer in each town and so tailor the service to the customers in those areas. Town A, the most affluent, will have a 1.5 per cent flat sales fee, whereas the customers in Town B will be charged 1 per cent plus advertising costs after the first month. To organize the advertising and promotion the retailer must determine the extent of each trading area.

Distance between Town A and Town B = 15 miles

The calculations are as follows:

Town B population   =   25 000
Town A population   =   65 000

$$\text{Distance of the breaking point from Town A} = \frac{15}{1 + \sqrt{(25\,000/65\,000)}}$$

$$= 9.3 \text{ miles}$$

The estate agent calculated that the breakpoint from Town A was 9.3 miles and using a scale map of the area, drew a dotted line to represent the boundary. Once established, the catchment and breakpoint was used to limit product promotion.

Reilly's approach is limited and relies on distance and population size to calculate breaking points in the catchment area. For example, the size of the population in a town is not necessarily a reflection of the shopping facilities available. Pull factors may be created by large multiples in an area stocking diverse product ranges. Sometimes, because of the popularity of a location, the relative density of retail businesses is high when compared with locations with less of a reputation as 'a place to go shopping'. This ties in with the earlier points we made about the *feel* of a place, and the impact this can have on whether or not it is desirable for retail location.

Another important drawback of the Reilly model approach is related to the distance, and the way it is measured. Several miles across a busy town or city can take a very long time, and may be considered quite daunting regardless of the time of day. In contrast, if the consumers just need to take the nearest motorway entrance and cruise along to the next exit, this may be far less stressful or time-consuming. In Europe, the distances to shops tend to be less than in the USA or Canada, and this also raises issues about the accuracy of gravity modelling. Finally, consumers are accustomed to large selections and the availability of stock (Verbeke, Farris and Thurik 1997). Choice and variety seeking are good reasons to shop around, or engage in outshopping.

> ⇨ Outshopping is the name given to the customer practice of trawling outside the regular shopping or trading area boundaries for products and services.

Huff's Model

The second gravity model we will explore is called Huff's probability model (Huff 1964). Like Reilly's model this also can be used to define a store's trading or catchment area. However, it recognizes that not everyone within a catchment area will travel to the store (or shopping centre). Instead it measures the probability that consumers will do their shopping at the store rather than travel to a different one.

The simplest way to describe Huff's approach is to think of it as a geographical map showing contours of demand round a central location or store. Figure 10.3 illustrates these contours or demand layers that stretch out from a central location like the contours of route map.

As we can see in Figure 10.3, each contour has been assigned a figure or probability value. This probability figure is the likelihood that a consumer within the area will go shopping at store A instead of a different location. For instance, a consumer living in the village of Weston will go shopping at store A 85 per cent of the time. So the 0.85 contour crosses the village.

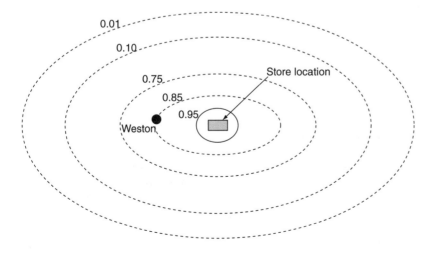

Figure 10.3   Contours of Customer Demand

Huff's model considers the pulling power of the store A relative to the total pulling power of all other stores within the region. The pulling power of the store depends on size, distance and types of products on sale. This means that there are three main factors in calculating the probability contours:

1 The size of the stores in the region. A larger store has a greater attraction for consumers, because they are more likely to find what they would like.

2 The time to travel to each store. For example, a store further away is less attractive than one close by, because of the time lost and inconvenience caused by travelling.

3 The type of product the customer is shopping for. People are willing to travel further for some products such as quality furniture than they are for other types of merchandise. The type of product affects the way that consumers balance the attraction of store size against the inconvenience of travel to the store. The extent to which consumers balance the two factors is symbolized by the Greek letter lambda (λ). (*Note*: different texts may use a different Greek letter instead of lambda.) This lambda factor is measured empirically from studies of consumer behaviour. A larger lambda means that customers are less willing to travel.

Figure 10.4 uses a numerical example to illustrate the calculation of probability contours for a very simple case. Actual cases are slightly more complicated. We can see that Huff's model is useful in identifying the number of shoppers from surrounding towns, cities or retail parks that may patronize a particular site or location.

Huff's model may also consider the percentage of potential customers that may be travelling through the area to patronize retailers in other shopping centres in the locality. These percentages are then included in the calculation. The mathematical formula does look a little daunting, but it is fairly straightforward. However, students are recommended to read further on the subject, as extended shopping and travel time scenarios are beyond the scope of this book.

Students who wish to delve deeper into this method of calculating catchment areas are recommended the following text: Lusch, Dunne and Gebhardt (1993), *Retail Marketing*.

A Concentric Zone Method

A very useful way of estimating how far your customers will travel to shop at the store is by using research data from maps to construct shopping, or *concentric zones*. These illustrate how far customers are likely to travel and whether they will pass in front of the retailer's store. Needless to say, the type of retail business will affect the travel time, as some stores like the chemist shop or anchor store will create a larger pull and, therefore, associated business.

We can use the following simple example to illustrate how we would use Huff's model to calculate the probability that someone in Weston (see Figure 10.3) would shop at store A. We suppose that Weston lies between two stores, A and B. There is no other store within reasonable distance. So what is the probability that residents shop at store A?

First we gather together the information we need:

Information required	Store A	Store B
Retail space in each store	36 sq m	57 sq m
Travel time	4 minutes	12 minutes
Lambda λ (this is the same for each centre)	2 (*estimated statistically*)	

Then we calculate the pulling power of each store:

Pull factor = Floor space (sq m)	36	57
Drag factor = (travel time) to the power of λ	$4^2 = 16$	$12^2 = 144$
Pulling power = Floor space ÷ drag factor (this is the weight for the store)	36 ÷ 16 = 2.25	570 ÷ 144 = 0.396

Next we calculate the probability of visiting store A:

Pulling power of all the stores = weight for store A + weight for store B	2.25 + 0.396 = 2.646 (this is same for both stores)	
Probability that customer shops at store A = pulling power of A ÷ pulling power of all the stores = weight for A ÷ total weight	2.25 ÷ 2.646 = 0.85 (to 2 dec.)	And for B also: 0.396 ÷ 2.646 = 0.15

Note: Probabilities should add up to 1; we can see that this is the case. Students can extend this model to include three or more centres by adding a column for each extra centre. We add up the weights as before. Obviously, the probability of visiting A declines as more centres are added.

Figure 10.4   Huff's Model: Calculating the Probability Contours – a Simple Example

> ⇨ Concentric zones are circles drawn on a map of the trading area and circle the retailer's store or shopping centre. Zones denote the primary, secondary and tertiary catchment areas.

For independent retailers, constructing concentric zones is a relatively easy way of estimating the likely catchment area. It is also reasonably straightforward to produce, and requires no specialist skills other than basic map reading. Other data is also required to estimate customers' propensity to travel to a store or shopping centre. For example, say a retailer finds that potential store customers in a given trading area will travel a maximum of 15 miles to shop. Of course, the distance people will travel to shop may well depend on the sorts of products sold. After consulting survey data from existing shops and data from census databases it will be possible to determine the profile of customers within the zone. Concentric zones are drawn around a central feature, which is usually a retail store.

However, as Figure 10.5 shows, there may be more than one zone. A primary zone could contain some 70 per cent of shoppers, with secondary zones of 20 per cent of shoppers and tertiary zones containing the occasional shoppers of around 10 per cent. These figures

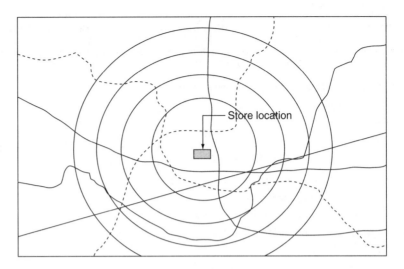

Figure 10.5   A Map of Concentric Zones

are examples and percentages that will vary with location and the nature of retailing. Percentages will also vary considerably across geographic and national boundaries.

The critical factor with this analysis is obtaining good quantities of reliable data about the target market. Clear profiles of potential customers and accurate estimates of travel times are needed or the projections will lack validity. Also, it is important to remember that populations change over time and consumer demands and expectations change with them. Urban and suburban areas (and rural ones) can alter considerably with the influx of new consumer groups, and especially if the incoming population is culturally diverse. This type of population shift can take place very quickly allowing retailers little room for planning.

Geographical Information Systems

The most common, and by far the most efficient, way of measuring the catchment area is using a purpose made information system, or a geographical information system (GIS). This provides a geodemographic picture of the areas around the store or shopping centre, marking out the main features and calculating break points.

> ⇨ Geodemographics is a computer-based information system that combines the demographics of the population with accurate geographical data for use in location analysis.

A GIS is a family of systems that draws on census and other market research data to construct digital maps, thus providing retailers with an easy-to-understand visual representation of data. Postcode data can produce maps of customer zones in precise detail, and clustered round socio-economic and lifestyle groupings. Retailers of all sizes can use this to calculate their markets, or market potential of a particular zone. Consumer profiling can be undertaken and the market potential of particular products assessed.

A key advantage of GIS is its ability to integrate a variety of information such as traffic counts, street maps and the socio-economic data for consumer groups. A typical system would include demographic information, census material and complete town maps showing out-of-town retail concentration with their associated catchment areas. Retailers can program a GIS system to calculate a given location very quickly, and estimate sizes of all the outlets or shopping centres in the locality. Modern systems have real-time links to the Internet and a global capability, and an increasing number of web-based specialists offer a GIS service, which is within the means of most retailers.

Revisiting Store Image

From our earlier discussions students will be aware of the dynamic nature of the retail environment. Retailers are frequently altering their image to help compete for a shrinking business market. Changing locations can alter the overall image of an organization, especially if the store is incompatible with the surrounding businesses. Does it inspire customers and do they want to shop there? For example, a high-class sportswear shop which charges high prices needs to locate in an upscale area. Customers will expect this.

Once the retailer can define with some accuracy who its customers are, it can then plan for the right location. Retail location is really about making strategic decisions. In many respects where retailers are is who they are. Retailers must learn to spot the essential characteristics of the best location and consider very carefully whether the store fits in.

References

Anderson, C.H. (1993) *Retailing: Concepts, Strategy and Information*, St Paul, MN: West Publishing, p. 328.

Ghosh, A. and McLafferty, S. (1987) *Location Strategies for Retail and Service Firms*, Lexington, MA: D. C. Heath.

Hasty, R. and Reardon, J. (1997) *Retail Management*, New York: McGraw-Hill, p. 216.

Huff, D.L. (1964) 'Defining and estimating a trading area' *Journal of Marketing*, July: 34–8.

Lusch, R. F., Dunne, P. and Gebhardt, R. (1993), *Retail Marketing*, Cincinnati, OH: South-Western Publishing.

Morris, N. (2000) 'Cover the service charge cracks', *Retail Week*, 23 June: 26.

Verbeke, W., Farris, P. and Thurik, R. (1997) 'Consumer response to the preferred brand out-of-stock situation', *European Journal of Marketing*, 32(11/12): 1008–28.

Retail Marketing: Operations

11 Store Design and Layout: Producing the Right Format

12 Managing Retail Services: Creating Quality Retail Services

13 Services Retailing: Creating Tangibility

14 Business Operations: Financial Development

15 Logistics and Distribution: Shipping the Goods to Market

PART

3

Store Design and Layout: Producing the Right Format

This chapter covers the following topics:

▶ The store and its image.

▶ The external store.

▶ The internal store.

▶ Display.

▶ Visual merchandising and atmospherics.

Store Design and Layout: Producing the Right Format

Introduction and Core Concepts

The store has traditionally occupied a central role in retailing as the direct point of contact between retailer and consumers. It is the place where the retailer can meet the customer's requirements and ensure continued business. The store is also an important extension of the retailer's image, and indicator of such things as price, quality and merchandise range. This helps the retailer position itself (see Chapter 6) and creates important differences between competitors. However, the major function of the store is to provide a basic storage and display for the merchandise offering, whether it is products or services or both. For most retailers this physical space is crucial to the business operation and is constantly manipulated to facilitate the customer.

11.1 The Store and its Image

The Role of the Store

For many retailers the store continues to be the only point of contact. However, the increase in non-store retailing, such as television and the Internet, has caused retailers to refine and relocate the role of the store. Some firms, such as computer retailers Gateway and Tiny, who started off largely using mail order, have now opened stores in major towns to support their mail order and Internet operations. This may, in part, be their attempt to compensate for the lack of direct contact with the customer, as the virtual store lacks the personal touch. Some firms, particularly furniture stores, tend to use their stores as showrooms that serve as conduits for customer orders to their factories. Supermarkets also use the central position of their stores in consumer shopping to provide other services.

The consumer, however, may visit a store as part of a wider shopping trip that may include competing stores and different retail formats. In most cases, shopping trips form part of a larger shopping programme over a period of time that may include non-store shopping. The retailer then must consider the consumer's shopping trips as a whole in order to:

▶ attract the customer into using the store

▶ inform the customer of how its products meet the customer's requirements

▶ persuade the customer that its products provide the best buy

▶ sell its products in a way that makes the customer feel good and comfortable

▶ influence the customer's decision-making using the displays and layout

There are several factors relating to the store and its environment that affect the consumer purchase process. These include:

▶ the location of the store

▶ the retail format

▶ the store image
  - the exterior of the store
  - the internal layout of the store
  - the methods of display
  - atmospherics, such as lighting, sounds, smells and colours (Kotler 1974).

Store Location

As we discussed in Chapter 10, the location of a particular store determines the range of potential customers. The store must also fit the general area and surroundings, which themselves may dictate the best type of retail format. Location may also determine the sorts of purchasing that the customers are expected to make. For example, customers often visit the small corner shop, as part of their wider shopping activity. This type of store is compact and offers the customer convenience rather than extensive merchandise displays. Out-of-town stores may provide enhanced facilities that attract customers, but the cost in time and money acts as a disincentive to travel there. Unless the features on offer attract them, consumers are less likely to visit a store the further away it is. In general, it is the image (incorporating the range and type of merchandise) created by the larger retail stores that entices customers.

Retail Format

The retail store format plays a compelling part in forming a consumer's image of the store. People tend to link the products they purchase with a particular retail format. For example, the traditional department store uses various departmental layouts to suggest the type of merchandise on offer and the price customers can expect to pay. Similarly, the discount warehouse presents images of value retailing and limited service levels. The format can thus influence the image of the store. When searching for a product or products customers may use the type of format as an indicator of shopping requirements.

Store Image

As discussed in Chapter 5, a retailer uses the store to establish a competitive advantage and communicate its offering to the consumer. The store image is how the consumer interprets that message. It is how the shopper perceives the store in terms of the products available in store, the store itself and the experience he or she expects when shopping at the store.

The key to success in retailing is to create a store image that is congruent with the lifestyles and expectations of the consumers that the retailer is targeting. Getting the right sort of image for its market is important for the retailer because it affects:

▶ the positioning of the store in the mind of the customer (see Chapter 5)

▶ the customer's choice of store

▶ how far a customer is willing to travel to the store

▶ how often a customer will travel to the store

▶ customer loyalty – the extent to which a customer uses the store.

This means that the retailer can attract more customers and increase sales by creating the right sort of image, regardless of the store's location.

Constructing an image of the store is a complex process, but the customer views the store as a total package. Individual customers have their own image of the store, but the process of market segmentation (see Chapter 6) means that we focus the store image on specific groups. This image consists of two major elements:

▶ The physical characteristics of the merchandise such as their quality and availability. These characteristics, together with price perceptions, affect the consumer's expectation of a successful shopping trip. A higher expectation of a successful shopping trip means that a consumer is more likely to shop at that store.

▶ The psychological effect of the store's physical characteristics. These include:
  – the exterior of the store
  – the interior design of the store, comprising internal layout of the store, the methods of display, and atmospherics such as lighting, sounds, smells and colours (Kotler 1974).

The customer's own self-image (see Chapter 6) determines the relative importance of these factors in choosing a store. Customers like to feel that they fit into the store surroundings. Social factors play a large part in building this sense of belonging and customers overtly survey their surroundings. Once the relationship has been established, retailers can build store loyalty and repeat business. A consumer shops more often at those stores whose image is congruent with the customer's own self-image. Thus, while the customer may be impressed by specific attributes of the products offered, the retailer must manage the physical attributes of the store and the method of service to create an image of the store that appeals to its target markets.

Purpose of Store Design

The store design has two basic purposes:

▶ To support the retailer's *market position* in maintaining its customer *image*, by relating to the needs and aspirations of the consumer.

▶ To meet the *operational needs* of the company in keeping costs down and maintaining sufficient stock to supply customers.

In order to create and sustain its consumer image, the store design has to:

▶ take account of customer aspirations, such as
  – a sense of status to confirm expectations of quality or fashion
  – a sense of entertainment or theatre in hedonistic shopping situations, particularly for clothing and restaurants

▶ recognize and resolve customer needs in accessing the store, such as
  – special facilities for the disabled
  – adequate parking for major grocery shopping

▶ make it easier for customers to access merchandise where appropriate, such as
  – clear labelling for the elderly
  – fitting rooms in clothing stores

▶ provide consumers with a sense of comfort and sense of belonging, such as
  – rest areas and refreshment facilities in large stores
  – store appearance conforming to local features and the surrounding area

▶ respect customers' ethical sense, such as making charity and fair trade shops appear efficient but not plush.

In order to keep costs down and maintain sufficient stock, store design has to:

▶ keep structure consistent with the retailer's general policy and market position

▶ relate store layout and display to the image of the store and the merchandise offered

▶ have the flexibility to adjust to changes in sales patterns and display methods

▶ support the sales methods used (such as self-service) and services provided

▶ use on-site storage and administration facilities efficiently

▶ be consistent with safety and security requirements.

Selling Space and Storage

The demand for appropriate trading locations and local authority restrictions on land use make good retailing property increasingly expensive to rent or buy. Retailers have to make efficient use of space, measured according to area, that is, square metres or square feet used. Some floor space must be used to provide for access and services such as lifts, stairwells, entrances, heating and ventilating plant, etc. The rest of the available area is the effective retail space.

The retailer has to divide the effective space into selling areas and non-selling areas (Lusch, Dunne and Gebhardt 1993). Selling areas are those parts of the store where the merchandise is displayed and customers can buy. Non-selling areas include stockrooms, toilets, rest rooms, administrative offices and storage. These are necessary to support the selling operation, but do not directly get the customer buying. Most retail units could sell more by increasing the selling area. In these cases, the real cost of the non-selling areas is the profit that the retailer could make by using the area for selling merchandise. The retailer therefore needs to balance the cost of non-selling space against the cost of alternative provision for storage or offices.

Retailers have been able to partly offset the increasing cost of land by using modern distribution technology and operating procedures to reduce non-selling space. The use of computer-based stock management systems allows stores to reduce their level of stocks and hold more of them in lower cost warehouses or distribution centres. Larger stores then replenish stock daily from these centres. Furniture stores stock merchandise off site in less expensive warehouse space and deliver direct to the home.

Most retailers have to provide on-site storage for some stock. They can do this through:

▶ *Direct selling storage* within the selling area. The retailer may combine storage with display by using showcases, counters or shelves, or it may store items in drawers or behind fixtures.

▶ *Stockrooms*. The retailer may have storerooms directly behind the selling area or in a nearby section of the store. This is useful in large department stores or variety stores selling a range of different items. Other stores may just have a single *central storage* area next to the receiving area for the goods.

We can divide the store into two aspects: the *external store* and the *internal store*. The external store is important in attracting customers and informing them of where the store fits into their aspirations and lifestyles. The internal store provides in-depth information on how the retailer's products fit with their aspirations and lifestyles and completes the process of persuasion and selling that begins when customers are first attracted to the store.

11.2 The External Store: Structure as Part of Image

Aspects of the External Store

The external store comprises the exterior of a store and its surrounding area (or environment). It has the following aspects, which affect consumer perception of the store:

▶ *The external environment.* This determines the setting for the store and includes:
  – the location of the store, such as in a shopping centre, high street or local parade
  – the surrounding area.

▶ *The external architecture* of the store building. This includes:
  – physical dimensions, such as height and depth
  – the visible materials used, such as brick, stone, metal and glass
  – structure and shape of the fascia or storefront
  – windows and window displays.

▶ *External features* such as:
  – car parking
  – horticulture, sculpture and lighting
  – other external buildings
  – outdoor seating, trolley parking and other miscellaneous works.

▶ *Entrances to the store*:
  – number, size and location near parking and other pedestrian traffic flows
  – walkways to and around entrances
  – types of doorways, entrance flooring, lighting.

▶ *Signage*:
  – marquee or logo that is displayed over the storefront
  – other signs and signals.

Requirements of the External Store

The external store is the first part of the store that the customer sees and has a significant impact on the consumer's image of the retailer. It can entice the consumer to enter the store, create empathy by adapting to consumer moods and introduce new products and categories.

The retailer can use the external store to best effect by relating its design to the following principles: *visibility, suitability, accessibility, welcoming* and *security*.

Visibility

Visibility is the prime mover in attracting customers in most retail situations. The only exception to this rule would be where invisibility is an important factor in maintaining the sense of status and exclusivity that the rich or members of an exclusive group may wish to foster, as with high-class bespoke tailoring or jewellery. The store retains its physical visibility through a location that conforms to the mindset of the appropriate group of people.

The retailer can increase the store's visibility in a number of positive ways, such as:

▶ using features to make the store stand out

▶ giving the store a distinct identity by use of materials, texture and colour

▶ having a fascia that is distinctive and appealing.

Suitability

The retailer needs to take into account the external physical and social environment of the store and present an image to customers, employees and the community that is appropriate to those surroundings. For instance, the store should adjust its external fabric, shopfront and signage according to:

▶ its situation within a shopping centre, retail park, high street or local shopping parade

▶ the images presented by surrounding stores, such as modern or traditional; high or low price

▶ the general perception of the local shopping area.

Accessibility

Store accessibility allows customers to get to the store and evaluate the merchandise. This splits into three considerations: parking; congestion; and entrances.

▶ *Parking*
  - For some stores such as supermarkets, a high percentage of customers travel by car, often to edge of town facilities. They require plenty of free parking nearby with adequately spaced places for easier parking.
  - There is a limit to the distance people will walk from public parking places. Poor or costly parking facilities within a shopping centre will also deter customers from the centre and reduce time spent shopping there.

▶ *Congestion*
  - A congested area can frustrate, injure and harass customers and makes them less likely to enter a store. Some stores, situated in new development blocks or in retail parks, can reduce congestion by implementing suitable walkways that guide people in and out of the store and to and from access points.
  - Town centres usually have crowded walkways. Where customers need to browse, as in jewellers, retailers can make use of recessed entrances. These give potential customers relief from the sense of congestion and provide browsing space within the store space. At the same time they relieve pressure on selling space and on the staff within the shop proper.

▶ *Entrances*

– A little attention to detail in the design of entrances can relieve stress on customers, particularly the elderly, the disabled and those with young children. This includes the provision of ramps instead of stairs where necessary for wheelchairs, safely opening doors to protect against accidents to young children and space for parking pushchairs in small specialist shops.

Welcoming

The external architecture can be inviting or intimidating. Retailers can design or refurbish their exteriors to make them more inviting. For instance, they can:

▶ use various forms of exterior decoration to lower the apparent height of an existing building to make it less daunting

▶ use fascia materials and colours suitable to the age group that they hope to attract

▶ widen entrances and walkways to reduce sense of crowding and provide a more comfortable atmosphere

▶ use window displays to promote seasonal empathy or lifestyle concepts, but maintain a balanced window display and entrance.

Security

Security considerations are important in an era of increasingly organized shoplifting. However, modern technology means that they do not need to be forbidding or intimidating to the consumer. Some retailers such as Boots use open-door systems for their stores within shopping centres.

Case 11.1 Changing Design in Supermarket Positioning

From the 1980s to the mid-1990s, the supermarket chains were building out-of-town stores as part of their competitive strategy. The emphasis was on location and convenience and less on building design. The result was a proliferation of traditional barn-style buildings that attracted derogatory epithets. However, during the mid-1990s, government restrictions on further greenfield development forced retailers to develop town or edge-of-town sites. The major supermarket chains also recognized the usefulness of store design in repositioning the retailers as modern, high-class brands. Local authorities usually restricted developments to conform to their surroundings, but some have allowed more modern styles, especially for brownfield developments (on reclaimed industrial land).

Tesco's new buildings combine modern design with a tight budget to convey value for money. It uses glass fronts to entice shoppers into the store. Sainsbury is now promoting its brand with cutting-edge designs and high-tech, environmentally friendly stores that fit well with many of Sainsbury's customer profiles. Asda has developed stores to create the feel and old-fashioned values of a Victorian market hall. Safeway, on the other hand, has been more cautious about modern architecture, on cost grounds. However, they have used a curved metal roof and rounded walls to soften the appearance of their new Canvey Island store.

Source: Cooke 1997: 28–31

11.3 Internal Store

The internal store comprises the interior of the store that the customer sees once he or she has entered the store. Its physical attributes consist of:

▶ *Envelope*: the internal structure and decoration of the building that provides the physical boundaries within which shopping takes place.

▶ *Internal layout*: the internal paths customers may use in order to view the merchandise.

▶ *Methods of display*: including the fittings and fixtures; their positioning; and the colour and texture within the products themselves.

▶ *Signage*: text, colour coding and other artefacts.

▶ *Visual merchandising*: displays of items on sale together with models, pictures and other items that illustrate product use or create lifestyle impressions relating to their use.

Managing the Consumer

The purpose of the internal store is to manage the consumer buying process within the secure environment of the store. This means that the design requirements for the internal store are similar to those for the external store, although we re-order them to make them consistent with the shopping process.

▶ *Welcoming* the customer and assuring him or her of a successful shopping trip. The physical environment provides clues as to the quality of merchandise and of service. Attractive displays of merchandise assure the customer that what he or she is looking for is available and the use of visual merchandising illustrates how the goods support the customer's desired lifestyle.

▶ *Visibility* of the products. The store should display its products effectively in appropriate locations.

▶ *Accessibility* of the products. The store should enable its customers to handle items as appropriate. For instance, in grocery stores, shelves must not be too high or low for elderly people.

▶ *Suitability* of merchandise, price and value. This is achieved through the use of appropriate layout and display techniques.

▶ *Security* of products, staff and customers. The store achieves this through appropriate store layout and product positioning. Even with the use of high-tech equipment, store staff are still the best defence against shoplifters. The retailer can reduce the risk of theft by having a design that allows salespersons between them to see any customer at all times.

The Envelope

The *envelope* is the internal structure of the store and provides the environment within which shopping takes place. It is partly determined by the external structure and may in parts blend with it. It can be used to create a sense of spaciousness and cleanliness essential for modern grocery stores or a sense of economy consistent with the ethics of charity shops. Floors and ceilings are part of the store envelope and have an integral role in conveying the image of the store.

Older stores used to have much higher ceilings, which meant that there was greater space to heat. Nowadays, many modern stores have much lower ceilings, some only about 3 metres high, which create a more intimate feel. Stores such as supermarkets can use a network of ceiling drops to identify goods and specific areas within stores. Modern discount superstores or warehouses and specialist hardware stores such as B&Q tend to have rather higher open-girder construction ceilings. These reduce the ambience of the store, but allow higher levels of on-floor storage and greater selection, which the shopper prefers.

Flooring can be used to convey a higher image and deep pile carpets generally suggest higher priced merchandise. Flooring choices are important and can muffle noise in high traffic areas. The retailer can choose from a range of different types such as carpets, wood, terrazzo, quarry tile, vinyl floor covering. Carpets are often the best choice for discounters and upscale stores.

Store Layout

Store layout is the way merchandise is laid out for inspection and accessed by consumers. It has two significant effects on the customer behaviour and buying activity:

▶ It determines the appearance of the store.

▶ It limits the way in which customers may negotiate their way round the store, which affects *customer traffic flow* or *circulation*.

These two aspects affect customer's impressions of the store and so level of customer spending within the store. Ideally, the layout should be consistent with the customer's mood in entering the store and work with the customer's natural inclinations in order to encourage sales.

Certain types of store layout have evolved over time and continue to be the basis for most store layouts. Textbooks identify between three and seven different basic models, but the difference in number usually occurs because some models are treated as variants of other basic layouts (Anderson 1993; Hasty and Reardon 1997; Lusch and Dunne 1993; McGoldrick 1990). This should not be a problem for students, as the idea is to get a feel for the different ways in which a store is laid out. Students should also remember that these are models only and real stores may have their own particular variants on them. Figure 11.1 illustrates some of these models of store layout.

The Grid

The grid or gridiron pattern usually has main, secondary and tertiary aisles. It was used in the early American supermarkets and has been copied worldwide. It is widely used today in supermarkets, variety and

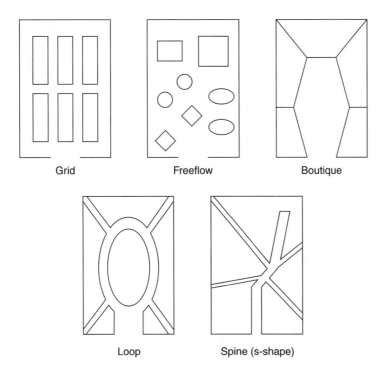

Figure 11.1   Models of Store Layout

discount stores. The purpose of the design was originally to steer the customer past the whole range of goods, which are displayed on the shelves. As consumers walk down each aisle, they are exposed to all the products and so are more likely to buy something they had not intended to buy, thus increasing their total spending. Larger stores tend to have two or more banks of shelving with a central aisle crossing the store. This relieves the intimidating appearance of long rows of shelving and allows customers to shortcut to aisles they want.

The advantages to the retailer are:

▶ It uses space efficiently. The horizontal and vertical pathways tend to maximize the amount of sales space and customer exposure to the products. The retailer can keep costs low by standardizing the fittings and aisles.

▶ It allows the easy siting of merchandise and the linking of products together throughout the store. The retailer can regulate the exposure to different products by allocating different amounts of shelf space to each product; usually good sellers are allocated more linear shelf space.

▶ It allows more customers in store at any one time (higher volume of traffic) and increases the rate at which they pass through the store (increased traffic flow). The grid supplies good orienting features that contribute to the efficiency of in-store movement.

▶ It allows staff to work easily alongside the customers without disrupting traffic circulation. Stock management is easier as the remaining stock out on the shelves is easily observed and the need for replenishment identified. The shelving plan makes the physical replenishment process easier.

▶ It allows for self-service, reducing the use of staff.

The corresponding disadvantages are:

▶ It makes displays rigid. Customers need to go past items they may not wish to buy and it increases the length of time required to shop in very large stores. The unsophisticated shopper may need to retrace steps several times in order to retrieve items. It also limits effective linking together of different items, as in concept shopping. Experienced consumers can bypass aisles. Non-pet owners obviously do not need pet food. However, some groups such as parents with children may skip certain aisles because of the pester power of children.

▶ It deters browsing. In order to maximize efficiency gains from the layout, stores limit the width of their aisles. However, modern stores have wider aisles to accommodate pallet trolleys used in restocking. They also allow easier movement of trolleys for disabled customers. Even so, people tend to get pushed along by the pressure of customers behind and two-way traffic is difficult. This discourages customers from a thorough viewing of products, which is more likely to discourage spending.

▶ It increases security risks. The highish shelving using in many layouts, particularly in some of the older stores can hide customers from view and may therefore encourage shoplifting. Security measures may be too expensive to install in older stores. Managers then need to protect frequently stolen items by displaying them near tills.

▶ It may leave customers feeling isolated. Large stores modelled on a grid pattern present a rather unappealing and soulless scene. The layout needs to provide the shopper with a sense of location and a recognizable focus point. For example, large supermarkets may have modified layouts that differentiate fresh fruit and vegetable and delicatessen counters from the rest of the store. These areas have a more spacious layout that identifies them as separate from the rest of the store and creates a collection of stores. This is also the case with the clothing sections in larger supermarkets.

Freeflow

The freeflow system is widely used in department and speciality stores. Its advantages to the retailer are:

▶ The pattern allows greater flexibility in a layout and reduces fixed areas. This means that structural elements such as columns and fixed partitions are less likely to intrude on the layout design.

▶ The retailer can arrange counters to give the maximum visual impact and focus customer attention on areas of merchandise. Counters can be positioned so that they capture customers in areas of high profit margin – Marks & Spencer do this in many of their stores.

▶ The use of 'cross aisles' makes shopping easier by increasing the width of aisles. This method also increases the number of 'end caps' (displays at the end of rows) in use.

▶ It encourages browsing. Customers enter department stores or speciality store for some substantial buying. Where purchases of items are made infrequently, the customer needs to spend more time searching the market. The customer spends part of the search in choosing the stores to shop at, but must continue the search within the chosen stores. Encouraging customers to browse allows them to be sure of their purchase and improves the prospects of repeat business.

▶ It encourages impulse buying. As customers can take the time to browse, the retailer can use linking displays to suggest to customers other clothing items or accessories that they had not originally intended to buy on their shopping trip.

The disadvantages of the layout, however, are:

▶ It is relatively expensive on space requirements.

▶ It makes stock control more difficult as there is less visual perception of items that need restocking. This should be lessened with the use of computer based stock control programs.

▶ The cost of fixtures is higher.

Boutique

The boutique or 'concept' pattern, as its name suggests, is widely used in small specialist shops and in speciality areas in department stores. It effectively adapts the freeflow system by creating departments to sell related merchandise. This is also called 'associated sales'. A sports retailer could use this type of design layout to sell trainers alongside sweaters, jogging pants and polo shirts.

This layout allows shops to appear as small intimate speciality stores within themselves. A major benefit of this layout allows customers to access various parts conveniently and with least effort. The retailer can then arrange the merchandise in the most appealing way for the customer, often around the walls or boundaries of the shop. The advantages for the retailer are:

▶ The layout can create a sense of space within a small area and conveys a sense of higher class.

▶ The customer can easily see the complete range of merchandise.

▶ There are spill-over benefits between sections as the customer can link items in different categories.

The disadvantages are, however:

▶ There is increased cost of using space, as the centre space is left empty.

▶ The boundaries between different categories of goods may become blurred and distract customers from their planned purchases.

Loop

This is also known as the racetrack in North American texts. It is useful in large stores to guide the customer round the store and increase exposure of the more distant parts from the entrance. Aisles lead off at various points on the loop to allow the customer to explore particular ranges of merchandise in more depth. The merchandise areas may be laid out in different ways according to the type of product sold.

The advantages to the retailer are:

▶ It guides customer round a large area while presenting a sense of order within the store.

▶ It exposes large amounts of merchandise.

The corresponding disadvantages are:

▶ Customers may see too much at once in a large store and not focus effectively on their intended purchases.

▶ The store may need to use internal walls or island screens in order to help customers focus on the particular ranges they are near to.

Spine

This layout uses a central walkway to access the various sections of the store, with branch lines, if required, leading into the various sections. It is similar to the loop except that the customer returns by the same path. It is therefore better suited to medium-sized specialist stores or stores with a narrow front but deep interior. The retailer can use various devices such as changes in flooring, lighting and display methods to indicate different sections of the store, if appropriate.

The spine layout is the basis for other shapes that may be appropriate for particular situations. For instance, some stores can use an S-shaped layout to accommodate different-sized departments or add variety and interest. Another approach uses extra central walkways to create different geometric shapes, such as the Y-shape (Lewison 1996), where the central aisle splits in two towards the back of the store.

The advantage to the retailer is that the layout can utilize the benefits of freeflow, grid and loop systems as appropriate.

The disadvantage is that the retailer may need to vary the shape of the central walkway and increase expenditure on fixtures and fittings in order to break monotony.

Department stores and some large variety retailers have merchandise across more than one floor. Many of these follow a traditional layout. Products such as cosmetics, accessories and impulse items are located on the ground floor. If the store has a basement, this will usually include bargain goods, groceries and housewares, together with children's clothes. Men's clothes are usually on the ground floor. Women's clothing is usually spread over two floors with higher priced items on the upper floor.

For small clothing stores in older buildings, men's and children's wear may be placed upstairs with women's clothing in the more prominent positions.

Changing Layouts

Store layout models reflect the experiences of retailers in managing customers and merchandise. Consequently, stores continue to adapt the various models to their own situation as retailers seek to provide better customer service and stock management.

For instance, there are very few supermarkets that adhere precisely to the grid layout as that would be inappropriate to the needs of the modern consumer. Fresh produce, for instance, and the delicatessen counters have become important areas within modern supermarkets. These are often laid out differently from the grid structure of the supermarket to create a more open environment that encourages people to dwell longer and spend more.

Many discount variety stores also adapt the grid principle to create a sense of variety. The store may be laid out in an L-shape, with offices and storage taking up the remaining space, or else a T-shape, with grids going across the far end of the store from the entrance.

The choice of layout is often dictated by the context within which the particular store is operating. However the principles behind the different layouts are the same and can be summarized as follows:

▶ *Support store image.* The external store creates expectations regarding quality, value and the shopping experience. The store layout is one of the signals customers receive that tells them whether they should go into rummage mode to look for bargains or into receptor mode waiting for the retailer to tempt them. For instance, narrow aisles in a supermarket indicate an old-fashioned store that stocks basic functional goods. Quality comes through the use of national brands rather than own brands. The customer does not expect special treatment and is encouraged to move on as quickly as possible. A modern supermarket has wider aisles that create a sense of space and leisureliness with connotations of quality. Similarly, a modern DIY store uses a grid layout for much of its tools, materials and equipment, with garden, kitchen and bathroom usually having their own display areas. This can be used with appropriate signage to demystify home projects and increase customer confidence, which reduces the need for in-store advice.

▶ *Manage space.* The retailer needs to create a suitable level of exposure of products. Increasing exposure of a product is likely to increase sales. However, space is costly and the retailer must balance the benefits of extra exposure of the product against the extra cost of space. For example, an upmarket supermarket uses more space to display its products to customers through wider aisles and various display techniques. This obviously puts up the cost per square metre of exposure, because there is less shelf space in relation to aisle space used. However, the retailer may recoup this higher cost in various ways. The wider aisles are more comfortable and improve the total shopping experience. Wider aisles can also be used to improve accessibility, particularly for the elderly and reduces stress. This also improves the store image and so more people return. The wider aisles also allow a more leisurely walk through the store, encourage dwell-time or time spent looking and increase spending accordingly. The improved sense of quality may reduce price resistance and allow the retailer to charge higher prices. In the case of supermarkets, it allows them to sell more of their own branded products, which usually carry higher margins than national brands, despite lower prices in most cases. This increases the return per unit of shelf space.

▶ *Manage customer flow.* Retailers can improve store layout to accommodate higher traffic counts. Widening aisles allows for browsing behaviour and inspection before purchase. This is useful where customers like to look at the merchandise adjoining the aisle. Customers tend to concentrate at entrances and exits and these are liable to become blocked at certain times for example during sales and peak periods. More space needs to be allowed for at these points, with reduced displays. In-store, the promotional merchandise and sale displays also create large concentrations of customers. Layout should be adjusted to allow for the clustering of interest round the displays, particularly in smaller stores. Retailers can use conditioned reflexes to control traffic and maximize the exposure of merchandise. For instance, most customers turn to the right when met by barriers. This makes the right-hand wall inside the store a good place to locate high concentration impulse goods. It also causes a counter-clockwise flow of traffic in many stores, in particular supermarkets.

▶ *Keep costs down.* This covers a number of different aspects, including efficient replenishment of stock on display. This means keeping check of what is on display, using labour efficiently to replenish stock without interrupting customers, protecting against theft and damage to stock.

One way to gauge the effectiveness of a store design and layout is to map out the flow of customers as they move through the store. Nowadays, this is a lot easier with the use of electronic tracking aids that use small sensors located in the ceiling and record the movement and pathway chosen. Observations of customer characteristics, time spent in-store, and overall spend by shoppers can be used to develop a customer flow map. The movement of each customer can be mapped on a separate layout sheet. These results can be transferred to a single master and the pattern analysed. If the results show that customer flow is unequal, management may correct this situation by relocating merchandise. It might be appropriate to improve the position of displays and signage, and reposition counters. This should improve customer flow and generate greater sales – shoppers will not buy what they cannot see.

11.4 Display

Image as well as the products displayed is important in attracting many customers and selling to them. All aspects of the store contribute to its image as perceived by customers. As shopping is an ongoing process rather than a predetermined activity, the store takes on the characteristics more of a theatre than an art museum. The staff and customers are the actors and the displays are part of the props that stimulate the imagination and contribute to the enjoyment of the play. Appropriate and imaginative displays are very important in developing customer enjoyment of the retail process and in supporting their interaction with the sales staff. Sound, smell and lighting all contribute to the atmosphere of the store and are important in enhancing the consumer experience.

Retail theory has identified two types of display: *visual merchandising* and *on-shelf merchandising* (Lusch, Dunne and Gebhardt 1993). *Visual merchandising* is the use of fixtures, decorations, signs and samples of the merchandise to create displays that increase consumer interest in and desire for the products offered for sale (the merchandise). *On-shelf merchandising* refers to the way the goods are displayed on shelves, racks and other types of fixtures in the store. Good on-shelf merchandising may also contribute to visual display and the general atmosphere of the store.

On-shelf Merchandising

Displaying the merchandise on offer provides the opportunity for customers to handle and examine the products directly before buying. In some stores, such as grocery and shoe shops, the customer may directly examine products on display before purchase. In other stores, such as electrical stores, the customer may handle particular items in a product range before buying identical items from stock.

The different methods and fixtures for displaying merchandise serve a number of purposes for the retailer and the customer. Understanding and working towards these purposes will enable the retailer to improve sales and profitability. Retailers also use different methods and fixtures to create microenvironments for the different lines of goods according to whether they are prestige, special value or end-of-line items.

Exposure

The first function of display is to show the customer what the retailer has to offer. The retailer should use display equipment to enable the customer to see as much as possible of the available stock. This saves the customer time and inconvenience, because in most stores now the customer has been trained (or conditioned) to know that if it is not out on the shelves, it probably is not available. Modern display methods also save the retailer time answering simple queries about availability and visual features of the products. This reduces the number of sales assistants required and allow the sales staff to concentrate on customer queries that are likely to lead to a sale.

The method of display should allow the customer to see the most important aspects of the product as well as the product itself, by taking account of the customer's *field of vision*. From a distance the walls of a store can be used to draw the customer in. Clothing chain stores for instance can use wall displays to create a sense of variety and depth of stock. This can be done using shelves or racks that use a well-planned mix of colours and designs.

The retailer arranges the displays to take account of customers' *sight-lines*. As customers walk up to the displays, through the aisles, they see more of the goods on display when they face them diagonally than when they are at right angles. Clothing stores make good use of this to allow customers to appreciate the shape, design and colours of items. Also the wider aisles of modern supermarkets allow customers to see goods before they come to them and prompt them to consider a wider range of items than they may have at first considered. The compact arrangement of displays, rather than broad horizontal ones, enables the retailer to present the products within the customers' effective field of vision as they come up close to displays (Lusch, Dunne and Gebhart 1993).

You should try these out for yourself next time you visit different types of store. When you go into a store, how far can you focus? How near can you focus? How far do you look up? How far do you look down? What catches your eye?

Displays should take account of customer *expectations*, as customers are more likely to see what they expect to see. Therefore, the arrangement of items should follow a clear pattern. Accessories or complementary items should be noticeable. Contrasting items should have a clear purpose for the customer, as well as being clearly visible, otherwise they will not register within the customer's shopping scheme.

Image

The items are displayed in a way that conforms to the image of the store. Well laid out items that create a sense of space and variety invite the customer to stay longer and consider their purchases in all their aspects – which is appropriate when you are buying and paying for quality. On the other hand, masses of the same item create a sense of limited variety and quality but relative cheapness. You do not need to spend a lot of time here if what you see is what you want. These displays that give the main message about store image need to be at strategic locations in the store. An example of this is the power aisle in a discount store. If there are masses of different items crowded together, the message comes across of low price – there may be some real bargains, but you, the customer, have to hunt for them.

As discussed in Chapter 7, displays play an important role in a retail store: an attractive and informative display can help to sell goods, but poorly designed displays can ruin the store's atmosphere and create an uncomfortable setting. The consistency of display with the image of the store requires the retail manager to stand back and take a holistic view of the pattern created. This should take account of the following factors in effective displays:

▶ *Balance* of the variety of items within an overall unity of purpose and harmony. Grouping merchandise is better than having long lines of items, which take up space and make it difficult for the customer to choose from. A good way to display goods is in themes such as 'back to school' or 'Christmas', with no slow-moving items in the displays.

▶ *Dominance.* Themes emerge around certain classes of items and displays should have a central point that attracts the customer. This should, preferably, be at eye level where merchandise display has greatest effect, as viewers tend to look straight ahead. The structure of the display should guide the customer by degrees to the rest of the display. For instance, small items should be placed at the front of displays and large ones at the rear.

▶ *Sales appeal.* The displays should always show the very best merchandise that the retailer has to choose from.

▶ *Simplicity.* Too many items in a display will confuse the customer and tend to create an atmosphere of chaos.

Consideration of balance and harmony within the microenvironment of each item mean that the store should also 'match the fixture to the merchandise' (Lusch, Dunne and Gebhart 1993: 429) not the other way around. This is important in bringing out the key selling points of the item.

Accessibility

The next function of the display is to allow the customer to examine the goods directly and appropriately. The customer wants to be able to touch and try on garments, see bedlinen out of its packets, read care labels on garments, test perfume and read the labels on food items. Single people and pensioners want to be able to buy appropriate quantities in the supermarket not oversized packets from which they will throw half away. The list of requirements is endless and varies with the products on offer. If the retailer is not sure what customers really want to be able to do, it can ask its customers.

Security and Damage Control

The retailer has to balance accessibility against security and damage control. A major problem within many stores is (non-)customer theft. Greater accessibility may increase the risk of theft. The retailer can use various general measures to protect against theft. It can also use various on-item devices, such as tagging or bar-coding devices. However, the display methods themselves can be used to increase security. For instance, jewellers have traditionally used plate glass cabinets to protect against theft. This does require greater use of staff to serve the customer, but the high value of the items justifies it. Another method is to relocate frequently stolen items to increase their visibility to staff.

For example, the traditional grid layout used in a small supermarket store in a Leeds shopping centre enabled frequent thefts of certain relatively valuable items, particularly coffee jars. Having analysed the pattern of loss, management reorganized the display so that these items were located facing the checkouts. As the checkouts were parallel to the display shelves this significantly raised the visibility of these items and noticeably reduced loss from theft. Damage to display goods is another problem stores have to deal with. For packaged textiles and clothing items having one sample of the product available for customers to handle is usually enough to stop further damage, but customers looking for different sizes or patterns need to access them fairly easily. Also the retailer needs to encourage the customer to replace items tidily.

Cost-effectiveness

It is, of course, important to make sure that each item in the retailer's portfolio contributes effectively to profit. It can only do that if the cost of labour, fixtures and display spaces is suitably controlled. Within a store, the profit margin on different items may vary. High profit margins are better able to bear the cost of larger display areas, more expensive fixtures and more labour in displaying them. Where there are alternative ways of displaying an item the retailer should always take into account the return on these costs and assign low margin items to lower cost display methods. Take for instance, a hardware chain store such as Wilkinson's or a large retailer such as B&Q. Packets of screws, shrink-wrapped handles and similar items that carry a relatively high margin or clearly need separating for customers are often displayed using peghooks from a freestanding unit in an aisle or hanging from a wall. However, lower valued items such as unbranded hinges are dumped in trays or boxes on tables below for the customer to sort. Dumping items in trays save a lot of effort in sorting out and keeping pegs tidy. At the same time it is not a deterrent for the customer.

Similar approaches are taken in the display of end-of-line CDs and tapes, which may be dumped in baskets for customers to find their own bargain. This saves on display space as well as labour in arranging and tidying displays.

Methods of Displaying Merchandise

The different layouts above divide the store into three areas: the walls, the margins by the walls and enclaves, and islands within the central part of the store. Each of these areas may be used to display goods for sale and for visual merchandising to promote the image of the store.

Walls

Walls are used in all layouts, though specialist clothing boutiques may not use any part of the wall in order to maintain the image of exclusivity. The walls can be used in different ways according to whether the products are *hard line* (such as groceries, pottery or televisions) or whether they are *soft line* (such as clothing or textiles).

Various *shelf systems* are widely used on walls to display many different kinds of items. Shelving must be compatible with the merchandise strategy and the overall image desired. Stainless steel shelving creates an entirely different image than natural wood cubes. China and glassware departments use shelf displays for the finer items and put the cheaper or more robust items on *display tables* that may also be laid against the walls. Such wall displays often use glass as it allows inspection from below and lighting to be used more effectively. When the glass shelving is framed in fine woods, it creates an incomparable sense of elegance. These displays may be complemented by stock from the storeroom to help maintain a sense of prestige while at the same time providing a measure of security. Wall cabinets may also be used, with glass-fronted doors. These can be had in a variety of finishes to suit the mood of the store, and serve to protect smaller items from theft and damage. They also enhance the perceived value of the products inside. Lower priced pottery sections can also use wall shelving, though with different styles to create the images of trendiness, exclusivity or value, according to the merchandise displayed.

Many other types of retailer use shelving that may be fixed to the wall or may be freestanding. Supermarkets, for instance, also use wall cabinets to stock and display higher priced packaged frozen products, especially ready meals or part-ready meals. Bagged or bulky frozen products are placed in chest freezers that may be against a wall or used to form aisles.

Soft-line goods may also be displayed from walls or wall-side tables or cabinets. Suits, for instance, are often hung sleeve-out on straight racks. This gives a sense of depth and value to the lines, while one item in the design will often be fully displayed to indicate the cut and pattern. More expensive or prestigious items will be displayed from *racks* that *face outward*, often downward sloping in a *waterfall* pattern. The full frontal display gives greater exposure and is more attractive. Similar techniques can be used for jumpers and the like. Here wall fixtures are often of the waterfall type so that the retailer can create messages using the different colours in stock and give a sense of depth to the merchandise. Younger-oriented fashion stores also use mixed display racks that alternately combine straight racks and outward facing racks to display sets of merchandise. These wall displays can be two or sometimes three levels, providing they are within customer reach to examine more closely.

Margins and Enclaves

The margins by the walls vary in size and width. Their usual purpose is to cordon off areas from customers and act as security barriers against opportunistic thieves. They may house cash tills and provide *counters* behind which the sales assistant stands and serves the customer, as in the case of pharmacies, jewellers and other specialist shops. These counters may also be used for display. Display shelves or cabinets may also form a backdrop to each of these margin areas.

Enclaves serve similar purposes but are situated within the body of the store. For instance, some supermarkets have customer service areas within their stores that are situated near the entrance but integrate with the rest of the store. They provide kiosk services for tobacco, perfume and higher price items that may be susceptible to theft.

Island Areas

These are display areas within the store and may be composed of a number of different display features. The most common one is the *gondola*. This is a long, narrow freestanding shelving system. The shelves are usually adjustable to accommodate different sizes of product. They are used in supermarkets such as Tesco, variety stores such as Wilkinson's, health stores such as Superdrug, and so on. They provide rigid, economical structures that are suitable for a wide range of boxed, packaged, bottled and tinned goods that can be closely displayed together. These usually have *end caps* that provide a short set of shelves at right angles to the main display. These can be used very effectively to run special promotions and their short length increases their impact on the customer as they turn the corner.

Various other forms of display equipment are used to create island displays. These include tables, decks and bins, again depending on the type of store. Tables are used for bulk display to promote special value products or end-of-line stock for both hard-line and soft-line goods. To create an upper value image for a soft-line product, the retailer can place items on a decked stand or on a wall display, where folding the product gives it enhanced value and where the range of colours can be used to create eye-catching displays.

Bins and baskets of various kinds are really used to signal low price and invite the customer to look for special bargains. However, they would look out of place in some mid- to upper-value clothing stores and are best left to supermarkets, variety stores and hardware stores.

Racks or rails of various sorts are widely used to display soft-line goods such as blouses, skirts, trousers and coats. Different racks are available and, as with similar wall fixtures, they provide different combinations of cost and exposure. The simplest rack is the straight-line rack. This provides the greatest economy in terms of space. They can hold large quantities of the garments. However, the customer only sees the sleeve of a top or the edge of a skirt or trouser. So they are best used where they display one variety of the garment ranged according to size. In this case the retailer can separate out different sizes using on-rail dividers. It is noticeable, however, that some small avant-garde fashion shops use straight rails in high rent areas of London, because shoppers there are prepared to search the rails for what they consider a bargain among the designs that are usually individualized variants on a theme.

Various feature racks are now widely used to combine economy of space with display effectiveness. Four-way designs permit the customer a front view of the garment. These are the equivalent of the straight out or waterfall type of wall fixture. Increasingly popular within young fashion stores is a mixed rail. These may be sturdy rectangular rails that combine straight out displays at the ends with straight rails along the length. This conveys the impression of good value, but also suggests excitement and value. They may also have displays on top.

11.5 Visual Merchandising and Atmospherics

Visual Merchandising

Visual merchandising uses various displays to increase consumer interest in and desire for the products offered for sale. These displays are like the backdrop in a theatre because they stimulate lifestyle images that support the sale of the products. In this sense, visual merchandising should permeate the whole aspect of the store from layout to individual displays.

On a more specific level, visual merchandising refers to displays to increase consumer interest in and desire for the products offered for sale. It includes the use of fixtures, decorations, signs and samples of the merchandise to create window and floor displays. The items used in visual merchandising are not normally for sale, although they may include items similar to those on sale. However, the items on sale may also contribute to the visual image of the store. For instance, displays of different coloured sweaters for sale may be used to create strong visual images in a certain part of the store and contribute to the total atmosphere of the store.

Visual merchandising may help divide the store into recognizably different areas, such as men and women's clothing and create different moods in each according to the target customer.

Visual merchandising should provide coherent themes. Uncluttered displays with good backgrounds help achieve this. Good backgrounds are important in giving coherence to a display. They require appropriate colour and texture of materials, such as silver for modernistic themes.

Window displays are an important means of communicating the retailer's self-image to the customer and as a way of attracting customers. The retailer can use window displays to get the customer's attention quickly and to convey a wide range of messages. For instance, in fashion retailing, window displays can convey the message of affordability of hitherto expensive designer clothes. Modern window designs can be very adventurous, but some store windows may retain their looks to appeal to a more traditional customer. Window displays should be in keeping with the products. They should be changed regularly to keep them looking fresh.

Aisle displays are necessary in a store to allow customers to look at the merchandise close up and touch it. It has to be a focal point, and yet not interfere with the flow of traffic. One way is to put stock on a dais or stand to make the display more prominent and be less of a hazard to customers.

Floor displays are usually within set areas, located in the high-traffic areas of the store. The indicate the type of merchandise available and help put them into lifestyle context.

Display equipment can be expensive and may require renewal or replacement to keep abreast of fashion. Mannequins are an important element in fashion and retailers have used them in windows and throughout the store to display apparel. Mannequins may look like a human being or a bust form without arms, legs or head. The design of mannequins changes over time. The modern mannequin suggests greater athleticism. The type of mannequin used varies with the products on display. Headless mannequins, busts and lower body models are suitable for displaying items such as jeans or sweatshirts, where uniformity rather than individuality is being expressed.

Other Atmospherics

There are a number of other aspects that form part of the atmosphere of the store and contribute to its image. These include signage, lighting, colours, music and scent as they can be used to control the customer. For instance, they can:

► enhance the customer's perception of the store

► structure the customer's decision-making and purchasing behaviour

► focus on certain aspects of goods or services offered

► steer the customer from one area of the store to the next.

Signage

Signage refers to the collection of signs, posters and labels that the retailer uses outside and inside the store to guide customers in their use of the store. These elements together fulfil a number of different functions:

► *Organizational.* The retailer uses signage to advertise the store; strengthen retailer's image; protect its market and promote the products on offer. It will also communicate the retailer's policy on various matters, such as the type of product, quality, price and customer services. This can also serve to support the retailer's planned high-brand/own-brand mix.

► *Locational.* The retailer can vary in-store signage to locate and identify the goods on offer. Large stores need to display directional signage in order to guide customers round the store and from one area to another. Directional signs should be large enough to be clearly seen by customers when entering a store. They should show customers where to go for any category of product or service. Even larger stores, particularly those on more than one level, also need to have a store guide. This should be clearly visible from the entrance and the path to the guide clearly marked out so that even the first-time customer can clearly see where to go. The store guide is often repeated on different floors for customer convenience. The colours used in directional signage should be easy to read and not clash with the store environment. The signs may also be visual, using symbols as well as words, particularly where the symbol is widely used. Large three dimensional signs are more easily visible and can be used to promote the image of the store as well. Hanging signs from the ceiling is often used to enhance the visibility of the signs.

► *Category signage* is used within the particular department or sector of the store. They are usually smaller than directional signs. Their purpose is to identify type of products on offer and they are usually located near to the goods they refer to. However, they can often be promotional of one or more categories of product.

► *Promotional signage* may refer specifically to special offers. These may be displayed in windows to entice the customer into the store. For instance, value fashion stores for the younger woman may display large posters in their windows of models wearing the items on special offer. This draws attention to the products and does not get in the way of the customer peeking through windows. With the right colour products, the posters can add to the attraction of the store.

▶ *Point of sale*. These signs are placed near the items they refer to. This is so that the customer can see the price and other detailed information. Some of this information may already be on product labels or packaging. However, point-of-sale signage can quickly identify for the customer those aspects likely to be of greater interest, such as whether the product is on special offer.

▶ *Lifestyle images*. The retailer may use various images, such as pictures of people and places to create moods that encourage customers to buy the products. These are part of the visual merchandising that the store uses.

To visualize the use of various signage we should begin with the customer entering the store and progress to the inspection of individual items. The marque or logo on the outside of the store is the first sign customers will see. This must be clear, distinctive and convey the image of the store in a manner attractive to its customers. Dark reserved greens with traditional lettering (in old book style) convey a no-nonsense approach to basic good quality products that is reassuring to young and old alike. This has been used to good effect by Marks & Spencer, with its dark green lettering on a creamy background. However, this can go too far and may persuade some of its younger customers that the store is not for them. This style can be contrasted with that of the supermarket chain Asda, which uses a bolder, lighter green logo in modern letters to welcome customers.

A wide variety of stores use red in name signs as it is eye-catching, stimulating and reinforces the message of good value that the bold lettering uses. Different types of store to use this approach are supermarkets (Tesco), food discounters (Lidl), electrical retailers (Dixons, Currys, Comet), variety stores (Woolworth) and similar stores. Some supermarkets, such as Morrison's and discounters such as Netto use black on yellow. These colours can be contrasted with the orange colour used by upper-end supermarket Sainsbury. Its colour and rather anonymous logo indicated the kind of clientele this supermarket was aiming for and placed the emphasis more on quality rather than on value. As Sainsbury was forced in the mid-1990s to take note of the value movement in supermarkets it also had to rethink its logo and use of colour.

Lighting

Lighting is a vital element of the store's interior and exterior design and creates a favourable first impression of the merchandise and its surroundings. Although a significant design feature in its own right, lighting is an integral part of the merchandising display and was examined earlier in Chapter 7.

Colour

The effects of colour on customer behaviour and the impact schemes have on store designs have already been discussed under merchandising in Chapter 7. We think it more useful to discuss colours in the context of retail merchandising rather than broader design issues.

Scent

Scent is perhaps one of the subtler and more surreptitious methods used by retailers to manage customers. The smell of freshly baked bread is one that attracts most people. However, supermarkets can enhance that smell and pipe it to other parts of the store to attract people from further away or simply just to enhance the feeling of freshness within the store. Department stores have similarly experimented with different odours near various clothing sections.

Music

Music is played in many stores from the local discount hardware store to the supermarket. Relaxing music or even something different from what customers normally experience tends to encourage people to stay and linger near displays, thus increasing exposure and sales.

Store Atmosphere and Customer Patronage

The atmosphere of a retail store is vital and will often determine whether customers are prepared to spend longer browsing and shopping (Kotler 1974), Retailers spend large amounts on designs and layouts to induce people to spend more money in their stores. Cues such as music, colours and smells are great inducements and can be used strategically to target particular customers. A number of specialist firms are available to advise on and implement these sorts of issues. Ultimately, the degree to which a retailer is able to get into the head of their customer will determine how successful these sorts of strategy are.

References

Anderson, C.H. (1993) *Retailing: Concepts, Strategy and Information*, St Paul, MN: West Publishing, p. 39.

Cooke, A. (1997) 'Star wars', *The Grocer*, 6 December: 28–31.

Hasty, R. and Reardon, J. (1997) *Retail Management*, New York: McGraw-Hill, p. 271.

Lusch, R.F., Dunne, P. and Gebhardt, R. (1993) *Retail Marketing*, Cincinnati, OH: South-Western Publishing, p. 34.

Kotler, P. (1974) 'Store atmospherics as a marketing tool', *Journal of Retailing*, 49, Winter: 48–65.

Lewison, D. (1996) *Retailing*, 6th edn, Upper Sadde River, NJ: Prentice–Hall International.

McGoldrick, P.J. (1990) *Retail Marketing*, London: McGraw-Hill.

Managing Retail Services: Creating Quality Retail Services

This chapter covers the following topics:

▶ Retail services.

▶ Service characteristics.

▶ Branding and service quality.

▶ Managing the service setting and the service encounter.

▶ Designing and improving service quality.

Managing Retail Services: Creating Quality Retail Services

Introduction and Core Concepts

Product retailers provide a variety of extra services to their customers as part of their positioning strategy. These retail services are important in meeting the different needs of the customer. Managing retail services is different from 'service retailing' which will be covered in Chapter 13. The quality of these retail services influences customers' judgement of the retailer. Retailers need to pay special attention to the service encounter, when the retailer meets the customer. This is of special importance to the customer and getting it right is crucial for the retailer. The retailer can make use of a number of approaches to design the delivery of their services and to continually improve the quality of the services they provide.

12.1 Retail Services

Retailing as a Service and Retail Services

Retailing is a service industry. This is because the essential economic function of retailers is to provide their customers with several basic and important services, including:

▶ accessibility of location

▶ convenience of timing

▶ choice of products

▶ information about the products

▶ convenience of size (appropriate quantities).

These services are part of the basic function of the retailer as the link in the supply chain between the producer and the consumer. They improve the efficiency of consumption and help consumers to be more effective in their working lives. Every retailer provides services as part of its retail offering and customers use them every time they go shopping. Different retailers can provide different levels of these services by varying the merchandise stocked, store format, design, layout and other facilities provided. The individual retailer decides on the level of services it offers its own target customers according to the various factors, including lifestyle, that affect their shopping behaviour.

The retailer also complements the merchandise offered with an appropriate service style. This includes additional services, such as advice and design, customer assistance, and home delivery that the retailer offers in response to consumer demand and competitive pressures. *Retail services* (or retailer services) are the set of services provided by the retailer to the customer in addition to the products offered.

We must be careful to distinguish retail services from *services retailing*. Services retailing occurs when the main product is a service itself, such as hotel accommodation, travel services, financial services and hospital services. The *service retailers* that provide these services face special challenges and these are discussed in the next chapter. This chapter, however, focuses on the retail services that product retailers provide as part of their retail offering.

Case 12.1 Home Delivery – Lifestyle Extra or Necessity

Go into a DIY, furniture or carpet store and buy some bulky items and you expect them to be delivered. Most people do not have vans or even large cars in which to carry home such purchases. Customers expect the store to provide a delivery service, although most of them would regard it as reasonable to pay for delivery.

Many furniture stores and electrical retailers have fixed rates within a 10 to 15 mile radius from the store. Do-it-yourself stores charge according to concentric zones from the store. Some charge according to tonnage delivered as well. Other retailers may offer free delivery as a bonus.

However, Iceland, the frozen food based retailer, offers a free delivery service as standard on orders over £40. Its stores are usually situated near to low-income estates and many of the families in the catchment area do not have a car, or the main shopper does not have the use of the car. Offering free delivery encourages shoppers to spend while they are there. It also widens the catchment area of the store by encouraging people to come from further away, knowing that they do not have to lug what they buy all the way home. This is particularly convenient for the frozen and chilled foods that form the bulk of sales.

The retailer must consider the elements of service when constructing its retail mix and tailor the services to its customers. This leads us to consider the types of services that different customers will require, which depend on the shopping experience desired or expected.

Service and the Shopping Experience

Our shopping experience has two basic elements. The first element relates to the *outcome* of the shopping trip in terms of the products that we buy. These should be appropriate to our lifestyle and current needs, and be value for money. So we may need a range of relevant services such as information on the product itself, delivery of bulky items, sometimes finance for major items and guarantees that appliances will continue to work.

The second element is the shopping *process* itself. Many people focus on the products they buy. They are concerned mostly with the outcome in terms of goods that are value for money and appropriate for their needs. So they just want shopping to be as stress-free as possible. Many people, however, particularly when not shopping for essential groceries, see shopping as an important leisure activity. So they positively want shopping to be an enjoyable activity in itself. Depending on what we are shopping for, we want pleasant surroundings, accessible products, friendly and helpful sales staff, and more.

In order to meet these two customer requirements the retailer must offer two different kinds of services:

▶ *outcome-related services* that are related to the products bought

▶ *process-related services* that are related to the shopping process.

Outcome-related services include various indirect and direct services to ensure the goods that the consumer buys continue to support the consumer's lifestyle. They may be offered before or after purchase and include:

▶ pre-purchase design and advice services, such as for kitchens

▶ refunds and exchanges for unwanted gifts or change of mind purchases

▶ extended warranties on appliances

▶ home delivery services

▶ arranging credit facilities

▶ helplines; and customer contact points, particularly through company websites.

Process-related services improve the customer shopping process and are directly linked to the *service encounter*, which is a vital part of the customer–retailer relationship. They include:

▶ in-store service, where sales assistants offer help and advice to customers

▶ providing product information, fact sheets and leaflets

▶ demonstrations and video displays

▶ product testing by the retailers and the customer, such as changing rooms for clothes or hands-on trials by customers of electronic products

▶ gift-wrapping

▶ a customer help desk.

The Importance of Service

The responsive retailer recognizes the importance of these additional services for the customer. High standards of living usually bring complex lifestyles, and retailers have an important part to play in helping customers manage their lifestyles. For instance:

▶ People need to make major purchases of durable goods such as a car, electrical appliances and household furniture. However, the complexity of modern technology and the relative infrequency of some major purchases mean that many customers are unsure as to what is appropriate to their own lifestyle. They need to assure themselves that their furniture purchases are value for money through informed selection. So they may gather information from various sources to guide them in their choices, but in many cases they look to retailers for final assurance in their purchases.

▶ Another service often marketed by retailers is the extended warranty on electrical appliances. For many customers, the pressure of time means that appliance reliability or swift repair is essential. Many customers are also averse to risk and want to be assured that they will not have to make further major expenditures on the item for a given period. These people are often on limited budgets and will willingly pay the retailer a high price to arrange these assurances. These extended warranties, as they are known, are often more expensive than similar ones offered by the product manufacturer or by other insurance providers. Retailers sell many warranties because customers often do not know which brand they will buy before they enter the store and may not like to ask what the manufacturer is offering. People often feel more comfortable dealing with the retailer and retailers can also offer other advantages such as cover against accidental damage (not always covered by other insurances).

Case 12.2 Extended Warranties – a Retailer Service or Ethical Dilemma?

All electrical products must now carry a one-year guarantee against defects. Electrical retailer Comet offers its own extended warranty for a further two or four years by offering accidental damage cover. It also encourages customers to take out extended warranties for an extra four years, rather than two, by offering money back if the customer does not make a claim within the five-year period. The customer would then only have spent the interest lost on not investing the money elsewhere or the interest on money borrowed to pay for the warranty.

However, some personal finance writers have advised consumers that they are not worth the money, and computer magazines often warn consumers against taking them out because they are too expensive. Suppliers have to give a year's warranty and most faults occur within that period. And who does not upgrade or replace their computer within three to five years anyway?

What would you advise?

▶ Shopping for clothes also requires its special customer service. For instance, the importance of the right dress codes for particular lifestyles and situations mean that customer service must reassure customers they are making appropriate purchases.

▶ People want to use their leisure time to shop in comfort and with a sense of individuality.

Competitive pressures force retailers to provide these extra services. However, the focused retailer will be proactive in providing those services that add perceived value for money for the target consumer. The retailer needs to communicate its additional services to its customers in such a way that customers identify those services with the retailer. The services then become embedded in the retailer brand and become part of the brand image. Viewed holistically, they guide the customers' expectations of the services offered. These services identify the retailer brand and clearly differentiate the retailer from its competitors. The retailer can then launch, enhance and position its brand in the market using these services as part of the overall retail offering.

Case 12.3 Privacy and Choice

Some fashion stores, aimed at young women, provide communal changing room facilities. This lack of privacy is hardly going to be liked by its target customers. On the other hand, the upscale fashion store Selfridges Manchester provides select customers with a personal shopper service. Part of the benefit for the customer is the use of specially enhanced room facilities away from the shop floor in complete privacy (Newman and Atkinson 2000).

Using Services as Part of the Brand

Customer service is more than just an element of the product mix. It extends the marketing functions after the sale of the product. A customer-oriented retailer embodies the principles and standards of service in its service policy. These policies are an important part of the company's strategy and help retail firms attain their goals. Some retailers, for example, are well known for the high-quality service they offer. This image helps them to gain significant competitive advantages.

A retailer can often use certain types of additional services to help them increase their market share. For instance, in the grocery sector, firms like Sainsbury introduced finance and mortgages as an additional service benefit for the customer. The issue of 'copy cat' policies may also contribute to the increasing move towards in-store services. In a bid to out-manoeuvre the competition, retailers frequently use the services they offer to encourage and sustain customer loyalty.

12.2 Service Characteristics

Service Problems for Management

Customers may pay for their services directly or indirectly. They pay for them directly when payment is specifically linked to the service, as in the case of home delivery charges. They may also pay for their services indirectly through higher product prices. Customers are willing to pay these higher prices when they receive some extra services, such as product knowledge and sales assistance that improve their shopping experience. In either case, retailers need to manage their service provision so that customers clearly perceive them to be value for money. Retailers also need to ensure that services cover costs or generate long-term improvements in profits through enhanced sales. This is quite difficult for a number of reasons.

The most problematic aspect of services is that it is difficult to manage what you cannot measure or even identify, and the very nature of services makes them difficult to identify. We experience a service but we cannot see or touch it. A product such as a television set is independent of the buyer and seller. Its physical specification stays the same whoever buys and sells it. On the other hand, a service changes with the person buying or using the service.

For instance, most clothing stores provide changing room facilities as a service to their customers. Customers benefit from being able to try on the clothes before buying them. This enables customers to reduce the risk of post-purchase unsuitability when buying clothes. Lowering the risks of unsuitable purchases effectively reduces the cost of purchase. This allows the store to charge a higher price than it would otherwise be able to and still increase its level of sales. It also helps to build a relationship of trust and so customers will increase their spending over time.

However, the extent to which different customers use the service and so the benefit they receive varies. Customers will also vary their use of the service according to the quality of the facilities and their availability. Two cubicles with curtains across in the corner of a store convey an image of low service and spoil customer care. Pleasantly decorated hard-wall cubicles in a separate area off the main selling area with an attendant service not only helps reduce shoplifting but conveys a sense of caring and belonging that enhances customer perceptions of the products.

Similarly, overcrowded facilities discourage people from using the service. If a customer sees a long queue, he or she may decide not to wait. The customer reckons the service is not readily available and so effectively is not there. A service must be available when the customer wants it, not an hour later. When a service is delayed the customer may not be able to use it and so it will have no value for the customer. The same problem applies in reverse when providers cannot entice customers to take the services when offered, and the customers then become unavailable later. Shops may encourage customers into the stores by offering special promotions during quiet, off-peak periods during the day or week. However, most stores seem to find promotions difficult to organize and communicate to customers.

Another problem is that the value of the service to the customer often varies with the store that provides the service or the sales assistant that delivers the service. This is partly because of the nature of the services themselves. When a customer buys a physical product, the physical specifications of the product are known. It is up to the customer to decide how and when the product is used. The customer pays the price and expects to use the product often enough or in such a way as to create a level of satisfaction that more than compensates for the price paid. The customer's use of the product largely determines the value of the product to the consumer – although the quality and serviceability of the product are important.

On the other hand, while a service provider can tailor the service to the customer, the service is then usually specified and is often consumed at the time of purchase. The two elements of the sale become inseparable. This requires the service to be properly marketed to the customer because customer satisfaction can be linked directly to the service provider.

The Nature of Services

Services, then, are different from products, although the difference between products and services continues to be the subject of much discussion. There are service definitions that have tried to capture the meaning of a service, but we use the following composite definition because of its usefulness in this context.

A service is an activity performed for a customer that:

► changes the customer or the customer's assets in some way (Hill 1987)

► may involve the customer's participation

► may use some of an organization's products or facilities without transferring ownership of them (Zikmund and d'Amico 1993).

An *instrumental service* is one where work performed by others to achieve a customer goal without direct involvement in the task. A *consummatory* service is one where the customer is directly involved in and immediately gratified by use of the service (Zikmund and d'Amico 1993). Various schemes have been drawn up to differentiate services from products. However, the four main differences that distinguish services from products are:

► intangibility

► heterogeneity

► perishability

► inseparability.

Intangibility

A service is intangible because the customer cannot see or otherwise physically sense it. This makes it difficult for the customer to measure the service and so evaluate the service properly.

The problem may be partly resolved by linking the service to a tangible product or to some measurable quantity. For instance, a fashion store provides changing facilities for customers who wish to try clothes on before purchase. The customer can then evaluate the service on the standard of the changing facilities, their capacity and the time to wait to use them.

Heterogeneity

Services are heterogeneous because the service provided to a customer is different from the service provided to every other customer. Products can be standardized so that one television set is exactly the same as the next. However, the delivery service that the retailer provides is different for each customer, because the customers have different requirements and levels of flexibility as regards timing of delivery and the place. This can add to the cost of maintaining the service and cause variation in the perceived quality of the service provided.

In order to control cost, the retailer may standardize the service as much as possible without noticeably affecting perceived customer value. One way is to standardize procedure. For instance, Currys, the electrical retailer, offers its customers a choice of delivery days, which is agreed at time of purchase. It will then telephone the customer the day before to confirm a time period within which delivery will take place the following day.

Another method is to standardize as much as possible of the service. For instance, electrical retailers often offer two levels of delivery service. For the basic delivery fee, the retailer will deliver the appliance. For an additional fee, the delivery people unpack and connect the product up as appropriate and ensure it is functioning.

Many aspects of a service are subjective and exist only in relation to specific customers who value them differently according to their own special requirements. However, a firm has to assess the value to each consumer, because these are the features that give the business its competitive edge.

Another example of standardization occurs in fast food, where an important quality characteristic is speed of service. A retailer can improve its service quality by reducing the time between ordering and delivery of the meal. McDonald's, for instance, anticipates demand and pre-prepares some of its products. Most customers do not notice any significant quality difference when the product has been held for a short time. So McDonald's can hold the product ready for a customer up to a certain time before throwing it away. This allows it to serve customers quickly, by having the product ready when the customer enters the restaurant.

Inseparability

Inseparability means that the service is produced and consumed at the same time: the buyer and seller must both be present for exchange to occur. The service provider is also a marketer and promotes both the service and the company that provides the service. The key to the success of the service, therefore, is competent service personnel. Some stores make up for the lack of interaction between staff and customers by providing electronic information points.

Perishability

Services are perishable because they cannot be stored. This makes it difficult for the retailer to provide the service as and when required. However, recent advances in technology make it possible for retailers to store some services. For instance, the latest type of store formats use systems that supply customers with information about products, out-of-stock items and waiting time.

Case 12.4 Storing Information as a Retail Service

Product information is retail service. You may know how to use a computer, but choosing the right one may be a difficult task. Computer retailers Time and Gateway are examples of retailers who supply product guidance to their customers, from the games player to the home office worker to the professional (power) user. The retailers standardize the information provided by anticipating the basic questions most customers will ask. They pre-prepare the information and store it in leaflets ready for the customer. These leaflets are available to customers before they come into, and when they are in, the store. Sales assistants can then concentrate their time on those aspects specific to each individual customer, thus improving the service offered.

Is your product in stock? Do you want the latest information on whether an item is in stock? Well,

you can ring up Argos to find out and you can reserve it for when you want to collect it – a service stored. Alternatively, you can go into the store and see if the item you want is in stock by using the computerized service screen. This saves time queuing when the product is not available. If the item is out of stock, you can then go to customer service and order it if you wish.

Queuing for shoes? You will be if you go to buy children's shoes on Saturdays at specialist stockist Clinkard's in Leeds. Take your numbered ticket and you will be able to gauge how long you will have to wait because the latest number being served is posted.

These examples show how different retailers have to approach customers in different ways in order to deal with different service problems.

12.3 Branding: Perceptions of Service Quality

Service Expectations and Service Perception

The customer has been led by the retailer to expect a certain level of service from the retailer brand. A *retailer services gap* exists when customer thinks or perceives he or she has received a lower level of service that he or she expected to receive. These problems arise when management fails to understand what the customer wants or is unable deliver what it has promised. For instance:

▶ Family shoppers may expect help with large quantity of groceries they have bought in Tesco, because television advertising may have given them the impression that this will take place. If the retailer fails to meet the customers' expectations this has a negative affect on the brand.

▶ When customers visit a shoe retailer they expect to find sufficient stock levels. If the retailer is out of stock, this leads to customer dissatisfaction and reduces the chance of return visits.

▶ Staff–customer interaction is an important part of the way the retailer delivers the products. If the sales person does not handle a question or a sale according to guidelines, problems arise with customer perception of the service received.

▶ Sometimes advertising promises more than sales personnel can deliver. A number of retailers use high-profile advertising to give the impression that staff are helpful, knowledgeable, worldly and friendly. However, experience suggests that product knowledge and knowledge about using the product are often deficient. Some retailers seem to have difficulty recruiting capable staff or in implementing their own training programmes to deliver promises.

The Service Encounter

The *service encounter* is the period of contact between the customer and the service provider during which the service transaction takes place. It is a crucial element in retailer services, but it can only be successful if the retailer supports it through appropriate behind-the-scenes activity.

Studies have shown that it is difficult to retain even satisfied customers, as a high proportion of them have no particular store loyalty. Keeping dissatisfied customers is even more difficult. Quality is nowadays a strategic element of retail services. Customers expect to receive a quality service and management must deliver it. Otherwise they will lose custom. The customer may balance a retailer's location, product range or store environment against other aspects of an unsatisfying shopping trip, but repeated incidents will surely drive many customers away. They will also tell several others of their unhappy experiences, which will reduce their perceptions of the quality of services received. However, retailers may improve relations with dissatisfied customers through appropriate *service recovery* procedures. These either deal with the problem – by, for instance, replacing faulty goods – or compensate the customer in some other way.

Defining Quality

The definition of quality is basic to developing a quality improvement programme, since the retailer needs to know what it is trying to achieve. However, there have been many different interpretations of the quality concept (Ghobadian, Speller and Jones 1994). A retailer, therefore, needs to select an approach to quality that recognizes the realities of the retailing process and the complexities of customer demand. One widely accepted definition is:

Quality is conformance to customer requirements.

This definition emphasizes the prime role of the consumer in determining what quality is. It also has a number of implicit aspects that are important for the retailer:

▶ *Quality depends on customer perceptions*. Retailers know that the image and presentation of the store have a significant impact on the perceived quality of products: there does not have to be real differences in product sold at different stores. Managing customer perceptions become an important part of quality management.

▶ *Quality also depends on customer expectations* of what they should get for their money. These expectations vary with the market segments that the retailer is targeting, and they affect the specification and finish of goods, the service setting and customer interaction. The retailer must determine customers' requirements and build them into the retail process, bearing in mind that quality must relate to the service outcome (satisfaction with the products acquired) and the service process (satisfaction with the service encounter).

There have been a number of different approaches to the development of service quality. These follow distinct lines and can be grouped into three different types:

▶ the total quality management approach

▶ the Nordic school

▶ the gap analysis school.

Total Quality Management

Total quality management (TQM) was originally developed in the manufacturing industry but the rapid growth of the service economy led to its highly developed techniques being applied there also. It has a set of straightforward principles that take full account of the process of implementation.

▶ *Quality is conformance to customer requirements.* The retailer has customer-driven quality standards, as discussed earlier. However, TQM requires the retailer to actually determine what these standards should be by doing the appropriate market research. For instance, many people find waiting in queues to be the most frustrating and annoying part of shopping, whether for groceries or for banking services. Supermarkets and banks need to determine an acceptable waiting time – not very long – and include it in their service standards when organizing customer service facilities.

▶ *Quality is company-wide.* Good customer service means more than sales staff being nice and attentive to the customer. The customer will not be happy unless the goods required are available, as with ice cream in a supermarket on a hot summer's day. Management has to be sure that customers can buy their ice cream. It has to forecast demand, buying weather forecasts for the area if appropriate; communicate demand to their suppliers and organize delivery and storage of the ice cream. In order to keep the customer satisfied the whole organization has to be on its toes. It goes further than that. You cannot supply your customers with what they want unless your suppliers do their part. Even visual merchandising requires mannequins, posters and three-dimensional objects to be reliable. This means that everybody should be geared to delivering quality services. This leads to the following rules:

  – *Everyone should be serving a customer or serving someone who is.* This introduces the idea of external and internal customers. Management is about service delivery. Within the organization, management control is a service to staff in general to help members of a team continue to work effectively together.

    – *Teamworking is essential.* Employees work together in delivering the services. The emphasis is on the team rather than on a hierarchy. Traditionally, management is seen at the top of a pyramid with the customers on the bottom. This is turned upside down. Managers now get paid more because they deliver greater service in supporting the workers and the customers.

    – *Self-monitoring of activities is important.* Working properly in a team means that each member of the team takes greater responsibility for his or her own performance.

▶ *Quality comes from the top.* This is a natural consequence of the previous principle. So:

    – *There must be commitment from the top.* Most authors on quality issues accept that at least 80 per cent, and perhaps up to 95 per cent, of problems are caused by bad management, not by bad workers. Managers often forget what quality is about in the day-to-day running of things. There are often problems within the system. However, when things go wrong, managers tend to blame the staff rather than look at their own effectiveness. As Dr Ishikawa pointed out, you can delegate authority to deal with problems but you cannot delegate responsibility for the problem (Ishikawa 1985). Another problem often encountered is that total quality management is often used to set higher standards, but management does not commit the necessary resources to achieve them. Instead of making life better for staff, this makes their employment conditions worse, which naturally leads to worsening of service in the long run. This is why TQM is so hard to implement in practice.

    – *There should be two-way communication.* Greater openness is important in decision-making. Japanese practice introduced the concept that proposals come from the top but are passed down through the company. It is important for the workforce to give detailed consideration to proposals, because they are more likely to have detailed understanding of how to best implement any ideas and whether they would be effective in achieving the desired outcome.

▶ *Zero defects.* This is perhaps one of the most difficult aspects of quality management to find acceptance, but is clearly embedded in its philosophy. It comes from the proposition that:

    – *Quality is free.* Service failure can be costly: the retailer has to pay the cost of re-doing the service or compensating the customer and suffers the loss of profit from customers who do not return or who never come because of the bad reports received. It is cheaper in the long run to ensure that the service is delivered properly by investing in the appropriate technology, procedures and training. This leads to the next rule:

    – *Get it right first time.* This is particularly appropriate for retailers because the inseparability of services means that you usually do not get to check the quality of the service before it is delivered. So the retailer has to plan things carefully to ensure that things go right every time. It may take years to build a reputation but minutes to destroy it. However, errors do occur, despite the best planning because it is difficult to take every factor into account. Rather than relying on periodic and fairly major evaluations of service provision, the retailer should have a positive attitude to the services it gives and implement the rule of

- *Continuous improvement.* This takes place through the implementation of continuous improvement programmes.

(Based on Oakland 1993.)

Total quality management developed within the framework of production and operational management approaches. This has given it a well-developed set of procedures and techniques that can be used to plan service operations effectively. Some of these are discussed later on in this chapter. However, it provides only a partial perspective on quality, because we need to understand more clearly how customers perceive quality. The service marketing approaches considered next help us understand some of the wider factors influencing service quality.

The Nordic School: Service Focus and Dimensions

The Nordic school is so called because its basic ideas were developed in Scandinavia. In this view, customers measure service quality according to the service they expect and the actual service they feel they have received (Grönroos 1984). The quality they expect and receive has three basic dimensions:

▶ *Technical quality of the outcome.* The customer measures the quality of the service in terms of what he or she receives at the end of the service transaction, relative to what the customer required. For instance, could the customer buy what he or she wanted at the hardware store at a reasonable price? The technical quality of the service depends on the technology, technical knowledge, equipment and systems used by the retailer and its suppliers.

▶ *Functional quality of the process.* The customer measures quality in terms of how he or she received the service. For instance, were the products easy to find, were the staff helpful and courteous, could he or she get through the checkout quickly? The functional quality of the service depends on factors such as accessibility, appearance of facilities, long-run customer contacts, internal relations, attitudes, behaviours and service-mindedness of service personnel.

▶ *Retailer image.* This reflects the customer's perception of the retailer. It is affected by technical and functional quality, price levels, external communication, physical location and appearance, and competence and behaviour of the retail staff.

This perspective adds to our understanding of service quality because it stresses the importance of outcome and process, and the importance of the retailer image. The different approaches contained within this school have also been successfully applied to customer care programmes such as with

Scandinavian Airways. However, there are problems in using this to build detailed procedures for improving services. The alternative gap approach has been widely used to develop insights into delivering service quality.

Services Gap Approach

The services gap approach is similar to the Nordic school in that service quality is defined in terms of the gap between customer expectations and the service received. It also sees quality as consisting of different dimensions. However, the approach has gained widespread application because of the development of the SERVQUAL model (Zeithaml, Parasuraman and Berry 1990). This is model for determining empirically the components of quality and conceptualizing the gaps that damage service quality.

The model identifies five dimensions of service quality (Zeithaml, Parasuraman and Berry 1990: 21–2) that the consumer uses to assess the quality of the service. They are: *tangibles*, *reliability*, *responsiveness*, *assurance* and *empathy*. Table 12.1 illustrates these dimensions.

Table 12.1 Service Quality Dimensions

Dimension	Measured by	Examples of questions in the customer's mind
Tangibles: Service is intangible, so the consumer assesses the quality of the service using clues provided by the physical environment	*Facilities* *Equipment* *Personnel* *Communication materials*	Is this an attractive store? Does the decor meet my expectations? Does the store use modern equipment? Does the cold-drinks cabinet really keep drinks cold? Are staff and managers appropriately and smartly dressed? Are direction signs easy to read? Are prices clearly displayed? Are displays interesting and informative?
Reliability: The retailer must do what it says it will do	*Dependability* *Accuracy*	Does/will the retailer deliver the goods on the specified day? Is my television repaired quickly and properly first time?
Responsiveness: Customers feel retail staff treat them as individuals by their helpfulness and individual attention	*Willingness to help* *Promptness in dealing with customer*	Does the sales assistant seem interested in finding what I wanted? When I go into the electrical shop, does anyone come to greet me? Does the supermarket try to keep checkout queues small?
Assurance: The customer needs to feel sure that s/he will receive a good service	*Competence* *Courtesy* *Credibility* *Security*	Can the salesperson tell me more about the different models than I can get from brochures? Can that assistant really help me choose the right perfume? Is the salesperson polite and attentive? Does he or she greet me in a friendly way? Does the salesperson help me and not pressure me to buy? Does the retailer have a good reputation? Can I be confident that salesperson has really helped me buy clothes that suit me best?
Empathy: Customers must feel that the retailer understands them and is on their side	*Accessibility* *Communication* *Understanding*	Is the store open at convenient times? Is there suitable provision for children, and the disabled? Does the computer salesperson explain details at my level? Does the computer salesperson try to understand my needs and what I can afford before advising me on what to buy?

Source: derived from Zeithaml, Parasuraman and Berry 1990

The model also identifies *four internal service-provider gaps* and *one external service gap*. These gaps occur at different stages in the service process. Identifying the service gaps allows management to use appropriate strategies to deal with the problem. Table 12.2 illustrates these service gaps and how the retailer can deal with them.

Table 12.2 Service Gaps

Service gap: the problem	Possible causes	What the retailer can do
Customer expectations – management perceptions gap: What the manager thinks the customer wants is different from what the customer expects	Managers do not have the information to determine what the customer expects. Managers are more concerned with the smooth running of the system than they are with the customer	Improve training of managers. Monitor complaints; use market research such as surveys and focus groups. Scan environment for changes in shopping behaviour and customer expectations
Management perception – service specification gap: Managers do not convert customer expectations into appropriate service specifications	Management lacks resources or sets unclear or unrealistic service standards; management controls may prevent a sales assistant from dealing with customer complaints	Have more open discussion between levels of staff that results in service design standards that serve as a model for all service operations
Service specification – service delivery gap: Retail staff may know the service standards expected but fail to deliver them	Staff insist on inappropriate interpretation of what the customer expects. Staff may lack training or facilities to deliver the service	Have a positive policy on clear communications; provide the resources and technology to facilitate the service; have appropriate staff training
Service delivery – external communication gap: The retailer does not deliver the service promised or implied in advertising or other external communications, such as the store location and positioning	This could be because of staff shortages or unavailability of advertised items	Retail marketers need to monitor promotional material to ensure consistency with the service that is actually being delivered
These four internal gaps lead to the fifth gap:		
The external gap between the customer's expected service and the perceived service: The customer does not believe that he or she is getting the service he or she should be getting	The retailer has not taken sufficient action to balance any internal service gap. The customer's expectations may be unrealistic: it may be too difficult or expensive to provide that level of service	Clearly communicate the service standards provided. Ensure that service staff make all reasonable effort to assure customers that the service is being provided

Source: derived from Zeithaml, Parasuraman and Berry 1990

The SERVQUAL model has been criticized as regards its theoretical perspective on customer satisfaction and the extent to which the five dimensions are really independent of each other. Despite these criticisms, the model provides useful insights into the service process and it, or variants of it, has been widely applied to many services. The model requires some sound empirical investigation to determine what is appropriate for each retailer, but it does indicate a basic direction in which quality programmes can be developed.

12.4 Managing the Service Setting and the Service Encounter

Implementing a service quality strategy requires appropriate management of the customer service environment, as this has a major impact on the customer's perception of service quality. The service environment has two important aspects:

▶ the service setting

▶ the service encounter.

Managing the Service Setting

The service setting is sometimes called the selling environment (McGoldrick 1990). This encompasses a large number of components including the setting itself, the people in the setting – customers and staff – and the merchandise. All these elements transmit coded messages to the customers when they enter the store – and often before they enter the store. They give clues to the customer about the nature of the retailer and the nature of the products that are available. Customers use these clues to guide them in their purchases. These clues are also very important in assuring customers that they have chosen the right place to shop and that they should not have gone down the street to the nearest competitor.

For instance, a high standard of fittings and fixtures in the service setting and an organized and efficient layout suggests a high-quality retailing service. By raising the standard of the service setting, the retailer improves the perceived quality of the service the customers can expect. Raising the standard involves considering the following:

▶ Design factors
  - Tidy and well-organized layouts suggest standards and quality.
  - Distinctive colours such as the Marks & Spencer's green denote reliability and quality (this is perhaps arguable today).
  - Distinctive signs and posters suggest brand image and lifestyles.
  - Technologically based displays imply the retailer is at the cutting edge of fashion or technology.

▶ Direction-finding
  - Clearly marked aisles and pathways provide orientation for the customer, as many stores are difficult to find your way around.
  - Points of reference, such as checkouts in supermarkets or paypoints in other stores provide a home base for customers.
  - Clearly visible entrances and exits to stores and escalators provide vertical circulation and good landmarks.

▶ Store atmosphere
  - Comfortable lighting and temperature levels improve the store environment and customer experience.

– Suitable spatial arrangements allow customers space to move comfortably about, privacy to browse and space to see and be seen as appropriate.

Case 12.5 Targeting the Setting to the Customer: The Emporium

In creating the store atmosphere, we must be careful to target the setting to the customer. We must not overdo things. For example, let us take the case of the Aladdin's cave type emporium. Customers expect all the merchandise to be piled high, and the store to have a dark and dusty, yet intriguing, atmosphere. Some of the merchandise is almost inaccessible and the entrances and aisles are crowded. This gives the store its distinctive feel and character. To obliterate this and replace it with chrome fixtures, functional shelving and high-quality floor covering would destroy the atmosphere and image of the store. The position of the store would then become ambiguous or uncertain and alienate existing customers.

Managing the Service Encounter

The *service encounter* is the period of contact between the customer and the service provider during which the service transaction takes place. It is during this period that the customer buys the product. There are four components that contribute to the service encounter:

▶ the *service setting* (such as furnishings, atmospherics, decor, equipment)

▶ the *service process* (such as routines, stages, complexity, queue length)

▶ the *customers* (such as patrons, clients, patients, guests)

▶ the *service staff* (such as counter staff, bank cashiers, hotel managers, tour guides).

We have already discussed how the service setting can be used in the provision of quality service. The service setting represents the stock of physical assets that is available to good quality services. The service process uses those assets to actually deliver services to the customer. However, as the previous section has shown, delivering good quality services involves managing the customer as well, because customer expectations have a significant effect on the customer's perception of the quality of services. Even today, the great majority of product retailing occurs in the store.

Stores are relatively open places and so service encounters can be high-visibility activities. Therefore, retailers should take account of the presence of other customers as they affect the experiences of all customers in the store. The astute retailer will understand when customers wish for low visibility – such as perhaps discussing the financing of a large purchase – and when they would wish for high visibility – to be seen acquiring or even considering acquiring certain expensive, fashionable or other desirable items. In the same way, the positive buying behaviour of a customer may influence other customers to buy. So the store needs to make its selling successes a visible activity.

These aspects are important in influencing the perceived quality of the service encounter, but we must recognize the varied roles service staff have to take on which become critical to the delivery of top-class service. We can see how important staff are as we envisage the service encounter process. We start from when the customer comes to the door of the store. We follow him or her into the store, through the service process and as he or she leaves having completed a mutually satisfactory deal with the retailer. If the customer does not make successful purchase, we can understand the reasons why so that we can do better next time.

Accessibility

One of the key elements in the service encounter is accessibility. For the basic retail store, it is important that the customer has clear access to the products and the purchasing of the products if the store is to be successful. The ease with which customers can enter the store and move round, locate the cash points and exit the store will have a big influence on their perceptions of the service encounter. Queuing is one of the least satisfying aspects of the purchase. Whether in a supermarket or a clothing store, if the customer has to queue for a long time in order to obtain their chosen products, this lessens the quality of the service experience. A long time in queuing terms need only be less than three minutes – less than two traffic light changes at a busy road junction. Various stores attempt to get round this:

▶ Supermarkets can have many tills that are fully staffed during busy periods.

▶ Catalogue shops such as Argos have a telephone enquiry and reservation system to speed up shopping time.

▶ Shoe shops, particularly specialist upmarket children's stockists (for instance, Clarks stockist with a well-defined and extremely loyal set of customers) may use a ticket system to ensure orderly waiting and to indicate to customers the expected waiting period.

Facilitating the Sale

Customer interaction with staff is important in the service process and the retailer's attitude to customers is an important facilitator of a good service encounter. Often the difference between closing the sale and losing the sale is in the hands of the service or counter staff.

▶ A good counter assistant can make up for failures in the system such as long queues or poor layouts. However, good service is not a substitute for poor or inappropriate merchandise.

▶ Knowledgeable sales staff would not wish to compensate for inadequate merchandise as this would damage long-term relationships with the customer.

▶ Experienced sales staff will understand their customers' needs and wish to maintain a good rapport for the benefit of future business.

The importance of this interaction varies with the type of retailer. It may also be more important for some customers than others. For example, when a customer goes into an electrical retailer like Dixons they expect to have a high degree of customer–staff interaction. In contrast, if the same person chooses to shop in Argos they expect little or no interaction other than for functional reasons such as:

▶ paying for goods

▶ collecting the goods

▶ returning faulty goods

▶ general enquiries.

The key to the success of any retail business is the retention and expansion of customers. Studies have shown that customers who are satisfied with the product are not necessarily going to return. It is the service encounter that makes the difference. It customizes the experience and by making customers feel special helps build customer loyalty. This is recognized by many service retailers such as hotels, restaurants, garages and travel agents. However, use of the service encounter as a means of building customer loyalty is also valid for product retailers.

Case 12.6 Making the Service Encounter Memorable

There are a number of ways of making the service encounter memorable:

▶ *Pleasant greetings*. Making the customer feel comfortable and at home in the store relaxes the customer. A relaxed customer is more likely to buy.

▶ *Good product knowledge*. Customers can open the washing machine and read the basic information but they are unable to access more detailed specifications. Customers expect sales people to provide informed opinions about the brand and its competitors.

▶ *Sensitive attention to detail*. The experienced salesperson knows when to stop with a sale and leave the customer to reflect on the choices. This is particularly important when the purchases affect the family, social or business position of the buyer. Stopping at the right moment increases customer trust and is more likely to generate repeat business.

▶ *Ability to demonstrate alternatives*. Good sales people empathize with their customers. They understand what the customer is looking for and use their knowledge to suggest alternative purchases. For example, customers wishing to buy personal computers may be dazed by the choice available. Good sales people will ascertain customers' needs and only sell them what they require, and make them feel comfortable with what they have bought. This is particularly important where a customer obviously cannot afford a high-specification product.

▶ *Taking the burden of responsibility*. At times purchasing can be difficult for the consumer and the sales person will be asked to take on the role of decision-maker. For example, the fashion store sales assistant will help the customer with words of encouragement: 'That suits you' and 'Try a larger size they aren't very generous'. They will also answer the question: 'Which one do you think I should buy?'

The Impact of the Service Encounter on Retailer Branding and Positioning

The retailer brand consists of lots of different things and when you buy an item from a retailer you also buy a bundle of benefits. The service encounter is an essential part of these benefits and provides:

▶ initial contact with the retailer

▶ prestige or status

▶ confidence

▶ measure of retailer effectiveness

▶ a means of comparing retailers.

In simple terms the service encounter provides the customer with an image of the retailer. The customer retains this mental picture and uses it as a basis for future expectations. Thus, the way the retailer manages the service encounter has a considerable effect on the customer's overall perceptions of the retail offering. For instance, if a customer does not receive the treatment they expect, or there is some other serious failure in the sales encounter, the retailer's brand image suffers. This increases the perceived risk that a repeat visit will be unsatisfactory. The end result may be that the customer uses a competitor.

In addition to the retained image of the retailer, many other factors inform customer expectations. For example, messages about the retailer are received from a number of sources such as word of mouth and advertising messages (as discussed in Chapter 9). These provide the necessary data prior to purchase. When there is a conflict between what the customer believes to be true and what actually happens this can harm the image of the retailer. Ideally, the retailer should project the sort of realistic image that is achievable. Otherwise it risks damage to its reputation, which could alter its position relative to its competitors and so lose it business in the medium and long term.

Improving the Service Encounter

First, it is important to know your customers through using market research. By investigating your customer you will find out their expectations generally, including the type of service they have come to expect. New customers may have different needs and so this has to be built into the service offering.

Advertising creates expectations through the process of communication. The customers recall various elements of the message and these guide their expectations. Retailer promotion should not make promises the retailer is unable to keep. For example, the image of very helpful supermarket packers is often inconsistent with in-store demands and staff available.

Case 12.7 Using Technology to Manage the Service Setting

Modern techniques are available to help retailers to organize and construct the selling environment. Modern sensor devices can be used to collect customer movement data from vantage points in the store. The information can be processed to provide customer data that can be used to construct graphical models of the store. These models include the persons in the setting (staff and customers) and the objects and various components that surround them. Once constructed these models can be used to run a real life simulation of the store. The results of these simulations can be used to fine-tune the setting. A true to life example of a store simulation is available at http://www.itp.co.uk/ for you to download at your convenience.

Source: Church and Newman 2000; Kirkup 1999

Designing and Improving Service Quality

Even small retailers may be able to make quality happen through their intuitive understanding, experience and commitment to customers. However, the complexities of operating a large organization mean that quality needs to be properly planned. This section looks at some of the methods available for improving service quality. It considers three aspects: planning for quality, analysing what goes wrong and making service better.

Planning the Service

Retail service is a process that is an activity which occurs during a period of time. It involves a number of steps such as the customer entering the store, selecting items, purchasing the items and leaving the store. We can draw a map of this process by using a *flow chart*. This shows the links between the different steps of the service process and, in particular, the interrelationships between the service encounter and the activities in the whole service process. Figure 12.1 shows a simplified flow chart for a discount grocery store, where all items are pre-packed and available for self-service (no bakery or delicatessen counters, for instance). Shostack (1984) adapted this technique from operations management and called it *blueprinting* the service process.

The flow chart in Figures 12.1 shows the different customer activities as boxes. The arrows show the sequence of customer actions. The lower area indicates the activities the retailer carries out to meet customer requirements. The lines between the customer and retailer show when the customer interacts with the retailer. This occurs for instance when the customer views the items on display, even though there is negligible direct interaction with staff when viewing displays in a catalogue shop.

The *line of visibility* separates those parts of the process, which involve customer interaction or presence and those where the consumer in not involved. For instance, a mail order retailer may accept an order by telephone. The telephone conversation takes place above the line of visibility. However, processing the order through to delivery of the product does not involve the customer and takes place below the line.

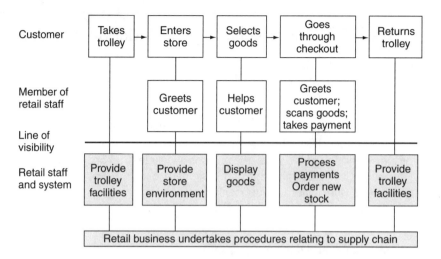

Figure 12.1   The Customer Service Flow Chart

When the activity takes place above the line of visibility, the customer should feel that it is geared to his or her requirements. Staff employed here should be good at working with customers. When the activity takes place below the line of visibility, the customer is not directly involved. The customer does not have to see what is going on, and sometimes the presence of the customer could hinder the activity. The work is done behind the scenes, if possible, so that modern production techniques can improve the quality of the service as much as possible. Staff employed in these areas should have the appropriate administrative and technical skills.

Blueprinting a service is useful in dealing with complex service procedures as it helps break them down into manageable parts. The retailer can use the blueprint to consider the extent to which it should alter the service. The model identifies the strategic choices to be made, such as increasing or reducing divergence and increasing or reducing the complexity of the service. For instance, putting more sales staff in the store helps the retailer give more attention to the needs of individual customers. However, if the greater individual attention increases sales per customer sufficiently, the extra staff will pay for themselves through the higher profit they generate. This is one of the changes Marks & Spencer introduced in 1999 in response to the decline in their market position.

The blueprint can also help the retailer identify *critical control points*. These are the stages in the process where the retailer must make sure everything is right and errors corrected before the next stage of the process is begun, otherwise the next set of activities cannot lead to the desired outcome. For instance, having stock available is critical for displaying the stock, which in turn leads to sales. The blueprint also allows the retailer to set tolerance standards such as time taken and quality of work, taking into account what has to be delivered to the customer at the end.

Service Recovery: Monitoring and Analysing problems

Service recovery is the procedures the retailer use to correct a problem in dealing with a particular customer. When something has gone wrong with the service process, the problem becomes obvious very quickly. The retailer needs to respond to these problems promptly and reliably. This means that sales staff should have the power to make decisions on behalf of retailer with little or no referral to their managers except in serious matters. However, the dissatisfied customer needs to be confident that the retailer will listen to and act on the complaint. They should be reassured that any changes taken will be lasting and management will take the necessary steps to prevent the problem reoccurring. The retailer should, however, monitor the service as part of the process of continuous improvement. This helps to identify significant problems and to deal with them.

Management, Staff and Customers

Service quality can only be effective when there is a tacit partnership between management, staff and customers. Most quality problems stem from bad management. This includes cases of the obstreperous customer. If we ask why the customer is like that, the answer very often is because of fear, frustration or uncertainty. The retailer can develop this partnership by focusing on some key points to improve service:

▶ *Reliability*. This is seen as the most important factor in perceived service quality. Promise only what you can deliver.

▶ *Time*. Time is increasingly valuable; there should be enough staff to meet customer requirements, even in busy periods. People hate queuing.

▶ *Convenience and ease of use.* Customers want staff that can use the necessary equipment, know procedures and have adequate product knowledge.

12.5 Analysing Service Problems: Some Techniques

When evaluating the service delivery system, we need a suitable method of analysis. You will find many techniques in general management texts. Two of the most popular techniques are:

▶ *Pareto analysis*. This is a statistical phenomenon that is crudely summed up by the phrase '80 per cent of problems are caused by 20 per cent of factors'. This may not always be exactly the case, but it indicates a good approach to dealing with a problem. A failure or problem in service delivery will usually have a number of possible causes. However, if the situations are analysed for reason of failure, we will find that perhaps three to five causes account for most of the problems. We should then focus on those, as solving them will make the most effective change in service quality.

▶ *Cause and effect diagram.* This is also known as the fishbone diagram, because if its shape (see Figure 12.2), or the Ishikawa diagram after its inventor. It identifies four major causes of a problem:

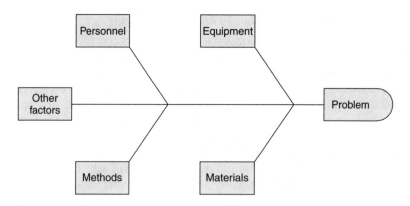

Figure 12.2   Cause and Effect Diagram

- personnel, such as lack of training, lack of attention, insufficient number
- methods, such as cumbersome procedures; orders not processed properly
- materials, such as faulty products
- equipment, such as inadequate number, faulty machines.

Each major cause can be subdivided according to the specific problems.

References

Church, I. and Newman, A.J. (2000) 'Using simulations in the optimisation of fast food service delivery', *British Food Journal*, 102(5/6): 398–405.

Ghobadian, A., Speller, S. and Jones, M. (1994) 'Service quality concepts and models', *International Journal of Quality & Reliability Management*, 11(9): 43–66.

Grönroos, C. (1984) *Strategic Management and Marketing in the Service Sector*, London: Chartwell-Bratt.

Hill, P. (1987) 'The service sector: current state of knowledge and research frontiers', in

H.G. Grubel (ed.) *Conceptual Issues in Service Sector Research: A Symposium*, Vancouver, BC: Fraser Institute.

Ishikawa, K. (1985) *What is Total Quality Control? The Japanese Way*, Englewood Cliffs, NJ: Prentice-Hall.

Kirkup, M. (1999) 'Electronic footfall monitoring: experiences among UK clothing multiples', *International Journal of Retail and Distribution Management*, 27(4): 166–73.

McGoldrick, P.J. (1990) *Retail Marketing*, London: McGraw-Hill.

Newman, A.J. and Atkinson, N. (2000) 'The re-branding of Selfridges: a framework for success', *Management Case Quarterly*, 5(1/2): 13–19.

Oakland, J.S. (1993) *Total Quality Management*, 2nd edn, Oxford: Butterworth-Heinemann.

Shostak, G.L. (1984) 'Designing services that deliver', *Harvard Business Review*, 62(1), January-February: 133–9.

Zeithaml, V.A., Parasuraman. A and Berry, L.L. (1990) *Delivering Service Quality: Balancing Customer Perceptions and Expectations*, Glencoe: Free Press.

Zikmund, W.G. and d'Amico, M. (1993) *Principles of Marketing*, 4th edn, St Paul, MN: West Publishing.

Services Retailing: Creating Tangibility

This chapter covers the following topics:

▶ The nature of service retailing.

▶ Key issues for retail management.

▶ Services and the systems that sell them.

Services Retailing: Creating Tangibility

Introduction and Core Concepts

Retailers selling services face different problems than their counterparts selling tangible goods or merchandise. The service retailer attempts to create *quality*, *value* and *tangibility*, and uses these factors to produce a point of difference. Many types of retail businesses sell services that are difficult to differentiate from those of their competitors. For example, insurance policies and banking account services are much the same wherever they are purchased. However, they may vary in price, standard of quality and the presentation of the service offered. The skill, consequently, lies in the way in which the merchandise is presented and sold. Experienced service retailers capitalize on this and gain competitive advantages.

Consumers tend to look upon services, and the retailers that sell them, in a different way than they might view conventional retailers. Although the nature of the products determines this attitude, it is also the retailers' approach that creates a different set of expectations. In general, customers expect to receive more substantial *evidence* of the suitability, quality and value for money that the service offers. Mainly this is because customers' purchasing services are constantly looking for evidence to confirm their purchase decision. Retailers work to make the intangible tangible and to compete successfully.

13.1 From Service Provider to Service Retailer

One of the more interesting phenomena of contemporary Western culture has been the widespread development of service retailers. Their journey reflects the changing political economic, social technological and cultural changes in Western society. Many of these retailers have grown from old-fashioned service providers and cover a wide range of services, from car repairs to insurance. Until the 1980s many of these service providers operated in highly regulated environments that limited the scope of service they provided. Where they enjoyed a local monopoly position, they were either state or local authority owned, or else they were heavily regulated. Their role was seen to be the provider of a particular service within fairly well-defined boundaries. Even countries such as the USA, regarded as the most market-oriented society at the time, had highly regulated transport, health, utilities and financial services.

The type of service provided was heavily determined by experts without intervention by the consumer. Typically, customers came to the service provider rather than the retailer taking the service to the customer. Services were dispensed from a depot or service centre, which was viewed as a cost centre. The aim was to make these services fit some norm, such as working within a budget or minimizing cost for a given standard of service. Even in the relatively free commercial sector, experts conventionally determined the type and quality of provision. For instance, the chef and the hotel manager through their professional networks, largely controlled what was available even though the customer may have been paying significant amounts of money.

Political, economic and social change have created a more fluid society. In traditional areas of government provision such as health and welfare, the rising cost of providing services has led to governments reducing their commitments and the encouragement of private provision. Service and utilities providers have been privatized or have been forced to accept greater quasi-market factors in order to improve their responsiveness to customer demand.

Large-scale deregulation has changed the focus of service production from cost centres to profit centres. Customer satisfaction became important. Greater mobility, higher incomes and the spread of information provided customers with the means of searching for service provision. Alternative suppliers and alternative forms of service provision appeared and consumers now became customers. Instead of charging consumers for services, the providers now had to sell services to customers.

Some service providers, such as fast food restaurants, operated in relatively free commercial environments, particularly in the USA. This allowed them to expand faster and develop new service provisions in response to commercial opportunities as social attitudes (to eating out, in this case) changed.

Other service providers had yet to make the journey from being transaction processors to a position where they saw themselves as marketing services, and still further to retailing them. Deregulation in the financial services industries came at a time when alternative methods of distribution were developing and retailers were intruding into the provision of financial services. This has led to a major restructuring within the sector. Financial institutions have had to refocus their operations. The traditional bank, for instance, has had to change from a producer-focused transactions operation to marketing a range of service to customers in competition with other financial institutions.

Consumers have also become much more demanding of their service providers. For instance, in the 1970s, when the Post Office was the sole provider of telephone services across most of the UK, obtaining a telephone was a slow and relatively costly process. The pace of investment in new technology was also subject to government approval and buying a telephone was an alien concept. The telephone service was partially privatized in 1984 as British Telecom (BT) and the market was opened up by stages to competition. This has encouraged the adoption of new technology and has provided the customer with a range of options. BT now responded with much greater effort at marketing and customer service.

Impact on Retailing

Service providers have gone further than adopting the marketing of their services. Many have now become service retailers by providing services on a large scale at locations that have responded to customer requirements. The increased demands on consumers' time has altered consumers' use of services. Consumers have also moved away from standardized lifestyles and this has changed their approach to services such as cinemas, swimming pools and travelling. Many of these issues have already been discussed in Chapter 6. Consumers also expect better links between the different types of services provided and the convenience of location. Timing and the service format have become more important. For instance, recreation centres are expected to provide a range of catering and other retail services to provide a fuller experience for the consumer.

This has meant that static retail businesses, once the mainstay of many industrial societies, have become less prevalent. In their place new methods of transaction have emerged.

> ⇨ Static retail business – we use this term to describe the classic retail shop in the high street that sells a variety of products, from holidays to newspapers. To purchase goods the consumer was obliged to travel to generic locations such as town centres. Many of today's retailers respond to movements in customer habits.

The retailer is more likely to reach out to facilitate the consumer, rather than the consumer having to travel to the retail outlet that uses the traditional counter and till. McDonald's and Burger King are two examples of food service retailers that have changed their offerings to suit the changing consumer market. They have also changed their location as new units have moved to suburban areas, retail parks, motorway and railway stations. Other service retailers, such as travel agents and insurance brokers, have made themselves more convenient and welcoming in response to changing market conditions.

Developments in technology and new management skills have contributed to the changes in the retailing of various services. They have also affected the attitudes of managers in the various sectors, who have now become much more retail oriented. For instance, a generation ago, hotel managers saw themselves as hotel professionals. Emphasis was on the special skills and culture of that particular business. The contemporary hotel manager, however, has much greater affinity with other leisure or retail managers and uses similar skills and knowledge in managing his or her establishment (Gilbert and Guerrier 1997).

There are numerous examples of retailers that sell services under various banners. Many are combinations of both the intangible and tangible. For this reason it is often difficult to see the difference between a retailer selling pure services, and one selling a mixture of both services and merchandise. For example, products that some retailers sell have a higher degree of service, or intangible component than the tangible or 'take away' element of the offering.

> ⇨ Services retailers often sell a mix of services and products. A key factor in the service is that the retailer provides some 'takeaway' element for the customer as evidence of quality, competence and value. For example, your own university will more than likely provide you with lots of physical evidence such as student handbooks and manuals.

For example, at car service centres there is a mix of products, such as oil, spark plugs and filters, and the labour time spent performing the service. Labour is the most important aspect of the offering and provides the essential difference between the service retailer and a product retailer that merely supplies the oil, spark plugs and filter. In the case of hotel accommodation, the degree of tangibility is very small and thus relies heavily on the service element to provide the evidence. Table 13.1 should help to bring these issues into focus and provides a guide for the discussion.

Table 13.1 Tangibility and Intangibility in Services Retailing

Retailer	Tangibility	Intangibility	Evidence
Takeaway restaurant	High – the food that the customer takes with them	Low – the retailer is located conveniently and open late	Some – menus and flyers announce the service location
High street insurance broker	Low – the policies are promises and rely on branding and a degree of trust built up over time	High – the provider's reputation is key and accessibility (offices in the high street) is vital	Usually prominent – the retailer relies on various types of advertising and word of mouth
Car maintenance centre	Variable and depends on the nature of the work – items used in the vehicle service and repair will be the tangible components of the service	Tends to be higher – feelings of security and confidence. Customers will tend to rely on results to measure competence	Some promotion and a good deal of word of mouth – the trade name and location are vital. Parts used in the vehicle service and repair will be important evidence
Hotel	Low – guests have the convenience of spending the night and the short-term ownership of quarters or dwelling	High – the dwelling has to be handed back at the checkout time, and the room and facilities are surrendered to other users	Hotels rely a good reputation, strong brands and promotional offers. Free soap, shampoo, coffee and tea in the room
University	Low – the student or customer is educated, has the opportunity to obtain a better career, and a memorable experience	Very high – late opening, drop-ins, workshops, library, counselling, and many other services. The university name will feature highly	Most educational institutions tend to use handbooks, diplomas and prospectuses to provide tangible evidence

13.2 Service retail sectors

When classifying services, it is sometimes difficult to determine the similarities between groups of services and common ways of delivering them. For example, with retail health services there are a number of historic issues that need to be considered. As health treatments have improved, and the systems that deliver them advance, the nature of the offering has changed. In the UK, health services have been production led, with little evidence of the concept of 'customer service'. The movement from technical provision to customer satisfaction has evolved in line with services elsewhere. In hospital waiting areas customer now enjoy high-class facilities, with branded outlets like 'Upper Crust' and McDonald's.

The peculiarities of the different services sold to consumers mean that there are many categories of service provider. However, there should be an underlying similarity between certain types of service retailers. For instance, for many consumers, banks provide quite different services from insurance companies, even though there may be some overlap in the services provided. However, from a consumer perspective, they provide financial services that enable consumers to improve the organization of their financial resources. We can also identify other service retailers, such as theme parks and museums, that appear to provide quite different services, but are basically concerned with a particular aspect of consumers' lives.

It is possible to group services into a small number of categories, according to the purposes for which consumers use the different services. This helps us to develop coherent approaches to their profitable planning and delivery. Table 13.2 illustrates how we can identity various categories of services, based on the type of services provided.

Challenges Facing Service Retailers

The basic commercial problems are similar for service and product retailers, but different responses may be required depending on the nature of the services provided. Competition among service retailers has increased and also changed its nature.

Changes in the regulatory framework and consumer behaviour has forced retailers to face up to competition on the consumers' terms, which may be a quite different perspective from the way service providers have up till now regarded their products.

A rapidly changing consumer environment and new dynamic competitors with innovative formats, may seriously threaten a traditional well-established product retailer such as Marks & Spencer. Similarly, new competitive situations and new forms of competition may also threaten service retailers.

For instance, the commercial and regulatory climate for financial services has been changing since the mid-1980s. This has encouraged competition between traditionally distinct areas of personal and small business finance. Such factors have had a significant impact on traditional high street banks such as Barclays. The changes opened up new

Table 13. 2   Service Retailer by Category of Customer Benefit

Service	Examples of providers
Financial services	Banks; building societies (mutual saving and loans funds)
	Insurance companies; investment companies; insurance brokers
	Investment fund mangers
Leisure services	Sports clubs; sport centres
	Holiday providers; tour operators; travel agents
	Restaurants
	Hotels; holiday camps
	Cinemas, theatres
Health services	GP; hospital; dentist
	Therapist
	Health spas
	Convalescent homes
Education and information services	Schools; colleges
	Libraries
	Specialist publishers
	Computer software manufacturers
Communication services	Telephone companies
	Internet service providers
	Post offices
Personal and repair services	Lawyers; product retailers
	Hairdressers
	Garages
	Domestic appliance repairer

areas for the high street banks and exposed them to competition from other financial institutions. Insurance companies have opened up new banks, using more direct approaches such as the telephone and Internet to attract customers. The credit card is no longer the preserve of the high street bank, and several US banks now offer their credit cards in the UK.

High street banks in the UK have also had to contend with competition from expanding building societies. Several of these building societies have converted into banks, some of which have merged with other banks. The effect of the changes has been to challenge the traditional activities of the high street banks and made it more difficult for them to compete in the growing markets for consumer financial products.

Case 13.1 Retailing Financial Services

The financial service industry today presents a range of overlapping retailers. High street banks (such as Barclays, LloydsTSB, and NatWest) remain at the centre of people's financial lives. Most people have their salaries and wages paid direct into their bank. (before the mid-1980s, it was often by cheque or in cash). They take money out through cash machines (or ATMs – automated teller machines) using their cash (or debit) card.

They pay many of their bills by standing order or direct debit and often transfer money to a savings account at 'the building society' (a mutual saving and loans association). Several building societies (such as the Halifax and the Alliance and Leicester) have converted into banks (sometimes called 'mortgage banks'), though they are not yet regarded in the same way as the traditional high street banks such as Barclays and LloydsTSB.

Banks these days offer a wide range of savings and loans vehicles, often as good as or better than alternative suppliers do. However, the banks still need to overcome their intimidating image for many people. This has led them to improve their store setting and visual merchandising.

Banks have also had to contend with the movement of large retailers, such as Tesco and Marks & Spencer, into banking and related financial services. These retailers have exploited the high consumer trust in their retail brand name to extend into financial services. They have also used their lower overheads and better costing to provide better deals for customers than available at high street banks or building societies.

Banks, on the other hand, have also expanded into other areas. Some banks have acquired or established mortgage banks, life insurance companies and estate agencies. Sometimes they have continued to operate them under their own established brand names. The latter have not always been successful and some banks have divested themselves of estate agents with heavy losses. Direct Line (owned by the Royal Bank of Scotland) is one example of a new approach to selling that has been highly successful. The company has used telephone selling to become the country's biggest motor insurer and led to a major change in the marketing and selling of insurance, now being extended into loans and mortgages. Consumers can now buy new and used cars through its website (http://www.directline.co.uk) which directly links the customer to its car sales subsidiary Jamjar (http://www.jamjar.com). The website works in conjunction with traditional suppliers. It has also partnered the large franchised dealer, Dixons, to offer car leasing through its fuel and go scheme.

Changes in the competitive environment have also occurred in other service sectors. For instance, tour operators and agents have had to respond to EU regulations designed to improve customer protection and increase competition. Many tour operators introduced direct booking services over the telephone or Internet with their 2000 brochures that they placed with travel agents. Faced with this challenge, travel agents have increased their customer awareness and focused on the need to improve the service they can offer the customer.

Museums also reflect the changing environment. Museum managers have been under increasing pressure since the late 1980s to attract larger and more diverse audiences. Most museums still rely on large subsidies, even those that charge for admission. However, they have to actively compete for funds against other areas of central or local government expenditure, by increasing their visitor numbers and achieving higher levels of customer satisfaction. This has forced museums to operate according to more commercial criteria and provide experiences that are more in tune with consumer standards and values (Goulding 2000).

Commercial and consumer pressures have also influenced the UK health sector. British consumers are now more aware of the limitations of the National Health Service and are supplementing the basic state provision with private facilities. Most provide for this through insurance companies, such as PPP. The insurance company often mediates in the choice of provider and this puts pressure on private health suppliers to improve customer satisfaction for the patient and lower costs for the insurance provider. Dentistry, however, is a part of the health service where the subsidy to the customer is relatively low and dentists have some freedom over the prices set, and level of care provided. Consequently, a more customer-oriented approach has become necessary in the area of health provision.

Competitive Advantage in Changing Consumer Markets

Retailers need to base the offering around the consumer. However, the intangibility and complex nature of the services provided make it difficult for the retailer to clearly identify its specific market. A service must, by definition, include some personal element prized by the customer. The customer is more sensitive to these aspects because they make the service more individual, at the same time reducing price sensitivity.

The services retailer should undertake research to identify those aspects that consumers regard as important This enables the retailer to identify its competitors better and thus focus more effectively on defining and improving its competitive advantage. However, service retailers also face fragmented and fickle consumer markets, particularly in areas such as financial services (Devlin and Ennew 1997). This creates problems for financial services retailers, because their relatively structured and orderly approach may make it difficult for them to compete effectively across a range of increasingly fragmented market sectors (Dawes and Brown 2000).

Service retailers, like product retailers, must also compete on a mix of price, convenience, quality and service. The convenience factor means that location is also an important element in choosing a service provider. Modern service retailers have responded to this by relocating to popular shopping areas and out of town areas (Jones and Pal 1998).

Retailing health or financial services also entails high involvement purchases that need careful planning and ongoing relationships. Encouraging impulse buying can damage reputation in the long term and may lead to regulatory fines, civil law suits or criminal prosecution.

Case 13.2 Boots Venture into Services Retailing

Boots is yet another product retailer that has moved into services. The company opened two Health and Beauty Stores in 2000. These combined beauty treatments with traditional Boots shops. In 2001 the company announced plans for a number of stand-alone health and fitness sites. These will extend the services offered in its Health and Beauty Stores to include a fitness suite, swimming pool, sauna and spa.

Another problem for many service retailers is that consumer markets are often mixed in with business markets and this adds to the difficulty of serving customers effectively. For instance, business-class (four-star) hotels in major cities, such as Leeds, usually enjoy high occupancy rates during the week, but have lower occupancy rates at the weekend. Hoteliers can use discounted packages to encourage the weekend leisure visitor as well as the use of facilities for local markets. The challenge is to provide suitable facilities for these growing markets without significantly raising costs.

13.3 Developing and Promoting the Service

The retailer needs to adopt a strategic approach to developing the service and maintaining its long-term acceptability. One aspect that some retailers need to develop is the branding of the service.

Branding is increasingly important in service retailing. The migration of retailers such as Tesco, Marks & Spencer and Boots into financial and health services demonstrates the power of brand extension. Some service retailers, such as McDonald's and Pizza Hut, have powerful brands that establish their position within the sector. Pizza Hut's distinctive logo is so well established that it has successfully resorted to legal action to prevent similar logos being used in signage and even in menu design. The McDonald's brand has been powerful enough to support the company as it developed its store format beyond its original burger service to its broad-based family restaurant image.

The major banks have also felt the need to extend the power of their brand in order to compete effectively in the market. However, several of the larger ones do not have powerful enough brands to support their development in the wider market for consumer financial services. Many of them have expanded under other names. For instance, Lloyds Bank retained the positive image of the Cheltenham and Gloucester brand when it acquired the former building society. However, when Lloyds and TSB merged into Lloyds TSB, the two parts retained their separate identity for some time. A separatist policy was also adopted for a period by the Hong Kong and Shanghai Banking Corporation when they acquired the Midland Bank. However, international development and the need to update the Midland's declining image in the UK led to the bank renaming itself HSBC. This partly followed the trend to use initialisms, company titles and logos, but it also helped the bank create a new identity in developing its international operations in areas not immediately connected with the original activity.

Branding has also played a part in the development of budget hotels. From the time the concept was introduced into the UK in 1985, budget hotels have emerged as one of the future formats in tourist accommodation. Originally introduced as a no-frills product charging basic flat-rate room prices, budget hotels have been attracting increasing numbers of business travellers and families. In line with these changes, the format has moved upmarket. The emphasis has switched from low-cost to value-for-money accommodation. Budget hotel chains are using highly visible signage and on-site branding to promote themselves. As the market has been developing, budget hotel companies have been extending their brands. For instance, Comfort Inns of the USA has established a range of brands, initially through franchises with Friendly hotels.

Other leisure retailers have renamed or rebranded themselves to develop their markets. The media, hotel and catering conglomerate Granada acquired Compass Catering in 2000. The merged company Granada Compass sold the hotels that Granada had previously acquired and then announced in 2001 its demerger into the catering group Compass, and the media company Granada. Compass is now rebranding its motorway service areas.

Promoting the Brand

The service retailer can promote the brand in various ways just like a product retailer. However, it is important to promote the service in an appropriate way and to those consumer groups that most influence decisions. For instance, children tend not to influence decisions regarding bargain break holidays. However, there are many aspects of leisure activity where they do have significant influence. Similarly, children are unlikely to take part in major financial decisions, but provision for children will influence parents' decisions about insurance and investments.

Case 13.3 Pester Power in Services Retailing

Service retailers are having to adapt the ways in which they promote their services, as family life continues to change and children get wise to methods of advertising. Fewer children later in life and dual income households means more leisure spending by families and a greater say for children on how money is spent. For example:

▶ A Butlins TV campaign use the strapline 'Come to Life, Come to Butlins' while showing a bored family transformed into a lively happy group of individuals, especially the children, on holiday at Butlins.

▶ Fast food operator KFC targets kids meal promotions at children aged 3–8 years. It also has a kids website, www.krazyforchicken.com. This has interactive games and competitions and is linked to the main company website at kfc.co.uk.

Leisure marketers also use links to children's characters, especially those that have a broad appeal across the family, to sell their products. However, they recognize that children eventually become bored with one gimmick and soon demand something more exciting.

Source: Michalczyk 2001: 15

Linking Developments: Managing the Mix

Service retailers can take a proactive approach to commercial developments. For instance, several relatively prosperous towns have schemes to attract people to move back into the town. These schemes mix retail units, leisure facilities and residential developments together. The planned Plaza 21 scheme in Swindon is a typical mixed-use development scheme. It is near to the main retail area and provides the sort of mix, including a health club, that would appeal to young professional living in the upmarket residential units (Perry 2001: 10).

Spectator sports have changed and have become a very competitive business. A club's success is built round the performance of its team. High-profile clubs incur significant costs in attracting the high-quality professionals required to generate competitive success. In order to meet these costs, the football or other club has to be a wide-ranging commercial enterprise. It has to undertake relevant merchandising and make good use of its fixed asset, the stadium. Fulham Football Club, is typical of the club that seeks to go further. It has plans to develop its ground to provide its supporters with off-pitch entertainment as well, using state-of-the-art technology. It will also open a new walkway by the Thames to provide spectacular views over the river.

13.4 Managing the Store

Services are fundamentally different to manage than conventional retailing. The intangible component means that retail store managers have to try that much harder to produce evidence of high standards and value for money. Even though some services are sold over the telephone from remote locations, for the purposes of this section we intend to discuss them as if they were conventional retail stores. This will make it easier to relate the various factors that influence the retail customer experience.

In conventional stores the merchandise arrangements and promotional displays tempt the customer, and provide very important clues about the nature of the offering. For example, when customers enter a grocery store they expect to *see* the fresh vegetables and fruit they have come into the shop to buy. The same shoppers will also expect to touch the produce and place the items in their shopping basket. When shopping for items of clothing or any other tangible product the same rule or situation applies. Services are intangible and are therefore by definition impossible to handle. However, in some cases there are aspects of the general offering that may be tangible, and therefore possible to handle.

Many retailers selling services have either set in place, or sell anyway, a number of tangible features. For example, Interflora, the UK florist, sells a mixture of services and products. The flowers are the tangible part of the offering and both the delivery and wrapping service are the intangible element. The store is arranged with fresh flowers to attract the customer, and this merchandise is available to the customer to take away or for delivery direct to another party. Service personnel provide an important function and their interaction with the customer make the service experience more pleasant. They also provide gift-wrapping and other important service items. In sharp contrast to this type of retailer the travel agent with an office in the high street sells mainly services. However, even the travel agent selling holidays and transportation provides tangible evidence of the transactions. Colourful brochures and ticket wallets help the customer to feel that they have in fact purchased something other than a promise.

The Setting: Raising Legibility

The physical evidence provided by the setting is a major part of the retail experience for the customer. In services retailing it is more important for management to provide visual information than in the conventional store. Take, for example, an accountant's office that offers a range of services to retailers. The retailer or customer will use things they see in the setting to evaluate such issues as quality, experience, efficiency and the likely cost of the service. A shabby suite of offices that are poorly organized with little or no customer service will generally indicate a low-cost fairly inefficient operation (Bitner 1990; 1992). The same could be said for the estate agent in the high street or the hairdresser shop. Retailers that sell services must raise the legibility of the setting to turn promises into something more certain.

> ⇨ Legibility – in this context we mean to make the store environment more noticeable. Introducing desirable features that symbolize key attributes such as quality, efficiency, experience and, of course, price can do this. Making the customer contact areas more noticeable will improve the customer's perceptions of the retailer and raise expectations at the same time.

There are many ways to change the store environment, some of which are covered in Chapter 11. A simple solution is to increase the level of space available to the customer by improving the waiting and reception areas. Refurbishment of seating, floor coverings and general decorations may be enough to alter customers' expectations of the retailer. Enhanced signage and the provision of tangible evidence of customer service are all evidence of quality.

Case 13.4 A Sprinkling of Reality Evokes the Holiday Experience

Some travel agents have gone to extreme lengths to counter the competitive effects of the Internet, and the attraction of on-line holiday bookings. For example, when Travelworld opened its third holiday superstore at Birstall retail park in West Yorkshire, its main aim was to create the most exciting retail travel experience.

Travelworld has created a store atmosphere that recreates holiday memories, and encourages customers to think about holidays to come. Some of the in-store attractions include a three-dimensional fixture that house video screens showing holiday destinations. Fibre-optic lighting features show scenes from a selection of capital cities, and areas are provided where customers may relax and absorb the atmosphere. Amongst the features in the store is a mock up of a train that holds 300 brochures in its four carriages. Emphasis is placed on customer experience and raising the legibility of the setting.

Source: Davis 2000: 14.

Stores that operate remotely are unable to show evidence or cues to the customer and are obliged to send these messages by other means. When financial services companies sell products to the consumer they often do so over the telephone, by post and via the Internet. The tangible cues they rely on are not as easy to establish as those found in static (bricks and mortar) retail stores. No deep-pile carpets are available and no upmarket furniture is on show to the customer. Instead, the retailer relies on evidence that they can send to the customer and recommendations by word of mouth. Recommendations by other consumers are crucial for all retailers but more so for services retailers. This is because of the intangible nature of services, which makes them much more difficult for consumers to evaluate compared with the merchandise that is placed in shopping baskets. Retail brands play a large part in providing the level of confidence needed for the customer to buy services and reduce feelings of uncertainty.

> ⇨ Services retailing brands and trusted names help customers to identify and choose between disparate offerings. For instance, when a customer orders takeaway food over the telephone they take the risk that the food will arrive when they want it and be of the desired quality. Paying for the food on arrival resolves only part of the risk, as the food may be inedible.

Strong brands and good reputations help customers through the decision-making process. If the local takeaway outlet is always reliable and offers quality and value for money, the customer will return. This principle applies throughout services retailing which is an area of retailing that relies heavily on reputation and image.

People and the Offering

Frequently it is the efforts of the service providers or sales people that customers experience prior to purchase that provides the only tangible evidence of the standard of services offered. These encounters with the retailer (service providers are an extension of the retailer) can make the difference between a good or bad impression. As we discussed in Chapter 6, customers evaluate alternatives and weigh up the various benefits of using services. They search for clues about the retailer and evaluate issues such as experience, credibility and ability to deliver the service. The performance of retail staff are therefore indicators of competence, and provide the insurance that customers *search* for in an attempt to eliminate risk.

> ⇨ Because services are intangible they are more risky. Customers must place trust in the retailer to deliver what they say they will. After all, how can the consumer be certain that the insurance or telephone company will deliver the service? Often consumers depend on their evaluations of the manner and knowledge of the sales agent who sells the service. Branding helps to reinforce the decision.

Retailers that sell products remotely, and are unable therefore to use the benefits of the physical setting, use their service personnel to reassure the customer that promises will be met. For instance, personnel are trained to make customers feel confident that each stage of the service will take place. Attentive sales staff ensure that no aspect of the service is neglected and reassure the customer that their decision to purchase was the right one. This interaction with the customer is very important and removes the sterility of remote selling. It also reintroduces the emotional side of purchasing, and this makes customers more attached to the service offered by the retailer.

Variability

The standard of service and interaction that the salesperson provides will vary from encounter to encounter.

> ⇨ The importance of service encounters – the all-important interaction between the retailer's representative and the customer can make the difference between satisfaction and dissatisfaction, or customer loyalty and loss of business.

This is because sales people are human and have the same feelings and emotions as the customers. For instance, the salesperson may have a headache or just handled an angry customer, and is therefore unable to offer the same helpful and interested approach to the service. Training helps to standardize service encounters and a strong team will generally lead to satisfied customers and repeat business. However, the calibre of sales people is also a factor and management is wise to maintain competitive levels of pay and working conditions. Services retailing is a high-contact business and relies greatly on a loyal dedicated team of sales people. This entire process is called the *delivery system* and is a crucial part of services retailing. If the delivery system breaks down the customer is not served, and retailers are obliged to constantly make adjustments and improvements. However, the system includes more than just staff. It includes other processes that convey the service to the customer.

Processes: Making Purchasing Easier

Accessibility

At its simplest, the service is a form of contact. For instance, the holiday flight has to be booked and this is usually accomplished by visiting a travel agent, ringing a number or visiting a website. The customers must be able to access this service and make contact with a service provider or services retailer. Accessibility is therefore a key factor and retailers must ensure that their products are readily available. This entails having a reliable and easy to use access point. Service retailers usually have many ways that customers can access their products. These may include some or all of the following:

► high street store

► Internet site with transactional capability

▶ telephone call centre with free or low-cost dial up for the customer

▶ television sales site with access through text based database (for example, in the UK Teletext).

Queuing

With services, a major part of customer time may be spent queuing to make contact with sales personnel. This is the point in the transaction when customers typically become impatient and can decide to shop elsewhere rather than wait for attention. Most types of shopping require customers to form queues of some sort. Buying products at the supermarket, for example, involves queuing at the checkout. Customers expect this and plan accordingly. With services the queue may take place at the end of the telephone while a customer waits for the retailer's salesperson to answer. Alternatively, there may be a tiered or staged system that the customer is required to navigate through, using the numbers on the telephone to select various options. Insurance and other service providers use this type of system to reduce the perceived length of the queue. Customers are shunted from department to department based on their own selections. In theory, this reduces the length of queuing time in the mind of the customer. This is important as the time spent queuing is generally associated in the mind of the customer with poor quality service.

Processes must be managed efficiently to ensure that overall process is made as easy as possible for the customer to use. It is also important that the customer has clear access to the service product if the service experience is to be successful.

Case 13.5 Chester Zoo: A Matter of Process

Most of us take a family day out to the local zoo for granted, but it can become quite complicated as it may involve a number of different processes. These can make the difference between mum, dad and the kids enjoying themselves or a nightmare of obstacles that make for a disastrous day out.

For instance, a family visit to Chester Zoo may start when they arrive at the zoo but are unable to park their car. Sufficient spaces must be available and the car park should be within easy reach of the entrance gates. Queues at the zoo entrance can be very wearing for a family, so the gates and processes they encounter when purchasing tickets

should be as easy as possible to deal with. After obtaining their tickets, and starting the tour, signage must be in place to show them where each segment of the attraction is located. Places like rest rooms, cafés and animal attractions must be clearly signposted. To make the visit as enjoyable as possible, tour guides and experts should be available at specific points to provide the educational and informational part of the service experience. Finally, the gift shop provides the family with souvenirs, and thus the memories and tangible aspects of the visit. Chester Zoo provides a great day out.

Perishability

The ease with which customers can enter a system and move round to the point where they can purchase the service, will influence their perceptions of the service encounter. Take for example the retailer selling a plumbing service. If the customer is obliged to join an extended and complex queuing process before speaking to, or obtaining someone who can arrange a service call, this tends to lessen the quality of the service experience. Moreover, they are more inclined to shop elsewhere next time. Purchasing an airline ticket is a case in point. Airlines have maximized the use of information technology to ensure a high standard of customer facilities with minimum customer waiting time.

The reservation systems used by major airlines are highly sophisticated customer facilities. They offer advance booking for the customer and measure issues such as yield and capacity for the retailer. Because services are produced and consumed at the same time this is important. Tracking production leads to reductions in losses due to unsold seats. Services are perishable and cannot be stored.

13.5 Delivering the Service

Using Price Differentials to Manage Demand and Capacity

The level of demand for services varies during the day, week and year. For instance, trains are crowded during the morning and evening rush hours as people travel to and from work. City centre hotels are busy during the week as people travel on business, but are quiet at the weekend. Some popular country hotels, on the other hand, are busy at weekends but are quiet during the week. Holiday resorts are busy during the summer and quiet during the winter.

This makes the service store busier at certain times and not so busy at others. A product retailer can vary the level of staffing and the amount of stock produced in order to provide customers with the required level of service. Many product retailers also offer discounts on their merchandise at various times of the year in order to maintain the level of customer interest. The service retailer can also manage staffing levels to maintain required service levels. However, the perishability of the services provided means that the service cannot be stored. For instance, a 50-(bed)room hotel has 50 rooms available every night, whether it has any customers or not. If only 30 people want accommodation on Sunday night and 70 people want accommodation on Monday night, the hotel has a problem. It cannot save the unused 20 rooms from Sunday to satisfy all its customers on Monday. In effect the hotelier is paying for and maintaining part of the hotel that he or she is not using for a lot of the time. This situation is typical of many service situations and it is the equivalent of a fashion store buying new stock every day and throwing away anything that is not sold by the end of the day. In some cases, demand varies so much that some facilities, such as theme parks and seaside hotels, shut down for several months of the year.

A hotel can reduce some of its costs by varying the level of staffing according to changes in the level of demand, although it may not be able to do so over the whole year. However, it can improve its profits by maintaining a more consistent level of demand for its facilities. General improvements in marketing can help in this direction.

However, one of the more useful ways of managing demand and profitability is to use *differential pricing*. Differential pricing varies the price charged according to the level of demand and type of customer. Price cuts should always be effectively promoted and they should only be made when the retailer expects the extra sales to increase revenue more than costs.

There are three techniques that the retailer may use: cost-based differentials, discounts for special groups and off-peak pricing.

Cost-based price differentials occur when there may be clear differences in supplying the services, as with servicing different types of car. Other service retailers may charge according to labour time used in providing the service.

Discounts for special groups are often used to improve the level of demand and profitability of the service. Some groups of consumers, such as families, may be more price sensitive than others. Charging lower prices to these groups of customer increases sales and profits. The retailer can build these different groups of customers into its long-term business plans. However, in the short term, the retailer will only offer these reductions if it has spare capacity, usually outside its busiest periods.

In order to make its discount policy work, the service retailer has to be able to identify appropriate groups. Price sensitivity is often related to income per head, which is why cheaper rail travel is offered to family groups. A similar scheme is practised at visitor attractions where children enjoy reduced rates during holiday periods.

Retailers often use *off-peak pricing* when there are regular variations in demand during a day, week or year. A retailer may for instance lower prices to encourage demand during quiet periods and raise prices to discourage demand during busy periods. Other examples of this practice are happy hours in pubs (time of day), cheaper room rates at the weekend in city hotels (time of week) and cheaper holidays during spring and autumn (time of year).

Case 13.6 Weekend Break Packages

A weekend break package is usually a mixture of off-peak and discount pricing. The off-peak pricing occurs because the price is usually based on the weekend rates opposed to the midweek rate. However, the price is reduced further still for staying two or three nights instead of one. Someone who stays for one night only is less price sensitive than the weekend-breaker, because they probably have to be in that area. People who take weekend breaks, however, are usually there for a mini-holiday. They are usually much more price sensitive, because:

▶ the weekend break is usually a second, third or fourth holiday and has to compete more strongly with other consumer products

▶ the holidaymaker spends some time looking for alternative locations and packages.

Off-peak pricing is based on the fact that the retailer has a limited capacity, such as the number of hotel bedrooms. When the hotel is busy, the opportunity cost of using a bedroom is very high, because every room can turn a profit for the night. However, when the hotel has spare rooms, the only cost of letting them is the small cost of servicing them. So it is more profitable for the hotel to let the rooms very cheaply, as long as it can cover this variable cost of servicing the rooms.

Discounts can also be bundled as part of a special package deal, such as weekend breaks. These special deals are widely used in leisure services. They are not necessarily aimed at lower-income groups, but at people who might easily spend their money elsewhere. Cheaper haircuts for pensioners on a certain day of the week are a mixture of discounting (low-income group) and off-peak pricing (because the hairdresser is not as busy on certain days).

Waiting a long time for a service discourages customers. So when a hairdresser charges pensioners less on Tuesdays, this is not just to encourage them to use the service more often. This practice also shifts some demand to another day and reduces waiting times for other customers.

Case 13.7 Using Special Discounts

There are a number of ways in which the retailer can apply discounts without losing profit from other customers. The retailer needs to use some means of identifying the more price-sensitive group. It can do this in various ways:

1 *By low income per head.* Students, pensioners and young families tend to fall into this category. The retailer can use various ways of identifying people who would respond to discounts by:

2 *Tagging the customer:* for instance, issuing a student card or family rail card. The card also prevents resale of the service, for example, a travel ticket.

3 *Using a visible identifier*, such as a child, to identity more price-sensitive groups. Hotel and travel companies offer children reduced rates when accompanying parents. They can sometimes limit the discount by offering reduced facilities so that only the most price sensitive will take them up, while well-off families will pay full price for better facilities. Retailers may also restrict the use of discounts to relatively quiet periods; otherwise they may risk turning away full-price customers. They can also restrict the geographic availability of discounts.

4 *Quality or category of the product.* People who are more time pressured will more likely pay for first-class travel on trains because they can use their laptops and they want to travel in higher levels of comfort.

Customizing the Service: Balancing Cost and Value

Services are relatively labour intensive and expensive to produce. The rising standard of living makes customers want a higher standard of service, to match their general lifestyle. Employees also want to receive higher levels of pay. These factors make the delivery of appropriate services increasingly expensive. This leads to changes in the way consumers want their services delivered and in the way that the retailer delivers them. In particular, retailers have to be more effective in tailoring their services to individual customers. They also have to fulfil services using less staff, which tends to reduce the level of service provided. The retailer can deal with these twin problems through the appropriate planning of its services.

Chapter 12 discussed the ways in which product retailers can standardize the services they offer to customers, while maintaining individual service to customers. Service retailers can apply the same principles in planning rather more complex services. As many as possible of the basic elements of the service, such as preparation, paperwork, processing and repair activity, should be done behind the scenes. Those elements that are special to the customer should be made as visible and as high profile as possible to increase their value to the customer.

Many retailers are using technology to encourage self-service among customers. In many cases, this actually improves the value to the customer because it increases the sense of freedom that the customer enjoys or expects.

Case 13.8 Standardizing Service Production Processes

When McDonald's identified growth in demand for a chicken alternative to beef, it needed a product that fitted in with the company's basic processes and could be cooked and served in the company's outlets without disturbing existing processes. The result was the McChicken chicken burger. Another response was the chicken nugget – dissimilar to the beef burger but retaining similar ease of handling.

Staffing and Quality

Service retailers have to recruit and train appropriate sales people and technical personnel. Some technical personnel, such as information technology (IT) specialists, may be recruited from a broad field, while others, such as hotel accountants, require specialist knowledge. However, service retailers must also hire and train people with the technical skills required to deliver the service. In some cases, such as car servicing, staff require physical skills and technical knowledge. In other cases, such as retail banking, staff need to be able to use modern credit-scoring techniques in order to manage the customer base. Service retailers have to ensure proper training so that technical staff understand customers even if they do not meet them. For instance, the car mechanic must be able to service the car without leaving dirty thumbprints. The financial adviser needs to be able to manage the client's expectations so that a positive outcome for both parties is achieved.

Quality is in the mind of the consumer. Quality also means different things in different situations. Tender loving care is what makes for good quality service for a hospital patient, and the patient does not always want to have to make contact with the staff. However, in other situations, being left alone is what people may require. For instance, in a museum, there is a very different social setting. The construction of displays and the deployment of staff should provide an appropriate balance between presentation, which decides what visitors see and learn, and exploration, where visitors find out for themselves (Goulding 2000).

References

Bitner, M.J. (1990) 'Evaluating service encounters: the effects of physical surroundings and employee responses', *Journal of Marketing*, 54, April: 69–82.

Bitner, M.J. (1992) 'Servicescapes: the impact of physical surroundings on customers and employees', *Journal of Marketing*, 56, April: 57–71.

Davis G. (2000) 'Travel agents come a long way', *Retail Week*, 18 August: 14.

Devlin, J. and Ennew, C.T. (1997) 'Understanding competitive advantage in retail financial services', *International Journal of Bank Marketing*, 15(3): 73–82.

Gilbert, D. and Guerrier, Y. (1997) 'UK hospitality managers past and present', *Service Industries Journal*, 17(1): 115–32.

Goulding, C. (2000), 'The museum environment and the visitor experience', *European Journal of Marketing*, 34(3/4): 261–78.

Jones P. and Pal, J. (1998) 'Retail services ride the waves', *International Journal of Retail and Distribution Management*, 26(9): 374–6.

Michalczyk, I. (2001) 'Kids, the key to family spend', *Leisure and Hospitality Business*, 4 June: 15.

Perry, C. (2001) 'Jewel in Wiltshire's crown', *Leisure and Hospitality Business*, 31 May: 10.

Business Operations: Financial Development

C H A P T E R

14

This chapter covers the following issues:

► The risks and financial requirements of firms during their early stages.

► The structure of the business.

► Investment activity.

► Financial planning.

Business Operations: Financial Development

Introduction and Core Concepts

In this chapter the image of the life cycle has been applied to retail businesses. This sees firms going through various stages of development from the young, vigorous and market-sensitive firm to the mature, cumbersome organization that cannot keep up with changing markets and gives way to or is absorbed by a younger more vigorous organization. However, many businesses do not make it beyond those vital first few years, because they lack the experience or expertise to deal with many of the problems that they encounter on the way.

14.1 Risks and Financial Requirements of a Business during Development

Small Firms in the Retail Industry

There are many small businesses in all sectors of the retail industry. Some of these are not registered for VAT and so are not included in official data. Even so, there were more than 200 000 firms in the retail industry in 2000 (Table 14.1), which was a significant decrease in the number of firms during the previous ten years.

Table 14.1   Number of Firms: VAT-registered UK Retail Businesses by Turnover

Turnover £000	1990	% of firms	2000	% of firms
1–99	135 241	53.6	70 460	35.1
100–499	101 531	40.2	104 190	51.9
500–999	9 849	3.9	15 815	7.9
1000–4999	4 846	1.9	8 830	4.4
5000 +	933	0.4	1 500	0.7
	252 400		200 795	

Source: National Statistics 2000a

The relative decline in the number of small business matches their declining share of retail sales, as illustrated in Table 14.2. These data are slightly affected by the reclassification of small and large firms by the Office of National Statistics during this period, which increased the upper sales limit for small firms to £5 million a year. This accentuates the decline in small firms. The final column shows that the change in sales at current price compared with the change in retail price index. Sales by small firms did not keep up with the increase in retail prices, which means that there was fall in the quantity of goods sold through small retail businesses.

Table 14.2 Sales of UK Retail Businesses at Current Prices (£000m)

| | 1990 sales | | 1997 sales | | % change |
	£000m	% of sales	(£000m)	% of sales	
Small businesses	41.4	32.3	42.6	23.9	2.9
Large businesses	86.6	67.7	135.6	76.1	56.6
Total	128.0	100.0	178.2	100.0	39.2
Retail Price Index 1990 = 100	100.0		126.0		26.0

Source: National Statistics 2000b

Most small firms are unincorporated businesses (see Chapter 1, section 1.4). Many have a limited life expectancy and a high exit rate from the industry. Therefore the development of these firms should be considered in the light of these telling statistics.

The Stages of Development of a Small Firm

The development experience of many retail businesses conforms to the following model:

▶ start up

▶ expansion

▶ maturity

▶ decline.

This model is illustrated in Figure 14.1, which describes the life of the firm over time and shows the progress of sales over this period. Using this model we can consider various functions within a typical retail organization in relation to the progress of that organization over its life. The model assumes that a retail business will reach a point at which it has to reappraise its direction, and renew itself. This is termed the *decline*, but in reality it is a point in the life of the company where new directions and strategies are adopted. In 1998/9, for example, Marks & Spencer had reached this juncture and saw the need to change its direction. This involved changing its merchandise, store formats and even store locations. For completeness we will start at the conception stage of the retail life cycle and work through the process to the later stages.

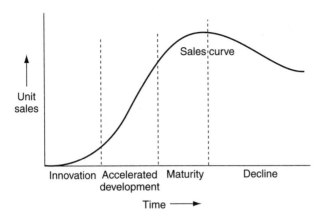

Figure 14.1   The Retail Life Cycle

Getting Started or Innovation

The major problems for most businesses come in the start-up phase. The would-be retailer often risks many thousands of pounds in cash during the first two years of operation, plus the loss of alternative income from working elsewhere. Many entrepreneurs suffer the loss of free time, as they may have to work a 12 to 14 hour day, seven days a week, during the initial period. These same entrepreneurs provide the momentum and creativity to set up the business and make it different from other competitors. Usually the young retail firm takes the lead in a field, such as the mobile phone retailers who first provided a distinct and innovative retail format and merchandising technique in their class. The Carphone Warehouse is one such retailer, which improved the selection available but also provided the badly needed customer advice in a technically challenging marketplace. This was backed up with a customer service guarantees and after-sales service for each purchaser of a mobile phone (http://www.carphonewarehouse.com).

At the start-up of any business finding suitable investment is crucial and key to the success of the venture. Investors and lenders such as banks and finance companies risk large sums of money but require a good business plan on which to base that risk. This is because experience has shown that too many firms go out of business within the first two years because their expectations about demand, costs and cash flow are overoptimistic. Some of these failures are genuine bad luck cases, but most failures could be predicted from the beginning. For example, choosing a bad location for the store or overestimating the customer demand can have a disastrous effect on a new business. This is symptomatic of small and inexperienced retailers. These people tend to focus on those issues with which they are familiar such as product knowledge and prior experience of renting property, and ignore the more complex and critical issue of location and marketing.

Banks, as major financiers, may pull back from financing many small retail projects. However, the evidence of many bankruptcies and insolvencies show that banks often back projects that are too risky, because they can average out losses over other projects. Many would-be retailers start their businesses as sole proprietors or as partnerships. However, unlimited liability means that business failure could leave them in a state of bankruptcy. So it is up to the small retailer to make sure that the business meets the five basic requirements for survival:

▶ *The product must be right for the market.* The retailer's positioning, location and pricing must be correct. Any entrepreneur should base his or her enterprise on what the market will support. Many successful small retailers identify gaps in the market for a particular collection of products. Others, however, identify a potential for a product range but choose poor locations in the mistaken belief that customers will beat a path to their door. For instance, a specialist fancy dress and novelty shop can successfully locate in a suburb with good road access, because there is limited competition in the town. However, a specialist handbag or leather accessories shop in the same location will find it difficult to attract sufficient customers against the competition from city centre or out-of-town stores.

▶ *The structure of the operation is appropriate.* The retailer needs to ensure that an appropriate supply chain exists and is functioning properly. Even the small independent retailer relies on a supply chain, which may be as simple as using the local wholesaler. Someone opening up a local convenience store can usually tap into an existing supply established by a wholesaler. However, retailers catering to a highly specialized market may have to establish their own links in the supply chain. This may require them to talk directly to manufacturers in order to have their product, such as food supplements, specially designed or made for them. Mail order retailers also need to ensure that they have a proper system for receiving and processing orders, and have appropriate replenishment and storage systems for their products (space).

▶ *The timing of investment is correct.* The firm should avoid major financial commitments at high costs at the peak of economic activity, just before the economy goes into a downturn. Timing is also important for markets and customer trends in purchasing. If, for example, a small retail business wishes to start up selling a specialized range of security products, such as alarm systems, the market for these products may vary with crime rates. One other key issue associated with retail business start-up is property rental or purchase. Prices are sensitive to the current level of demand and can alter the cash profile of the business. Alternatively, strategic property acquisition can have a very positive effect on the business and add to the value when businesses are sold.

▶ *The staff has the appropriate mix of skills and abilities.* The founders of new retail businesses come from a variety of backgrounds. Some may have a trade background, such as appliance repair or clothing design. Others may have worked in retailing or marketing, while others come into the trade because it is relatively easy to set up a small retail business. The problem in many cases is that the proprietor may have a good understanding of the product lines, but lack sufficient financial and marketing skills. People are also unduly optimistic at all stages as regards finance, cash flow and the physical practicalities of the supply chain. This can lead to serious problems that can sink the business. The retailer needs to ensure:

- *clear identification of target markets*
- *proper contingency planning*
- *strict cost control over the initial investment and the timing of payments*
- *clear specification of products and the delivery of the requisite stocks.*

Where building work is involved, the retailer needs to be clear about design specifications and there has to be proper control over the progress of building and shopfitting work. Delays in getting the business up and running means that business is lost and the cash flow problems greater.

▶ *Management structure and style is appropriate.* The management structure in small firms is often informal with the owners getting closely involved with staff in the business. Their close involvement with customers creates an advantage, which only the independent operator can genuinely offer. This often strikes a difference in customer service that compels customers to use the small retailer rather than the large multiple. However, even new retail businesses may require several staff, perhaps on a part-time basis. Management structure and style need to ensure good cost control and service style.

It is likely that the management style fails to recognize the importance of marketing and the marketing concept. This frequently results in a lack of focus on issues that encourage repeat business and long-term prof-itability. In general, the major problems are due to the inexperience of the proprietors who invest in a business with little knowledge of how they are to run it. Running a small business requires appropriate support and advice and a range of skills. Problems arise when people with narrow experience in retailing try to take on the running of a business without re-skilling. A limited perspective inhibits the general running of the business.

Planning the First Year

A properly constructed *business plan* covers these basic requirements as well as specifying how the project is to be funded over the first five or more years. Essentially the business plan explains how the business will develop during the first five years and provides a net cash flow forecast for that period. Commercial lenders require a business plan to assess the chances of success and whether to risk money on the venture. However, the large number of failures of new businesses during the first two years of trading suggests that commercial lenders are unable or unwilling to provide the necessary advice and control to minimize risks. Therefore, it is important to check the business plan carefully and guard against overoptimism. This also goes for opening new branches of a company and major refurbishment.

There are three major problems in establishing successful operations:

▶ *Understanding the market well enough.* The new business owner needs to know where and how the retail outlet should be located. Locations have to be carefully selected and the appropriate planning consent is required. The catchment areas need to be researched and the customer base fully understood. The merchandise range must fit the customer. A new retailer needs to offer something distinctly better than what was previously available to overcome the loyalty, or even inertia, of consumers to their existing retailers.

▶ *Bringing the business on stream within the given time at the stated cost.* Inadequate allocation of resources to planning, design and control over development cause time and cost overruns, which increase the deadloss of rent and other costs incurred. Overruns occur because architects, designers and builders are inadequately instructed and schedules are not adhered to.

▶ *Establishing and maintaining the projected cash flow during the first year of operation.* The retailer should be careful of reading too much into an initial consumer interest. New restaurants, for instance, almost always experience a steep surge in customer spending during the first two months or so of opening, as the novelty factor diffuses through the local population. As the novelty factor wears off, demand declines significantly during the year, unless the restaurant provides sufficiently strong attractions to counter consumers' natural desire for variety of experience. When taking over an existing business, the new retailer needs to retain those services that customers like and signal to potential customers that improvements in decor, merchandise and service will be made where they are required.

In the majority of cases, turnover is below that projected. Costs are often kept down simply because the owners and their families provide, in effect, unpaid labour, often working much longer than the normal working week during the first two years of operation. Even so, costs are usually higher than expected. Rising consumer standards and the increased burden of government control have also increased the investment required for any given customer base. This reduces the net cash flow and increases the liquidity problems of firms.

14.2 The Growing Firm

Continuing Growth

If the business can survive comfortably its first year, then it has a good chance of survival. However, the owners must now consider how to continue its development. If the retailer has not already done so, he or she may need to consider forming a private limited company. This requires involving at least one other person, often a family member, as a director and giving more serious attention to accounts and the development of more formal management systems.

Moving a store beyond its fifth birthday will almost certainly require some thought as to the redevelopment of its format as consumer tastes and the competitive situation change. It is at this stage that many owners of small stores sell their businesses after a few years, because they want to relocate their activity or move on to other businesses. Even where a business has enjoyed phenomenal growth, the founders of the business may wish to sell out to a larger firm and realize some of the wealth that they have accrued in the business. In either case, their concern is to be able to sell a thriving business with a good turnover and trading profit in order to keep the sale price high.

Changing Stores

As a retail business continues to grow, it may need to increase the size of its store. Sometimes competitive forces determine this. The small retailer may be able to redesign and refit the property it currently owns or leases. It may be able to relocate to a larger store within a parade of shops or shopping centre, or relocate to one nearby. Much of the funds required for the redevelopment come from reinvestment of profits, supplemented by loans from the bank or other finance company.

However, continued growth will eventually require the addition of extra branches of the store. At this stage the position and image of the retailer changes significantly. The retailer will now find it difficult to remain a small player and must continue to grow, decline or sell out.

The Changing Role of Management

Management also has to change, with the founder taking a less active role in each branch. As chairman of the board of directors, the founder can use his or her entrepreneurial skills to focus on the strategic development of the company, identifying the direction of change and developing strategic responses. Even those responsible for the rapid development of existing companies are often ill at ease with a more stable situation, and either leave or are forced out as their style no longer fits in with the needs of management. For instance, the supermarket chain Asda rose from the brink of disaster in 1991 to be a high-performing company in 1998. This reflected the talents of Archie Norman as chief executive and then chairman in changing the culture of the company, Allan Leighton in delivering efficient operations and George Davies in developing the George brand. All three left within 18 months of its sale to the US retailer Wal-Mart to pursue other activities. George Davies had previously founded and successfully developed Next as a revolutionary high street fashion company in the 1980s. However, his ambitious and unsuccessful attempts at diversification caused significant problems during the recession at the end of the 1980s and he was forced from the company.

The board of directors takes the responsibility for developing appropriate strategies for the retailer and for ensuring adequate financing. They are also responsible for ensuring an appropriate management structure through which strategy can be implemented through efficient operational management.

There is a natural shift from focusing almost entirely on strategic issues at board level down through the management structure, to concentrating entirely on operational issues at the departmental supervisor level. However, the too rigid separation of management level and functions creates problems that can damage retailing performance. Management becomes remote from operational realities, with a lack of proper communication inside the organization and failure to think through the implementation of policy.

A number of organizations recognize this and attempt to deal with it in various ways. Some retailers require their managers to get back to reality through a stint on the shop floor, serving customers and promoting one culture and open door policies. Other companies such as the LloydsTSB bank focus on shareholder value (McKinsey 1998). This is translated into targets for its staff, many of whom are shareholders through its share-save scheme. This is linked with building long-term customer relationships. Emphasis on customer service provides a way of keeping an organization focused, because it emphasizes the integration of activities and the role of communication between the different parts of the organization.

Finance

Where the company enters a phase of rapid growth or has grown on a large scale, it will almost certainly find the conventional bank funding inadequate. It is at this stage that the retailer may look to venture capital investment from specialist organizations or large private investors. The provision of government-sponsored business enterprise schemes may be useful for relatively small companies that need a few hundred thousand pounds for branch development. However, the rapidly growing company will look to venture capital firms specializing in this kind of finance. These firms will usually take a majority stake in the company, with the intention of taking the company public within five to seven years and selling their stake to a wider public or to other large investment companies.

If the company establishes itself as a rising star, it may open itself to wider public funding through being listed on the London Stock Exchange. This provides an established marketplace where its shares can be traded and makes holding them more attractive.

In order to get a full listing or to be a quoted stock, the business has to satisfy various requirements concerning trading history and disclosure of accounts and other aspects of the business. The business must also conform to certain rules regarding the conduct of its business and needs to be open to analysts from various stockbroker companies, to provide the public with fair assessments of performance. The bulk of the finance still comes from large institutional investors such as pension funds and insurance companies.

The Stock Exchange is really only for very large companies that raise millions of pounds of finance at a time, and fewer than 2800 firms have a listing, 500 of which are foreign firms. The London Stock Exchange, however, provides an alternative facility for smaller companies called the Alternative Investment Market or AIM.

The AIM does not require the same level of market capitalization, experience or availability of shares that a Stock Exchange quotation does. Instead, it is up to investors to decide whether to invest on the basis of what the company has made available. The typical market value of the companies using this market lies between £5 million and £15 million, although the range is from £2 million to over £200 million (Alternative Markets Review 2000). There are just over 300 firms using AIM, 50 of them foreign, which is a small proportion of the 40 000 or so small public companies. Table 14.3 shows the number of retail and related industry companies with a full quotation or AIM listing.

Table 14.3   Listed Companies in Retailing and Related Trades, November 2000

Sector	London Stock Exchange Quoted companies	AIM companies
Food & drug retailers	19	4
Retailers – hardlines	24	8
Retailers – multidepartment	22	3
Retailers – soft goods	32	0
Discount, superstores and warehouses	3	0
Retailers – e-commerce	2	4
Vehicle distribution	17	2
Distributors – other	23	0
Hotels	16	2
Restaurants, pubs and breweries	30	18
Laundries and cleaners	1	0
All	2443	307

Source: London Stock Exchange 2000

An alternative to AIM for smaller companies is OFEX. This is a privately run facility that enables unlisted companies to raise capital of £100 000 and upwards through issue of share capital, mainly to private investors. OFEX is a source of venture capital for companies that will eventually go on to raise larger sums of development capital though AIM or a full Stock Exchange quotation. Companies can also use it to trade existing share capital publicly. The number of OFEX companies was 211 in November 2000 (http://www.jpjenkins.co.uk/).

14.3 The Structure of the Business

The successful small retailer develops a distinctive format for its store or service that proves a success locally and gives a high return on investment. Some small retailers may be happy with this situation and even sell up and start again in order to remain small. However, success may encourage a small retailer to expand beyond its locality:

► to develop a regional or national brand

► to forestall imitators who may destroy the firm's intellectual property and to head off rivals with alternative formats

▶ to gain important scale and experience economies that enable it to compete effectively on price once the product enters the maturity phase.

In order to expand, the store-based retail firm has to open more units. This will lead to changes in the structure of the retail business and can affect the range of products it sells and how it sells them. It can undertake the *intensive* development of its market by opening more units close to its existing ones. This is suitable for outlets such as convenience stores because there are substantial economies of scale in distribution and organization; marketing communication is less formal. It also makes it easier for the retailer to grow the company's management organically to maintain the ethos of the business and protect its strategic development.

Alternatively, the retailer can also undertake the *extensive* development of its market by opening branches in new population centres some distance away from the existing one. This would be appropriate where the retailer is selling in a highly segmented or specialized market, which limits the potential for initial development locally. However, this kind of development in the early growth and rapid expansion of the brand means that retail units become relatively dispersed. This makes it more difficult for management to oversee the development of the market and ensure the quality of service. This may lead the retailer to consider franchising its retail format by developing a franchise system.

Franchising

A franchise system occurs when one firm, the *franchiser*, allows another firm, the *franchisee*, the right to supply its brand exclusively within a defined territory for a specified period of time, usually five years or more. The territory could be a region, such as Greater Manchester, or a type of facility, such as railway stations. The types of franchise structure can vary according to the products or services provided (see Key Note 1998b). In most cases, however, the franchisee is prohibited from selling other products or services from the same outlet.

Franchisees have to make the following commitments:

▶ Operate to specified service standards. This means:
  – supplying goods and services approved by the franchiser
  – operating specified hours of business
  – maintaining standard prices
  – conforming to standardized promotional messages and methods.

▶ Pay a fixed initial royalty fee plus a percentage of total sales revenue (turnover).

▶ Make some specific investment, which can include:
  – buying merchandise from the franchiser
  – leasing the premises from the franchiser
  – using the franchiser's approved design services.

▶ Only sell the business with the consent of the franchiser and (usually) give first refusal to the franchiser.

The franchiser in return:

▶ provides advertising and marketing services

▶ provides training programmes, especially management training

▶ monitors franchisees' performance and may terminate a franchise if the franchisee is underperforming.

The number of franchises in retailing grew from 84 in 1993 to 100 in 1997, and the number of franchised stores increased from 3385 to 4785 (Key Note 1998).

Reasons for a Franchise Sharing the Risks and Profits with Other Firms

A successful retailer with limited capital funds can use a franchise to expand more quickly, by franchising its format. Internal finance from even profitable firms is usually insufficient to finance the large-scale developments required to grow and stabilize the product in the market fast enough to forestall imitation and other competition. External finance is expensive to raise. Lenders are usually less optimistic than the firm's managers and so debt financing is restricted. Franchisees effectively provide equity investment that does not dilute control of the franchiser firm.

Of course, the franchisee will only buy the franchise if he or she expects to make surplus profit or the investment risk is reduced. The evidence suggests, however, that failure rates are lower and profitability higher for franchised than non-franchised businesses (Key Note 1998b). This makes a franchise a useful way of setting up in business. High street banks now actively support franchise development and the Department of Trade and Industry have established a Loan Guarantee Scheme to help in financing franchises.

The Structure of the Franchise

The franchiser owns the right to the retail format and chooses a franchise system to extract the maximum profit. The advantageous position of the franchiser is one reason why franchise agreements have to be registered with the Office of Fair Trading.

The structure of the franchise should improve joint profit-sharing. The franchiser charges fees to the franchisee as a way of transferring a lot of the extra profit of the successful retail brand to the franchiser. However, the franchiser must keep the fees reasonable otherwise the more capable prospective franchisees may take up alternative franchises or set up their own independent businesses. Franchisers must also provide active support to their franchisers in order to maintain their loyalty and encourage other prospective franchisees.

The franchisee usually pays an initial fee plus annual royalty of a percentage of turnover. This system helps to protect the retail brand by discouraging any *cheating* by franchisees that do not maintain the required level of service. The royalty payment is charged on turnover and not on profit. This encourages the franchisee to keep control of its costs, as it has to bear the full effects of any inefficiency in its operations.

The initial fee is also based on the expected profitability over the life of the franchise. The initial fee encourages the franchisee to work harder to generate that extra profit to recover the initial expenditure. However, if the franchiser takes its share of the profits as an up-front payment, it loses the incentive to deliver brand support to the franchisee. This would lead to dissatisfied franchisees and longer-term damage to the brand. The franchiser assures franchisees of its support by reducing the initial payment and taking part of the profit after it has been made, in the form of a royalty payment. However, well-established franchises tend to have relatively high lump sums and relatively low royalty payments.

Franchisees usually have to make some investment in specific equipment, signage and sometimes property sub-leases from the franchiser. These have relatively little value elsewhere if the franchiser terminates the franchise because the franchisee fails to maintain quality standards. This helps to maintain the franchisee's efforts for the retail brand and reduces the cost of monitoring franchisees.

Vertical Integration

Retailing is part of the supply chain that delivers a product or service to the consumer. The supply chain is made up of a series of production processes, such as the rearing of cattle and their processing into various cuts of meat or meat products. Historically, retailers such as butchers, grocers and tailors once performed many of the processes that are now carried out in factories. They carried processes that were technically linked at the time, such as measuring and fitting clothes before the development of standardized garment-cutting procedures. However, the large-scale standardization of production processes removed the need for the retailer to be directly involved. Retailers increasingly concentrated on the end processes of distribution, while other firms made the products. For instance, modern bread-making technology has improved the shelf-life of products and distribution planning has meant quick delivery of all kinds of special breads to local supermarkets. Specialist bakers that have their own in-store bakery are therefore *vertically integrated* because there is a sequence of technically distinct activities carried out in the same business.

Backward or *upstream integration* occurs when a firm takes over a supplier: for instance, when a retailer owns a food manufacturer from which it buys some of its food. *Forward* or *downstream integration* occurs when a firm takes over a customer or outlet: for instance, when a bakery owns a shop. There are also cases of quasi-integration where there are long-term supply relationships or joint product development.

Vertical integration also occurs for other reasons. For instance, a retailer may own a fleet of vehicles for distribution to increase control over the distribution process to minimize cost or exploit their market position. Vertical integration also occurs where there are highly specific products. Examples of this include factory outlets, selling seconds and overruns, and craft shops in tourist areas.

Mergers and Acquisitions

Firms can expand their business by merger or acquisition as well as by organic growth. A firm will try to acquire another business when it believes it can put the assets of the business to better use than the existing management. In this sense the threat of acquisition encourages management to work more actively in the interests of the shareholders by increasing the value of the firm.

However, the directors of successful firms that are growing quickly may also welcome the opportunity of selling the business to a larger firm that has the resources to expand the business. This can happen at all levels in the industry firms. Asda, for instance, recognized that its sector of retailing was changing fast and competitive forces were putting great pressure even on large firms in the sector. So it was actively looking for a merger with another retailer for several years before selling out to the American giant Wal-Mart.

Merger and takeover activity in retailing and distribution has reflected the effects of technological, social and economic changes. The decline in the relative costs of transport and communications costs has led to the development of international markets. Foreign competition has increased and changing consumer tastes have led to shorter product cycles. Pressures to meet competition have required lower cost structures, better products and broadened managerial capabilities.

Shareholders in the business that is being taken over do reasonably well (Reekie 1989), because the acquiring firm makes a bid above the current market value of the company. The acquiring firm often makes a less than satisfactory return because its management is overoptimistic about the future, particularly in its ability to use the increase in market power. However, there is some evidence to suggest that planned programmes of acquisition can yield shareholder benefit over the longer term, provided the acquisitions fit in with the takeover firm's culture (Weston and Jawien 1999).

Horizontal mergers and acquisitions take place when a firm merges with or acquires another firm in the same line of business. These may take place for a number of reasons. Where the industry is growing more slowly because of demographic or other long-term factors, there is a tendency to consolidate smaller firms into larger ones. This is beneficial if advancing technology provides substantial economies of scale. The process of consolidation may also be speeded up by the competitive movement into a broader range of services, as has been the case with retail banking and financial services. The high street banks such as Lloyds and TSB merged to gain cost economies but also because this strengthened their positions in the high street. The acquisition of the Cheltenham and Gloucester building society expanded the bank's skills to help it market comprehensive financial services to their customers. However, successful mergers require the firm to be strong in its core activities as well as finding organizations that fit in with its ethos.

Diversification

A retailer may *diversify* its activities by extending its operations into other products lines where there is either some marketing or production relationship. Food retailers may add non-food lines if they fit in with their customers' shopping habits. Convenience stores by their nature need to stock a variety of products. Alternatively, diversification may take place into unrelated products, so giving pure conglomerate activity. *Conglomerate mergers* occur when a firm uses acquisitions or takeovers to diversify into a different line of business.

A variety of reasons have been suggested for conglomerate activity, such as:

▶ *More profitable opportunities elsewhere.* Retailers may take this approach when their existing markets are maturing and the returns on investment look higher elsewhere. However, the firm has to be sure that it has the necessary management skills to manage different types of operation.

▶ *Economies of scope.* In essence, however, this requires the retailer to have a special expertise that is common to both activities, rather than in an area that is heavily product specific.

▶ *Risk reduction.* Increasing the size and range of the retailer's activity may make it a more attractive proposition for investors. This makes funding cheaper. It also makes it easier to raise more capital in the form of debt, which increases the return to shareholders in good times.

However, experience shows that many conglomerate mergers do not become fully integrated and can hold back the profitable operation of a group. This is particularly so when one or more of the sectors has matured, or in tougher economic times when the strain on management becomes too great. Mature or declining sectors of retailing tend to have more cases of relatively unprofitable firms whose value has fallen sufficiently to make a takeover attractive to other firms. Other firms find it useful to demerge parts of the business and sell them off. For instance, Sears sold off its underperforming shoe division in 1996 to concentrate on its Selfridges store in London and open other stores around the country. The troubled Storehouse group is another example of a conglomerate that did not have a long-term future. It comprised three loosely related and somewhat dated formats of Habitat, Bhs and Mothercare. Habitat was sold off to IKEA in 1994, Bhs was sold in 1999 to the independent entrepreneur Howard Greene and Mothercare downplayed its unsuccessful attempts to develop Children's World stores.

Core Competences

The problems of diversification and whether to acquire other businesses can be expressed in terms of *core competence* of the organization. This is the set of particular skills and aspects of culture that provide the organization with its competitive advantage in the market. They are defined in terms of customer benefits rather than in strict product lines. For instance, a supermarket may define itself as being in the grocery business. Its focus is on selling groceries efficiently through supply chain management and creating value through range and store image. However, its focus on grocery lines limits its future direction and makes the task of competing effectively in a changing city market very difficult. For the supermarket chain to be a success it needs to reinvent itself by extending its skills in food merchandising to support customers in other products opening up new areas of development. This strategy is also likely to encourage one-stop shopping.

Other retail stores may have different competencies that allow them to expand in different directions. It is important for a retailer to define its business in terms of the skills that are of benefit to its customers. This enables it to get the best out of (optimize) its investments. If the retailer does not understand its core competence, it may miss opportunities for improving shareholder value or worse still may lead into disastrous mergers or expansion to inappropriate areas.

14. 4 Investment Decisions

A retailer provides its services to consumers through a complex series of activities using various resources. Some resources are bought in as the retailer requires them. These include the products it retails, distribution services and the services of its employees. It also owns or leases for substantial periods other resources to use as and when required in providing its services. Such resources include land, buildings and equipment. These resources are the *assets* or *capital* of the business and provide an essential flow of services over time to the retailer.

The assets of a business have traditionally been seen as its *physical capital* stock, such as its stores and vehicles, and its *financial capital* consisting of cash and other financial assets. However, management and labour skills also represent considerable capital resources because they have those specialized skills, attitudes and knowledge of company practices that enable the retailer to survive and prosper in a competitive world. These skilled and experienced workers can be worth far more to the retailer than their wages indicate and they should be discarded only with reluctance. It is also important to invest resources in updating those skills as the needs of the company change.

Investment and the Cost of Funds

Once the retailer has decided on its correct market and the products appropriate to that market, it has to invest in the assets required to provide the planned services. Some investment replaces worn out capital; the rest is net investment in new or updated capital. The strategic direction of the retailer should determine the general quality of particular alternative courses of action. This general evaluation usually reduces the acceptable alternatives to a few, perhaps only one. Once this is done, however, the retailer should make a financial evaluation of the project in order to ensure that money committed to the investment will bring adequate returns. The approach is the same whether the *investment project* is a major one, such as new store development, or a small project such as the choice of a particular piece of cost-saving equipment.

The investment project generates a series of costs and benefits over time, called an *income stream*. Some of these costs and benefits are financial, whereas others may be more difficult to express, such as increased customer satisfaction. Where possible, the retailer should estimate the types of costs and benefits in their financial equivalent. Where this is definitely not possible, they should be regarded as extra factors to be taken into account along with the financial evaluation when making the final decision.

The timing of the money flows is important because £1 today is not worth the same as £1 in a year's time. If the retailer borrows money for investment, it has to repay it with interest. If it is investing money it already has, it will not be able to invest it somewhere else and must make as good a return as it could in some alternative, relatively safe, investment. Finance, like any resource, is in relatively short supply and financial markets ration out the available supply through the rate of interest. The rate of interest that the retailer has to pay in order to get additional funds for investment is its *cost of capital*. This represents the minimum return it has to make on its investments in order to make them worthwhile. In practice, the cost of capital has to take into account the different sources of funds, including shareholder investment, the return or interest rate to be paid to each source and the possibilities for further borrowing from each source.

When the retailer has calculated the cost of capital, it can use it to compare the costs and returns of the project on the same basis. It does this by setting out the surplus (positive cash flow) or deficit (negative cash flow) for each period (such as a year). It then calculates the *present value* of each item using the appropriate *discount factor*. In the simple case of annual cash flows, the discount factor is $(1 + i)^{-n}$ or $1/(1 + i)^n$, where i is the cost of capital (expressed as a decimal) and n is the number of years in the future in which the surplus is received or deficit incurred.

⇨ To find the present value of a surplus of £100 received in two years' time when the cost of capital is 10 per cent per annum:

The present value	$= £100 \times$ discount factor
In this case, the cost of capital, i	$= 0.1$ (that is 10 per cent)
and the period n	$= 2$
So the discount factor	$= 1/(1 + 0.1)^2 \quad = 0.8245$
So the present value	$= £100 \times 0.8245$
	$= £82.45$

Computer spreadsheet packages (such as Excel) provide standard procedures for applying this factor as appropriate and for calculating the present value of a project. Present values can also be calculated using a calculator or using tables of discount factors that are available commercially.

Case 14.1 Compounding, Discounting and Present Values

The discount factor is derived from the formula for compound interest. We use the cost of capital to *compound* a present sum of money to its *future value* at a given point in the future. We do the reverse to *discount* a future sum of money to its *present value* now. If the rate of interest is 10 per cent (or 0.1) per annum, and we invest £100 now, the sum will grow as:

Year	Amount (£) at beginning of year	Interest for year (£) = rate of interest × amount	Amount (£) at the end of the year
1	100	$100 \times 0.1 = 10$	$100 + 10 = 110$
2	110	$110 \times 0.1 = 11$	$110 + 11 = 121$
3	121	$121 \times 0.1 = 12.1$	$121 + 12.1 = 133.1$

Conversely, in this case, £133.1 in three years' time is worth £100 now, its present value. The general formula for compound interest replaces the numbers by general terms. We use A for the sum of money and i for the cost of capital:

Year	Amount at start of year	Interest = cost of capital × amount	Amount at end of the year
1	A	$A \times i = A.i$	$A + A.i = A(1 + i)$
2	$A(1 + i)$	$A(1 + i) \times i = A(1 + i)i$	$A(1 + i) + A(1 + i)i = A(1 + i)(1 + i) = A(1 + i)^2$
3	$A(1 + i)^2$	$A(1 + i)^2 \times i = A(1 + i)^2$	$A(1 + i)^2 + A(1 + i)^2 i = A(1 + i)^2(1 + i) = A(1 + i)^3$
n	$A(1 + i)^{n-1}$		$A(1 + i)^n$

The future value of money now n years in the future = its present value × compound factor $(1 + i)^n$. This means that we can find the present value of a sum of money n years in the future by dividing by the amount $(1 + i)^n$. This is the same as multiplying it by the term $1/(1 + i)^n$ or $(1 + i)^{-n}$, which is the *discount factor*.

Investment Decision

We calculate the *net present value* of the project as,

Net present value = *Sum of present values of all future sums of money to be paid or received* minus *the initial outlay.*

If the present value of the project is greater than 0, this means that the investor would be better off in the future by doing the project. So the decision rule is simple:

Accept the project if the present value of the project is greater than 0.

It is important to remember that if rate of interest in the economy increases, it will lower the present value of an investment in two ways:

▶ by raising the cost of funds and so reducing the present value of returns in the future

▶ by decreasing the level of demand in the economy and so reducing future cash flows.

Investment Alternatives

We can also use the present value criterion when we have to select a project or set of projects from a range of alternatives. In such cases, however, we have to establish the options available before applying the present value criterion. The decision rule becomes to choose the project with the highest net present value.

When looking at alternative investments, there are a number of aspects to the problem and they should be approached systematically:

▶ *Identify all feasible options.* Some options can be ruled out at this stage because they do not fit in with the style or ethos of the organization or the capital expenditure cannot be funded from any source.

▶ *Determine the time horizon.* This is the period of time over which any investment is going to be considered. This should reflect the degree of structural work to buildings required and the life of the equipment (including replacements). For some operations, five years may be adequate, but for other operations the period may be ten or more years. This will depend on the retail life cycle.

▶ *Estimating the present value of each alternative.* All future cash flows should be discounted at the rate of interest that reflects the cost of borrowing to the firm.

▶ *The alternative with the highest present value provides the base from which decisions can be made.* Any alternative must then generate sufficient extra long-term benefits to offset the lower present value. These extra revenues are, however, usually more difficult to estimate.

Financial Constraints

When there is no limit on the availability of funds, the decision can be made according to the above procedure. However, most retailers do not have sufficient funds to undertake all profitable investments. There are various techniques that the retailer can use to ensure that the available funds are allocated in such a way as to maximize the net present value for the retailer over all projects undertaken. These can be found in books on capital budgeting or investment appraisal.

Risk in Investment

A business must retain sufficient liquid assets such as cash and bank credit so that it can make payments as they fall due. These include the ongoing costs of the premises, for example, rent and business rates, gas, water and electricity, continuing costs such as wages and telephone bills, provision for tax payments, particularly value added tax, and being able to buy more stock as required.

The cash flow forecast is a useful way of working out the likelihood of meeting these payments. The future is so uncertain that, in practice, it is difficult to forecast the increased revenue or reduced costs resulting from an investment with any great deal of certainty. There is a natural tendency to be overoptimistic as to sales and expenses and to make assumptions that may be comfortable rather than realistic. The retailer should use *sensitivity analysis* to deal with these problems by analysing the effect of possible changes in interest rates or other factors affecting demand and costs. By looking at a worst case, a best case and an expected case, the retailer can get a broader picture of what might happen. In these situations, it may choose a project with a lower expected return if it provides a significantly better return in a worst-case scenario. There are various methods for dealing with risk, but the usefulness of any method depends ultimately on whether possible losses from any investment can be sustained without the firm going bankrupt or being taken over. Small retailers should not rely too much on the cash flow forecasts. Sales may not occur at the prices expected, payment may be late and costs may be higher than expected.

Other Methods of Investment Appraisal

Maximizing net present value provides the best return for any investment programme. However, the practicalities of business life and the uncertainty surrounding the investment process have led to other traditional accounting practices being used by many firms. These include the *payback* method, which measure the time required to get back the original sum invested, but neglect the cost of capital. With the difficulty of seeing even five years into the future and the need in modern retailing to refurbish and reinvest regularly, this rather naive method may not be all that bad and it can be a useful consideration when making the final decision.

14.5 Financial Evaluation

Assessing the Business's Financial Position

It is important to keep a check on the general performance of the business. This is done at two levels, at the level of the department and of the business as a whole. The performance of each department can be undertaken as part of the general merchandising covered in Chapter 7. A useful way of looking at the business as a whole is through the use of various financial indicators. These are usually expressed in the form of ratios derived from the balance sheet, profit and loss account and cash flow statements.

The accounts of a business must be prepared under a specific accounting convention. This may be the historical cost convention, which records items at the prices paid not their current worth, but may be modified by the revaluation of land and buildings to give a more accurate representation of the assets of the business. The accounts must also be in accordance with all the relevant accounting standards as given out by the various accounting bodies.

These include statements as to how assets are depreciated, for instance, by the straight-line method that reduces the value of the asset by equal amounts over the life of the asset. This is fairly arbitrary and may be more or less than the actual loss of value.

The company's balance sheet details the company's assets and the method of funding them (called liabilities). These assets consist of:

▶ *Fixed assets.* These comprise physical capital (land, buildings and vehicles) *plus* financial investments. However, the valuation of these items can be problematical, particularly for retail companies, as the value of property can change significantly between booms and slumps in the economy.

▶ *Current assets.* These are usually listed as the sum of stocks plus debtors (owing money to the firm) *minus* creditors (to whom the firm owes money) *plus* cash. However, these assets may also be difficult to value as stock may lose value and debtors do not always pay up.

Assets are financed from a mixture of sources (denoted as liabilities in the company accounts). They fall into two main categories: long-term capital funds and working capital. *Long-term capital funds* consist of:

▶ *Equity capital.* This comprises the original investment by the owners, or shareholders in companies, *plus* retained profits (listed as reserves in the accounts). In companies this equity capital comprises:

▶ *Debt (loan) capital.* The major form of loan stock is the debenture. This is usually a fixed-term loan sold in specified units of nominal value such as £1000. The firm pays interest on the loan, normally at a fixed rate, until the *maturity* date, when the loan has to be repaid. The firm may then issue further loan stock to repay this debt. Failure to meet interest payment can lead to insolvency. Debentures may be secured against particular assets of the company (mortgage debentures) or against the business as a whole.

Working capital finances day-to-day operations of the business. In practice the difference between working capital and fixed capital funding is blurred. Increases in material costs increase the amount of money that the firm requires to maintain operations and necessarily reduces the amount of funding available for fixed investment.

Debt

The importance of debt, profitability and liquidity to the business was mentioned in Chapter 1 and appropriate indicators should be used by the company to keep track of these. Gearing or the debt level is measured by the debt ratio. This may be calculated as either:

$$\frac{\text{Total debt}}{\text{Total assets}}$$

or as

$$\frac{\text{Total debt}}{\text{Equity}}$$

A ratio of more than 1 is not considered healthy in most circumstances.

The burden of debt is reflected in the ability to meet interest payments. This is measured by *times interest earned*, which is defined as:

$$\frac{\text{Gross income (Profit + Interest)}}{\text{Interest charges}}$$

However, where there are other fixed expenses, particularly leased property rentals, the fixed charge cover gives a better measure of the company's stability. This is measured by:

$$\frac{\text{Profit before tax + Interest charges + Lease charges}}{\text{Interest charges + Lease charges}}$$

Profitability

There are a number of factors to consider in profit. Administration and other costs can be excessively high, particularly in a large group with several units. This can be particularly damaging during the early stages of a recession when interest rates are also high. The group may become insolvent even though individual stores are operating at a profit. A firm can improve its profitability through:

▶ the appropriate timing of investment over the macroeconomic cycle

▶ slimming down its organization with management focused on delivering the product

▶ maintaining product quality and long-term customer relationships

▶ good financial management which can reduce interest payments and taxation.

The balance on the profit and loss account after payment of dividends to shareholders is transferred to the balance sheet.

Liquidity

The firm must have sufficient *liquid assets* (cash or credit) to pay its bills as and when required. It must have a suitable cash flow profile through the appropriate timing of investment and its returns. Importantly, the liquidity of the company increases when:

▶ profits go up

▶ fixed assets are sold

▶ shares are issued for cash

▶ creditors increase (the firm makes use of trade credit more).

On the other hand, the liquidity of the firm decreases when:

▶ dividends are increased

▶ taxes are paid

▶ assets are bought

▶ the company is reorganized

▶ stocks are increased

▶ debtors (people owing money) are increased.

Stocks and debtors appear to be part of the financial assets of the company, but can badly affect liquidity if excessive and may not convert into actual cash. Financial evaluation uses various ratios to assess the liquidity of the organization, though the appropriate range of values may conventionally differ according to the modes of operation and payment practices in that particular sector of the industry.

Conventional measures of liquidity include *current liquidity ratio*, which is defined as

$$\frac{\text{Current assets}}{\text{Current liabilities}}$$

or the alternative *quick (acid) ratio*, which is defined as

$$\frac{\text{Current assets} - \text{Stocks}}{\text{Current liabilities}}$$

These should be well in excess of 1 to allow for normal trade problems.

References

Alternative Markets Review (2000) http://www.amreview.co.uk

Carphone Warehouse, http://www.carphonewarehouse.com

Key Note (1998) *Franchising 1998 Market Report*, 6th edn, Hampton: Key Note Publications.

London Stock Exchange (2000),http://www.londonstockex.co.uk/

McKinsey (1998) 'Putting economic profit into practice', *McKinsey Quarterly*, June: 100–1.

National Statistics (2000a) *Business Monitor PA1003*, London: The Stationery Office.

National Statistics (2000b) *Business Monitor SDM28*, London: The Stationery Office.

Reekie, W.D. (1989) *Industrial Economics: A Critical Introduction to Corporate Enterprise in Europe and America*, Aldershot: Edward Elgar.

Weston, F.J. and Jawien, P.S. (1999) 'Perspectives on mergers and restructuring', *Business Economics*, January: 29–33.

Logistics and Distribution: Shipping the Goods to Market

CHAPTER 15

This chapter covers the following issues:

▶ The distribution process.

▶ The stages of distribution.

▶ Trends in supply chain management.

▶ Physical distribution, information and inventories.

▶ Warehousing.

Logistics and Distribution: Shipping the Goods to Market

Introduction and Core Concepts

Logistics and supply chain management are important aspects of modern retailing. Modern developments in the retailing supply chain have led to the improved management of inventory, distribution networks and vehicle scheduling. Retailers need the timely delivery of suitable products if they are to satisfy and retain their customers.

15.1 The Distribution Process

If it's not in store, you can't show it! If you can't show it, you can't sell it! This is the case for those small products and services that customers buy as part of their regular weekly or monthly shopping. When this happens, the retailer loses a sale and profit. Worse still, when a product or service is a key brand for the customer, the retailer will not be able to sell a substitute. Customers expect the retailer to have the product or service available, and the retailer's communications have told them so. The retailer has damaged its reputation and the shopper will be more inclined to look elsewhere next time.

Yet often the customer comes out dissatisfied. For instance, UK grocery distribution is regarded as one of the most efficient in the world, but on average 6 per cent of major product lines are out of stock (Brunfaut and Shipley 1999). Even on the top-selling items, the goods are on the supermarket shelves less than 98 per cent of the time (Bruun-Jensen and Shipley 2000). For larger and occasional items of purchase, such as electrical appliances, customers may still want to see them in-store although they may be prepared to wait for delivery. However, *the longer the delivery van takes, the fewer repeat visits the customer will make.*

These points remind us that when we say '*at the right time*' we mean when the customer wants it. And in the '*right place*' means at the point of sale or point of delivery. *Distribution* is the process of ensuring that these two requirements are met. However, distribution is more than the physical movement of products from the point of production to where the consumer wants them. It is an integral part of the supply side of retailing and has become one of the key drivers in improving profitability for many retailers. Effective management of distribution is important to a retailer's competitive position. Some retailers use distribution strategically to win customers and others make a point of incorporating delivery claims in their communication strategy. Service retailers guarantee appointment times and the availability of service items. The car hire firm Avis, for example, guarantee a car on arrival at major airports.

The distribution process incurs a number of extra costs that must be passed on to the retailer and then on to its customers. These costs include transport costs, warehouse storage costs and other costs associated with stocks or *inventory* of products that retailers hold. Transport and warehouse storage costs are clearly visible costs, because there is a direct monetary element. Reducing these costs is now a major concern for retailers and specialist distribution firms. This is partly because of the rising costs associated with transportation and the general clutter on the roads.

Other inventory costs are less visible, but still important. Retailers see an increasing need to maintain their competitive position by stocking lines that customers demand. Customers are less loyal than in years gone by and they are quite prepared to switch stores for the goods or services they require. The retailer has to hold some stocks to be sure of having the product available when customers want them. Demand is uncertain and the retailer does not know precisely when customers will require the product. So the retailer has to hold some stocks as a precaution. The retailer also has to hold a certain amount of display stocks to fill its shelves or have a wide display in the shop in order to inspire confidence in customers.

However, holding more stocks than necessary takes up expensive retail space that could be used for selling and generating extra profit. This loss of profits from reduced selling space is one cost of excess stock. When the retailer eliminates its excess stocks, it also releases the money that is tied up in excess stocks. The retailer can use the extra money to improve its liquidity, or it could invest in better equipment or facilities to improve its profits, or it could reduce interest payments by reducing its outstanding debt. Many retailers have attempted to solve the increasing pressure on space and margins by introducing more efficient distribution systems.

Managing distribution systems is now part of *logistics* and *supply chain management*. These processes are closely interconnected and very often the terms are used interchangeably (see Bnet). They focus on stripping out unnecessary costs and improving availability of products for customers. The following definitions illustrate the closeness of meaning:

> *Supply chain management is a strategy to reduce costs and improve the level of consumer service by removing excess stocks and other inefficiencies in the supply process. It does this by working back through each stage of the supply chain from consumer to retailer, to supplier and supplier's suppliers and so on.* (Based on Supply-Chain Today 2001)

Logistics plans, implements, and controls the efficient, effective flow and storage of goods, services and related information from the point of origin to the point of consumption in order to meet customers' requirements. (From *The Council of Logistics Management* definition)

In practical terms, logistics is about the level of customer service or product availability and cost between a supplier and its customer, such as material supplier and manufacturer, or manufacturer and retailer. Supply chain management coordinates the supply process to ensure a smooth flow from raw materials to finished goods in the hands of the consumer.

The organization has traditionally approached product availability through the management of stocks of materials and finished products in transit on trains, planes, boats and trucks, in warehouses and in stores. Producers had to buy enough materials far enough in advance so that they would have enough components for long steady production runs. Retailers had to buy large quantities to ensure sufficient stocks between long delivery periods and larger retailers often booked extra production time with manufacturers just in case they needed the extra supplies.

The modern competitive environment and changes in technology and consumer demand have led to shorter product life cycles. This has placed more stress on getting products in store and on the shelf at lower cost and to improve the level of customer service. Supply chain management is important for those companies that assemble products in large quantities and also for those retailers that supply large quantities for many customers.

In practice the lead player heavily influences the supply chain. For instance, the major grocery retailers have taken control of the supply chains for most products that they stock, but major suppliers, such as Heinz or one of the large distribution firms, increasingly manage the supply chain for their products for smaller retailers. This naturally alters the selling focus of the stores concerned.

15.2 The Stages of Distribution

The Distribution Channel

The *distribution channel*, or supply chain, is the method used to bring a product to consumers. The basic structure of a traditional retail distribution channel consists of several stages that take the product through *production*, *wholesale distribution* and *retail distribution*. Each stage is linked to the next through the physical movement of the product from farm, factory or workshop to the wholesale warehouse to the retailer's store and thence to the consumer's home. Some of these stages may be combined together or may be split into further sub-stages. Figure 15.1 describes the basic distribution process.

Stage 1: Materials Sourcing

This stage includes the specification, ordering and delivery of materials to the production facility. This stage is remote from the traditional

Main activity	Main institution	Other activities include
Sourcing materials	Materials suppliers ⇓	Warehousing Transport to firm using materials
Producing the product	Producer ⇓ ⇓	Design Warehousing; selling through agents; brokers; importer Transport to wholesaler
Wholesale distribution	Wholesaler ⇓ ⇓	Warehousing; consolidation Transport; cash and carry depot
Retail distribution	Retailer ⇓ ⇓	Regional and local distribution centres Transport to store and/or transport to home
	Consumer	

Figure 15.1   Basic Elements of a Supply Chain for a Product

retailer, particularly if the product is made overseas. However, some larger retailers take an active part in this process. For instance, most fashion retailers such as Marks & Spencer and Dorothy Perkins will specify the quality of materials to be used as part of their design specifications. Mail order companies often do likewise for their own branded products. Similarly, Marks & Spencer and supermarket chains may lay down fairly specific requirements for a food product in terms of ingredients, such as absence of genetically modified foods or their derivatives that the supplier can use.

Manufacturers also take an active interest in their material suppliers through *material resource planning* (MRP-II), *just-in-time* (JIT) production management methods, while some firms are moving towards integrated enterprise resource planning (ERP). These methods help manufacturers meet increasing competitive pressure by cutting costs and production delays. This has increased cooperation at the upper end or beginning of the supply chain and helped to integrate transportation within the supply chain. Suppliers usually provided much of their own transport, but firms are increasingly using third party distributors to deliver materials.

Stage 2: Production

This stage includes the design of products, the organization of production facilities, management of production operations and the delivery of products to the initial customers. The initial customers are usually wholesalers or shippers in the case of food and clothing items sold through small retailers. However, many producers often deliver direct to retailers, as in the case of car dealerships and mail order companies, and a small proportion, such as furniture suppliers, may sell direct to customers. The producer also holds stocks of the finished products in warehouses for the following reasons:

▶ There is some involuntary or forced inventory because of unanticipated falls in demand.

▶ The producer holds some stock as a buffer against the natural fluctuations in demand within a period. These fluctuations are difficult to forecast and so safety stocks are held.

▶ The producer sometimes holds stocks because the demand for the product is seasonal, but production is more efficient when it is at a steady level. As long as the saving in cost is less than the cost of storage, the producer will maintain these extra seasonal stocks.

This traditional approach to production is very producer focused. The producer decides what it can sell to the customer and determines product specification accordingly. It then uses various forms of promotional and selling activity to get retailers or customers to buy what it has produced.

Producers often take this approach when they are selling products to distant markets, as in a foreign country, or the market is highly fragmented with many small retailers, and consumer information is relatively scarce. The producer may also use various intermediaries for its promotion activities, such as agents, brokers and export and import agents. For instance, an overseas manufacturer who produces very attractive consumer products may distribute them through manufacturer's agents in this country. A retailer may wish to reach a distant geographic market and employ a sales agent to make their products available to distant customer groups. Many agents deal with specific product lines; others may work on behalf of certain firms. *Brokers* are more opportunistic and will negotiate on behalf of any manufacturer in dealing with wholesalers or retailers. Service providers, such as insurance companies, may also use brokers to facilitate the distribution of services.

Changing consumer demand and rapid developments in technology have a significant effect on manufacturing. Modern production systems emphasize speed to market, cost reduction and improved customer value. These systems require manufacturers to integrate the distribution of their products more closely with their production processes, and develop greater involvement with their customers.

This has changed the attitude of manufacturers to delivery and storage of their products. Firms used to deliver their own products or they may have used transport firms as *carriers* to deliver lorry loads under contract to them. However, several large transport operators have developed specialist logistics support systems. A manufacturer (or wholesaler or retailer) can acquire these services under long-term contract, often up to five, sometimes ten, years. When this happens, the carrier (or *logistics firm*) provides a *dedicated* logistics service to the manufacturer. Many large manufacturers, especially those selling to widely dispersed markets, now make use of these dedicated logistics services. The logistics provider may operate the manufacturer's own fleet of vehicles, or it may provide its own fleet of vehicles painted to the manufacturer's specification or it may use its own-label distribution fleet, such as the Eddie Stobart classic vehicles.

The growth of large firms in several sectors of retailing has shifted the balance of power from manufacturer to retailer in those sectors and has led retailers to become actively involved in the production stage of the supply chain. For instance, many large retailers employ their own designers in order to improve the range of products that they offer to their customers. The extreme case of this is when they supply own-label products. They also take an active role in the production processes involved.

Similarly, supermarkets take an active interest in new food product development. The same food manufacturer may produce a range of sandwich fillings or beefburgers for Asda, Sainsbury, Safeway, Morrison and Somerfield as well as their own brand. Each supermarket brand will have a slightly different set of ingredient mix that has been negotiated between the companies concerned. Some retailers may own their own production facilities. For instance, fast food retailer McDonald's owns its own meat-processing plant. Similarly some manufacturers, such as Timberland and Benetton, integrate forward into their own stand-alone shops as well as directly supplying other retailers, through their own distribution system.

Stage 3: Wholesaling

The wholesaler still remains an indispensable part of their supply process for many thousands of small retailers. The main function is to provide a halfway house between manufacturers and retailers. There are a few thousand manufacturers, but these are widely dispersed and undertake the dedicated large-scale production of goods. However, the many thousands of retailers need a convenient means of selecting relatively small amounts of the various products to build the appropriate product assortments for their stores. The wholesaler provides a gathering point for many different products and performs a bulk-breaking service for the retailer so that it can make up its required assortment of products. The wholesaler provides warehousing services where this process takes place. These include:

▶ storage of items until the retailers require them

▶ picking of items from stock to make the retailer's assortment

▶ consolidation of the items into a load for distribution to the retailer

▶ transport of the consolidated load to the retailer's store.

The wholesaler may alternatively provide a cash and carry depot. This still provides storage facilities, but retailers may carry out the other functions themselves.

The wholesaler also takes ownership of the goods and so assumes some of the producer's risks of non-saleability caused by damage, obsolescence or lack of customer demand. The wholesaler also speeds up the process of payment to the producer.

The transport of items to the retailer's store is often contracted out to third party carriers, but larger wholesalers now lease this out to dedicated logistics suppliers, much in the same way that manufacturers do.

However, a high proportion of independent retailers still make weekly or monthly trips to wholesalers during slack times at their shops, and wholesalers are continuing to streamline their cash and carry provision to reduce costs to the retailer.

Retailers pay for the wholesaler's services by the difference in price per unit that they pay and the price per unit that the wholesaler pays. Part of the difference in price goes to covering some of the costs incurred by selling in small quantities. These costs include the extra labour and storage space required and the cost of the money tied up in slower-moving stock. However, there are some buying co-operatives to improve the purchasing power of the independent retailers and reduce their delivery costs. Some of these co-operatives are owned and managed by retailers. Others, such as Spar, are buying co-operatives that are managed by a wholesaler.

Stage 4: Retailing

In the case of retailing, this is the final stage between the producer and the customer. The role of the retailer is to make the assortment of products available to consumers so that they can make their purchases. However, the presence of large multiple retailers in modern retailing has seen the development of intermediate stages in retail distribution. Large multiple retailers now use local and regional distribution centres. Manufacturers deliver to these centres, where loads are reassigned and consolidated for delivery to the individual stores. Retailers may contract out the management of these centres to dedicated logistics providers.

The retailer may run its own fleet of vehicles to transport goods from its consolidation centre, but they are increasingly using dedicated logistics firms to do so plus additional short-term contract hire to move goods. The retailer may also use similar logistical arrangements for delivering products direct to the customer's home. Some products, such as furniture and bulky electrical appliances are delivered straight from the warehouse or even from the factory to the customer's home using similar transport systems.

Retailers carry stocks of products or inventory in order to meet customer demand. As stocks are sold, the retailer orders more stock according to its own replenishment system. The time taken for the manufacturer to deliver the items is the manufacturing response time. It includes time to process the order, produce the goods and deliver them. Improving the manufacturer's response time can substantially reduce the inventories that a retailer has to carry.

Adversarial and Cooperative supply Chain Activity

Figure 15.1 indicates the links between different stages of the supply chain and the various functions. However, as some of the examples above show, the different stages do not need to be separate from each other, and there have always been different combinations of the various stages. For instance, mail order companies have combined the whole-saling and retailing functions.

Many small independent retailers and some large discounters still have to work in this traditional environment, where the retail stage is independent of the other. In this case, the retailer aims to buy as cheap as it can and sell for as much as it can. The retailer has an *adversarial* or *win–lose* relationship with the wholesaler or producer that it is buying from. This is because the retailer can only improve its profit from a deal by reducing the price it pays for products, which would reduce the profit to the wholesaler or producer.

Each member of the supply chain tries to *optimize* its own position, which is to get the best position it can for itself. This includes reducing its own supply and distribution costs as far as possible. It can save some costs by being more efficient, but it may also push some of its costs on to another firm either further up or further down the supply chain. As a result, the supply process may be *suboptimal* or less than the best that could be obtained. The consumer must ultimately pay the price for these inefficiencies. It is only the competition between suppliers for consumer business that drives out inefficiencies over time.

These competitive pressures to reduce supply costs may lead to *vertical integration* of the supply chain. This is when one member of the supply chain takes over some of the other activities of the supply chain. For instance, mail order firms combine the functions of wholesaler and retailer. Alternatively, large retailers, such as Marks & Spencer, gain greater control over the cost of supply through long-term contracts with suppliers and transport firms.

A more radical approach to cutting distribution costs has been the development of *cooperative* relationships through supply chain partnerships. Retailers and their suppliers share information and use information technology to reduce total costs and improve the availability of the product (the *customer service level*) to the final consumer. This results in a *win–win* situation, where each organization reduces its costs and increases its profits.

Another development in cooperative relationships has been *partnership sourcing*, where suppliers and retailers actively search for long-term partnerships. Tesco, for instance, actively cooperates with selected suppliers to develop and improve the quality and distinctiveness of their products. This encourages longer-term investment in product quality and development, lowers total cost by reducing wastage and selection costs, and improves delivery of the product.

15.3 Trends in Supply Chain Management

The Retail Supply Loop

The term 'supply chain' uses the analogy of a physical chain to link the different stages of the supply process together in delivering products to the customer. However, modern supply chain management treats the supply chain as a *loop* or pipeline: goods flow forward and recyclable material returns, and there are two-way information flows between all the parties including the final customer. Within this flow important relationships maintain the efficiency and effectiveness of the chain.

The supply chain comprises two parts: the external supply chain and the internal supply chain. The *external supply chain* involves the different members of the supply chain dealing with one another. The *internal supply chain* is the process of moving goods through the firm's own organization. In the case of the retailer, this includes everything from the receipt of the goods at the retailer's warehouse or consolidation centre to delivery to the customer in the store or at the customer's home.

Retailers, like manufacturers, hold stock because of the uncertainty about the level of demand and the delay or lead-time between ordering more stock and its arrival from the suppliers. However, the traditional methods of delivering and storing stock ate up a substantial proportion of revenue earned in the supply chain. Since the 1970s, the larger retailers and other supply chain firms have used new methods to cut down on stocks of items and passing them through the system quicker, with very substantial cost savings. Larger manufacturers and retailers undertook much of the early development within their own internal supply chains. Retailers made use of improved computer technology and point of sale (POS) equipment to track stock in store and reduce the level of uncertainty about requirements. Larger retailers also centralized their buying processes and set up national or regional distribution or consolidation centres from which they could supply their stores.

As the larger retailers increased their share of the market, they extended their control over their channels of supply, and the relationships within them. As part of this process they required more frequent and smaller deliveries tailored to the needs of their own stores. This helped the retailers reduce their own costs. However, the smaller order quantities and the variability of demand increased uncertainty and costs for their suppliers. Retailers could push these hidden costs back up the supply chain, but these costs had to eventually come through to the consumer by making prices higher in the long term than they would have been.

By the 1990s however, stronger competition in the market and declining levels of customer loyalty had forced retailers and producers to consider more radical ways of reducing distribution costs and improving customer service. New European Union environmental regulations that required suppliers and retailers to recycle more of the packaging increased the existing market pressure on costs.

Supply chain cooperation offered the chance to reduce the total cost of supplying the consumer, by reducing the level of stocks and the time for which they are held. Cooperation required the sharing of accurate information on consumer demand. It also allowed suppliers and retailers to use new efficient replenishment methods to improve the availability of products to consumers (or *customer service level*), which would give those suppliers and retailers a competitive advantage. Supply chain management depends on the following key elements (Anderson and Lee 1999; Billington and Amaral 1999):

▶ *Synchronizing interacting activities through information exchange.*

▶ *Synchronizing interacting activities through order postponement.*

▶ *Using technology and the Internet in new supply chain strategies.*

▶ *Restructuring and re-skilling supply chain organizations.*

The core of the supply chain is the set of *interacting activities* of the different members of the supply chain. For example, the quantity of green jumpers (as opposed to red jumpers or green cardigans) a manufacturer produces *interacts* with the quantity that the retailer orders to determine whether there is any excess stock of the product or not enough to satisfy the final consumer.

Supply chain synchronization occurs when the retailer collaborates with its channel partners to make their operations *consistent in timing and direction*. This means that the retailer sends out its order to get just the right amount of stock for its intended sales, because its supplier will deliver just the right quantity at the best time for the retailer to slot it into its appropriate space in the store. The supplier will also have the same consistency with its materials suppliers. This reduces the amount of stocks of the product that are held *anywhere in the supply chain* to the minimum required to satisfy the consumer. This collaboration can take two different forms: information exchange and order postponement.

Synchronizing Activities through Information Exchange

Information exchange uses investment in information technology to improve the quality of information to be shared with supply chain partners. Sharing information improves the ability to forecast customer demand accurately. This enables manufacturers to anticipate orders from the retailer. Alternatively, in manufacturer-led systems, retailers can order appropriate quantities ahead of demand.

The systematic sharing of information came with electronic data interchange (EDI).

Case 15.1 Electronic Data Interchange

Electronic data interchange is an electronic link between the manufacturer, supplier and the retailer. It allows one trading partner to transmit information directly from its computer application (software) to the other trading partner's computer application (software) through the appropriate computer application software.

For instance, a retailer's product caries a bar code (that little label with the black lines and a number). The customer sees the sales assistant use a scanner to identify the product, note the price, add it to the customer's bill and tot up the final bill. Meanwhile, the information is sent to the retailer's head office or distribution control centre. It identifies each product, where it is sold and the variety (green jumper/red jumper, summer fruits/exotics yoghurt). This tells the retailer the remaining stock level of the particular product at that particular store. This information is conveyed to the supplier's computer system.

The supplier's computer application (software package) periodically (once/twice a day or other appropriate frequency) determines the amount of each product that is to be shipped to each store, or where appropriate, to each distribution centre. A distribution centre will also have the information and know what amounts need to go to each store on each day.

The amounts to be shipped and where they are to be shipped to are decided automatically according to rules written into the computer programs.

Retailers and other firms in the supply chain first developed EDI as part of their *intranets* in order to improve their own internal supply systems. This was particularly useful for the larger multiple retailers who were using centralized buying and distribution to supply their stores. It was some time before firms tried to extend these systems to provide extranets to include their own supply chain partners in the mid to late 1990s.

The full use of EDI should include the disclosure of information regarding consumer demand for products so that producers can anticipate the retailer's order and plan production accordingly. Conversely, producer-supplied information allows retailers to anticipate supplies of the products. This enables them to plan promotions, price and orders accordingly and without the need to overbook production time.

Electronic data interchange is associated with dedicated systems between the retailer and its suppliers. However, there is now a move towards the use of the Internet to exchange information. The Internet allows greater traffic of information and the improvement in technology. This means that costs will be less. The improvement in security provides adequate data protection and individual firms can be restricted to accessing only data on their own products. However, many firms that have adopted EDI have not achieved the results expected for several reasons:

▶ Collaboration can only work properly when the different organizations are prepared to trust one another. In order to integrate the relevant operations, some organizations, particularly large retailers, have to relax some of their control over the supply chain and also divulge highly confidential information about themselves.

▶ There have been technical problems in integrating information systems within the organization. Many producers have different systems for different parts of their organization and integration is still some way off (Kilgore 1999).

▶ A large amount of data is required to provide a comprehensive picture, but there are difficulties in using the data effectively.

Synchronizing Activities through Order Postponement

Order postponement uses investment in designing and developing *postponable products*. These are standard (or generic) products that can be configured or differentiated quickly and inexpensively once actual customer demand is known. There is a wide range of postponable products, for example:

▶ *Paint mixing.* Decorating stores offer colour shading of standard base paints. This allows the paint producer to provide a very large number of shades at a reasonable cost and high value added. In this case the retailer completes the ordered product.

▶ *Computer assembly.* A computer is based around a particular processor and motherboard. However, for each processor speed, there are several practical alternative specifications for the other compatible components, such as hard drive, CD-ROM/DVD, memory, graphics card and sound card. With just two alternatives for each of these components, the manufacturer can supply 32 (= 2 × 2 × 2 × 2 × 2) different models, although to most people they are very similar. Building a range of models would add to the stock of products, in this case with a high degree of obsolescence. However, since the same component can be used across different models, the variability in demand for any component is going to be less than the variability in demand for a particular model, so that buffer stocks can be reduced.

▶ *Benetton* is an example of a manufacturer that has used up-to-the minute information and quick dispatch of items to determine colour quantities of its knitwear. Other manufacturers of furnishing items, such as curtains or furniture cover, complete to order, either at the factory or through the reseller.

Case 15.2 Order Postponement in the Computer Industry

Computer manufacturer and reseller Dell developed rapidly as a cost-effective supplier of computers by completing orders at its own regional assembly plants. Similarly, Hewlett Packard produces its desk-jet printers and sends them to four worldwide distribution centres. It completes the final configuration of the printers, including packaging and manuals at these centres. This reduces it total manufacturing, shipping and inventory costs by 25 per cent (Billington and Amaral, 1999).

Order postponement may also lead to in-store completion by a retailer, as with many computer shops that customize computers at their stores.

The purpose of postponement is to enable the manufacturer or final seller to respond effectively to changes in product mix. It avoids the need for detailed forecasts for each individual variety of a product (*end-item* or *retailer's stock-keeping unit*). However, the cost of a lost sale is high, so this approach is most valuable when:

▶ The manufacturer supplies a large number of similar products, but where the demand for particular varieties may be variable.

▶ The cost of holding a postponable product is low. The producer or retailer can reduce these costs by using standard parts that can be used elsewhere at the end of the product life cycle.

▶ Capacity cannot respond quickly to changes in demand because there are delays in materials from suppliers or it is difficult to reschedule production plans. The manufacturer can produce the basic model (or generic sub-assembly) using standard parts. This keeps production scheduling simpler and reduces the delay (or *lead-time*) between order and delivery.

Using Technology and the Internet in New Supply Chain Strategies

Improvements in information and distribution technology have improved collaborative planning. The use of the Internet has improved access to overseas markets and also enabled retailers to source products from more distant locations. These have affected the way retailers and other supply chain members operate. For instance, information technology enables increasing numbers of retailers or their suppliers to deliver customized products that can be delivered within a short time. Information can be processed automatically as it is received so that a retailer can respond within a specified time to a customer order:

▶ Computer supplier Dell can translate data supplied by telephone into a computerized order that is acted on immediately in its assembly factory. This allows Dell to deliver custom-configured computers within a few days.

▶ A woman's computerized measurements can be sent from its specialist shop in the UK to Levi's US factory, downloaded into the computerized garment process and the custom-made jeans will be delivered within days.

▶ Larger opticians can also provide some on-site lens services.

▶ New computer hardware and software in warehouse management has improved the time taken to select and load product assortments. New technology has also affected the physical storage and selection of products. Supply chain collaboration has also led to reduced inventories in warehouses and *cross-docking* of products, where the items are transferred directly from a supplier's wagon to the retailer's or distributor's wagon.

▶ New transport methods, such as multi-temperature vehicles for grocery distribution have reduced lorry journeys, improved delivery schedules and reduced costs. The use of satellite positioning technology has enabled some retailers to be more precise in delivery times and improved the inflow of goods.

▶ New methods of product packaging, such as vacuum packaging in fashion distribution, have reduced handling costs including damage. Food packaging of instantly microwavable foods has improved the competitiveness of manufacturers in supplying retailers.

Restructuring and Re-skilling Supply Chain Organizations

Supply chain management has been changing to take advantage of new technology. Retailers, major wholesalers, logistics firms and manufacturers have been re-evaluating their activities. Each stage of the supply chain can be seen as a separate business. The various firms in the process have been focusing on their core competencies or key skills and how they can transfer across businesses. Working in those areas in which it does not have a relative advantage over other firms reduces the level of profitability. The alternative is to *outsource* the activity to a supply chain partner.

For instance, some large retailers own their regional distributions centres, but outsource or contract out the operation of the facility to a specialist logistics firm. That is they hand over day-to-day management to a specialist firm. In the case of distribution centres, this would include inventory management and delivery scheduling. Outsourcing in these cases may be the subject of a five- or ten-year contract. This makes outsourcing different from the normal contracting out of jobs, such as lorry capacity or for delivering certain types of goods. This type of contract is for a specific limited task or time and is often used to supplement the retailer's own resources but the detailed management of the operation is firmly within the retailer's control.

15.3 Physical Distribution and Inventory Management

Physical Distribution

Physical distribution is the movement of a product from the producer to consumers in one or more stages. Physical distribution may be direct as when a furniture manufacturer receives an order from a retail outlet or by mail order and delivers the furniture directly to the final consumer. However, the physical distribution of many goods goes indirectly from the producer through the retailer, sometimes also through a wholesaler.

Large retail chains have developed a more indirect method of distribution, by creating an extra step in their own internal distribution. For instance, a manufacturer selling to a major retail chain normally sends large quantities of one or more of its products from its factory to the retailer's *consolidation centre*. The consolidation centre takes the various loads from different suppliers and breaks them down into the quantities required at its different stores. It then combines the different products into the mixed loads that are required at its different stores. These loads may also pass through regional distribution centres before finally arriving at the store. Large wholesalers also perform similar services for small retailers.

This indirect distribution method reduces costs for retailers and improves their product offering in various ways:

► It reduces costs because producers send a smaller number of fully laden lorries to the consolidation centre instead of to scattered stores. Retailers locate their consolidation and distribution centres near to major roads and motorways so that suppliers can send very large, fully laden vehicles to these centres. Retailers can use a much smaller vehicle for round town distribution.

► Large-scale distribution centres can afford sophisticated handling systems, which may be partially automated and are supported by computerized warehouse management systems. These reduce the time and labour involved in handling the goods.

► Individual stores can order smaller quantities and order them more frequently from distribution centres. This reduces inventory costs because the store needs less expensive retail space to support the large number of product lines on display. The smaller quantities also reduce the problems of congestion in the loading bays.

► Smaller quantities of different items are delivered more frequently. This lets a store use a sales-based ordering system based on forecast sales. This requires fewer stocks and saves money compared with the traditional stock-based system, which orders further quantities according to existing stock levels.

▶ Customers perceive the store to carry a much larger range and assortment of merchandise than the store actually carries in its stock room.

Transport Mode

Transport mode refers to the way in which goods are distributed. They may be defined in different ways. In this textbook we define them as *primary* and *secondary*. The *primary* modes are air, sea, road, rail and waterways (rivers and canals). In the UK the last mode is rarely used because of the good road and rail networks. Practically all goods must go by road for part of their journey to the store, but other modes may be used for part of the journey.

Sea transport is also unimportant for internal distribution within the UK, although most goods still arrive in the UK by sea, because of the lower cost. However, where speed is important, air transport may be used, as with flowers from Europe and Africa for instance. Benetton is an example of a producer that combines order postponement with the speed of air transport to supply its shops with the right coloured clothing. Marks & Spencer also uses air transport to send part of its clothing supplies to Hong Kong in order to respond quickly to demand changes there.

The size and geographical structure of the UK mean that suppliers and retailers rely solely on road transport for internal distribution, because of reliability, speed and cost. Air transport is usually too expensive and unnecessary for deliveries to the main centres of population. Rail transport is also unsuitable for many products, although it is used more extensively for certain industrial products. However, political, economic and environmental considerations are leading to studies aimed at increasing the use of rail transport for some consumer goods, particularly for supplies from remoter areas of the UK.

Rail freight has advantages over road for large-scale haulage over long distances and through congested areas. An important factor is the legal limit placed on the driving time of lorry drivers. Sainsbury ships large loads between Colchester in Essex and East Kilbride near Edinburgh. Safeway runs a trainload between Wakefield in West Yorkshire and Kent. Tesco imports wine from France and Italy by train through the channel tunnel. The continental piggyback system of putting trucks on trains cannot yet be used in Britain because railway tunnels are too low (Cull 1998). It seems likely, however, that European Union harmonization will make it easier for rail freight to pass more easily through Europe and will lead to greater use of rail deliveries from Europe.

Forms of Road Transport

Secondary modes of transport mean the specific types of transport within the primary form. Road transport, for instance, offers a wide range of alternative transport forms such as articulated lorries, rigid trucks and light vans. The retailer or distributor needs to select an appropriate form of road transport to suit delivery requirements.

Most deliveries from the supplier or consolidation centre use large articulated trucks. These trucks are commonly seen on major roads and consist of a tractor unit with a large detachable container-like body. There is an increasing use of drawbar vehicles, which have a shorter body with a separate trailer unit. This allows the containers to be directly transferred to smaller wagon chassis for urban distribution. However, retailers with fast response systems may use small vans for speed. For example, mail order retailers widely use the firm White Arrow, which operates fast 1.5 ton vans.

Case 15.3 Drawbar Vehicles

Exel Logistics is using drawbar vehicles to distribute Kellogg's products. It is using five fewer vehicles and saving 400 000 miles in travel and £512 000 in running costs per year. The vehicles also carry other products on the return journey.

Source: The Grocer 1997: 57

Suppliers and retailers may need to use special vehicles for delivering products to the store and also to the customer's home. For instance, specially constructed van bodies can allow clothes to be transported on clothing rails ready for transfer into the shop. Food transport requires three different temperatures to carry goods at ordinary or *ambient* temperature, *chilled* products and *frozen* items. Modern distribution methods now use multi-temperature vehicles to deliver combined loads of these goods from distribution centres to stores.

Grocery home delivery services use large vans with specially built bodies to provide deliveries of ambient, frozen and chilled products. Tesco uses multi-temperature vehicles in its home delivery service. Iceland, the frozen food supermarket chain, will deliver large purchase quantities to customers' homes. Since these are often in the locality, and frozen foods are a major component, it uses simpler single temperature insulated vehicles for its deliveries.

Marketing the retail chain may dictate the mode or even the route of the logistics operation. Public awareness of green issues means that large supermarkets and discount stores restrict delivery times and routes to avoid both pollution and noise. The avoidance of traffic congestion is usually part of any planning agreement the retailer engages in before roll out. Retailers also use their vehicles to promote the image of their store. For instance, variety retailer Marks & Spencer use a fleet of dedicated vehicles, which carry the M&S logo. These are visual evidence of the quality and ubiquitous of the brand. This is especially so when the vehicles are highly visible on the main roads and on motorways.

Managing Transport Operations

A retailer needs to have a transport strategy that is closely linked with its product and inventory policies. There are two stages of the transport operation: *supply to the store*, or warehouse in the case of mail order or Internet retailing, and *delivery to the customer* of the product or service once ordered or purchased.

Transportation to the store depends very much on the relationship between supplier and retailer. Small retailers tend to have to less control over when and how often supplies are delivered. This affects their inventory management and they tend to carry proportionately higher level of stocks. Larger retailers that have established their own consolidation or distribution centres have more control over the transport system. Larger suppliers have also established more retailer-oriented supply systems and more frequent deliveries.

Case 15.4 Heinz Introduces Shared Distribution in the UK

Global food manufacturer Heinz introduced the first shared grocery distribution operation in the UK, following a review of its operations in 1996. Changing market conditions meant that it needed to upgrade its distribution facilities to improve customer service and integrate its system more closely with retailers' own systems.

Heinz used to subcontract haulage, but it chose Wincanton Logistics to provide all its distribution services. It uses curtain-sider trailers, most of them in the Heinz livery to distribute over 500 product lines from factories in Lancashire, and London, to retailers' distribution centres across the country.

Wincanton uses its Net Logistics system to allow other non-competing manufacturers to use the same vehicles to carry their own high volume product ranges on return journeys.

Source: Murphy 1997: 53

A major question for retailers is the extent to which they should own and manage their own vehicles to carry goods to the store and to the customer. The supplier usually undertakes delivery to the retailer's distribution centre, warehouse or storeroom, while the retailer undertakes delivery from the warehouse to the store. We should note, however, that large successful producers and retailers are increasingly contracting out their transport, warehouse and inventory management to specialist logistics firm. This is usually done on the basis of a five- to ten-year contract, which means that the retailer or supplier knows or can easily calculate the cost of transport over this period. It also allows the retailer or supplier to concentrate on their *core competencies* or skills of customer and product management.

Secondary distribution from the store is an important part of the retail process for some retailers. Customers usually expect home delivery of furniture, electrical and large DIY items. Many retailers use small contractors to make deliveries as this relieves them of the problems of maintaining their own vehicles. Even large retailers may use this system because it allows the local store to concentrate on store management rather than delivery services. Additionally, some DIY stores provide a customer self-drive, self-help, service to take home bulky or heavy items.

There may, however, be strong reasons for a retailer to provide its own home distribution fleet. Small retailers that provide a delivery service may need direct control over their vehicles to ensure service quality. Similarly, larger firms such as Carpetright that provides an in-home ordering service may want to use their own vehicles. However, even in these circumstances, firms may lease vehicles to avoid tying up large amounts of capital. They may also have contract servicing of vehicles to reduce risks of unexpected cost increases.

Case 15.5 Nisa-Today's New Combined Delivery Facility

Nisa-Today is Britain's largest retail buying consortium, supplying about 2000 independent retailers and wholesalers. Increasing deliveries led the consortium to commission Exel, its frozen and chilled distributor since 1990, to develop a new combined facility to deliver frozen and chilled food, which had been previously delivered from two separately run centres. It decided to increase warehouse capacity and change its operating methods to meet demand and give members greater flexibility to maintain their competitiveness against larger retailers.

Exel undertook the conversion of a 1 600 000 sq ft warehouse in Stoke into a dedicated operation. The new facility has dual temperature operation and an annual capacity of 26 million cases. Exel has replaced its fleet with dual temperature urban articulated lorries. These have 25 per cent more capacity than comparable rigid trucks, but with the same turning circle to cope with limited loading space at members' stores. Deliveries now take place over six

days instead of five. These improvements have reduced vehicle requirements by 25 per cent.

Retailers can now place a single order and receive combined single delivery. They can also order smaller quantities of frozen and chilled foods, which has enabled some retailers to increase their deliveries from two to three a week, while other are receiving six deliveries a week. This makes chilled produce fresher on shelves.

Cost savings have been used to invest in new equipment and increase service levels.

The consortium uses an in-cab communications system to track the vehicles and real-time communications to update retailers on when vehicles will arrive.

Nisa-Today uses Bibby Distribution Services to supply ambient temperature goods from its Scunthorpe depot. It added a second site in 1999 for wines and spirits, also run by Bibby and can now supply these along with groceries.

Source: The Grocer 2000a: 53

Case 15.6 Growing Use of Multiuser Centres

Multiuser centres distinguish themselves from common or public warehouses through the development of partnerships with their customers within the supply chain. Multiuser centres were formerly used mainly by smaller or specialist suppliers. Now large manufacturers and retailers are using them. Large retailers are asking suppliers to deliver full loads within tight delivery windows. They also want shorter lead-times, smaller order quantities and lower costs. Many suppliers would find this uneconomic to provide their own dedicated facilities and need the facilities offered by multiuser centres.

MSAS decided several years ago to concentrate parts of its business on multiuser centres for the grocery sector because this was the most feasible way for many manufacturers to meet retailers'

delivery requirements. It now has several larger companies among its customers. These include pharmaceutical firm Roche, which contracted them in 1996 to handle 250 lines for major multiples. They also signed up Reckitt & Colman in 1998 with a contract worth £5.5 million a year to provide a full range of storage handling facilities in a designated warehouse in Bawtry, shared transport facilities nationwide and for export to the Middle East and Africa.

Its Bawtry, Doncaster, centre provides real multiuser facilities: clients can share its transport network with the flexibility to cover seasonal peaks and troughs. It offers full load benefits for multiples and independents, 24 hours a day with 15-minute delivery time windows. It also works closely with retailers to develop new consolidations or delivery and uses the grocers' haul back systems.

The staff only have access to data on a need-to-know basis. They also work in teams dedicated to specific users to heighten sense of ownership. Each client has its own area and the company can conceal product lines if required.

Meanwhile, Boughey Distribution has 90 suppliers, ten sharing ambient grocery warehousing and distribution sites from 20 000 to 40 000 sq ft. It expects to add another 25 after expanding its site in Wardle, Cheshire. It also provides repackaging, labelling and bar-coding and other services. The company works with retailers to attain the status of an intermediate warehouse and has been chosen by Sainsbury as the NW England consolidation centre for its small regional suppliers.

Source: The Grocer 1999: 56

15.5 Warehouse Management

The Warehouse

The warehouse is traditionally a storage centre for products until they move further down the supply chain. There are different types of warehouse according to their position in the supply chain:

▶ A product supplier may own or lease a warehouse to store stocks of its products. The warehouse is usually adjacent to the factory but it may also be a major distribution centre some distance from the factory. The producer may also use a warehouse to stock spare parts for appliances and also parts and materials from its suppliers.

▶ A wholesaler may own or lease a warehouse to store goods from various manufacturers. It may then be some distance from the retailers that the wholesaler serves.

▶ A specialist distributor may own or lease a warehouse to store goods for different producers as part of their distribution services.

▶ An independent warehousing company may rent out space in a public warehouse to various producers, wholesalers and retailers on short-term contract. It may also undertake additional services for producers of retailers.

▶ A retailer may own or lease a warehouse to supply several stores. The warehouse will usually be some distance from the retail outlets in order to save on expensive retail space. Many retailer-owed warehouses are now contracted out to specialist distribution firms who undertake the complete management of the warehouse as part of an integrated logistics and distribution service.

Retailers often have some storage space attached to the store, though the trend is to reduce this area. Large grocery retailers only use this area for receiving and short-term holding of deliveries, which are often made daily and sometimes twice daily. Many furniture retailers, including discount supplier MFI, have moved to fulfilling orders from a distribution centre. Electrical retailers deliver large appliances from central depots and keep only small quantities of smaller appliances in the storage area.

Some warehouses perform mixed functions. For instance, the large grocery retailers may use consolidation centres for smaller suppliers. Deliveries from these small suppliers are then consolidated into larger mixed loads and sent to regional distribution centres. Larger suppliers may supply the regional distribution centres direct from their own warehouses or factories.

Warehouse Design and Layout

In the traditional warehouse operation, goods are stored in rows or aisles in a rectangular grid pattern. The type of product and the ease and efficiency of handling them determines the type of physical storage system used, such as stacking in boxes on pallets, on racks or in bin shelving.

Warehouse management determines the height, depth, length and space between the rows. It has to balance the greater utilization of the available space against the extra time taken to store and collect items. The warehouse can save space by increasing the height of a row, but this makes it more difficult to reach some items and increases the average time to collect items. Similarly, if the warehouse increases the number of transverse or cross-aisles, this reduces the time an operator takes to store or collect items but also reduces the available storage space. The depth of an aisle is sufficient to store large items or one or two pallets on which the goods are stored. The aisles usually allow goods to be picked from the back or the front and they should be wide enough to allow the two-way travel of warehouse vehicles.

Storage and Picking of Goods

Deliveries of goods are made to the *drop-off point*. This often serves as the *pick-up point*, where goods are loaded onto wagons for delivery to customers. The operators unload the goods and take them to their pre-assigned storage *location*.

When an order is received, a *picker* has to identify the storage locations, travel to the locations, *pick* the required quantity of each product, confirm the picking on the list, and bring the items to the pick-up point for loading. The time spent on picking orders is a major cost in warehouse operations. It depends on the distance the picker has to travel and how items are selected and made up into the customer order.

The distance that the picker has to travel depends on the location of the items and the route taken by the picker. Many warehouses decide on the locations of items largely at random, depending on the space required and the space available, but they usually group similar items together. This usually uses more of the whole warehouse and reduces congestion in the aisles as it spaces out the flow of vehicles. However, it may cause excessive travel time for pickers, particularly when items in frequent or heavy demand are long distances from the pick-up point. An alternative approach is to use *volume-based storage*, where frequently required items or products that are demanded in large quantities are placed. This significantly reduces the average distance pickers have to travel to pick an order, but can cause problems through increased traffic congestion as pickers get in one another's way (Petersen 1999).

The picker usually adopts a simple rule of thumb or heuristic approach to work his or her way round the warehouse. For instance, one simple approach is for the picker to walk across the top of the aisles and go down the first aisle containing any required items. The picker continues down the aisle picking the required items and leaves the aisle at the other end. He or she then moves to the next aisle containing any required items and repeats the process. The picker avoids those aisles not containing any required items. The picker will also have gone along the back aisle. More sophisticated procedures take into account the gap between different picks, but any such procedure must be kept simple in order to ensure that no item is missed. Nowadays, computer-based warehouse management programs may be used, although the routes need to be easy for pickers to follow. The management of very large warehouses may also find it worthwhile investing in automatic picking equipment.

Case 15.7 New Automated National Distribution Centre for SmithKline Beecham

SmithKline Beecham opened a new automated national distribution centre in Gloucester in 1999 to distribute 600 nutritional and consumer healthcare products to 4000 retail outlets.

The centre replaces the previous network of 11 warehouses and was designed and built by Wincanton Logistics. Wincanton also manage the centre and use Wincanton's own warehouse management system to control the automated handling equipment. This stores, locates and collects products for dispatch automatically and reduces handling to maintain better product quality. Products are also scanned repeatedly during the various processes to achieve picking accuracy of 99.9 per cent.

The centre does 24-hour, five-day delivery, but can operate seven days a week if customers require it. It also delivers at night and weekends to smooth loads for multiples.

Source: The Grocer 2000b: 56

The Impact of Supply Chain Collaboration on Warehouse Management

Modern supply chain planning has developed in order to reduce waste and excess inventory between trading partners and improve the availability of products to the final consumer. As a result, there have been several developments that have affected warehouse management.

There is a trend to increasing numbers of small orders and daily deliveries. Technological developments and competitive pressures have seen the trend towards *mass customization*, with deliveries tailored precisely to customer (retailer) demand. Regional distribution centres may operate postponement programmes for certain consumer goods. These include, for instance, the final configuration, labelling and packaging of different variants of computer printers or of computers for delivery either to a retailer or direct to a consumer. Products such as fashion items and CDs can also be finally labelled and packaged at warehouses.

Many warehouses now have to support *continuous flow distribution*, where the aim is to minimize the time goods are in storage. This is the result of many retailers moving to just-in-time deliveries. *Cross-docking* facilities exist in many warehouses to allow the direct transfer of batches of products from suppliers' lorries to distributor's lorries for transport to the retailer's outlets or distribution centre.

Some suppliers and retailers have been developing collaborative planning, forecasting and replenishment (CPFR) methods. This calls for the sharing of relevant information between the supply chain partners. These methods require warehouses to use computer technology to provide information in *real time* to its supply chain partners. This means that the warehouse processes information as soon as it is received and constantly provides up-to-date information to other supply chain members.

Competitive pressures are forcing businesses to reduce the cycle time from production to consumption and improve the availability of the product. One effect of this is to increase the use of time-definite delivery, which is to provide specific slot times when specific deliveries are to be made. This applies also to goods being shipped out of the warehouse to meet specified delivery times at the next stage of the supply chain.

The outsourcing of distribution operations by the retailer also leads to several logistics operators effectively providing vendor-managed inventory services. This means that with the transmission of sales data from the retailer, the logistics provider determines timing and quantity of orders from suppliers. Vendor-managed inventories are one way of improving the flow of goods through the system, although few suppliers have been able to progress to even co-managed inventory with retailers.

Case 15.8 New Technology in the Warehouse: Automated Fast Frozen

Bird's Eye Walls opened the UK's largest automated frozen food warehouse at Hams Hall near Birmingham in May 1999. The warehouse replaces two warehouses in Norfolk and Humberside and handles the national distribution of all Bird's Eye Walls' frozen food. The only exception is ice cream for the impulse sector, which is serviced from its Gloucester cold store.

Bird's Eye Walls has outsourced the management of the entire operation: Power Europe manages the centre and the Frigoscandia handles the distribution. This leaves Bird's Eye Walls free to concentrate on its core activities of frozen food manufacture and marketing.

The centre operates 24 hours a day, seven days a week and provides improved service for its customers:

▶ Retailers can place a single order and receive single delivery. Previously they had to place orders at Lowestoft and Humberside depots and receive two deliveries. Customers also gain the cost efficiency of fuller vehicles.

▶ Lead-times are being reduced from a minimum of 48 hours to 24 hours. This helps retailers at holiday periods, because they can now leave ordering to nearer the time.

▶ The warehouse is meeting retailer's requirements for smaller more frequent deliveries, It can deliver any time within the 24-hour cycle so it can fit within the retailers' receiving slot.

Source: The Grocer 2000c: 56

Computerized stock rotation and traceability is an increasingly important technique. These can use radio data terminal technology to allow every item and pallet to be bar-coded and scanned. This allows for full traceability of products from production through to the supermarket shelf, which is increasingly important in modern food retailing.

References

Anderson, D. L. and Lee, H. (1999) 'Synchronized supply chains: the new frontier', http://anderson.ascet.com/

Billington, C. and Amaral, J. (1999) Investment in product design to maximize profitability through postponement, ASCET 1, http://billington.ascet.com

BNet Management guides: logistics and supply chain management, http://www.bnet.co.uk

Brunfaut, O. and Shipley, J. (1999) 'The solution to that six percent', *The Grocer,* 13 February: 58.

Bruun-Jensen, J. and Shipley, J. (2000) 'Net: Picking the right option' *The Grocer,* 5 February: 44–7.

The Council of Logistics Management (2000) http://www.clm1.org/

Cull, C. (1998) 'It's time to deliver', *The Grocer,* 31 January: 30–2.

The Grocer (1997) 'Drawing lessons from drawbars', 8 February: 53.

The Grocer (1999) 'Flexible base cost solution', 13 February: 56.

The Grocer (2000a) 'Nisa-Today's new combined deliveries benefit stores', 5 February: 53.

The Grocer (2000b) 'National centre panacea for SmithKline Beecham', 5 February: 56.

The Grocer (2000c) 'BEW fast frozen success', 5 February: 56.

Kilgore, S. (1999) 'Dynamic supply chains alter traditional models', http://kilgore.ascet.com/

Murphy, Y. (1997) 'Heinz meanz shared distribution first', *The Grocer,* 8 February: 57.

Petersen, C. G. (1999) 'The impact of routing and storage policies on warehouse efficiency', *International Journal of Operations & Production Management,* 19(10): 1053–64.

Supply-Chain Today (2001) Glossary/reference, http://supplychaintoday.com

Delivering the Product

16 Rolling Out the Goods: Developing New
    Relationships

17 People in Retailing: Making People
    Matter

18 Out-of-Store Retailing: Buy by Wire

19 International Retailing
    Internationalization and Globalization

20 A Review of Retailing: Environment and
    Operations

P
A
R
T

4

Rolling Out the Goods: Developing New Relationships

This chapter covers the following topics:

► Controlling merchandise as part of a strategy.

► Retailers' use of information systems.

► Relationship management.

From lifestyle to enthusiast
This garden centre uses visual merchandising to broaden its appeal to many different customers.

New Ways in Old England
The charm of an English country town invites shoppers to stay and spend in this modern factory outlet.

Elegance breathes quality
Understated displays create the sense of elegance in this modern department store

Rolling Out the Goods: Developing New Relationships

Introduction and Core Concepts

Some unique possibilities are available to retailers as a result of progress in thinking, technology and shopping culture. In particular the technological change that has swept through developed economies in Europe, Asia and the USA has transformed the way retailers operate. The advent of cheap and easy-to-use computer systems has made it possible for retailers to centralize key functions such as sales, purchasing and ordering. The small independent retailer has also benefited from computer technology, which has automated some of the more laborious and repetitive tasks like accounting and invoicing. The rethinking of these processes has brought retailers closer to their suppliers and the manufacturers that produce their merchandise.

Other techniques surrounding the arranging and buying of merchandise produce a detailed plan and strategy for retailers to manage their merchandise in distinct categories. This type of approach has meant that the larger retail business can manage and plan merchandise very precisely, thus gaining considerable competitive advantages.

16.1 Retail Information Systems

For all retail businesses, information systems (IS) are vital to maximize the efficiency of the operation. Even the small independent business needs to keep up with the competition by creating efficiencies and automating the more mundane processes. This may be something straightforward like using a personal computer for simple accounting functions and routine transactions. For example, sales or order processing provides a cheap way of handling many transactions at the same time. Invoices can be generated simply by using templates and provide a cheap way of storing data at low cost, and with great accuracy. When the time comes to produce the end-of-year accounts the data are simply called up and printed out. For the larger retailer, electronic transactions are vital to the existence of the business. Computing power is used to handle automated tills linked to stock replenishment and purchasing. Wages and salaries are also handled by the system. Modern retail operations are unable to function efficiently without computers and information systems.

All types of retail business use information systems and in particular the retailing of services. This is where efficiencies are arguably more crucial because of the lack of tangible products. In the hotel sector, systems are used to great advantage to track enquiries from potential customers and make bookings. The UK hotel chain Travel Inn, for example, employs a reservations system that enables a booking clerk to view the availability of rooms when a customer telephones the reservations *hot line*. Because of the information at their disposal, the clerk is able to offer different types and classes of rooms, such as smoking and non-smoking family, executive, or even a large suite. Customers expect to be informed of this information and to have the room available when they arrive. The hotel can meet the customer's expectations by ensuring that the room is cleaned and that the linen and tea and coffee facilities are in the room when the customer arrives.

Another retailer of services that relies heavily on information systems is an airline business. For example, the British Airways reservations system will help a booking agent to advise a customer whether or not a seat is available on a particular flight and day of their choice. For the customer, this is highly important and will make the difference between using British Airways or shopping elsewhere. For the airline, it means the difference between making a sale or loss of business. In addition, the system provides accurate and timely information about the number and nature of the passengers booked on its flights. This makes it possible to maximize loads thereby keeping the costs of tickets down. It also means that they can if they wish offer special discounts when expected loads are down, as it is better to make some money than none at all. Without an information system a modern airline could not function.

Bar-code Scanning

In the retail trade generally, information systems are crucial to the day-to-day operation. Food retailing has seen the most use of information systems because of the fast-moving and competitive nature of the merchandise. Retailers like Tesco and Asda use systems to track sales transactions that are processed at the checkout with bar-code scanners.

> ⇨ Bar-code scanning – the term 'scanning' refers to a laser system that identifies bar codes on products. Each bar code relates to information held on computer about the product being scanned. As the scanner is passed over the bar code the price and description of the item are called up from the central information system and the sale is registered. The scanning system used in Tesco stores, for example, is known as 'Checkout Plus', which stands for 'Price Look-Up System'.

These provide the retailer with a minute-by-minute account of the sale of products, and the available stocks held at the back of the store. Held on computer, this information is also linked to loyalty cards. The retailer can therefore check things like which products and special offers appeal to particular customers. Promotional offers such as mailshots are timed and targeted more efficiently. Customers feel more in tune or connected to the retailer, as their needs are catered for specifically. This means that the retailer offers customers a better service and retains their loyalty in the longer term.

> ⇨ Bar codes and EAN numbers – every product has a bar code as a representation of its European Article Number or EAN. The EAN number of a product can be found below the bar code. It normally has 13 digits but may have only eight on smaller products. The first two numbers represent the marketing country; the next five identify the suppliers of the product, and the following five identify the product. The final figure acts as a check digit for the previous 12 numbers so that the computer can validate the code.

Supermarket scanning systems, or EPOS which stands for electronic point of sale, came into being following the introduction of the small but powerful personal computers in the early 1970s. Most of the retail application development took place in the USA and the first installation in the UK was in 1981. Previous trials helped to develop the bar-code numbers for product labels, and the equipment to be installed in the supermarkets. By 1992 the system had been implemented in all of Tesco's UK stores.

The Benefits of EPOS

There are a number of benefits that stem from the use of scanning systems and these not only benefit the retailer but the customer as well. The following is an example of some of the various advantages of using scanning at the checkout.

For the Customer

▶ Improved efficiency.

▶ Automatic printing of cheques.

▶ Cash back facility.

▶ Improved promotions.

▶ Itemized till receipts.

There are of course many reasons why retailers use these types of scanning systems. The benefits of a modern scanning system can be divided into two main categories: hard and soft benefits.

> ⇨ Hard benefits are likely to be quantifiable and for this reason they are easily identified.

> ⇨ Soft benefits – difficult to quantify like, for example, some type of public relations exercise. Soft benefits may increase sales and profitability but in a manner that is difficult to demonstrate.

For the Retailer

Soft benefits include:

▶ sales-based ordering

▶ reduced stock levels

▶ reduced wastage

▶ promotional analysis and sales analysis.

Hard benefits include:

▶ improved transaction accuracy (reduces checkout error)

▶ faster and more efficient throughput

▶ improved customer service

▶ improved staff productivity

▶ scanning systems allow checkouts to give discounts and provide coupons.

Retailers use EPOS systems to track sales via scanned bar codes. This enables the retailer to provide the products that are in demand and make other products more attractive by offering price discounts.

Computer Systems and the Supply Chain

The extent to which data transfer systems are embedded in modern retail organizations are now taken for granted by most people . However, the data that retailers collect and analyse are essential and permit them to survive and grow. For the large retailer, using an information system enables them to plan and control their business to provide a better service to their customers at a lower cost. However, information systems are used throughout the entire supply chain, from the sourcing of basic materials to the final customer.

At the product manufacturers, for example, as soon as the retailer or wholesaler transmits the sales order, and they have been accepted by a sales order processing system, the data can be analysed to predict patterns of demand. This helps the company to plan for the future. Also, these data can be sent across to other systems, such as production planning, to help ensure that the right goods are produced at the right time and in the right place. This enables the company to deliver the specification asked for by the buyer; in this case the retailer.

Many retailers now share EPOS data with their suppliers so that the suppliers can have the merchandise most in demand available in their warehouses. In this way, the retailer and supplier can plan for the right type and quantity of merchandise at the lowest possible cost. This inevitably benefits the customer.

Internet technology has increased the possibilities for the use of shared systems, as the public networks can be used to allow the different systems to communicate (or talk) with each other. This is not normally possible with corporate networks, as they tend to be restricted for use inside the business. The freedom of public networks not only aids the supplier with their task of calculating the retailer's demand, but it also creates wider access. For example, Sainsbury's management can have access to a supplier's stock levels and availability, and the space available in Sainsbury's distribution centre at the same time. The end user, or the customer, is the beneficiary because the retailer is able to maintain customer loyalty by making sure the product is always in the store.

16.2 Category Management

The increasing use of retail information systems has meant that retailers have been able to develop methods that focus the business very specifically on the customer. In particular, the way in which groups or categories of merchandise are managed to maximize customer satisfaction and retail store efficiency, is of major importance to retailers. We learnt about the importance of planning merchandise and assortment mixes in Chapter 7. This covered some of the major merchandising issues, such as space planning and assortments linked to customers' buying patterns. Here we introduce category management, which is a relatively new method of controlling and managing merchandise groupings, using a vertical rather than functional approach.

Case 16.1 Category management as a strategy in grocery retailing

Developed in 1993 for the US grocery distribution channel, category management has been effective in various retail situations across the US, Europe, South Africa and Latin America. Category management provides a strategic benefit by organizing the grocery retailer's merchandise into a set of 150–250 product categories. These categories are treated individually and have their own function with regard to issues such as sales, profit and productivity objectives. Categories are typically distinct and manageable groups such as health and beauty products that consumers perceive to be related. This may introduce some innovative categories such as 'snack shops' and 'winter remedies' (Croft 1998). Retailers are thus able to gain sustainable competitive advantages and differentiation by competing on the basis of each category. Another important function is to stop the erosion of sales of these types of products to 'category killers'. For customers, this approach brings greater benefits and value than they could otherwise through the traditional retail approach. Software programs have been developed that can analyze the data necessary to operate the category management process. This has made the task of implementing a category management strategy much less complex and reduced the time required to review new categories (Gruen 1998). Large manufacturers, such as Robertson's, also manage specific categories for retailers, which can benefit all the products in the category (*The Grocer*, 1999: 42).

Category management differs from the traditional way of running a retail business, as it treats each major merchandise category as a business in itself. This alters the orientation of the retail business to a more vertical arrangement. The retailer runs the business as a series of integrated business units, and each unit represents a merchandise category. Advantages to this approach centre on the ability to target the customer's needs more effectively.

There are a number of basic characteristics of category management that sets it apart from the more conventional retailing approach. Some of the key issues are contained within Table 16.1.

Table 16.1 Some Characteristics of Category Management

Function	Action
Build a target group of customers	Attract by destination categories, e.g. breakfast cereals, pet food
Create unique consumer value and protect market segments	Stock what the consumer wants and how they want it, in advance of the competition
Enhance image to target groups	Employ special promotional displays and techniques
Develop a powerful retail strategy	Use category management to build store traffic and generate excitement through character products. Establish assortment, and placement of stock-keeping unit (SKU) based on the best way to satisfy the customer
The employment of practical in-store management	Each SKU is allocated a category. Use IT to manage the merchandise and employ data-driven, fact-based decision-making

The Category Management Process

As the list in Table 16.1 suggests, category management is a significant step toward balancing a store's merchandise to consumer demand, and greatly reducing stock outs. Although category management is labour intensive, the benefits far outweigh the costs in terms of time and effort to implement the system. The following stages are typical of the steps that a retailer may take towards the in-store implementation of category management:

1 Generate a report by category of all sales in the last three months. Some stores may have to approach each supplier for these data.

2 Identify the best-selling items in the category (for example, health and beauty). This is usually the top 20 per cent to 30 per cent of the total merchandise mix.

3 Single out merchandise with little or no sales in the last three months. This will vary depending on the size of the store and its sales volume.

4 Discontinue any merchandise with minimal sales by removing the product from the shelves.

5 Using the additional free space, double up on the top-selling items in the category, making sure these products are close as possible to eye level.

6 Repeat this review and inventory balancing by category throughout the store every three months.

We can see that the fundamental goal of category management is to produce a more efficient consumer-driven approach to the business. This will increase profits and customer loyalty, because the retailer's customers will be provided with exactly the right merchandise. By moving through the above stages the retailer will rethink the way merchandise is selected for sale in the store, and allocate space to best-selling lines, therefore, maximizing sales and reducing stock outs.

However, for retail management to assess categories requires a variety of analytical tools designed to determine the category's strengths, weaknesses, opportunities and threats. For example, producing an analysis will involve comparisons of sales data scanned in the store, and market data obtained from external sources and based on consumer, distributor, supplier and market information. This will provide a detailed assessment of such factors as market segments, brands and the retailer's SKUs. Spreadsheets are normally used for this type of analysis and calculations would determine such factors as contribution to margin, gross margin return on investment, gross margin profitability and annual inventory turns.

Information Technology and Category Management

Employing category management techniques requires retailers to adopt a 'scientific' approach to managing the business. Because category management is driven by data collection and analysis, the process relies on the use of information systems. Advances in information technology and decision-support software have changed the way retailers manage their businesses. For example, the huge amounts of data that retail scanning collects are changed into useful information. This helps the retailer to target their customers in a precise manner never dreamed of in the early days of the supermarket. The average retail system now collects, manages and analyses huge volumes of data from multiple sources, all of which requires an investment in hardware, software and often specialized personnel.

> ⇨ The level of investment required for category management precludes the small independent retailers, who are restricted by the cost and scale of this type of operation. However, a small retailer may wish to operate a form of category management functioning on a basic level. This may use a simple information system, and track sales of merchandise and the profit generated and contribution to margin.

We can see that the implementation of category management is made possible and less complex by the use of software programs that integrate various data sources, and then automatically analyse the results. Many of these software programs are available through consultants or large data providers.

> ⇨ Example – Procter & Gamble and Coca-Cola have developed their own custom-made category management software analysis tools.

Using retail information systems allows retail managers to produce summaries of categories very quickly. Response times are therefore shortened as conducting a category review is far less difficult. Customer requirements can be met speedily and loyalty is maintained.

A significant feature of category management is the shift to a fact-based decision-making approach that effectively changes the role of the retail buyer. As category business planning is about finding the best way to satisfy the consumer, the merchandise assortments and placement of SKUs are determined by what the data reveals. This makes for an objective approach that relegates the traditional buying function to more of a logistical role. For buyers the emphasis is to minimize distribution and stock holding while ensuring that there is enough stock to satisfy customer needs. Relationships between suppliers and retailers are therefore crucial to the success of the category management process.

Supply Chain Benefits

Similar to the supply chain partnerships that EPOS provides, category management makes it possible for retailers to reach forward and backward within the supply chain. For instance, a retailer can move forward towards the customer to gain insight into shoppers' needs and preferences. This allows retail management to align merchandise categories more accurately to the market and customers' expectations. It also makes it possible to target promotional campaigns specifically and improve the performance of individual categories.

16.3 Integrating the Supply Chain

Category management is one of the modern techniques retailers are using to provide customers with the right products at the right time in the right place. Improved computer technology and point-of-sale equipment track stock in store and reduce the level of uncertainty about requirements. Developments in logistics have also contributed to reduction in costs and the availability of products to the consumer, as discussed in Chapter 15.

These improvements to the retailing process make use of advances in information technology. They also rely for their effectiveness on increased cooperation and the sharing of information between organizations in the supply chain. This cooperation helps to overcome the problems of suboptimization in the supply chain, when the various members operate in isolation from their suppliers or customers.

The application of these techniques is based on the view that the only value is that created by the consumer and that holding stocks is a cost not an asset. However, unless the whole supply chain is coordinated, consumer information will not be effectively translated into appropriate production and stocks will be greater than strictly necessary, leading to reduced value and greater costs across the chain as a whole. Several large firms have recognized the advantages of integrating these methods so that suppliers could provide sufficient quantities according to consumer demand. This new approach underlies the two closely related activities of *quick response* and *efficient consumer response* that represent a revolution in modern retailing.

Quick response was developed in the US clothing industry in order to shorten the retail order cycle.

> ⇨ The retail order cycle is the time between the retailer identifying merchandise requirements and the time taken for the merchandise to be in store.

Quick Response and Efficient Consumer Response

Quick response (QR) uses point-of-sale data and other consumer data to determine consumer demand automatically. The information is passed back up the supply chain through electronic data interchange (EDI) to enter the order, which is based on actual consumer demand. Further cooperation between retailers and manufacturers would improve the efficiency of distribution to the end consumer. Application of these methods has greatly reduced the order cycle. The process reduces the time taken to make the appropriate merchandise available to customers and reduces the amount of stocks held and the capital tied up in them.

Efficient consumer response develops and extends the underlying idea of quick response to increase efficiency and reduce costs in the grocery supply chain.

> ⇨ Efficient consumer response (ECR) is a consumer-demand based system in which supply chain members work together to satisfy consumer needs with the lowest possible cost.

Efficient consumer response integrates retailing with distribution, warehousing and manufacturing so that the retailer can provide a better service to customers. It uses technology to improve the speed and accuracy of each step of the supply process. It also uses any form of collaborative relationships to eliminate inefficiencies and reduce costs for all partners. Efficient consumer response was developed for the grocery trade, but its basic concepts can be applied to the whole range of consumer goods retailing.

Efficient consumer response has come about because of major changes in supply and consumer markets that threatened the position of major retailers and producers. For consumers, the issue of convenience is of major importance and stores that stock the right level and type of merchandise secure a competitive edge. Making sure the merchandise is in the store is key to maintaining customer loyalty. Partly this is because consumers are facing increasing time constraints and require high levels of convenience. Thus, shoppers will habitually tie themselves to particular retailers for grocery shopping. However, if customers are inconvenienced with stock outs, they are far more likely to switch stores.

When retaining stock levels the retailer must avoid overstocking because of issues like margins, space management and wastage. This type of operation makes for a very competitive and dynamic environment, where one multiple competes against the other for a limited customer base.

Electronic retail information systems have provided retailers with a means of managing the supply chain activities. Integrated systems provide the crucial link back to the suppliers, and join the supply chain partners with the retailer's own distribution system. Far more efficient retail systems have increased customer expectations regarding the nature of the offering, and the replenishment of the stock. As a result, customers have become far more sophisticated in their needs, and what they expect from the outcomes of their shopping strategies. For example, customers come to expect reductions or sale items whatever the time of day, or day of the week.

Increasing customer sophistication and changing consumer requirements have necessitated changes in the retail offering. The short-term marketing activities of suppliers and retailers have led to a proliferation of brands and product extensions. This has been criticized as offering an illusion of choice, without providing real choice for consumers. Continuous promotions tend to confuse the customer rather than create a real understanding of the range of items available. This can add to the confusion and discourage loyal customers from maintaining their shopping patterns. Less stable consumption patterns lead to increased costs. As a result suppliers and retailers have now begun reducing the number of SKUs in a product category, particularly in the grocery trade.

The Nature of Efficient Consumer Response

Efficient consumer response has a number of objectives:

▶ To improve the supply process. This can be achieved by reducing distribution costs, removing costs that do not add value, and reducing the response time. Within this context, stockholding increases costs and so reducing stocks held within the system is now important.

▶ To improve the value to the customer. This can be achieved by improving the quality of products and services to consumers. Again, removing costs that do not add value means careful investigation of the market to ensure that products are effectively specified without undue frills.

▶ To improve the efficiency of the distribution system. Streamlining the information required to run the system.

The Components of Efficient Consumer Response

In order to achieve its objectives, ECR uses three interrelated strategies (Coopers & Lybrand 1996):

1 *Category management*. Within the context of ECR, category management also includes the efficient promotion of products such as special

offers. This will eliminate those promotional practices that lead to higher than necessary stocks and so costs in the supply chain. It will also eliminate unnecessary promotions that do not significantly generate extra sales. This also takes a more cautious approach to new product introductions. The high failure rate of new products often leads to unreasonably high stock levels.

2 *Product replenishment.* The supply chain needs to respond quickly to changes in demand. This reduces the amount of stocks required across the whole supply chain in order to meet the customer demand. Electronic point of sale data are used to plan the order cycle thus eliminating unnecessary costs. The retailer will support this system through efficient warehouse and distribution management.

3 *Enabling technologies.* This requires the effective use of systems such as:
   (a) The bar-coding of SKUs that is linked to an efficient database management system.
   (b) EDI and electronic funds transfer.
   (c) Using activity-based costing (ABC) methods to track costs accurately.

Implementing Efficient Consumer Response

A retailer wishing to get involved with ECR may visit the ECR Europe website for advice and information. Efficient consumer response activity may start with any part of the business and select an appropriate trading partner to form a strategic alliance. Continuous replenishment programmes (CRP) and category management are typically two areas of frequent collaboration. The partnership must establish an open relationship that may seem unnerving to businesses operating in highly competitive markets. The basis of this openness must be a shared objective, backed by a combination of pooled resources.

Implementing the partnership requires both parties to establish a smooth flow of information and products, with the supplier and retailer working together to forecast and plan activities. In these situations, both partners may undertake tasks traditionally undertaken by the other, depending on their relative efficiency.

16.4 Customer Relationship Management

For all retailers, the structure and members of the supply chain are crucial factors in running the business. The small independent retailer, for example, will give careful consideration to the nature of the wholesaler before a decision to use it is made. Practical considerations such as the type of merchandise the wholesaler stocks, its availability and prices charged will be high up on the list. However, the retailer will also take into account issues such as contact with people and personal service. Having selected a satisfactory wholesaler, the retailer will develop a relationship with it over time that will help to bond the retailer to the supplier.

Consumers develop similar types of relationships that bond them to their favourite retailer. Building relationships is one of the traditional but often hidden skills of the small retailer. It is also important in retaining customers who could just as easily bond with competitors. A thriving independent retailer understands the financial reward from identifying and cultivating potential long-term customers. The retailer understands what they value and is constantly alert for snippets of information to develop personalized offerings to the customer. The retailer becomes the customer's greengrocer, cobbler, insurance broker, pub or tea shop, because it can empathize with the customer.

The growth of large-scale retailing across many sectors replaced these customer relationship skills by methods of mass marketing and standardized customer service. These segment customers according to price sensitivity and quality requirements. However, increasingly competitive markets and the growing sophistication of the consumer are now forcing many large retailers (and their suppliers) to increase the level of personalization in the services provided. Individual consumer requirements that were previously neglected are now recognized as having a high impact on customer loyalty and spending. They are important in situations where:

▶ The retailer needs to be able to relate the service to the customer's requirements, as in financial services and travel services.

▶ The staff who deal with the customer may change and the customer's details may need to be accessed quickly, as in call centres and after-sales services.

▶ The retailer, such as a supermarket or mail order retailer, needs a relatively lost-cost method of targeting promotional campaigns for supermarkets.

▶ The retailer wishes to use automatic processing of sales and order fulfilment, such as in Internet sales.

In each of these examples, the retailer makes use of a 'collective memory' of its customers (Thompson 1999) in order to market its products or services more effectively. This collective memory requires an appropriate database of customers. The database would include any relevant customer information, provided it is permitted by data protection legislation. The retailer's *customer relationship management* (CRM) programme determines the information required in the database and how that information should be used. The CRM programme will also use an appropriate computer-based CRM package in order to deliver these improved services to the customer.

The Nature of Customer Relationship Management

> ⇨ Customer relationship management is a business strategy that puts the customer at the centre of a company's sales and marketing practices in order to increase the number of customers and serve them more effectively. It uses appropriate computer-based system to support this strategy.
> *Source*: adapted from the CRMGuru.com definition in Sims (1999)

Customer relationship management recognizes that even satisfied customers will not return if they find other retailers providing greater value. One of the objectives of CRM is to use appropriate technology to collect information that will help the retailer to understand what its consumers value and thereby turn them into profitable customers. A CRM system can be used in different ways. For instance:

▶ A retailer can use it to automate its marketing. A CRM system can be used to gather data on customer spending when customers use loyalty cards and automated payment systems. Product and service information can be sent automatically to customers according to specifically tailored mailing lists, which reduce the amount of staff time involved. The direct computer sellers, Dell, use their automatic emailing to inform potential customers of special offers on their factory outlet website.

▶ A retailer can use it to automate its selling. Selling over the net is one example. This is particularly useful for service retailers as diverse as coach operators and insurance companies. It can also be used to support store sales. For instance, domestic appliance retailers such as Currys can hold a limited stock in store. However, a salesperson can instantly check the regional availability of a washing machine and provide a delivery date using the store's computer system.

▶ Call centres can instantly categorize enquiries. For instance, large hotel groups use call centres to improve reservations services. Once the call centre operator has the requisite data, the customer's query can be answered within seconds and suitable alternative accommodation may be offered if the requested accommodation is unavailable.

▶ Service enquiries to call centres can be dealt with more quickly because the relevant information can be viewed on a screen in front of the operator.

▶ Field service personnel can access information directly relating to the customer, including any technical information required or the availability of parts.

Information systems can also be used to improve the internal links within the organization, so that the retailer can respond more effectively to individual customer requirements. This is particularly important in the growing areas of services retailing. Services by their nature are often sold to market segments of size one, but may go through different stages. Internal tracking of the service will focus attention on final satisfaction for the consumer. In product retailing, additional services are becoming more important and these also provide opportunities to market to specific segments.

Using Information

Electronic point of sale (EPOS) terminals collect a vast amount of data about products and customer buying patterns. Conventional analytical methods can be used to ask questions such as: what do people who buy product X also buy in the store? This can yield some useful answers for in-store merchandising. For instance, a supermarket is likely to eliminate a product that sells very slowly. However, if it finds that the store's biggest customers usually buy that item, then it would make sense to retain the item. Similarly, if people who regularly buy product X also buy product Y in significant quantities, this may lead the store to place the items closer together.

The large number of different SKUs stocked by a supermarket or other large store means that there are billions of possible relationships or hypotheses that could be investigated. This is more than computer technology has been able to handle so far.

Data mining is one method being developed to deal with this problem. It sets out to discover relationships using a more general method of searching through the large amounts of information to discover empirical relationships that are unusual or unexpected. A retailer can also use data mining to identify emerging trends so that it can react rapidly to them. The retailer can also improve stock, staff and shop layout if it knows what customers buy during a single shopping trip (Banks 1996).

Computer-based technology is constantly improving its power and range of support for CRM. Database management and order tracking are just two areas. Another development occurs in computer telephony integration (CTI) and associated developments such as interactive voice response. At its simplest, this brings up customer details on to the computer screen in response to specific telephone numbers or other identifying factors, which improve the speed with which customer enquiries can be dealt with. Call centre representatives (for example, Direct Line Insurance) can quickly and easily relate to the customer and serve the customer more efficiently.

More sophisticated procedures allow repeat callers to be connected automatically to the specific member of staff who dealt with the original enquiry. The major benefit of this technology is that the retailer can track the flow of calls and analyse the pattern of revenue generated.

Implications of Customer Relationship Management for Marketing

The purpose of CRM is to boost profitability by focusing on improving customer value. Customer relationship management can give the retailer a competitive edge by identifying those offers that are most likely to be attractive to which group of customers. The retailer can use databases to test and refine offers to help in the development of this strategy.

Customer relationship management focuses on the customer groups according to the value they generate over their life cycle as customers. It does not necessarily require large, complex systems. Financial services retailers have been successful by keeping their focus narrow and selling through inexpensive direct delivery channels. This simplifies system design and maintenance, and it keeps marketing focused (Ruediger *et al.* 1997).

Customer relationship management systems should be able to track results of a particular promotion and analyse results statistically in order to discover patterns and opportunities.

Implementing Customer Relationship Managment

Customer relationship management seeks to improve profitability by giving customers better service. In this way it is an extension of service quality management. This means that the approach to effective design and implementation is similar:

▶ Implementation must come from the top. Customer relationship management relies on company-wide cooperation and the breaking down of barriers to cooperation.

▶ Plan the system around what the customer wants. Plan the system round the customer life cycle with the retailer: provide the system with the means of listening to customers so that promotional activity responds to dialogue with the customer.

▶ A CRM system will use computer technology and the temptation is to restrict involvement to a few knowledgeable users in order to speed up its introduction. This runs the risk that others would find it difficult to tune in to the system and end up not using it effectively.

▶ The retailer should focus on customer throughput from the beginning to the end of the marketing process. Taking this viewpoint will prevent various departments or sections from improving their own efficiency by pushing problems up or down the line.

▶ Choose appropriate software. This means identifying the technology requirements at each stage of the customer process and having a system appropriate to each stage. Service retailers may have service engineers or field sale people who have direct personal contact with customers in their own homes. They require laptop computers loaded with customer and product details, linked to the retailer's main system. Call centre operators, on the other hand, require a link into the main system so that customer details are brought up on to a screen for updating or amending.

▶ Ensure that sales personnel have adequate support so that they can get fast answers to any question. This includes appropriate enhancements to the system when the sales and marketing system is upgraded. In practice, CRM should be seen as a developmental process rather than a once and for all grand design.

16.5 Retail Security and Information Systems

A retailer may develop a strong competitive position through its marketing and supply chain management. However, its profitability can be significantly damaged through extra losses as a result of various forms of criminal activity perpetrated against it. Most losses are the direct result of criminal action by suppliers, staff, customers and members of the public. Retail crime accounts for about 1 per cent of total retail sales in the UK and rather more than that in the USA (Tonglet and Bamfield 1997). This figure has declined from a much higher level, partly because of more sophisticated technology being used to detect and prevent crime. In addition, a significant amount of losses may occur as a result of damage to stock caused by negligent behaviour or administrative error.

Some crime, such as burglary, is detected at the time it occurs, but most theft by employees, customers and suppliers is detected much later. This requires the retailer to invest in appropriate technology in order to detect and prevent such crime. Selecting appropriate security measures can reduce crime and significantly improve profitability. Spending on security in the UK accounts for about 0.5 per cent of turnover.

Case 16.2 Strategic Partnership in Crime Prevention

Scotland Yard's Counter Action has been helping retailers to combat crime in London since 1994. This has contributed to the drop in commercial robberies in London, which are often well organized with planned escape routes. The police have been working closely with retailers and the business community to provide them with information on combating crime. They promoted the scheme through Crime Prevention Forums, which were originally aimed at senior managers and business owners. Now the programme has been expanded to help middle and junior managers, who are the people that have to face robbers in retail stores. The initiative achieved a reduction of over 6 per cent in commercial robberies in 1998 compared with 1997.

Because of better protective measures, such as closed circuit television and small quantities of cash held on the premises, there has been a shift from traditional targets such as post offices towards small independent retailers. Smaller retailers are more vulnerable because of late night opening, less security and the fact that fewer people are about. Small retailers can now phone free of charge the 'Business Crime Check'. This UK-wide initiative has a large database of crime prevention information to help callers. Among the measures they recommend is the use of professional cash collection carriers. This can be done cheaply and saves valuable staff time.

Source: Hyams 1999a: 8–10

In order to make best use of its security budget the retailer needs to understand the sources of crime and the relative costs and benefits of the various detection and prevention systems available. Increasing security in the past has often meant reducing the visibility and accessibility of the merchandise to the customer, which reduced the level of sales. However, some of the newer security systems improve display and accessibility and can enhance sales and profitability compared with older systems.

Types of Retail Crime

Retail crime may be classified according to its immediate visibility and its direct relationship to the supply chain and store operations of the retailer. Table 16.2 provides one such classification.

Table 16.2 Types of Retail Crime

	Immediately visible	**Not immediately visible**
Not related to retail operations procedures	Arson; criminal damage; burglary	Supplier (vendor) theft (supply chain problem)
Related to retail operations procedures	Sabotage (including wilful damage to stocks); robbery	Shoplifting; employee theft; employee–customer collusive theft (sweethearting)

Research studies have shown that retailers detect less than 3 per cent of conventional crime at the time it occurs (Tonglet and Bamfield 1997). Retailers can only assess the level of crime through an audit of stocks. The stock audit allows the retailer to calculate the amount of *shrinkage* of stock. This is the difference between the retail value of the goods that the retailers receives (or is supposed to have received) and the actual sales value realized when the goods are sold. Shrinkage is expressed as a percentage of gross sales volume.

It is estimated that 70 per cent or more of the shrinkage occurs because of theft by employees, customers and suppliers. Shoplifting appears to be more serious in Britain than in the USA (Tonglet and Bamfield 1997). However, this may be because the use of sophisticated anti-theft devices is more widespread in the USA and also because more effort has been put into detecting staff theft than in Britain.

Retail theft has always had a low rate of detection, arrest and prosecution. Police forces have also reduced the priority the police give to non-violent retail crime. Stores and shopping centres may provide their own security staff but these have limited powers in dealing with criminals. These factors and the advent of new technology have been changing security policy from detection and punishment to managing losses through various methods of prevention and deterrence. Security management is now part of general retail management and figures routinely in staff recruitment and training, store design and operating procedures, equipment programmes and supply chain cooperation.

Shoplifting

Shoplifters fall into different categories: drug addicts who steal to fund their activities, professional gangs that steal for resale and profit as a business, and ordinary people who have a psychological need to steal from shops to get something for nothing (Lin, Hastings and Martin 1994). It is difficult to prevent such activities, but the retailer can take steps to reduce the scale of theft.

Retail staff have a positive security role to play, as they are responsible for the majority of arrests of shoplifters in the UK. Their success in controlling theft by other employees, however, is less effective as this requires the use of sophisticated technology (Tonglet and Bamfield 1997).

A retailer can also reduce the risk of theft by reducing the accessibility of the merchandise. For instance, jewellers have traditionally used glass cases to protect high-value items. Electrical retailers use alarms in order to prevent theft. However, in each case, there is some restriction of the consumer's ability to touch and physically assess the product.

Shoplifters are also naturally deterred by the risk of being seen and identified. As part of its security management, the retailer can plan the layout of the store so that a small number of strategically placed staff have sufficient lines of sight as to be able to cover the whole store area. Closed circuit television is useful, but may be ignored by many thieves. Organized groups use techniques of diversion and intimidation to distract staff attention. Staff training should also help sales staff to identify high-risk situations, such as groups of people for professional shoplifters and groups of youths for juvenile crime. Customer service improvements can also reduce the risk of theft. For instance, the use of greeters in supermarkets and other stores is known to reduce the level of theft because there is greater supervision of customer activity.

Benefit Denial

Physical denial of products to shoplifters is also widely used in clothing and textiles through the use of ink tags. These tags are attached to the garments and need a special tool to remove them. Trying to remove tags will lead to them spilling indelible ink over the clothes denying shoplifters the benefit of the stolen merchandise. This method has some deterrent effect but more organized thieves have learnt how to counter this technique. Tag makers have therefore to increase the strength of the locking pins and make them more difficult to remove.

Electronic Article Surveillance

A major advance in retail security has been the development and deployment of electronic article surveillance (EAS). This system uses electronic tags or labels on items. The tag or label is deactivated when the customer pays for the item. A customer must pass by a *pedestal* or between two pedestals (depending on the system used) when leaving the store. If the tag or label has not been deactivated, the alarm will sound. This system has now improved to the extent that it provides a very cheap means of guarding items.

Case 16.3 Supply Partnership in Security

Boots the Chemist has built a close working relationship with its security supplier. It decided to install electronic article surveillance equipment in its stores. It experimented with acoustic-magnetic, radio frequency and electromagnetic EAS systems. It finally chose the acousto-magnetic system as best fitting in with its store environment. Boots then developed a close relationship with its supplier, Sensormatic, in order to get the best system for its stores. Using key performance targets to manage the relationship, Boots extended the implementation of the security system in stages. This enabled it to test the latest improvements to blend with the open retail environment it wanted to maintain in its stores.

Source: Hyams 1999b: 11

Electronic tagging has been growing slowly and the great majority of products are not routinely tagged. However, certain high value or high-risk items across a range of retailers are being tagged. Some tagging takes place at the store, but this is relatively costly in time. On the other hand, some large retailers and manufacturers are having products tagged at source. The miniaturization of technology has enabled tags or electronic labels to be applied very cheaply. This frees up time for retail staff to concentrate on selling and managing the store environment.

The rapid development of anti-theft technologies for source tagging allows anti-theft labels to be deactivated and reactivated as often as necessary. Manufacturers can now apply inactive labels to merchandise in the factory, thus keeping tagging costs to a minimum. These labels can then be activated as the goods go through the distribution process, if the retailer has the appropriate deactivating system, or left inactive for those retailers that do not have the system installed. Alternatively, the store may activate labels itself.

Dealing with Staff and Supplier Theft

Staff crime is a serious and increasing problem for retailers. Retail employees have many opportunities to steal money and goods from their employers and may also damage the retailer's reputation. Within the store, staff may steal goods directly or through sweethearting.

> ⇨ Sweethearting occurs, for instance, when a supermarket cashier slides items past a scanner to an accomplice who is pretending to buy it.

Employees may also steal money through fraudulent refunds, cancelled transactions and cash thefts. They can also steal security codes, credit card numbers and other information that could expose the retailer or its customers to other types of fraud.

The drive to increasing efficiency has reduced staffing and meant the reduction in procedural controls related to receiving and cash handling. These problems are often difficult to detect, but point of sale (POS) systems are available that can now deal with many of these problems cost-effectively for high-volume retailers. Point of sale systems alert the retailer to possible theft situations using exception reporting.

> ⇨ Exception reporting: a system of identifying problems by unusual occurrences.

An example of exception could be the scanning time at a supermarket checkout. The management may investigate every delay of more than 10 seconds between the scanning of different items in a customer's shopping basket. The delay could mean that the cashier is passing an item to the customer without scanning it in (Muzzi 2000).

Where staff theft is perceived as a problem these POS systems can be integrated with high-resolution cameras, videos and data-tracking systems. Suspect situations over a period of time can be reviewed (Muzzi 2000).

The system can also show where staff procedures are weak and where staff need more training. This not only improves performance but also increases awareness of monitoring, which serves as a deterrent to illegal activity.

Retailers may suffer shrinkage in the delivery system. Problems can occur in receiving and storing of goods, inventory control, and the refrigeration and proper rotation of perishable merchandise. These can be partly avoided through proper monitoring procedures. Accurate systems for aligning supplier and retailer activity are important so that the correct orders are delivered and checked through and the right level of payments charged. For instance, modern computer-controlled procedures with bar-coded products can reduce problems at the distribution centres. Individual grocery suppliers can now make up orders for distribution centres that are already pre-coded to the different supermarkets operated by a retailer. This reduces the effective number of stages merchandise passes through, reduces the probability of error in the distribution chain and enables orders to be traced through to their destination.

In spite of modern technology, security considerations are important in the recruitment and training of staff. The integrity testing and screening of potential employees is widely used in recruiting staff in the USA. This approach is gaining wider acceptance in the UK, although the high level of part-time employment may be seen as a limiting factor in its application. Induction and training programmes should also stress the general benefits of a positive culture of honesty. They should also increase staff awareness of how they can attune their behaviour so that they are alert to the problems of theft and other causes of shrinkage.

References

Banks, M. (1996) 'Valuable discoveries mined from raw data – the amount of data on retailing operations is doubling each year. Review of information technology (17)', *Financial Times*, 7 February: xvii.

Coopers & Lybrand (1996), *Efficient Consumer Response – Europe: Value Chain Analysis Project Overview*, London: Coopers & Lybrand.

Croft, M. (1998) 'Trading Spaces', *Marketing Week*, 5 February: 47–52.

The Grocer (1999) 'Delisting your own products', 16 January: 42.

Gruen, T. (1998) 'Category management: the new science of retailing', *Financial Times*, 26 October: 1.

Hyams, J. (1999a) 'Commercial Flying Squad', *Retail Week*, Retail Crime Report, September: 8–10.

Hyams, J. (1999b) 'Open door policy', *Retail Week*, Retail Crime Report, September: 11.

Lin, B., Hastings, D.A. and Martin, C. (1994) 'Shoplifting in retail clothing outlets: an exploratory research', *International Journal of Retail & Distribution Management*, 22(7): 24–9.

Muzzi, J. (2000) 'All the fixin's', *Security Management*, 44(12): 50–5.

Ruediger, A., Grant-Thompson, S., Harrington, W. and Singer, M. (1997) 'What leading banks are learning about big databases and marketing', *McKinsey Quarterly*, September, issue 3: 187–92.

Sims, D. (2000) 'What is CRM?' CRMGuru.com, 21 March.

Thompson, B. (1999) 'What is CRM? It's not the shoes!' CRMGuru.com, 30 July.

People in Retailing: Making People Matter

This chapter considers the following issues:

▶ Employment in retailing.

▶ Employing the right type of staff.

▶ Planning the workforce.

▶ Developing the team spirit.

People in Retailing: Making People Matter

Introduction and Core Concepts

This chapter pulls together the social dimension of the retail business and identifies the main issues that create a successful retail enterprise. Retailing is about people and their aspirations. Staff are an important asset in meeting those aspirations and laying the foundations for a successful business. A good team of staff and an appropriate working relationship create an important and invaluable asset. The benefits of this are measured in improved customer interaction and, therefore, customer service. These factors are crucial to the long-term profitability and success of the retail organization.

17.1 Retail Employment

Retail employment accounts for about 2.4 million people or about 9 per cent of all employment in the UK (Table 17.1). However, a significant proportion of people employed in retailing is working part-time. Retailing also has a high proportion of female employees and many of these work part-time. There are also a significant number of people self-employed in running the large number of small businesses.

Table 17.1 Employment in Retailing

	1984	1990	2000
Total employment	2.0 m	2.4 m	2.4 m

Source: National Statistics 1996 and 2001

Changes in Employment

The increase in retail employment in the 1980s and the relative stability of employment in the 1990s does not give a full picture of the changing employment situation. The traditional independent retail operator has been in continuous decline since the 1960s. Many firms in this sector, particularly in the grocery sector, had relied on unpaid family labour and small numbers of full-time employees. Part-time employees were a minority. In many larger firms, sales assistants could progress to management as they became more experienced and were willing to take on more responsibility. Larger retailers often decentralized much of their management to their individual stores. Managers made many of decisions as to what to stock and many products were supplied directly to the stores.

However, the pattern of employment changed with the changes in retailing. The growth of the larger firms led to more formal and hierarchical management structures. Part-time employment increased, particularly for women who were increasingly seeking employment, largely on a part-time basis, during this period. Larger retailers could use this part-time employment as a cheap and flexible source of labour that they could adjust to suit prevailing market conditions (Freathy 1997). Part-time employees were also denied many of the benefits, including training and career development that were accorded to full-time employees.

Careers in Retailing

Case 17.1 The Changing Distribution Worker

The amount of floor space used to sell groceries varies significantly across the UK. Relative to the population, London, Cambridgeshire and South Yorkshire have the lowest levels, while Hertfordshire, Cheshire and Tayside have the highest provision. These variations clearly affect the employment opportunities for people who live and work in these regions.
Source: *Economist* 1997: 59.

Retailing is a fast-moving and exciting sector that requires strong leaders and energetic employees. Most staff employed in retail businesses need to be prepared to work longer hours than in other comparable occupations. Modern thinking about the importance of a career in retailing has boosted the job market. Retailers demand better-trained employees and educational institutions have responded with better and a variety of courses that cater for different levels of staff and industry experience.

Traditional attitudes in retailing still persist, however, and this has led to two different career paths: one at the core of the industry and the other on the fringes. The core consists of full-time workers at various grades, who are usually better paid, better trained and have a distinct career path within the organization. Part-time workers have until recently been kept at the fringes. Fringe workers may work at different levels in the company, depending on their previously acquired skills, but will not usually be able to access the development that core workers can.

Core workers gain specific company skills and attitudes during the course of their employment, which make them more valuable to the company. Employers recognize this and, in order to attract talented people, provide career structures that, starting with trainee management positions, enable progression up through the company. Management training programmes are an important means of recruitment to such companies, which tend to promote from within to many posts. However, as a manager progresses through the company, the required skills and attributes change as that manager takes on broader responsibilities. This allows more flexibility in recruiting people from outside to fill more senior posts in the organization.

Similarly, at a lower level, a store supervisor or team leader has to understand how the company works. So supervisors tend to be appointed from within the existing workforce. Direct appointment to supervisor from outside would be unusual, though not impossible. However, progression from supervisor to manager level requires a range of additional skills that are more important than specific abilities. These more general skills are normally acquired through education or a wider employment experience. They limit the chances of progression from supervisor level and open up other opportunities for more highly educated people as trainee or assistant managers. Experienced managers can then transfer across companies as deputy or store manager, or even at senior management level.

In order to attract people into the company, retailers have to set pay and conditions at levels comparable to those generally available. The company also operates an internal staff structure, which determines pay and promotion to various grades within the workforce according to the company's own specific requirements. However, there are likely to be significant barriers to promotion at various entry levels. So, women who make up the vast number of sales assistants find it difficult to climb further up the company. This also makes it difficult for women managers to progress further.

Traditional attitudes have limited progression of women through the management system (Broadbridge 1999). They have also deterred men from seeking promotion because of the commitment required and the need to relocate in national chains. The position of women is likely to change only slowly, partly because one inhibitor to their development is the small number of women in senior managerial positions who can act as role models for aspiring women managers. This situation is likely to continue for some time as a breaking the barriers will take 20 to 30 years to work its way through the system.

Company Ethos and Career Development

The attitude towards staff and customers is part of the ethos of the organization. For the purposes of this discussion we will use the word *ethos* to explain the attitudes beneath the way a retail organization functions. Ethos is the prevailing view or collective thinking that drives the stakeholders of the company. Company ethos can be very strong and well known and may be an important part of the company's reputation. For example, some organizations pride themselves on their longstanding ethos of customer service, or their treatment of staff.

This ethos determines the type of selling approach and strategy employed. For instance, large multiples will have a prevailing view regarding price, location, merchandise and so on that focus on maintaining and developing market share and profitability. In contrast, many small independent retailers have a different predisposition towards their retailing activities: to stay small and maintain a low-cost base. Ethos has, therefore, a significant impact on the way a retailer operates across a range of activities, including the management of staff.

> ⇨ Students may wish to look up the difference between ethos and culture. Culture may be described as the sum of the morally forceful understandings acquired by learning and shared with the members of the group to which the learner belongs (de Blij 1982).

Case 17.2 illustrates the importance of staff to the company's goals as the staff are key to all activities in the organization. For example, staff interaction with customers and merchandise replenishment are important components of the Marks & Spencer image. Equally, the uniform appearance of staff and the manner in which they address customers are key gauges of quality. Staff are motivated to perform by the ethos of the organization.

Case 17.2 Marks & Spencer: The Firm to Work For?

Marks & Spencer built its business on a number of key principles that placed quality, value and service at the heart of the business. These principles influenced the way it treated its customers, staff and shareholders and were an important part of the company ethos. For customers this meant a high standard of merchandise and service with guaranteed quality. The staff valued these principles and were encouraged to do by the excellent working conditions and management commitment. Marks & Spencer backed this commitment with a unique supplier relationship that developed close partnerships on a long-term basis. These excellent systems supplied stores and supported the customers and staff. Simon Marks, who led the company for nearly 50 years until his death in 1964, instilled a culture of 'Quality, Value and Service', which continued to dominate company thinking and planning. But times change and retail organizations need to change also.

Source: Nickolds 1997

Quality and value depend on the perception of the customer (see Chapter 12). As times change, the retailer needs all its management and staff from the top down to be alert to changing customer requirements. This applies to buyers and other behind-the-scenes staff as well as sales staff. Since 1997, the market changed and Marks & Spencer was seen to have lost touch with its customers. This has forced Marks & Spencer to reappraise its position, which led to the use of more front-line sales staff. In 2001, the company commissioned a substantial market research programme to investigate the customers' perceptions of staff generally. Case 17.3 also illustrates the importance placed on staff.

Case 17.3 Sears: A Focused, Evolving Strategy

Sears, Roebuck in the USA had been undergoing a regeneration of its activities to improve profitability. Its guiding principles are:

▶ Customers
 – take very good care of the customers
 – make the stores a pleasant place to shop for merchandise and service

▶ Employees
 – make them feel that Sears is a compelling place to work

 – give employees a sense of satisfaction in the work
 – make them feel working for Sears is a personal opportunity as well as a financial opportunity
 – make pay structures reflect this approach.

Source: Martinez 1997

In the first case, there is a sense of something from the past, continuity and staidness, but staff are almost passive in the process. In the second case, however, there is a feeling of change, of staff doing things to better themselves and the company by being alert to the customer. There is a sense of risk, but also of reward when the employee delivers benefit to the company. These cases illustrate the importance of the workforce, and the need for flexible attitudes, in meeting customer requirements.

A Flexible Workforce

Retailers need to take a long-term view of their labour force rather than rely on casual temporary labour. Short-term employment contracts leave the manager with some discretion as to the level at particular times, but they discourage enthusiasm and diligence on the part of the employee. This raises a number of issues and frequently creates a dilemma for retail management. For example, a retail company has policies in place that lay down the number of staff needed at given times. This may take precedence over more practical issues such as wage bills. However, managers are constantly encouraged to reduce the costs of delivering the retail offering (the store, its merchandise and other benefits). Meanwhile, the retail customer is led to expect a degree of expertise, and service quality from the promotional efforts of the retail company. The solution is often to use part-time and temporary staff to fill gaps in service demand.

Part-time employees can be a useful means of creating flexibility in the workforce. For example, no retail store has a constant demand on its sales staff but is forced to cope with peaks and troughs in the daily operation and in weekly cycles. The part-time employee allows the retail manager to fill in when needed and maintain levels of customer service. This allows the retailers to fulfil the promises they make to their customers, by maintaining the same level of service.

One type of part-time employment offered is the zero-hours contract. This does not guarantee the employee any specific number of hours' work, but allows the retailer to decide how many hours are worked each week. Part-time work is often associated with temporary work contracts, which allow the retailer to tap into the constantly changing market of young people, particularly school and college students, as well as the large part-time market of working mothers. These temporary contracts are often used to meet seasonal peaks in demand or when the level of customer demand (and so staff requirements) is relatively uncertain.

However, larger retailers that have used these methods of flexible working in the past have been reconsidering their methods as the longer-term costs and benefits have become apparent. After reviewing their employment policies, the two largest food retailers, Tesco and Sainsbury, made thousands of their temporary workers permanent and cut the proportion of temporary staff from 10 per cent to 3 per cent of their workforce. Keeping staff too long on temporary contracts affected motivation and discouraged investment in training, which in turn had an adverse effect on customer service. This trend reflected the changing pattern of part-time working. Employers had to respond to the growing demand from skilled people for regular part-time employment (Pickard 1998).

Part-time sales positions are often filled with more mature applicants who are known for their reliability and experience. This additional factor makes them popular with customers and committed to their job. In comparison to full-time personnel, part-time workers are more likely to be flexible about the mode of operation, unsociable hours, salary and type of work. The use of part-time staff may, however, fail to deliver in areas of expertise and quality. Many retailers tend to confine part-time workers to low-paid jobs. However, the experience of some retailers has shown that part-time workers can fill supervisory positions. In particular, women whose family commitments prevent them from working full-time often have the skills and qualifications to undertake senior roles.

Changing Attitudes to the Workforce

Retailing is making an increasing use of technology. This brings new demands on the workforce and retailers require a better-educated workforce equipped with more modern skills in merchandise preparation, information processing and decision-making. The increasing emphasis on quality and customer service as competitive instruments also requires higher levels of skill in customer service, teamworking and managing people. As economic prospects continue to improve in the future (see Chapter 4), it will become more difficult for retailers to recruit appropriate staff. Retailers will have to compete more effectively for the limited supply of an educated and skilled workforce. They will also have to invest more in recruiting, training and retaining people with the appropriate talent (Summer *et al.* 2000). Workers today expect more openness from employers and the opportunity for personal development and job satisfaction. This may include flexible working arrangements.

Building a Vision: People are the Most Important Resource

Image is part of the overall offering and as such is sold together with the merchandise or service on offer. When customers buy a product or service they buy into a total (holistic) image and the reputation of the retailer. A good reputation is built up over time through a succession of satisfied customers who receive an appropriate combination of price, quality and service. Increasingly, customer satisfaction depends on the level of service received and the way staff treat the customer. Many large and successful retailers recognize that they have to be customer focused: good service increases customer spending and poor service accounts for the majority of lost customers.

Good service, however, is delivered through people. This extends beyond the direct service personnel who come directly into contact with customers. It includes all those people who are involved in bringing the products or services to the customer. Customer satisfaction is now critical to the success of most retail organizations. Management of the organization must give practical meaning to the idea of customer-focused service so that each employee clearly understands it and his or her role in delivering that service (Denton and Richardson 1997).

In practical terms, successful retailers encourage a company ethos that recognizes the importance of customers, shareholders, employees and suppliers as key players. Management must provide clarity of direction, support the effective integration of activities by getting people to work as part of a cohesive unit, and be aware of the changing situation in the market. This requires the development of teamwork and openness in management.

> ⇨ Openness – staff are encouraged to perform when managers share information and are genuinely open to staff suggestions and comments. Staff will accept change more readily when they are aware of the reasons for the change. By operating in an open fashion, managers encourage teamwork and break down traditional barriers.

Organizing for Customer Service

The retailer has to structure its organization so that it focuses on 'customer-based transactions' (Denton and Richardson 1997), such as tracking the flow of information or products necessary for delivery to the customer. This helps break down internal barriers between different departments and the organization becomes a system of internal suppliers and customers. These are the individual workers that make the difference to service quality (see Chapter 12). However, the system can only function effectively if members of staff feel in control and accept responsibility. This increases staff involvement and commitment to the retailer's goals and improves performance.

Case 17.4 Sainsbury's Organized Divisions

Supermarket giant J. Sainsbury had been organized along traditional divisional lines. Each division was responsible for a particular function such as property management, finance and store management. However, in the mid-1990s the company underwent reorganization in order to improve cooperation across the different divisions and focus more effectively on customer service.

The first step was to get staff to recognize that the most important people in the business were those who have direct contact with the customer. It also introduced the principle of internal customers and service levels between departments (see Chapter 12). A comprehensive management development programme emphasized teamwork leadership to replace the old *command and tell* management style.

Source: Dandy 1996

Empowerment

The need to share power with the workforce is a difficult concept for management to accept. It is even more difficult to put into practice within a commercial environment that constantly demands further reduction in operating costs. However, particularly in US service retailing, there have been numerous and longstanding examples of successful empowerment that have helped the reputation and financial success of the organization.

Empowerment means that an employee can take whatever action is necessary to take care of a customer to that customer's satisfaction. This means that the employee can bend and break the rules to do whatever has to be done for the customer (Tschohl 1998). It is understandable that management shies away from this concept in practice and usually only allows staff to operate within defined rules. Trust is a significant factor in this sort of manager–employee relationship. However, in a well-run organization, the times when expensive action needs to be taken should be few and far between, and the hidden cost of not taking the appropriate action may be significant. If a supermarket loses a customer because of poor service, it will lose thousands of pounds in future sales. It may also lose further sales because other potential consumers may hear of the incident by word of mouth (WOM). As Disney World put it: 'Management must not only support the front line, but it must trust it as well . . . front-line employees should be the first, and the last, contact for customers' (Tschohl 1998: 421–5).

Employees are an important part of the image of a retail organization. They are in many cases a reflection of the retailer. In the case of contact personnel, they are the first port of call and in the customer's eyes they *are* the retailer. It is the contact personnel that respond to the customers' needs and determine the level of satisfaction. Improved levels of customer satisfaction tend to lead to repeat purchases, which mean customers come back for more (Bitner 1990). The key to maintaining high standards of customer service is highly committed staff. Company ethos and management style are important drivers of customer service.

Keeping Staff Happy

Staff who enjoy their job have a high level of job satisfaction; staff who do not enjoy their job have a low level of job satisfaction. Job satisfaction can depend on a number of factors at work and outside work. However, important factors that can be managed are *role conflict*, *role clarity* and *job tension*.

> ⇨ Role clarity is the degree to which an individual has enough information to know his or her role in the organization, and to perform their job proficiently. Clear job roles minimize conflicts among employees, between employees and management, and between employees and customers. Frustration and unhappiness with the job occur when employees are unclear as to their roles in an organization.

> ⇨ Role conflict occurs when the employee receives contradictory demands from different superiors or from management and customers. Staff suffer role conflict when they are unsure what they are allowed to do to solve particular customer problems. However, staff that empathize with customers and fellow employees can often reduce these problems (Rogers, Clow and Kash 1994).

> ⇨ Job tension reflects the extent to which employees are bothered by work-related matters, such as role conflict. The resulting tension reduces job satisfaction.

Retail managers need to ensure that contact personnel, particularly, receive clear guidelines as to their responsibilities and freedom of action. It is also the manager's responsibility to set realistic goals and fairly distribute workloads. Contact personnel are directly in the middle of the demands of the customers and the requirements of management to improve company profitability. Hiring the right kind of people, providing them with clear job descriptions and giving them appropriate training in customer service, can improve customer service and job satisfaction among employees. Failure to consider these issues can lead to low job satisfaction and high levels of job tension. A contented workforce will deliver better customer service. When staff are dissatisfied, the quality of the service encounter declines and customers and revenue are lost. Dissatisfied staff are also more likely to leave and the increase in staff turnover increases the annual costs of recruitment and training.

17.2 Planning the Workforce

Workforce planning is about matching people to the organization. Independent retailers will have very different requirements from multiples, mainly because their goals are different. Independents tend to require staff that are multiskilled and will fill in when required to. For some individuals seeking employment in retailing this may be a distinct advantage. Working for a large multiple retailer can require more commitment to career development, and to the company's ethos. It follows that this type of occupation is more controlling and allows a less flexible lifestyle. When selecting suitable candidates a retailer must consider individual expectations.

Retail managers need to define the type of knowledge, skills and orientations needed for a particular position, and the standard of performance required by the job. It is useful to model the job and project the ideal candidate and general criteria for the suitable applicant. Skills will vary with organizational size, but in many ways planning for staff skills is similar regardless of the organization. This is because organizational goals and the mission statement will determine the need for focus on specific skills. For example, the large travel agency chain will need staff that can project a professional and pleasant manner. They must also demonstrate a high degree of expertise and have the appropriate IT skills. These criteria may be similar for an independent travel agency, but staff may need to possess a personable attitude and less of a corporate approach to customer service.

The workforce requirements can be refined into a list or table, which determines the exact needs of a particular business. These should contain the key skills and requirements identified by the retail business or policy document. In the case of a department store the requirements are more specialized and centre on areas of the store operation. For example, window dressers will need very special design-oriented skills whereas the sales staff must possess product knowledge and interpersonal skills of a high order.

> ⇨ Students may wish to draw up their own table of staff requirements, using a fictitious retail organization. Try to employ the principles you have learnt so far.

Stores may recruit new employees to cope with an increase in customers or to replace employees that are leaving. A large organization with a fairly complex structure will usually have well-defined job titles and structures. The retailer tends to fit the person to an already existing job specification. These maintain organizational conformity, but may prevent the retailer from adapting appropriately to the changing market. In such situations, large organizations must periodically review the different staff roles. Smaller stores, however, may use such occasions to reassess the role of their staff and use the new member of staff to improve the retailer's ability to adapt to changes in the market and customer priorities.

Specifying Jobs

There are a number of aspects that need to be considered in drawing up a job specification. One aspect relates to the formal position of the job in the organization. An organization can be described in terms of its personnel structure, which lays out the position of different jobs in the organization. A particular job is expected to perform certain functions and require the employee to bring specific skills and attributes to the organization. These primary skills identify the position of the individual in the organization, the job title and whom the person will report to and be responsible for. The recruiter should be able to identify the key duties and tasks that have to be carried out.

Another aspect of the job relates to the person required to fill the job in terms of the range of activities he or she will undertake. The retailer today requires staff that are multi-skilled and flexible, who are able and willing to work across job boundaries and focus on new ways of working together to achieve solutions. This aspect can form part of the person specification for the job.

The job description should specify the role of the jobholder within a particular department, what the jobholder is responsible for. It should also describe what the person is expected to achieve or how performance will be measured. A fuller understanding of what a potential employee can bring to the organization often happens informally when a store manager interviews or reads the applications of prospective candidates. From these data the manager will identify suitable recruits.

Recruitment agencies may in some cases be used to handle the analysis of jobs and other recruitment services for retail management. Sometimes this outsourcing may include writing the job description and composing an advertisement or internal vacancy notice. A clear job description and person specification are essential if these tasks are sourced from outside the organization. Small independents will undertake all these tasks themselves and many of the processes will be reduced. However, the smaller business character means that the recruiter will use more intuitive methods of selection.

The Selection Process

The employer uses one or more selection processes in order to select the right person for the job. The selection process should make some assessment about how the candidate will perform on the job, but this is difficult to achieve. The job application form is a preliminary method and should avoid asking questions that may be construed as discriminatory in terms of gender, race or religion or (by 2005 in the European Union) age. Interviews are almost always held and some selection processes may require two or three interviews. Interviews, however, are often used to confirm previous expectations and do not necessarily relate to on-the-job performance. Psychometric tests are increasingly popular, but, as with other selection procedures, candidates can obtain coaching in the various techniques.

> ⇨ Psychometric testing – the practice of psychological profiling candidates using known measures or constructs that are indicative of a person's behaviour.

Induction

A successful candidate needs time and training to familiarize himself or herself with the new job. The organization needs to provide an appropriate induction programme, according to the type of job. This will help new employees to quickly understand how the retail organization works and how they fit in. This will help to enhance commitment to the business and improve customer satisfaction.

Training

Selling is the retailer's main function and is certainly the most important. Personal selling must reflect the standard and quality desired by customers and is consistent with the image of the retailer. Training should be focused on developing these skills among contact personnel. Staff that do not have a direct selling role, such as in customer services, should be trained to see the potentially positive influence they can bring to bear on the customer. The increasing use of call centres in various areas of retailing demands the development of supplementary skills. These include, for instance, courtesy, patience, telephone skills and focusing on solving problems (Mouawad and Kleiner 1996). Major organizations recognize the need for customer service training and the ability to use the latest technology. Tesco, for instance, appointed a learning director in 2000.

17.3 Management and Organizational Culture

There is a wide range of retailing organizations depending on the sector. The implications of this for retailing are that there are many different types of organizational structure and management. Organizational structure can be described using an organization chart that sets out who is responsible to whom. Figure 17.1 shows part of the management structure of a retail store. It shows the *line of authority* between a member of staff and the general manager.

In this example, the member of staff is directly responsible to his or her departmental manager. Only the general manager can override the authority of the departmental manager. The deputy manager undertakes various tasks that have been agreed with the manager. However, he or she has direct authority over members of staff only when it has been expressly delegated to him or her, such as when the manager is absent.

A small independent store has a simple structure centred on selling. There is a direct line of authority between the owner of the store and staff. Large independent department and variety stores have a more complex structure, with additional specialized functions such as accounts. At the other extreme, a large regional or national chain will have a complex structure. Each store may have several departments, each with its own head. These heads of department report to the store manager. Each store manager will report to a regional manager who reports in turn to the operations manager at head office. However, the

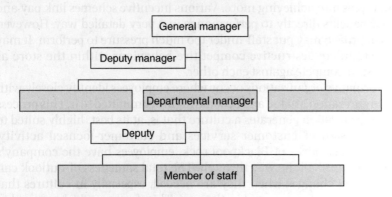

Figure 17.1   The Line of Authority

availability of advanced technology has enabled large groups to centralize many decisions relating to buying and distribution, as well as the additional personnel functions such as payroll, and the property management function. Small independent chains, on the other hand, may have less well-developed structures.

The model in Figure 17.1 illustrates a very simple chain of command and facilitates communication between senior management and front-line staff. This is essential for delivering quality customer service, and was the approach taken by Archie Norman when he stripped out layers of management and revitalized Asda in the 1990s.

Organizational Culture

Retail organizations, as with any other organizations, develop their own special cultures or ways of doing things. The culture of the organization is the set of values and characteristics that affect its behaviour and those of its employees and managers. This culture reflects the commercial environment of the organization and is largely influenced by the perceived factors in past successes. It is transmitted to succeeding generations of employees through its management, and reinforced by the collective attitudes of its employees. The methods used by management, to keep employees in tune with the company's objectives reflect the underlying culture of the organization. This culture may be classed as *coercive*, *calculative*, or *normative* (Jarvis 2000).

A coercive culture pushes its employees into doing what is demanded of them. Those who underperform face the loss of their job or status. Staff are driven to achieve more than they would otherwise do. However, they will stick to tried and tested ways of doing things, for fear of losing what they have already. This attitude may work in a relatively stable and well-defined environment, but it discourages risk-taking and enterprise within the organization (sometimes known as *intraprise*). This type of culture is inappropriate for retailers, as they need employees who are confident enough to adapt to the changing requirements of their customers.

A calculative or instrumental approach, on the other hand, pulls employees into achieving more. Various incentive schemes link pay and other benefits directly to performance in a very detailed way. However, this approach may put staff under too much pressure to perform. It may also stimulate destructive competitive behaviour within the store as sales staff compete against each other.

Normative organizations occur where employees identify closely with the organization's value and become highly committed to it. This process of internalization generates a culture that is, at its best, highly suited to the provision of customer services and customer-focused activity. However, like sticks of Blackpool rock, employees have the company's name stamped all the way through. The total sameness of outlook can inhibit real changes when they are needed, especially in cultures that have been highly successful in the past. This, for example, happened to Marks & Spencer in the late 1990s.

Leadership

Leadership is an important part of management. It can critically affect the success of an organization. When Archie Norman took over as chief executive of the supermarket chain, Asda, the company was on the brink of collapse. His style of leadership was to make himself accessible by going out to talk to the low-paid sales staff. He restructured the organization and the tasks to be done. Sales assistants became colleagues who saw that teamworking and customer orientation were the way to keep the Asda name going. Within five years he had reimbued the organization with a new sense of purpose and turned it into a recognizably successful chain before leading it to a takeover by Wal-Mart in 1999.

Norman's style of management at Asda typifies Adair's "action-centred leader" (Jarvis 2000). Such a leader embodies the norms of quality management and customer-orientation that are increasingly required in the retail industry today. This leader leads from the front. He or she clearly identifies the company's aims and tasks required, communicates these clearly to the staff, chooses appropriate team members and delegates effectively, involves the team in decision-making and supports the work team doing the job.

Not all leadership situations are as dramatic as Norman's at Asda, but Sam Walton, who founded Wal-Mart, showed similar traits. He used the theatrical device of driving everywhere in an old truck to meet employees, while driving forward a mix of shrewd business sense and social control over the workforce. As with many other business leaders, he could build a following of low-paid workers through encouragement, support and recognition as a 'valued' member of the team.

Motivation

These cases demonstrate one of the key skills of leadership, the ability to motivate staff. Motivating staff means getting them to do more than they would otherwise do from a purely personal and self-interested point of view. Within the service context of retailing, many employees are motivated when they come to the job. We are all aware of the keen, dedicated and enthusiastic employee for whom serving the customer is a pleasure. They want to help people and are motivated by more than money, which for many employees is relatively poor. Not all employees, however, are highly motivated and we often experience the rude, cold and dismissive employee who would find the job all right if there were no customers. Most people probably fall somewhere in between.

Early management theorists such as F.W. Taylor saw the worker as calculating for their own benefit. Money was then the main *instrument* used to motivate employees. Money is an important aspect of a job and most people expect to get a reasonable wage, taking into account the type of job they do and what other people get paid as well. However, most people do not do a job merely for the money and wish to receive some intrinsic satisfaction from the job they are doing.

A shop assistant working in a small shop may be attracted to working for one of the larger retailers that pay significantly more. However, he or she will take other factors into account and may prefer the smaller store and easier-going atmosphere that can allow greater flexibility in work arrangements. The shop assistant has other psychological and social *needs* besides the economic need for money. The Maslow model of lower- and higher-order needs is widely used to illustrate this. Herzberg's two-factor model takes a more sophisticated approach. A number of job elements, such as pay, constitute basic need. These affect the level of job satisfaction and must be at an acceptable level. However, improving them beyond a certain reasonable level does not increase job satisfaction or motivate employees to work harder. People are instead motivated by *satisfiers*, which may include a range of things such as the type of job, a sense of achievement and recognition (Stredwick 2000).

Managers have to recognize employees' need to belong, receive recognition and praise. These factors are often more important than extra money. This has been shown time and again by retailers such as Asda, Tesco, Wal-Mart and Marks & Spencer during the successful periods of their history. What is praised and recognized will more likely be repeated. People also need to be supported in what they are doing through training and a sense of worth.

Employees gain a sense of self-worth through the job they do. The employee's *cognition* or perception of the job includes the tasks involved and the various social, psychological and financials costs and rewards. Proper training can give employees the confidence to tackle the tasks required and also engender a sense of achievement in what they have done. Employees want to be recognized for their achievements in an appropriate way. This does not always mean more money, but basic pay and the employee's own individual rewards should be seen to be fair relative to other jobs. This has obvious implications for the way managers select their staff, train them, empower them and reward them.

Management today has to continue to motivate their staff: how they treat staff affects the way staff treat their customers. A manager's approach to motivating staff reflects his or her attitude to employees. Many managers are dynamic leaders who show genuine concern for the well being of their team. They often reflect McGregor's Theory Y approach (see Handy 1985: 33). When management respond with the appropriate conditions, staff will exercise self-direction and self-control in working towards the retailer's objectives. Successful leadership motivates employees to take on responsibility for the success of the company as if it were their own success. The manager has to respond accordingly and build up two-way communication and trust. This approach is consistent with modern service quality theory (see Chapter 12).

There are, however, other managers, relics from a bygone age, who are authoritarian power trippers that see staff as instruments for their own advancement. They usually reflect McGregor's Theory X approach. They see staff as rarely taking the initiative and who are committed only as far as the stick and carrot can get them to be. These managers see themselves as having to structure jobs in detail and closely supervise staff. The result is an atmosphere of low trust on both sides.

Retailers can encourage general involvement of staff through participation in decision-making. Tesco do this through their representative councils, following their agreement with the Union of Shop Distributive and Allied Workers (USDAW) in 1998. John Lewis Partnership effectively makes its staff its partners. More modern systems include the share-save scheme. This allows employees to save for a period of three or five years. At the end of this period they may take their savings with added tax-free interest, or they may buy shares in the company at a discounted price that was set at the start date of the scheme. If the company has been successful, the shares will have risen significantly and the employees stand to make significant tax-free gains.

Case 17.5 Tesco SAYE Savers Get Bumper Returns

Over 33 000 Tesco staff shared in a £123 million share option windfall when two SAYE schemes matured in 2000. Thirty people who put away the maximum £250 a month for five years received shares valued at £53 000.

Tesco chief executive Terry Leahy was proud to say that staff have again been able to share in the company's phenomenal success, with a record number of staff signing up for the scheme.

17.4 Personnel Management and Administration

The Personnel Function

The retailer needs to keep adequate and effective personnel records. These enable the retailer to track the performance of the member of staff during their time at the company and plan the effective development of that member of staff. There also needs to be practical, consistent and efficient administrative procedures that support the management of the workforce. These must be consistent with all legal requirements, be clearly notified to staff and properly implemented.

These tasks form part of the personnel function. The personnel function may be undertaken by a line manager in a small store or organization. Usually, however, retailers have a specialist personnel department.

Personnel officers and managers may come from a variety of backgrounds. Some retailers develop personnel staff from general retail staff who choose to specialize in personnel management. Other retailers recruit personnel specialists from other industries.

Wherever the personnel function is located, it has to support the organization in achieving its objectives. Maintaining the administrative framework is important to ensure consistent practice across the organization. This can protect the retailer from some of the errors of its managers. The personnel specialist may also contribute to the development of policies and ensure compliance with government regulations. The personnel function also extends to recruitment, selection and training. It should support employees through the changes that the organization regularly undergoes, which may require specialist knowledge of employment law. These are some of the ways in which the personnel function can maintain the sensitivity of senior managers and prevent them from becoming too distant from their staff.

Maintaining Records

Keeping records is an important aspect of personnel management. However, the widespread availability of computers and database software allow personnel managers to store and amend large quantities of data relatively easily. However, they need to restrain information gathering to what is useful to the company while maintaining the privacy of the individual member of staff. Table 17.2 lists some suitable personal details.

Table 17.2   Personnel Files

Personal details	
Personal and contact details	Including home and work contact details
Employment details	Contract of employment; previous posts in the company
Pay and attendance	
Earnings and benefits	Pay and benefits; taxation, pensions, expenses, deductions
Holidays	Holidays taken; holidays remaining
Work record	Time sheets, attendances; rota
Health and accident records	Sickness certificates
Discipline and grievances	Disciplinary action; grievances raised
Training and development	
Competencies	Formal qualifications; appraisal reports
Training and development	Training undertaken; needs identified; training planned
Other verifiable information	Team roles and contributions; career aspirations

Source: Adapted from Jarvis 2000

17.5 Health and Safety

The health and safety of employees and customers may seem a fairly humdrum matter. However, there are many dangerous situations in retailing and distribution. Some of these constantly pose threats to life, such as the use of forklift trucks in hardware retailing, shopping trolleys in supermarkets (over-turning trolleys have killed or seriously injured children inside them) and various types of cutting equipment. There are also dangerous substances such as cleaning materials and situations such as lifting heavy objects that frequently pose the risk of injury.

Retail managers must take account of the increasing amount of legislation and parliamentary orders that detail their responsibility for the health and safety of their staff. These matters are now vitally important, because neglecting them can affect the long-term profitability and viability of the business. From the point of view of the retailer, these problems of health and safety all create costs, without a visible return in greater customer sales. There is a natural tendency to skimp on the time and money required to make the workplace safer. However, failure to comply with these regulations can lead to significant fines on the business or may prevent it from trading.

As has happened in other countries, the UK has been building up a comprehensive and complex system of health and safety legislation and regulation that covers practically all places of work. This places a duty on employers to provide a safe working environment for all employees. All retail managers at unit and head office level must now become familiar with many detailed aspects of health and safety regulation. Managers now bear significant legal responsibility for health and safety and must manage staff and customers to ensure that the retailer's image of a safe environment is protected (Coventry Occupational Accident Prevention Group 1999).

Administration of Health and Safety Regulation

The administration of health and safety in the UK is divided between the Health and Safety Executive (HSE) and local authorities. Shops, offices and warehouses come under local authority inspection and control, while manufacturing and transport operations come under the control of the Health and Safety Executive. The Health and Safety Executive website (www.hsedirect.com) contains all the relevant legislation, HSE guides, approved codes of practice, updates on EU directives, case summaries and HSE press releases. Employers can access the site through an on-line subscription or buy the information on a CD-ROM. Other commercial organizations, such as Jordan's Health and Safety Management provide various materials to help in the administration of health and safety in the workplace.

Health and Safety at Work Policy Statement

The Health and Safety at Work Act 1974 and the Management of Health and Safety at Work Regulations 1992 provide the basis for health and safety policies in the workplace. They give expression to common-sense notions of looking after employees and taking care of fellow workers. Everyone in the workplace has a general duty to promote safe working practices. Employers must provide safe working conditions and employees have a duty to protect themselves and fellow workers. Suppliers of equipment and substances used in the workplace also have duties towards their customers and their employees. Employers must appoint competent people to carry out the proper planning and implementation of safety measures (Jordan's Health and Safety Management, BNet, 1999).

Any firm employing five or more workers must produce a company health and safety policy statement and provide appropriate training for its workers in health and safety. The policy statement should assign clear responsibility for implementing policy. Retailers will usually designate the manager of the relevant store, even where there is also a designated health and safety officer for the store. More information can be had from the Health and Safety Executive guide, *Writing a Safety Policy Statement: Advice to Employers,* and a pro forma, *Writing your Health and Safety Policy,* is also available. The safety policy should also include detailed procedures for safe working, dealing with emergencies and reporting accidents. It should also include training requirements and procedures for the safety of those who are not employed by the firm but who are likely to visit its premises, such as customers.

The retailer must take all reasonable steps to eliminate or reduce risks, taking into account the costs of doing so. What is reasonable depends on the circumstances: not all risks can be eliminated and reducing risks below a certain level would be excessively expensive. In general terms, however, the retailer has to make sure that any equipment is safe to operate. It must devise safe working practices for the handling, storage, transport and use of articles and substances, and it must supervise them properly. It should also train all employees in the safe use of equipment and dangerous substances.

Risk Assessment

Employers must carry out risk assessments where there is a possibility of injury to their employees or customers. There are two elements of risk assessment: *hazard* and *risk*. A hazard is anything that causes harm to people. It can be associated with particular activities, such as injury when lifting goods, or situations, such as breakage and spillage in the storage of cleaning materials. A risk is the chance that a hazard will occur and how bad the injury could be. The manager or safety officer should record the findings of the risk assessment. He or she should:

▶ Identify the hazards.

▶ Evaluate the risk for each hazard.

▶ Implement measures to control the risks. The manager must do what is required to reduce the risk to an acceptable level, particularly for pregnant women, new mothers and young people. The manager, however, does not have to implement measures that are impracticable or are prohibitively expensive.

▶ Continually check that staff are following correct safety procedures. The risk assessment must be carried out again regularly and especially when there has been a change in the equipment or working methods.

There are many other health and safety regulations that employers must comply with. These include: fire safety; accidents and dangerous occurrences; electrical inspection and safety; control of substances hazardous to health (COSHH); noise; manual handling; equipment; personal protective clothing; workplace conditions, breaks, holidays; insurance and administration. Table 17.3 provides a summary of these areas:

Table 17.3 Areas of Health and Safety

Fire safety	The owner or sole occupier of a building must obtain a fire certificate when: a) there are more than 20 workers in the building; or b) more than 10 working on different floors from the ground floor; or the business is storing or using flammable material They require a special certificate to store large amounts of flammable or explosive material. Fire certificate must be kept Building must have unobstructed doorways and exits Regular fire drills should be held; staff should be trained in emergency procedures. Business must have appropriate equipment for dealing with small fires
Accidents and dangerous occurrences	The Reporting Injuries, Diseases and Dangerous Occurrences Regulations (RIDDOR) 1995 govern recording and reporting these events. An accident book must be kept Suitable first aid equipment must be held in appropriate places. Regulations specify the minimum contents of first aid equipment There must be 1 designated and qualified first-aider for every 50 low-risk employees, or 1 for every 20 high-risk employees
Hazardous substances	These are governed by the Control of Substances Hazardous to Health Regulations (COSHH) 1994 Hazardous substances include chemicals and substantial amounts of dust
Electricity	General electrical safety and inspection of equipment is required. In addition, portable appliance testing (PAT) must be carried out periodically, for which there are specific recommendations
Noise	Noise is subject to the Noise At Work Regulations 1989. Although not a major problem for retailers, some services and facilities may have high noise levels. There are two actions level of 85 and 90 decibels [dB(A)] Employers must reduce the risk of exposure and provide proper training and instruction to prevent long-term injury
Work equipment	Periodic inspection of work equipment is required. This is particularly so in the case of equipment if it is liable to deteriorate and cause a significant risk
General employee protection	Regulations cover manual handling: safe limits are prescribed Personal protective equipment must be provided and training given, where appropriate
Welfare	The Workplace (Health, Safety and Welfare) Regulations, 1992, require adequate toilet and handwashing facilities, rest areas and drinking water Weekly working hour limits of an average of 48 hours per week now apply
Administration	Retailers must register with the local authority environmental health department. Employers' Liability (Compulsory Insurance) Act 1969 requires employers to have insurance against work-related accidents and disease. The certificate must be displayed at the place of work Businesses must keep adequate records including their Safety Policy, risk assessments, and other assessments where they are required. They should also keep records of health and safety training, maintenance and safety checks, and some statutory accident notification forms (F2508) in case of a notifiable accident

The responsible manager, however, should obtain details of requirements and regular updates by consulting the appropriate government body and subscribing to one of the commercial services available that can provide detailed interpretation of the regulations through specific case material.

References

Bitner, M.J. (1990) 'Evaluating service encounters: the effects of physical surroundings and employee responses', *Journal of Marketing*, 54, April: 69–82.

Blij de H.J. (1982) *Human Geography*, New York: John Wiley and Sons, p. 179.

BNet (1999) http://www.bnet.co.uk.

Broadbridge A. (1999), 'A profile of female retail managers: some insights'. *The Service Industries Journal*, 19(3): 135–61.

Coventry Occupational Accident Prevention Group (1999) 'Health and safety at work', available through *BNet*, http://www.bnet.co.uk/bnet/documents/bndd00001/bndd000012.phtml

Dandy, J. (1996) 'Jonathan Dandy interviews Terry Wells, director of Customer Service, J. Sainsbury plc', *Managing Service Quality*, 6(3): 16–22.

Denton, D.K. and Richardson, P. (1997) 'A unifying approach to management', *Management Decision*, 35(5): 398–403.

Economist (1997) 'More in store', 21 June: 59.

Freathy, P. (1997) 'Employment theory and the wheel of retailing: segmenting the circle', *Service Industries Journal*, 17(3): 413–31.

Handy, C. (1985) *Understanding Organisations*, 3rd edn, London: Penguin.

Jarvis, C. (2000) 'Management, business open learning' http: //sol.brunel.ac.uk/~jarvis/bola/

Martinez, A. (1997) 'Sears: a focused, evolving strategy', *Inside Retailing*, http://chainstoreage.com/news_desk/inside_retailing/inside_retail_arch_1.htm.

Mouawad, M. and Kleiner, B.H. (1996) 'New developments in customer service training' *Management Service Quality*, 16(2): 49–56.

National Statistics (1996) *Annual Abstract of Statistics*, London: The Stationery Office.

National Statistics (2001) *Annual Abstract of Statistics*, London: The Stationery Office.

Nickolds, C. (1997) 'Marks & Spencer: old hands in the global market', *Inside Retailing*, http://chainstoreage.com/newsdesk/inside_retailing/inside_retail_arch_1.htm.

Pickard, J. (1998) 'Retail giants view temping as past its sell-by date', *People Management*, 4(12): 14.

Rogers, J.D., Clow, K.E. and Kash, T.J. (1994) 'Increasing job satisfaction of service personnel', *Journal of Services Marketing*, 8(1): 14–26.

Stredwick, J. (2000) *An Introduction to Human Resource Management*, Oxford: Butterworth-Heinemann.

Summer, J. with Cardinale, C., Kaplan, S.L. and Jones, J.M. (2000) 'The talent search: attracting and retaining people with the skills your business needs', *Retail Insights*, 9(1), Deloitte Touche Tohmatsu, http: //www.dttus.deloitte.com/PUB/Retail/vol0901/vol90101.htm.

Tschohl, J. (1998) 'Empowerment – the key to quality service', *Managing Service Quality*, 8(6): 421–5.

Out-of-Store Retailing: Buy by Wire

This chapter considers the following issues:

- ► The nature of the virtual store.

- ► How retailers currently use virtual stores.

- ► Other types of remote retailing.

Out-of-Store Retailing: Buy by Wire

Introduction and Core Concepts

This chapter provides students with the different models that retailers employ to display and sell products and services without using the conventional (bricks and mortar) retail store. The term often used to describe this type of retailing is *out of store*. The implications for the retailer and customer are considerable as many of the normal rules discussed so far in this book do not apply. Customer behaviour tends to be different and the retail operation is far less people intensive. Buying away from the conventional store environment means that the traditional physical and social factors that affect the customer's purchase situation are no longer in place. In the out-of-store situation the merchandise and services are remote from the customer and this reduces control, and cost for the retailer.

18.1 Out-of-Store Retailing

The virtual store is a concept that was first developed in the USA. In this fast-moving consumer marketplace several alternative methods of shopping away from the conventional store environment became extremely popular for retailers and customers alike. There are three main types of out-of-store retailing: Internet shopping, television shopping and mail order shopping. Others such as the vending machine and electronic kiosk form part of this family of retail operations. All these approaches share one major characteristic; none of them rely on conventional store exteriors and interiors. No buildings or sales staff are required for the customer to interface with.

The idea of out of store is fairly new and has taken on new meaning with the spread of the Internet. In this book we will define out-of-store retailing as any retailing (whether product or services) that takes place outside an actual retail space. However, there are number of complications when we attempt to define retail space. For example, catalogue retailers are technically out of store. These companies sell to the customer through a remote system of agents and customers. They do not sell from a defined retail space. However, there are catalogue shops such as Argos, which sells from a defined retail space. Market traders who sell their wares from an open-air market are out of store, but they have a defined retail space. Clearly, it is hard to provide a definition to help us focus on the exact nature of out-of-store retailing. For this reason we have decided to use the term 'virtual store' to mean any store where the retailer communicates directly through a computer program. This allows us to use the term 'out of store' to refer to retailers who trade from catalogues and stalls.

> ⇨ Retail space is where the business of retailing to the customer takes place. However, we wish to create a distinction between an actual retail space and a virtual retail space. For example, the web page of Debenhams (see Chapter 5) is virtual retail space and customers are able to buy goods and services. However, using the website does not allow customers to touch or interact with products and services.

Major Differences in Operation

In the conventional retail store the retailer is constricted by the location, layout and visible operating systems (sales staff, checkouts, stockrooms, etc.) and must work within these constraints. Customers must visit the physical store and buy goods and services when the store is open. In some cases, such as food shopping, retailers have implemented a 24-hour opening policy to negate the disadvantage of time-dependent customer access. There are advantages, however, to this type of operation. For example, the customer may well purchase additional (associated) items during the time they spend in the store. This has become known as customer *dwell time* in certain specialized retail operations. In airports and retail malls, for example, the retailer has a *captured audience* and capitalizes on this situation. Stores cater for the leisure shopper and the types and layouts encourage browsing behaviour.

Case 18.1 Barclays Personal Internet Banking

An advertising campaign for Barclays Bank plc in late 2000 emphasized the flexibility of the personal bank account. In the advertisement message, British actor Robbie Coltrane was pictured sitting in a hotel room in an overseas hotel location and using a laptop computer to 'key in' transaction details. The dialogue reinforced the importance of accessibility and the remote nature of the virtual store: in this case bank retailing. Great emphasis was placed on opening accounts and paying bills at any time of day or night. As the advertisement points out, there is no need to conform and transactions can be undertaken sitting on a hotel bed in your pyjamas. Therefore, conventional banking (store) behaviour was not necessary and a more private and privileged interaction with the bank was possible. This fundamental point demonstrates the main difference between actual and virtual stores.

In contrast, the virtual store is not time dependent. Customers can shop or just browse whenever they have the desire, time, and energy. Shopping may take place after normal opening hours. For example, a customer may wish to visit a virtual store at 4.00 a.m. to make a purchase, or undertake a personal banking transaction.

The Distribution of Products

With a credit card and a computer modem the customer can buy goods at any time. Freephone numbers and express delivery services mean that the items can even arrive overnight at the customer's home address. This is very different from the conventional store where the customers form part of the distribution channel by collecting their purchases in the store. The Internet shopper does not need to be mobile or allocate time for the collection of goods. There are of course many non-store retailers in existence such as catalogue companies and door-to-door selling organizations. Retail companies or distributors sell merchandise such as music tapes and disks from mailing lists and book clubs, which operate in similar way to the Internet-based websites. Many retailers are now starting to sell goods only over the Internet and use this medium exclusively.

Electronic commerce such as this is having a tremendous impact on the supply chain. In particular, the proliferation of electronic delivery channels, such as electronic kiosks to the telephone, EDI and email, provides a wealth of new ways for companies to interact in real time with customers. Manufacturers can sell direct, for example, and new partners can be brought on board with relative ease.

These new channels of distribution make the task of pleasing the customer more important than ever. For example, a retailer that sells direct via the Internet is actually entering a new arena. The company has probably had no real experience of this type of operation, other than where the retailer owns catalogue shopping networks. Retailers must therefore proceed with caution, making sure front-line employees and logistics systems are able to deal with customers competently. Also, the retailer must be able to target, understand and serve the 'right' profitable customers. Failure to fulfil customer needs and expectations will certainly harm the retailer's image and reputation. This will have a similar effect to service delivery failures and stock outs in conventional store environments.

With the advent of electronic commerce, retailers may choose to trade directly or locate their businesses away from the customer and work solely through a website. For example, a clothing retailer such as Matalan could reach remote, rural customers by using an online ordering service. Local distributors of the goods would handle all aspects of customer contact. The risk involved using this type of operation is high as quality control is not securely in the hands of the retailer. Issues such as packaging, selection of merchandise and carriage to home are sourced and handled by another company. The problems are varied as, for example, when alternative grocery products are selected in the event of stock outs. Customers may suffer a great deal of dissatisfaction when undesirable products are sent as replacements.

As retailers take advantage of electronic channels they must also find ways to manage across all the channels they operate. A given customer will typically use more than one channel (actual stores and virtual stores) and channels must be managed in a coordinated fashion so that customers receive consistent quality and service. Coordination is also necessary to provide an accurate view of customer purchase activity, and to deliver differentiated service to different sets of customers. This means that the promotional information must be consistent across channels, and any 'promises' made need to be kept.

Pockets of Growth

Many retailers are now offering customers a better choice and service by integrating high street stores with home shopping facilities. Home shopping is an area of growth that is likely to gain in popularity and account for a much greater proportion of retail revenue in the future. However, there are some areas of retail provision that seem to fare better than others. This may be because in these sectors there is much less need for customer contact with the products. For example, books and computers tend to be more widely accepted as product groups that customers may purchase from virtual stores. Other areas are insurance, computers, computer supplies and ticketing facilities. Like banking, insurance has been well received as a product/service area that can be dealt with remotely. Change in customers' needs and expectations (see 'postmodern consumers' in Chapter 6) mean traditional transactions involving personal contact are less important.

Case 18.2 Amazon.com

Since opening in October 1998, Amazon.co.uk has sold in the UK market around 1.5 million books. No traditional high street chain book retailer can really compete because of Amazon's massive range. This makes the Internet retailer very popular with customers who may order from a large number of titles. The other important advantage for customers is that they can order from their armchair, and expect delivery in two or three days. Books are fairly standard items and do not require a great deal of deliberation during purchase. As long as customers have a clear idea of the content, and can rely on the delivery, books are highly suitable items to purchase from virtual stores. Amazon offers a complete range of books (in 2000 some 2 million titles) and is diversifying into videos, music and pet products. The latter is an interesting departure from the company's core areas.

The Internet website offers small independent retailers distinct advantages as a place from which to trade. This is because the size of the organization is not always apparent to the visitor and, unless the retail brand is known, small and large retailers are indistinguishable. Because of this, and the relatively low start-up cost of sites, many smaller firms have been encouraged to sell 'online'. Small retail operations such as specialized services and historic sites are examples of successful Internet-based operations. For these retail businesses the website is more a means of disseminating product knowledge and building customer bases, than important selling areas.

Other larger retailers, and in particular computer suppliers, have developed an almost unstoppable advantage over conventional retailing using Internet selling. Jungle.com and dabs.com are examples of Internet retailers that offer large ranges of computers and computer-related items to an ever-widening audience. For the customer, the advantage is the immediate processing of an order, which can leave the warehouse before the customer's modem line has been disconnected. The ranges of computer products and accessories available are virtually unlimited with immediate dispatch possible. Backed up by 100 per cent credit card security guarantees, and reimbursements of total order value, these retailers are posing a real threat to conventional store retailing. Firms such as PC World and Tiny tend to be more expensive on the consumer's pocket and the time spent travelling to the store and locating merchandise in-store.

Case 18.3 Dabs.com the Mail Order Computer Dealer

Dabs.com is a long-established British traditional mail order computer dealer, which has moved assertively into e-tailing, or selling computer products using a website. The company's primary business is the sale of computers, peripherals, software, office supplies, telephones and audio-visual (brown) goods via the Internet. Dabs.com also has a traditional call centre where telephone, fax, or in person orders can be placed. The retailer employs around 200 staff and is an e-tailer of technology products which has dealt with nearly 500 000 customers to date. The company enjoys sales of about £100 million per annum which places them in the top 20 of UK dealers of this type. Dabs promises that orders placed on the World Wide Web are secure and there is no retention of confidential information.

Source: http://www.dabs.com

⇨ Students may wish to try out online computer purchasing using the following website: http://www.novatech.co.uk/NOVATECH/Home.html
    Examine the range of merchandise, methods of purchasing and payment systems.

Another product or service that seems to be favoured by consumers when sold from a website is tickets for travel and leisure. In particular, tickets for trains or aeroplanes and leisure activities such as the theatre and popular events. For example, the Internet-based train travel site called TheTrainLine.com has enjoyed a great deal of success. TheTrainLine.com provides impartial information on train times and tickets on mainland UK routes. It is generally accurate and up to date, using current timetables and fares information. The service enables customers to make travel plans and ticket choices online, using a simple step-by-step electronic form. Secure online booking and payment is part of the attraction of this site. Also, the convenience of immediate bookings with following-day dispatch reduces travel risks. This reduction in risk is a key attraction of the service.

The Online Ordering Process

Most retail websites work in the same way by offering the visitor a variety of different services, which are readily accessible. The home page is a vital part of Internet and acts as the gateway, or front door, of the virtual store. In fact the various parts of the website such as doorways, shopping baskets and order forms are modelled on the conventional store experience. For the retailer, regardless of size, the order system tends to work as follows:

▶ Stage 1 Accept the order.

▶ Stage 2 Validate the customer.

▶ Stage 3 Wait until stock is present or with the supplier.

▶ Stage 4 If stock is present, attempt to process the payment.

▶ Stage 5 If payment correct, produce delivery note or direct shipment purchase order.

▶ Stage 6 Pack and ship to customer.

These processes are similar to those employed in conventional retail stores with one major difference: in the virtual store there is no actual customer–employee contact. This creates a significant difference in operation and simplifies the retailer's job. However, as some retailers have discovered, the lack of personal contact places greater strain on ordering and delivery systems. The reason for this is obvious. Customers rely on lots of visual information when they walk into an actual store. A major part of this data evaluation is usually based on the attitude, approach and knowledge displayed by the sales staff. This important data source and confirmation of the purchase decision is absent in the virtual store.

In financial services retailing, where the level of customer service is crucial, the problems associated with the lack of personal contact has been overcome with the help of more efficient systems. The fact that this has worked is surprising as retail services are traditionally people focused and results hinge on the quality of sales personnel. However, in some areas of retailing there appears to be a greater level of acceptance for remote selling. For example, Direct Line Insurance provides a range of products including car and home insurance. To counteract the lack of personal contact they operate a high-speed order processing service, which provides on-the-spot quotes. The need for personal contact is removed with a mixture of overnight delivery of documents, immediate debit or switch card payments and reliable product information.

Case 18.4 Direct Line Insurance: Developing the Business

Direct Line began in 1984 when four businessmen used their experiences in the insurance and IT industries to take a fresh look at private motor insurance. The founders saw that traditional insurance companies had become complacent which was typified by overpricing and low-quality service. It was these factors that provided the stimulus for a new outlook on the industry. Direct Line focused on the consumer and developed an idea that brought new standards for simplicity, service and value for money into the industry. The Royal Bank of Scotland provided the initial funding of £20 million on 2 April 1985. Currently, the Direct Line Group remains a wholly owned subsidiary of the Royal Bank of Scotland and has over 3 million customers. In September 1999, Direct Line launched the fastest 'quote and buy' Internet service, enabling customers to purchase motor, home and breakdown insurance online in under two minutes, for 365 days of the year.

One of the main advantages of the Internet is the uniformity of image across most websites. The entrances to sites are much the same regardless of the company. Even big names like Next, Tesco and B&Q have similar site formats that are governed by the software and the computer screens we operate. This means that, for customers, small independent retailers can appear similar, as the conventional method of evaluation, namely the bricks and mortar, is absent. However, where well-known retailer brands are involved a good knowledge of the retailer will reduce the level of risk for the customer when making a purchase. In other words, the Tesco website, for example, is an extension of Tesco's conventional store (and brand) and inspires similar confidence and reduces the risk of purchase. For the lesser known independent retailer, new customers may be reluctant to buy unknown brands, or they may have some concerns over delivery.

18.2 Retail Strategy and the Internet

A huge range of products and services are available on the World Wide Web, ranging from books and clothes, to cars and music and holidays. For retailers the vast quantities of goods being sold are unparalleled in the retail sector. Because of this many retailers have chosen to launch Internet sites that either supplement business, or spearhead parts of the business. The Internet and home shopping is the most significant format development affecting retailers, and most companies see it as a major priority.

Internet home shopping is being developed by many of the leading multiples in the clothing sector on the principle that it complements rather than competes with conventional store trading. This has been inspired in part by the success of the Next Directory clothing catalogue, which is seen as a major growth area in the future and one that retailers cannot afford to ignore. Arcadia and Marks & Spencer are currently offering printed catalogues and telephone ordering, but they are likely to take advantage of the Internet in the near future. Also in the clothing sector, a number of new Internet-based stores have appeared such as Readytoshop.co.uk and whyfronts.com. However, no Internet start-up companies appear to be succeeding in the womenswear sector. This is because women still like to visit conventional stores and actually experience clothes shopping. Even those consumers who prefer to shop at home find the task of searching the Internet time-consuming, and browsing extensive catalogues of womenswear on screen has low appeal.

Case 18.5 Boo.com: A major Boo Boo

Boo.com is a high-profile e-commerce company that was established with the intention of selling clothing over the World Wide Web. From the outset, the website had problems due to the slow shopping process that customers were forced to take moving through graphics and virtual advisers. For site users this meant it took a long time to browse the ranges. There were also various launch delays and technical problems, with the inevitable negative media, and uncertain advertising that failed to explain Boo's intention.

A major problem in home shopping is that it takes a long time for a brand to become accepted, and to build trust among consumers. Home shopping is all about trust, and it is much easier for established retail brands to expand into home shopping. Boo started from cold and the site, backed by Benetton and French entrepreneur Bernard Arnault, closed down after only six months. In June 2000 the US company fashionmall.com announced the re-launch of boo.com. The re-launch will start in the UK, and then move to other areas of Europe and eventually into 18 other trading countries.

Buying clothes on the Internet is likely to grow but it will probably never replace the experience of shopping for clothes. This is because consumers need to see, feel, smell and even hear the material that garments are made of. The advantage then of the Internet to most retailers is that it offers a secondary channel from which to sell ranges. This allows customers to view the wide variety of merchandise on offer. It is also important for retailers to be part of the drive towards Internet home shopping, although the value of trading over the Internet has yet to be established. In time this will change.

Non-store book selling is an area where major change is taking place. The benefits of the Internet are enormous as it enables book retailers to offer huge databases of titles without actually having to stock or display them. It is common for retailers to stock over 1 million titles, giving these Internet-based sellers a huge advantage over operators in conventional retail premises.

Quick Response Services

In financial service retailing Egg.com the Internet banker, and a division of Prudential Banking plc, have reaped huge rewards with strategic use of the Internet. Offering low interest (typically 2.5 per cent APR) and a range of service products such as mortgages and loans, Egg are attractive to new customers. Key benefits of the service are online transactions with password-protected secure areas from which to conduct business. All transactions including issue of statements are conducted online, with simple to view arrangements for customers. Like Direct Line, Egg operates a quick decision service.

In segments of the retail sector that do not fall into the conventional categories, new retail businesses have sprung up. We will call this 'grey retailing'.

> ⇨ Grey retailing – these are parts of the retail sector like car boot sales, informal auctions, entrepreneurial activities. Many independent businesses start up and fold because they have no traditional customers or lack knowledge of the market. The main stumbling block is often the substantial running costs incurred during start-up.

The low cost of Internet start-up has created a new breed of retailer and provided a new range of offerings for the customer. Numerous sites are now offering a range of services and products which provide opportunities that were previously unattainable. For example, consumers can buy and download music direct from the websites of popular and famous bands and pop groups. This type of business activity is an excellent way of building loyalty through the wide dissemination of a product or products.

The influence of MP3.com, the complete music service provider, which offers free products and services, means that music may be downloaded direct from the Internet site. A major feature of this service is that it is free of charge. The hope is that customers interested in the music will subsequently purchase a CD from the site, or in a conventional store. Other retailing areas include auctions such as Letsbuyit.com, where visitors to the site may enter a bid for items sold through the site. Goods include video cameras, televisions, washing machines and computers. Also the annual holiday may be purchased in this manner and there are plentiful sites, such as Bargainholidays.com, that offer last minute bargains at knock-down prices. For the airlines and travel agents this is a great means of selling off large quantities of holiday bookings or airline seats. Customers obtain good value for money and are able to travel abroad more often due to the low costs involved.

Reaching New Markets

Currently, leading retailers are directing their efforts at growing in less well-established retail markets. This is, in part, because of the gradual *saturation* of existing markets. The Internet crosses traditional boundaries and opens up new markets.

> ⇨ Saturation – first considered in Chapter 10, this is a concept that is used to determine the extent to which a market may have sufficient store facilities for the population, or customer base. The terms 'under-stored' and 'over-stored' are used to describe too many or too few stores to satisfy the needs of the customer, and a return for the retailer. Students may wish to use the index of retail saturation (IRS) to test their local retail provision (Applebaum and Cohen 1962).

For example, both Tesco and Sainsbury have introduced website links to home deliveries as a way of attracting new business. Existing and potential customers are reached using direct mailings (we explained these in Chapter 9) and encouraged to 'log on' to their websites. For customers this form of shopping promises to be trouble-free with ease of ordering and express service when needed. The retailer gains in a number of ways:

▶ Customers who normally shop in-store may wish to *supplement* their weekly purchases.

▶ The novel approach and appealing advertising encourages *new* customers to use the virtual store.

▶ A record of customer visits and purchases permits a more accurate prediction of stock levels, thereby reducing stock outs.

There are other implications for retailers and these will vary from sector to sector. For example, tempting customers away from conventional store visits may be advantageous or disadvantageous. Lower volumes of store traffic reduce congestion and variable costs (staff, wages, etc.) but may also affect long-term customer behaviour. In addition, the lack of direct contact with sales staff may give the impression of lower standards of customer service. Broken delivery promises and poor selections of merchandise could lead to lost custom.

For the customer there are considerable benefits, some of which may attract people away from conventional store shopping. Tesco, for example, offer choice of delivery times over a seven-day period for just £5. This is backed up with the same prices, bonus points and multi-save promotions as the conventional stores. Customers have everything to gain from using Tesco's online service that provides recipes and *favourites* based on a customer's buying profile.

> ⇨ Favourites are those items that the shopper buys most frequently. The retailer's use of this term suggests the virtual shopping experience, and is similar to the *favourites* list on a web browser like Internet Explorer.

In the financial services sector, Direct Line Insurance has recently extended their product range (you can read about this in Case 18.4) to include car sales. This is comparable to the approach adopted by food multiples offering customers more convenience and low-cost alternatives. Jamjar.com provides visitors with money off deals on new cars, advantageous trade-ins, and delivery straight to the door. For customers using the online service this is an extension of existing services, and for Direct Line the new service joins their car insurance products to car purchase.

In an attempt to draw customers in and sell more products and services, some retailers have moved into the provision of Internet services. For instance, many leading retailers have offered free Internet connection, and even the removal of phone charges, to encourage customers to join their in-house Internet service, or Internet service provider (ISP). Electrical retailer Dixons became an ISP in September 1998 and offers free Internet access to customers. Using its two retail businesses, The Link and PC World, this allowed Dixons to move into the rapidly growing personal communications and personal and business computing market, thus extending the Dixons empire into new markets.

Virtual Trading Posts

Other ways of attracting new and existing customers by way of the Internet have brought into being new methods of sourcing. At the supply side of the business, highly developed ways of purchasing are making the old supply chains obsolete. The Internet provides a simple and efficient way of bringing many suppliers together with little physical effort. Retailers call these *trading exchanges*.

> ⇨ Trading exchanges are a way for retail companies to buy from and/or sell to each other using the Internet as a trading post. Buyers and sellers are drawn from a vertical or horizontal marketplace, or across many interrelated marketplaces, with the idea of uniting them in trade. This results in a highly efficient supply chain.

Trading exchanges have become increasingly important to retail businesses as they provide a way of trading more efficiently from business to business. As supply chains need to be driven by consumer demand a lean, robust and flexible supply chain is highly desirable. This means a synchronization and coordination of activities with trading partners. Trading exchanges are a way of developing the supply chain strategy to achieve this, and lowering the costs of executing that strategy (Hotchkiss and Woodall 2000).

Trading exchange services provide retailers with important information and access to online product databases, auctions, discussion forums and transactional systems. These facilities help the individual traders by making activities such as ordering and information gathering fully automated. This provides benefits to both suppliers and retailers in the following ways:

▶ Participants have real-time access to opportunities in the market, which reduces their response time.

▶ Retail buyers have a better understanding of prices which leads to greater negotiating power (this was discussed in Chapter 7).

Trading in a Virtual Market

The Internet trading exchanges permit suppliers and retailers to extend their supply chain management processes to a much wider audience. This may lead to the elimination of older and sometimes excessive systems used in some retail sectors. In the future, trading exchanges could handle the full trading life cycle, which stretches from the purchase of raw materials to end consumer. In particular, trading exchanges improve the retailer's relationship management between suppliers and manufacturers. This helps to improve and sustain the flow of merchandise for the customer. As there is anonymity in the marketplace, trading partners will no longer touch or take ownership of merchandise down the supply chain. Instead, virtual manufacturers and distributors will play an ever-increasing role. For the independent retailer this means similar treatment as the large multiples. All businesses appear equal as far as their relative size is concerned.

There are, however, some disadvantages associated with the use of virtual trading. For example, a retailer's brand may suffer if the service standards to the customer are not maintained. This is because virtual trading can be more difficult to manage due to the lack of direct control. With virtual intermediaries processing only information there is a tendency to treat transactions in an impersonal way.

Some key advantages for retailers are flexibility and control. For instance, the Internet simplifies pricing enormously and any changes can be implemented in seconds. Because information is so readily available, and on tap, real-time pricing analyses and adjustments are possible. This makes the task of establishing a pricing strategy easier and more effective. Customers are happier as the prices reflect real value for money, and compare favourably with the competition. Most websites have order tracking so customer are able to track the progress of their purchases. This system also provides control for the retailers as the communication is two-way and retailers also obtain information about the customer. Reduced handling means greater control over supply and delivery.

> ⇨ Coca-Cola is using an automated computer price link to outside temperatures. The higher the temperature rises, the higher the price.

> ⇨ In France, the average delivery time for goods ordered on the Internet is five or six days, compared with a maximum two days in the USA. Timescales for delivering fresh produce are reducing all the time. For example, orders placed before noon on one day will be delivered next morning anywhere in the USA.

18.3 Mail Order Catalogue Shopping

This section deals with mail order catalogue retailing, which is another area of home shopping. However, unlike Internet shopping which is fairly new, mail order has been popular with consumers for many years. Mail order catalogue shopping is different than conventional store shopping, but similar in process to Internet shopping. A major appeal of the home catalogue lies in its versatility. Customers may purchase merchandise from the comfort of their armchairs, and do not need to travel to the store. Catalogue retailers are major companies operating from central locations, which are essentially large distribution warehouses. Some merchandise is sent from factory to customer, with the mail order company acting as an intermediary. This type of operation is open to the independent retailer as it requires a large investment in infrastructure and supply chain.

A major part of the mail order process is the speedy distribution of goods from the retailer's premises to the agent's home. The mail order agent replaces the conventional store functions by acting as salesperson and merchandiser. Agents are recruited from existing customers and act as sales people, to sell on the merchandise to their personal customer base. These may be friends, neighbours or acquaintances.

The success of the mail order agent hinges on the relationships developed with clients or customers. Customers have the advantage of *seeing* and *trying out* the merchandise before purchase. Hire purchase arrangements make buying merchandise easier for customers, and particularly for the lower socio-economic groups. However, the higher cost of the credit arrangements makes the merchandise more expensive than on the high street.

> ⇨ The higher cost of mail order merchandise – customers are prepared to accept this in exchange for the benefits derived from mail order catalogue shopping. These consist of armchair ordering, easy return of goods, low weekly payments, large range of sizes available, wide variety of merchandise, discreet ordering and commission for agents.

Accessibility is one of the main reasons why consumers use a mail order catalogue. For example, in the high street, fashion items such as clothing may be available but some sizes are frequently in short supply. Stock outs are a major reason for customers switching to another retailer. In mail order retailing, however, because the merchandise is stored in the warehouse, or by the manufacturer, the retailer is nearly always able to supply the desired item. The allocation of storage space is less of an issue than in the high street where space is at a premium. Moreover, the customer does not have to travel to the store to view and likely purchase the item or items. Mail order shopping is available at any time of the day or night and places no demands on a customer's mobility.

Historical Factors

Mail order shopping that was easily accessible was a distinct advantage in Britain during the early 1900s as the population was less mobile, and lacked both the means and the will to travel. Also, there were fewer variety stores and limited choice available at that time. Across the Atlantic, in 1930s USA, the size of the country and great distances involved created a need for remote shopping facilities (Ornstien 1990). In the UK, there was a steady rise in popularity of catalogue shopping from 1950 to 1970. During this period catalogue shopping increased market share to 4.2 per cent of the total consumer market.

Britain was enjoying a period of social change and consumers wanted to express themselves with new fashions and consumer products. Mail order provided this new market for consumer goods with an easy access to credit, with weekly payment through an agent who was often a neighbour. In general, the merchandise obtained through mail order catalogues was not of high quality and targeted the less well off consumer groups. Mail order has come a long way since then, and the quality of goods and service offered through mail order catalogues has improved considerably.

The Modern Mail Order Shopper

Modern mail order consumers tend to be called 'reluctant shoppers'. This means that they probably dislike going shopping in general. There are several reasons for this reluctance but the most likely is because they are time poor, and use mail order as a way of reducing the time they spend shopping. Of course, some consumers dislike shopping and seek ways of avoiding it all together. For older consumers, however, mail order provides convenience and especially for less mobile older or retired consumers. As we have already discussed, the more practical reason for the popularity of mail order are that most catalogues offer a much wider range of stock. For example, because the mail order company is not bound by the conventional store, they can offer numerous sizes, models, etc. For consumers, this means less frustration in stores when they find that items are out of stock or unavailable. Modern mail order consumers are just as demanding and discerning as conventional store shoppers.

Several developments have been shaping the marketplace over recent years. For example, there is a move away from traditional agents and higher purchase agreements, to direct and value-for-money mail order. This is customer driven and is due to changing attitudes towards expensive credit and the convenience of home shopping offered by the new Internet operations. With the increasing expansion into home shopping, alliances between mail order and multiple retailers such as Tesco and Grattan are increasing. On the high street, retailers have moved towards mail order as a way of complementing their normal offering.

Case 18.6 Grattan Links to Tesco

Trading under the corporate name Grattan and 'Look Again', the Grattan catalogue. targets agency customers in the mass market. Grattan is not as fashionable as Freemans, but does carry brands such as Morgan, Lipsy, Sacha, Cat and Kangol. The catalogue has a range of stylish womenswear appealing to customers in the 25+ age group. In general, this range is moderately priced and similar in positioning to Marks & Spencer. At the end of 1999 the company announced that it would begin to trade on the Internet, and forged links with Tesco Direct. This is a similar move to that made between Littlewoods the mail order retailer and the Arcadia group.

The mail order industry structure is not straightforward and dominated by several corporate giants. There are just six retailers in the UK market, and these account for 69 per cent of sales. This figure does not account for direct retail sales from those retailers that trade from a factory or other premises other than conventional mail order traders. Table 18.1 illustrates the rise in sales from 1993 to 1997.

Table 18.1   Percentage of Mail Order Sales by Leading Retailers from 1993 to 1997

	1993	1994	1995	1996	1997
GUS	30.6	30.6	33.3	32.3	29.4
Freemans	8.9	8.2	8.5	8.4	7.3
Grattan	6.7	6.7	6.8	7.3	7.3
N Brown	2.8	2.9	3.4	3.7	4.1
Empire Stores	3.8	3.7	4.1	4.7	N/A
Littlewoods	14.8	14.7	15.9	N/A	20.5
Total	67.5	66.9	72.2	56.8	69.4

Source: Annual Company Reports and Accounts, ONS and Mintel

However the list in Table 18.1 is a little misleading as the corporate names own and operate a number of smaller (but not independent) mail order retailers. For instance, N Brown owns JD Williams which operates a variety of catalogues that include: JD Williams, Ambrose Wilson, Oxendale, Heather Valley, Dale House, Hartington House, Fashion World, Candid Collections, Special Collection, Country Garden and The Classic Combination. Great Universal Stores, or GUS as it is commonly known, controls Kays, Great Universal and Choice. Great Universal Stores also owns Argos, the high street catalogue store and Marshall Ward the direct-purchasing showroom.

Strategic Moves and Initiatives

Mail order retailing is important in the UK marketplace and currently accounts for around 11 per cent of womenswear. Many of the high street retailers have viewed mail order as an area of potential expansion in a saturated market. They have in some cases complemented their retail operations with mail order, as a means of extending sales and reaching new markets. For example, the Next Directory and Marks & Spencer catalogues have led the development in this area and other high street retailers have followed.

Case 18.7 Next Directory Leads the Market

Next Directory helped to revolutionize the mail order industry with quality of service and high delivery standards, and many other retailers have since followed suit. Next catalogue is well presented with high-quality photography and page layouts, fewer items per page than conventional merchandise directories in the same market. It followed this up with a 48-hour delivery promise which became the industry standard. All these attributes have provided Next with much more upmarket appeal, and one that is in keeping with its retail store image. This has maintained the customers' expectations.

A number of retailers have become more involved with traditional mail order as a result of strategic moves and take-overs. For instance, Argos was bought by GUS in 1998 and the Argos Gift Directory was born. This is a direct order catalogue, which will be independent of the agency type operations associated with the traditional mail order companies. Other retailers have also come together to create a 'new look' in mail order retailing. For example, Littlewoods mail order, which owns Index the high street catalogue retailer, launched a new direct mail order catalogue called Index Extra in 1998. This group now trades under the name of Littlewoods Index shops and has entered the high street with conventional stores carrying the Littlewoods brand.

Many of the conventional mail order retailers like Littlewoods and Grattan are in the process of developing direct response catalogues, due to competitive pressure from the high street. For instance, Marks & Spencer has cultivated catalogue-based home-shopping services. Retailers are very conscious that electronic shopping is a major goal for the future, and that home-shopping specialists have the service infrastructure to support electronic retailing or e-tailing. There are several examples of big high street names developing strategic links with mail order, such as Littlewoods extending its expertise in home shopping through a tie-in with the Arcadia Group. Littlewoods has also moved into digital television shopping services jointly with Granada Television, to produce television output with home shopping on digital television channels.

A major issue for all retailers is which of the new technologies offer the best medium for electronic shopping. Many experts believe that the Internet is less suited to mass market retailing than television. There are many factors that define the future of retailing and one of these is the development and take-up of television and Internet retailing. It is clear that embracing technological change is vital to retailers achieving and maintaining a competitive advantage. The same is true for both independent and chain retailers.

18.4 Television Shopping

Retailing may never be the same again as the result of interactive television. This is certainly what happened in the USA where home shopping channels have become very popular. Similar to the PC-based transaction, direct response or interactive television allows the consumer to make a direct purchase without leaving their armchair. Interactive television shows the items to be purchased in detail, and actually being worn in the case of clothing and jewellery.

> ⇨ Interactive television is a system that allows the customer to select whenever they want the programme or product to be viewed, as well as controlling and participating in product demonstrations.

> ⇨ Direct response television – using this medium, customers may respond to an advertisement message on the television by making a direct purchase.

In the UK, recent developments in digital television may well increase the popularity of interactive shopping considerably. The main reason for this is that digital television will offer customers huge variety and greater accessibility.

> ⇨ Digital television owes its success, in the main, to the developments in the user-friendly multimedia interface, which can be found in computer games. Using this type of presentation for customer shopping transforms the Internet into a virtual shopping world. Digital technology converts text, sound and images into 'digital bits' of information. This information can be delivered down telephone lines or, in the near future, using terrestrial broadcasts. Using this compression technology will help retailers to communicate their offering in an efficient and attractive manner.

Digital television uses a connection to a network similar to that offered by the British Broadcasting Corporation (BBC). A binary code is sent from a broadcasting centre to a household television set (Driscoll 1999). The technology is simple and similar to that used for compact disc (CD) players, radios and many other devices that involve transmissions. Other countries such as Germany, the USA and France already possess digital television networks. However, the service that is to be provided in Britain by BSkyB, ITV Digital and Cable and Wireless (CW) offers more channels, better sound and better quality pictures. More importantly, the UK system will offer greater *interactivity*, which makes it an altogether more sophisticated service (Ody 2000). The new system will allow levels of interactivity controlled by a handset similar to a normal television control or computer games console.

The introduction of home shopping through digital television and the Internet is likely to raise the following issues for retailers:

▶ Cutting out the middlemen or the removal of traditional retailers may take place.

▶ Existing retailers have the greatest relevant knowledge and experience to capitalize on digital television.

▶ Customers will expect to see high street retailers becoming highly proficient in online selling.

▶ Those retailers that are able to continue normal operations whilst developing additional trade over the Internet will have the greatest chance to maintain their market share (Newman, Bailey and Heptinstall 2000).

It is in the UK clothing sector where interactive television has seen most growth. Unlike the USA, British consumers have a different approach to television-based shopping. British and many European consumers need to feel that they are actually *inside* the store, and need to touch and experience the merchandise. Nevertheless, in the UK the plan is to provide numerous shopping networks so consumers will be able to order merchandise by using a hand-held remote control. This will provide shoppers with a far richer range of home shopping options than currently available. For example, the mail order catalogue offers wide ranges of merchandise but may have difficulty competing with a television shopping channel. The fact that consumers can actually see the merchandise being demonstrated creates an edge that is hard to follow. The visual sense is a very persuasive element in consumer decision-making. However, there is still speculation over the likely level of acceptance in the UK market.

Digital television considerably improves a retailer's chances of launching interactive television shopping, and can provide hundreds of channels of output and interactive services. Home shopping, educational activities such as home tutoring, and regional information services are likely to be the most popular interactive services in the future. Research suggests that one in five households now have digital television and it is likely to spread rapidly in the UK. People will become more familiar with interactive services and expect to access online activities from the comfort of the home. Ultimately, the digital format will be the sole television system as the government switches off analogue television services around the year 2010.

The Digital Divide

As we might expect, usage is lowest among the unemployed, older people, and small family units. Table 18.2 illustrates the typical services a digital television subscriber is likely to use around the year 2001.

Table 18.2   Which Key Services Do Digital Television Subscribers Use?

Total UK penetration of digital television	Online banking	Online shopping	Internet access	Playing games	Email
19%	6%	18%	9%	44%	13%

Source: OFTEL 2000

We can see from Table 18.2 the relatively small number of consumers that use shopping services. However, it would seem that this is not because of a reluctance to use technology, as the take-up of other services such as email and the Internet shows. This raises some interesting issues about the types of interfaces that may be used for shopping services.

> ⇨ Interface – in simple terms, this means the point of contact or the device that the customer actually touches, views and uses for connection to the virtual store.

Trends in Television Internet Shopping

As the communication bandwidths increase, the hardware equipment is likely to become more powerful, sophisticated, easier to use, affordable and portable. For example, WAP telephones and interactive digital television seem to be the most popular Internet access methods. If these prove to be popular with customers they may provide an alternative to the personal computer (PC) and increase the number of online customers. There is another much larger group of mobile computing devices led by Psion's palmtop computer. These 'smart' and 'small' devices will ultimately be the main interfaces for mobile e-commerce. Using the mobile phone to interact and perform shopping transactions with anyone, at any time and anywhere, eliminates the barriers of time and location.

Developments in digital television have improved Internet access and retailers can now reach customers anytime when a television receiver is turned on. Customers 'click' the icon to dial up the Internet and then place an order. Given the dependency on television, there is little doubt that Internet access via the television is likely to become important to consumers and suppliers. However, the question of which medium consumers will choose, digital television or the PC, is yet to be determined.

Case 18.8 SkyDigital Launch Virtual High Street

Retailers GUS, Woolworths, Iceland, Argos, Somerfield and Dixons have joined up with SkyDigital to provide an interactive television service. Viewers with a set-top box linked to their telephone will be able to spontaneously buy merchandise. The service offers consumers an opportunity to select and pay for their weekly groceries, and view and purchase the latest high street fashions.

Called the 'Open' service, the facility is accessed when a customer presses the 'interactive' button on their remote control. The interactive element can only work if there is a telephone connection to the set-top box, but there is no cost to the customer for the use of the line. A menu comes up on the television screen offering five options – shopping, banking, information, games and email. When the customer chooses to go shopping, they can pick which retailer they want to visit and view the goods on offer. The service offers the benefit of digital sound and images and a secure credit facility.

Source: Clements 1999: 12–13

New technology is likely to continue to widen the choices for customers and therefore the potential for home shopping on the Internet. In fashion retailing, for example, the unique tailoring of clothes is taken to a whole new level with the mass access to digital television and the Internet. Levi Strauss, the jeans manufacturer, are leading the way in the textiles and fashion industry in terms of technological innovation. Their customers can customize and adjust selected garments, by adjusting clothing on a computer model. This template can be accessed whenever they wish to purchase a new pair of jeans, and allows the consumer to select the style of jeans with a choice of leg openings, colours and fastenings. Future versions will bring increased functions, allowing rotation on the screen and be adjustable to the same figure as the customer to provide a more realistic three-dimensional view of how the clothes will appear. This facility should help to reduce returns and their associated problems, as the customer decision is based on more detailed information. As technology develops the potential for mass customization and access to global markets becomes even greater (Newman, Bailey and Heptinstall 2000).

Electronic Kiosks: Operating Procedures

Much more common in the US marketplace, the electronic kiosk is becoming a very useful format for some retailers. In particular, small independent operators may well move into this type of format, as lower capital investment is required. For example, a small retailer could operate a branded concession inside a department store or supermarket chain.

> ⇨ An electronic kiosk is a free-standing unit linked to an interactive computer system. This provides consumers with information about merchandise features and prices and makes it possible for them to purchase without the help of sales people.

Key benefits for the small retailer apart from costs are location and access. An independent would be able to enjoy the high levels of footfall, and access the customer profiles offered by the chain operator's location. Another real advantage of the electronic kiosk is the ability to expand the product lines *immediately*, with no consequence for space and inventory. For a small retailer this is crucial.

The electronic kiosk concept has been seen for some time in bank retailing where the automatic teller machine, or ATM, has become an important part of our lives. Developments of the ATM have extended the service to include withdrawals, statements, receipts, and other bank-related services. In the future we may well see this type of format extended to include travel information and product information. Travel agents selling holidays and other services will be able to inform, persuade, remind and train/educate customers. Already some airport operators are offering catalogue-type purchases and this may well be extended to include luxury goods such as motor cars. In general, however, British consumers do not readily accept this type of shopping medium for products linked to extensive problem-solving, and favour the personal touch. Things may well change with the new technological advances.

18.5 The Future of Out-of-Store Retailing

> ⇨ Whether we call it e-commerce, e-shopping, e-tailing, cybershopping or virtual retailing, the technology is unlikely to change why consumers buy. Consumers may not evolve into different shoppers but just learn to use the new technology as an aid to shopping more effectively.

Over time, every factor of store operations has been affected by the advance of technology. Today more than ever before retailers have the opportunity to expand into different retail formats. New technologies are enhancing the out-of-store experience making it more realistic, faster and much more convenient. We are likely to be purchasing in a global marketplace of information, combining goods, services and the exchange of ideas. The Internet websites are becoming more and more inviting with features that mimic conventional store environments. In fact, the website is now accepted as an extension of the retailers' operation, and part of their brand image.

The idea of virtual store shopping has increased in popularity more so in the UK than in other European countries. Some of the reasons for this growth are time pressure and competition, which we have already discussed. One other factor is advertising clutter. The increased variety on the shelves that consumers have come to expect, and the associated retail promotions, just add to the confusion. All these messages create uncertainty and can in some cases reduce shopping trips, as consumers find themselves overcome by the array of choice. However, students of retailing must not forget that consumers come to the shops, malls and retail parks for enjoyment, not simply because of the range and depth of merchandise available. It is sometimes the social and cultural factors that boost revenues in these locations, rather than markdowns and multi-saver offers. Consumers who choose to use Internet shopping as an alternative will not encounter the same experiences.

Virtual Store Patronage

Several factors are likely to influence the growth of home shopping and use of the Internet. The most obvious factor is access, or the number of households purchasing interactive televisions and personal computers. However, the increasing popularity of electronic mail as a means of communication is also helping to fuel the growth of the virtual store. Advertising has also had a similar positive impact on this growth, as it can be measured directly by counting the number of 'hits' on a page. However, we should point out that a customer can access a page several times, and currently there is no way of differentiating between customers.

Web advertising pays for the increased number of retail sites which, in turn, attract a greater number of customers. The rising number of sales stimulates other retail businesses to start up new sites. Web start-ups are relatively inexpensive and by starting a web page small retailers can reach potential customers around the world. Selling on the Web is fairly straightforward and a low-cost option compared to conventional 'start-ups'.

Outside the UK, continental Europe is catching up with increases in online activity. However, telephone connection rates in this market are still triple those in the USA and the UK, where unlimited access is allowed on free and fixed-charge local lines (the UK currently operates fixed-charge connections). Increasing competition and technological advances and cheaper telephone, cable and satellite connections will encourage consumers to use Internet shopping facilities. However, there are some features of home shopping that retailers will need to perfect if consumers are to switch to the virtual store for part or all of their shopping needs. For many consumers, the decision to use the Internet for shopping will depend on whether home delivery is included. Bulky furniture, clothes, electrical products and food are the most popular types of merchandise for home delivery.

The potential growth of the Internet remains huge when compared with the current dominance of mail order we considered earlier in this chapter. Retailers that encourage customers to deal with them in a number of different ways (for example, virtual store, conventional store and telephone) will stand out. The biggest challenge of all for retailers is to make all these channels appear to be one of the same image. However, an even greater challenge is overcoming concerns about privacy, and the confidentiality of business transactions.

Fraud and Home Shopping

Some Internet retailers have gone to extreme lengths to reassure customers about the risks associated with fraud on the Internet. In fact, the risk of credit card fraud is greater on the Internet but modern encryption technology is rapidly reducing this type of fraud.

> ⇨ Encryption technology – used in the purchase area of a virtual store, the technology utilizes what is called Secure Sockets Layer (SSL) to allow for the encryption of potentially sensitive information, such as the customer's name, address and other critically sensitive data like credit card details. Information passed between the customer's computer and the website cannot be read if someone other than the retailer intercepts it.

Vast amounts of time and money have been spent on making e-commerce secure. Customers are naturally worried that transactions will fall into the wrong hands as soon as they enter details on the Internet. The main worry is that credit card details will be taken off and used to acquire goods that customers did not order. This worries both consumers and retailers, and security is one of the most debated issues in e-commerce. The Internet is, by definition, an open-access medium. As a result, determined individuals and teams of organized criminals hack into websites and commit fraud. It is the publicity about these escapades that have generated so much concern. In response some retailers like jungle.com will refund the value of any fraudulent order, and offer a 100 per cent guarantee to customers if they ever suffer from fraudulent use of their credit card.

Unlike traditional transactions taking place in a retail store, which works upon the basis of secure networks, the Internet can cause problems. There are four main reasons why this is so: confidentiality, authentication, integrity and non-repudiation. These relate to the following functions:

▶ stopping 'eavesdropping' on data

▶ checking the credentials of individuals

▶ ensuring that data is not tampered with

▶ confirming the dispatch and receipt of material.

The smart card could well be the total security key of the future, not only holding vital information such as digital signatures, but also providing the holder with access to everything from computer networks to bank teller machines and building security systems.

> ⇨ Smart cards – a credit card sized device containing a micro-computer processor which can store large amounts of information.

Once the transaction has been completed, the transmission can be encrypted for increased security so that, even if it is intercepted, the message cannot be unscrambled. It remains to be said, however, that when customers can be certain that doing business over the Internet is as safe and secure as the conventional store, then the virtual store will become a major commercial alternative to actual store shopping.

Moving Out of the Store

For retailers, moving out of the store is about diversifying into new retail formats, which take the next step towards multiple access. With this approach retailers will be able to sell to customers who do not wish or cannot come to the store. This may be the result of a reduction in consumer time or an unwillingness to visit the conventional store. Future consumers will expect technological advances to change the way they shop, and buy merchandise without leaving their homes.

This idea is in contrast to conventional stores, which tend to limit consumers' options and determine when and where they shop. Customers must go where the store is located and, of course, they have to shop when the store is open. Out-of-store retail is available anywhere and open at any time. This requires a mix of conventional and virtual retail formats. Figure 18.1 illustrates the evolution from conventional to the multiple format stores. By offering a variety of formats the retailer is able to offer flexible time, location and merchandise range.

Future Developments

It is very unlikely that conventional retailing will disappear in the near future. The reason for this is because retailing is all about discovery, fun and social interaction. Not to mention the functional side of retailing: convenience, selection and value for money. However, customers of the future will be fully accustomed to searching the store and paying with virtual money.

Today the Internet is just a shadow of what the information super-highway is likely to be in the future. Interactive systems will provide many functions in real time, or as things take place. Many more information-based transactions will help retail customers to develop their knowledge of products, and buy more expertly. Smart cards that can store huge amounts of information about customers will become commonplace. For retailers, the smart card will provide economic, demographic and lifestyle information about their customers. Control is likely to be a key feature of retailing in the future. For businesses up and down the supply chain, the emphasis is on bringing customers and suppliers together more efficiently. For instance, an independent retailer will be able to use Internet-based systems to replace the order and trans-action function, making the business far more efficient. Multiples will

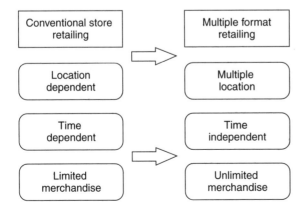

Figure 18.1   Conventional Store versus Multiple Format Retailing

make continued use of database retailing and focus more on the personalized service to the customer.

Virtual reality (VR) will be the next step forward in the use of technology in home shopping. Already used by kitchen retailers for planning and design, VR can be used for enhancing the shopping experience. Potential shoppers will be able to sit at a screen and watch images of three-dimensional products. This technique can also be used for store design and layout and in-store promotions. With a click the customer will be able to move up and down retail aisles. It will be possible to zoom in and out of any shelf and pick up products to examine them, and then place them in the virtual shopping basket. The future is likely to bring sound and three-dimensional animation to the shopping experience. More than ever before, going shopping on the Web will be much more attractive and places the customer in control.

References

Applebaum, W. and Cohen, S.B. (1962) 'Trading area networks and problems of store saturation', *Journal of Retailing*, Winter: 35–6.

Clements, A. (1999) 'Open all hours', *Retail Week*, 5 March: 12–13.

Driscoll, G. (1999) *The Essential Guide to Digital Set-top Boxes and Interactive TV*, London: Prentice-Hall International.

Hotchkiss, C. and Woodall, S. (2000) 'Infomediaries enter the chain', *Retail Week*, 2 June: 42.

Newman, A.J., Bailey J.M. and Heptinstall A.K. (2000) 'The impact of digital television and the Internet on the fashion industry', *Management Case Quarterly*, 5(1/2): 33–7

Ody, P. (2000) 'Still a novel experience: sales via interactive TV', *Financial Times*, 6 December: 5.

OFTEL (Office Telecommunications) (2000) *Consumers' Use of Digital TV – Summary of OFTEL Residential Survey Q1*, July, http://www.oftel.gov.uk/publications/research/digi0800.htm/

Ornstien E.J. (1990) *Mail Order Marketing*, Aldershot: Gower, pp. 48–60.

International Retailing Internationalization and Globalization

This chapter will cover the following topics:

- ► The extent of internationalization.

- ► The reasons for international development.

- ► The different methods of international expansion.

- ► Cultural adaptation.

International Retailing Internationalization and Globalization

Introduction and Core Concepts

Modern consumers are internationally focused as the result of their experiences and technological developments that have taken place. Young people today are much more in tune with the broader world beyond their countries' borders. They are familiar with the sights, sounds and ideas of many countries. Retailing is, in many ways, the medium that creates this outlook, because it draws goods and services from across the world.

The shrinking global market now allows retailers to reach markets not previously considered. Many large retailers have responded by establishing a significant and growing international presence that depends on a sophisticated marketing and distribution system. This means that international retailers have come mainly from the USA, Western Europe and Japan. In order to succeed, many of these retailers have had to adapt their business methods: the merchandise they sell, their stores and distribution, their labour management and their relations with government and the business sector generally.

19.1 Shopping at World Stores

People constantly seek new experiences and products to improve their lifestyles. They gather increasing amounts of information from around the world directly through travel and contact with visitors, and indirectly through the Internet, television and other media. This leads to the rapid communication of what is considered appropriate and socially acceptable among large groups of consumers in different countries.

Consumers learn how to consume from the range of information available that provides insight into the symbolic meanings of products and services. Although products and services differ across cultures, and the images they evoke may not be similar, global purchasing patterns and lifestyle indicators are generally the same. Consumer tastes in food, clothing and other products are growing closer together around the world. Young Europeans are even more similar in their views than their parents' generation. This displays an interesting contrast with earlier societies that watched the industrial revolution create the widespread dispersion of manufactured goods in countries across the world. The result is that people increasingly embrace an internationally accepted view that determines how they consume.

Retailing is the medium that creates this outlook because it draws goods and services from across the world. The fact that the global market has shrunk makes it possible for retailers to reach markets not previously considered. Consumers in these markets search hungrily for positional goods that are can be identified as *world products*.

> ⇨ World product – product that has a worldwide market that transcends national cultures. The product may be used in different ways across countries but it has been assimilated into national cultures.

Table 19.1 lists some examples of world products.

Table 19.1 World Products

Product	Brand
Soft drinks	Coca-Cola
Disney products	Walt Disney
Audio-visual	Sony
Razors	Gillette

Sometimes product and retailer brands have become household names and entered the English language. These are called *generic* brands. For example, McDonald's and Levi jeans and are both used to denote shopping activities, such as 'going for a big Mac' or 'going for some Levi's'. Similarly, everyday merchandise may be associated with particular retailers such as Woolworth, Boots and Marks & Spencer.

Lifestyles are also denoted by brand names. For example, Levi jeans and the Nike flash are icons of a young and socially aware generation. Young people today increasingly purchase similar products and the stores they buy them from have international links. This promotes the international development of retailing. Table 19.2 uses a sample of consumer purchases in the UK to illustrate the increasingly international nature of our shopping.

Table 19.2 Shopping at International Stores in the UK

Item	Typical retailer	Group and international connections
Jeans	GAP	US retailer; stores in Europe; Canada
	Levi	US manufacturer with specialist stores
Shoes	Brantano	Belgian retailer
Outdoorwear	Timberland	US manufacturer with own stores

Table 19.2 continued

Item	Typical retailer	Group and international connections
Weekly food shopping	Sainsbury	UK retailer with US subsidiary
	Tesco	UK retailer; European and Asian subsidiaries
	Asda	Wal-Mart; US retailer with stores across the world
Electrical products	Comet	Kingfisher – UK retailer; owns Darty (France)
	Dixons	UK retailer; subsidiary operates across Scandinavia
Computers	Dell	US manufacturer with direct retail operation
	Dixons	UK retailer; subsidiary operates across Scandinavia
Fast food	McDonald's	US organization; stores worldwide
Toiletries and cosmetics	Boots	UK retailer; has stores and linked operations abroad
	Body Shop	UK retailer; has international operations
Books	Borders	US retailer
Stationery	Staples	US retailer with European subsidiaries
Furniture	IKEA	Swedish retailer; stores in Europe and America
DIY	B&Q	Kingfisher – UK retailer with European subsidiaries
Toys	Toys 'Я' Us	US retailer; also has stores in other countries

Cultural Differences and the Consumer

A key reason for the homogenization of retailing is that consumers are becoming similar in the way they shop. Comparable patterns of shopping are developing across the world. There are several reasons for this, such as the pressures on consumers' time that has resulted in increased demand for convenience formats. Petrol forecourt retailing and new style convenience stores, as well as Internet shopping, have increased in countries such as the USA, the UK and Japan. Global awareness has also increased the demand for value-based pricing of quality goods and services. This enables retailers who have developed these formats in one region of the world to transplant their concepts into another region. For instance the European value clothing retailer H&M can instantly find success in its New York store and the US jeans retailer Gap can quickly establish itself in Europe.

Consumers across the world also respond similarly to changing economic conditions. Less favourable economic conditions at the turn of the century have been associated with an increasing emphasis on value-based retailing. This increased emphasis on value-based retailing has meant that even the discerning Japanese shoppers are looking for value-for-money as well as quality. This illustrates the growing acceptance across the world of retailer brands and encourages the growth of international operations (Kutyla 2000).

However, consumers in different countries can still respond differently to brands and retailers and the messages they send out. As countries proceed with their economic development, younger, better-educated and more sophisticated consumer markets develop. However, the international retailer has to recognize that the majority of consumers will continue to shop with different motives and look for different products, because of important cultural differences between countries and sometimes within small geographical regions. These differences will affect the way in which retailers can trade in different countries across the world, right down to store format and visual merchandising. Consequently, when identifying potential markets, the retailer needs to consider the influence of culture on shopping behaviour. Cultural characteristics (such as Finnish *sisu* and passion for *sauna*) reflect a region's geography, history, religion and economic development. Language is also important in the way that ideas and concepts are expressed and messages transmitted and received. Promotional material in Western, individualistic countries can ignore religious sensibilities in ways that are forbidden in traditionalist Muslim countries.

Retailers need to recognize the impact of a country's culture on the practical and symbolic values of different products, services and modes of shopping. These in turn influence ability of retailers to market themselves effectively.

Implications for Retailers

There are broad cultural differences across geographic regions, and the consumption of goods is normally determined by a society's beliefs. For example, Westerners are used to the idea that lifestyles should usually improve, and this is likely to come about as a result of the acquisition of ever more sophisticated goods and services. Significant differences in the buying process exist across the world, and the basic approaches to buying outlined in Chapter 6 do not necessarily apply universally. Theories of purchasing behaviour will, therefore, vary as the motives for buying goods in Western cultures does not necessarily hold in non-Western countries.

Retailers must be aware of ethnocentricity and the rationalistic model that assumes that consumers engage in uniform patterns of thought.

> ⇨ Ethnocentricity – the practice of imposing a biased set of standards that emanate from one particular prevalent culture. For example, some companies design merchandise that reflects their own personal values, without considering others.

Mapping Out International Societies

Retailers need to understand their markets and break them down into clearly defined segments they can target (see Chapter 6). When a retailer engages in an international venture it needs to understand the foreign market on its own terms. This requires its decision-makers and planners to undergo a learning process of *acculturation* so that they can empathize with their new market.

Lifestyles and Values

Western retailers have problems in adjusting to a new culture. Even in neighbouring countries they may find consumer behaviour different.

Sometimes, the idea of a consumer is an alien concept and Eastern European countries lack a well-developed understanding of consumerism. Within the UK, there is a distinct difference between Scottish attitudes and those just across the border in England as regards living accommodation, pubs, entertainment and food. The traditional haggis is made from the stomach of a sheep, which is, generally speaking, distasteful to the English. The English taste for Scottish woollen products that suggest high quality and status, is considered strange to the Scots.

There are many products that evoke special feelings because of their nationalistic links. For example, in France red wine is a totem drink that is considered to have healing properties. This is similar to the English habit of drinking tea whenever they feel sick, in need of sustenance or to stimulate social discourse. Types of fast food may be considered multinational in some contexts and yet, when displayed alongside other goods, take on a nationalistic form. The real challenge for retailers is to take a product or idea from one country and package it so that it is acceptable to another culture. Food service retailers provide classic examples of this technique. 'Chinese' dishes sold in many takeaways may be very distant from the original, but they suit Western palettes and social situations.

Another important area of cultural difference for retailers lies in the use and symbolism of colour. Some colours evoke universal responses, but the psychological perception of colour is subjective, and the implications of different hues of the colour vary between cultures. American and Japanese cultures recognize red and orange as stimulating warm colours, but blue and green as cool colours that evoke calm. However, they have differences in their perception of 'good' and 'bad' colour ranges (*Encyclopaedia Britannica* 2001). Colour perception varies across regions. Some languages, for instance, use words that could mean blue or green, whereas some African languages use several words to distinguish the many naturally occurring shades of green. Black is the colour of mourning in the West, but China also uses white.

Retailers should not expect consumers to behave according to Western marketing norms. For the Chinese consumer, self-esteem is an important driver of behaviour whereas other factors are important in Western culture. The Western consumer has become very individualistic, which is in sharp contrast to more traditional or less economically developed countries where family or social ties are taken very heavily into account when making purchases. The traditional aspects of family, social conventions and self-esteem are reflected in greater consumer loyalty rather than the Western expectation of the self-seeking and disloyal consumer (Doole and Lowe 2001).

These factors can make it hard for retailers to break into new markets because each function in the organization requires re-thinking. Even in markets that appear culturally very close, such as adjacent European countries or the USA, British retailers have experienced significant difficulties in establishing themselves. Experiences such as these suggest that retailers entering or extending their international operations need to carefully consider the process of internationalization.

Case 19.1 American Gap?

The simple clean lines of American retailer Gap appealed to youth across the world in the early 1990s. The worldwide growth of its format led to Gap merging its domestic and international operations in 1999. However, by 2000 profitability was falling in the United States and even more so in its international stores. As a result, the company decided to expand but not at the same rate (Business Wire, 2000).

The relative decline in the profitability of its international stores indicated that Gap needed to rethink its ambition as a global brand.

19.2 Internationalization and Globalization

A retailer internationalizes its operations when it carries them in two or more states (nations or countries) of the world.

> ⇨ Internationalization is the act of crossing international boundaries with business interests. An international retailer is one that sells directly to consumers through shops or other form of distribution in more than one country.

'Country', 'state' and 'nation' have different meanings and connotations across the English-speaking world and we need to clarify their use when discussing international retailers We use the word 'state' in the context of internationalization to mean a legally independent state. Thus, we would not describe a retailer that operates only in Scotland and England as an international retailer, because these two countries lie within the same state, the UK. The different legal systems of England and Scotland and other cultural factors do not present major difficulties for most retail operations. Similarly, retailers such as Marks & Spencer may have a store in the Isle of Man or in the Channel Islands. These are small associated states that are close to Britain geographically and culturally. Operating in these countries does not constitute internationalization.

However, a retailer operating in two or more countries of the European Union, such as France and Germany, is an international retailer. This is because the political ties in the European Union are still loose and the various members still have considerable independence. Commercial and legal harmonization is also far from complete. These differences and language barriers still make extending operations into another EU country a significant step for retailers.

The USA is only one 'country' even though it is made up of 50 states and represents a vast market with very different cultures contained within it. So, a retailer operating stores in California and New York is not an international retailer, even though the cultural difference between the two states is quite significant. On the other hand, a small retailer that operates in two towns either side of the US-Canadian border is, technically, an international retailer, even though the cultural difference between the two local communities is very small. (For a brief economic and cultural analysis of the US-Canadian markets, see Anderson 1993.)

Different Perceptions of International Activity

The previous discussion spells out the *geopolitical* criterion of internationalization. However, we have to consider other aspects of the retailer's operations that make the criterion a little fuzzy. Most retail stores sell mainly to customers resident within the same country, but may sell to foreign visitors or may export products directly. Where a retailer sells mostly to residents of the country, the business is essentially a domestic retailer. However, some stores rely on the tourist trade and a significant part of their sales may be to customers from abroad. This is not important for many stores in large island communities like Britain, but cross-border shopping may have a significant impact in some areas of Europe and North America. Airport retailing is another important example of cross-border shopping, where the retailer needs to take specific account of the requirements of the international customer.

In these cases, the distinction between domestic and international retailer becomes harder to draw. Its customers may be international, but the retailer operates within the jurisdiction of the country containing the store or airport. In terms of planning controls, labour management and distribution, the retailer is essentially a domestic retailer. So we do not use the term 'international' to describe this type of retailer unless the retailer also has stores in anther country.

Retailers by their nature supply products from around the world. However, most retailers acquire these products through international distribution channels, so that their operations only start from within the boundaries of their own country. In this sense these retailers remain national operators. However, some retailers also undertake the direct sourcing of their products from abroad. Some large retailers maintain their own international distribution facilities and even small fashion retailers may make trips abroad to buy directly. These retailers have become international operators because they also operate directly within the jurisdiction of another country. However, we do not count them as international retailers unless they also sell abroad.

The practicalities of operating in different countries vary with the geopolitical structure of the country. A large country such as the USA that is divided into many smaller semi-autonomous states provides two major levels of regulation. However, the geographically and demographically smaller Federal Republic of Germany is divided into a number of states (*lander*) that also have their own regulatory systems. Germany is also a member of the European Union, which may also take an active regulatory role, particularly in relation to competition and trading practices that further limit the freedom of retail operators. The USA is also a member of the North American Free Trade Agreement (NAFTA), but this has a more limited regulatory impact.

These have an impact on the attractiveness of expansion into other countries and the rate of expansion once within the new country (Alexander 1997).

Globalization

Many international retailers can be identified with their country of origin and undertake limited international activity. Their stores and sales abroad are only a fraction of those at home. The initial venture abroad will be either through opening a store or acquiring a retail business in another country. If the retailer opens a store under its existing brand, the natural experience of many retailers has been to reproduce the store formats developed for their domestic markets. In such cases, retailers project their domestic surroundings abroad and sell a concept that can be distinctly identified with their own native country.

However, as the retailer develops across several countries it has to decide on the essential format for development. Where the retailer continues the development of its international stores in line with its domestic formats, the retailer is globalizing. When it has established its standard format in several countries, it may then be recognized as a global retailer. In practice, retailers learn to adapt ideas to, and sometimes adopt ideas from, their international stores in order to be more effective. Whether a firm is globalizing or merely internationalizing depends on whether the retailer makes any significant adaptation of its standard format.

> ⇨ Globalizing produces a standard offering for all markets, whereas internationalizing produces an adaptation of the home market's offering.

> ⇨ A global retailer does not modify its home market's offering to any significant extent as a result of opening branches abroad.

For example, the US retailer Toys 'Я' Us attempted to develop as a global retailer and it used essentially the same format across the world. However, its has now become less of a global retailer because it has been forced to alter the merchandise and format according to regional requirements.

Multinational and Transnational Retailers

The initial success of a retailer abroad depends on an innovative format and effective supply chain. If the retailer can identify and fill a gap in the market it may be able to expand rapidly. Fairly rapid expansion will encourage the retailer to persist with its domestic formats. If it can export its format to several countries, particularly in different continents, it becomes a global retailer. However, sooner or later the retailer will find that the growth will slow down. It will then have to explore new ways of growing in its chosen markets. It will also find that its home market is also changing and will have to develop its initial format. This provides the environment for learning and re-evaluation.

The retailer may then develop increasing individualization of its formats with different merchandise, service procedures and layouts for each country. This is likely to be the case where the retailer has built up an effective local supply chain and is increasing its use of local managers. The retail organization appears to lose much of its distinctive national identity and becomes a *multinational* retailer.

Alternatively, a retailer may use very different formats to expand into different countries. For example, a retail bank like Barclays trades under Barclays International and has a very different format in overseas locations than it does in the UK.

The retailer may also become a multinational through the acquisition of a foreign retailer. The retailer may rebrand its foreign subsidiary or seek to improve its value by introducing those skills and systems that gave it success at home. For instance, the UK food retailer Sainsbury has kept its US food chain under its original name, while improving its format. This process will pull the subsidiary towards the retailer's original home model. Rebranding moves the retailer towards globalization, while reorganizing the brand will pull it towards being a multinational retailer.

A highly successful retailer may, however, develop a format that transcends its national origin and becomes accepted as part of the shopping culture of the various host countries. The retail brand becomes a world-class format, which is the retail equivalent of a world good (as discussed in section 19.1). The format is usually the result of adapting a global brand significantly to take account of local conditions, without losing the similarity of format. The similarity of format enables the retailer to take advantage of economies of large-scale organization. The retailer may then be described as a *transnational* retailer.

> ⇨ Multinational retailer: the retailer operates in more than one country and adapts its offering to fit that country.

> ⇨ Transnational retailer: the retailer develops a world-class format that is flexible enough to adapt to local markets.

The various concepts of international, multinational, global and transnational retailers are not always used consistently and may have more than one meaning (Alexander 1997). Ideas such as internationalization and globalization can express a *process* of change within a retail organization as well as the outcome of that process. Figure 19.1 illustrates the use of the terms to describe the extent to which a retailer's offering changes as it expands its international activities. The diagram uses two dimensions to describe a retailer's international development: the relative impact of the home country on the format used (shown along the vertical axis); and the extent to which the retailer adapts the format to each of the countries it operates in (shown along the horizontal axis).

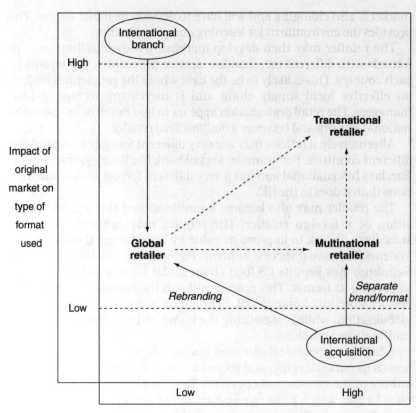

Figure 19.1   Classification of Retailers' International Behaviour

The placing of a particular retailer within this framework should take account of the fact that particular formats are associated with particular cultures. For instance, hypermarkets originated in France and superstores and fast food outlets in the USA. However, these formats are now accepted around the world and so have become transnational or world-class formats. Just as Levi's and Coca-Cola symbolize world goods, so shopping at Wal-Mart and eating at a McDonald's are their retailing counterparts.

The fast food chain McDonald's illustrates the change from globalization towards transnationalization. The company started out in the USA as a chain of standardized hamburger restaurants. It originally adopted a globalization programme but has since adapted its offering to local conditions. In addition, the company has acquired other food retailers as part of its worldwide expansion programme. In the process, it has been losing much of its distinctive American *feel* as it adapts to *local* culture. However, it manages to retain its brand image through the use of core attributes like the clown, the 'golden arches' and toy promotions. Tesco has developed the supermarket format and distribution system that has been flexible to adapt to its local markets. This enables Tesco to expresses itself within the context of the host country, although it is recognized as coming from Britain.

19.3 Going International

Many retailers only consider internationalization after they have established a very substantial presence in their home market. Their international ventures initially are heavily dominated by their domestic operations. Although they may expand cautiously one country at a time, some take a global attitude, because they try to transplant their successful format into other countries. However, they have been unsuccessful in many cases. Marks & Spencer opened stores in Canada but found that the apparent similarity of language and culture did not translate into customer behaviour and after a disastrous period scaled down its operations (Nickolds 1997). Several large retailers have also taken an international approach by acquiring retail businesses abroad, hoping to use British management styles to run them more successfully. Major UK retailers, such as Dixons, Marks & Spencer, Boots and Tesco have acquired American and West European retailers only to find their operations return low or negative profits and have ended up disposing of their acquisitions at a loss. Part of the failure comes about through the complacency of not doing proper market research or assuming they understood the business and consumer culture of the host county (Nickolds 1997).

Another area where success has been elusive has been the attempt by many American fast food operations to enter the UK. Many have come and gone, but few have been really successful. McDonald's and Burger King have been two spectacularly successful examples. Burger King has used a master franchisee to develop operations that fit in with the UK way of doing things. McDonald's initially started with company-owned outlets but then extended its operations using franchises. In contrast to this, the larger US fast food group Wendy's has entered the UK on two occasions and failed to catch on. By the second time it entered the UK, McDonald's and Burger King had already dominated this part of the UK market.

Some retailers use a mixed strategy for international development. The US retailer Wal-Mart, for instance, as part of its growth strategy, has acquired large retail businesses in Germany and Britain. In Germany, it converted its store acquisitions into the Wal-Mart format. However, in Britain, its successful Asda stores for the moment retain their own format. Over time, Asda is becoming more closely integrated with Wal-Mart's European operations, particularly in the supply chain areas. This may suggest that Asda will eventually conform to Wal-Mart's global strategy. The largest UK retailer Tesco has similarly expanded in different ways. It has disposed of the unsuccessful French businesses it acquired. In Eastern Europe it has developed the Tesco brand in some countries and established partnerships with others.

Reasons for Internationalization

Internationalization tends to be the next step up for large retailers that have a significant share of the domestic market. Part of this process may have taken the retailer from regional to national coverage. Going international provides an opportunity to further exploit the assets of the business, which include the brand name, store format and merchandise as well as important skills in store management, merchandising and distribution. When the retailer develops an international presence it invests these assets into new areas in the hope of getting a proper return. However, the move from purely domestic retailer to international retailer is a significant step, for three reasons:

▶ The retailer is moving into a different business environment. In many situations the regulatory environment can be very different from what the retailers has hitherto experienced.

▶ The retailer needs to make a long-term commitment of a substantial amount of resources in order to establish the brand in the foreign market.

▶ Investing abroad will eventually require a significant internal reorganization of the company.

These factors mean that size has an important influence on the whether a retailer will internationalize. Most of the largest retailers in the world have an international presence. The exceptions are some US retailers that operate within the USA only, or limit their international operations to US territories or Canada. Ten of the 20 largest retailers in the world are from the USA, but five of these ten operate only within the USA or its territories and another two limit their international activities to Canada (Kytula 2000). All the other large retailers undertake some international activity.

We can measure the degree of internationalization by the number of countries that the retailer is operating in. On this basis, the origin of the retailer affects the degree of internationalization of large retailers. This is illustrated in Table 19.3, which shows the changes between 1996 and 1999 for the world's largest retailers. It shows greater initial degree of internationalization of European retailers. It also shows that European retailers have grown more international (by an average 1.9 countries) than the USA (by an average 0.8 country) However, American retailers have increased their international expansion *relatively* faster during this period.

Table 19.3   International Operations of World's Largest Retailers

Country/region of origin	Average number of countries operating in	
	1996	1999
USA	2.0	2.8
Europe	5.0	6.9
Asia/Australia	3.4	3.6

Source: Kutyla 2000

Push and Pull Factors

A retailer will take the decision to internationalize according to its assessment of the relative profitability of international development. Two sets of forces act on this decision-making: *push* factors driving the retailer to expand abroad and *pull* factors that encourage retailers to develop new opportunities abroad.

The retailer may feel *pushed* into international development in order to anticipate or forestall competitive action by other firms in its market segment. Retailing is a mature industry in most industrialized countries and growth in particular market segments may be slow. A retailer may foresee the approaching saturation of its market segment as preventing further profitable opportunities. Where a retailer already has a dominant market share, it may need new ways of growing the business. The retailer may then consider internationalization as a more appealing prospect than reshaping its domestic format or investing in new developments at home. Thus market saturation pushes the larger retailers and smaller specialist retailers into expanding abroad. The retailer may also see international expansion as a way of countering the perceived threat from international retailers that may enter the country.

Expanding abroad may allow the retailer to achieve various scale economies and drive down costs, thus making it more competitive against other international retailers. One of the attractions of expanding into Europe, for example, is a well-developed distribution infrastructure. In areas such as the USA, this factor is less important because the large internal market provides sufficient scope for most US retailers to develop scale economies.

The retailer may feel *pulled* by the favourable response of foreign interest or an identified gap in foreign markets. Foreign tourists, journalists and others may encourage this by spreading the reputation of the store. This spurs the retailer on to consider new possibilities. The 'pull' factor is increased by the rapid spread of taste and fashion. This gives a retail business with quality standards the opportunity to take advantage of expanding markets abroad. Smaller speciality retailers can also expand successfully by exploiting particular niche markets. Other retailers may see the chance to exploit some special skill or competence, such as the experience of using up-to-date systems or the ability to organize supply chains.

Push factors are important, but they do not play a major part in international expansion by themselves (Alexander 1997). Retailers will not expand abroad successfully unless there are positive factors that are pulling retailers abroad. For instance, much of the early internationalization efforts of West European retailers centred on Western Europe and North America. Since the 1990s, political, socio-economic, cultural and technological changes have continued to improve the climate for international expansion across the world. A major political change has been the greater freedom for investment in Eastern Europe and Asia. Despite the various economic difficulties of the late 1990s, government regulation of the market has declined. Foreign investment is now freer of controls, and wholly owned subsidiaries have been permitted in many countries (Kytula 2000).

There has also been a wider acceptance of Western-style shopping. Malaysia, Thailand and Indonesia have all developed a thriving modern retail sector. By 2000, between 30 per cent and 45 per cent of retail sales in these countries were through supermarkets, convenience stores, and department stores. In Taiwan, which had started earlier, 80 per cent of retail sales were through these formats. China has also been rapidly expanding the proportion of goods sold through these formats. The exception to these developments has been India, which has been slow to liberalize its highly regulated economy and remains culturally committed to small businesses, regulated prices and low competition (Fernandes et al. 2000). Even here, however, some retailers can support their efforts through the Internet as this appeals directly to the more Western-oriented and wealthier classes.

19.4 The Internationalization Process

A successful international retailer needs to have a sufficiently strong competitive advantage across the markets in which it is operating. In practical terms this competitive advantage must operate through a strong customer-focused offering and appropriate supply chain skills. Most successful retailers do not bring new products to the market. They establish their position through an innovative format that carries an appropriate merchandise assortment and supporting retail facilities and services (Vida, Reardon and Fairhurst, 2000). In order to establish this advantage, the retailer should take the effort to get to know its market and its different customer profiles through good customer research. Lack of good customer research has often caused well-established quality retailers in the UK to be unsuccessful abroad.

An innovative international format also requires a distinctive skill in distribution and inventory management (Vida, Reardon and Fairhurst, 2000). The retailer's skills in building up appropriate supply chain relationships is important in competing effectively on both quality and price, and gaining the confidence of foreign customers. This is illustrated by the success of Tesco and Carrefour in Eastern Europe and South East Asia, where they are emerging as major rivals.

Developing an International Presence

A retailer can develop its international profile in many ways. These are illustrated in Table 19.4. The list is comprehensive and includes methods that may be more suited to service retailers rather than product retailers. For instance, an insurance retailer intending to sell consumer policies in an international market may choose an agent rather than take the costly decision to locate overseas.

Table 19.4   Method of Internationalization

Method	The retailers' action	Method is useful for/when	Investment cost and risk	Market growth
Exporting	Receives order from abroad; sends product abroad	Premium brands from high-class retailer; easier with website	Very low extra cost; very low risk	Very slow
Licensing product brand	Sells brand through another store in foreign country	Recognized brand in niche or undeveloped markets	Low-cost; low risk	Slow

Table 19.4 continued

Method	The retailer 's action	Method is useful for/when	Investment cost and risk	Market growth
Licensing process	Allows another retailer to use store brand or format for a fee	Service element usually makes this method inappropriate for retailing	Low-cost investment; has to monitor licensee	Variable, but usually slow
Agents	Uses an individual or company to represent its interests	Cost of alliances is too high, or market potential is limited	Low cost; need to monitor agent	Variable, limited growth
Management contract	Manages a business for another company; it receives a fee plus a percentage of profit	Hotel sector; in newly developing regions; where ownership restricted to national firms	Low cost; low risk; provides experience in new markets	Slow growth
Franchising	Allows another business to operate under its name	Fast food (Burger King); cosmetics (Body Shop); hotels (Marriott); fashion products (Marks & Spencer)	Low cost; low risk; more of profit shared; when political or economic stability uncertain	May be rapid (Body Shop)
Strategic alliance	Has partnership with another retailer or distributor to work together	Entry into some markets for political or cultural reasons	High cost; high risk of failure after short period	Enables more rapid expansion
Joint venture	Setting up jointly owned subsidiary to develop new market	Host country's laws regulate ownership or require indigenous partner	Moderate to high cost; moderate (shared) risk	Expansion depends on capital investment
Acquisition	Buys existing retail business. May convert to own format (Tesco in SE Asia) or keep existing brand (Sainsbury in the USA)	Quick entry to local markets; useful where there are significant restrictions on market competition or store development	High investment; moderate to high risk	Early quick growth, but may be slow afterwards
Establish subsidiary abroad	The firm has an equity stake in the business	'Organic growth'; used by Tesco in Eastern Europe	High cost; high risk; but retains all profits	Usually slows growth

Each method of internationalization presents its own advantages and disadvantages as regards cost and funding of new investment, how quickly the retailer wants or needs to establish itself abroad and the risk factors involved. The retailer can maintain full control by owning its own subsidiary. This form of organic growth allows the retailer to keep all the profits, but it also increases the amount of capital funding required. It will also slow the process of expansion, unless the retailer expands through the expensive acquisition of well-established retailers, as Wal-Mart did with Asda in the UK. This may be very important in some markets that are attractive to other foreign retailers. The lack of local partnership may mean lower understanding of local culture that reduces the chances of success.

There are also other risks related to the general business environment, some of which are indicated in Table 19.5.

Table 19.5 Host Country Factors Affecting Method of International Expansion

Factor	Examples
Political	Foreign firms may be restricted in ownership of businesses
Planning	Restrictions on large store development
Commercial	Low consumer-orientation; networking important; attitudes to risk
Economic	Level of income and rates of market growth
Managerial	Work patterns; language differences
Cultural	Consumer market not well developed

Internal and External Factors in Internationalization

There are two aspects to the process of internationalization. Most retailers develop their international operations through an incremental approach (Vida, Reardon and Fairhurst, 2000). Retailers go through some preliminary stage, usually testing the waters in one foreign country. The retailer will tend to follow up its initial success by further developments within the chosen country, as its management becomes more comfortable with operating abroad. Growing confidence among the retailer's management will lead to further expansion into another country even before it has established broad coverage within one country. The same applies, of course, with expansion or filling in market areas within the retailer's country of origin.

The above approach to internationalization focuses on the internal process within the firm's organization, such as the firm's competitive advantages, its resources, and the knowledge and attitudes of the management. However, the broader commercial environment, or macroenvironment, has an important impact on the location of international activity and the types of retail format that are successful. The types of factors and their impact are illustrated in Table 19.6.

Table 19.6 Macroenvironmental Influences in Internationalization

Factor	Includes
Political and legal	Deregulation of markets. Less restrictions on foreign investment
Economic	Long-term prospects for growth in disposable income
Sociocultural	Emergence or growth of more cosmopolitan social classes
Technological	Gaps where technology transfer is required in improving range and delivery of products
Demographic	Rapidly growing population changing lifestyle and domestic structures, in particular parts of the world
Physical	Product availability, air and water quality, visual clutter, noise pollution

The impact of these environmental factors can be seen in the development of international retailing in Eastern Europe and South East Asia from the 1990s. The decline of communism in Eastern Europe brought about a change in the retail environment. In Poland, for instance, the previous economic system had a poorly developed concept of the consumer, with demand often exceeding supply. Modern retailing and distribution systems had to start from scratch. Privatization and deregulation was accompanied by the positive encouragement given to foreign retailers to set up in business, thus enabling massive technology transfer (Waters 1999).

In South East Asia, economic growth, foreign travel, media and Internet exposure had created a sizeable class of the population that had acquired modern shopping habits and expectations of the shopping experience. The existence of a large market with high growth potential encouraged a scramble for retailing space within several countries. An important element in this were the advantages to be gained from being first in the market with the type of retail format required. Other retailers joined in so that they would not be left behind. Even the Asian crisis of 1997 worked to the advantage of some retailers from Europe and the USA. Some retailers saw this as an opportune time to fund investment relatively cheaply at a time when Asian property and equity prices were being depressed by the crisis. Carrefour, for instance, took advantage of low property prices in Japan to expand into that market (Ganesan 2001).

Locating International Expansion

A retailer contemplating international expansion needs to evaluate the different areas into which it can expand. The retailer can judge a candidate region on a number of basic factors (Alexander 1997) as illustrated in Figure 19.2.

The political climate is important in guaranteeing a positive environment in which assets may be deployed and protected. Income and population growth may encourage firms to view the market favourably. Common language is a major attractant. Many British retailers turned to expansion in the USA during the second half of the twentieth

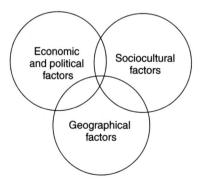

Figure 19.2   Factors Affecting International Location Decision

century, in the expectation that a common language and superficial cultural similarities would enable success. Many of these ventures were unsuccessful and retailers then turned their attention to geographically closer continental countries. Success here was mixed. Major retailers such as Boots and Tesco have been unsuccessful in their ventures into neighbouring continental countries during the last quarter of the twentieth century. The opening up of Eastern Europe has provided UK retailers with strong supply chain management skills the opportunity to expand further still. Similarly the rapid economic development of South East Asia during the 1980s and early 1990s proved a major attractant to retailers. The opening up of the Chinese market to foreign investment is likely to be a major attraction for many large retailers from Europe, Japan and the USA, as long as economic growth and political stability continues.

The process of balancing these factors in making a location decision is illustrated in Table 19.7. The comments are suggestions only and show how advantages can be identified. The strategic disadvantages are often tied up with political and cultural changes and so further consideration is left to the reader as appropriate.

Table 19.7 Evaluating Attractiveness of Potential Regions for a UK Retailer, 2001

Region	Cultural/social	Strategic factor Geographic	Economic/political
Western Europe	Similar habits Dominance of world-class formats and specialist retailers	Very close; densely populated	One of the most affluent markets; EU membership/ trade links
Eastern Europe	Growing sense of consumer Acceptance of world-class formats and specialist retailers	Relatively close; improving access	Improving political stability and economic development Format and distribution skills needed
North America	Shared language Dominance of world-class formats and specialist retailers	Some areas densely populated	Affluent; strong economy
Latin America	Growing sense of consumer Acceptance of world-class formats and specialist retailers	Potential for developing distribution networks	Improving political stability and economic development Format and distribution skills needed
China	Growing sense of consumer	Improving access	Improving political stability and economic development Format and distribution skills needed
India	Gradually changing culture Internationally oriented elite	Densely populated areas	Opportunities for supply chain skills
SE Asia/Japan	Growing sense of consumer Acceptance of world-class formats and specialist retailers	Some densely populated areas	One of fastest growing regions in world Opportunities for supply chain skills

Table 19.7 continued

Region	Strategic factor		
	Cultural/social	Geographic	Economic/political
Australasia	Acceptance of world-class formats and specialist retailers	Some densely populated areas	Economic stability
Strategic cities/ centres across the world	Internationally oriented elite class	Strategic transport networks	Effective for niche markets/travel retailing

Case 19.2 The M&S experience

When Marks & Spencer (M&S) opened its first stores in Canada in 1974, its British format was unsuccessful. However, M&S learnt the lessons of expansion abroad: a solid base of good property in the right location, and a thorough understanding of local conditions, culture and people. By 1997 it had stores in Europe, Canada, North America and Hong Kong, and continued to export merchandise to 20 other countries around the world.

M&S felt the 'pull' of increasingly global fashion together with the opportunity to extend its format abroad based on quality, value, customer service; good staff management and close supplier relationships. There was also the 'push' of its dominant market share threatened by increasing international competition. M&S expanded by acquisition in the USA; by slow organic growth in Europe, but used a local partner in Spain. Elsewhere, where market potential was too low or uncertain, it used franchises (Nickolds 1997). However, in 2001, with major problems in the home market, M&S announced that it was to close overseas stores and export only through its franchise operations.

19. 5 Culture, Business and International Management

Improved communications and the increasing internationalization of business and consumption activity generally are major influences in the development of international retailing. They also mean that retail managers and other professionals are more likely to deal with international suppliers or customers and staff in more than one country.

Retailers that are considering expanding into other countries should be aware of the painful lessons learnt by some earlier adventurers. They should be aware that proper market research is needed before expanding into foreign markets and that, in many cases, partners or franchisees provide a useful means of getting to understand the consumer culture of the destination market.

However, the retailer should also be aware that general management styles vary between countries as much as they do between businesses. Management styles can be described in terms of organizational culture, leadership and decision-making styles (Wilderom, Glunk and Inzererilli 1996). Understanding aspects of a foreign market's culture will remove many misunderstandings within the supply chain, in negotiation with government and consumer bodies and also in managing the workforce.

Each organization has its own culture or set of values and characteristics that largely reflects the social, political and economic environment within which the organization operates. This culture can affect the organization in three important aspects (Schneider and Barsoux 1997). The *first* aspect is how people use ideas of time, space and language in their activities. A culture may be described as *linear-active* or *multi-active* cultures (Lewis 1996; described as *monochronic* or *polychronic* by Schneider and Barsoux 1997). Linear-active cultures include North American and North European societies. Their use of time is relatively sequential – dealing with one thing at a time. In contrast, South American and Southern European cultures tend to be multi-active. For them, time is flexible and expandable to deal with many activities at a time, so appointment times are flexible and meetings may be interrupted for other things.

Both linear-active and multi-active cultures communicate through dialogue, that is, the continual mutual exchange of information. Linear-active cultures tend to be more orderly so that meetings should stick to the agenda, whereas multi-active cultures can jump about a little more. Lewis also identifies *reactive* or listening cultures such as in Turkey and Finland. People listen and reflect before they speak, but then go in for monologues in response and may therefore appear rather rigid and inflexible.

The *second* aspect concerns the way in which managers deal with other organizations and uncertainty in their external environment. The *third* aspect concerns internal relationships within the organization and includes attitudes to management, competitiveness and cooperation. These two aspects of behaviour can be considered using ideas devised by Hofstede (1991). Hofstede identified four basic dimensions to describe the culture of an organization:

▶ *Power-distance*. This measures the extent to which people accept an unequal distribution of power. High power-distance countries such as those in East Asia and Latin Europe are more status and power driven, they have more hierarchical organizations and more centralized decision-making with less employee participation in decision-making. North Americans naturally have low power distance, as do Scandinavians, and they expect a corresponding management structure. A retailer moving into a high power-distance country will tend to find that employees distrust participative management styles and may regard managers who engage in it as incompetent.

▶ *Uncertainty-avoidance*. High uncertainty-avoidance leads to greater preference for rules and procedures, greater specialization of roles and managerial control. Europeans vary in their higher uncertainty avoidance but are more cautious than Americans. Thus they prefer clear policies and procedures, and systems.

▶ *Individualism-collectivism*. Individualistic cultures occur in countries where English is the dominant language, as in Britain, Ireland Australasia, Canada and the USA. These cultures expect individuals to stand on their own two feet and they are regarded in terms of what they achieve. Within organizations, this leads to greater individual autonomy and responsibility.

Collectivist cultures occur in East Asian countries. Their culture expects the group to support the individual and the individual to support the group. In organizations, the group decision-making, consensus and cooperation are more important than individual initiative. This can cause confusion across European organizations as some countries, such as Sweden, exhibit a moderately high collectivist tendency and an emphasis on conformance to the group.

▶ *Masculinity-femininity*. This reflects the leaning towards the more masculine values of assertiveness, competitiveness and materialism or towards the more feminine values of nurturing, quality of life and relationships. The masculine societies of the USA and Germany are more task oriented, whereas the feminine Nordic countries emphasize the quality of interpersonal relations and quality of working life.

Seeing Eye to Eye

Cultural differences affect the way in which people see or discuss situations and problems. Any situation can thus be seen as two points of view where certain concepts and values overlap, but where certain differences are inevitably difficult to resolve and where some aspects may be completely overlooked (Lewis 1996: 86–91). A similar way of looking at what people have in common is the Johari window exercise (Schneider and Barsoux 1997: 11–12). This looks at what people have in common and identifies four areas of perception of a situation:

▶ Things I see and you see → we can discuss these.

▶ Things I see but you don't see → your blind spots.

▶ Things I don't see but you see → my blind spots.

▶ Things I don't see and you don't see → our shared blind spots.

Understanding the different cultural origins allows us to describe these situations more fully. This should help to anticipate difficulties and may also find novel paths to agreement.

Developing International Management

The retailer's operations and the formats used will have a significant influence on the appropriate style of management. However, an international retailer needs a group of managers that can cope with the diversity generated by international operations. The managers need to be able to work within a unifying framework but be flexible enough to fit in with the local cultures.

There are three important types of local diversity in attitudes and practices (Boone and van den Bosch 1996) that international retail managers need to deal with:

▶ Those caused by differences in the legal and regulatory environment.

▶ Those caused by different accounting rules, information systems and production and supply systems.

▶ Those caused by the historical cultural differences.

The first two differences will tend to lessen over time as international trade develops. However, historic cultural differences will last for some, even in areas such as Western Europe where economic and political integration is continuing. These will affect customer preferences, the behaviour and attitudes of employees and the relationship between business and government. Managers in Europe and elsewhere will have to develop skills at managing integration and differentiation.

These differences are severe enough for European retailers, but they are more challenging for retailers expanding further abroad. International retailers must therefore recruit managers from the host country because they will understand the local culture, particularly the attitudes of the workforce. However, their training needs to ensure that they are acculturated to the company ethos, so that they can implement and if necessary effectively modify company policies in a manner appropriate to the local area. The retailer will also have to ensure that managers and other appropriate staff in the original country also undergo adequate internal training in order to be able to deal effectively with international activities. The question arises as to whether the retailer can develop a common style of management that its managers can apply flexibly within regions such as Europe that house a diversity of cultures and outlooks.

References

Alexander, N. (1997) *International Retailing*, Oxford: Blackwell.

Anderson, C.H., (1993) *Retailing: Concepts, Strategy and Information*, St Paul, MN: West Publishing.

Boone, P.F. and van den Bosch, F.A.J. (1996) *Discerning a Key Characteristic of a European Style of Management, International Studies of Management and Organizations*, Fall: 109–27.

Business Wire (2000) 'Gap Inc. Reports August Sales Flat to Last Year; Comparable Store Sales Down 17 Percent', Business Wire, 6 September, http://www.businesswire.com.

Doole, I. and Lowe, R. (2001) *International Marketing Strategy: Analysis, Development and Implementation*, 3rd edn, London: Thomson Learning.

Encyclopaedia Britannica (2001) 'Colour', http://www.britannica.com

Fernandes, M., Gadi, C., Khanna, A., Mitra, P. and Narayanswamy, S. (2000) 'India's retailing comes of age', *McKinsey Quarterly*, special edition (4): 92–100.

Ganesan, V. (2001) 'Multinationals scrambling to enter Asian retailing mart', *Business Times* (Malaysia), 4 January: 14.

Hofstede, G. (1991) *Cultures and Organizations: Software of the Mind*, Maidenhead: McGraw-Hill.

Kutyla, D.M. (2000) 'Moving into the 21st century at Internet speed', *Retail Insights*, 9(3), http://www.us.deloitte.com/PUB/Retail/vol0903/vol90301.htm

Lewis, R.D. (1996) *When Cultures Collide: Managing Successfully Across Cultures*, London: Nicholas Brearley.

Nickolds, C. (1997) 'Marks & Spencer: old hands in the global arena', *Inside Retailing*, http://www.chainstoreage.com/news_desk/inside_retailing/inside_retail_arch_1.

Schneider, S.C. and Barsoux, J.-L. (1997) *Managing Across Cultures*, London: Pearson Education.

Vida, I., Reardon, J. and Fairhurst, A. (2000) 'Determinants of international retail involvement: the case of large U.S. retail chains', *Journal of International Marketing*, 8: 37–60.

Waters, C.D.J. (1999) 'Changing role of the retail sector in Poland', *International Journal of Retail & Distribution Management*, 27(8): 319–27.

Wilderom, C., Glunk, U. and Inzererilli, G. (1996) 'European management as a construct', *International Studies of Management and Organizations*, Fall: 3–12.

Review of Retailing: Environment and Operations

This chapter covers the following topics:

- ► Cultural transformation and retailing.

- ► Emerging retailing themes and niches.

- ► Consolidating for the future.

A Review of Retailing: Environment and Operations

Introduction and Core Concepts

This chapter is concerned with consolidating some of the ideas dealt with in this book. In this chapter we will bring together many perspectives to help readers form conclusions about the way retailing could change in the future. However, rather than predict that future, we intend to draw on past events and current trends to provide an intellectual basis from which students may themselves identify retail changes. Modern retailing has evolved into a much more sophisticated experience for customers. It is these customers, or to be more explicit their expectations, that have driven retail businesses to offer increasingly diverse ranges of merchandise and more exciting retail store designs. Other external and internal forces, such as new technology and social change, have played a significant role in this transformation. Retailing would seem to be at a crossroads that offers some unique possibilities. Which direction the industry, or arguably its customers, will take is a matter for retailing students to decide, for it is they who are the retailers of the future.

20.1 Retail Change: A Review

From the preceding chapters we can see that there are a number of areas where traditional retailing has altered as a result of various types of change. A popular view is that the greatest change has been brought about by the revolution in technology that swept before it old-style retailing approaches.

⇨ Students may wish to form groups to brainstorm the many technological advances that have influenced retail change. To start you off we suggest the discussion should centre round Chapter 15, Logistics and Distribution: Shipping the Goods to Market.

However, other shifts in the retail environment (both internal and external) have contributed and formed the catalyst for retailing to reinvent itself time and time again.

The big topic of the 1990s was how information technology would change the way retailers operate, and the manner in which consumers consume.

> ⇨ Example – according to the market research company Verdict, UK consumer spending on the Internet for retail goods (excluding services) will grow by more than 1000 per cent in the years up to 2004. Around this time the projection is that consumers will be spending £7.4 billion shopping on the Internet and interactive television. This is a considerable increase on the 1999 figure of £581 million. As this figure is over 3 per cent of all retail sales it is likely to have a major impact on the retail sector (http://www.verdict.co.uk/fcpr.htm).

However, this was not the first time that big changes had swept through the retail industry, as we discussed in Chapter 3, past retailing approaches would appear far too basic for modern consumers. For example, in the 1970s UK retailers thought that all they needed was an *adequate* range of goods and straightforward selling techniques. The most popular approach was to pile the goods up high. Customers, however, became far more discerning and informed about the availability and allure of products. In part, this was the result of social changes in the UK that stemmed from the following areas:

▶ mass tourism

▶ becoming a member of the European Union

▶ greater spending power.

When the population of a country has the opportunity to travel widely, this alters people's expectations through experiences. The number of people in the UK, and for that matter worldwide, using air travel has continuously increased over the last 50 years. In the past, the high relative cost of air travel restricted this type of transport to the higher socio-economic groups. In more recent years, as a result of higher living standards and greater disposable incomes, more people have travelled by air. In addition, the significant advances made in aircraft technology have provided larger and more fuel-efficient aeroplanes. This factor has impacted on the cost of air fares bringing them down. In the UK, this upsurge in commercial passenger traffic has had a pronounced social effect. People are more experienced, worldly, and knowledgeable about the range of merchandise available in other countries. Expectations are higher as a result.

> ⇨ Tip – strengths can become liabilities because the retail environment is in a constant state of flux. Case 20.1 considers two great UK retailer brands, Boots and Marks & Spencer, and the reasons why they have lost their customers' loyalty and suffered a downturn as a result.

Case 20.1 Boots and Marks & Spencer: Icons of British Retailing?

Boots had enjoyed a long and successful period helping to mend the ills of the British public, and attending to their beauty needs. The company had dominated the market, producing high-quality drugs and cosmetics that it manufactured itself. This gave Boots an edge over the competition, and ensured consistent quality, innovation and large returns. As Boots were unrivalled they could charge high prices. However, things changed in the mid-1990s when supermarket chains began selling core health products, cosmetics and toiletries. Because of their buying power and strong brand image, supermarkets could offer lower prices and gain market share. In five years, Tesco became Britain's second biggest health and beauty retailer with a 12.5 per cent share of the market. Others like Asda, owned by Wal-Mart the US retailer, will follow suit.

Source: Anonymous 2001: 68

'Marks and Sparks' is one of the most well-known truly *British* retailers. This Britishness, and the nature and quality of the merchandise it sold, made M&S a generic brand in the UK high street. The same could be said for some European countries. For example, when M&S closed all its French stores as part of a cost-cutting exercise in 2001, there was a huge outcry from the French public. In its best years M&S produced clothing that appealed widely but in the late 1990s a fashion-conscious and more demanding British consumer began to switch to other more exciting retailer brands. This led to a gradual fall in sales and a worsening financial position. In an attempt to buy back the consumers' favour, M&S chose to move its clothing mix to what it called a 'classically stylish customer'. Changing the nature of the merchandise was an attempt to buy back the loyalty it had lost. However, lost customers are difficult to replace and expectations difficult to provide for.

Source: Morrell 2001: 6

The European Union and Retailing

For the UK, entry into the European Union led to a process of cultural change for the UK consumer, and for the retailers that served them. A new and different way of looking at things altered customers' tastes and habits and therefore the merchandise in the shops. Entering new markets presented the opportunity for retailers to expand into different product areas, and for consumers to try out these new products. This greater open-mindedness towards the acceptance of new types of food, clothing, and consumer products in general fostered social and economic change. This change was inevitable and part of joining the EU. Europe's policies affect a whole range of business activities, and cover the following:

► competition

► social

► environmental

► industrial.

⇨ Try to relate each of the above policy areas to the retail sector. For example, EU industrial policy actively encourages small and medium-sized enterprises. The small independent retailer may thus benefit from EU membership.

The effect of this transformation on grocery giants like Sainsbury and Tesco was the gradual expansion of their ranges to include *continental* products. Greater flexibility across international boundaries meant the freer movement of goods, and more items on the shelves. For the British consumer this meant greater choice and higher expectations of the retailer. As part of the European Community, British consumers expect greater variety.

20.2 Cultural Transformation and Retailing

Greater experience and a more diverse knowledge of what merchandise is available in other countries creates needs, wants and desires in consumers. For example, holidaymakers that visit the USA will note the greater availability of low cost denim jeans and other clothing; and wonder why they are so expensive in Europe. Such is the power of the consumer that it can compel retailers in the home market to match ranges in other markets.

> ⇨ Tip – it is important to remember that the UK population is ageing and older consumers spend a lower proportion of their disposable income in the shops. Retailers have traditionally focused on the young consumers, in particular the 18 to 25 age group, and tend not to consider the mature consumer. In the main, this practice is driven by the retailers' propensity to copy each other in an attempt to gain competitive advantage. A major challenge facing UK retailers is to focus more on older people without loss of image. Encouraging older consumers to spend more will provide the retail sector with essential growth, and may provide new opportunities in a changing competitive environment (http://www.verdict.co.uk/fcpr.htm).

Without the economic means, however, consumers are unable to buy and this affects demand. The substantial rise in consumer spending power in the 1980s had a big impact on retail expansion. Greater disposable incomes, and so spending power, will create the demand for the new merchandise. As new goods from overseas become available the prices will be fairly high as demand is usually inelastic in the early stages. When consumer demand rises the prices tend to fall and, as we discussed in Chapter 8, there is constant pressure on retailers to reduce prices and remain competitive. Competition also creates the wide availability of the new merchandise. The new lines thus become part of what is on general offer in most shops.

> ⇨ Tip – a major challenge facing retailers is to produce innovative ways to add value to the shopping experience, making it more pleasurable and attractive. The majority of consumers are experienced and fully aware of the available merchandise. Shoppers know what is on offer in the shops and the attraction of goods and services. However, the retailers must persuade the customer that it is worth spending more on consumer items like fashion clothing, microwaves and DVD players. As in the past, retailers focus on status goods and desirable and well-known brands. However, this strategy assumes that consumers only buy products at the exclusion of other intangible factors. Retailers have therefore sought to increase their levels of customer service and present their customers with eye-catching store environments (http://www.verdict.co.uk/fcpr.htm).

Other Factors of Change

There are, however, other views and opinions that suggest very different explanations for the development of UK retailing. Some of these are not confined to consumers' shopping requirements. For example, out-of-town shopping which is a process of moving retailing out of the central areas in suburban locations has contributed to the change in retail provision. The following are some of the reasons for that change:

▶ the huge rise in car ownership that has made it much easier for consumers to access out-of-town locations

▶ cheaper store rents in out-of-town locations

▶ the expansion of the road system in the 1980s

▶ the reduced shopping appeal of many town centres

▶ the development of new large hyper or superstore formats

▶ changes in shopping patterns and the growth of females within the labour force (Jones and Pal 1998).

Out-of-Town Retailing

The huge and continuing growth of out-of-town retail sites reflect a change in the way consumers now shop. Looking back in time, shoppers favoured the local stores that were often 'just around the corner'. This was a time when part of the shopping experience was meeting others, who may be friends or just acquaintances, in an atmosphere of familiarity. As consumers moved towards the highly practical and sanitized buying experience in retail parks, the essence of which focuses on obtaining value for money, this announced a fundamental shift in shopping behaviour. There were, of course, additional reasons for this shift that arose out of fundamental changes to the British way of life. We relied more on the ownership of products as a means of expressing our social position (see Chapter 6). These greater expectations pushed retailers to expand the ranges of merchandise, and build larger stores to accommodate them.

Many social factors have fuelled retail change and the location of retail businesses; such as increasing numbers of women in work, the length of the working day and the escalating importance of shopping as a leisure activity. These and other factors in particular stand out as highly visible areas of transformation. Another example of changing attitudes stems from the rising number of motor cars in use since the 1970s, and the perceptions of travel times. Shoppers are now able and willing to travel further in order to shop at more exciting and interesting places. Mobility also impacts on where people choose to live.

In the search for better lifestyles, people have switched from living in the towns and cities to choosing a suburban setting. This has created large areas of purchasing power within these locations. This movement of the population from the cities to the suburbs has also narrowed the gap between cities and countryside. Commuter belts provide the businessperson with 'a place in the country' or rural surroundings.

Case 20.2 Focus on England and the English Way of Life

The majority of English people would prefer to live in the countryside and feel more at home in these sorts of surroundings. However, there are not enough cottages to go round so modern suburbia was invented for those who could afford it. Green belts suit the rich, and the English vice of snobbery plays an important role. A prerequisite of this rural-type utopia is the retail park or shopping mall, which provides all the comforts of home. Local people can thus purchase lifestyle goods in complete comfort and protected from the rigours (or smells) of country life.

Source: Barker 1998: 7–11

Retail parks and shopping malls have continued to spring up all around the UK. Most of the sites used are brownfield. For example, Gateshead Metrocentre, which opened in 1986, was built on an old power station ash dump, and Meadowhall is located on the old Hadfield Steel mill site in the lower Don Valley. The shopping mall at Lakeside Thurrock (Essex) is built in a disused cement quarry site in North Kent. Unlike in the USA, most of the UK's retail parks and malls have been built on low-grade reclaimed land. Table 20.1 shows some of these and other out-of-town centres in the UK.

Table 20.1   Some Out-of-Town Shopping Centres in the UK

Name of centre	Opening date
Metro Centre (Tyneside)	1986
Merry Hill Centre (Dudley)	1989
Lakeside (Thurrock)	1990
Meadowhall (Sheffield)	1990
White Rose Centre (Leeds)	1997
Trafford Centre (Manchester)	1998
Cribbs Causeway (Bristol)	1998
Bluewater (North Kent)	1999
Braehead (Glasgow)	1999

Source: adapted from Mintel 1999

Back to the Towns and Cities

Consumers' expectations of shopping facilities have undergone considerable transformation and we seek more pleasing areas in which to shop. Markets and town centres, however, have fought back with new and elaborate schemes to attract the shopper. In an attempt to create more visually attractive places, town and city developers have made radical changes to architectural and structural layout. This has produced tree-lined boulevards and sophisticated shopping to go with it, for example, reviving the medieval part of a city and creating a magnificent shopping area in the process.

⇨ Are there any other factors you can think of that have changed retailing in recent times? You may wish to consult Chapter 6 and Chapter 18 to help you form some conclusions.

20.3 New Approaches in Retailing

The food sector has seen a great deal of change in the face of severe competition for market share. The branching out of supermarkets chains into non-food activities is a response to the intensifying competition and the need to grow volume by adding other merchandise lines. The two supermarket chains, Adsa and Tesco, that have moved boldly and decisively into non-food retailing as part of their core operations have shown significant positive performance in recent years relative to their competitors. These two chains have added significant non-food lines in clothing and household textiles, as well as kitchenware and, increasingly, domestic appliances. Sainsbury has also been experimenting with various non-food lines within its supermarkets.

Case 20.3 The Big Supermarkets Go Non-food

Tesco, Asda and Sainsbury are increasingly dedicating shelf space to non-food items in the rush to please customers. Not long ago it was rare to see anything other than basic crockery and utensils on the supermarket shelves. More and more non-food is taking over from the traditional supermarket fare, which is being replaced with PC monitors, printers, wide-screen televisions and other domestic white goods. This is a strategic move on the part of retailers.

In general, when retailers improve their space utilization it can lead to significant growth in the operating performance of their businesses. Good planning provides the flexibility needed to allow for any fluctuations in the day-to-day running of the operation. Retailers are thus obliged to constantly monitor key product categories and the amount of retail space allocated between ranges. Space management is concerned, therefore, with placing merchandise within the store in the most profitable manner. Retailers tend to copy each other and produce similar ranges within product classes. Children's clothing is a case in point with most clothing stores offering similar product ranges, colours and even similar styles.

Expectations of Retail Space

Consumers' changing expectations are also responsible for the allocation of space in some sectors. For example, in food retailing the space allocated in respect of the mix of food and non-food product areas, and the redistribution of priorities as traditional retailer policies and strategies become transformed by consumer demands. This is largely due to competitive forces. Being one step in front of the competition is about 'providing the right products at the right place at the right time'. The retail food sector is intensely competitive and no serious contender can afford to relax, and should where possible pioneer new ideas by listening and responding to customer needs. Clearly, these needs will change over time.

Changing consumer habits and the wider dispersion of consumer goods means that a greater proportion of consumer non-food spending has been brought within the range of convenience or everyday shopping. However, there are other equally important factors for this shift in retailer strategy that stem from altering consumer lifestyles, and retailers' strategic use of merchandise arrangements. The following factors influence the changing nature of retail space:

▶ time

▶ location

▶ merchandising.

Time

Time has become increasingly important for people for a number of reasons. A key factor has been the increase in incomes, which has improved the range of opportunities for consumers to spend time. New working routines and the greater number of working women and single households, and longer working hours, mean that the traditional shop opening hours no longer apply. Greater flexibility in working practices and the ability to work at home has led to a more flexible and fluid attitude towards shopping in general.

For the consumer, days are crowded with tasks and social obligations that become more complex and require more frequent servicing. This has pushed consumers to search for better methods of shopping in order to save time. New buying methods such as home catalogue shopping and Internet websites bring new and better ways to deal with time shortages (Mai and Ness 1999; Murray and McCormack 2000). To help the consumer with these new shopping priorities many supermarket multiples have moved into adjacent products such as fashion and white goods. Retailers have also started to install convenience-style retail formats that accommodate products and services that save time and reduce household work.

Location

Government policy affects where stores can locate or relocate. Extended opening hours make it possible for most consumers, those who have the mobility, to shop at their convenience. New skills in information gathering, due in part to the use of Internet search strategies, have created new and better informed consumers. Anxious to obtain value for money and the best possible deals, consumers are more inclined to 'switch' retailers to buy the merchandise of their choice. Shoppers, and especially food shoppers, can be very fickle when purchasing some products and services, particularly when brand loyalty is at stake. So customers will switch to other stores to obtain their preferred brands if their favourite supermarket or store is out of stock.

Food supermarkets have therefore been encouraged to locate closer to each other in an attempt to attract fickle consumers searching for bargains. The notion of the anchor store, and the retail theory of associated sales (for example, Marks & Spencer and Tesco located in close proximity), seems less credible where food supermarkets are clustered together. In the near future, the same Internet technology that provides consumers with their information about stores and food products may well alter the way stores locate. Whilst the nature of the retail sector will influence the format used, Tesco's recent move towards smaller formats and high street locations could herald the beginning of a new wave of retail development.

Merchandising

Food retailers in particular have reduced their ranges overall to account for switching behaviour. The tendency is to diversify into other consumer goods to improve turnover and subsequent conversion rates. As in most strategic planning efforts, developing an assortment is not a one-time activity. Retailers update the range periodically and add merchandise details based on business trends, product sourcing issues and changes in customer preferences. The retailer tailors the product mix to meet customer needs, tastes and expectations and, as a result, improves profitability.

New purchasing patterns have provided competitive advantages for supermarkets through merchandise extension, as consumers view them as a major conduit for non-food products. Extended displays of compact discs, stationery, books and similar goods that the shopper observes during the normal shopping process provide a reminder for special purchases, particularly when purchases are made during extended opening hours. Advertising in non-food areas has capitalized on this consumer tendency to buy goods that were not originally specified on the shopping list, for example, the Woolworth 1999 and 2000 Christmas campaign.

Multiple Format Retailing

Different approaches to merchandising and the rapid take-up of virtual shopping has helped to foster new outlooks towards retail format designs. With the conventional store, the format presents the shopper with as complete a selection of merchandise as possible. This presumes that the shopper will buy all their goods under one roof, providing those goods are available. The fixed layouts of the bricks-and-mortar store assume that customers visit or patronize the store for certain types of goods, and need to be tempted into buying others goods while browsing. Customers are thus presented with the merchandise displays as they pass through the store, and select items for their shopping trolleys or baskets. Shoppers need to focus on this selection process or risk forgetting the items they came in for. This process is similar for small independents but because of the store location, and smaller selections available, the level of risk for the customer is reduced.

As we discussed in Chapter 18, retailers are moving towards multiple format operations that necessitate a very different approach to selling merchandise. New technology driving the virtual store is within the reach of all retailers, from large multiples to small independents. Anyone can have websites and sell products from more than one location, whether it is a conventional store or a virtual store. The traditional store–customer interaction seems to be undergoing a transformation. It is conceivable that the conventional retail experience will be supplanted with an eclectic mix of different shopping experiences that can be offered to a global audience of eager shoppers.

20.4 Emerging Themes and Niches

There are types of retailing that have been mentioned in this book that may well emerge as important new areas of expansion. Airport retailing has previously been relegated to an area called niche retailing.

> ⇨ Niche retailing refers to smaller more specialized segments of the retail market as a whole, and contrasts with the core areas such as the electrical, grocery and clothing sectors.

However, this may well change as retailers extend their corporate boundaries to include multiple locations. This strategy draws the retailer away from the more traditional structures. Airport retailing, for example, may well become an extension of the chain retailer's business as they aspire to establish a network of customer access points. Just as the home PC or digital television acts a portal to the virtual store, the airport retail provision is just another gateway for the shopper. When returning from holiday the family can therefore purchase their grocery shopping before returning home.

> ⇨ Compile an audit of the different types of store found in major airport retail malls. Some of these data may come from a recent holiday or interviews with others who have flown in the last year. Differences between provincial and major hub airports can be evaluated, as can the differences in provision in other countries.

Airport Retailing

In the UK, international airports have become highly commercialized and have looked towards retailing as a means of expanding profits. Travellers are consumers and they tend to wait around airport buildings for long periods of time. This is called 'dwell time' and is an important consideration when designing and operating an airport terminal of any size. Passengers can be left to sit around bored or be entertained with enhanced passenger facilities that incorporate a high-quality retail provision. At London airports, for example, which include London Heathrow and Gatwick, both owned and operated by the British Airports Authority (BAA), a great deal of space has been allocated to retailing. This is because BAA earns more from retailing than from landing fees, which is the more traditional and core side of the business. This change happened in 1993 when for the first time revenues raised from the company's airport shops exceeded income from traffic charges (Doganis 1992). BAA, for example, increased their retail space by 175 000 sq ft from 1991 to 1994.

Most airports in the UK and overseas have been transformed into shopping malls, with pavilion-like atmospheres, incorporating well-known high street retailers. An increasing number of outlets, consisting of major retail brands and well-known high street names, compete eagerly for these sites in anticipation of large returns on their high investments. At the London airports, for example, shoppers can buy from major brands such as Bally, Benetton, Haagen-Dazs, Garfunkels, Upper Crust, Burger King, Body Shop and Sock Shop. The introduction of high-priced indulgence brands means that Burberry, Aquascutum, Harrods, and Jaeger are all under one roof. Sales in these malls far outstrip consumer spending on the high street, and adds another dimension to the shopping environment. In fact, many consumers visit airport malls just to go shopping and this practice is likely to continue (Newman 1998).

In the USA there has been tremendous change in the nature and provision of retailing in US airports. This changing trend is due partly because of the economics of running airport facilities, which changed due to rising costs and deregulation in the industry. Operators were obliged to become more cost-effective and competitive. Pittsburgh International and Portland International airports set the trend with retail provision and now an increasing number of high-profile national brand stores are situated in terminals. Retailers enjoy some of the most profitable business in the country, with high sales per square foot. The average air passenger spends US$8.3 per annum at the airport. In 1999 there were 1.5 billion air passengers, which is a worldwide market of US$12 billion (Reuters Business Insight 1998).

> ⇨ Retailing students from all countries may wish to go to their local airport and browse around the retail outlets. Return to Chapter 10 and consider how to use the BPI Index and evaluate the trading area. Is the population easy to define and catogorize? Also, would it be possible to define and research the catchment area? Set out your research findings and evaluate the airport mall as a potential location.

In part, the expansion of US airport retail provision has stemmed from the success of the UK airport retailing operation. This is because UK-based companies that were eager to extend their horizons offered design and management expertise to operators in the USA. However, the expansion of the airport retailing experience is something that no manufacturer or retailer can afford to ignore. For example, Japan's New Tokyo International Airport encompasses 3.02 million square feet. In the Netherlands, Amsterdam Schiphol has a shopping complex comprising 5400 m^2 of floorspace. In Asia, the new Karachi Terminal in Pakistan includes a 1.3 million square foot building, and in Toronto, Canada, the passenger terminal 3 at Lester B. Pearson International Airport, occupies 1.4 million square feet. The future may bring more change and airports are growing retail spaces in the UK and overseas.

Factory Outlets

First mentioned in Chapters 3 and 5, the factory outlet is a way in which UK retailers can integrate more efficient methods of merchandise management, with elements of format development. These stores operate in a different way and are far more functional than regular stores. Factory outlets are additional out-of-town retail space that enables the retailer to sell off goods at a substantial discount without affecting store image. Well-known retail brands that operate within the outlet *boundaries* do so without affecting their reputation relative to the high street. In many respects, consumers expect some brands to be represented in a similar way to the retail park and high street locations. However, the changing shopping culture has made it possible for retailers to sell branded merchandise, in a manner that would have been considered inappropriate years before.

The arrival and popularity of the factory outlet has been linked to other issues such as the relaxed planning regulations during the 1980s and early 1990s. This encouraged developers to build out-of-town retail parks in locations that required consumers to use the motor car for their shopping trips. The British shopper saw this as an opportunity to obtain high status brands, at a value retailing price, in a post-recession period. Towards the end of the 1980s in the UK, the out-of-town retail site appeared more and more on the retail landscape.

Although the popularity of factory outlets is driven by the consumers' desire for quality and well-known branded products at value prices, the additional benefits of the factory outlet format to manufacturers and retailers has been a major factor in the growth of these centres. Here are several reasons why manufacturers and retailers need factory outlet centre operations:

▶ the disposal of surplus stock

▶ increased control of the merchandising function

▶ an additional promotional medium

▶ an additional source of income for retailers and manufacturers.

Factory outlets have played an important role in changing the way UK consumers shop, and in particular for clothing products. Factory outlets have a strong heritage or leisure park theme that encourages families to spend a day at these factory outlet centres. There are usually other attractions such as cinemas nearby or on site. The problem for developers is that they must look for sites away from established shopping centres, as there would be a conflict of interest between the provision of conventional branded goods in specialist shops and the factory outlet brands in a nearby off-centre shopping mall. There are multiple forces driving the development of factory outlet centres in the UK.

⇨ Conduct a piece of research into the popularity of factory outlets. Design a short questionnaire and use a small sample of typical consumers (see Mintel 'Factory Outlet Centres' March 2001 report). Distribute the survey and from the analysis try to establish other reasons for the popularity of these retail outlets.

Case 20.4 Stop Press! – Expanding Outlet Space

▶ The fashion retailer Logo is to invest £3 million on a chain of 15 discount clothing factory outlets, and is also planning to expand its network of high street shops (21 March 2001).

▶ Tweedmill Factory Outlets is to expand its discount clothing retail complex (13 March 2001)

▶ BAA McArthurGlen is to spend up to £900 million opening factory outlets in Germany, Italy,

Spain and the Netherlands, and it will sell stakes in existing UK outlets to help fund the project (11 September 1998).

▶ Marks & Spencer has announced plans to set up its first discount outlets at retail parks in Ashford, Cheshire Oaks and Livingston (5 September 2000).

Source: http://www.ukactivityreport.co.uk/

Factory outlets had enjoyed great success over the last two decades across the Atlantic in the highly competitive US market. United States developers seeking new opportunities to apply their successful formats in foreign markets, and facing saturation at home, moved towards the UK. The UK had a growing number of shopping centres (see Table 20.2), malls and retail parks, and so consumers had experience with this type of retail format. The UK was therefore quite attractive to potential factory outlet developers with American experience. Also, Britain's position within the EU created added appeal for US developers wishing to extend their concept on a global scale.

Table 20.2 The Growth of Factory Outlets in the UK

	1995	2000
Outlets	10	34
Operators	8	18
Space sq. metres	78 040	406 485

Source: Adapted from Mintel 2001

20.5 Building for the Future: Learning from the Past

As demonstrated throughout this book, the retail industry is in a constant state of flux driven by numerous factors. Consumers play a major part in this development process, and there is no reason to suggest that the customer will have any less influence in the future. We can see evidence of consumer-led retail change in the way in which stores have extended their offering to include the service element. Service is now a major issue for most retailers and frequently provides the differentiating factor. Smaller independent retailers are very familiar with this strategy and rely on the personal touch to attract their custom. It is this same small business approach or mentality that larger multiples have adopted in pursuit of greater differentiation. By making the service encounter pleasurable and memorable retailers are one step closer to retaining customers. Of course, the successful chain multiple must still demonstrate an adequate range of *high-quality* merchandise.

Losing Sight of Customers

The retail business is secure as long as its customers continue to patronize it. To ensure a continued presence in the high street, or other location, retailers are obliged to adapt and evolve or go under. The changing fortunes of Marks & Spencer in 2000 are testimony to the importance of tracking customers' needs and behaviour. Social change promotes different attitudes towards a whole range of issues such as fashions, communications, products and shopping experiences. As society changes so does retailing as retailing is society. When a retailer fails to make that connection the result is often quite devastating. In the case of Marks & Spencer the time for change had come and gone, and the management missed the message. Britain's favourite store failed to move with its customers' aspirations and so its customers moved on.

Image, Design and Space

Some well-established retailers have made marked changes to both their image and general offering to survive and prosper. In many respects, environmental trends and patterns mirror the feeling of the society that inspire them. In the 1990s, the UK was enjoying a renaissance, and return to the more classical layouts and designs of the nineteenth century. City planners emphasized this with the use of street architecture and the refurbishment of old dilapidated buildings, which focused on nostalgic themes. The old was now in and the 1970s modernist architecture was definitely out. The London department store, Selfridges, still had a tired and dusty image and profits were falling. A new layout provided the store, and the Selfridges brand, with a new image in keeping with the period and customers' expectations. Refurbishment provided the London store with an extra 7 per cent selling space and led to an increase in sales and profits.

In 2001, Selfridges sought the option to buy half of a Marks & Spencer flagship store in the heart of Manchester for the sum of £25 million. A further £15 million was allotted to refitting the interior.

Size Matters!

Newcomers to retailing make a greater mark as they have the distinct advantage of leanness. The larger the retailer the more difficult it is to control and organize. For example, the small independent can make changes to the merchandise range and store layouts relatively quickly. Larger retail structures are less able to respond quickly to customers' demands, as changes take longer to implement. There are exceptions, however, and some large retailers retain their small business culture because they are immature and have yet to develop the infrastructure and layers of bureaucracy that slows the business down. An example of this is the value-for-money fashion retailer Matalan, which boasts a strong and decisive management team. An in-house approach to store layout and design, merchandising and distribution ensures a quick response, and retains customers. Good quality merchandise, keen prices and retail park locations produce high-volume sales and lucrative margins. The company's considerable rate of growth fuels the number of store openings.

However, at some point the company must change and move away from its small business culture. This is because it will reach a situation where it is unable to respond technically or managerially to its expanding operation, and lose customers as a result.

Reinventing Retailing

> ⇨ To what extent is retailing about an assortment of service offerings rather than merchandise assortments?

For most retailers, including the small independent, the level and quality of customer contact and standards of service will impact on future business. Every retail business works to increase the likelihood that customers will come back to shop in their store. For example, the main reason for the extended use of loyalty or reward cards in super-markets and other chains is to tie customers into long-standing rela-tionships. This type of strategy has a number of benefits. First, the retailer is able to understand the customers' patterns of consumption, and plan accordingly. Furthermore, a good knowledge of customer habits and requirements make the task of merchandising less uncertain, and in tune with customer perceptions. This helps the business to be more effective and the retailer becomes far more responsive to customer needs. Customer service plays a key role in this retail strategy.

> ⇨ Students may wish to place themselves in the role of a small inde-pendent retailer and develop a retail strategy that employs customer service. Think about the types of services you could offer to tempt local customers away from the major supermarket chains. Remember that the business needs to be cost-effective so account for any additional benefits in the pricing strategy. You may wish to use special offers as loss leaders!

Levels of service are the glue that bonds various parts of the retail offering together and creates a persuasive and desirable package for the shopper. For example, the family shoppers in Tesco are treated as special guests at the checkout by the till operator who asks for their loyalty card. The data captured by the system as a result of the loyalty card ensures the right merchandise is in the store at the right time. Customers therefore feel special and tend to *own* the store or retail brand. It becomes *their* store to shop in, whatever the retailer or retail sector. Lifestyle advertisements reinforce this idea with family scenarios and reassurances that reflect the brand. Customer loyalty is the lifeblood of the retailer.

Case 20.5 Loyalty from Service: Lessons from Tourism Retailing

First established in 1987, the UK holiday village Center Parcs offers a short break holiday experience, which is fairly unique. The focus is on 'the leisure lifestyle of the country club, the exhilaration of the sports complex, the flexibility of the villa holiday and the indulgence of the health farm'. Guests are free to choose how they wish to gain relaxation and exhilaration (Ashton 1998). This type of holiday experience offers more than just a good mixture of facilities: it caters for the customer's lifestyle needs. The company targets ABC consumer groups and taps into their values and attitudes (see Chapter 6).

Center Parcs operates in a marketplace where customers expect better service and there is pressure to raise the quality of service constantly. Much of the service process is visible to the customer and requires additional attention to detail. For example, the villa complexes need to be kept clean, but in a way that does not adversely affect the village atmosphere. Eating facilities must be delivered in a manner that makes them an enjoyable experience rather than a sequence of tasks. Quality service is about staff. Staff must understand the brand and the expectations and needs of guests to ensure their continued loyalty. Competitors can imitate physical surroundings but high-quality service is very difficult to replicate. By 1998 Center Parcs was catering for over one million guests per year with a 90 per cent or more occupancy rate.

Source: http://www.erconsultants.co.uk/contact.html

Consumers of the new millennium are seeking a quality experience. To deliver this the retailer must provide more than just products and retail environments. Quality is also about how the service is provided by staff. This part of the offering is difficult for competitors to imitate unlike the physical surroundings such as store design and visual merchandising. The service delivery and the brand culture are far more difficult to replicate. Contact staff must understand the core values of the brand and the expectations and needs of customers. It is only by exceeding these expectations that customers will remain loyal to the retailer brand.

Back to the Future!

In many respects this last chapter of the book was a *new* introduction to retailing, in light of earlier discussions. Points from the preceding chapters helped us to set the scene in the reader's mind, and create a picture of the external and internal factors that change over time. As everything in the retail environment is subject to these changes, the rules we observe today, at the time of writing, have altered by tomorrow. This means that retailers must constantly update their knowledge of the retail environment to survive. Sometimes this variation may be incremental and seem too small to be worthy of consideration. For students of retailing these small but noticeable shifts are the alarm bells of change, and suggest the need for action of one form or another. In the UK market, two poignant examples of this are Marks & Spencer and C&A. Both retailers failed to identify the changing expectations of the consumer and the cultural move away from traditional merchandise.

New methods of tempting customers seem to be dominating retail strategy, with most retailers adopting the latest information technology. There is no real alternative to offering an online service, if for no other reason than to scoop up the incremental sales from customers that might otherwise use alternative retailers. It is, after all, the ultimate goal of the retailer to boost sales and become more competitive. The extent of this competitiveness alters with the expansion plans of competitors. Retailers of all sizes must therefore be available on as many channels as possible so that their customers can have access to merchandise at any time of the day or night. Even for the small independent retailer, managing a multi-channel business presents a challenge. It is the fulfilment issue that may well prove the most difficult to overcome. However, the mail order companies we mentioned in Chapter 18 have a significant advantage because of the logistics and distribution infrastructure.

The new retail environment will produce casualties, and it is undoubtedly the consumer that dictates what retailers have to offer in order to survive. The balance of power, therefore, remains with the customer.

References

Ashton, G. (1998) 'Topics, volume 1', http://www.erconsultants.co.uk/contact.html

Barker, P. (1998) 'Malls are wonderful', *Independent on Sunday*, 25 October: 7, 9, 11–12.

Behind the scenes: The airport (2000), American Express Publishing.

Doganis, R. (1992) *The Airport Business*, London: Routledge.

Financial Times (2000) 'Success of the new unorthodoxy: management online retailing', 13 September.

Jones, P. and Pal, J. (1998) 'Retail services ride the waves', *International Journal of Retail & Distribution Management*, 26(9): 374–6.

Mai, L.-W. and Ness, M.R. (1999) 'Canonical correlation analysis of customer satisfaction and future purchase of mail-order speciality food' *British Food Journal*, 101(11): 857–70.

Mintel (1999) *Retail Review 1999*, London: Mintel International Group Ltd.

Mintel (2001) *Factory Outlet Centres 2001*, London: Mintel International Group Ltd.

Morrel, L. (2001) 'An identity in crisis', *Drapers Record*, 16.

Murray, R. and McCormack, L. (2000) 'Click on to a shopping trolley; supermarket shopping online is timesaving and convenient, but there are pitfalls', *Daily Telegraph*, 21 October: 6.

Newman, A.J. (1998) 'Consumption and the airport setting: "Find" the time to go shopping', Fifth International Conference on Recent Advances in Retailing and Services Science, Baveno, Italy, August.

Reuters Business Insight (1998) *Global Airport Retailing 5th January 1998* (RETIZ), n.p: Reuters Business Insight Publications.

Index

accessibility 14, 247–9, 286
  in services retailing 308–9
accounts 22, 25, 322, 324, 335, 336,
  370
acculturation 444
acquisitions
  absorbing 451
  disposal 451
  and shareholder value 431
adjacencies, merchandising 165
advertising 121, 125, 127–8, 131–3,
  138, 204, 206–8, 277, 283, 288,
  298, 304, 416, 422–3, 434–5
  budget 208
  children 304
  clutter 434
  consumer expectations 277–8, 283,
  288
  consumer involvement 138
  consumer motivation 131–2
  direct mail 431
  effectiveness 128
  formats 206
  image 129, 132–3
  media selection 207
  non-foods 475
  objectives 204
  sales promotions 206
  strategy 206–7
  television 435
  website 423
affect (evaluation), consumer 129
age, income and lifestyles 121–2
airlines 370
airport retailing 38, 476–7
Aldi 69, 190
Allders 61, 201
Alternative Investment Market (AIM)
  22, 324–5
Amazon.co.uk 418
anchor stores 218
Arcadia 59, 430
Argos 62, 66, 73–4, 75, 429
  Decision making at 138
Ariel (brand) 197

arranging and displays 157–60
Asda 248, 265, 329, 403, 404, 451,
  473
  Davis, G. 323
  Norman, A. 323, 403–4
assets of business
  current 336
  fixed 336
  location of 165
associated sales, location of 165
assortment 26, 145–8
  balanced 142
assortment plan
  retail strategy 146–8
ATM 434
atmospherics 263–4
attitude 126–30
  measurement 130
  motivation 128–30
  to shopping 126–8
  and values 127
attribute ratings 130
Avis 342

B&Q 75, 163, 194
backward integration 66, 112–13
balance of payments 83
balance sheet 336–7
balanced assortment *see* assortment
bankruptcies and insolvencies 89, 319
bar code
  EAN 371
  and promotional offers 371
  scanning 370–1
  stock management 370–1
Barclays bank 416
Beales (retailer) 61
Beanie Babies 111
behavioural variable 125
Ben & Jerry's 174
benefit denial 386
Benetton 174, 346, 352
Bhs 330
birth rate and retailing 33
block plan 169

Body Shop   173, 174, 206
    Roddick, A.   173, 206
Bon Marche   68
Boo.com   421
Boots (The Chemist)   75, 174, 200, 202,
    302, 386, 451, 469
Boughey Distribution   359
boutique layout   253–4
BP (British Petroleum)   74
brand   197–203
    added value of   198–9
    development   201–3
    franchise   202
    name   197
    nature of   197–8
    producer   201
    retailer   199–200
branding   201, 277, 303–4, 307
    in differentiation   201
    logo   197
    in segmentation   201
    in service retailing   303–4, 307
break-even analysis   180–1
breakpoint (trading area)   229–31
British Airways   370
brokers   345
Brown and Jackson   35
brownfield sites   222
browsing   247, 252, 254, 421
BSC   58
BT (British Telecom)   297
Budgen's   60
budget hotels   303–4
buffer stock   345
building societies
    conversion to banks   300
Burger King   68, 297, 451
business confidence   86
business interception, strength of   220
business objectives   98–104
business plans   319, 321
business strategy   20
business to business   13, 15
butchers   11
Butlins   304
buyers
    planned gross margin   154
buying   153–7
    at discount   155–6
    cycle   156–7
    negotiation in   155
    steps in process   154
    types of   155–6
buying power
    consumer   221
buying power index   221

C&A   203
capacity management   310–12
car parking   223, 224, 226, 250

car service centres   298
careers in retailing   392–4
Carpetright   357–8
Carphone Warehouse   185, 206, 319
Carrefour   457
cash flow
    business operations   319, 322, 335
cash machine *see* ATM
catalogue retailers   62
catalogue shops   73, 286
    see also mail order
catchment area   227–35
    methods for determining   229–35
category killer   70–1, 200
category management   373–8
    characteristics   374
    information technology   375
    process   374–5
    strategy, customer targeting   373,
        376, 378
cause and effect diagrams   291–2
ceilings   160
cellular phones *see* mobile phones
census   38, 234
Center Parcs   482
charity shops   127
Chester Zoo   309
circulation
    Layout, merchandising   250–1
closed circuit television (CCTV)
    store security, costs   385
clothing retailing   60–2
Coca-Cola   197, 198, 199, 375, 426
cognition   405
cognitive process   132, 134–5
colour   160, 265–6, 445
    perception, international differences
        445
combined deliveries *see* shared
        distribution
Comet   61, 66, 73, 188, 200, 217, 265
Communication Effects Model   196–7
communication in promotion   195–7
communication process
    advertising, strategy, targeting   195–6
community   16, 20, 194
company   22–3
    private   22
    public   22
    public corporation   23
Compass   304
competition and change   66–76
competition policy   64–66
competitive advantage   302–3
competitive environment   59–64
complementary merchandise   161
computer retailing, order postponement
        in   351–2
concentric zone method
    store location, catchment areas   232–4

consolidation centre   354
constant price values   9
consumer
   shopping   6
   social obligations   128
consumer behaviour   48, 124, 128,
      130–1, 134–6, 472–3
   decision-making   134–6
   expectations   48, 128, 472, 473
   influences on   134–5
   motivation   130–1
   reference groups   124, 135
   willingness to buy   122–4
consumer involvement
   brands and advertising   135–8
consumer spending   35–6, 79–81, 86,
      470
   changes in   79–81
   and consumer confidence   35, 86
   effect of building society conversion
      35–6
   patterns   470
consumer supply chain   47–8
consumerism, types of
   international differences   443
consummatory service   275
continuous flow distribution   361
continuous improvement
   service quality   285
convenience goods   144
convenience of size   14
convenience of timing   14
convenience store   18, 60, 128,190
Co-op village store   218
co-operatives   23
   retailer sponsored   113
core competencies   331, 335, 337
COSHH *see* Health and Safety
cost of capital
   in investment   331
cost per thousand (CPM) method   209
cost-based
   services retailing, demand   311
costs
   fixed   181
   variable   181
Cotton Trader   112
CPFR (collaborative planning,
      forecasting and replenishment)
      362
critical control points   290
CTN (confectionery, tobacco, news) store
      17, 205
cues in stores *see* image and display
cultural change
   and retailing   470–6
cultural differences, international
      443–6
   adaptation of goods   445
   individualism-collectivism   461

masculinity-femininity   461
   power-distance   460
   uncertainty-avoidance   460–1
cultures
   linear and multi-active   460
current price values   8, 66, 73
Currys   73, 75, 200, 217, 265
customer-based transactions   397
customer, keeping sight of the   480
customer behaviour *see* browsing
customer loyalty
   and service   481–2
customer relationship management
      102, 379–83
   implementing   383
   implications for marketing   382
   nature   380–1
   using information in   382
customer service
   and employee empowerment   398
   and internal customers   279, 398
   and retail staff   397–9
customer spotting, spot map   228
customer switching   147

Dabs.com   419
Darwinism
   natural selection, competition   71–3
data management   106
data mining
   customer satisfaction, retail strategy
      382
Debenhams   61, 102–4
debt
   business finance   24, 336
   debt ratio   336
   gearing, financial   24
Decathlon   162,170–1
decision-making   134–7
   high involvement, process   135
   routine, process   136–7
dedicated logistics   345–6
Dell   352, 353
demand   27–9, 175–7
   change in   27–9
   and demand curve   175–6
   and revenue   176–7
demographic change   36, 38–9, 122
department, in-store specialised   72
department stores   61–2, 69, 71–2,
      242, 453
   multi-line   69–70, 72
deregulation of services   296
design factors   248, 284
developing services   303
dialectic model
   price wars   73–5
dialectic process competition, copy cat
      policies   73–5
digital television   430–1

Direct Line Insurance   301, 420, 424
direct mail order   437
direct response television   430
direct selling storage   245
direction finding   284
discount factor, in investment appraisal
    332–3
discount prices, by type of consumer
    311, 312
discount retailers   18, 70, 144, 190
discount store   18, 190
discounts in buying   155–6
Disney World   70, 398
display   158–63, 165, 256–63
    associated sales   165
    balance   258–9
    dominance   259
    equipment   261–2, 263
    effective use of   159–60
    exposure   257–8
    fixtures   161–3
    gondola   261–2
    image   258–9
    islands   261–2
    margins and enclaves   261
    security   259–60
    store design   160–1
    themed   158
    walls   260–1
distribution   345–6, 353
    combined deliveries   358
    contract, third party carrier   345, 346
    dedicated logistics services   345–7
    draw bar vehicles   356
    multi-temperature vehicles   353
    integration with production   345
    satellite positioning in   353
    shared distribution, Heinz   357
distribution centre   358–62
    automated   361, 362
    multi-user centres   358–9
    postponement programmes   361
distribution channel   343–7
distribution process   5, 341–3
Dixons   61, 66, 75, 199, 265, 424, 451
Dorothy Perkins   67, 344
dwell time   255, 416, 476

EAN number *see* bar code
economies of scale   56–8
    in marketing   57
economic activity, related to retailing
    25–6, 36–40, 80–91
    aggregate demand   81
economic fluctuations   25–6, 80–4
    managing during   89–91
economic indicators   87, 89–90
economies of scope   56–8, 331
Eddie Stobart (distribution company)
    345

efficient consumer response   377–9
    components   378–9
    development   377–8
    objectives   378
Egg.com   422
elasticity of demand   180
electrical retailing   74
electronic article surveillance (EAS)
    386
electronic data interchange (EDI)
    350–1
electronic funds transfer   379
electronic kiosks   433–4
Electronics Boutique   72
employee theft   387
employee welfare *see* health and safety
employment in retailing   8, 391–8
    attitudes towards staff   392–4, 395–7
    changes   391–2
    core and fringe workers   392–3
    empowerment   398
    part-time employment   391–2, 395–6
    regional variation   392
    temporary staff   396
    women's careers, management   393
employment in wholesaling   8
emporium   285
encryption technology   436
English, way of life   472
enterprise resource planning   344
envelope, store   249–50
EPOS   114, 371–3
    benefits to customer   371–2
    benefits to retailer   372
    use in the supply chain   372–3
equity   336
equity investment   21
Esso   74
ethics   175–6
ethnocentricity   444
ethos   393–5
European Union, cultural transformation,
    355, 469–70
exception reporting
    security   387
exchange rate   83–4
Exel (logistics)   358
exposure *see* display
extended warranties   272
external benefits and costs   29

facilitating the sale   286
factory outlets   108–9, 186–7, 477–9
fashion retailing   35, 37, 42, 60–1,
    67–8, 76, 111, 116
fashion followers pricing strategy   187
fashion forward retailer   116
    inventory   111
fast food sector   6, 68, 296
feature fixture   261–2

field of vision   257
financial evaluation of business   335–6
financial service retailing   299–301, 302,
financing business growth   319, 324–5
fire safety   410
Fishbein
    attitude measurement   130
fixtures   161–3
floor covering   160
floor space   72
florists   13, 76
food retailing   9, 59–60
    food stores   9
franchising   113, 326–8
fraud
    costs, image, business operations
        435–6
freeflow layout
    circulation system, image   252–3
full sourcing package (FSP)   151–2

Games Workshop   73
Gap   200, 201, 203, 446
Gateway (computer manufacturer)   241
gender
    and consumption   126
    and segmentation   124
general store   17
generic brands   443
genetically modified (GM) food   174
geodemographics
    population, store location   234–5
geographical information systems (GIS)
    234–5
global retailer   448
globalization   448
gondola *see* display
government policy   64-6
government regulation   26, 65
Granada   304
Grattan   428, 429
gravity models   229–2
greenfield sites   222
grey retailing   422
grid layout   250–2
gross domestic product   7
group pressure
    influence on consumer purchasing
        135

Halfords   75, 107–8
Harvey Nichols   122, 172, 211
health and safety   407–11
    accidents and dangerous occurrences
        410
    administration   407–9, 410
    COSHH   410
    employee welfare   410
    electricity   410
    fire safety   410

noise   410
    regulation   408–11
    risk assessment   408–9
health services   297, 301–2
Herzberg, F.   405
heterogeneity
    consumers   121
    of a service   276
Hewlett Packard   352
high involvement
    decisions   135–6
    and low involvement goods   137–8
high street banks   300–1
HMV   104, 105, 106
Hofstede, G.   460
home delivery   270, 356, 357, 423
Homebase   75, 221
homogeneous customer groups   122
homogenization
    brands, consumer tastes   443
Hoopers   61
Hoover   199
hot spots
    store design, merchandising   184
hotels   297, 303–4, 370
household
    impact on retailing   36, 39–40,
        79–80
    size and structure   36, 39–40
    spending   79–80
HSBC   303
Huff's model of trading areas   231–3
human resource management *see*
        managing staff
human senses   133
hypermarkets   69, 450

Iceland (retailer)   16, 174, 270
identity
    and shopping   126
IKEA   200
image
    and display   258, 480
impulse goods   144
impulse purchase   144
independent retailers   11–12, 60, 61,
        75–6
Index (catalogue retailer)   62, 66, 73–4,
        75
index numbers   41
index of retail saturation   226–7
information
    as retail service   277
information technology   468
innovation   319
inseparability
    of a service   276
in-store colours *see* visual merchandising
in-store simulations
    store design, customer behaviour   289

instrumental service 275
intangibility
    and risk 307
    of a service 275–6, 307
integrated marketing system 110–13
interactive television 430
interface 432
Interflora 76
intermediate products 12
international stores 442–55
internationalization
    degree of 452
    internal and external factors in 456
    interpretation 446–8
    joint ventures 455
    methods 454–5
    pull factors 453
    push factors 452–3
    strategic alliances 455
Internet
    banking 416
    retailing 419–46, 437–8
        on-line ordering 419–26
        retail strategy 421–2
        trading exchanges 424–6
    shopping 128, 416–19, 423–4
    spending 468
Internet service provider (ISP)
    shopping on-line 424
intranet 350–1
intraprise 403
inventory
    costs 342
    management 111
    and manufacturing response time
        347
investment 331–4
Ishikawa diagram see cause and effect
    diagrams

James Beattie 61
Johari window
    cultural differences 461
John Lewis 61
Johnson's the Cleaners 67
joint ventures see internationalization
    455

Key Note (market intelligence company)
    35
KFC 68, 100, 304
Kingfisher (retail group) 203–4
KitKat 197, 198
knock-on sales 184
KwikSave 69, 190

large retailers
    advantages for 56–8
layout of merchandise 164, 250
leadership 404

learning attitudes 128–9
leasing retail property 223–5
leasing
    warehouse 358–9
legibility 306–7
Levi Strauss 199, 353, 433
Lidl 265
lifestyle classification
    Mosaic system 124
    VALS2 125
lifestyles 15, 124–6
lighting 160
limited liability 22
line of authority 402–3
line planning 147–8
linear space 163–4, 251
liquid assets 25
liquidity 25, 337–8
listed company 325
Littlewoods Index 61, 66, 73, 74, 429
LloydsTSB 303, 323, 324, 329–30
location 216–42, 474
    customer satisfaction see assortment
    market position 216–27, 221–2, 474
    price wars 217–18
    planning restrictions 222
    store image 235, 242
    site analysis 221–2
    strategy 215–16
    supermarkets 474
logistics, definition of 343
logo see branding
London Stock Exchange see stock market
loop layout 254
low involvement decisions 136–7

macroenvironmental influences 53
mail order 128, 426–30
management culture
    internationalization 460
management style 321, 323–4
managing staff
    employee requirements 400
    employee selection 401
    induction 402
    job satisfaction 399
    job specification 400–1
    job tension 399
    planning the workforce 399–402
    training 402
    see also employment in retailing
manufacturer's agent 345
marginal cost 177–8
marginal revenue 176–7
markdown 148
market adjustment 27, 28–9
market opportunity 108
market positioning 26, 101–2, 123
market process 27–9
market research 35, 109, 122

market segmentation 122–6, 201
  lifestyles 124–6
  psychographic analysis 124–6
  retailer brands 201
marketing audit 105
Marks & Spencer 63, 67, 98, 174, 199,
    200, 201, 203, 265, 290, 301, 318,
    344, 394, 451, 459, 469, 474
mark-up 148
Mars (brand) 199
Maslow, A.H. 405
mass customization and the supply chain
    361
mass market, pricing for 172
Matalan 116, 122
materials sourcing 344
McDonalds 6, 68, 100–1, 218, 297,
    313, 450
McGregor, D. 405–6
Meadowhall 71
media selection
  customers, strategy targeting 209
melting pot theory *see* dialectic process
merchandise 17, 148–50, 164–5, 170
  budget 148–9
  layout planning methods 164–5
  performance 150
  replenishment 147
  see also atmospherics
merchandise assortment 110
merchandise characteristics 144
merchandise planning 144–50
merchandise sourcing *see* sourcing
merchandising
  changes in 475
  merchant 14
  stages 143–4
  strategy 110, 141–3
merchandising cycle
  planning, strategy, buying 157
mergers and acquisitions 185, 329–30
MFI 61, 113, 206, 359
microenvironmental influences 54
middleman 14
Migros 202
Mintel 35
Miss Selfridge 61
mission statement 21, 100–1
mobile phones 137, 174–5
  see also WAP phones
Morrison's 265
Mothercare 330
motivation 131, 404–6
  and advertising 131
motives 131–4
  consumer behaviour 134
  rational and emotional 131
  psychological and social 131
MP3.com 423
MSAS (distribution services) 358

multinational retailer 449
multiple format retailing 475
multiple retailers 11
multi-line department stores *see*
    department stores
multi-save pricing
  value retailing 184, 434
multi-user centres 358–9
museum services 301
music 266

national chains, evolution of 61
natural selection 71
needs, psychological and social 131
neighbourhood stores 17
net output and value added 8
Netto 190, 265
new product development
  supermarket involvement in 346
Next 60, 75, 172, 186–7, 201
  Directory 110–11, 429
niche markets
  targeting 173
  retailing 476
Nisa-Today 218, 358
Noise 410
non-food in supermarkets 473
non-food stores 9
non-store retailing and repairs 10
Nordic School 285–6
Norman, A. *see* Asda
NTS (newpapers, tobacco and sweets)
    147

OFEX 325
off-peak pricing 313
off-price store 18
one-stop shopping stores 18
online ordering process 419–20
on-shelf merchandising 257
on-site production
  by retailers 13
open merchandising
  customer interaction 158
opportunity costs 311
order postponement 351–2
order takers 211
organizational culture
  retailer, sector, retail policies 403–6
  calculative 403
  coercive 403
  normative 403
  leadership 404
  large and small retailers 402–3
organizational structure
  line of authority 402–3
out-of-store retailing 415–21
  types 415–16
  differences from conventional store
      retailing 416

distribution 417–18
growth 418–19
out-of-town retailing 471–2
outshopping
location, strategy, customer 231
outsourcing
distribution 353
overstored
location strategy 226
ownership *see* retail outlets
Oxford, city centre 218

Pareto analysis 291
Park and Ride 218
partnership 21
perception
of retailer and consumer 133
perceptual selectivity
advertising effectiveness 133
perishability
of a service 276–7, 309–10
personal computers
market for 174
personal selling 204, 210–11
personality
measurement 130
personnel
function 406–7
management and administration
406–7
records 407
PEST analysis 20, 106
pester power 304
petrol station retailing 57, 74
physical distribution 354–9
consolidation centre 354–5
transport mode, see transport
picking centres
distribution strategy 346, 360
Pizza Hut 218, 303
planning, definition of 98
point of purchase (POP) displays 164
point of sale 265
polarization
size of retail businesses 75–6
political change 36
in international expansion 453
population changes 36, 3839
Porter's generic strategy model
115–17
Post Office 296
postmodernism
and consumers 126–7
Poundstretcher 35
powerbrand
Boots 202
present value 332
price changes 29
price differentials
in capacity management 310–12

price lining 189
price premium
of a brand 198
pricing 170–89
bait 188–9
and competition 179, 180
and customer service 188
decisions 170
to define a market 172
and demand fluctuations 179
effect of location 172–3
ethics
effects of 173–4
strategy, image 189–90
leader 188
luxury goods 176
and product developments 174–6
macroeconomic influences on 175
multiple unit 189
niche markets 173
objectives 169–71
psychological 187
pricing policy 183–5
and market segments 183–4
and merchandise 184
and promotions 184–5
and geographic location 185
pricing strategy 185–6
above the market 186
at the market 186
below the market 186
own brand 170–1, 187
privacy 273
privatisation 296–7
Procter & Gamble 375
product replenishment 379
production methods
capital-intensive, labour intensive
41–2
profit maximization, rules for 178–9
profit, operating 24
profitability 337
profits
distributed and retained 22
promotion
cost-effectiveness 205–6
in-channel 205
pull strategy 205
push strategy 205
of retail brand 201–4
store, reasons for 193–4
types 202–6, 303–5
promotional goals *see* retailer
promotional mix
branding, customers, strategy 193,
202–4, 206
psychographics 126–8
psychological pricing 187–8
psychometric testing 401
publicity 204, 209–10

pulling power
    store location, competition 217–18,
        221
purchasing and distribution
    economies of scale in 56–7

quality
    and the consumer 278
quality management *see* total quality
        management
queuing
    and services 309
quick ratio 338
quick response *see* retail order cycle
quotation, Stock Exchange 23

recession
    managing during 91
Reilly's Law of retail gravitation 230
replenishment and stock rotation
        145
reservation systems
    airlines, hotels 370
reserves
    in accounts 22
retail
    crime 384–8
    environment changes 25, 33–7,
        44–9, 66, 295–301, 467–3
    security 384, 385–6
    services 269–70
    space 416
Retail Accordion Theory 69–71
retail activity
    changes in the level of 37–8
retail business success
    factors in planning 19–20
retail formats 16–20, 115–17,
        242–3
retail industry
    measuring 7–8
    structure 9–10
retail information system
    and security 387–8
    strategy, business operations 106–7,
        369–73
retail inventories
    and manufacturing response time
        347
retail life cycle 319
retail offering 54
retail order cycle 376–7
retail outlets
    ownership of 11, 55
retail parks 472
Retail Saturation, Index of 226
retail supply loop 347–48
retailer
    promotional goals 203–4
    services 271–5

retailer brand
    strategy, international 196,
        199–206, 443
retailer involvement
    production, design 344–6
retailing
    changes in 48–9, 54–5, 69–70
    forms of 16
    functions 14
    and the retail industry 7, 12
    significance in society 6, 7, 9, 16, 25
    as social institution 6
retailing information system
    planning, strategy, trends 106,
        369–73
RIDDOR 410
risk
    assessment 409–10
    and purchasing behaviour 58, 136,
        334, 346
River Island 61, 67
Roddick, A. *see* Body Shop
role clarity 399
role conflict 399
role of government 64–5
Royal Bank of Scotland 101

Safeway 248, 355
Sainsbury 57, 58, 69, 73, 122, 128,
        174, 190, 217, 248, 265, 355, 359,
        396, 398, 473
sale or return
    costs, strategy 147
sales based ordering 354
sales promotions 204, 208–9
saturated locations 226
SAYE (save as you earn) schemes 406
scent 266
Sears 58
Sears, Roebuck 395
seasonal change 35
seasonal departments 161
secondary distribution 357–9
security 248, 249, 259
    tagging 386
Selfridges 58, 127, 157, 172, 184, 480
self-service 42–3
self-worth 405
selling space 245
Sensormatic 386
service 270–308
    blueprinting 289–90
    brands 307
    characteristics 273–5
    encounter 278, 285–9, 308
    planning 289–90
    problems, analysing 291–2
    process 285
    and the shopping experience 270–2
service charges 223

service provider
  and service retailer 14, 295–7
service quality 282–91
  dimensions 282
  Nordic school 281–2
  services gap approach 282–4
  recovery 291
  see also total quality management
service retailers 6–7, 297–305
  and changing technology 297–8
  sectors 299
  commercial developments 305
service setting 284–5, 289, 306
service staff 313–14
service store 305–7
service variability 308
services
  nature of 275
  outcome-related, process-related 271
  as part of brand 273
services gap 277–8, 283, 286–8
services retailing
  tangibility and intangibility in 298–9
  impact of personnel 307–8
SERVQUAL model 282–4
shared distribution see distribution
shares in company
  dividend 22
  value 22
share-save schemes 324
Shell 74
shelving 160–1, 162, 165, 260–1
shoplifting see retail security
shopping
  analysing trends 43–5
  behaviours 125–6
  and changing lifestyles 470–4, 476
  experience 270–1
  home shopping see mail order; Internet
  leisure 46, 55
shopping centres (malls) 71
shopping goods 144
shrinkage 385, 387
sightlines see visual merchandising
signage 264–5
site analysis 222
size of business 55–8
SKU 146, 352, 374, 376
SkyDigital 433
small retailer 58–9, 317–22
  adaptability 480
  competition 58
  requirements for survival 320–1
  stages of development 318–19
  surviving first year 322
smart cards 436
SmithKline Beecham 361
social change 36
social class
  categories of 124

mapping out society 124–6
sociodemographic change 38
Sock Shop 70
sole trader 21
Somerfield 60, 69
Sony 199
sourcing 143, 151–4
  competitive advantage 152
  exploitation and social responsibility 153
  global 153
  stages in the process 151
space allocation in store 157–8, 164–5
  criteria 164–5
  measurement of 164
space management 144, 163–6
  computer-based 166
Spar 190, 347
specialist multiples 61
specialist retailers 9–10, 18, 73
speciality goods 144
spectator sports 305
spine layout 254
sponsorship 210
sports see spectator sports
spreadsheets
  business planning 333, 375
stakeholders 173, 193–4
standardizing services provided 313
Staples (office supplies) 15
static retail business 297
stock market 324
stock rotation
  computerized, product traceability 363
stock turnover 162
stockouts 26, 148, 341
stockrooms
  storage space, store design 245
storage space 163, 245
store
  architecture 248
  atmosphere 284–5
  design 162–3, 244–5
    see also atmospherics
  external 245–8
  fixtures 161–3
  format 242–3
  image 243–4
  internal 245, 249–50
  layout 250, 255–6
    see also layout of merchandise
  patronage 134
  role of 241–2
  types of 17–18
strategic alliances see internationalization
strategic planning 99–100
strategy 98–9
  see also promotion
strength of business interception
  of trading area 220

structural change   25, 36–7
subjective value   14
success factors in retailing   19
suitability   247, 249
supermarkets   14, 15, 19, 46, 57, 75,
        122, 128, 171, 190, 473, 475
superstores   69, 450
supplier relationship   102–3, 114–5,
        347–8
supplier theft   387
supply, change in   28–9
supply chain   5
    development   349–50, 352–3
    European environmental regulation
        349
    external   349–50
    integration and category management
        376–9
    internal   349
    information and distribution
        technology   352–3
    as loop   348
    management   342–3, 348–54
    partnership   347
    and product life cycle   343
    synchronization
        competitive advantages   349–52
        information exchange in   350–1
        postponement in   351–2
survey questionnaire   229
sweethearting   387
switching behaviour
    store loyalty   128–9, 144, 427,
        474
SWOT analysis   108–10

tactics   99
tagging *see* security
tangibility and intangibility in services
        298
teamwork   397, 398
technological change   36, 42
television Internet shopping   432
television shopping   430–3
Tesco   7, 58, 73, 75, 98–9, 101, 122,
        128, 137, 174, 190, 201, 217, 248,
        265, 301, 355, 371, 396, 406, 423,
        424, 428, 450, 451, 455, 473, 474
themed displays   158
Theory X   406
Theory Y   405–6
third party carriers   346
Thorntons   172
Tie Rack   70, 201
Timberland   115, 346
time, consumer use of   43–5, 128, 474
Tiny   241
Top Shop   201
top-up shopping
    specialist retailers   60

total quality management   279–81
tour operators   301
tourist market   38
Toys 'Я' Us   70, 116, 200, 448
trademark   197
trading area   219
    and accessibility   219–20
    and consumer profile   220–1
    consumer profile data   220
    doing research on   225–9
    and retail concentration   225–6
trading exchanges   424–5
training
    customer service   402
transnational retailer   449
transport
    air   355
    inland waterway   355
    rail   355
        piggy-back system   355
        European Union   355
    road   355–6, 357–8
    routes, marketing considerations   356
    sea   355
transport mode
    primary   355
    secondary   355–6
transport strategy   356–9
    outsourcing   357–8
travel agents   163, 301, 306, 434
Travel Inn   370
Travelworld   306

umbrella brand   202
understored
    location   226
unincorporated businesses   21
unpredictable events, effect on retailing
        34
upstream integration   328

VALS ™ 2 (Values and Lifestyles)
    SRI International   125
value of a business   23
values
    and attitudes   127
    in shopping for clothes   123
variability in service standards   308
variety   26
variety stores   17, 61–4
vendor managed inventory   362
venture capital
    business start up   328, 329
vertical integration   328, 346, 348
vertical marketing system
    contractual   113
    corporate   112
    forging links, customer satisfaction
        112–13
    integrated   112

Viking 15
virtual reality
    customer interfaces, merchandise
        438
virtual shopping 434–5
virtual trading 425–6
visibility 246–7, 249
visual displays *see* visual merchandising
visual merchandising 158 -9, 262–3
    in-store colours 160

Wal-Mart 323, 329, 450, 451, 455
    Walton, S. 404
WAP phones
    Internet shopping 432
warehouse
    design and layout 360
    drop-off point 360
    leasing 358-9
    pick-up point 360
    picking 360–1
    storage, volume based 360
    public, common 358, 359
    types 359–60
    see also distribution centre
warehouse club 18
warehouse management
    and continuous flow distribution
        361–2
    cross docking 362
    impact of supply chain co-operation
        361–3

and mass customization of deliveries
    361
and real time information systems
    362
technology 353, 361
warehouses 344–5
warehousing services 346
weather
    effect on retailing 34
weekend breaks 311
welcoming 248, 249
What Everyone Wants 35
Wheel of Retailing 66–9
wholesaler 14, 15
wholesaling functions 346–7
Wilkinsons 186
Wimpy 68
Wincanton Logistics 357, 361
window display 263
women
    impact of changing role 45–7
    as managers 393
Woolworth 72, 265
workforce
    flexibility 395
    management attitudes 396–7
    planning 399–400
world class formats 450
world products
    international generic brands 442

zero-hours contracts 396